RUSSIAN RESEARCH CENTER
Study No. 37

CENTER FOR INTERNATIONAL AFFAIRS

Original Edition Written under the Auspices of
THE RUSSIAN RESEARCH CENTER
AND THE CENTER FOR INTERNATIONAL AFFAIRS
HARVARD UNIVERSITY
Revised Edition Prepared under the Auspices of
THE RESEARCH INSTITUTE ON COMMUNIST AFFAIRS
COLUMBIA UNIVERSITY

THE SOVIET BLOC
UNITY AND CONFLICT

THE SOVIET BLOC

UNITY AND CONFLICT

By Zbigniew K. Brzezinski

REVISED AND ENLARGED EDITION

Harvard University Press · Cambridge, Massachusetts
and London, England

This volume was prepared under grants from the Carnegie Corporation and t Rockefeller Foundation of New York. These institutions are not, however, the a thors, owners, publishers, or proprietors of this publication and are not to be unde stood as approving by virtue of their grants any of the statements made or vie expressed therein.

Library of Congress Catalog Card Number 67-12531

ISBN 0-674-82548-9

Printed in the United States of America

To
Merle Fainsod

PREFACE

THE events of recent years have made it plain that the Communist camp is neither homogeneous, monolithic, nor unchanging. Underneath the external façade of unity a continuing process of change is taking place through evolution as well as through the internal clash of "antagonistic contradictions," to use a popular Marxist expression. Evolution is part of life; political systems, be they states or empires, are not immune to it. A scholar's task in observing such gradual change is to determine, if possible, its direction and its likely future significance. In time even gradual evolution may produce a real discontinuity: there is a qualitative difference between a boy and a man even though they are still the very same person. Similarly with the Communist camp.

The "antagonistic contradictions" are a different problem. The Communist camp as a collective entity is guided by purposes which are said to reflect its collective interest. At the same time, within these dominant, universal objectives there are also the specific, particular interests of the component units. Occasionally, and almost inescapably, a clash between the universal and particular takes place, and much of the history of relations between Communist states has to be written in terms of such conflicts. Even with the best of intentions and even with a conscious desire on the part of its members to adjust their interests, a collective organization of states produces strains and tensions. In the case of the Communist camp the disparity between the dominant power and the dependent Communist regimes resulted from the very start in the imposition of a one-sided priority of interests which ultimately was conducive to the emergence of open antagonisms and contradictory objectives.

Some of these conflicts might have been avoided had the Soviet leaders been more skilled in managing an international empire. Initially at least, they were limited by their own inexperience. Having viewed international affairs in terms of the hostile external world ranged against the Soviet Union, they could not think of the new Communist camp in any other way except as a slightly more expanded Soviet system. In the interwar period international Communism had become identified with the interests of Soviet power, and the Soviet leaders had become accustomed to think of Communists from other nations primarily as agents of that power. This tendency was especially marked after the purges of 1937–1938 which had liquidated many prominent foreign Communists (including almost the entire leadership of the Polish Communist Party). The majority of the survivors continued to serve the Soviet Union as employees of the Comintern or in the international branch of the NKVD. After 1945 it was difficult for Moscow to consider them as equals, especially since most of the new regimes were still largely dependent on Soviet backing. The new leaders who had come from the USSR experienced a similar difficulty in adjusting their perspectives. It was hard for many of them to think of themselves as national leaders and no longer as agents of the center.

In time, however, the responsibility of leadership and the complexity of building Communism under specific national conditions began to assert themselves, and both Moscow and the local leaders had to learn by trial and error that organizing relations among Communist-ruled states is more intricate than running the Comintern's various national bureaus. The story of these relations is thus also the story of the education of Soviet and other Communist leaders in making "agonizing reappraisals" and in seeking new ties for inter-Communist unity. The concluding chapter specifically examines this Communist "learning process."

In undertaking this study I have tried, whenever possible, to approach the question of relations among Communist states from the standpoint of the regimes concerned, either in Moscow or in the Communist capitals.* In so doing, I have assumed that the Communist leaders by-and-large are dedicated to "the construction of Communism" though, as we shall repeatedly see, that objective does not mean precisely the same thing to all of them. In attempting to construct Communism (or initially socialism) they make political judgments which reflect their ideology as well as their special interest in maintaining their political power, the power without which the ideology would be only an empty shell. As a result, the policy of a given Communist regime involves an intricate balance between its universal ideological values and particular power imperatives. My concluding chapter attempts to develop further the nature of this interdependent relationship between ideology and power on the basis of the evidence pre-

---

* For this reason words such as "socialism" or "People's Democracy" will often be employed in the sense used by the Communists.

sented in the book. For the moment, suffice it to say that, viewed purely from an "outside" perspective, the Communist camp is necessarily overshadowed by the steep wall dividing the Communist and the non-Communist political systems. That shadow, accordingly, obscures the many differences in approach and interpretation which manifest themselves within the Communist system. To an outsider, a particular church may appear homogeneous until he becomes aware of the various theological or institutional conflicts which operate within the organization.

My primary purpose is to examine how the Soviet bloc has changed over the years, which problems faced and continue to face its Soviet and other Communist leaders, and how they go about solving them in terms of their general ideological orientation. The book will also try to show how internal changes in the USSR affected political developments within the other Communist states and eventually changed the pattern of relations among them. In so doing, the study will point to the forces which make for unity within the Soviet bloc as well as the pressures making for diversity. To the extent possible, it will do so in terms of the Communist regimes and not in terms of the nations concerned. This book, therefore, is not meant to be either a history of the Communist take-over or of Communist rule, although some of these domestic aspects are summarized when relevant to external relations. Individual or factional struggles, as important as they are, are not extracted for the purpose of historical narrative or minute examination but are treated within the context of the general pattern of interacting domestic and external pressures, aspirations, institutions, and outlooks that at once shape the camp and change it. More hopefully perhaps, this book is meant to be a modest contribution to the study of the interaction of ideology and institutions of power of several states within the same ideological context. A general theory of ideology-institution relationships among states awaits further study and thought, but my hope is that this might provide the nucleus for some generalizations.

This revised edition of the book originally published in 1960 is organized into five major historical phases, each corresponding to a distinctive pattern in ideological and institutional relations among the Communist states. Even though the primary emphasis of the book remains focused on the problem of relations between the Soviet Union and the East European states, in recent years the Sino-Soviet relationship has loomed large on the East European horizons. Accordingly, this revised edition contains a new phase, one dominated by the Sino-Soviet dispute, while the Chinese role in the post-1956 turmoils of the camp is also discussed in several other chapters. Although the basic structure of the book remains unchanged, specific factual corrections and some interpretative ones have been made throughout.

The historical method of organizing the material was retained in preference to a topical division (for instance, economic relations, political relations, military relations, and such), since it lends itself more readily to a study of the dynamic factors changing the structure of the camp. However, one new chapter dealing with the contemporary institutional state of the Soviet alliance-system was added to the revised edition in order to provide an up-to-date, topical analysis of recent Communist efforts to institutionalize their relationships.

Since the appearance of the original edition of this volume, the study of Communist relations has come into its own. As a result, I have been able to take advantage of the excellent works that have appeared either on international Communism in general or on specific aspects of Communist relations. My debt to these works and to their authors is reflected by the footnotes to the new chapters. Moreover, the availability of studies dealing specifically either with the Sino-Soviet relationship or with, say, the Rumanian-Soviet relationship has permitted me to treat some of these problems in a more analytical fashion than is the case with the pre-1960 period.

In reviewing the past I have tried to resist the temptation to see now the earlier period in the light of all the conflicts that have recently surfaced. Just as formerly there was a tendency to be sceptical about the proposition that the Communist camp is really not homogeneous, today there is an inclination to minimize the degree of unity that once existed and to push back in time the different conflicts that are now so apparent. In my treatment of some of these conflicts I have tried to show how they evolved and why they did eventually become so important. Although I do not know if they could have been avoided, I do feel that the way they were handled by the Communist leaders, largely inexperienced in the art of compromise, contributed materially to their intensification. By the same token, greater sophistication of the Communist leaders in ordering their relations may have some important and relevant implications for the future.

The sources on which this volume is based fall roughly into five categories: (1) official statements and speeches of Communist leaders;

(2) Communist press and books dealing with the problem of relations among Communist states, as well as some unpublished Communist documents; (3) my own interviews with Communist officials in Communist states and abroad, personal observations from frequent travel in Communist states, and statements and depositions by former Communist officials now abroad; (4) summaries and reports of various Western institutes, including the excellent research materials of Radio Free Europe; (5) secondary sources dealing with the problem of relations among Communist states, especially for the post-1960 period, and with East Europe, useful particularly in the early portions of the book.

The original edition of the book was sponsored by the Russian Research Center and the Center for International Affairs, both of Harvard University. Their support is again gratefully acknowledged, as is also the invaluable counsel of Professors Merle Fainsod, Robert R. Bowie, Adam Ulam, Benjamin Schwartz, Ferenc Vali, Andrew Gyorgy, and Albert Mavrinac, and the help of my research assistant, Peter Kolar.

The revised edition was prepared under the auspices of the Research Institute on Communist Affairs at Columbia University. I particularly benefited from the work and comments of my colleagues Professors Alexander Dallin, A. Doak Barnett, George Heltai, Joseph Rothschild, and Donald Zagoria. I have a special obligation to Professor William E. Griffith of the Massachusetts Institute of Technology who most generously made available to me both his files and the manuscript of his own work on the Sino-Soviet dispute. I am also grateful to Professor Stephen Kertesz of Notre Dame for sending me a detailed critique of the original edition. In my work I was most ably assisted by Mrs. Christine Dodson, who supervised the over-all preparation of the manuscript, by David Williams, whose special contribution is acknowledged in Chapter 18, and by Misses Sonia Sluzar and Reet Varnik, whose linguistic skills and indefatigable research closed many a gap. Finally, to repeat what was said in the original edition, to my wife, but for whom this book might have appeared much earlier though with the inconsistencies and semantic monstrosities that she so unrelentingly combatted through countless evenings, I owe a special debt which I affectionately acknowledge.

ZBIGNIEW BRZEZINSKI

May 1, 1966

CONTENTS

The First Phase: 1945–1947

THE PEOPLE'S DEMOCRACY
INSTITUTIONAL AND IDEOLOGICAL DIVERSITY

1   THE POLITICAL BACKGROUND   3

The Communist Involvement — The Polish Pattern — The
Bulgarian, Rumanian, and Hungarian Variants — The Yugoslav and Czechoslovak Extremes

2   PROBLEMS OF THEORY   22

Emergence of the People's Democracy — Relations with the
USSR — The Dissidents

3   PROBLEMS OF DIVERSITY   41

The Soviet Scene — The People's Democracy: A Transitional
Phase — The Strains of Diversity: Domesticism — The Cominform: An Antithesis

The Second Phase: 1947–1953

STALINISM
INSTITUTIONAL AND IDEOLOGICAL
UNIFORMITY

4   THE THEORY RECONSIDERED   67

The Reassessment — The Soviet Model — Impact on Constitutions

5   LAYING THE SOCIALIST FOUNDATIONS   84
    *The Supremacy of the Party and the Dictatorship of the
    Proletariat — Purge Patterns — Transformation of the Material
    Environment*

6   STALINISM: A PATTERN FOR THE
    COMMUNIST INTERSTATE SYSTEM   105
    *The Formal Devices — The Informal Devices — Economic
    Aspects — China: The First Ally — The Interaction of Domes-
    tic and International Pressures*

7   THE STALINIST LEGACY   139
    Communist Testimony — Stalin's Testament

The Third Phase: 1953–1956

FROM THAW TO DELUGE
INSTITUTIONAL AND IDEOLOGICAL DIVERSITY

8   THE NEW COURSE: STALINISM DISSIPATED   155
    *Problems of Soviet Succession — The Malenkov New Course
    — Khrushchev's Conception of the Communist Camp — The
    Issue of Yugoslavia — The Twentieth Party Congress*

9   THE IMPACT OF YUGOSLAVIA   185
    *The Yugoslav Road to Socialism — The Emergence of the
    Anti-Stalinist Axis — Titoism for Export — Soviet Second
    Thoughts*

10 HUNGARY: THE TEST CASE OF NATIONAL
    COMMUNISM   210
    *Power versus Ideology — The Meaning of the Rakosi Phase —
    Crystallization of an Alternative: National Communism — The
    Failure of Controlled Transition — The Soviet Response —
    Tito's Dilemma*

11 THE POLISH OCTOBER: THE CHALLENGE
    OF DOMESTICISM   230
    *The Controlled Transition: A Summary — The Paralysis of
    Evolution — Gomulka and Power — The Revolutionary Dy-
    namic — The Problematics of Intervention — Conclusion:
    Domesticism and National Communism*

The Fourth Phase: 1957–1959

THE COMMUNIST "COMMONWEALTH"
INSTITUTIONAL DIVERSITY AND IDEOLOGICAL
UNIFORMITY

12   THE MAOIST EFFORT TO RECONSTRUCT
A CENTER   271

*The Inter-Communist Dialogue — Diversity in Unity: The
Chinese Solution — The Economics and Politics of Unity —
Poland and the Principle of Soviet Leadership — The Dialec-
tics of Unanimity*

13   UNITY THROUGH THE STRUGGLE AGAINST
REVISIONISM   309

*Noninstitutionalized Revisionism — The Quest for Unity: Tito
Outmaneuvered — Institutional and International Revisionism
— The Dynamics of Leadership*

14   THE POLISH WAY TO SOCIALISM   338

*Gomulka and the October Upheaval — The Period of Re-
strained Spontaneity — Restoration of Control — The Limits
of Polish Autonomy*

15   DIVERGENT UNITY   367

*The Silent Split — The Neo-Stalinist Loyalists — The Price
of Primacy*

The Fifth Phase: 1960–1965

COMMUNIST PLURALISM
INSTITUTIONAL AND IDEOLOGICAL DIVERSITY

16   THE SINO-SOVIET CONFLICT   397

*Issues and Origins — Dynamic Escalation — The Fate of the
Alliance*

17   SATELLITES INTO JUNIOR ALLIES   433

*De-satellitization, De-Stalinization, and Ideological Nationaliza-
tion — The Rumanian Self-Assertion — Emancipation and Interdependence*

18 THE SOVIET ALLIANCE SYSTEM   456
    *Multilateral Institutional Ties — Bilateral Agreements — In-
    formal Arrangements and Dynamic Patterns*

19 IDEOLOGY AND POWER IN RELATIONS
    AMONG COMMUNIST STATES   484
    *Policy and Ideology — Patterns of Inter-Communist Relations
    — The Communist Learning Process — Ideological Relativiza-
    tion and Erosion*

    APPENDIX   515

    NOTES   517

    BIBLIOGRAPHY   559

    INDEX   577

The First Phase: 1945-1947

THE PEOPLE'S DEMOCRACY — INSTITUTIONAL AND IDEOLOGICAL DIVERSITY

Those politicians of the revolutionary class who are unable "to maneuver, to compromise" in order to avoid an obviously disadvantageous battle are good for nothing. — V. I. Lenin, *"Left-Wing" Communism: An Infantile Disorder*

1 / THE POLITICAL BACKGROUND

> To tie one's hands beforehand, openly to tell the enemy, who is now
> better armed than we are, whether and when we shall fight him is be-
> ing stupid, not revolutionary. To accept battle at a time when it is
> obviously advantageous to the enemy and not to us is a crime. — V. I.
> Lenin

HISTORY has been playing cruel tricks on its most dedicated apos-
tles, the Marxists-Leninists. Both their defeats and their victories have
been "unhistorical": they have failed where they thought they ought
to have succeeded and they succeeded where they ought to have
failed. What is more, they were often defeated when acting "historically," and they often prevailed when acting "unhistorically." The
revolutionary activity of industrial proletarians resulted in one failure
after another, from Hamburg to Shanghai. The conspiratorial activity
of the elite of the proletariat, symbolically embodying that proletariat
but not actually composed of it, succeeded in largely rural Russia,
compressing two separate stages of history into one. Subsequently that
elite initiated the accelerated processes of industrialization which
should have provided the historical foundations for their victory.
Basing itself on the power of the state which it had created, that same
elite then sponsored, through military occupation, the setting up of
Communist governments in East Central Europe. Finally, in China,
a revolution led by the Marxist-Leninist elite, but based on the peasantry, completed the process of standing "history" on its head. Historical dogma in its pristine form could not comprehend the unpredictability of the historical process.

The purpose of this chapter is to summarize the political problems
which the Communists encountered in East Central Europe between
1945 and 1947. The next chapter addresses itself to the special ideological issues which arose as a consequence and which interacted with
the strategic and tactical adjustments the Communists had to make in
view of the East European situation. During these early years the
problem of "relations between Communist states" was still, strictly
speaking, nonexistent, except in the case of Yugoslavia. The new po-

3

litical structures of the various East European states were still only being erected. In some of the countries the Communists were acquiring power; in some they were just consolidating it; and only in one were they in a firm position independent of Soviet support. Under the protective shield of Soviet armies stationed in Central Europe, the local Communists were initiating patterns of domestic transformation: the domestic pattern was one of reform, reconstruction, and political realignment.

THE COMMUNIST INVOLVEMENT

The immediate objectives dictating the Soviet policy in East Europe during the war and immediately afterwards, and affecting the pattern of Soviet relations with it, may be broken down into five major areas of presumed Soviet interest. The first involved the desire to exert influence on the lands immediately west of the Russian frontier in order to deny the area to Germany — in the past a source of major threat to Russian security. There is no doubt that from the perspective of the *prenuclear* age the Soviet leaders could not feel certain that the mere defeat of Germany would ensure Soviet security and that the post-World War I situation would not be repeated. Moscow's emphasis on security was readily understood by the Western powers, especially in view of Russia's war effort. Prime Minister Winston Churchill frequently stated in the Commons during the war that the West was willing to go to some lengths to guarantee Soviet security from Germany on terms satisfactory to the Russians. As a result, the Western leaders were also inclined to grant the Soviet Union the benefit of the doubt insofar as the second broad Soviet objective was concerned: to ensure that East Europe would not be controlled by domestic elements which, while hostile to Germany, would also be hostile to the Soviet Union. Stalin encountered little difficulty in demonstrating that East Europe could not shield the USSR against a resurgent Germany if simultaneously it was unwilling to collaborate very closely with the USSR. Hence, he argued, it is essential that East Europe not only be denied to Germany but also that it be governed by regimes which were purged of all opponents of the USSR. Given the prevailing power balance, it was up to Stalin to decide what criteria would determine just who was an enemy of the USSR.

The remaining three probable Soviet objectives for East Europe seemed at the time less apparent to the West; or perhaps it was that the West simply felt unable to oppose them.[1] The first of these was to use the area for purposes of Soviet economic recovery. The war damages inflicted on the USSR by the Germans could be healed much more rapidly by extracting capital from East Central Europe through the removal of enterprises and resources. Insofar as the former Axis powers were concerned — that is Bulgaria, Hungary, and Rumania as well as Germany — the Western powers concurred and a policy of reparations was endorsed. The situation differed sharply in the case of Poland, Czechoslovakia, and Yugoslavia, all Allied powers. There could be no question of direct reparations, but at least in the case of Poland and Yugoslavia the Soviet Union extracted some economic advantages. In Poland there was the matter of the incorporation of eastern Poland into the USSR and the removal of industrial equipment from those parts of Germany assigned to Poland as compensation for the German occupation and for the loss of territory to the USSR.[2] In the case of Yugoslavia joint companies were established which, according to the Yugoslavs, the USSR found profitable.

The fourth objective, we may surmise, was to deny the area to the capitalist world since it was likely to plot hostile moves against the USSR. No doubt the Soviet leaders, even at the height of the Grand Alliance, must have considered the possibility that some day after the conclusion of the war the capitalist world would again be arrayed against the USSR. Many of the wartime Soviet suspicions about alleged British or American contacts with German anti-Nazi groups were derived from such general ideological assumptions about capitalist behavior. As a result, Anglo-American declarations to the effect that postwar governments in East Central Europe must be democratic were presumably viewed in Moscow with a great deal of mistrust. The Kremlin undoubtedly suspected that such governments were meant to be the springboard for an eventual capitalist onslaught against the USSR.

The fifth probable objective was related to the preceding one. If ideological assumptions played a role in the crystallization of Soviet defensive interests in East Europe, then it is likely that the other part of the ideological orientation, namely its offensive component, was also present. Leninist-Stalinist strategic concepts have always emphasized the importance of a strong basis for expansive operations, and it is inevitable that any accretion of territory to the base of socialism in itself was regarded as reflecting the march of socialism toward its eventual victory. It would be impossible not to relate the new political situation in East Europe to this historical process, especially since the prevailing situation was already clearly suggesting that the area had become divorced from capitalist domination in space and from the capitalist era in time. It would be inconceivable not to consider the establishment of Soviet power in East Europe as another revolutionary turning point in a process which *must go forward.*

The objectives of the local Communists were much more precise: to attain firm control over the levers of power and to consolidate that power. This achievement would relieve the Soviet Union of the obligation to maintain its influence by direct force, which might eventually provoke the West and which, in any case, was contrary to the basic Communist belief that external domination must be supported by domestic efforts to change the existing society. For this reason, East Central Europe was not to be considered as an occupied area but as a zone of eventual revolution, carried out by indigenous elements but backed, to the degree necessary, by Soviet power. The processes of obtaining domestic power were therefore linked to a series of internal programs, postulated by the Communists, to which progressive and democratic elements could not object. These programs stressed reform, political, social, and economic, for which there was great need.

Indeed, enlightened public opinion could not oppose many of the measures recommended. Some of the politically active liberal elements in East Europe undertook at least partial collaboration with the Communists since it appeared that democratization went hand in hand with Communist reform programs. Moreover, a certain tradition of cooperation between some liberal-democratic groups and the Communists had developed in the anti-Nazi undergrounds. But what appeared to many a liberal as a desirable end was to the Communist leadership merely a means, and a means which in itself set social forces in motion toward the ultimate Communist objective. The democratic forces were further handicapped in that they often lacked defined programs which could justify explicitly their purposes and draw clear lines between them and the Communists'. This absence of clarity both in purpose and action hindered the non-Communists, as did the decisive factor of Soviet strength backing the Communist parties.

The Communist challenge to these non-Communists favoring reform amounted, in substance, to this: collaborate with us or oppose progress which you also desire. The challenge was well calculated, given the prevailing attitudes among the dominant social groups: the intelligentsia, the peasantry, and the workers. The intelligentsia, always a group of great importance in a revolutionary period, had been deeply disillusioned by what they construed to be the failure of the democratic world to evolve a clear-cut program designed to create a better life for war-torn Europe. Much of this intelligentsia, hounded by the Nazis and wooed by the Communists, had become alienated from the prewar governments because of their failure to cope with existing ills. A minority of them, drawn to Marxism sometimes by curiosity, sometimes by the appeal of a doctrine which seemed to know where history is pointing, were willing to give this ideology a chance to build a better world.[3]

To the peasants, prospects of land reform held out a vision of the fulfilment of their most cherished dream, and one much too long denied. The peasantry, while rarely politically active, was the backbone of the various peasant parties which could conceivably contest the Communist control of power, and plans for land reform forced these parties to endorse at least some part of the economic program of the Communists. It is true that fears of ultimate collectivization persisted and neutralized much of the political capital that the Communists might have hoped to gain among the peasants; nonetheless, land reform did serve to alienate the peasantry from some of the influential, landowning, anti-Communist elements in the predominantly rural areas.

The workers and industrial engineers were primarily interested in getting their factories going again. Unlike the peasants who can live off the land, the workers were especially dependent on the economic recovery programs. Their primary concern was to make certain that smoke was again pouring from the factory smokestacks. To most people in war-devastated East Europe, rapid economic reconstruction was the most vital issue, even more so than politics. And to a majority of them state planning appeared necessary and logical.[4]

The Communists, even though a small minority, were thus able to exploit a situation in which to oppose their programs of reconstruction was to engage in what amounted to sabotage of the national interest. Politically, it meant isolating oneself from the mainstream of public opinion. Faced with this dilemma, the politically active non-Communist elements split into three groups. First there were those who believed that despite everything the only course open was that of underground resistance. Between 1945 and 1947 this policy was pursued by the remnants of the anti-Nazi underground in Poland — organized into the generally liberal group "Freedom and Independence" (WIN) and the right-wing "National Armed Forces" (NSZ) — and in Yugoslavia by scattered units of the Chetniks. Such activity was based on the calculation that war between the USSR and the United States was inevitable and, in fact, imminent. Gradually, however, these lonely fighters found themselves more and more isolated, with the people tired of war and the West uninterested in the area. By 1948 most of them had been liquidated and only sporadic and isolated groups carried on.* The second, and largest, group consisted of those who decided to work within the framework of the system and organize democratic parties. Expecting Western insistence on free elections, they calculated that through the democratic process they would succeed in defeating the Communist minority, and they assumed that the USSR would not dare to oppose such powerful democratic states as the United States or the United Kingdom. This course was pursued particularly by the leaders of the various peasant parties. However, the price of open electoral contests was the repudiation of the more violent opposition to the Communists, and hence the anti-Communist camp was split from the start. Finally, the third group was composed of those who felt that collaboration with the Communists was justified because the Communist domestic programs were desirable and because the Communists were a guarantee against the return of "right-wing" governments. Members of this group entertained no illusions about an East-West war or about some Western intervention on behalf of free elections. Recognizing Soviet domination of the area as the determining factor, they conceded that the future belonged to the Communists and that the reasonable thing to do was to join them. Some of them might have also hoped that by joining the Communist ranks they would mollify the more extreme or brutal Communist programs. Much of the left wing of the various socialist parties, as well as radical agrarians, oscillated in this direction.

These general considerations may be briefly examined in terms of some of the individual countries concerned. Conditions in each varied significantly, but three varying patterns of Communist activity may be broadly discerned: (1) consolidation of power already obtained through Soviet occupation by 1945, and the initiation of domestic re-

---

* The scale of the Polish resistance can be seen from the following figures. In the spring of 1947 the Communist regime acknowledged that it was imprisoning 21,176 persons for political reasons; during the "amnesty" period concluded in April 1947 some 55,277 members of anti-Communist organizations stepped forward, handing over close to 15,000 weapons (including, for example, 10 cannons and 904 machine guns); Communist losses amounted to 1,427 security men and 2,000 party members killed in 1945 and to about 30,000 between 1945 and 1948. (S. Korbonski, *W Imieniu Kremla*, Paris, 1956, pp. 268, 290; *Po Prostu*, October 14, 1956; *Polityka*, February 15, 1958; *Glos Koszalinski*, May 23, 1956.) For a detailed account of Communist "counter-insurgency" efforts, including the fact that at one point some 15–17 divisions of troops and police were involved, see I. Blum, in *Kultura i Spoleczenstwo*, January–March 1965.

forms not necessarily doctrinaire in form; (2) efforts to obtain power through participation in the political process and through active encouragement of internal reform; and (3) consolidation of power obtained by their own efforts, and the launching of a radical totalitarian revolution. There was occasional overlapping, but on the whole the first pattern applied to two former enemy states, Bulgaria and Rumania, and also to Poland which the USSR initially treated as if it had been an enemy power (occupation, arrests, deportations). The second pattern applied to Czechoslovakia, and the third to Yugoslavia. Hungary was a marginal case, partially fitting the first and partially the second category. External Soviet protection prevented outside interference from disturbing the unfolding of these patterns and doubtlessly also constituted an element of psychological support to those engaged in furthering them.

THE POLISH PATTERN

There appears to be little doubt that Poland, due to its geographical position, was the primary objective of Soviet policy in East Central Europe. A non-Communist Poland would have resulted in the exclusion of the USSR from Central Europe. The Polish fear of Germany, however, was a major Soviet asset. The overwhelming hatred for the Germans was a legacy of Nazi rule which the Communists could easily manipulate, particularly in terms of the necessity for close Polish-Soviet collaboration. The territorial changes made at the Potsdam Conference, setting the Polish western borders on the Oder and Neisse (Odra and Nysa) rivers, made such an alliance imperative to Poland's future. The Nazi and Soviet extermination policies, which had decimated the Polish intelligentsia, the usual source of the political elite, had badly weakened the nation as a whole, decreasing its capacity for resistance.* The Red Army on entering Poland pursued a policy of wiping out political and military centers controlled

* According to available statistics, about 700 university professors and academic workers were exterminated; about 1000 gymnasium and professional school teachers perished, as did 4000 primary school teachers. About 43 per cent of the various cultural and educational resources were totally destroyed; 60 per cent of the educational facilities. Over 6 million Polish citizens perished as a result of the German attack and occupation; of these 5.3 million died through various forms of terror (executions, pacifications, death camps, starvation or exhaustion in concentration camps) and 0.6 million through direct hostilities. For every 1000 citizens in prewar Poland, 220 perished, a much higher percentage than even in Yugoslavia (108 per 1000) or the USSR (40 per 1000). *Zachodnia Agencja Prasowa*, bulletin no. 3, 1957. To the above totals, about 1.5 million should be added to account for those deported to the USSR and who subsequently never returned, and the 10,000 officers killed by the Russians in Katyn and elsewhere.

by the underground and by the Polish government in exile, and set up its own body, the Committee of National Liberation, controlled by the Communists. The Committee represented a fusion of the underground Polish Workers' Party founded in 1942 on instructions of the Comintern with the Committee of Polish Patriots, founded in Moscow in 1941, and it was recognized on January 5, 1945, by its sponsor, the USSR, as the provisional government of Poland. The Czechoslovak government of Eduard Benes followed suit with recognition on January 31. In keeping with the Yalta agreements and following the inclusion in the provisional government of four Polish non-Communists from abroad — including the Peasant Party leader, Stanislaw Mikolajczyk — this body was recognized on July 5 as the government of Poland by the major Western powers. The government, in which the four "imports" were outnumbered by sixteen incumbents from the Soviet-sponsored body, was to hold free elections in which all "democratic" parties were to participate.[5] With most of the important governmental positions under their control, the commitment to elections did not change the fundamental facts of the Communist position, openly stated in October 1945 by Wladyslaw Gomulka, the Communist Secretary and former underground head of the Workers' Party. The "commanding heights" of the political system were well in hand.

The Polish Communist Party, dissolved by the Comintern in 1938 and rebuilt in the late months of 1941 and early in 1942 as the Polish Workers' Party, emerged from the war with limited cadres.[6] Its early 1944 membership was between 20,000 and 30,000,[7] but its ranks grew rapidly with the influx of Polish Communists from the USSR and through local recruitment. Apart from the party's self-identification with some of the more important national causes (such as the western frontiers), the very fact that it was wielding power made it more attractive to some elements. By the end of 1945 its numbers grew to 235,296, a year later to 555, 888; and by the end of 1947 it numbered 820,786.[8] The majority of the membership at this time was recruited from the workers with whom the policies of industrial recovery, nationalization, and development of the former German enterprises were popular. The proportion of peasant membership was also appreciably higher at this period than after the party had consolidated its power and had launched its collectivization policies. As might be expected, the majority of the peasants enrolled in the party were from among the very poor strata of the peasantry.*

* In December 1945, the social composition of the party was as follows: Workers

The party at the same time applied pressure on the left wing of the Polish Socialist Party in order to have it join in an electoral alliance against Mikolajczyk and eventually to fuse it with the Workers' Party. The Socialist Party was badly split and handicapped by the absence of able leadership. Its most prominent leaders, well known in the international labor movement, had perished during the war, or were in exile, or under arrest.* The party was in the hands of second-string leadership, less known among the rank and file (which still equaled the Communists in number). Its opposition to Communist invitations was made on two grounds: the question of Polish independence from Russia (much in keeping with the patriotic traditions of the Socialist Party) and that of internal democracy. But the economic programs of the Communists and the need to close national ranks for the purpose of reconstruction could not be opposed. Under these circumstances, and aided by terrorism, arrests, and pressure, the splinter left-wing faction led by such men as Jozef Cyrankiewicz and Oskar Lange gradually was able to assert its control over the Socialist Party and, from the very beginning, to prevent it from supporting the democratic forces led by Mikolajczyk.

The task of liquidating Mikolajczyk's opposition was more closely linked to the international situation. It could be argued that his position was doomed from the very start and that it was only a matter of time before the full measure of Western disengagement in East Europe would reveal the extent of Mikolajczyk's weakness. His only *real* source of power was the assumption widely made by the Poles,[9] and presumably shared even by the Communists, that Mikolajczyk was returning to Poland with some Western guarantees of support in the event Soviet promises to allow free elections in Poland were violated. Beyond that, his political power was almost nothing from the

— 62.2 per cent, Peasants — 28.2 per cent (W. Zaleski, *The Pattern of Life in Poland*, Paris, 1952, p. 56). According to Zambrowski, a member of the Politburo, 68.7 per cent of the peasant membership was composed of peasants owning average or below-average land plots ("On the Realization of the Leading Party Slogan in the Countryside," *Nowe Drogi*, no. 5, 1955, p. 55). There is striking correspondence between these figures and comparable data on peasant membership in the French and Italian Communist parties. In France, of the peasant membership, 69 per cent come from the average or poor economic level (which can broadly be equated with land ownership); in Italy 88 per cent of peasant membership is recruited from among the tenant farmers and laborers. S. M. Lipset, "Socialism — Left and Right — East and West" (mimeographed, 1958); figures based on P. Williams, *Politics in Post-War France* (London, 1954), and *Italian Political Party Preferences* (New York, 1953).

* Dubois and Niedzialkowski were shot by the Germans; Puzak and Pajak perished in Stalin's prisons; Erlich and Alter were executed by the NKVD; Arciszewski was heading the free Polish government in London.

day of his arrival in Poland (as Vice Premier of the newly constituted government) to his departure two years later. True, he enjoyed great popularity among the peasantry, and most democratic and even conservative forces considered him their only source of salvation from Soviet and Communist domination. In a free election he most certainly would have won a sweeping victory, with possibly even the majority of the Communist membership voting for him. But free elections were not likely to occur. In Poland of 1945 (and to a greater extent later), all the levers of power were in Communist hands, the Red Army was on the scene, and the NKVD was active. Mikolajczyk's popularity under these conditions had no political significance, while the growing awareness of the absence of effective Western support made it possible to apply increasing doses of terror against the Polish Peasant Party. In 1947, after the manipulated elections formalized the liquidation of his party, Mikolajczyk escaped abroad.[10] From the point of view of the Communists this concluded yet another chapter in the process of sweeping away the remnants of the preceding historical phase — that of bourgeois rule.

At least as important to the Communist strategy as these political developments were the economic and social measures which the Communists were able to launch. The series of economic and social problems besetting Poland even before the war, and deeply aggravated by the German oppression, gave the Communists a golden opportunity to take advantage of what they themselves considered to be "the objective processes" of history. Seizing the initiative in these fields meant again that all democratic forces which emerged with Western encouragement to compete in the promised free elections had to endorse major parts of the Communist program and to associate themselves with it. The greatest impact of the reforms was felt, naturally enough, in agriculture, where need for land reform was genuine, and in industry, which was badly devastated and which was now more important because of the recovery by Poland of the Silesian basin.

Radical land reform was initiated even while the hostilities were in progress. On September 6, 1944, a decree on the expropriation of landholdings exceeding 100 hectares (247 acres) of total area or 50 hectares in cases of purely agricultural land was announced. No compensation was provided, and in the execution of the land reform properties even below the proscribed maximums were also seized. Since political considerations were paramount, the land reform in the old parts of Poland resulted in the proliferation of uneconomically

Size and number of private and public farms

Size of farm (in hectares)	Prewar area of Poland, 1931 Holdings		Postwar area of Poland, 1949 Holdings	
	In thousands	% of total	In thousands	% of total
Less than 2	747.1	25.5	962.1	28.7
2–5	1,136.1	38.7	1,084.0	32.3
5–10	728.7	24.8	906.3	27.0
10–50	309.1	10.5	392.6	11.7
Over 50	14.7	0.5	10.3	0.3[a]

[a] 90 per cent of the land owned by farms over 50 hectares was in state or collective ownership.

Source: *Foreign Agriculture*, no. 7–8 (1953), p. 143.

small landholdings.* The accompanying table gives a statistical picture of the situation. In the former German territories, more medium-sized farms — about 60 per cent of all farms were from five to twenty hectares in size — were created for the new Polish settlers through the expulsion of the Germans and the division of former German estates.[11] However, the reform did have the effect of liquidating the formerly influential landowning gentry and of stimulating a measure of class conflict in the countryside. It resulted in the curious paradox of the peasants supporting Mikolajczyk in the hope that he would defend their soil against the Communists and the landowners supporting him in the hope of less radical expropriations.

Nationalization of industry already applied since 1944 through the seizure of former German plants and the setting in motion of frequently abandoned enterprises in the prewar Polish territories, was decreed in the law of January 3, 1946, entitled "Concerning the Seizure of Basic Branches of the National Economy." [12] The decree provided for the seizure "with compensation" of the mines, the petroleum industry, the power, gas, and water works in the public service, all

* "This form of parcelling was inexpensive in terms of new investment, because most of the former laborers continued to live in their laborers' quarters on the estate . . . It did little for the farmers on the old dwarf farms who received additional land, since they could not make a complete living on either the original or the slightly increased holdings. It did not provide a surplus of grain or other food stuffs for the non-farm population." *Report of the F.A.O. Mission to Poland* (Washington, 1948), p. 39; cf. Iwanska, cited in note 8, pp. 468ff.

synthetic-fuel industries, foundaries for ferrous and nonferrous metals, armament industries, cokeries, sugar factories, flour mills of a given capacity, cold-storage facilities, and printing establishments — as well as any other industrial undertaking "capable of employing more than 50 workers per shift." [13] As Boleslaw Bierut, the Communist leader of the government, explained, since the law really sanctioned the existing state of affairs, compensation was not actually paid to domestic owners affected by the decree. This measure, while enlarging appreciably the role of the state, again was viewed by many as a necessary consequence of the war and dictated by the imperatives of recovery. And the Communists stressed throughout, particularly in the Three Year Plan of Economic Reconstruction (adopted in July 1947 but effective as of January 1), that the Polish economy would be based on the "coexistence" of three fundamental sectors: public, private, and cooperative. In this manner they distinguished Poland from the Soviet model. [14]

The sum total of these measures, launched by a regime already under Communist control and directly sponsored by the Soviet Union, was to create in Poland new patterns of economic and social relations. The foundations for a "People's Democracy" were thus laid through a blend of political and economic policies: through terror and reform, by giving land to the peasants and expropriating the large and medium entrepreneurs, by appealing to Polish nationalism against the Germans and destroying those wishing to assert Polish independence against the USSR. The acquisition of the lands east of the Oder and Neisse rivers and the opportunities created by the availability of ownerless farms, homesteads, and factories gave the Communists unique patronage opportunities, and Gomulka himself took charge of the development of these territories. The consolidation of power was in this manner linked with the initiation of an internal transformation. But both had to proceed at a relatively cautious pace because Western attention was focused on Poland to a far greater degree than on any other country in East Europe. The Communists in Poland were secure enough through Soviet support to be able to afford a certain amount of restraint.

THE BULGARIAN, RUMANIAN, AND HUNGARIAN VARIANTS

The Polish pattern, involving a party in effect already in power at the conclusion of the war, might be considered as a case example also applicable basically to Bulgaria and Rumania, and partially to Hungary. Some differences, however, must be noted. International complications played a lesser role in Bulgaria and Rumania, both former Axis powers, although the negotiation of peace treaties did give the Western powers the opportunity to express continued interest in the internal affairs of these countries. Also, unlike Poland, the institutions of government had not been destroyed by the war and did not have to be rebuilt in their entirety. While not challenging Communist control, these institutional factors did constitute an impediment which the Polish comrades did not have to face. The case of Hungary, also a former enemy power, was somewhat complicated by its proximity to Austria and Czechoslovakia. In these two states the Communist parties still entertained certain aspirations, and possibly as a result the Hungarian Communist Party moved with greater caution. However, in Hungary a more drastic break with the past took place through the destruction of the Horthy regime and the establishment of a republic. "National committees," set up by the Soviets, undertook the initial tasks of government and screened former government officials. Thus in different ways each party could plead a variety of difficulties, external or internal, which delayed or rendered more difficult its rapid consolidation of power.

In Bulgaria, the Communist Party had the advantage of having enjoyed some measure of popularity in the past and was not handicapped, as in the cases of Poland, Rumania, and Hungary, by nationalist anti-Russian feelings. In 1919, the Bulgarian Communist Party succeeded in electing over one fifth of the deputies to the parliament and was, until outlawed, the country's second largest party. Subsequently, operating under the label of Independent Workers' Party, the Communists managed to elect 31 of the 274 deputies in the 1931 elections. During the war they were instrumental in setting up the Fatherland Front, an organization of anti-Fascist parties dedicated to the overthrow of King Boris' dictatorship. When the Soviet Union suddenly declared war on Bulgaria in September 1944, on the eve of a Bulgarian decision to join the Allies, the Fatherland Front seized power. In the coalition government the Communist Party obtained control of the important Ministry of the Interior and played a major role in the "purge" of public officials which was immediately launched. The purge amounted simply to a terror operation, designed to destroy the political cadres of the "bourgeoisie" which had not been decimated by the war (as was the case in Poland). Within six months of the entrance of Soviet troops into Bulgaria, the special courts had condemned 11,667 persons, 2,138 of whom were actually executed.[15]

In July 1946 a decree on "Leadership and Control of the Army" paved the way for a thorough purge of the armed forces. When the elections for the National Assembly were held on October 27, 1946, it came as no surprise that only 99 deputies out of 465 did not belong to the Communist-dominated Fatherland Front. Eleven days later, Georgi Dimitrov, the former head of the Communist International, became the Premier of Bulgaria, having just renounced his Soviet citizenship. The year that followed was marked by the liquidation of the opposition which had refrained from joining the Fatherland Front, most notably the peasant movement under Petkov. Symptomatic of the general caution exercised against a premature union with the socialists (to be distinguished, however, from the close cooperation which was stressed from the start and which was used to split the socialists), it was only early in 1948 that the Bulgarian Social Democrats were formally absorbed into the Communist Party.* [16]

This initial period (September 1944–1947) was highlighted by an economic recovery drive organically linked with social reform. However, unlike the other East Central European states, Bulgaria did not have to cope with large-scale private property either in industry (a minor sector in the Bulgarian economy until the post-1948 industrialization) or in agriculture. Land reform had been carried out already in the twenties, and the postwar decree limiting private land holdings to a maximum of 20 hectares by 1947 affected only 3 per cent of a total of 7.8 million hectares of arable land.[17] Collectivization of the agricultural sector was left on a "voluntary" basis until after the September 1947 peace-treaty ratification removed the Allied Control Commission from Bulgaria.

In Rumania the situation might be considered as already heavily weighted in favor of the Communists by March 1945, when the young Rumanian monarch, acting under duress applied by the Soviet representative, Andrei Vishinsky, commissioned a cabinet headed by Petro Groza, a Communist sympathizer, and dominated by the Communists. The monarchy persisted for two more years, acting as a passive restraint (the Communist daily *Scinteia* even wished the king on November 8, 1946 "a long life, good health, and a reign rich in democratic achievements"), but was powerless to prevent the Communist consolidation of power. The Communists benefited from the Soviet willingness to entertain Rumanian claims to Transylvania, and

---

* In fact, there is reason to believe that Moscow generally discouraged the rapid absorption by the Communists of the local socialist parties on the sound ground that a premature merger might result in Social Democratic predominance. To the more eager Communists, this might have appeared as excessive caution or, at least, as indicating a certain lack of confidence in their ability to handle the situation.

the Rumanian Communists were able to argue that only they could obtain such Soviet support. "The unhealthy state of Rumanian agriculture, the persistence of extensive cereal cultivation and low level of productivity, the failure of the 1918–1921 land reforms to establish a prosperous peasantry, the persistence of metayage and other semiservitudes, the proletarianization of the poorer peasantry, and the inability of a great number of Rumanian peasants to support themselves on their meager holdings" [18] — all these factors played into the hands of the Communists who decreed an extensive land reform on March 22, 1945, twenty days after the formation of the Groza government.[19] The "war crimes" trials of Rumanian leaders responsible for Rumania's support of the Axis paralyzed the right wing and the officer corps, preventing an anti-Communist coalition with the liberal and peasant groups. By 1946–47 the latter were powerless.

In Hungary the Communists encountered greater difficulty than either in Bulgaria or Rumania, partially because of the strong anti-Russian prejudice of the people and partially because of their greater restraint. The latter was in part due to Hungarian Communist interpretation of postwar Soviet policies. Matyas Rakosi, who had returned to Hungary with the Red Army, was anxious to demonstrate that Communist rule was not incompatible with a democratic system. Another element in the picture might have been the strong impression created on the Hungarian Communists by the failure in 1919 of Bela Kun's Soviet Hungarian Republic, which was in part due to excessive revolutionary zeal. In any case, the Hungarian Party actually experienced a sharp electoral reversal in the relatively free elections held in November 1945, polling only 17 per cent of the vote as opposed to 57 per cent for the Smallholders' (Peasant) Party. In the Hungarian case, the land reform, carried out in the spring of 1945 and affecting about 33 per cent of the arable land — Hungary's prewar agricultural system was the most antiquated in East Europe — actually worked against the Communists by removing rapidly a legitimate grievance. The Hungarian Communists were also severely handicapped by Hungary's territorial losses, blamed by the people on the USSR. This hurt the effort of the Hungarian Communists to pose as protectors of the national interest, which they attempted to do in 1946 by trying to obtain some adjustment of the frontier with Rumania.

The Communist response to this electoral setback was to intensify the terror against "war criminals," broadly interpreting that category, and to sponsor a coalition of the "democratic" parties against the allegedly reactionary Smallholders. A Leftist Bloc was formed, composed of the Communists, the Social Democrats, and the National Peasant Party, the latter comprising rural radicals and the populist writers who had been in the forefront of the anti-Horthy intelligentsia. In 1947, taking advantage of the temporary absence from the country of Ferenc Nagy, the Smallholder Prime Minister, the Communists succeeded in forcing his resignation, and they quickly followed up their advantage by revising the electoral law. In the August 1947 elections, the Leftist Bloc "polled" 60 per cent of the votes, although the Communist share still remained a meager 22 per cent. During this period, nationalization was not actively pushed, and until March 1948 about a quarter of the heavy industry and four fifths of all other industry remained in private hands. In this respect the pattern also varied from that in Poland and more closely resembled the Rumanian example.

Looking at the situation from the perspective of the Polish, Rumanian, Bulgarian, and Hungarian Communists, their goals accordingly had the following priority: (1) creation of an effective political organization, which would contain a hard core of disciplined supporters and an outer rim of allied groups sharing most of the immediate goals even if not the ultimate ends (which were at the time not made explicit); (2) crystallization of a pattern of action designed to undermine the legal opposition usually led by the peasant parties and in Poland tacitly supported by the remnants of the anti-Nazi underground; (3) economic reconstruction on patterns compatible with the political end of consolidating power; (4) social reforms which would be popular and which would weaken the anti-Communist elements; (5) identification of Communism with nationalism through emphasis on popular national issues, typically territorial ones. The cumulative effect of these measures, the Communist leadership probably calculated, would produce a sufficiently profound internal transformation of society to make for a qualitative difference both in the character of the society and in its relations with the USSR.

THE YUGOSLAV AND CZECHOSLOVAK EXTREMES

Czechoslovakia and Yugoslavia are the two countries deviating from the broad pattern of Communist action. In both cases the Communist Party had strong indigenous roots and support, and in both cases it came to power largely on its own, although benefiting from Soviet backing. In Czechoslovakia a variety of factors favored the Communist Party. The republic, modeled on the Western type, suffered a disastrous loss of prestige in 1938, and many of the returned leaders were held to have been responsible for Czechoslovakia's fall to Hitler. Many others had collaborated with the Germans. The country was badly split by an intensified sense of nationalism in Slovakia, fed by the wartime existence of a separate Slovak state. Soviet prestige was high, both because the USSR was not blamed for Munich and because of its wartime role. The Communist Party gained further acceptance by exercising great moderation after 1945. At the same time as it posed as a champion of decentralization, the party was able gradually to consolidate its position on the local level by gaining control of the "people's committees" established in December 1944. A special factor in the postwar Czechoslovak scene was the rapid ouster of the Sudeten Germans, as well as portions of the Magyar minority. This operation, carried out ruthlessly, resulted in a considerable shift in property relations, already badly undermined by German expropriations, killings of Jewish owners, and postwar confiscations. Large-scale nationalization was decreed in October 1945, involving banks, insurance companies, and so on.

The rapid growth of its membership (see the table in Chapter 5) soon made the Communist Party the leading party. It justified its claim to this distinction by polling 38 per cent of the vote in the free elections held in 1946. The party's leader, Klement Gottwald, was then asked by President Benes to accept the premiership. The following year was accordingly marked by the consolidation of the Communist influence, particularly in the police, in the army, and in a workers' militia, set up once control had been gained in the Central Trade Union Council. Although the final take-over did not take place until February 1948, on the eve of the national elections, the Communist grip on the instrumentalities of power was by then sufficiently secure to allow Czechoslovakia to join rapidly the other Communist-ruled states in initiating more radical domestic programs and, in time, even surpassing them.

The events in Yugoslavia followed a much more revolutionary pattern, and during the first postwar years Yugoslavia's Communists outdistanced the other parties in their common march toward socialism. Already in the November 1945 "elections," the Yugoslav voters had been presented with a single slate, and this plebiscite was meant to be merely a formal confirmation of the fact that power was firmly in the hands of the Communist-led partisans of Josip Broz-Tito. His partisan movement, deriving its hard-core leadership from the illegal prewar Communist Party (which early in the twenties was able to obtain some measure of peasant support) and ably capitalizing on Croat-Serb animosities, was able to defeat the Serb nationalist and anti-Communist Chetnik forces of General Draja Mihailovic. Power was firmly in its hands by the war's end. The new Yugoslav constitution of January 1946 was unashamedly patterned on the Soviet constitution of 1936, and the regime pushed forward with a radical socioeconomic program. Between November 1944 and December 1946 a series of decrees transferred to state ownership all industry, as well as banking and other enterprises, while in the fall of 1945 a land reform was carried out. Shortly afterwards, the regime began to lay the groundwork for collectivization.

These patterns of development in the immediate postwar period were thus in keeping with the fivefold syndrome of Soviet interests in the area, suggested briefly at the outset of this background chapter. That these interests were closely interrelated is cogently illustrated by the fate of the Benes government in Czechoslovakia which was not spared from Communist subversion even though Benes' policies satisfied the first two Soviet *desiderata:* he was prepared to consider East Central Europe as falling primarily within the Soviet sphere of influence, and he was determined to be, above all else, a staunch ally of the USSR. As events proved, that was not enough. In the case of Tito, the determination of the Yugoslav leader to pursue a radical domestic policy, accompanied by a certain hesitation in fully subordinating his state to the USSR, was already in 1947 placing strains on an otherwise warm and close relationship.[20]

Elsewhere, the Communist regimes were highly dependent on Soviet support, even while consolidating their power. The worst Soviet abuses, such as the dismantling of industry and other unfavorable economic measures (see Chapter 6 for further detail), at this time took second place to the paramount objective of cementing power. Dependence on Moscow was further heightened by the relative isolation and inexperience of the Communist leaders; violently hostile to the West, which was giving moral support to their domestic enemies, they also frequently vented their traditional national animosities toward one another, with the result that Moscow was their only rallying point and arbiter. Seeking ways and means to power and then to the fulfilment of many years of waiting, many of the Communist leaders, returning after decades of exile — fighting in Spain, waiting and debating in wartime London, or undergoing disciplined service in the USSR — must have felt somewhat out of touch and must have derived a certain sense of comfort from the thought that they were backed by a central leadership, powerful, purposeful, and experienced. Outwardly united against the common enemy, their various origins necessarily created cliques and competition between the "Spanish" veterans, the London intellectuals, the Moscow *apparatchiki*, the graduates of the German concentration camps (the *Kazetniki*), or the domestic hard core which survived the German occupation. But to all of them Moscow was a common frame of reference.

Within this early pattern of development, there was thus both a broad congruence of interests between the local Communists and Moscow and a considerable range of diversity in action. The diversity meant that, within the framework of Soviet interests, the local Communists were able to make adjustments which to some may have been only tactical but which to others represented a more suitable way of building Communism. The Soviet Union acted as a decisive buttress without which they would fail, but it was not yet fully subordinating local interests to its own. At this stage the Soviet policy, which occasionally even restrained the local Communists against excessive zeal (see Chapter 3 for cases of greater Moscow restraint), seemed to be guided by a sound strategic consideration: "the whole task of the Communists is to be able to *convince* the backward elements, to be able to work *among* them, and not to *fence themselves off* from them by artificial and childishly 'Left-wing' slogans." [21] Thus it is clear that even in this early period problems of theory were being related to problems of action.

2 / PROBLEMS OF THEORY

> There is one absolute demand which Marxist theory makes in connection with the analysis of any social problem whatsoever: that is to place it within its *specific* historical framework and then, if the problem concerns one particular country (for example, the national program for that given country), to take account of the concrete particular traits distinguishing that country from others within the framework of the same historical period. — V. I. Lenin

IN 1945 a new political and socioeconomic reality was in the making in East Central Europe. To the Communists, who believe that popular consciousness tends to lag behind changes in material reality and that their strength lies in keeping up with history, and even in outpacing it, the critical questions now were: What are the theoretical implications of the new situation? How does it fit the established categories which guide political action? What practical considerations does it portend? They noted that, thanks to the decisive factor of Soviet power, a series of states were about to rise in which they would have a dominant voice. Yet, for a variety of reasons, these new states could hardly be classified as Soviet Republics, pure and simple, even though to have done so would have simplified the theoretical and political issues a great deal. At the same time, the important role played by the Communists in these new states seemed to suggest some new and distinctive features which required evaluation as a springboard for further Soviet action.

The doctrinal problem facing the Communists was to extract from the existing ideological arsenal of Marxism-Leninism meaningful categories for *analyzing* and *directing* contemporary political dynamics in East Europe. Assuming that the local Communists also tended to think in Marxist categories, their immediate purpose was somehow to provide a program of action which in itself would promote the impending transformation of East Europe into a Communist society but which would also facilitate the short-range tasks at hand. The task of the doctrine was, as always, to crystallize a conceptual framework which would provide an understanding of the existing reality and be a useful guide to action for the Communists actually engaged in shaping that reality.

Stalin and his local Communist associates realized that the very presence of the Red Army (as well as the acquiescence of the West) guaranteed the Communists a major voice in the various governments about to be established. They would participate in restoring the ravaged economies, in healing the wounds inflicted by Nazi brutalities, and in setting up political institutions to direct the process of peacetime recovery. Nonetheless, the local Communists and Moscow realized that the situation was not free from complications. As one might have expected from the Marxist-Leninist doctrine, to set up a series of republics on the Soviet model would have meant coming up against other considerations which a Communist, even if only thinking theoretically, could not ignore. Apart from the uncertain element of Big Power relations and the need to mollify the United States and the United Kingdom, it seemed that in East Europe itself, the situation was still not ripe for the duplication of Soviet experience. The bourgeoisie still had its own political forces; the workers were to some extent under the influence of "right-wing" socialists; the peasantry was controlled by peasant parties openly hostile to the Communists. This resistance would have to be undermined and ultimately crushed, but within the framework of the states which the Communists would now help to construct. The implicit necessity of some kind of transitional phase raised serious problems of theory.[1]

According to well-known Marxist-Leninist doctrines, the collapse of the bourgeois states must lead to the setting up of a dictatorship of the proletariat as a prelude to the transition to socialism. Lenin stated in 1920 that "the dictatorship of the proletariat is the fundamental question of the modern working class movement in all capitalist countries without exception."[2] This view was in keeping with his strong conviction that there was no middle ground between the old forms of the dictatorship of the bourgeoisie — the last state form before the revolution — and the dictatorship of the proletariat. While it is risky to prove a "Leninist" position on the basis of Lenin's chameleonic statements, the following citation is characteristic:

The forms of the bourgeois state are extremely varied, but in essence they are all the same: in one way or another in the last analysis, all these states are inevitably the *dictatorship of the bourgeoisie*. The transition from capitalism to communism will certainly create a great variety and abundance of political forms, but in essence there will inevitably be only one: the dictatorship of the *proletariat*.[3]

Stalin frequently reasserted these tenets, maintaining that the dictatorship of the proletariat had to be created by revolutionary violence and that "to overthrow capitalism it was not only necessary to remove the bourgeoisie from power, it was not only necessary to expropriate the capitalists, but also to smash completely the bourgeois state machinery." [4] Clearly, then, the collapse of the "bourgeois dictatorship" had to involve the violent destruction of its institutions, the expropriation of its dominant class, and the setting up of the proletarian dictatorship. As far as the actual form that the dictatorship of the proletariat was to take, Lenin, and later Stalin, maintained that the Soviet type (based on the 1905, and subsequently 1917, experience) was the most suitable and represented a general norm. "The Soviets are a higher form of democracy, and even more they are the beginning of the socialist form of democracy." [5] In turn, according to Stalin, the political essence of the proletarian dictatorship was the rule of the Communist Party: "it could be said that the dictatorship of the proletariat is in essence the 'dictatorship' of its vanguard, the 'dictatorship' of its party, as the main guiding force of the proletariat." [6]

Earlier revolutionary practice outside the USSR had accordingly been grounded on the assumption that the overthrow of the bourgeois state results in the creation of a dictatorship of the proletariat in the form of a Soviet state. When, shortly after the Bolshevik revolution, the Communists succeeded in seizing power in Hungary and in Bavaria (March and April 1919, respectively), Soviet Republics were proclaimed in both cases, and in Hungary land socialization was immediately attempted. This was also the policy adopted in Slovakia where an abortive Soviet Republic was proclaimed in June 1919, and declared to be a dictatorship of the proletariat. [7] Similar doctrinal rigidity characterized attempted Communist coups in the Baltic state during 1918 and 1919, and during the Polish-Soviet war of 1920 a group of Polish Communists also proclaimed a Polish Soviet Republic. [8] The pattern everywhere was to imitate the October Revolution particularly in terms of doctrinal precepts.

Although the failure of these early endeavors resulted in remarkably little theorizing about the problem during the interwar period,

---

* A somewhat more flexible line was suggested by the Fourth Congress of the Comintern which introduced the following gradations of "real labor governments": (1) a government of workers and poor peasants, such as may develop in the Balkan, Czechoslovakia, and so on; (2) a workers' government with the participation of the Communists; (3) a genuine proletarian workers' government, which in its pure form can be realized only by the Communist Party. *Protokoll des Vierten Kongresses der kommunistischen Internationale* (Hamburg, 1923), p. 1017, as quoted in R. Fischer *Stalin and German Communism* (Cambridge, 1948), p. 213.

it did leave behind a feeling that rigid application of the theory could be harmful in that it failed to take into account the many particular factors varying from country to country.* The post-World War II situation in East Europe certainly appeared to require more elastic concepts than rigid attempts to fit the East European situation into the early Bolshevik categories. In post-1945 East Europe "bourgeois" parties and forces were still strong and were actively participating in coalition governments. Thus the situation differed sharply from that of Russia in 1905 when, in Lenin's view, a "revolutionary democratic dictatorship of workers and peasants" had taken power, not to speak of the seizure of power by the Bolsheviks in 1917. The governments created with the assistance of the Red Army were obviously no longer dictatorships of the bourgeoisie. The important role played in these governments by the Communists and their measures of land reform and nationalization excluded the application of the standard categories of analysis derived from the experience of the bourgeois states. On the other hand, for reasons already suggested, they could not qualify as dictatorships of the proletariat. In some of them, the Communists were clearly minority partners in coalition governments — hardly the dominant role which the party is to play in a true dictatorship of the proletariat — and in all of them, "hostile" political forces were still organized and politically active. To the Communists, the "objective" circumstances, and not just the Yalta and Potsdam agreements which spoke broadly of democratic governments, required a reconsideration of standard formulas, and a "creative" application of Marxism-Leninism to the new and complex environment.

EMERGENCE OF THE PEOPLE'S DEMOCRACY

The concept which seemed to answer this need was that of the People's Democracy. The term was used by Tito in 1945 at the Congress of the Yugoslav Fatherland Front, and in this early period the term "New Democracy," formulated by Mao Tse-tung during the thirties, was also occasionally cited. However, apart from the specific Chinese significance of Mao's concept,[9] in the early forties the Chinese

* The feeling that the early foreign Communists might have been a little too "sectarian" is conveyed by the *ex post facto* Soviet efforts to rewrite the history of the Lithuanian Communists, making them appear somewhat more responsive to the need of gaining popular support. Thus even the name of the revolutionary Lithuanian regime which in 1920 was describing itself as "the Provisional Revolutionary Workers' Government" (*Politika Sovetskoi Vlasti po natsional'nym delam za try goda, 1917–XI–1920*, Moscow, 1920), in 1954 was changed retroactively to "the Provisional Workers'-Peasants' Government of Lithuania" (A. M. Andreev, *Borba Litovskogo Naroda za Sovetskuiu Vlast*, Moscow, 1954) to stress the need for a broad popular base.

Communist Party was virtually unknown to the East Europeans, and it may be assumed that Stalin also did not encourage the East European Communists to borrow Chinese concepts. The term "People's Democracy" thus gained acceptance. It was to serve as a theoretical insight into the existing phase of development and as a policy plank for the various East European Communists and fellow travelers in whose eyes the concept of the Soviet dictatorship of the proletariat was not only theoretically inapplicable but also a political liability. Preoccupation with ideology was clearly linked again with efforts to isolate those elements which would favor the desirable (and hence inevitable) political ends. As a result, and under the benign shield of Stalin's vague remarks about the democratization of East Europe, after 1945 the local Communists provided the impetus for the conceptual development of the People's Democracy as a new form of state organization.

Their new concepts, partially influenced by the wartime alliance between the USSR and the capitalist powers and partially based on observation of domestic processes, stressed the need for a broad democratic front, including the progressive bourgeoisie. This was not only for the earlier purpose of defeating Nazi Germany but also for the construction of new democratic states in which power would be shared with the Communists. As early as the fall of 1941, this was the consensus reached by the surviving Polish Communists in the USSR (Stalin had most of them shot in 1938) in the course of lengthy discussions with Georgi Dimitrov, the Comintern head.[10] As a result, and given the factors of the postwar East European situation as they saw it, the leaders of the local Communist parties were forced to conclude that the hitherto universally valid concept of the dictatorship of the proletariat was inapplicable to the new state forms. Gomulka, the Secretary of the Polish Workers' Party, asserted explicitly in November 1946 that the Polish People's Democracy was not a dictatorship of the proletariat and that Poland would reach socialism by avoiding it altogether. "Our democracy is also not similar to Soviet democracy, just as our social system is not similar to the Soviet system," Gomulka explained.[11] It followed logically from this that the Soviet type of state also could not be applied in the new East European context. This point was repeatedly stressed by some of the most prominent Communist leaders, with long Moscow associations. Bierut, the Communist President of Poland, asserted in June 1946 that "this specific order is not based on any existing model. It is not similar to the Soviet socialist order or to the classical economic system of the West."[12]

Dimitrov, speaking in Sofia three months later, was even more direct:

Bulgaria will not be a Soviet republic but a people's republic in which the functions of government will be performed by an enormous majority of the people — workers, peasants, craftsmen, and the people's intelligentsia. In this republic there will be no dictatorship of any kind.[13]

Furthermore, the origins of the People's Democracy were not to be traced to the revolutionary consequences of a domestic upheaval, fitting the classical Marxist-Leninist concepts of intensified class conflict leading ultimately to a revolution. It was, first of all, the direct consequence of the presence of the Soviet Army. Thus Gomulka, while stressing that the changes which were occurring in East Europe had "the character of deep revolutionary transformation," acknowledged that they had been effected without a revolution because of the presence of the Red Army, in the face of which "the forces of reaction were inhibited and paralyzed in their activity." [14] Second, the revolutionary processes produced by the dislocations of war and by the presence of the Red forces were still not a true socialist revolution, but rather a "national democratic" one, as the Communists were fond of calling it. The idea of a socialist revolution was not mentioned, and Gottwald, in a confidential speech in May 1945 outlining party tactics to Communist functionaries, warned: "We must continually remind ourselves that in the present phase we are following the line of the national and democratic . . . and not the line of the socialist revolution." [15]

Leninist strictures notwithstanding, the conclusion that the People's Democracy was something entirely new under the sun seemed inescapable. It was no longer the classical oppressive bourgeois state; yet it was not therefore its antithesis, the dictatorship of the proletariat. What was it then? Bierut gave a rather lame explanation: "the People's Democracy is a special form of revolutionary authority which came into being under new relations among classes in the international arena." [16] The very vagueness of the statement is mute testimony to the ideological embarrassment which this old Comintern *apparatchik* must have felt. "A special form of revolutionary authority" does not tell much about such simple issues as whether a state has ceased to be a bourgeois state and is now a proletarian one, or in whose hands the power rests. The issue was stated in a more precise, but also more extreme, fashion by a member of the Hungarian Central Committee. Martin Horvath asserted that "in view of the fact that a People's Democracy does not destroy the right to own the means of production, it can simply be regarded as the most progressive form of bourgeois democracy (or, to put it more correctly, its only progressive form)." *

Unlike the orthodox view of the dictatorship of the proletariat, in which its vanguard wields the effective power, the political power of the People's Democracy was to be shared in a formal sense by national coalitions and in the real sense (if we may use these distinctions of Marx) by an alliance of the working and peasant classes, but with neither exercising a hegemony. The reason, of course, was that in a People's Democracy the former exploiting classes, while no longer enjoying a monopoly on power and gradually losing it altogether, still continued to exist. "In the state of People's Democracy there still exist classes which live by exploiting the work of others; these are the capitalists — various entrepreneurs, well-to-do merchants, factory owners employing a certain number of workers, rich peasants, speculators and other non-workers," explained Bierut.[17] Power is wielded by a broad coalition of the working class, the peasantry, the middle strata of the urban population, the working intelligentsia and a portion of the bourgeoisie,[18] all of whom are said to be opposed by the remnants of reaction. Under these circumstances the usual Leninist concept of a unified, single-class state authority was both theoretically and practically inapplicable.† "There is nothing more false than accusing the Polish Workers' Party of mono-party tendencies, of the desire to subordinate other democratic parties," Gomulka was frequently assuring the Poles,[19] even adding that "an evolutionary way of social change and an evolutionary transition to a socialist order is entirely possible."[20] A further and consequent tenet in this line of reasoning was the assertion that domestic violence was unnecessary and that it might be

---

* *Tarsadalni — andomanyi szemle*, October 1948 (Kardelj, *On People's Democracy in Yugoslavia*, p. 8; Kardelj distorted the spelling of the publication. The correct version was *tarsadalomtudomanyi szemle*). In this state, private property was to enjoy the benevolent protection of the authorities of the People's Democracy. For instance, Dimitrov: "Bulgaria will be a People's Republic in which private property acquired by labor will be protected by the state authorities." (Chervenkov, as cited in note 12.) Bierut was almost whimsical on the subject of free enterprise; stressing the newness of the People's Democracy, he attributed it to the "specific harmony of the two factors; on the one side the leading role of the state . . . on the other side, the spirit of enterprise, the energy and free initiative of the mass of independent entrepreneurs" (speech in Cracow, June 1946).

† This was explicitly stated by Joseph Revai, one of the leading "ideologues" of the Hungarian party. Cf. his speech quoted in the *Information Bulletin of the Central Committee of the Hungarian Party*, no. 8, 1948. Revai has always been identified as one of the staunchest Stalinists in the committee, and after the October 1956 events he led the struggle for the most severe condemnation of Nagy and Lukacs.

possible to avoid it because of the overwhelming power of Soviet support. Stalin's notions about the intensification of class struggle after the seizure of power were discreetly not mentioned.

The crux of this type of evaluation was the frequent insistence of the local Communists that in every situation Marxian policy had to be shaped in accordance with the specific circumstances. These circumstances varied from country to country in 1945, and they certainly also differed from those encountered by the Bolsheviks after the 1917 Revolution. No wonder then that many local Communists stressed the specific character of their individual countries. Rakosi, who was to become the scourge of the "national Communists" during the anti-Tito phase, expressed this rather well:

> During the last 25 years the Communist Parties of the world learned that there are several roads which lead to Socialism and accordingly we cannot build Socialism if we do not build our own road, taking into account the special conditions prevailing in the country. We have learned that lesson, and, while we are strengthening the Hungarian democracy, we are not doing this because of tactical reasons or in order to achieve some secret aim, but because of our deep Communist convictions, and we will do whatever we can to fill the frame of the democracy with the largest possible Socialist content. That will speed up the progress which leads mankind into Socialism. We also know that, although Socialism utilizes a multitude of international experiences, our Socialism can be created only as a result of the development of Hungarian history and Hungarian economic, political and social forces. That will be Socialism born on Hungarian soil and adapted to Hungarian conditions.[21]

Quotations to this effect could be cited for Gomulka, Gottwald, and many others.

One must note, however, that a clear-cut, theoretical, and well-reasoned analysis of the People's Democracy, made within the context of Marxian ideology, was not elucidated systematically by the East European Communist leaders. It may well have been that most of them were not, trained as they were in the Stalinist Comintern or in local undergrounds, theoretically equipped or so inclined. In addition to this, they were faced with the many daily tasks inherent in the unfolding struggle for power and could hardly be expected to devote themselves to a serious formulation of an admittedly ticklish subject. Finally, they probably preferred to leave the field of theory, with all its dangerous quicksands, to their Soviet senior colleagues and limit themselves to mere elaborations of formulas shaped in Moscow.

During this initial period, the Soviet leaders themselves also refrained from making any definitive programmatic statements. Stalin's assertions were rather vague and stressed such broad considerations as "democracy," "democratic governments friendly to the Soviet Union," and the like. It was only in the latter part of 1947 (to be dealt with subsequently) that Soviet leaders made public *ex cathedra* pronouncements.* Soviet scholars, however, were less reticent, and it is to them that we owe a more systematic treatment of the theoretical problem presented by the People's Democracy. It may be safely assumed that their reflections corresponded to the broad lines of analysis of the top Soviet leadership and that it was not mere intellectual curiosity that prompted their preoccupation with the subject. It was probably from them, as well as from the informal channels of party communications, that the East European Communists drew their ideological inspiration. Consistency in broad outlook was hence properly maintained.

The view of the Soviet scholars, as developed between 1945 and 1947,[22] may be briefly summarized as follows: The People's Democracy was not to be confused with a proletarian democracy, the latter being essentially "identical with the dictatorship of the proletariat which does not share its power with any other class." [23] This could hardly be the case in Eastern Europe where the class rule of the proletariat was, at best, incipient,† and where the other classes were still economically and politically active. A true Marxist had to conclude,

* In what appears to this writer to be an accurate statement for all the East European parties, Joseph Revai, writing in 1949 about this early period in reference to Hungary, stated: "The Party didn't possess a unified, clarified, elaborated attitude in respect to the character of the People's Democracy and its future development." He also implied that Stalin was not very helpful before the autumn of 1947. "The Character of a 'People's Democracy,'" as translated in *Foreign Affairs* (October 1949), p. 147. See also Chapter 4 for further discussion.

† There seems to have been some disagreement among Soviet scholars on the degree of class rule of the proletariat already in existence. Varga, as cited in note 21, p. 13, spoke vaguely of "the political rule of the toilers," while Trainin (note 21) was inclined to claim that the political hegemony of the proletariat was already operative, although in a somewhat different form than in a Soviet type of state. "The hegemony of the proletariat is expressed in the fact that the proletariat, in the shape of its vanguard — the Communist Party — tends toward finding solutions for these tasks not through the strengthening of capitalism, but through the gradual consolidation of the principles of real democracy, which correspond to the interests of the working class and all working people, that is, the overwhelming majority of the people" (p. 3). Trainin's views were backed by A. Schaff, a leading Polish Marxist theoretician. In his book, *Wstep do teorii marksizmu* (Warsaw, 1948), Schaff maintained that Poland, while not a dictatorship of the proletariat, already was under the hegemony of the proletariat for reasons outlined by Trainin.

therefore, that the existing order was neither bourgeois nor socialist, although the proletariat was able to influence sufficiently the political organization of society to ensure that a "real democracy" was realized. The theoretical journal of the Communist Party of the Soviet Union (CPSU) accordingly held that:

There have arisen in these countries new, higher forms of democracy as compared to the old, bourgeois-parliamentarian democracy. These countries have so developed and expanded democracy as to signify the participation of workers and peasants in the state administration and make the benefits of democracy accessible to the broadest masses. Thus new forms of state polity have been created which are a big step forward in comparison with the bourgeois democratic states and which offer possibilities for further progress by these countries in the economic and political fields.[24]

These new People's Democracies, insofar as their administrative structures were concerned, were to be a hybrid between the forms of the old bourgeois state (presumably with its instruments of class oppression) and the forms of the socialist state as created by the USSR. Academician Eugene Varga, for instance, explicitly stated that the old state had not been demolished in its entirety, but that some of its institutions were being creatively reshaped, through the infusion of new class content, to fit the existing requirements. In an actual institutional sense, the constitutional picture of East Europe was at this time remarkably diversified. Two of the states, Rumania and Bulgaria, were still monarchies. The Bulgarian and Rumanian constitutional structures were not changed, although by 1946 the Communists began to agitate against the "antiquated" constitutions, demanding particularly that a national system of people's councils be established to "democratize" the state. Nonetheless, it was not until after the creation of the Cominform that the old forms gave way to new constitutions. In Hungary, where a provisional government was set up after the expulsion of the Germans, a new constitution was proclaimed on January 31, 1946, and Hungary became a republic. The constitution provided for a President, somewhat on the Western model, and a parliamentary form of government.[25] In Czechoslovakia and Poland the prewar constitutions were essentially retained, although in Czechoslovakia a provisional national assembly was to prepare the groundwork for a constituent assembly which would draft a new constitution. This undermined Benes' claim of legitimacy, replacing it with a "revolutionary conception" of legality.[26] In Poland, the 1935 constitution was ignored, and the government was said to base itself on the 1921 constitution framed on the French model. Only in Yugoslavia and Albania were truly new constitutions adopted.

Varga could thus maintain that in the People's Democracies "the old state apparatus is not destroyed, as was the case in the Soviet Union, but is being renovated with the steady absorption of the followers of the new regime. Those are not capitalist states in the ordinary meaning of the word. But neither are they socialist states. Their development in the direction of Socialism is based on the nationalization of the chief means of production and on the very character of those states." [27] Eventually, it was stated, the capitalist sector was to disappear, but at the same time it could not avoid having some temporary effects on the political scene. Hence, the presence of bourgeois parties associated in the government through coalitions or through national fronts was explained. The specific degrees of adjustment between the socialist and capitalist sectors depended, of course, on the specifics of each country's situation. In brief, what the Soviet theorists were suggesting was a form of permanent revolution in which the transitional phase developed a distinct institutional identity. But if this was the case, then the Communists had to ask in turn: what are to be the relations of this new type of state with the only true socialist state, the USSR?

RELATIONS WITH THE USSR

From the standpoint of international politics, the postwar relationship of East Europe to the USSR was defined in a number of documents usually identified by the name of the location in which each had been signed. The Teheran, Yalta, Potsdam agreements, in one way or another, all expressed the view that postwar East Europe was to be governed by regimes "democratic and friendly" to the USSR. These broad statements of purpose never clearly defined what the link between the two norms (democratic and friendly) was: whether both were of equal importance or whether one was to serve as a basis for the other. Yet it should have been clear that one of the basic assumptions of Marxists, who think in dichotomic terms,[28] was that there exists a basic hostility between capitalists and socialist states. We may therefore conclude that if East Europe was to develop along the lines of "bourgeois democracy" (which Churchill and Roosevelt presumably had in mind), there could be no question that, in the Russian view, its relations with the USSR would have to be fundamentally hostile, even if some form of coexistence were possible. East Europe could be truly friendly to the USSR only if some significant *internal* transformation were to occur, lifting East Europe out of the "bourgeois democratic" orbit, which, as Lenin stressed, was essentially identical with the dictatorship of the bourgeoisie. The People's Democracy was such a transformation. This put the question of relations on an entirely different plane.

Thus, the problem of relations between the People's Democracy and the USSR could be approached from the standpoint of relations between states which were not mutually antagonistic by their very definition. The task of defining the relationship was at least free of this particular complication. However, a major political liability encumbering the Communists in East Europe was the widespread popular belief that their ultimate objective was the incorporation of the area into Russia. This prospect was loathsome to practically all East Europeans, from the conservative to the most progressive, and charges of this type could be supported by documented precedents. The fate of the Baltic republics, once they embarked on the road of "socialist construction," was one striking case in point. The left-socialist faction in Poland, which originally founded the Polish Communist Party, had split away from the Polish Socialist Party (PPS) precisely on that issue: it did not wish to identify itself with the cause of Polish nationalism. This was the case elsewhere in East Europe.[29] The Communists during the war and immediately afterwards had to labor against this apprehension.

There is no doubt that in the past East European Communists had taken a violent stand against nationalism, which they identified with bourgeois rule. They tended to emphasize their international character and their contempt for national traditions and habits. Nonetheless, a careful reading of Lenin and other Bolsheviks[30] reveals that their approach to problems of nationalism and of international relations was purely a *tactical* one, based on certain more general theoretical assumptions. It seems clear that Lenin and others condemned nationalism as one of the many subterfuges designed to obscure the development of class consciousness, to obliterate the international sense of solidarity of the proletariat rooted in its common relationship to the means of production. Thus it was the task of the Communist to struggle against nationalistic feelings — to remove this smoke screen obscuring the vision of the working class. Ideally, a socialist society would be composed of many nationalities living side by side without national animosities.

However, Lenin and others stressed that the attitude of the Communist toward nationalist feelings had to be derived in every case from a proper appreciation of the major factors involved. The setting up of Communist rule, after all, was not an end in itself but only a means to the final end. Therefore, a Communist, while being very careful not to subordinate his class ends to a temporary nationalist zeal, also had to consider the depth of the nationalist feelings in society lest he lose touch with the situation. He always had to bear in mind Marx's warning: "We know that we must reckon with the institutions, the customs and traditions of various individual countries." [31] Lenin elaborated this into a clear principle in his "First Draft Theses Concerning the National and Colonial Question," addressed to the Second Comintern Congress (1920):

The more undeveloped a given country is, the stronger also are its small agriculturists, its patriarchical sentiments, and its backwardness — all of which inevitably give particular strength and tenacity to the most profound small bourgeois prejudices, i.e., the prejudices of national egotism, national narrowmindedness. Since these prejudices can only disappear after the disappearance of imperialism and capitalism in advanced countries and after a radical change of the entire basis of economic life in backward countries, the extinction of these prejudices cannot but be very slow. Therefore the duty of fully conscious communist proletarians of all countries is *to handle with particular caution* and particular attention the remnants of these nationalist sentiments in the case of the countries and nationalities which have been oppressed longest; likewise their duty is *to make certain concessions* for the sake of the quickest possible extinction of these feelings of mistrust and these prejudices. [32]

It follows that an important corollary of this principle was the insistence on the right of secession and self-determination. These rights, again, were still only relative. The idea was that the very granting of the right would take the sting out of much of the nationalist appeal and would thereby permit the workingman to attend to his true interest. As long as the bourgeoisie was able to claim that its dominance was required by some national cause, such as liberation or expansion, the tasks of the social revolution would be delayed.* The Communists were accordingly justified in supporting national emancipation of oppressed nations, thereby linking even the processes of national liberation with social revolution under certain conditions. The long-run objective, of course, did not change, and in each case the question

---

* "Just as mankind can achieve the abolition of classes only by passing through the transition period of the dictatorship of the oppressed class, so mankind can achieve the inevitable merging of nations only by passing through the transition period of complete liberation of all the oppressed nations, i.e., their freedom to secede." Lenin, "Right of Nations to Self-Determination," *Selected Works* (New York, 1943), V, 271

of self-determination, or secession in the case of a multinational state, had to be resolved in terms "of social progress as a whole and the interests of the class struggle of the proletariat for socialism." [33]

In the case of Russia, the Communists felt justified in insisting that the unity of the state be preserved, albeit in federal form. The problem of nationalism, they felt, was solved by granting the right of secession. But to attempt to exercise it in the Russian context was to go against history. "There are instances," Stalin explained, "when the right to self-determination comes into conflict with another higher right, the right of the working class which attained power to fortify its power. In such cases, it must be stated frankly, the right of self-determination cannot be and must not serve as an obstacle to the realization of the right of the working class to its own dictatorship. The first must recede before the second." [34] The Bolshevik leaders also felt that the Russian federation had shown itself to be a desirable form of expressing relations among socialist states, since presumably in the future they would all have the same institutional form: the dictatorship of the proletariat. However, at best this was the eventual prospect, and in the more immediate future it could be expected that some states might wish to preserve their complete independence. Stalin, in commenting to Lenin on the latter's "Draft Theses," emphasized that a major distinction must be made between nations and nationalities which had been part of the Russian Empire, for which "our own (Soviet) type of federation can and must be considered a suitable way toward international unification," and nations with long traditions of separate statehood. The latter, even if already under Soviet-modeled institutions would, Stalin thought, prefer to maintain their distinct identity, and it would be erroneous to fit them into some federal mold.[35] Communists would have to accept the idea that separate statehood for these states was desirable for the time being.* For this reason separate national Communist parties would have to be maintained, although the Soviet leaders were quick to assert that it was the task of every national party to strive for Communism by giving continuous support to the Soviet state. They categorically rejected any suggestions that there could be a conflict of interest between a national party and the Soviet party and its state.†

---

* The long-range goal remained, in the words of the Second Comintern Congress, a "World Federation of Soviet Republics." *Kommunisticheskii Internatsional v Dokumentakh, 1919–1932* (Moscow, 1933), p. 88.

† A suggestion to this effect had been made in the German Communist Party paper, *Roter Kurier*, early in 1924 and most violently condemned in a letter from Comintern head Zinoviev. Fischer, *Stalin and German Communism*, p. 395.

In East Europe, as noted already, nationalism was very intense as a result of the war. To ignore nationalism would have been to hand it to the bourgeoisie, who could exploit it for their own class interests. In keeping with Bolshevik notions, to enflame nationalist feelings was a prelude to true internationalism. The brighter the flames of nationalism, the sooner they would burn out. Accordingly, the local Communists thoroughly identified themselves with nationalism. Such identification to them did not involve either an ideological zig-zag or a theoretical capitulation. It was, instead, a sensible adjustment to the requirements of the situation, quite compatible with basic doctrinal assumptions. Local Communists became the most vociferous spokesmen for national interests. They took every opportunity to wave the flag (and it was rarely the Red one), to associate themselves with any cause enjoying nationalist appeal. Talk of any union with the USSR was condemned as bourgeois slander. The founding declaration of the Polish Workers' (Communist) Party reads almost like a nationalist harangue.[36] The reconstruction and maintenance of independent statehood was one of the chief planks in all Communist programs in East Europe. The new states were to be sovereign — not Soviet. Their relations with the USSR were to be, naturally, "friendly" but founded on mutual recognition of the principles of independence and noninterference in internal affairs.

The Soviets, for their part, also felt compelled to adjust not only to their own international commitments but also to the problems faced by their local agents in East Europe. Moscow's role was to make the process of acquisition of power within the existing framework easier, not through direct help alone but also by assuming the proper ideological stance. In the spirit of Lenin's injunction (quoted at the beginning of this chapter), Stalin was fond of repeating his dedication to the task of reconstructing independent states in East Europe and frequently asserted that the Soviet Union would pursue a policy of friendship and alliance toward them. This friendship was said to be possible due to the internal transformations in process. Federation, or even a confederation (which in 1920 had been considered as an eventual alternative), was not mentioned. Formal ties along traditional lines were established between the USSR and some People's Democracies: state treaties of friendship and alliance on the basis of equality between the cosignatories (see Chapter 6). But beyond this formal equality, a convenient theoretical element of historical inequality was implied in the very definition of a People's Democracy. Since the People's Democracy was only at the threshold of socialist development, the more advanced USSR implicitly enjoyed the position of a guide, even if roads to socialism varied. Thus, within the essential meaning of People's Democracy and the formal nature of official links with the USSR, the seeds of future ideological subordination were planted.

THE DISSIDENTS

In the immediate postwar period, which saw both the theoretical and the practical birth of the People's Democracy, all the local Communists save one group labored under the major handicap of having been brought in on the coattails of the Red Army. Many of the theoretical problems inherent in the attempts to define the People's Democracy were due to the fact that the acquisition of power did not quite fit the ideal notions of a genuine proletarian revolution. Difficulties of interpretation were maximized by the international commitments of the USSR and by the presence of domestic forces capable of offering the Communists at least a temporary challenge.

In one country, Yugoslavia, the situation differed radically. The Yugoslav Communist Party, proudly bearing that name and scoffing at those who hid themselves under the euphemistic label of workers' party, had won power through its own resources, though aided in the last stages of the war by the entrance of the Red Army. In the course of their partisan activities the Yugoslav Communists had crushed the bourgeoisie and had thus effected what they considered to be a revolution not unlike the Bolshevik Revolution of 1917. In the words of Kardelj: "In view of the fact that our Revolution began to develop in the conditions of the National Liberation War, in its first phase it possessed the form of a People's Democracy, but, in view of its class forces and the internal relationship of these forces, it could in fact only be a Socialist revolution." [37]

There was no reason, therefore, to think that the power wielded by the Yugoslav Communist Party differed in its essentials from the dictatorship of the proletariat as set up in Petrograd some twenty-eight years earlier. Though willing to adopt the label of a People's Democracy, the Yugoslavs asserted that this was merely another form of the dictatorship of the proletariat and very much similar to the Soviet type of republic. The Yugoslav constitution of January 1946 and the Albanian constitution, passed a month and a half later, explicitly broke with the "bourgeois-democratic" forms of state organization, proclaimed the states to be People's Democracies, and unabashedly copied the Soviet constitution of 1936. [38] By adopting a constitution markedly like the Soviet, Tito again rejected the more moderate practices of his Communist neighbors and underlined the fact that the old state had been destroyed in substance and in form. This was another way of expressing what the Yugoslavs felt other East European comrades were neglecting to assert — that the People's Democracy did not differ in essentials from the Soviet system. Even after Tito's expulsion from the Cominform in 1948, the Yugoslavs heaped scorn on their East European colleagues for the latter's efforts to define the People's Democracy as some new type of state.

Speaking after the 1948 break to the People's Assembly, Kardelj made the following modest claims:

We owe the victory of our People's Revolution precisely to the fact that we nurtured no illusions as to the "new paths in principle" which lead to Socialism. We were the only ones to set out this attitude clearly at the first session of the Informbureau. Contrary to it, the leaders of the Communist Parties of the other People's Democracies constantly made some kind of "discoveries" about their own — in principle — "new path" to Socialism, about various "specific harmonies" between socialist and capitalist elements, and about the especial worth of some vestiges of bourgeois democracy, which they glorified as a singular aspect of a People's Democracy. And all of them were unendingly claiming patents for these "discoveries" of theirs. Then the Soviet professors repeated these phrases in countless variations. That is why the Soviet press always gave more prominence to various opportunistic absurdities from the other People's Democracies than to facts about the new Yugoslavia, *which stood far ahead of the others*. And we, who contended that we had won our Socialist revolution, *that our People's Democracy was of the Soviet type*, we were told that we were narrowminded sectarians and entirely incapable of inventing something new, despite the fact that practically everything that is really new in the present People's Democracy had been created in our country.[39]

The Yugoslav argument was based on Marx's discussion of the transitional period (in his "Critique of the Gotha Programme") during which some remnants of the capitalist era would persist, although eventually giving way to the socialist order. It was the dictatorship of the proletariat which politically expressed this transition. Hence, the Yugoslavs reasoned, the People's Democracies could not be anything but a dictatorship of the proletariat — as developed in Russia in 1917 and in Yugoslavia in 1945, and as should be the case in East Europe also. In the strictest sense, they were probably right but their perspective was rather provincial. Viewing the area through the prism of their own experience they could not help but be somewhat contemptuous of their comrades elsewhere, who were organizing coalitions, talking about a new type of democracy, stressing distinctive patterns of development, even playing court to kings and attempting to stage elections. Impatient and somewhat doctrinaire, the Yugoslavs at this stage were ideologically more Stalinist than Stalin.

The Yugoslav thinking on the nature of their state naturally impinged on the problem of interstate relations within the Soviet bloc. Like their colleagues elsewhere in East Europe, the Yugoslavs endorsed nationalist sentiments and gave free vent to their sense of national pride. They felt justified in doing this because of their wartime struggles and successes. In fact, they most likely felt that their subjective sentiments were in keeping with the objective requirements of the moment. Yugoslavia, like the rest, had to go through the nationalist phase, and Yugoslav Communists, unlike the rest, were fully justified in enjoying the fruits of national pride. However, they never lost sight of the fact that this was to be only a temporary phase. And since Yugoslavia was already a dictatorship of the proletariat, ultimate socialist unity was not as distant as assumed by those who made "erroneous" assertions about the uniqueness of the People's Democracy. If we are to trust the June 5, 1945, dispatches of the Soviet Minister in Belgrade, and they seem to be in keeping with the general tenor of the prevailing Yugoslav thinking, Kardelj considered himself and Tito to be leaders *conscious* of the course that history had to take, their national pride notwithstanding. In the Soviet Minister's words:

We would like, continued Kardelj, the Soviet Union to look at us as representatives of one of the future Soviet Republics, and not as upon representatives of another country, capable of independently solving questions . . . [They] consider the Communist Party of Yugoslavia as being a part of the All-Union Communist Party, that is to say, that our relationship . . . [should emphasize] that Yugoslavia in the future would be admitted a constituent part of the USSR. Therefore they would like us to criticize them directly and openly, and to give them advice in what way to conduct the home and foreign policy of Yugoslavia in the right direction.*

But even though the Yugoslavs deviated by overinsistence on

* *The Correspondence between the Central Committee of the CPJ and the Central Committee of the AUCP(b)* (Belgrade), p. 49. Stalin and Molotov, in their May 1948 correspondence with Tito, gleefully branded these views as "primitive and incorrect." They certainly raised a point on which the Yugoslavs were particularly touchy but which, in terms of dialectical thinking, had not been incorrectly put. Nonetheless, by 1948 Kardelj's early views seemed somehow strangely romantic, naive, and provincial.

orthodoxy, they were not, initially at least, viewed as harmful. They represented a higher stage of development to which the other parties could ultimately aspire. Stalin paid special tributes to Tito, and Yugoslav Communists were even convinced that Tito would succeed Stalin as the leader of the international Communist movement. In the meantime, the responsibility of Communists everywhere in East Europe was to obtain and consolidate a firm grip on power. Since the reigning doctrine stressed a form of harmonious diversity, the occasional Yugoslav outbursts of super-loyalty could be viewed with that benign tolerance which is occasionally granted to a precocious child. It was only when these views began to develop a political import of their own — that is, when they began to affect broader problems of power outside Yugoslavia and to imply theoretical equality with the USSR — that the need arose for Moscow to cope with them. For the time being, however, the People's Democracy was an adequate theoretical reply to the questions asked by local Communists; it was a guide to action sufficiently doctrinaire to maintain over-all unity of purpose and elastic enough to deal with the existing diversity.

3 / PROBLEMS OF DIVERSITY

THE Soviet leadership, surveying the East European scene in 1947, had some cause for gratification. In all the capitals, including even Czechoslovakia's, the most powerful offices of state were occupied by Communists. Democratic forces were everywhere either defeated or very much on the defensive. Internal changes in East European societies were undermining the remaining "hostile class elements," most of which had already been deprived of effective political power. The Western states were implicitly accepting Soviet hegemony over the area, despite occasional verbal outbursts. The Soviet leadership, viewing American disinterest and Anglo-French impotence, could gaze serenely on its new dominions.

The institutional and ideological diversity which characterized the Communist world at this time was the natural outcome of the complex and fluctuating postwar conditions. In 1945 the Soviet leadership could not be certain what limits the West would attempt to set on Communist control and at what point the West might possibly react to excessive and rapid Sovietization of the area. It was not yet clear how strong the anti-Communist forces in the area were. Furthermore, at that time it looked as if revolutionary situations might develop further west. The task of the Communists, therefore, was to act so as not to activate their enemies by excessively peremptory measures. This was the time for caution, for elasticity, for camouflage. By 1947, however, even if the potentially revolutionary prospects in the West were not unfolding quite as rapidly as desired, the stabilization of Soviet control in East Europe was moving apace, and the uncertainties of the initial picture were beginning to give way to a clearer image of the postwar phase of development. A reassessment of this phase was becoming necessary.

THE SOVIET SCENE

Soviet internal developments undoubtedly had something to do with the need for reassessment. In the Soviet Union itself the political aftereffects of the war — the blurring of clear-cut political and ideological lines — had also resulted in a measure of theoretical and insti-

41

tutional diversity. This diversity had been tolerated as a concomitant of the peculiar historical phase in which the USSR had found itself. Some expressions of this phase were purposely tolerated for the sake of the immediate goal of winning the war. Others had sprung up by themselves, as a spontaneous outgrowth of the USSR's engagement in a total conflict. The most serious of these was the decline in party zeal, the lowering of party morale, and the relaxation of the tight organizational bonds so necessary to the efficient operations of a ruling totalitarian party. The war produced a tremendous turnover in party membership — with many hundreds of thousands admitted each year, and almost as many dying each year on the battlefield. The exigencies of an obvious emergency situation meant that normal procedures of training, indoctrination, and discipline had to be suspended. Party membership for quite a few ceased to be a privilege and became mere routine. The consequence was that the CPSU emerged from the war with an organization badly in need of reform and very much in need of new political fervor.

The impact of the war on the party produced another consequence of vital significance to the leadership. The very same factors which undermined the qualities that the Communist leadership considers so central led to the appearance of the army on the Soviet political scene. The army emerged from the war considerably more powerful than it had been at the beginning. While the CPSU went into the war in 1941 with a more disciplined membership, with every indication of being the central organ of the Soviet system, and emerged with these qualities somewhat blurred, just the opposite happened with the army. It went into the war disgraced by the Finnish defeats, still licking its wounds from the great purges, even having to reach into the concentration camps to replenish its depleted command staffs; it emerged blazoned with glory, with a powerful fighting machine, with decorated marshals — the victors of Stalingrad, Budapest, and Berlin. In a May 1 photograph they were shown surrounding their generalissimo, thereby almost symbolizing new domestic realities.

It would be misleading, however, to exaggerate the significance of this development. Despite a certain measure of degeneration, the party still remained the key political instrument and, above all else, its leadership was still the leadership of the country, controlling the secret police. The latter's power was enhanced by the wartime pressures for internal security and the responsibilities of coping with enemies in the occupied countries. The army lacked a political purpose, a "political sense," and a politically oriented leadership. It did not therefore constitute a purposeful challenge to the party's supremacy. It did, however, create strains by its very presence and popularity. It was to these problems that the party leadership had to turn its attention in the immediate postwar period, and it resolved them by downgrading the military and by revitalizing the party.

The symbolic gesture indicating that the role of the military would differ in peacetime was the removal in March 1946 of Marshal Georgi Zhukov from his prominent position in Berlin and his reassignment to an obscure command post. Politically even more significant to those "in the know" in the Soviet political system, though not at the time a matter of public record, was Zhukov's removal in the same year from the party's Central Committee. At the same time, organizational measures were taken in the military forces to activate political controls and party indoctrination.[1]

Insofar as the party machinery and ideology were concerned, the measures adopted involved, first of all, a far-reaching, though unheralded, membership purge in the territories recovered from German occupation. For the upper echelons of the party, and also of the state administration, a resolution of the Central Committee (of August 2, 1946) envisaged a thorough reorganization of the training and indoctrination programs under the direction of the Higher Party School and the Academy of Social Sciences, attached directly to the Central Committee. Similar institutes were to be established on the lower organizational levels.[2] In the realm of ideological concerns the party cracked down on certain publications accused of pursuing a "nonideological, apolitical line." This was followed by similar measures with respect to the theatrical world.[3]

A return to more orthodox patterns also took place in the agricultural sector of the national economy. The war had resulted in the destruction of the collective farm system in the German-occupied parts of the USSR, and this had aroused widespread hope in many peasants that collectivization would not be rigorously applied and might even be given up altogether. In the parts of the Soviet Union not reached by the Germans, the collective farm system operated during the war in a somewhat more relaxed fashion. Possibly due to the weakness of party controls and discipline, to the desire of the regime to obtain the maximum of foodstuffs from the peasants, and possibly also due to the premeditated effort to cultivate the good will of the populace, the Draconic application of existing agricultural regulations gave way to a semiofficial policy of ignoring the growing expansion of private plots and private herds, clearly at the expense of the collective sector. But on September 19, 1946, the Soviet peasant population learned that socialist construction in the countryside was to continue and that the regime would insist on strict adherence to its programmatic goals.[4] This, together with the measures to revitalize the rural party organizations, marked the return of totalitarian conformity to the Soviet countryside.

By late 1946 and early 1947 the process of coping with the internal relaxation which had developed in the USSR during the war was well under way. The outside world was also beginning to emerge in sharper focus. Major revolutionary upheavals in Greece had been suppressed as early as 1945, although a renewed attempt was made on the fringes of the Greek mountain ranges in 1946-1947. In Italy and France the non-Communist forces had consolidated their position, and the Communist partisans had been disarmed. In May 1946, De Gaulle scored a major electoral victory in France on the constitutional issue and it was becoming apparent that a seizure of power by the French Communist Party through pseudo-legal means was no longer feasible.

The crystallization of Soviet thinking about the nature of the postwar phase probably occurred in this period.* The peaceful, and indeed friendly, coexistence which had been the recurring theme of Soviet declarations in 1945 began to give way to more and more explicit assertions of the fundamental difference between Soviet socialism and the capitalist world. Stalin himself signaled the shift in Supreme Soviet campaign speech in February 1946. Forcefully, he extolled the superiorities of the Soviet system and contrasted it with the capitalistic world torn by internal contradictions. Thereafter the Soviet press directed a steadily intensifying campaign against the West. From the Soviet point of view, Churchill's speech in Fulton, Missouri, in March 1946, calling for an Anglo-American alliance in view of Soviet violations of the Yalta Agreement and continued Soviet efforts to expand, constituted capitalism's last-ditch effort to alla

---

* The Varga debate was one of its later symptoms. Late in 1945 Yevgeni Samoilevich Varga concluded his book *Change in the Capitalist Economy after World W. II.* The book was published in the early part of 1946. In it Varga took a sanguine view of capitalism's postwar prospects. Based on Varga's book, three lively debates took place among Soviet economists in May 1947, with the purpose of clarifying the general line for the continuing analysis of the Western economy and of the entire economic and political system of the Western world. As a result of these debates and subsequent discussions, Varga was expelled from most of his posts. However, at the beginning of 1949 he announced that he would revise the theme of his book. Finally in 1953 his new book appeared, *Basic Questions of Economy and Politics of Imperialism after World War II.*

internal contradictions through emphasis on the common enemy, Communism. At the twenty-ninth anniversary celebration of the Bolshevik revolution (November 7, 1946), the restoration of the old dichotomic approach toward world affairs was affirmed by Zhdanov who delivered the main address. Reasserting in most emphatic terms the need for internal discipline and ideological indoctrination, Zhdanov militantly condemned the Western attitude toward the USSR and its East European policies. Not only did he make frequent references to "reactionary circles" in England and the United States; he also made repeated use of such phrases as "the Soviet Union leading the democratic countries," "USSR — the vanguard of the democratic movement," and so forth.[5] Implicit in all of this was the vision of a world rapidly splitting into two fundamentally hostile camps, with the Soviet Union asserting its leadership over one of them.

THE PEOPLE'S DEMOCRACY: A TRANSITIONAL PHASE

Stalin's and Zhdanov's speeches had special pertinence to the future development of the People's Democracies. The changes in the internal and theoretical character of these states which followed after the founding of the Cominform in 1947 (see Chapters 4 and 5) have consequently led some observers to assert that this entire period of relative institutional and ideological flexibility had been a well-timed hoax. They have been able to point effectively to certain clearly definable stages of development in the Soviet pattern of domination and consequently feel justified in asserting that a plot had been effectively carried out according to a preconceived blueprint, its ultimate objective being the stage-by-stage total subjugation of East Europe.

Some evidence to buttress this type of approach is readily available. It would certainly be rash to take at face value, considering past behavior and the postwar record, Soviet statements about the truly democratic and unique character of the People's Democracy and the Soviet assertions of their dedication to the maintenance of free states in East Europe. Statements of that type could well have been designed to lessen Western suspicions and to pave the way for the processes which subsequently followed. From the very beginning of the Soviet participation in the war, duplicity in speech and action had been faithfully practiced by Moscow. Soviet policy toward Poland is a case in point. On the one hand, in July 1941 Stalin signed an agreement with the Polish government in exile, recognizing it as the legal spokesman of the Polish nation and giving it the power to organize a Polish army in Soviet territory. The army was to be recruited from the Polish

POW's taken during the Hitler-Stalin pact. Almost simultaneously, however, a Union of Polish Patriots was set up in Moscow, composed of Polish Communists and extreme left-wingers. This Union, which rejected the Polish government, was then given broadcasting facilities (the Kosciuszko Station) and, following the Soviet rupture of relations with Poland early in 1943, it began to organize a Polish army under Soviet sponsorship. The subsequent transformation of this Union into a Soviet-sponsored government of Poland is a matter of public record.

In addition to the Union of Polish Patriots, the Soviet Union took measures to reactivate the Polish Communists even while the Nazi Armies were driving on Moscow and Stalin was entertaining General Wladyslaw Sikorski, the Polish Prime Minister. Communist elite groups were gathered together and prepared for parachute drops into Poland. After a short period of training and indoctrination, the first of such groups was ready for an air drop as early as September 1941. Following a special briefing by Dimitrov, the Comintern head, the group proceeded to Vyazma, west of Moscow. However, a plane accident prevented the departure, and the rapid Nazi advance prevented a rescheduling of the flight. The uninjured members of the team were evacuated east of Kuibyshev, to a small locality called Kusharenkovo, just north of Ufa. There they met another Polish Communist group which had been similarly trained at the Comintern school in Pushkino near Moscow and which had also been evacuated. They were headed by Jakob Berman, at the time a Comintern instructor, who now assumed direction over both groups. After the Nazi offensive had been halted, the two groups returned to Moscow and were dropped near Warsaw and some Silesian centers on December 28, 1941, and January 3, 1942, respectively.[6] Their task was to prepare for participation in a postwar Polish regime on the assumption that Poland would be freed by Red and not Western armies.[7]

Similarly, evidence could be cited in support of the argument that from the very beginning the other People's Democracies were mere shams. In the case of those parties which, unlike the Yugoslavs,[8] did not have domestic forces at their disposal, the Polish pattern was followed. For instance, a Hungarian committee was set up to direct the Kossuth Radio (a patriotic name, much like the one selected for the Poles) under the control of Matyas Rakosi who, with several colleagues, was charged with drafting plans for postwar Hungarian policies.[9] The Czech Communists, particularly Gottwald, Sverma, Slansky, and Kopecky, all of whom were destined to play major roles in setting up the Communist regime, also were actively involved in drafting Czech postwar programs. In addition, they directed the propaganda campaign from Moscow and published a Czech-language journal.[10] Planned action designed to seize power everywhere seems evident.[11]

However, there is a danger of distortion present in any *ex post facto* interpretation of events, assigning with the wisdom of hindsight both purpose and foresight which at the time might have been less clear. History begins to acquire a logic which in the immediate perspective it could not conceivably have possessed. Events begin to take on a meaning because of the significance they subsequently acquired. It would be more appropriate, therefore, to inquire into what the Soviet extrapolations of the nature of the postwar period were, irrespective of subsequent events which necessarily infused them with further content. Evidence on this is extremely scanty, but a few tentative judgments can be essayed.

Looking more closely at this particular phase and even at the events preceding it, one notices aspects which suggest that the People's Democracy phase, certainly never an end in itself, *was* considered to be a meaningful political expression of the peculiar relationships of domestic and external forces which the Communists felt would exist in postwar Europe. The argument that Soviet domination was the ultimate objective of the People's Democracy phase does not in itself mean that the People's Democracy did not have content of its own, and it certainly does not prove that this phase had to last the three years that it did rather than one, five, or ten.

It would appear that Stalin and his associates, reconsidering their original idea that the World War was essentially a crisis between capitalist states, initially accepted the notion that the anti-Nazi alliance would have some significant implications for Communist conduct in Europe not only during the war but also afterwards. Of course, they probably continued to assume that events would generally unfold in the direction of an eventual Communist triumph, but that during the war and immediately following it a popular-front political situation would reflect most closely the underlying social and economic conditions. How long these conditions would last no one could tell in advance, but as long as they did, caution, flexibility, and "guided democracy" ought to be the essential qualities of Communist conduct lest the West be prematurely jolted into upsetting the developing patterns.

Soviet commitment to such a policy of flexibility is well expressed in their wartime instructions to the Yugoslav and Polish Communists. Moscow, for instance, criticized Tito on March 5, 1942, for allowing the partisan movement to acquire "a communist character" and for not joining in the common struggle with "other Yugoslav patriots" who were not Communists or Communist sympathizers. On another occasion, Moscow eliminated some pro-Soviet slogans from a Tito proclamation which the Soviets were broadcasting on his behalf.[12] Later in the same year, in November, Tito informed Moscow that he was setting up "something like a government, which is to be called the National Liberation Committee of Yugoslavia." Moscow immediately became concerned that this might smack of a Communist takeover and advised Tito "not to fail" to give this committee a broad political character and not to consider it as a government. The message went on: "Do not put it [the committee] in opposition to the Yugoslav government in London. At the present stage, do not raise the question of abolition of the monarchy. Do not put forward any slogan of a republic."[13] In brief, Tito was enjoined not to deviate from the "democratic alliance" formula which, the Soviet leaders felt, represented the political embodiment of the existing pattern of basic forces.

An almost identical situation arose with the Polish Communists. Those who happened to be in the USSR at the outbreak of the Soviet-Nazi war proceeded to hold discussions among themselves and with Dimitrov about the nature of the existing phase of world affairs. Noting that the USSR had abandoned its earlier assessments and was now a partner in an anti-Nazi alliance, the Polish group decided that the "fundamental principle of tactics of all Communist parties in the occupied countries" must be the achievement of mutual understanding with the progressive bourgeois forces for the eventual democratization of the socioeconomic order. The Polish Communists, accordingly, even favored naming their party the Polish Worker-Peasant Party and it was only after some further discussion with Dimitrov that the label of the Polish Workers' Party (PWP) was adopted as the most suitable. After the Polish groups had been dispatched to Poland, they encountered among the local Communists a more "provincial" orientation, not unlike Tito's. Some of the local Communists, viewing the matter from the standpoint of their own local experience, were rather disturbed by the new line and by the new name. They favored the open restoration of the Polish Communist Party under the old name. To some, the new program, which stressed a democratic state with

Communist participation in the government and a peaceful transition to the social revolution, appeared to be "incorrect" and possibly even "some new form of provocation." It was only after a series of lengthy and heated discussions that the local Communists accepted the instructions brought by the parachutists, and the Polish Workers' Party was officially launched on the new platform. To underscore its new character, it did not become a section of the Comintern but an entirely separate party. Shortly after, when the Comintern was abolished, the leaders of the PWP dispatched a telegram hailing this development as a factor which would further aid their work among the Polish masses.[14] It was, however, the Moscow-trained and indoctrinated group which helped to set the Polish party on this course.*

None of the above, of course, could be interpreted to mean that Stalin and East European Communists were forever committed to the new analysis on which, subsequently, the People's Democracy was founded. To a Communist, every situation is fluid — the important thing is to detect the speed and direction of the flow of events. Once a new situation arises, or is in the process of arising, the preceding phase must give way and a new phase, with its own imperatives of action, begins.† It seems clear that in East Europe the policy of caution, pursued in rapidly diminishing degrees as time went on, was predicated on an analysis which stressed both the internal and the ex-

---

* Some evidence of wartime tension between the groups in Poland and Polish Communists in the USSR is provided by a recently published text of a report sent by the Warsaw Communist leadership to Moscow on January 12, 1944. The report complains of insufficient support for Communist activity in Poland, and at the same time gently protests the decision of the Moscow Communist group to set up a committee with the powers of a provisional government. Noting that matters pertaining to domestic Polish affairs should be decided in Poland, the Warsaw group offered to consider the Moscow committee as its foreign representative. *Ksztaltowanie sie Podstaw Programowych Polskiej Partii Robotniczej* (Warsaw, 1958), pp. 205–221.

† A good example of this type of thinking is provided by Gomulka's answer in May 1945 to those critics who accused the party of either abandoning or masking its Marxist character by putting main stress on popular democracy: "Our slogans and the political line of our party can be incomprehensible only to those to whom the science and theory of Marxism-Leninism is basically distant and foreign, to whom the concepts of democracy and socialism are incomprehensible . . . The Polish Workers' Party applies most consistently the policy of uniting all the democratic forces of the nation, precisely because it is a Marxist party. And Marxism is not some soulless dogma and Marxist science is not some Talmudistic petrification . . . The dialectical Marxist method of analyzing phenomena occurring in human society allows the Marxist parties to apply the most correct evaluation of the situation at every stage of the class struggle and in every historical phase. And the correct line of the party depends on the proper evaluation of the political situation." *W Walce o Demokracje Ludowa*, I, 150.

ternal complexity of the picture and which presumably assumed that domestic non-Communist forces would be more powerful and get greater support from the West than actually turned out to be the case.

The wartime policy probably had involved assessments stressing both minimum and maximum Soviet objectives. The minimum Soviet expectations, which grew as the battlefields shifted westward, were predicated on a belief that the postwar European situation would present the Communist movement with certain revolutionary opportunities, either through the direct assumption of power or through participation in democratic governments. Stalin's behavior and his communications to the Yugoslav and Polish comrades suggest, however, that the Soviet leaders feared that rash actions might precipitate a Western reaction or even induce the West to sign a separate agreement with some "bourgeois" anti-Nazi German elements, thereby depriving the USSR of its rightful share of the spoils of victory. In order to prevent concerted efforts to contain the Soviet Union, the tasks of the Communists outside the USSR were to make themselves an inseparable part of any postwar political structure and to participate in the reconstruction of the occupied states. A form of popular front was the very minimum which the USSR expected in East Europe.

Addressing a closed meeting of the party's agit-prop workers of Budapest in May 1945, even before the term People's Democracy had been devised, Rakosi presented an analysis of world affairs which substantiates the interpretation suggested above. Rakosi, undoubtedly reflecting Soviet thinking, suggested that the postwar phase would be dominated by the collapse of the British Empire and by weakened Anglo-American relations. This would allow, in turn, the gradual expansion of the Communist sphere. However, to prevent a mobilization of capitalist resistance, such expansion would have to avoid a radical, revolutionary character. By the same token, internal policy in East Europe, and Hungary in particular, would have to eschew revolutionary measures and would require a "great compromise" with the middle class and the peasantry. He drew the attention of his audience to Lenin's warnings in *"Left-Wing" Communism — An Infantile Disorder*, and estimated that such a transitional phase might last a decade or more.[15]

The USSR's maximum expectations took on greater significance as the West's fundamental disinterest in the area was revealed and as the westward march of the Soviet Armies was creating opportunities for *faits accomplis*. The various satellite organizations sponsored in the

USSR gradually ceased being mere candidates for partnerships in postwar governments and became the embryos for such governments. "Revolutionary" manifestations would be certain to arise not only in areas under Soviet control but even beyond, where the popular-front phase would lead to a rapid accumulation of Communist strength. The setting up of Communist-dominated governments in East Europe and possibly even farther west was not an unreasonable maximum expectation, given the general international picture as it was emerging in 1944 and 1945. The unresolved question, however, still remained: when, and how?

To the Soviets, the pleasantly surprising factors in the postwar European picture were: (1) the overwhelming Soviet strength; (2) the weakness of the non-Communist forces in East Europe; and (3) the rapid demobilization and disengagement of the West. As long as hopes existed for revolutionary situations elsewhere, and as long as the internal Soviet picture made direct Soviet involvement in the management of East Europe less immediately desirable, the phase of diversity and flexibility was the most rational policy to adhere to. Its very vagueness was its strength, and it also freed the USSR from premature ideological commitments.* By 1946, however, both the international picture and Soviet domestic developments called for a return to a more dichotomic image of the world and to an accelerating revolutionary pace. The transition was to be shorter than originally expected.

THE STRAINS OF DIVERSITY: DOMESTICISM

Zhdanov's 1946 evaluation accordingly had ominous implications for the existing pattern in East Europe. True, the initial tasks were yet

* Wladyslaw Bienkowski, a close associate of Gomulka, was one of the chief theoreticians of the evolutionary patterns of change, based on alliance with other social forces, and it might well have been from him that Gomulka derived some of his views. Bienkowski's views were expressed during the war in Communist underground publications and endorsed by Gomulka who, in his speeches, explicitly referred to the "lengthy" struggle necessary before socialism is achieved, and specifically stated: "The road to socialism is neither short nor can it be simplified. For these reasons the Polish Workers' Party fought and fights for a Democratic Poland." He warned against "gross oversimplifications" which suggest that Poland can pass through the transitional stage rapidly. (Gomulka, *W Walce o Demokracje Ludowa*, I, 155.) Revai's article (cited on p. 30), frequently mentioned as proof of the "plot" interpretation, makes it clear that in the case of Hungary it was not until the Cominform sessions in the fall of 1947 and the summer of 1948 that the Hungarian Communists were "taught . . . that a People's Democracy could not stop at any but the final stage of its destruction of the capitalist elements." This again suggests that Communist thinking was essentially in terms of relative phases and the question was only one of how long it would last.

to be fully accomplished in Czechoslovakia; true, in some countries the remnants of hostile political movements were still on the scene. The substance of the situation, however, pointed to the indisputable conclusion that effective power was in Communist hands and that the area was in the Soviet camp. Yet the existing institutional and ideological diversity was by 1946, and even more so by 1947, tending to produce what, from the Soviet standpoint, were disquieting symptoms. These symptoms appeared to be precisely the product of the doctrinal and practical insistence on recognizing the specific requirements of each individual situation. The various Communist leaders, most of whom had been either Comintern or NKVD agents and had always displayed the deepest loyalty to Soviet interests, were now becoming too engrossed in their own domestic tasks. The Soviet leaders, on the other hand, were finding that it was more difficult to run several Communist states than to run one. What had begun as an operation based on the complete identification of Soviet objectives with the objectives of the local Communists was now developing certain, admittedly very minor, but potentially significant, crevices.

This development might be described as involving the onset of a form of parochialism, or, more broadly, a malaise of "domesticism" in orientation and emphasis. Such a domestic perspective was not the same thing as the later phenomenon of national Communism or Titoism.[16] Domesticism is merely a certain implicit perspective which is inevitably acquired by even the most loyal Soviet functionaries when they are assigned to specific tasks within the framework of more loosely defined ideological conceptions. It may involve a frequently unconscious preoccupation with local, domestic Communist objectives, at the expense of broader, international Soviet goals. Absence of direct external purpose, such as struggle against world capitalism, or of direct Soviet involvement in the management of a given country, generates the domestic orientation in many local Communists. But once the issue is obvious and the priorities are again clearly stated, this type of Communist should adjust to the new values without hesitation. In East Europe, the acceptance of transitional diversity was closely linked to the problem of the domestic perspective, for the principle which accepted flexibility implied the need to adjust to the varying internal conditions. The Communist *apparatchiki*, entering with the Red Army, were originally dedicated to what appeared to be, at least conceptually, a simple proposition: to attain and consolidate power in keeping with the ideological insights into the unfolding events (this being linked closely with the interests of the USSR). But as their power began to jell more firmly, some of them began to realize that the task of building Communism is complex, that there is an absence of clearcut, detailed ideological guides to every specific situation, that human inventiveness and initiative must complement the broad ideological framework. Under these circumstances, and given the ideological definition stressing the uniqueness and peculiarities of the People's Democracy, many of them gravitated toward domesticism.

Domesticism expressed itself in a number of ways. The hard-boiled, wholly unsentimental Secretary of the Polish Workers' Party, Gomulka — who did not hesitate to exterminate the opposition or to endorse the Soviet deportations of thousands of young anti-German underground fighters — by 1947 found himself defending the nationalist traditions of the Polish Socialist Party against critics upholding the relatively weak Rosa Luxembourg faction in the Polish working-class movement. It is doubtful that Gomulka had become infected by the romantic notions of patriotism, especially since it was clear that Communist efforts to attract the socialists were encountering resistance among the highly nationally conscious proletariat which viewed the Communists with suspicion. Gomulka's appeal, however, does not seem to have been based entirely on expediency. He apparently shared the feeling of many left-wing Poles that the Communist Party had erred in the past by divorcing itself from the mainstream of patriotism, thereby appearing to be purely a Soviet agency. "The fundamental error of the Communists was that, while fully appreciating the question of the struggle for the social emancipation of the working masses, they did not sufficiently appreciate the question of independence . . . The struggle for social emancipation cannot be separated from struggle for national emancipation," Gomulka warned his comrades.[17] Seeing no basic incompatibility between Polish national interests and those of world Communism, Gomulka presumably felt both ideologically and politically justified in his stand.

The commitment to building socialism in Poland by a maximum of domestic effort also affected some of Poland's relations with her Communist-ruled neighbors. In the case of the Germans, where the SED was only in organizational stages, the Polish Communists preached and practiced a fanatical national hatred somewhat out of step with the doctrinal concepts of relations between nationalities. In this they were echoed by the Czechs, while the SED leadership, anxious not to be saddled with responsibility for the Oder-Neisse line, at first even hinted broadly to the Germans that it was not committed in favor of this line.*

Relations between the Polish Communist regime, grasping for domestic popularity, and the Czech government of Klement Gottwald, who was to prove himself Stalin's most loyal shield-bearer in East Europe but who was also concerned at this time with enhancing the popularity of the Czech Communist Party, were similarly uneasy. They reached the point that the Communist Prime Minister felt compelled to imply publicly that the two regimes did not quite see eye to eye. In a speech which stressed, above all, Czechoslovakia's friendship for an alliance with the USSR and, secondly, Tito's Yugoslavia, Gottwald expressed the Czech willingness to enter into similar arrangements "with other States with the same interests, if the relations of such States with us warrant it." And then he added: "This applies in particular to Poland. However, it is necessary that our vital interests, which we cannot sacrifice, should find the fullest recognition and respect on the Polish side." [18] (The Czechs at the time were making claims to areas around Kladzko, while the Poles were unhappy about the Cieszyn settlement.) † The relations between the Hungarian and Rumanian Communists were even worse, and at the Paris Peace Conference the two sides had a sharp altercation after which their relations were characterized by marked coolness.[19] The Hungarian Communists had hoped that a nominal concession on the Transylvania issue would improve their domestic position.

The natural preoccupation of the East European Communists with the consolidation of their power within the individual states led some of them to lose sight of the broader international considerations. Again, this was not necessarily a matter of pursuing an independent, "national" line; it was rather the consequence of their instructions to take advantage of the domestic situation and to manipulate it accord-

---

* Cf. *Neues Deutschland*, September 14, 1946, in which a lead article, entitled "Clarity on the Eastern Question," quoted Wilhelm Pieck as stating that the frontier is only provisional and that "the necessities of life of our people will be taken into account" if "democratic" Germans represent German interests. The paper also quoted Max Fechner, the leading SED candidate in Berlin: "I would like to declare that the SED will oppose any diminution (*Verkleinerung*) of German territory. The eastern frontier is a provisional frontier and can be fixed only at the peace conference." The SED conducted at the time a whispering campaign to the effect that it, if supported by the Germans, would be more effective in gaining Russian support for a revision of the frontier, a tack very disturbing to the Polish Communists.

† The southern Cieszyn (Teschen) area had been seized by Poland during the Munich crisis; it had been taken by force by the Czechs in 1919, when Poland was embroiled in war with Russia. In 1945 the Czechs regained this territory.

ingly so that, under the external protection of the USSR, domestic power consolidation would take place. Interpreting this to mean that they should take advantage of every opportunity to build up socialism, the Polish and Czech Communists reacted favorably in July 1947 to the American invitation to participate in the Marshall Plan. They presumably felt that the economic advantages accruing to their countries through such participation would make their political tasks easier, thereby furthering their own and Soviet objectives. They apparently did not read Zhdanov's speech of the preceding November very carefully. The Soviet leadership had developed by then a "deeper" insight into American motives. Accordingly, the Soviet leadership reacted violently, condemning the plan and peremptorily announcing in Moscow that Poland had decided not to participate. In the case of the Czechs, a delegation went to Moscow, and shortly afterwards the Czech position was clarified.[20] The leaderships of the two parties were thus forcefully reminded that in their own domestic pursuits they must not forget the implications of the division of the world into hostile camps.

In some respects, the most glaring example of domesticism in theory and practice was supplied by what appears to have been the most orthodox, the most Stalinist, the most Soviet type of regime in East Europe at the time: Tito's. His domestic orthodoxy, his insistence on considering the Yugoslav People's Democracy as merely a Soviet Republic, led him not only to adopt a rather condescending attitude toward his East European comrades but also to identify the interests of world Communism with his own, rather than the other way around. As a result, Tito became increasingly insistent that the USSR, and presumably the Soviet bloc in general, endorse his territorial ambitions in Austria and Italy, and that they consider them as crucial interests of international Communism as well.[21] This reversal in values must have been somewhat discomforting to Stalin, though possibly, given Tito's wartime behavior, not surprising. Nonetheless, the rather thinly veiled Yugoslav suggestions that the Communist alliance be prepared to go to war against the West for the sake of Yugoslav claims to Trieste — thereby throwing on the scales of history everything which had been built up at such cost through so many years — must have appeared as the height of provincialism. And it could have occurred only within the flexible framework of institutional and ideological diversity.

The Balkan Union scheme, originally encouraged by Moscow and planned by Tito and Dimitrov, can also be viewed from the perspective of domesticism. At first a scheme designed to weld together some of the Balkan states under the hegemony of Dimitrov and Tito, certainly tried and trusted Stalinists, it must have appeared to Moscow as a desirable arrangement, quite in keeping with the ideological assumptions about the ultimate pattern of relations among socialist states. In both countries the Communist parties enjoyed a measure of popular appeal unparalleled elsewhere in East Europe with the exception of Czechoslovakia, while their leaders were unusually distinguished Communists. In fact, according to Dedijer, Tito's court biographer, Stalin whetted Tito's vanity with veiled hints about bequeathing to him, some day, the mantle of leadership of international Communism, and as a token of his esteem (and also as a convenient arrangement) encouraged Tito to dominate Albania, where the Yugoslavs could be trusted to set up an orthodox regime.[22] A Balkan Union would have accordingly constituted a solid unit, self-supporting but loyal, and more able on its own to withstand effectively possible Western pressure.

However, by 1947 a Western challenge was unlikely, and Soviet control over the area was uncontested. At the same time, Tito's and Dimitrov's enthusiasm for the Balkan Union appeared to be dominated more by considerations derived from their domestic concerns and from purely personal factors (for example, Tito's rather flattering image of himself as the second-ranking Communist leader in the world)* than by broader perspectives. There is no doubt that some of the economic difficulties encountered at home in both countries could partially have been resolved through closer ties.[23] Their missionary zeal — Tito made a number of trips to the other neighboring capitals, failing in one instance to inform Moscow about it,[24] and signed treaties of friendship with his former enemy neighbors even before the USSR did † — began to bear fruit: favorable reactions to a Balkan Union, eventually even expanded into an East European one, came from the Poles and the Rumanians. Both Dimitrov and Tito must have viewed this as a desirable and a normal historical development. To both of them, this larger framework seemed dictated both by doctrine and by good politics. It would be the first stage in the construction of a multinational Communist society. To these flamboyant

* Dimitrov, too, given his Comintern position, may have had personal ambitions on this score. Ruth Fischer, for instance, felt that if there should ever be "a Stalinist United States of Europe, one of its principal officers may be Georgi Dimitrov." *Stalin and German Communism*, p. 309.

† With Bulgaria, November 27, 1947; with Hungary, December 8, 1947; with Rumania, December 19, 1947. Cf. table on p. 110, Chapter 6.

and fiery leaders with rich revolutionary histories, this offered a larger stage on which to gain Communist virtue and to be acclaimed for it. Whatever the motives, in late 1947 the two leaders were furthering the Union not only in response to Soviet prodding but with an increment of personal enthusiasm which rapidly transformed the venture into their own private little enterprise.

By that time, however, the scheme of a more rational and solid organization for Communist-controlled states in the Balkans no longer suited the requirements of the situation as the Soviet leadership probably saw it. In January 1948, after Dimitrov's public press interview in Sofia of January 23 in which he envisaged a future federation embracing even Poland and Czechoslovakia (and Greece, should the Greek Communist partisans succeed), *Pravda* published an explicit critique that left no interpretative doubts. Federation or confederation was not desirable, *Pravda* stressed, and it was much more important to develop internal forces in the individual states "as correctly stated in the known declaration of the nine Communist Parties" (referring to the Cominform declaration).[25] The original imprimatur for the project was thus withdrawn. Following this, both the Yugoslavs and the Bulgarians were invited to Moscow where they were charged with conduct, in Molotov's words, "inadmissible either from the Party or from the state point of view," while Stalin personally castigated Dimitrov for behaving "as if you are still the Secretary of the Comintern."[26] The crux of the matter, however, was again the problem of diversity's having outlived its usefulness and actually creating difficulties. Stalin stated it bluntly: "Mistakes are not the issue: the issue is conceptions different from our own." *[27]

A similar, though less directly political, instance involved the Polish-Czech efforts to establish closely knit economic collaboration, the territorial conflict notwithstanding. The Polish-Czech Economic Collaboration Convention of July 1947 provided for a permanent economic council, with eight specialized commissions, to guide industrial development collaboration in the Silesian basin, jointly develop energy resources, and eventually establish a waterways system linking the Oder with the Danube. Hungary was to be included subsequently, especially in view of its bauxite resources. If effected, such collaboration would have materially strengthened the Polish and Czech posi-

---

* One upshot of this incident was the formal commitment made by Belgrade on Moscow's insistence that Belgrade would consult Moscow before taking any foreign-policy steps. Such a formal arrangement was hardly needed in the case of the other parties, which were much more dependent on Soviet support. Dedijer, p. 324.

tion in Central Europe, and its failure to materialize was related closely to the potential political implications.

In brief, what in 1945 and 1946 had been a sensible adjustment to the complexities of the new situation was tending by 1947 to drive a wedge in the community of interests of the Soviet leadership and the East European leaderships. The local Communist leaders were taking their domestic tasks too seriously, and, in their search for the best possible solutions to the problems facing them at home, they were not always sufficiently conscious of broader Soviet goals. Even a Dimitrov or a Bierut, faced with truly overwhelming burdens not only of political consolidation but also of economic reconstruction, naturally tended in time to interpret his role in terms of the various forces and elements that he had to cope with. Considering the Soviet unwillingness to step in and set up open Soviet occupation authorities, and considering the Soviet insistence that they would supply help only to prevent a domestic revolt against the Communists and only minimal help in launching internal Communist operations, the local Communists could not avoid developing a certain domestic perspective in the execution of their tasks.

Despite various acts of Soviet interference, considerable areas of initiative were left to the local Communists during this phase. They had to justify ideologically to themselves and to others the roles they were playing; they had to build up their organizations; they had to control the patterns of reconstruction so that they would proceed in the desirable direction; they had to define the position of their particular states not only vis-à-vis the Soviet Union but also to one another. The Soviet Union could remove or paralyze the anti-Communist threat, but the consolidation of Communist power was still in large measure up to the Communists themselves. Under these circumstances, a Polish-Czech economic collaboration, or even Marshall Plan aid, might have appeared to the Communists involved as the most desirable way of achieving their domestic political and economic goals, and as in keeping with their ideological notions about interstate relations. "National Communism" was not yet involved: no choice was being made between the interests of the larger unit and those of the particular state involved. In fact, in every case it was assumed that the larger unit would benefit from such decisions, since a community of interests was said to exist on all levels.

THE COMINFORM: AN ANTITHESIS

To Stalin, viewing the situation from the perspective of his own efforts to re-establish totalitarian unity at home and noticing the growing external tensions, the phase of diversity must have seemed to have reached the stage of its own antithesis: having fulfilled its general purposes, it now made imperative a greater emphasis on unity. This unity would be attained through a more conscious perception of the objectives of all Communist power at home and abroad, through a common discussion of practices to eliminate the excessive commitment to narrow national interests, and through the drawing of a common ideological line which would de-emphasize the existing diversities in theory and practice.

The founding of the Cominform was the Soviet response to the challenge presented by the phase of diversity. It was to initiate the transition to more common patterns of development for which the necessary basis had been laid by the popular fronts, by national appeals, by the mobilization of the working class and by the beginning of social and economic transformation. Ironically, it was the Yugoslavs, with their distaste for compromise, who, as early as 1945 had first suggested that some sort of international organization be revived to further the "exchange of views and . . . the exchange of the wealth of experience" between Communist parties.[28] It is not difficult to surmise that from the standpoint of the zealous Yugoslavs such an institutional device would have served to assert more violent revolutionary patterns in East Europe. To the Soviet leaders, however, the application of such violent patterns in countries without strong indigenous parties would have meant a more direct and a more costly Soviet involvement in domestic affairs, not to mention international complications. This inhibition was less marked by mid-1946, when Stalin himself broached the issue of a new Communist International to Tito, encouraging him to take the initiative in organizing it.[29] Stalin's logic in choosing the Yugoslavs for this undertaking was commendable: if the phase of diversity was now to give way to its logical antithesis, the Yugoslavs could play a significant role in encouraging the other states to adopt, not only on the Soviet but also on the Yugoslav example, more uniform political and economic patterns. And such community of behavior would necessarily induce a more common ideological perspective in which the primacy of universal goals (equated necessarily with the USSR's) would be asserted. Conversely, the assertion of a common perspective would help establish more common patterns of action. In both, the Yugoslavs were far ahead of the rest and close to the USSR.

After some months of consultations, the formal inauguration of the new International took place in September 1947 at Szklarska Poreba, a small resort town in southwestern Poland. Zhdanov, the chief Soviet spokesman, delivered to the assembled representatives of the ruling Communist parties (except Albania's), and of France and Italy, a broad analysis of the international scene. He indicted the United States on charges of conspiring for world supremacy by exploiting the destruction of its two capitalist rivals, Germany and Japan, as well as by exploiting weakened France and Great Britain. The consequence of this American design was the division of mankind into two camps, Zhdanov noted. For this reason the relations among Communist parties, particularly those in power, must be especially intimate, although, Zhdanov hastened to add, they must be based on "equality and mutual respect." The Soviet spokesman felt further that:

the present position of the Communist Parties has its shortcomings. Some comrades understood the dissolution of the Comintern to imply the elimination of all ties, of all contact between the fraternal Communist Parties. But experience has shown that such mutual isolation of the Communist Parties is wrong, harmful, and in fact unnatural.[30]

This theme was echoed in the first resolution passed by the new Cominform, "Resolution on the Interchange of Experience and Coordination of Activities of the Parties Represented at the Conference":

The Conference states that the absence of contacts among the Communist Parties participating at this Conference is a serious shortcoming in the present situation. Experience has shown that such lack of contacts among the Communist Parties is wrong and harmful . . . [It was decided to] charge the Information Bureau with the organization of interchange of experience and, if need be, coordination of the activities of the Communist Parties on the basis of mutual agreement.[31]

The other Soviet delegate, Malenkov, devoted a good part of his report to the internal Soviet scene, and his emphasis on the need for internal ideological uniformity in the USSR itself left no doubt as to the close links between domestic Soviet developments and the reassessment of the East European scene. Of the East Europeans, all of whom "informed" one another of their domestic programs and progress, the most assertive tone was taken by the Yugoslavs, who again took the opportunity to assert their ideological orthodoxy, repeatedly stressing the social-revolutionary content of their activities and the great similarity in Soviet and Yugoslav patterns.[32]

There is probably little reason to doubt that to many East European Communist leaders, and not only to the Yugoslavs, the founding of the Cominform was a welcome development. The very process of forced internal change and the sharpening of conflicts was creating increasing pressure toward dependence on the USSR. Those who had originally held to an image of a People's Democracy in which social progress and change would be furthered by the cooperation of all good-willed citizens were rapidly finding that the realities of politics were shattering their dreams.* For the Moscow-trained *apparatchiki*, furthermore, there was a certain security to be gained from conformity. Liberated from the tensions and strains of diversity which frequently served to reveal their own domestic weakness, the East European Communists could now expect the transitional period of Soviet noninvolvement to give way to more direct Soviet participation in the "socialist construction." The situation would be much less blurred. The compromises and conciliatory gestures which the preceding phase required — and which Stalinist cadets like Rakosi or Bierut or Gottwald probably found distasteful — could now be jettisoned. They would no longer need to plead for the support of the "progressive" non-Communist forces while at the same time fearing being swamped by them. Moderation, which to a fanatic Bolshevik is a sacrifice greater than any suffering for the cause, could now give way to class struggle, to violence, to real revolution, the victory of which would be assured by greater Soviet involvement.

As far as is known, the founding of the Cominform was opposed by only one prominent leader, Wladyslaw Gomulka. His opposition did not evaporate into thin air once the line between domestic and "larger" (hence Soviet) interests was drawn.† He himself subsequently admitted having opposed the organization of the Information Bureau, and, in the deliberations of the constituent meetings, took a somewhat deviant position on such matters as collectivization and the relationship of the Communists to Polish socialists whom Gomulka,

* Some of the left-wing socialists might have subscribed to this point of view, and even among some Communists there were those who believed that a maximum of diversity and a minimum of violence were necessary to build a popular program of reform. Also, some well-known intellectuals belonged to this category of non-Communist idealists, Czeslaw Milosz for one.

† Gomulka's orientation is revealed by the following statement made at the First Congress of the Polish Workers' Party: "There are those among the former members of the Polish Communist Party [i.e., the one abolished in 1938 by the Comintern] who have not been able to feel themselves into the new situation, have not been able to understand it, have not ceased being narrow sectarians. It is necessary that they also begin to think with the categories *of the nation, of the state* in which we now co-govern." *W Walce o Demokracje Ludowa*, I, 323; italics added.

even in his published report, defended by implication.* This came at a time when, according to Zhdanov, the world was divided into two camps and the socialists were "objectively" the agents of imperialism. Gomulka is also said to have taken the position that no resolution of the meeting should be made public and that the meeting itself be kept secret.[33] With the memories of the Polish Communist Party's dissolution by the Comintern in 1938 apparently still fresh in his mind,† and presumably fearful lest the Cominform give a new, arbitrary shape to his "Polish way to socialism," Gomulka's independent line meant the transformation of his domesticism into the first case of what came to be known as national Communism — that is, the explicit assignment of priority to internal considerations even if openly challenged by those who consider themselves to be the central spokesmen of international Communism.‡

The founding of the Cominform, much more than the subsequent break with Tito, meant the end of the phase of diversity and the beginnings of what is most satisfactorily identified as Stalinism — a period of total conformity in the relations among Communist states. For a while afterwards, a certain degree of diversity inevitably lingered on and expressed itself in such incidents as the Balkan Union affair, or the opposition of the Polish Politburo to the June 1948 Cominform resolution enjoining collectivization,§ but the mounting

---

* There are striking parallels between Gomulka's behavior here and at the fortieth anniversary meeting commemorating the Bolshevik revolution, November 1957 (see Chapter 12). In the words of one of the participants at the Cominform founding (E. Reale, *Nascita del Cominform*, Mondadori, 1958, p. 35), Gomulka's report "was most noteworthy for the reservations which the chief of the Polish Party advanced against collectivization of land in which he underlined the difficulties in a country such as Poland which is fundamentally agricultural . . . I was struck by the complete absence of any rhetoric and above all by the absence of these exaggerated fountains of gratitude, expressions of recognition, etc. for the Soviets which characterized the other speeches. I was struck, moreover, by a certain tone of coldness toward the proposition of activating a permanent consultative organization among the various parties, truly a strange thing on the part of those who had, at least officially, taken the initiative for bringing about the meeting."

† This writer was particularly impressed in the course of his conversations with Polish Communists to learn to what extent this single incident colored Soviet-Polish Communist relations.

‡ The 1948 Gomulka deviation was caused by "his lack of understanding of the essential idea of the mutual relationship between the countries of the People's Democracy and the USSR and the leading role of the All-Union Communist Party in the international front of the struggle against imperialism." *Pravda*, September 9, 1948, accounts of the Resolution of the Polish Workers' Party.

§ The Polish delegation even opposed the use of the word "collectivization" but finally voted for the resolution. Gomulka was no longer a delegate. See *Nowe Drogi*, no. 10 (1956), p. 90.

assertion of the Cominform's control over the Communist power structures meant a rapid acceleration in the direction of uniformity. The problem of Titoism arose as a consequence of this effort to establish hierarchy and coordination. As long as the phase of diversity existed, Titoism — at that time a form of premature Stalinism — could be tolerated. It was no longer tolerable once conformity was established because the essence of that conformity was a clear-cut institutional and ideological hierarchy. Without that hierarchy, compliance, discipline, and single-minded unity of purpose could not be achieved. The situation can be compared to that of a successful guerrilla army which is eventually organized into a professional military establishment. As long as operations are conducted by relatively self-contained units, strategic and, especially, tactical elasticity is essential. Decisions, in keeping with the grand conception of purpose, are made on the spot in terms of the conditions encountered. But once the enemy is on the run and the guerrilla units begin to be merged with the professional army which had finally made its appearance on the scene, the bravest, the most successful, and hence the proudest guerrilla units may be a far greater source of difficulty than those which have done less or in fact little.

The various incidents cited in the Soviet-Yugoslav correspondence, involving the role of the Soviet ambassador, the Soviet officers, the Soviet efforts to organize spy networks,[34] were expressions of tension inherent in this situation which came to the fore once the processes of unification were launched. It is ironic to recall that the formation of the Cominform had first been urged by Tito himself because of his orthodoxy in behavior and aspirations. What he had forgotten was that imitation within diversity did not imply the same political consequences as imitation within uniformity. In the former, imitation was an act of independent decision made in terms of one's own specific situation. In the latter case, imitation led to subordination to the center and that subordination Tito was not willing to acknowledge. But until the very end of their association with Stalin, Tito and his colleagues trusted that an arrangement providing for their local autonomy could be worked out and that an open conflict with Moscow could be averted. Hence an ideological content in Tito's position was lacking at the time of the break.* Their domesticism, which

---

* Tito admitted as much in speaking to the Central Committee session which, on April 12, 1948, upheld his resistance to Moscow: "Comrades, remember, this is not a matter here of any theoretical discussion . . . Comrades, the point here, first and foremost, is the relations between one state and another." Dedijer, p. 338.

only Stalin transformed into national Communism by his expulsion of the Yugoslavs from the Cominform, blinded them to the nature of Stalinism, which they had practiced domestically, as an international system. They failed to perceive that subordination was an essential quality of Stalinism.

On Stalin's side, the decision to launch the Cominform meant that a new phase in Communist relations was beginning, and that, given the Yugoslavs' devotion to himself and to the Soviet Union, the achievement of Yugoslav subordination would not be a difficult task. He was, therefore, obviously willing to bring the undersurface conflict out into the open on the assumption that the Yugoslavs would submit. But Stalin overlooked — maybe because of Tito's ideological orthodoxy — Tito's independent power. This miscalculation, which was revealed in the aftermath of Tito's expulsion from the Cominform, later sharpened the trends toward conformity in East Europe.

Titoism, however, had not begun the new phase; it was its first symptom. The new phase started because diversity in theory and practice seemed dangerous and no longer properly reflected the times. Domestic consolidation of the Communist parties, which had been the Soviet goal, had required various internal adjustments which necessarily called for some measure of diversity. Stalin's decision to insist on conformity meant that a far greater degree of Soviet involvement would be necessary, with one of its costs being a further decline in the domestic sources of support for the Communist parties. For reasons already sketched, Stalin was prepared to pay this price. Titoism, Stalin's inadvertent creation, added to this calculation a further dimension: that internal practices on the Soviet model did not guarantee loyalty to the USSR and that premature Communist power, even on the Stalinist model, could have a corrupting influence on the Communist leaders. This fear and suspicion of Communist power abroad was what the experience with Tito bequeathed to the Stalinist era, thereby intensifying Stalin's insistence that ideology and power must have a common and undisputed source.

The Second Phase: 1947-1953

STALINISM — INSTITUTIONAL AND IDEOLOGICAL UNIFORMITY

The cult of personality cannot be confined solely to the person of Stalin. The cult of personality is a certain system which prevailed in the Soviet Union and which was grafted to probably all Communist Parties . . .

The essence of this system consisted in the fact that an individual, hierarchic ladder of cults was created. Each such cult comprised a given area in which it functioned. In the bloc of socialist states it was Stalin who stood at the top of this hierarchic ladder of cults. All those who stood on lower rungs of the ladder bowed their heads before him. Those who bowed their heads were not only the other leaders of the Communist Party of the Soviet Union and the leaders of the Soviet Union, but all the leaders of Communist and Workers' Parties of the countries of the socialist camp. The latter, that is, the First Secretaries of the Central Committees of the Parties of the various countries who sat on the second rung of the ladder of the cult of personality, in turn donned the robes of infallibility and wisdom. But their cult radiated only on the territory of the countries where they stood at the top of the national cult ladder. This cult could be called only a reflected brilliance, a borrowed light. It shone as the moon does.

— Wladyslaw Gomulka, 1956

4 / THE THEORY RECONSIDERED

Love of the Soviet Union does not tolerate the slightest reservation. The road into the morass of treason indeed begins on the inclined plane of reservations and doubts regarding the correctness of the policy of the Soviet Union. — *Rude Pravo*, May 25, 1952

THE previous diversity of views and constitutional arrangements could not be maintained in an era characterized by the omniscience of a single individual whose views were considered to be a universally applicable dogma. "So calm, wise, human, sincere and illuminated by the stars . . . Behold! This is Stalin!" mused a Czech broadcast.[1]

The imposition of doctrinal uniformity took place over a period of about two years, from mid-1947 to some time in 1949, although its aftermath lasted much longer as the new doctrines continued to be elaborated in fuller detail. The major change, however, was not merely a matter of asserting Stalin's position of infallibility and universality. While that certainly played a role, the theoretical changes were also a response to the dictates of the actual situation and a guide to actions designed to shape the future. In other words, the theory changed because the requirements of power had changed; but, in addition, the requirements of power changed because the conceptions of the type of power desirable also changed. Ideology and power again interacted.

THE REASSESSMENT

In time, the new reassessments developed a reality of their own, particularly since individuals often tend to associate themselves with certain policies in order also to promote their own interests. Gradually, the very process of shaping a policy begins to affect the individuals themselves and in turn to shape their thinking and actions. When this happens in an organized group, the impact on thought and behavior is that much intensified. The concept of the class struggle may serve as an example. Among the East European Communist leaders there were certainly many whose firm belief in the need of intensified class struggle even after the seizure of power (a classical Stalinist contribution to Marxism-Leninism) was based on a combination of "rational" assumptions about the nature of rapid social transformation and of deep personal animosity toward the former ruling classes. Many of them had been alienated from their societies and harbored bitter hatreds. Some of the Jewish Communists had been exposed to anti-Semitism. The Stalinist notions of the class struggle could, therefore, be quite appealing and provide the justification of historical inevitability for actions which the Communist leaders also might have wished to carry out for reasons of personal gratification. That in waging such class struggle they would be acquiring Communist "virtue" was, of course, gratuitous; and moral problems were resolved by this historical inevitability: "when one chops wood, chips must fly."

During the earlier transitional period of diversity, some measure of differentiation of views among the various leaderships was inescapable. Faced with a variety of postwar challenges, each leadership had to devise its own ideological concepts and political weapons. Within the limits imposed by Soviet sponsorship, this meant a certain amount of creative debate. But once the diversity began to narrow down, the previous divisions of opinion gave some leaders a welcome opportunity to castigate those whose views had least approached the newly established and more militant standard. They could now assert that their own earlier differences in tone had been a method of expressing their misgivings with the policy of neomoderation, and they could now claim credit for having deviated least from a standard which then only potentially existed. Competition in loyalty to the USSR, a vehicle for advancement and the fulfillment of one's own views, thus rapidly developed and accelerated the process of redefining some of the basic domestic assumptions of the East European Communists. A few held to their original views and had to be removed. Some had always viewed the preceding phase with a measure of suspicion and were now triumphant. Some shifted their position out of fear and desire to accommodate. Some shifted because they genuinely believed that the situation itself had changed sufficiently to warrant some new evaluations.

That the domestic scene in East Europe had shifted appreciably in the direction of more common patterns is undeniable, and this, considering the Marxian assumptions about the relation between reality and ideology, was bound to affect the ideology. Between the founding of the Cominform and the expulsion of Tito, the Communist parties completed the elimination of the articulate opposition and were ready to pass from the stage of consolidation to a stage of "socialist construction" (see Chapter 5). The differences between the Communist-ruled states diminished; the similarities became more marked. The Soviet Union was displaying a more active attitude toward the domestic affairs of the People's Democracies, culminating in the establishment of the Cominform. On a larger plane, these shifts and developments were certainly not immune to the growing international tension and the accumulating evidence that Communist parties in France and Italy could come to power only through violent means. A more militant Communist bloc seemed dictated by history.

The initial reconsideration of the meaning of the People's Democracy, and of the pertinent ideological problems, proceeded at an uneven pace. The stimuli which came from the Cominform meeting found the Hungarians and the Bulgarians most responsive. They were gradually joined by the Polish party, while the Rumanians and the Czechs lagged somewhat behind. Apart from the very important consideration that clear ideological guidance was at this time still unavailable, there were the obvious domestic reasons for this initial variety in response. In Rumania, the Communist Party was barely completing the consolidation of its internal power and, shortly after the first Cominform session, had unburdened itself of the monarchy. (A People's Republic was proclaimed on December 30, 1947.) There even might have been some genuine doubt as to whether Rumania had yet become a People's Democracy — Zhdanov certainly implied as much in his first speech to the Cominform when he made a vague distinction between People's Democracies and countries like Rumania which had just "broken with imperialism." In Czechoslovakia, where the Communist Party had been heading the ruling coalition since 1946, it was not until the February coup of 1948 that Communist power was firmly consolidated and the Communist leaders could devote their attention to broader problems. In the meantime, they maintained a cautious silence. In Poland, where the ideological problem was linked with the person of Gomulka, the conflict was sharpened by an internal power struggle which came to the fore immediately after Tito's expulsion.[2]

The patterns of reassessment seem to fall into the following chronological order:

(1) From the 1947 creation of the Cominform to about the time of Tito's expulsion — assertion of certain basic principles common to all People's Democracies.

(2) From Tito's expulsion to late 1948 — negation of the most ex-

treme aspects of the formerly alleged uniqueness of the People's Democracy and the assertion of certain common programs of action.

(3) After late 1948 and in early 1949 — elaboration of a common
interpretation of the People's Democracy, of its "constitutional" forms
and its pattern of growth.

Although the change can be dated to the 1947 Cominform meeting, that gathering did not lay down an explicit new line for all to
follow, other than to stress the need for close collaboration between
parties and "exchange of experience." In his report to the meeting,
Vulko Chervenkov even repeated Dimitrov's earlier adjurations about
the Bulgarian road to socialism and the irrelevance of the dictatorship
of the proletariat insofar as Bulgaria was concerned. His remarks, it
seems, were still considered perfectly proper and received due publicity. Shortly afterwards, however, once Stalin's two-camp theory
had made its impact, a spate of pronouncements appeared in which
the first shifts in the existing ideological framework became apparent.
The reconsideration of the theory was under way.

Matyas Rakosi and Vulko Chervenkov, the latter soon to become
Dimitrov's successor, were at the time the most active discussants of
Communist-bloc affairs and frequent contributors to the Cominform
journal. Rakosi, an opportunistic Stalinist *apparatchik*, eager to get on
with the job and anxious to take advantage of the avenue opened to
him by the Cominform sessions, might have also aspired to Tito's
mantle as the most trusted East European Stalinist. For Chervenkov,
the question of the ailing and aged Dimitrov's successor was probably
not irrelevant, and rapid identification of his fate with the new trends
was not likely to harm his prospects. They were aided by occasional
hints from the chief editor of the Cominform journal (*For a Lasting
Peace, for a People's Democracy*), P. F. Yudin, a CPSU *apparatchik*
personally selected for the job by Stalin. Initially, the emphasis was
put on two major aspects: the role of the party and the role of the
USSR. It was stressed that the Communist Party was the mainspring
in the process of "democratization" which East Europe was experiencing and that, therefore, its role must not be equated with that of
the "other democratic" parties with which it happened to be col-
laborating. True, the Communist Party was a member of a coalition,
or a national or patriotic front (depending on the given country), but
while enjoying equality with the other parties, it stood above them
because of its sense of purpose, which went far beyond the more
limited perspectives of the other parties.[3] The claim to one-party
hegemony was incipient in these views.

THE SOVIET MODEL

The growing and articulate emphasis on the leading role of the Communist Party was accompanied by mounting stress on the ideological significance and relevance of the Soviet system itself. The earlier tendency not to stress Soviet experience, which, indeed, most East Europeans did not view with much admiration, gave way more and more to an insistence on the leadership of the Soviet Union.[4] But this aspect was not yet interpreted to mean that ways to socialism may not differ; in fact, some parties continued early in 1948 to stress their own way to socialism while acknowledging Soviet leadership — a balance which was to be re-established only in 1957.[5] That the concept of Soviet primacy, however, had certain theoretical and practical content soon became apparent from several hints dropped by the editors of the Cominform journal. On February 15, 1948, Yudin published a lengthy missive on the occasion of the centenary of the Communist Manifesto, which he used to lay particular stress on the general applicability of the Soviet experience. A month later, an editorial in the same publication, entitled "The Ideological Weapon of the Communist Parties," explicitly called upon the parties to "generalize" their experience, and severely admonished those party organizations whose leaders "are lukewarm propagandists of Marxist theory" and who, therefore, "inevitably lose all sense of perspective, and from whom one can expect the most extravagant and pseudo-Marxist 'ideas' and 'theories.' " The editorial then flatly asserted:

> The Communist Party of the Soviet Union (Bolsheviks), created and educated by the great geniuses of revolutionary theory, Lenin and Stalin, serves as an example to all fraternal Communist Parties of how to approach the development of Marxist theory . . .[6]

During the summer of 1948 events began to move more rapidly, particularly in view of the mounting tension with the Yugoslavs. The Cominform met and, apart from dealing with the Yugoslav case, established certain general principles for the construction of socialism along the lines of known Stalinist precepts. The meeting adopted the position that socialist transformation cannot be limited to the towns, but must be pushed into the countryside where Soviet experience can fruitfully be applied.[7] At the end of August and beginning of September, the Central Committee of the Polish Workers' Party convened to deal with the problem posed by Gomulka's persistence in holding to his "antiquated" positions (already debated at an earlier

July meeting). The full account of this deviation has been presented elsewhere.[8] For our purposes, it is particularly relevant to note that Gomulka was charged with distorting the role played by the party and undermining the class struggle content of the socialist transformation of the countryside. Gomulka was accused of having recommended that the Polish delegation to the Cominform's June meeting refuse to endorse the agricultural resolution and of having refused to support the struggle against the kulak, which was stated to be the very basis of the socialist transformation.[9] The charges pertaining to these domestic errors were buttressed by an accusation which, in years to come, was to have an increasingly ominous ring: inadequate understanding of the role of the USSR, the attitude toward which, "given the increasing polarization of forces in the world between the imperialist and the anti-imperialist camps," is in fact "the test of true internationalism, the test of devotion to the cause of socialism." [10]

The Polish plenum helped to focus more sharply on what the central issues facing the Communists in East Europe were and to spell out the broad outlines of the *correct* position. By bringing the Gomulka case out into the open, the Polish party performed the service of placing in bold relief the borderline between orthodoxy and heresy. From now on, to err by omission would be more difficult. Nonetheless, even the Polish plenum did not achieve the task of a systematic revision of the ideological basis for the People's Democracy. It did not indicate with precision what was and what was not still sacred. The urgency created by the conflict with Tito, and the ideological confusion resultant from the fact that Tito's position in many respects had been ideologically closest to the prevailing Soviet notions, made a more formal guideline imperative. It came forth in two forms: an article by Yudin in the Cominform journal in October 1948,[11] and a speech by Dimitrov in December to the Fifth Congress of the Bulgarian Communist Party.[12]

Yudin's article took as its point of departure the tenth anniversary of the publication of the "Short Course History of the CPSU," authorship of which had been generously credited to Stalin. Hailing this work as "a classical creation of scientific Communism," Yudin stressed that the central themes of the book, which described the Soviet experience with the socialist transformation, were a "universal source of inspiration" to all Communist parties. The article emphasized repeatedly the widespread applicability of the specifics of Soviet experience, castigated leaders like Gomulka (explicitly named) for committing "a big mistake by ignoring the experience of the USSR,' and left little doubt as to the dangers inherent in attempting to follow one's own road to socialism. As if to underscore the point, prominent space was also given in the same issue to an article by a member of the leadership of the Hungarian party, Z. Biro (Rakosi's brother), entitled "Learn from the CPSU(b) How to Struggle and Win."

Dimitrov's speech, which became a classic frequently quoted by other leaders, went beyond the questions of the role of the party, the primacy of the USSR, and the universal applicability of the Soviet experience. It was a systematic effort to revise most of the earlier assumptions concerning the People's Democracy. He categorized Bulgarian postwar experience into two phases: the first, from September 9, 1944, to the execution of the peasant leader Nikola Petkov in September 1947, as the struggle of all democratic forces against Fascism in the process of which domestic "malicious opposition" was eliminated; the second, which followed, as the beginning of the socialist transformation. Dimitrov pointed out that in the present phase the People's Democracy was performing the functions of a dictatorship of the proletariat in order to eliminate the remnants of capitalism within the framework of a world democratic coalition headed by the USSR, on whom "the very basis of the existence of People's Democracy" depends. Friendly relations with the USSR were thus a fundamental aspect of the People's Democracy itself.* The general effect of his speech was to initiate a full-scale revision of the concept of People's Democracy. Under the existing circumstances the various leaders hastened forward with their own contributions to the construction of theoretical uniformity.

The East European leaders now had the advantage of generous Soviet ideological assistance. Apart from the programmatic statements of Zhdanov or Yudin's articles, the Soviet scholars themselves elaborated during 1948 and 1949 a new conception of the People's Democracy.[13] Out of these re-evaluations emerged a new theoretical framework which not only shaped and rationalized the domestic policies but which also served as the basis for the new constitutions which followed. For this reason, in discussing the ideological changes effected after Dimitrov's speech it may not be inappropriate also to refer oc-

---

* Dimitrov's categorization of Bulgarian events survived the various post-Stalin vicissitudes. Thus, for instance, in a discussion of "Our Development on the Path of Socialism" on April 11, 1956, Radio Sofia emphasized the two stages (September 9, 1944–1947: "solution of democratic problems"; 1947 on: "nationalization and building of socialism") and pointed out that the presence of a "coalition" of parties "did not mean that this democracy was basically different from the Soviet form of proletarian dictatorship."

casionally to one of the most significant collections pertaining to the
Stalinist notions of the People's Democracy — namely, a three-volume
collection of papers, articles, and discussions, amounting to 1589 pages
and entitled (in English translation), "The Legal Problems of the
Constitution of the Polish People's Republic." The collection was the
product of a conference planned early in 1953, but actually held in
July 1953, to discuss all the pertinent aspects of Marxist-Leninist
thinking on the problems of the state and constitution in a People's
Democracy.[14] It represents the quintessence of Stalinist thinking, for
the few months which had passed since Stalin's death were too brief
materially to affect the views presented and undoubtedly prepared
earlier.

On the fundamental questions of internal democracy, democratic
coalitions, and the dictatorship of the proletariat, Dimitrov in his
speech, Revai in his oft-cited article, and the Soviet theorists[15] all
now maintained that the People's Democracy was a new *form* of the
dictatorship of the proletariat which, depending on the given historical circumstances, "can mean different qualitative conditions of the
state: it can initially be a state building socialism or subsequently a
state of victorious socialism." [16] Thus, even in its early stage of historical development, "the content of the People's Democracy is the
dictatorship of the proletariat." The People's Democracy, in Yudin's
words, is one of the two historically established forms of the proletarian dictatorship, the other being the Soviet form.[17] Among the reasons explaining why the People's Democracy was a different form
were cited the favorable conditions under which it had been established which rendered unnecessary the disenfranchisement of the old
exploiting classes.[18] At the same time, however, the existence of democratic coalitions meant that the hegemony of the working class was
not expressed directly through the one-party system, as in the USSR.
The democratic coalitions were said to be the aftermath of the anti-
Fascist struggle and, thanks to the presence of Soviet power, they did
not constitute a challenge to the role of the party.* As one leading

* This was stressed by all concerned. Revai: "We must liquidate the concept that
the working class shares its power with other classes. In this concept we find the remnants of a viewpoint according to which a People's Democracy is some quite specific
kind of state which differs from the Soviet not only in its form, but also in its essence and functions" (p. 150). Sobolev: "A multi-party system is characteristic of the
political life of the countries of People's Democracy. . . . Experience has shown that
the system of People's Democracy can perform the functions of the dictatorship of
the proletariat also under conditions of the existence of several parties, but with this
imperative condition, that the leading and directing state power is the vanguard of the
working class — the Communist Party" (pp. 94–95).

Soviet scholar put it, this was merely a special application to the East European scene of Stalin's concepts of the alliance between the proletariat and the working classes. He then noted: "The content of a People's Democracy, as also of Soviet power, is determined by the Marxist-Leninist leadership of the Communist Party." [19]

At the Polish constitutional conference, held several years later, the supremacy of the party was not only firmly asserted but made the basis for the sovereignty of the People's Democracy on the grounds that party leadership guarantees the maintenance of the dictatorship of the proletariat which is the foundation of sovereign national power.[20] The party is not only supreme insofar as the other "democratic" parties are concerned, it also rejects any institutional limits on its power. Separation of powers, which in feudal times was a progressive arrangement, was pointedly criticized as having lost all its progressive character and for serving as a bourgeois device to suppress the people. "In a real people's state there is no room for any 'competition' of organs." [21]

The nature of the East European states was said to reflect a sharp break with the past, a break which involved the complete replacement of old state forms by new ones. Previously, it had been held (see Chapter 2) that the retention of some of the old bourgeois forms constituted one of the unique features of the People's Democracy. This view was now rejected, although it was conceded that the smashing of the old forms had not been performed in one violent sweep, as during the Russian revolution.[22] "It must be openly acknowledged that from the first moment of the existence of People's Poland we have a completely new form, although one cannot ignore the fact that in specific fragments of our system we temporarily used the old forms which subsequently, through the inflow of the new content, were liquidated in the course of intensifying class struggle," declared a Polish constitutional expert.[23] Even in Czechoslovakia, where the state had not been as disrupted by the war as in Poland and where the Communists took over the machinery of the state almost intact, similar change in *content*, and gradually in form, was alleged.[24]

The class struggle was now held to be a common denominator in the transitional period after consolidation of power. After the Soviet break with Tito, the Yugoslavs and Gomulka as well were castigated for underestimating or ignoring its importance as a "law of development." [25] They were charged with failing to understand that the bourgeoisie cannot be patriotic and cannot cooperate sincerely in the task of national reconstruction.[26] Insofar as the People's Democracies were held to be now entering on the stage of laying the foundations of socialism, and last-ditch desperate resistance of the former "oppressors" could be expected, this was a particularly serious charge. The earlier definition of the revolution as a democratic, but not a socialist, one was accordingly broadened to include a struggle against world imperialism, thereby making the early stage more "historically meaningful" than a mere bourgeois revolution and allowing its rapid transformation into a revolution "of the socialist type." * The class struggle would be imperative in this phase.

The arrival of the People's Democracies at this higher historical plateau raised the question of the relation between their development and that of the USSR. They were all forms of the dictatorship of the proletariat, but admittedly they were not identical. The reason for that was history. The People's Democracies were still at an earlier stage of development, and even the process of the complete liquidation of the former exploiters was not finished. The above conditions notwithstanding, Soviet support was said to have made possible the creation of the dictatorships of the proletariat under conditions considerably more favorable than in 1917. They could hence pass almost immediately to the internal fulfillment of the three basic tasks of a proletarian dictatorship: to liquidate the exploiters, to strengthen the alliance of the proletariat with the masses, and to lead toward a socialist society.[27]

It would be a grievous error, however, to conclude that because of more advantageous circumstances the People's Democracies could pursue a distinct path of their own. While acknowledging that Leninism requires recognition of "individual characteristics, conditioned by differences in historical development," [28] both the Soviet theorists and the East European politicians warned against any excesses. The Soviet scholar, N. P. Farberov, stressed that "it would be incorrect to maintain that 'as many countries as many roads to socialism.' This kind of statement means the negation of the international significance of the experience of the USSR and of the basic laws of the transitional period." He therefore felt that "the countries of People's Democracy do not march along some new, distinct road from that which the Soviet Union took to reach socialism." [29] That his

---

* There was some disagreement on whether the two phases together were a "socialist revolution." See Skilling, p. 28, for a contrast between some Soviet scholars; for later views, see Sobolev, pp. 91–92, and *Zagadnienia Prawne*, I, 352–353, where a difference is made between mere bourgeois revolutions and "popular democratic" revolutions, the latter having occurred in East Europe and leading directly into the proletarian dictatorship.

views reflected the official Soviet thinking is suggested by the following citation from the theoretical journal of the CPSU, *Bolshevik:* "The general laws of transition from capitalism to socialism, discovered by Marx and Engels, and tested, put to concrete use, and developed by Lenin and Stalin on the basis of the experience of the Bolshevik Party and the Soviet State, are binding upon all countries." [30]

The East European leaders, under the existing political pressures, soon found it necessary to move from mere assertions of the relevance of Soviet experience to stringent proclamations of blind devotion to the USSR. Starting with declarations that in all fundamental questions the USSR was a model for the People's Democracies,[31] the various leaders were soon competing in proclaiming their determination to apply the Soviet example and in minimizing the particularities of their countries. This was extended to mean that the basic criterion for judging an individual or a policy was its relation to the USSR, and that any underestimating of the relevance of Soviet experience was a bona fide indication of dangerous nationalist or even proimperialist leanings.[32] Soviet classics, particularly Stalin's, were described as "brilliant" contributions which had to be applied in East Europe through the adoption of the Soviet type of central planning, collectivization, and heavy industrial development.[33] To remove any last doubts, the emergence of the new theoretical uniformity, which served as the basis for policies which characterized the East European scene after 1948, was said to have been assisted through the personal contributions of Stalin himself.[34]

IMPACT ON CONSTITUTIONS

The new theoretical uniformity also found expression in East European constitutions and constitutional thinking. To a Communist, a constitution is not an intricate legal arrangement organizing and limiting power and expressing certain societal norms. Rather it is a reflection of existing reality and a means of furthering the transformation of society. It is both passive and active, meaningful only within its own historical phase, and can be altered when circumstances dictate. Given the actual environment changes that had taken place, particularly since the formation of the Cominform, and given the recent theoretical reassessments, the emergence of more commonly shared constitutional forms seemed unavoidable. Without going into a detailed structural discussion,[35] it is noteworthy that in short order all the states adopted new constitutions.

Bulgaria led the way with a new constitution proclaimed on November 4, 1947. Its provisions testified to the impact of the July Cominform meeting, for they differed significantly from the May 1947 draft.[36] Unlike the earlier version, it was modeled closely on the Stalin constitution and abandoned the planned post of President on the Western model. Rumania followed suit on April 13, 1948; Czechoslovakia on May 9, 1948; Hungary on August 20, 1949; and finally Poland on July 22, 1952. All these states declared themselves in their constitutions to be People's Democracies and drew heavily on the Soviet constitution for their legal, administrative, and local government provisions. This indebtedness was considered to be one of their particular excellences, and the parental relationship was not denied. "All the basic principles and institutions of the people's democratic states bear on them the stamp of the beneficent influence of the Stalin Constitution," one Soviet scholar asserted.[37] Two of the constitutions, those of Hungary and Poland, both products of a more ripened Stalinism (1949 and 1952, respectively), actually praised the USSR in their texts — not a frequent procedure among sovereign states. Although no one would admit it, the People's Democracies had finally reached the stage attained already in 1947 by the Yugoslavs.

The spirit behind the new constitutions was fully revealed in the Polish constitutional lawyers' discussions. The basis for political power was the alliance between the working class and the toiling peasantry, with the former playing the leading role on the basis of the victorious socialist construction in the USSR.[38] The state apparatus was said to express the transformation of the "popular anti-imperialist" revolution into a socialist one,[39] and the restriction and liquidation of exploiters was one of the purposes of the institutional framework. For this reason, such operations as the state budget would serve as one of the means for socialist transformation and elimination of exploiting classes.[40] Similarly, the criminal code had to evolve according to the actual objectives on the political and economic front, "depending on the form and intensity of class struggle."[41] Thus the evolution of the criminal code after the war was said to have gone through three main stages: (1) struggle against imperialism and Fascism, against survivals of feudalism; (2) suppression of the resistance of internal class enemies; (3) protection of socialist property.[42] The law, according to the Polish constitution, reflects at all times the interests and purpose of the working class and, for this reason, all acts injurious to socialist property can be equated with sabotage or diversion (article 77) (Czech legal thought went even further and maintained that it can be equated with treason.[43]) These considerations, expressing the dominant themes of established Stalinist thought, as well as the adoption of local institutions modeled on the Soviets, gave the constitutions of the People's Democracies a "socialist character," making them "after the great Stalin Constitution, the most progressive and democratic constitutions in the world." [44]

The only exception was East Germany which had been granted a constitution in October 1949 after the West German state had been set up. Up to this point East Germany had not entered into consideration because it constituted an occupied territory, without any pretense of independent statehood. The broad outlines of East German thinking, however, followed the pattern already traced. In 1945 the founding proclamation of the German Communist Party declared: "We are of the opinion that the course of forcing the Soviet system on Germany would be incorrect, since this course does not fit the current conditions of development in Germany." It then stated itself to be in favor of a "parliamentary-democratic republic." [45] Walter Ulbricht expressed similar sentiments on numerous occasions.

The 1949 constitution was based on a draft proposed by the SED in November 1946 and which had been meant for all of Germany. East Germany was proclaimed to be a "Democratic Republic" rather than a People's Democracy. This distinction was emphasized for essentially two reasons: Germany was still divided and the new East German institutions were meant some day to apply to West Germany where capitalism was still supreme; furthermore, internal changes in East Germany were lagging behind those in the People's Democracies. Colonel Tulpanov, the *politruk* of the Soviet Military Administration, used the following striking analogy to draw the difference between the various satellites insofar as their "socialist transformation" was concerned: "Yugoslavia has already reached the other bank [a socialist state]; Bulgaria is taking the last few strokes to reach it; Poland and Czechoslovakia are about in the middle of the river followed by Rumania and Hungary, which have gone about a third of the way; while the Soviet Occupation Zone has just taken the first few strokes away from the bourgeois bank." [46]

The GDR was thus said to be a democratic state ruled by an alliance between the workers and peasants. This was no longer a bourgeois type of state, but it was not yet a People's Democracy because power was shared with other social groups.[47] It was not listed among the People's Democracies, although on July 23, 1952, it too significantly revamped its constitutional structure in the Soviet image. The five component *länder* which had existed until that time were deprived of their constitutional functions. They were dissolved and replaced by 14 *Bezirke* (districts) which were controlled from the central government. Thus by 1952, with the adoption of administrative centralism, the content of the East German system was very similar to the People's Democracies though the label, for external reasons primarily, was not adopted. The SED openly assumed the posture of the ruling party, thereby paralleling the role played by the Communist parties elsewhere. In Otto Grotewohl's words: "The Workers' and Peasants' Authority in the GDR is the state form of the dictatorship of the proletariat under our special national conditions." [48]

The People's Democracies, together with the "more advanced" Soviet society, were thus in a class by themselves. In the eyes of the Communists they had outstripped other forms of political organization, particularly the Western democratic type, and had attained in short order a higher stage in historical development on the road to the eventual socialist society. Together with the Soviet Union, they were the only countries in the world which were basing their domestic organization on certain conscious insights into the laws of societal development and, armed with that understanding, which were creating a society that was in keeping with history. Recognition of Soviet leadership, given the Soviet Union's more advanced stage of socialist development, was accordingly a natural consequence of this perception of the real state of affairs. Similarly, there had to be intimate friendship with the USSR, given the fact that the People's Democracies were following so closely the Soviet road, a road which was said to lead away from traditions of national hostility, class oppression, artificially stimulated nationalism, and trite territorial ambitions. All of these vices faded, it was claimed, once the internal transformation of the People's Democracies gathered momentum. Friendship with the USSR, which in the earlier stage had been stressed as a matter of policy, now became an *organic* quality of the People's Democracy, maturing and strengthening as the People's Democracy transformed itself.

This "natural" development, inherent in the very process of transformation, was abetted, however, by external stimuli which could not be ignored. The splitting of the world into two camps was to the convinced Communist another proof of the need for maintaining Leninist-Stalinist norms of discipline, not only within each individual party but among them also. It meant that "democratic centralism" had to be applied on the interparty level, that hierarchy of command had to be respected, that the Cominform and ultimately Stalin himself had to be obeyed in every instance. Personal qualms about the ethics of any given policy had to give way in face of the external challenge lest the dreaded Leninist standard be applied: "does the enemy benefit from your stand, view, or policy?" Subjective motives then became irrelevant; the question pointedly raised the issue of the objective consequences of doubting the established line. Even the best domestic cause had to yield if the enemy were to benefit, if the international solidarity of the socialist camp were to suffer. Since the focal point of East-West tensions was the relationship between the USSR and the capitalist powers, the enemy would benefit from anything which could be construed as damaging to the USSR. Since the Soviet leadership would know best what was and what was not damaging to it, the primacy of its views on domestic affairs in East Europe was hence again justified and sanctified. To many Communists this line of reasoning was irresistible and for many years provided the crucible of their attitude.

In fact, the revisions in the ideological conceptions of the People's Democracy, the rapid advances made by them on the road toward "socialism," the emergence of fundamental characteristics common to all of them and to the USSR, and the need to close ranks in face of external threat brought the People's Democracies closer to the USSR than ever before. Given the known Marxist conceptions concerning relations between states and the basis for separate statehood, the stage was now reached when the very purpose of separate statehood could be questioned legitimately. The differences that still distinguished the People's Democracies from the Soviet Union were less significant than the similarities which involved some of the more crucial aspects of the nature of a state or society. The facts that they were already dictatorships of the proletariat, that the party was wielding power, that the "exploiting class" was defeated, were much more important than the specifics of the various temporary adjustments in some of these states. Considering this, and also considering the circumstances prevailing in the Soviet Union (the reassertion of monolithic party control, ideological conformity, industrial drives, and so on), was not the merger of the People's Democracies with the USSR not only theoretically justifiable but indeed dictated by the laws of historical development?

The ideological objections that might have been raised could have stressed a fact which has already been noted — namely, the differences in the stages of development between the satellites and the Soviet

Union. For this reason a union, federation, or confederation would have been premature. But such considerations had not prevented the formation of the USSR itself, with its component units ranging in stages of development from the industrial to the almost prefeudal; nor did they prevent the incorporation of the Baltic states, which had no prior "socialist transformation." Clearly then, the problem of relative stages was not crucial.

Probably much more important in this question of a merger were the presence of Titoism and the emergence of Communist China. Paradoxical as it seems, it may have been Tito's earlier hints about eventual union with the USSR that now helped to delay what seemed so timely. The Soviet government had gone to considerable lengths to discredit the Belgrade regime as a betrayer of both international Communism and the Yugoslav people. Kardelj's pious hope for a Union of Soviet Socialist Republics including the People's Democracies was ridiculed, reviled, and rejected. Every emphasis was placed on the significance of the sovereignty of each individual People's Democracy even while that sovereignty was being drained away. After 1949, a further consideration might have been the creation of a Communist state in China which probably would not have viewed with enthusiasm the idea that the launching of domestic socialist transformation is tantamount to formal union with the USSR.

Finally, practical considerations were involved. Incorporation, or even federation, would not have increased by much, if at all, the existing ideological and political supremacy of the USSR. But it might have caused domestic complications in East Europe, weakened the Communist appeal abroad, provoked resentment among some East European Communists and caused suspicion among the Chinese, while providing the Yugoslavs and the capitalists with additional ammunition. The dotting of the *i* could well be delayed, for it would have involved no significant gains since relations with the People's Democracies were already based on the ideological principle of the universality of Soviet experience, expressed politically through the acceptance of Soviet primacy. The forms of independence were hence maintained.

The reconsideration of the theory of the People's Democracy, aided by growing Soviet intrusion, ended the most creative period in postwar Communist thought and led to a rapid decline in the importance of theory. The dynamic interrelationship between ideological disputes and political problems, which had been at least embryonic in East Europe, was eliminated. Politics began to dictate ideology and to manifest the general unwillingness to go beyond the limits of already established doctrine. Thus, ideology ceased to be what it had been for those Communists who had been so genuinely motivated by it — a method of understanding reality, thereby creatively guiding and shaping political action while also serving as a source of mass appeal. It became instead the ideology of a state, with its content determined by reason of state or, more correctly, by the interests of specific groups within the ruling class.

But to many East European Communists, dependent for their position and new privileges on Soviet support, the reconsidered theory represented a much less complicated insight into their existence. Reliance on Soviet experience was the safest way of coping with any new problems which might bring on interpretative difficulties and consequent political pitfalls. Those internal problems which flew in the face of the state ideology were viewed as expressions of hostile activity or, at the very least, as manifestations of a lag in social consciousness left over from the bourgeois period. The operational formula was to take a Stalinist dictum or action and apply it rigidly to the domestic circumstance. Sterility in thought and policy was the consequence.

5 / LAYING THE SOCIALIST FOUNDATIONS

AS the theory was being reconsidered, the construction of the foundations for socialism was beginning in earnest. The situation was no longer obscured by the need to adjust, to compromise, to take one step backward before leaping two steps forward. The internal transformation of society was based on tried Stalinist patterns and reflected Stalin's apparent conviction that the political-economic course he had pursued in the USSR during the thirties had been essentially correct and had saved the Soviet Union. The Soviet dictator, aging and growing more suspicious with each passing day, seemed no longer willing to relate the experience of the past and the perception of what is new to the existing situation. Like many old tyrants, he now sought security in rigidly applying *his* past experience to every new circumstance. He was fortunate in possessing the power to make the new circumstances fit his established and well-tried criteria. Fearing that war with capitalism was a real and immediate possibility, he probably felt that loyalty would be best achieved by duplicating the Soviet structure in East Europe. He believed that in so doing he was creating the material conditions for close liaison between his socialist state and the People's Democracies while eliminating those sources of diversity which might ultimately lead to disunity.

The new pattern, which was to serve as a basis for the relations between the USSR and East Europe and which was applied uniformly to the area, stressed: (1) the implementation of the theory of the Communist Party's political supremacy and the assertion of the dictatorship of the proletariat; (2) the intensification of the class struggle not only to seek out the known hostile classes but also to unmask the enemies which had infiltrated the Communist movement; (3) the carrying of the class struggle into the countryside to break the resistance of the peasants, particularly the more prosperous ones, to the socialist transformation of agriculture without which both effective industrialization and real socialism were said to be impossible; (4) the launching of rapid and large-scale industrialization of each People'

Democracy. The result would be a uniformity in existing conditions which inevitably would produce conformity in behavior and interests. The Stalinist formula had the virtues of simplicity and directness.

THE SUPREMACY OF THE PARTY AND THE DICTATORSHIP OF THE PROLETARIAT

The assertion of the party's supremacy was merely a matter of openly acknowledging the prevailing state of affairs and mopping up the remnants of the former opposition. By 1948 in every People's Democracy the Socialist Party had been absorbed into the Communist Party,* and open opposition had been dispersed, imprisoned, or liquidated.† The Communist parties, which had enjoyed a spectacular growth in membership, by 1948 had reached a plateau in their number (see accompanying table) on which, like the CPSU, they were to remain for the next ten years. In fact, the leaderships had just cause to fear that their efforts to increase memberships rapidly, a political necessity during the earlier stage, had resulted in the influx of many questionable elements. Accordingly, paralleling Soviet postwar practice, they sharply reduced any further recruitment. The non-Communist parties, when not actually abolished, were emasculated and merged in the patriotic or national fronts (National Front in Poland, Czechoslovakia, East Germany; People's Independent Front in Hungary; People's Democratic Front in Rumania, and Fatherland Front in Bulgaria); they were given the task of transmitting to their members and sympathizers the directives of the ruling party. The Communist Party openly assumed state leadership and abandoned the pretense of partnership with the other parties. In Poland, Bierut, the First Secretary, also held the office of President and, after that was abolished, that of Premier; in Czechoslovakia the First Secretary, Gottwald, was also President; elsewhere the posts of Premier and First Secretary were combined.

There is no need to trace in detail the penetration of each society by party controls. Suffice it to say that the Soviet model was duplicated,¹ and in every factory, enterprise, town, or village it was the party committee which was the source of authority, no matter how

---

* Rumania: February 23, 1948; Hungary: June 14, 1948; Czechoslovakia: June 27, 1948; Bulgaria: August 11, 1948; Poland: December 15, 1948.

† The process, of course, never had a clear cut-off date, but the symbolic end of effective opposition may be set as October 1947 for Poland (Mikolajczyk's flight abroad); October 1947 for Rumania (Maniu's trial); February 1947 for Hungary (Bela Kovacs' arrest); and September 1947 for Bulgaria (Petkov's execution).

Growth of Communist Party membership from the seizure of power to the New Course

Poland 1956 pop. 27.5 million		Czechoslovakia 1955 pop. 13 million		Hungary 1955 pop. 9.8 million		Yugoslavia 1953 pop. 16.9 million		Bulgaria 1955 pop. 7.5 million		Rumania 1956 pop. 17.5 million		GDR 1950 pop. 18.4 million	
Dec. 1945	235,296	Aug. 1945	712,776	May 1945	150,000	Dec. 1945	141,066	Sept. 1944	25,000	Sept. 1945	217,000	Feb. 1946	511,000
Dec. 1946	555,888	Mar. 1946	1,081,554	Sept. 1946	653,000	July 1948	468,175	Mar. 1945	254,000	June 1947	710,000	Apr. 1946	1,298,415 [a]
Dec. 1947	820,786	Nov. 1947	1,281,138	May 1947	700,000	Dec. 1949	470,379	Mar. 1946	500,000 (approx.)	Sept. 1948	937,846 [a]	June 1948	2,000,000 (approx.)
Dec. 1948	1,368,873 [a]	May 1948	2,000,048	May 1948	884,000	Nov. 1952	779,382	June 1948	495,658 [a]	July 1950	720,000	Jan. 1949	1,773,689
Dec. 1949	1,200,000 (approx.)	May 1949	2,311,066 [a]	Mar. 1949	1,200,000 [a]	Dec. 1953	716,985	Dec. 1949	460,000	June 1956	580,000	Apr. 1950	1,750,000
Dec. 1953	1,226,716	Feb. 1951	1,677,443	Mar. 1952	880,000	June 1955	624,806	June 1950	367,000			Sept. 1953	1,230,000
Mar. 1954	1,297,000	Aug. 1954	1,489,234	May 1954	864,607	June 1956	635,984	June 1954	455,251			Apr. 1954	1,272,987 [b]

[a] Following absorption of the Social Democrats.
[b] Figure excludes 140,326 candidates.

Note: We may make the following observations: (1) There was a rapid growth in party memberships during the early phase, preliminary to complete liquidation of the opposition. (2) Following the consolidation of power, the membership remained relatively stable. (3) The parties contained a relatively high proportion of the population, as compared to the CPSU where the total never went above 3.5 per cent of the total population. (4) The more totalitarianized the regimes, the smaller, relatively, the parties.

Sources: For Poland: Iwanska, p. 316; for Czechoslovakia: Hajda, p. 324; for Hungary: Rakosi, *Valogatott Beszedek es Cikkek* (Budapest, 1953), pp. 60–61, 229, 295; for Yugoslavia: *Komunist*, no. 11–12, 1956, no. 7–8, 1956, pp. 754–765; for Bulgaria: *Materiali po istoriia na bulgarskata komunisticheska partiia* (Sofia, 1956), p. 391; for Rumania: S. Fisher-Galati, ed., *Romania* (New York, 1957), pp. 69–76; for GDR: C. Stern, *Die SED* (Germany, 1954), pp. 152–3, and Ulbricht, *Tagesspiegel*, March 5, 1946.

trivial the issue, no matter how unimportant the problem. With this accumulation of power the party soon became the source of privilege and corruption. With the growing shortage of housing and consumer goods, special facilities for party members were made available, and the heavily curtained stores without names became a source of public scandal and indignation. In time this was to cause serious demoralization, but in the first flush of victory it seemed like justifiable spoils. Subsidiary party organizations were established to embrace the youth, the women, the university students, and so on, much on the Soviet model.[2] Party controls reached into the universities through Communist youth organizations, through the introduction of new curricula (particularly courses on Marxism-Leninism), and finally through appointment of new professors and purges of the old ones. Those disciplines which represented an inherent challenge to the official doctrine, such as mathematical logic, sociology, and psychology, were eliminated altogether. Universities were deprived of their academic independence; promotions were made on the basis of political criteria; the Soviet academic system of *kandidaty* replaced the Western doctorate. By 1952 party controls on education had been imposed in all the states. Yet even after Stalin died, in a typical example of the competition in imitating, the organ of the Czech Party complained that "it is still a frequent phenomenon in our country that while we proclaim in our slogans that the Soviet Union is our example, at the same time we are very often satisfied merely with the proclamation. Therefore it is now necessary to study more concretely and systematically the life of Soviet universities."[3] Within the various states, academic and scientific activity was coordinated by academies of science, modeled again on the Soviet and controlled by the ruling party.*

In other fields of creative endeavor the party also asserted its domination and articulated its expectations. Socialist realism was proclaimed to be the norm in the arts, and at the World Congress in De-

* In a remarkable exposé published in Poland after October 1956, a distinguished Polish professor revealed that the presidium of the Polish Academy of Science played a purely fictional role and that all power was vested in the scientific secretariat which was an agency of the party's control. In fact, elections of the secretariat's membership were so nominal that once the election of a member to it was announced immediately after the party's Central Committee had made its selection and before the formal vote in the Academy had taken place. Of the Academy's 107 members, only 27 belonged to the party; of its presidium's 26 members, 12 belonged to the party; of the secretariat's 12 members, 10 belonged to the party. The article, by J. Chalasinski, "Ways and Byways of Socialism in Polish Science (1949–1954)," *Kultura i Spoleczenstwo*, no. 1, 1957, is a broad indictment of Communist policies in the field of scholarship and science.

fense of Peace (August 25–28, 1948) the Soviet spokesman in literature, A. Fadeiev, drew a sharp and distinct line between those who are
for socialism and those who are against it. In architecture, a field
especially important since its achievements cannot disappear as easily
as a bad book, particular stress was laid by the Communist parties on
emulating the Soviet "gingerbread" style. Architectural journals were
filled with discussions of the socialist city, the socialist style, and the
Soviet architectural experience. Party ideologues, such as Revai in
Hungary, took an active part in urging and cajoling architects to learn
from the USSR.[4] In Poland, Bierut himself participated in the discussions on the reconstruction of Warsaw and severely castigated, as
"cosmopolitan and bourgeois aberrations," the modernistic tendencies
of the Warsaw architects.[5] The symbol of the new era, and of the
close Polish ties to the USSR, was the Stalin palace constructed in the
center of the city. Statues to Stalin dominated the horizon elsewhere.

The party was to be omnipotent and omnipresent. The pervasive-
ness of its controls was to leave no doubt that it, the vanguard of the
proletariat, was directing the life of society toward the ultimate utopia.
The previous emphasis on reconstruction and reform, which in its
very essence implies some relation to existing reality, gave way to
shrill insistence on the need for revolutionary change — to be effected
within and through the institutional framework of the dictatorship of
the proletariat which the People's Democracies were now said to be.
This insistence was not merely a case of ideological ritualism. The dictatorship of the proletariat was a conception not devoid of political
content, and the Soviet and East European leaders must have been
fully aware of it. Its implementation was bound to speed up those historical processes which to a Communist must naturally seem desirable
and inevitable. At the same time, the fulfillment of such objectives
could not help, it seemed, but narrow the gap between the USSR and
the People's Democracies in the historical progression toward Communism.

A concomitant development was the decline in importance of state
institutions. The most dramatic expression of this trend was the reduction of the assemblies to a purely nominal role, both on the national
and the local levels. The popular councils, adopted with so much fan-
fare as another step forward in "democratization," became at their
very inception mere appendages to the local party committees and
the instruments of endorsement of administrative *fiats*.[6] The decline
in the importance of the administrative structure, however, was not
tantamount to a withering away of the bureaucracy. On the contrary,

particularly with the large-scale nationalization and industrialization, the bureaucracy grew even as the ultimate decisions slipped from its hands.* The additional factor of fear of "hostile penetration" meant that extensive controls were instituted on all levels, thereby further expanding the bureaucratic apparatus. Cross-checking and interpenetrating organs were designed to exercise "proletarian vigilance" against diversion, sabotage, and other forms of hostile class activity. The atmosphere of the state administration soon lost the character of a public-service organization and became dominated by internal militancy, suspicion, and almost paranoiac secrecy.†

By 1950–1951 the administrative structure of the People's Democracies began to assume what was labeled as the forms of socialist administration. This usually followed the adoption of the new constitutions reflecting the new ideological concepts (see preceding chapter). The ministries were broken down into smaller, more specialized units directing specific economic branches. By 1953 the adoption of long-range planning — Bulgaria: Five Year Plan, 1949–1953; Czechoslovakia: Five Year Plan, 1949–1953; Hungary: Five Year Plan, 1950–1954; Poland: Six Year Plan, 1950–1955; Rumania: Five Year Plan, 1951–1955; East Germany: Five Year Plan, 1951–1955[7] — made possible the introduction of "the socialist forms of state budget," [8] in which the turnover tax, on the Soviet model, became the most important source of state revenue.[9] These fiscal arrangements of the dictatorship of the proletariat were, however, construed as being pri-

---

* The prewar size of the Polish state administration was estimated at 172,000 (Spulber, p. 21). In postwar Poland, with its population decreased by 30 per cent, the number of purely state administrative officials was 348,500 (B. Minc, "The Problem of Bureaucracy," *Nowa Kultura*, May 27, 1956). These figures do not include officials of state enterprises or full-time Communist Party functionaries (roughly 15,000 in Poland). In prewar Czechoslovakia there were 345,300 officials, including state officials (200,800), teachers, and officials of state enterprises and monopolies (Spulber, *ibid.*). In 1956, the figure was 792,000 for "public administration and the courts, banks and insurance companies, in social organizations, science, research" (*Predvoj*, February 27, 1958). The prewar Czech ratio of productive workers to administrative personnel declined from 4:1 to 2.32:1 under the Communists (*East Europe*, VII, no. 8). The number of state officials and teachers in prewar Bulgaria was 63,000 (Spulber, *ibid.*). In 1952 the number was 91,000 (*Statisticheski Godishnik na Narodna Republika Bulgariya*, 1956, p. 100).

† The Bulgarian *State Journal*, December 6, 1948, included the following items as military information and therefore state secrets: number and distribution of workers, fulfillment of the Plan in absolute figures, absolute figure on sowing, livestock, and agricultural production, results of research work, and so on. In Polish scientific institutions even geological and botanical findings were classified as state secrets and suppressed. W. Szafer, "On Some Unfulfilled Aims of the Polish Academy of Science," *Kultura i Społeczenstwo*, no. 1 (1957), pp. 61–62.

marily designed to facilitate the historical dialectic of the class struggle. For this reason, in the words of an East European planning journal, "in the people's democracies, taxes serve the ends of the dictatorship of the proletariat. They are an efficient tool of class warfare and are devised to help in the process of limiting and ousting capitalist elements from the national economy." [10]

The class conflict was broadly interpreted and therefore broadly applied. "The means which the enemies use are varied: from destroying and damaging machines and installations to the systematic disorganization of production through the false preparation of plans, erroneous decisions, misleading accounting, statistical frauds; from premeditated negligence of fire prevention measures, of security regulations and labor hygiene — to the organization of arson and causing catastrophes and accidents in places of employment; from ordinary theft or illegal sale of rationed items to the cutting up for scrap of useful machines." [11] Such a definition of hostile activity on the economic front embraced in one sweep both subjective and objective guilt and made it possible, as frequently became the case, to try for sabotage individuals guilty of a simple mistake. It also resulted in increased security measures at places of employment, with a consequent component of fear and suspicion.

Terror as a form of public policy in the USSR and East Europe is a matter of generally familiar record, and it had an impressive history even during the earlier period when the Communist parties were just seizing or consolidating their power. However, the emphasis on class struggle made organized violence an integral characteristic of the People's Democracy as a social system. It was expressed in a continuous series of public and secret trials of various real and imagined enemies of the system.* These ranged from former underground leaders in Poland or the "White Legion" trials in Czechoslovakia[12] — involving, in both cases, manifestations of organized resistance to the system — to a variety of economic sabotage charges, frequently involving people who merely happened to have been engaged in some state venture which failed. The growing number of arrests throughout the area resulted in the establishment of a regular system of concentration camps, usually utilized for purposes of forced labor. For

---

* It is estimated that in Poland between 1945 and 1949 some 6,000 people were secretly executed. Most of them were former members of the anti-Nazi underground, including some of the most heroic figures of the war. (A detailed analysis, with many hitherto unknown facts, is in *Na Antenie*, July 10, 1966.) Although after 1956 the Gomulka regime repudiated Stalinist terror, most of these victims were not rehabilitated and their executioners were not punished.

instance, in Rumania, the Danube–Black Sea Canal project employed prisoners; in Poland, special penal battalions were formed for the most exposed and deadly coal shafts in Silesia. The number of *identified* camps suggests the scale of this operation: 124 in Czechoslovakia, 199 in Hungary, 97 in Poland.[13] The first country to institute this procedure, as early as 1945, was Bulgaria. It was then used against former Fascists, but its scope was enlarged in March 1948 to embrace "alien class enemies." Czechoslovakia followed suit in October 1948. Other Soviet police controls were also adopted: between 1950 and 1952, for example, internal passports issued by the police became obligatory throughout the area. Mass deportations from some of the large urban centers were enforced (particularly in Budapest, Bucharest, and Sofia) to eliminate former industrialists, soldiers, and professionals, thereby vacating sorely needed space for the new elite.

But far more important, as the future was to show, in the connection of these regimes to the USSR was the changing relationship between the secret police and the Communist Party. In the USSR, the secret police under Yezhov had run amuck during the Great Purges, and Stalin finally had to purge it.[14] After the war, the Soviet secret police regained some of its influence, and Stalin seemed to be using Beria as a lever to insure the monolithic unity of the party, occasionally unchaining the police to exact the party's unquestioning loyalty. The Voznesensky case and the Leningrad affair, both tangled and complicated matters of intraparty strife, are still, broadly speaking, cases in point.[15] In East Europe, following the decision to establish conformity through the intensification of class struggle, the secret police inevitably began to assume greater political significance as the "shield of the revolution," defending the People's Democracy against all forms of subversion. Its operations gradually slipped out from under the party's control, and the secret police became semiautonomous, subject only to direct Soviet control (see next chapter). The police became a state within a state, feared by both the population and the party membership.[16]

PURGE PATTERNS

The stature of the secret police was particularly enhanced by the purges and the purge trials of various party leaders and members. The purges were closely related to the new phase of development, marked by new theories and policies. The East European purges, much like the earlier Soviet ones, were a product of organizational and doctrinal pressures. With power seized, all sorts of elements not identified with the objectives of the movement flocked into the ruling party (see membership table). The absence of competition resulted in internal stagnation, decay, and loss of revolutionary zeal. Various "mutual-admiration societies" developed, sponsoring one another within the movement purely for reasons of self-interest. Power, in brief, corrupts, and a totalitarian system lacks the competitive qualities of democratic party struggle to minimize the corruption. The method of resolving these dilemmas was the purge.

Inherent in these general considerations was the growing Soviet fear of Titoism — both of the "national Stalinism" variety (which might be described as the left wing) and of the more moderate right-wing variety which insisted that existing domestic situations be a primary consideration in shaping Communist policies. As it happened, Soviet fears of the right-wing type of orientation were largely exaggerated — only Gomulka in Poland and Patrascanu in Rumania really fitted this category, and it is extremely unlikely that either Rajk, Slansky, or Kostov could have been accused of plotting a policy geared more to domestic requirements than to Soviet ones. Rather, they seemed to have originally favored a revolutionary policy and, in this respect, reflected the more extreme earlier Titoist position. It may be surmised that the left wing drew some of its inspiration from the Zhdanov policy of ideological and political radicalism. Its liquidation coincided with the purge of the Zhdanovites in the USSR following Zhdanov's death in the summer of 1948.

Whatever the motives, the elimination of alternatives was bound to improve coordination and unity, especially since in East Europe the Communist parties were much less monolithic than the Soviet party. They had only recently acquired power, and it is sometimes forgotten that these parties were initially amalgams of very diverse groups, held together only by a commitment to the usually unarticulated Communist image of tomorrow. After the war all kinds of individuals, ranging from the most hard-boiled party veterans to starry-eyed fellow travelers, came together from many parts of the globe. The new ruling parties were split into a variety of overlapping factions (for instance, the Moscow Communists versus the domestic ones, the Soviet stooges versus "our own road to socialism" believers, the former Spanish Civil War veterans, the wartime London refugees). Held together by common hostility to the non-Communists, they differed on the positive program to be pursued once power was won. Indeed, from the Soviet point of view, these diverse backgrounds were sufficient proof of the "objective" existence of an unhealthy diversity among the ruling groups. In November 1949 a resolution of the Cominform accordingly warned the Communist leaders that they must "increase by all possible means revolutionary vigilance in their own ranks."

The purges were especially violent in Bulgaria, Hungary, and Czechoslovakia. In these countries some of the leading Communist figures were tried and executed. They were accused not only of ideological deviations; the defendants were also charged with treason. The victims came from diverse backgrounds: some were old Communists, now accused of having been Gestapo agents; some had fought against Franco, now called "cosmopolitan" traitors; many were Jews, now accused of being Zionist infiltrators; some were even Moscow-trained *apparatchiki*, now supposed to have betrayed the movement. The pattern of the Soviet purge of 1936–1938 was thus being closely imitated. With the elimination of such "factions" as the Spanish Civil War veterans who had a special sense of group identity, the party could become monolithic.

The first violent purge took place in Hungary. In September 1949, Laszlo Rajk, Politburo member and Minister of the Interior, a Communist with many years of devoted service, faced a People's Court accused of being an employee of Allen Dulles and Alexander Rankovic (head of Tito's secret police). Sharing the dock were several important party and army functionaries (including, for instance, General Palffy, who engineered the communization of the armed forces). In a trial remarkable for the fantastic content of the confessions (after the Hungarian revolt it was revealed that the defendants had been tortured and promised clemency for confessing), the chief defendants were condemned to death and duly executed by garroting. Rajk's execution and the resulting atmosphere of fear did much to strengthen the hand of Rakosi, who, unlike Rajk, had spent the war years in the USSR. And it made the policy of blind imitation of Soviet forced industrialization and collectivization a matter above discussion. Dependence on Soviet support naturally increased, and any Titoist alternatives (whether such had ever been considered by Rajk is doubtful) were out of the question.

A similarly violent operation was almost simultaneously performed on the upper echelons of the Bulgarian Communist Party. The political picture was complicated by the previous Bulgarian negotiations with Tito about the Balkan Union, which resulted in opportunities among Bulgarian leaders for charging each other with complicity with Belgrade. The undisputed chief, Dimitrov, had been ailing for some time, and this necessarily generated a struggle for succession. In March 1949, Traicho Kostov, a Deputy Prime Minister and Politburo member, was summarily removed from his posts. He had previously been one of the contenders for power and was associated with the rapid economic revolution being pushed in Bulgaria. According to some reports, he became so enthusiastic over his tasks that he tended, despite his known anti-Titoism, to develop a "Bulgaria-first" outlook. His fall was followed by the rapid advance of one of his chief rivals, Vulko Chervenkov, who succeeded to Dimitrov's mantle. In December 1949, Kostov, together with several high party functionaries, was indicted on charges which might have been borrowed directly from the Rajk trial. The only sensation of the trial was Kostov's sudden repudiation of his alleged confession. Kostov, as a matter of course, was executed, and the official party organ, *Rabotnichesko Delo*, reported that after the sentencing he repudiated his repudiation. His associates received severe prison sentences and the top party echelons were thoroughly purged. Of the forty members of the Central Committee, seventeen were removed.

The most extensive purge swept the leadership of the Czechoslovak party. The purge gradually gained momentum between the years 1950 and 1952. Individual leaders were dropped from their high posts; others then accused them of treason. In turn the accusers were dropped and accused. The first to go, early in 1950, were some high officials handling foreign policy and trade, such as Vilem Novy (editor-in-chief of *Rude Pravo*, the official organ, and chairman of the Foreign Affairs Committee of the National Assembly) and Evzen Loebl (Deputy Minister of Foreign Trade). They were followed by Vladimir Clementis, the Foreign Minister and a high-ranking Slovak Communist, suspected of "right-wing" leanings. The purge then covered the top echelons of the Slovak Communist Party. By late 1950 and 1951 it began to embrace the Czech Communist leadership itself, and finally reached its zenith in November 1951, with the announcement that Rudolf Slansky, a Deputy Prime Minister and formerly the powerful Secretary General of the Central Committee, had been arrested. It is noteworthy that, among Communists, Slansky was considered to have been close to Zhdanov. President Gottwald stated: "New disclosures have proved Slansky guilty of a direct, active and, one might say, leading part in the anti-Party and anti-state conspiracy." [17]

The purge then proceeded to cleanse the Secretariat of the Central Committee and the Central Committee itself. Gottwald's primacy wa now consolidated. Fifty of the ninety-seven members of the Central Committee and six of the seven members of the Secretariat were removed, and the purge reached deep into the bureaucracy and the army. Insofar as Slansky and Clementis were concerned, their cases were linked even though they appeared to have been at opposite ends of the political spectrum, and a typical Soviet-style show trial was staged. The Minister of Justice drew explicit parallels between the Slansky trial and the Soviet purge trials of the late thirties. The special feature of the trial held in November 1952 was its openly anti-Semitic character, which paralleled the campaign being then waged in the USSR in the form of special press emphasis on the execution of "Jewish speculators" and which culminated in the Doctors' Plot. Since a high proportion of the defendants in the Slansky-Clementis trial were Jews (including Slansky himself), the prosecution repeatedly stressed the alleged links of the defendants with Israel, mocking some of them for their Jewish accents and accusing them of a "cosmopolitan" orientation. Eleven of the accused, headed by Slansky and Clementis, were hanged on December 3, 1952.

Less violent purges occurred in Rumania, Poland, and East Germany. In May 1952, several high Rumanian Communists (including Ana Pauker and Vasile Luca) were dropped from the Politburo, but recourse to violence was delayed until April 1954 when Patrascanu (purged in 1948 for alleged nationalism) was executed. It seems that the dismissed Politburo members constituted an internal clique, which in the phase of uniformity was incompatible with Stalinist leadership. Pauker and Luca represented the old Moscow faction in the Rumanian leadership, and moreover Pauker was Jewish. Their elimination thus had the effect of establishing in power a solid national, Stalinist leadership under Gheorghiu-Dej's personal direction. Patrascanu's elimination lacked the staging of the Rajk, Kostov, and Slansky performances. Clearly, 1954 was no longer the season, and apparently the Rumanian leadership wanted to get rid of an inconvenient skeleton in its closet.

Less violent purges occurred within the Communist leaderships of Poland and East Germany. In 1950 the East Germans expelled Paul Merker, a member of the SED Politburo, and the top functionaries Leo Bauer, Bruno Goldhammer, Willi Kreykemeyer, Lex Ende, and Maria Weiterer from the party. Four other high officials were dismissed from their party posts. In May 1953 Franz Dahlem lost his position in the party leadership. After the June uprising Wilhelm Zaisser, Minister of State Security, Rudolf Herrnstadt, editor of *Neues*

Deutschland, as well as three other members of the party leadership and several high state officials were expelled from the party for their opposition to Ulbricht. These moves, however, were relatively *sub rosa* and did not produce any openly significant ideological cleavage or any major show trials, although several of the officials concerned were imprisoned for a lengthy period of time and one of them, Leo Bauer, was even sentenced to death by the Soviets and only subsequently pardoned. The absence of an explicitly ideological aspect distinguished the German purge from the also relatively nonviolent Polish pattern.

In Poland, the removal of Gomulka occurred in the context of a power struggle between him and Bierut which, under the circumstances, was almost predetermined in favor of Bierut. It also occurred, however, in the context of an ideological cleavage in which Gomulka favored a delay in collectivization as well as greater autonomy, and hence diversity, in domestic policy. The ideological discussions, with Gomulka gradually giving way and being demoted step by step, lasted from the late summer of 1948 to November 1949. Gomulka and his associates were then expelled. The Soviet pattern of development was now obligatory for Poland — Stalinism was the official path. Nonetheless, initially Gomulka was not even arrested (he was taken into custody in 1951) and never tried. No show trials of Polish Communists were staged.

What are the reasons for this distinct pattern in Poland and East Germany (though of course in Germany no one of Gomulka's stature was involved)? No definite answer can be given without access to party archives, but we do know that Stalin had insisted that purge trials be held and that severe methods be used. Polish observers were "invited" to the various show trials abroad and presented with evidence "implicating" Gomulka. At the Eighth Plenum (October 1956), Berman, the Politburo member most responsible for the secret-police terror in Poland, explicitly took credit (with the Politburo) for having resisted Soviet pressures to do away with Gomulka.[18] There is no way of checking Berman's veracity, but since none of his enemies belied him at that session we may assume an element of truth in his account. Why did the Polish party resist Stalin's pressures and, more important, how was it able to procrastinate until his death, thereby saving Gomulka?

The causes might possibly be linked with the fact the Polish Communist Party labored under the bitter legacy of Stalin's 1938 accusation that the party was an agency of Polish espionage. At that time, the Comintern abolished the Polish Communist Party, and Stalin completed the process by shooting almost all of its leaders, many of whom had served with Lenin. The reconstituted party, according to the accounts of some of its well-informed members, consequently went out of its way to avoid any further executions of its leaders. Furthermore, the openly anti-Semitic character of the Slansky trial might have frightened Berman, the Politburo member directly responsible for such matters. On a more general level, Stalin's pressures for violence were combined elsewhere in East Europe with domestic needs for a purge. The Czech party might have actually needed a violent shake-up of its leadership, once the democratic elements had been crushed. Security tends to breed disunity and factionalism, and Stalinists know only one way of resolving such difficulties. Paradoxically, the relative weakness of the Polish and East German parties might have enabled them to avoid a violent purge by pleading that such violence would further undermine their position and harm the unfinished process of consolidation. (In East Germany there was, of course, the further need to appeal to some left-wing West German elements.) Weakness might have thus been a source of evasion insofar as responding to Stalin's pressure was concerned.

In addition, all of the East European Communist parties adopted during this period broader measures to reassert the monolithic quality of their organizations. These took the form of purging their memberships of real or alleged "unhealthy," "alien," or "hostile" elements, more or less on the basis of the categories established in the purging of the prominent deviationists. Since very large numbers were involved, the degree of violence was less intense than in the more spectacular individual cases. But the scope is suggested by the following data on Communists purged in this period:

Poland	Czechoslovakia	Rumania	Hungary	East Germany	Bulgaria
70,000	550,000	200,000	200,000	300,000	90,000

On the average, about one of every four party members was purged in each of the East European parties.[19]

TRANSFORMATION OF THE MATERIAL ENVIRONMENT

The reliance on Stalinist experience in the socialist transformation of the People's Democracy also led the regimes into extending the class struggle into the agricultural sector. This policy was one of the most glaring examples of dogmatic application of alien experience. Some of the previously existing social inequities had been resolved by land reform, and most of the land holdings were now concentrated in the small and medium categories, while the large landowners had all but disappeared. The policy of collectivization, adopted in 1948–49 and launched in 1950, was justified by reference to Stalin's "law of

Private agricultural holdings: percentage distribution

Holdings (in hectares)	Czecho-slovakia	Poland	Hungary	Rumania	Bulgaria
Small					
0–2	46.5	28.8	68.6	53.1	29.2
2–5	23.5	32.5	18.9	22.9	38.6
Medium					
5–10	17.1	27.1	8.5	17.9	25.4
Large					
10–20	10.6	10.1	3.4	5.0	6.8
20–50	2.3	1.2	0.6	1.1	—

Source: Spulber, p. 245.

development" which categorically stated that socialist industrializa-tion must be accompanied by a socialist transformation of the country side. At the Fifth Congress of the Bulgarian Communist Party (1948) Dimitrov stressed that nationalization of land is the inescapable enc of the process of socialist transformation,[20] while the Polish constitu tional discussions stressed that the persistence of private-land owner ship is "the most important factor" delaying "the tempo of socia change." [21] It was argued that by reducing the peasant to the status o a hired laborer, the socialist transformation of the countryside woul assure state control over food supply, provide surplus labor throug] the introduction of mechanization, squeeze out of the agricultura sector some of the funds necessary for capital investment, and preven the peasants from wielding political influence. Since these considera tions, abstracted from the problem of their actual social and economi validity, seemed important to the regimes' survival, they felt justifie in using the means necessary to achieve the desired consequences.

The policy of collectivization, applied with a considerable amour of coercion,* relied on the following devices for inducing the peasan to join either the collective farms or the state farms: heavy taxe forced state deliveries, moral pressure through repeated visits fro

* For example, it was officially admitted that during the Rumanian collectiviz tion of 1950–1952 approximately 80,000 peasants were imprisoned. Scinteia, Decemb 13, 1961.

party activists, a certain amount of local violence usually pitting the poor peasants or the landless rural proletariat against the richer farmers, punitive expeditions of urban party activists and police whose task would be to "socialize" rapidly a given district. The collective farms as established in East Europe ranged from the pooling of privately owned machinery and property to common ownership of land and machinery. Most, however, were of the latter, more "advanced," type and for this reason provoked a high degree of peasant resentment. Unlike an American farmer, say, who tends to think of his land as a commodity which is a source of income, to the peasant land has also the properties of tradition and sentiment which vest it with a certain mystical quality. Efforts to deprive him of it were hence considered as measures directed at the very essence of his being. No wonder then that even among those peasants belonging to the party, the majority were unwilling to join the collectives. In Poland, for instance, only 31 per cent of peasant party members had joined by 1953.[22]

Generally speaking, the progress in collectivization was roughly equivalent to the degree of violence applied. The table below suggests

Per cent of arable land in the socialist sector[23]

	1950	1952	1953	1954	1956	1957	1958
Poland	12	13	17	19	24	14	15
Czechoslovakia	25	24	48	44	45	70	77
Rumania	12	19	21	26	35	50	51
Hungary	19	25	37	32	33	22	23
Bulgaria	44	50	62	60	62	90	92
East Germany	—	5	8	30	33	40	—
Yugoslavia	18	—	24	—	9	—	—

significant differences in the various states in this regard. In fact, it could be claimed that the internal strength of the regime was reflected by its ability to push collectivization forward and overcome internal resistance to it. In every country, with the exception of Bulgaria and to a lesser extent Czechoslovakia, the progress made was considerably slower than in the USSR during the 1930–1938 period. The rate of progress notwithstanding, a consequence of this policy was the rapid alienation of a good part of the peasantry. From the standpoint of larger ideological perspectives, this was not as important as the fact that the People's Democracies were going forward in eliminating what was considered to be the chief block to the socialist transformation. With this transformation progressing, material differences between

East Europe and the USSR were lessening and the bonds for a close relationship strengthening.

The launching of the collectivization policy followed the earlier nationalization policy and paralleled the intensified efforts to industrialize the region. The nationalization policy, particularly in industry but also in handicrafts, by 1950 had resulted in the fairly general adoption of state ownership throughout the area, thereby breaking with the former pattern of diversification.* As a result, at the beginning of the long-range socialist planning, all the People's Democracies could boast that the major means of production, save the agricultural sector, were in the hands of the proletariat. Socialist transformation was now to be accompanied, according to the tried Stalinist experi-

---

* The patterns of establishing uniform state ownership in nonagricultural production in East Europe may be briefly summarized as follows. At the end of the war, and following the first nationalization acts, in Czechoslovakia the nationalized sector contained about 57.7 per cent of the industrial labor force. Two years later, just before the February coup, the state sector had grown through minor nationalizations and adjustments to 63.9 per cent of the labor force. The new Communist regime immediately launched further state ownership schemes, and within a year, by January 1949, the state sector had grown to 89.2 per cent. Thus, to all intents and purposes, by 1949 nationalization had been achieved and the regime had attained direct control over the productive processes. In industry it went even further, taking in 96 per cent of the total industrial workers. In the next four years, the Communist regime successfully completed the eradication of the handicrafts and the imposition of its controls over retail trading.

In Rumania, another state in which nationalization had initially lagged, in June 1948 a broadly conceived nationalization law swept away most privately owned industries, and by 1949 the state sector included 85 per cent of the total industrial production; by 1952, 95 per cent.

In Hungary, after the postwar nationalization acts, by the beginning of 1948 about half of the industrial labor force was in the state sector, and, two years later, upon the launching of the first Five Year Plan, the state could boast that its sector contained 90.5 per cent of the labor force.

In Bulgaria the industrial sector was nationalized in one major act in December 1947, and the state sector as far as production was concerned jumped from 6 per cent to 93 per cent.

In Poland, much of the initial nationalization was dictated by the wartime destruction and geographical changes, and already by 1946 the private sector in industry controlled a mere 11 per cent of the labor force. Two years later it was only 7 per cent, and by 1949, after further nationalization, in keeping with prevailing area trends, it decreased to 4.6 per cent.

Nationalization of domestic trade, which by 1947 had reached the level of 13 per cent in Hungary, 22 per cent in Poland, 42 per cent in Czechoslovakia, and 43 per cent in Bulgaria, moved apace and by 1950 reached 40 per cent in Hungary, 80 per cent in Poland, and about 98 per cent in the other two states. Elimination of private enterprise was thus rapidly accomplished. Based on Spulber, pp. 49–50, 64, 78, 80, 82, 90; Roberts, p. 322; *Wykonanie Narodowych Planow Gospodarczych 1948–1952* (Warsaw, 1952), p. 10; *News from Behind the Iron Curtain*, August 1952, p. 21; *Razvitie Ekonomiki Stran Narodnoi Demokratii* (Moscow, 1958), especially chapters 2–4, 6, 9–11, and the statistical appendix.

ence, by a radical and rapid industrialization of the individual states, unhindered by private enterprise. This industrialization would result, together with collectivization, in a radical destruction of the old ways of life, bring to the cities hundreds of thousands of new laborers, produce extensive urban development, and shatter once and for all the remnants of former habits, traditions, and nonsocialist characteristics. The repetition of the Soviet experience of the thirties would be bound to create an environment essentially like the Soviet environment.

The plans, admittedly prepared with the assistance of Soviet economic advisers,[24] emphasized the priority of the development of heavy industry, to which the major investments would be assigned.* The funds were to be used to expand the existing industrial plants and also to launch several spectacular schemes which were to symbolize the new socialist era and stand as lasting monuments to the socialist order. Each People's Democracy boasted of some such project: the Nowa Huta Steel Works in Poland, the Gottwald Steel Plants in Czechoslovakia, the Stalin Works at Dunapentele in Hungary, and the Dimitrovo Steel Plant in Bulgaria.[25]

Without evaluating the plans and their fulfillment, it is worth noting that within a few years of almost superhuman effort and tremendous social sacrifice the various countries of East Europe could point to certain genuine achievements. Considerable strides were made in such sectors as steel production and coal extraction, and by 1953, total steel production was roughly equal to West Germany's and about twice as much as before the war. The area's hydroelectric capacity was more than doubled, and by 1953 Czechoslovakia, Poland, and Hungary roughly tripled their engineering production as compared to the prewar level.[26] By 1952, Poland's annual industrial production reached 194.8 per cent of the 1949 level (by comparison, in agriculture the total was only 104.9 per cent),[27] and in Czechoslovakia the comparable percentage was 198.9 per cent.[28] The area, with all its deficiencies and problems, was emerging into the industrial age even though its economies were still largely unintegrated and developed on a semiautarkic pattern.[29]

---

* The percentages of total investment assigned to heavy industry according to the national plans were: 34.5 per cent in the case of Poland; 37 per cent in Czechoslovakia, which represented an increase of more than 5 per cent over the initial version of the plan; 47.6 per cent in Hungary, an increase of more than 11 per cent over the initial plan; 44.1 per cent in Rumania; 36 per cent in Bulgaria. Economic Commission for Europe, *Etude sur la situation économique de l'Europe depuis la guerre* (Geneva, 1953), p. 25, as quoted in Marczewski, *Planification et croissance économique des democraties populaires*, p. 200.

Internally, the *politically* significant consequence of this process of industrialization was the rapid increase in bringing the nonagricultural labor force into the organized, and hence more politically controllable, industrial process and urban life. According to the most exhaustive study available on the economics of East Europe, "between 1948 and 1953 there was a net increase of the nonagricultural labor force of about 400,000 in Bulgaria, 465,000 in Yugoslavia, close to 600,000 in Czechoslovakia, 750,000 in Hungary, 825,000 in Rumania, and over 1.9 million in Poland." [30] This amounted to an increase of about 33 per cent in the industrial labor force, telescoped into the remarkably short time of five years. During this period the rural population, while remaining generally stable in absolute numbers (with some small decreases), declined in terms of ratios between urban and rural populations as the new industries drained off the rural youth, having previously absorbed whatever surplus town labor had existed (in the form of the unemployed and the female labor force).

The new proletariat, housed in temporary barracks and workers' hotels, with no privacy, individuality, or family ties, was to help build the new tomorrow, the socialist society. The conditions under which it labored have been best described by the poets and novelists. But to many of these workers, the new environment did at first offer an improvement over previous conditions, or at least an opportunity of breaking away from a life which many of them no longer thought meaningful or desirable. Many of them did not have a clear image of what tomorrow would bring, but many did have a vague feeling that today was no longer for them — a feeling which Communist agitation stimulated. The masses flocking to the cities and industrial work sites were hoping for something they did not clearly grasp; but by coming they were helping to weaken the existing social bonds, to undermine the social institutions of the past which the Communists felt had to fall. The effect of industrialization was to create a revolutionary social situation in which the only source of cohesion would be the party, the only source of direction the leadership's will.

Under these conditions, the Soviet methods of labor discipline and organization were rapidly adopted. The trade unions were usually subordinated with the absorption of the Social Democratic parties and with the nationalization of the last areas of private enterprise. One man management assisted by party committees became the norm, and the factory became merely a unit within a hierarchically organized industrial pyramid, characterized by the strictest discipline and subordination. Laws of labor regulation, such as penalties for absenteeism and lateness, and a system of sanctions patterned on the Soviet model were adopted, together with specified norms, "socialist competitions," and premiums. Labor discipline was strictly enforced and labor recruitment subjected to state control. Announcing the introduction of strict state surveillance over employment, the Czech Minister of Labor stated:

By this new regulation the entire existing system, which was based on the voluntary movement of labor under state supervision, will be abandoned, and a new system applied which will directly control labor recruitment for the most important sectors of our industry in the same manner as our entire Socialist economy is directed.[31]

The submerging of society in the state, a process characteristic of totalitarian development, was accordingly to be one of the major by-products of the internal transformation.

The application of these new concepts meant that the People's Democracies were becoming replicas of the Soviet system, though somewhat less advanced (in the Marxist historical sense). In effect, they duplicated the Stalinist pattern of "economic war communism," that is, a rigid system of limited priorities to be achieved at the cost of other, less essential, economic sectors, particularly agriculture, housing, and light industry. The previous diversity among East European states was giving way not only to common patterns but also to a fundamental affinity between their domestic patterns and those of the USSR.

At this stage one might again raise the question: which of these changes had been motivated by ideology and which by power considerations? Power alone cannot explain the emphasis put on rapid collectivization unless the peasant is considered by those in power to be an imminent political threat. But if he is, then the very act of such consideration is colored by ideological assumptions about the implications of private enterprise. Industrialization was badly needed by the area — and Communist power was admittedly strengthened by it, initially at least. But the nature of the industrial development, based on Soviet experience, again was affected by the image of the society desired and the forces said to oppose it. In this manner policy reflected the impact of a peculiar normative perspective on reality as well as the assumed existential imperatives of that reality for those in policy-making positions.

As far as relations among Communist powers were concerned, it followed from Marxist thinking that these necessary internal changes were also creating political and economic bonds between the Soviet and East European societies. The result would be a solid, spirited, and single-minded phalanx which would stand together under any circumstances. The parties, by becoming Stalinized, by purging themselves and destroying such sources of deviationism as the Social Democrats, would tend to be more oriented toward the USSR. Terror used against the population at large would destroy any sources of potential opposition to the regime and introduce such fear that compliance with the policies and purposes of the system would be assured. Collectivization would carry the class struggle into the countryside and weed out the normally conservative orientation of the peasants, driving them into collective institutions where they could be subjected to organized political and economic control. Economic transformation through nationalization and, more significantly, through industrialization would create the objective basis for socialism while ripping apart the social fabric to such an extent that the Communist Party — Stalinist and dependent on the Soviet Union — would be the only source of social cohesion, the only organization to which the youth, in particular, could turn for guidance. The revised theory as applied would create the material bases for an internally cohesive socialist bloc. It would serve as a solid foundation for Stalinism as an interstate system.

6 / STALINISM: A PATTERN FOR THE COMMUNIST INTERSTATE SYSTEM

STALIN never underestimated the historical significance of political power. Entertaining a marked Bolshevik distaste for those Marxists who wished to rely on spontaneous material processes for the achievement of the desired goals, the Soviet leader throughout his spectacular career displayed a remarkable talent for wielding political instruments and employing organizational devices in the promotion of his ends. This was as true in the case of his personal political career as in the broader area of the development of the Soviet state and the "socialist transformation" effected in Soviet society. He unquestionably believed that the role of the state in a socialist society must be that of an indispensable tool for the acceleration of inevitable historical trends and that this positive role of the state deserved ample recognition in Soviet ideological perspectives. The practical expression of such an orientation was Stalin's growing reliance, particularly in his later years, on state institutions and the administrative structure — a reliance symbolized by Stalin's dual capacity as Premier and Secretary General and effected through the appointment of most Politburo members to responsible bureaucratic posts. Following the Second World War, the line pursued in domestic propaganda was to glorify the Soviet state as an almost coequal agent with the CPSU of historical progress.* In theory this meant the assignment to the state — to the political superstructure — of an important, positive, and conscious role.

Stalin's most elaborate statement concerning his views on the functions of the socialist state came at the twilight of his career, when his

---

* This attitude, as was to be expected, was duly imitated in the People's Democracies. In his memorandum to the Central Committee of the Hungarian Communist Party, Imre Nagy noted: "It is well known among Party leaders that when Matyas Rakosi became Premier he alluded to Stalin in voicing the view within the Political Committee that it was necessary to increase the role of the state vis-à-vis the Party; that it was necessary to place the government more in the foreground. . . . He indicated that placing the state and the government more in the foreground and increasing respect for them was an important task of the Party when the Council of Ministers came to the fore." *On Communism*, pp. 251–252.

dependence on the administrative structure had placed the state in an exalted position in the Soviet system. In an oft-cited pronouncement, "Regarding Marxism in Linguistics," Stalin restated the basic assumptions of Marxism concerning the relation between change in the socioeconomic realm and change in the political sphere:

Every base has its corresponding superstructure . . . the capitalist base has its superstructure, the socialist base has its superstructure. If the base changes and is eliminated, then its superstructure changes and is eliminated after it; if a new base is born, then a superstructure corresponding to it is born after it.[1]

This, however, was not to be interpreted literally. To do so could lead to a dangerous underestimation of the role of the state and, particularly, to erroneous conclusions regarding its historical significance once the socialist changes had taken place. Stalin duly amplified his views, explaining that:

The superstructure is generated by the base but this by no means signifies that it merely reflects the base, that it is passive, neutral and indifferent to the fate of its base, to the fate of classes, to the character of the system. On the contrary, having put in an appearance, it then becomes a *most active* force which contributes vigorously to the formation and consolidation of its base, takes all steps to assist the new order to drive the old base and the former classes into the dust and liquidate them.[2]

It follows from this categorical assertion that for anyone to minimize the role of the Soviet state would be tantamount to a betrayal of the interests of the socioeconomic base — to a betrayal of socialism, in fact. The interests of the Soviet state are hence considered inseparable from the cause of socialism.

Stalin's insistence on the fundamental importance of the state, even for effecting a revolutionary upheaval in the material base, is illustrated by his discussion of collectivization. Pointing out that collectivization was a revolution which had set up a new socialist order in the countryside, Stalin explained that it still did not require, as might have been expected from usual Marxist thought, the creation of a new regime because it had been "a revolution from above" carried out by the state with the support of the majority of the peasantry.[3] The socialist state, established by a revolution, could thus in turn become an instrument of positive reform, creating further changes in the base through political devices. It could do so effectively because, unlike a bourgeois state, it was no longer plagued by internal contradictions which would ultimately spell its doom. The socialist state could be an agent of history without fearing that history would inevitably turn around to devour the state.

The very nature of the Soviet bloc involved similar principles. The People's Democracy as a political institution represented a superstructure resting on an only partially transformed base. The bloc's task, therefore, was to complete the process of the socioeconomic transformation of the base, but it would be rash, or at least premature, to depend purely on a community of patterns in the socioeconomic base for the maintenance of close ties between it and the USSR. For this reason, it was essential that political ties be firmly established as part of the creative contribution which the superstructure has to make in each historical phase to "the formation and consolidation of its base." [4] Stalinism as an interstate system in the existing phase had to be, given Stalin's categories of analysis, an essentially political system.

The construction of the Soviet bloc, however, could not be carried on at a sacrifice to the Soviet state. In fact, since what harmed the Soviet state harmed socialism and what aided it could not help but aid socialism, the construction of the Soviet bloc was only meaningful if it strengthened the USSR. The strength of the Soviet state, in turn, was bound to aid the People's Democracies in their "construction of socialism." This meant, simply, that no conflict of interest was possible as long as a consistent policy of assigning priority to the interests of the Soviet state was pursued. Temporary difficulties caused as a result of this were more than compensated for by the strengthening of the Soviet state; this state in turn would strengthen the states of the People's Democracies which in turn could then proceed to reconstruct those parts of the base which still needed it. According to this neatly circular argument, if temporary difficulties arose as a consequence, for instance, of economic arrangements favoring the USSR, these difficulties were outweighed by the resultant increased might of the political instrumentality.

Stalinism as an interstate system, then, rested on the primacy of the political factor and on the priority of Soviet interests, derived logically from Stalin's concepts of the relation between the material and the political, between the base and the superstructure.

THE FORMAL DEVICES

The vital political "superstructure" had relatively few formal institutional devices. Much like the Soviet political system itself, the formal arrangements were meaningful only when infused with the more dynamic content of informal leadership, controls, and ideological zeal. Without this content the Soviet government would be a far different kind of system. This is also true in the case of Soviet-satellite relations. Without the informal content, the outward forms of that relationship would be radically different in practice, as the future, at least in part, was to show.

The formal ties binding the People's Democracies to the USSR and to one another were expressed through a series of bilateral state agreements, usually in the form of a treaty of friendship, collaboration and mutual aid, and cultural cooperation agreements.[5] The treaties were all bilateral — no multilateral agreement existed — and, significantly, the Soviet Union refrained from signing cultural cooperation agreements with the People's Democracies although the latter did conclude such agreements among themselves. However, the ties among the various People's Democracies were never as close as between any one of them individually and the USSR. No special political schemes bringing, say, Rumania or Bulgaria closer together, or Poland and Czechoslovakia (which had planned a federation during the war), were implemented in the treaty structure. After the creation of the German Democratic Republic, the People's Democracies signed cultural and political treaties with it, but the latter, since Germany was still formally demilitarized, were carefully called treaties of friendship, not mutual aid (see table, p. 110), and the Soviet Union still hopeful of exerting influence in West Germany, refrained from concluding such a treaty until West Germany joined NATO.

All of the political treaties emphasized the determination of the signatories to assist each other in case of external attack, with a rearmed Germany or some state allied to it usually singled out for specific mention.[6] The anti-German orientation of the defense treaties effectively played on the vivid memories which most Central and East Europeans had of the German occupation and supplied one of the very few popular aspects of the treaties. This was especially the case with the Soviet-Polish treaty which gave formal protection to the Oder-Neisse line. Similarly, the Polish-Czech treaty, despite the fairly widespread dislike of the respective populations for each other, did contain a genuine element of national interest insofar as the German problem was concerned. When the Polish-East German agreement of 1950 was signed, it was hailed by Polish-German official circles as the first instance of formal German recognition for the new frontier[7] and, despite the known limitations of the East German regime, it was welcomed by Polish public opinion as another impediment in the way of any future German designs on this territory.

Beyond this persistent concern of the East European states with the German question, the treaties could hardly be accepted as politically meaningful arrangements reached by equal and sovereign partners and with reference to their own specific national interests. They did, however, serve as symbolic expression of the Marxist position that states building socialism cannot harbor aggressive designs against one another and are, by definition, friendly. States with bitter and still vibrant traditions of hatred went through the motions of signing friendship treaties even while unresolved territorial issues were keeping the passions aflame. And certainly the East German Communists were not helped by Grotewohl's renunciation of the lands east of the Oder and Neisse rivers, nor was Rakosi's popularity enhanced by his approval of the loss of Transylvania or parts of Slovakia. The Polish Communists similarly labored under the handicap of having sanctioned the Soviet seizure of East Poland, although this bitter pill was made easier to swallow through the Oder-Neisse line and the Soviet support for it.

The timing of the treaties deserves comment. The accompanying table suggests that in the initial phase the construction of formal links applied primarily to the USSR, Czechoslovakia, and Poland. Yugoslavia at that time was also an active treaty partner, having signed a political alliance with the USSR on April 11, 1945, with Poland on March 16, 1946, and with Czechoslovakia on May 9 of the same year. These treaties were abrogated following Tito's expulsion from the Cominform. At this time, however, Hungary, Rumania, and Bulgaria were not included in the bilateral network since technically they were former enemy states subject to armistice arrangements. Following the 1947 Paris Treaty, Yugoslavia was the first to conclude formal treaties with them (see Chapter 3), thereby beating the USSR to the punch. In the course of one year, however, these states were included in the treaty structure while the agreements with Yugoslavia were declared null and void.

The treaties followed a set pattern. First, they created so-called defense alliances between the cosignatories and prohibited them from entering into any coalitions opposing the interests of one of the signatories. Second, they bound the signatories to participate in all efforts to protect the peace and particularly enjoined them to oppose any and all aggressive designs on the part of a rearmed German state and its allies. Third, they made explicit the positive qualities of the friendship existing between the cosignatories by emphasizing mutual respect for sovereignty, noninterference in domestic affairs, and equality in their relations. Fourth, they either provided for future economic cooperation or endorsed it if it had already been established. Finally, in the case of treaties among the People's Democracies, provision was made for cultural cooperation between them.[8] The treaties were hailed as expressing a new type of state relations, confirming Stalin's thesis that new social content seeks new political forms. They were

Bilateral political treaties and cultural treaties

	USSR	Poland	Czecho-slovakia	Hungary	Rumania	Bulgaria	East Germany
USSR		FMA 4/21/45	FMA 12/12/43	FMA 2/18/48	FMA 2/4/48	FMA 3/18/48	
Poland	FMA 4/21/45		FMA 3/10/47	FMA 6/18/48	FMA 1/26/49	FMA 5/29/48	F 6/6/50
			CC 7/4/47	CC 1/31/48	CC 2/27/48	CC 6/28/47	CC 1/8/52
Czecho-slovakia	FMA 12/12/43	FMA 3/10/47		FMA 4/16/49	FMA 7/21/48	FMA 4/23/48	F 6/23/50
		CC 7/4/47			CC 10/14/47	CC 6/20/47	
Hungary	FMA 2/18/48	FMA 6/18/48	FMA 4/16/49		FMA 1/24/48	FMA 7/16/48	F 6/26/50
		CC 1/31/48			CC 11/25/47	CC 10/29/47	
Rumania	FMA 2/4/48	FMA 1/26/49	FMA 7/21/48	FMA 1/24/48		FMA 1/16/48	F 8/22/50
		CC 2/27/48	CC 10/14/47	CC 11/25/47		CC 6/20/47	CC 9/20/50
Bulgaria	FMA 3/18/48	FMA 5/29/48	FMA 4/23/48	FMA 7/16/48	FMA 1/16/48		F 8/25/50
		CC 6/28/47	CC 6/20/47	CC 10/29/47	CC 6/20/47		CC 5/5/52
East Germany		F 6/6/50	F 6/23/50	F 6/26/50	F 8/22/50	F 8/25/50	
		CC 1/8/52			CC 9/20/50	CC 5/5/52	

Key: FMA: Friendship and Mutual Aid; CC: Cultural Cooperation; F: Friendship Treaty.

said to represent a community of interests based on common socio-economic forces as well as a new form of international behavior.

The formal relations between the USSR and the People's Democracies went quite far in stressing the latter's sovereignty, equality, and independence. Nothing in the treaties sanctioned either Soviet leadership or direct Soviet interference in the domestic affairs of the allied states. Soviet supremacy, stressed ideologically, was thus not given a formal basis and could not, in the future, justify itself by any reliance on formal arrangements. On the contrary, the egalitarian forms, once power began to waver, could begin to exert some slight influence of their own — at least a point of departure for those who may have wanted actual relations to be compatible with the formal. The latter declined in importance as the Soviet bloc more and more took on the character of the Stalinist system. During the earlier phase of diversity, the agreements signed with Czechoslovakia, Yugoslavia, and Poland were actually meaningful links in the chain tying these states to the USSR. Yugoslav efforts in the Balkans also took advantage of these more traditional methods. The agreements reached between 1948 and 1950 merely completed the initial process, and there are good grounds for assuming that an agreement of friendship reached between the USSR and, let us say, Rumania in 1948 had far less political significance than did similar agreements signed with Czechoslovakia in 1943 or even with Yugoslavia in 1945. Its value was now essentially symbolic and propagandistic and to some extent required by local Communists who wished to maintain a formal position no less dignified than that of the Poles or Czechs. The treaties also served to regularize the relationships established earlier and internationally symbolized the formal equality of Communist states. However, after 1950 no political treaty of any significance was signed between Stalin and the People's Democracies since there was no useful political task to be served by doing so.*

* A minor but very characteristic corollary of this was the disappearance of traditional diplomatic activity in the Soviet camp. With the exception of periodic Foreign Ministers' conferences called to take a united stand on some issue, politically significant contact was not maintained through diplomatic channels, with the exception of the role played by Soviet ambassadors. The Foreign Ministry was not considered to be an important position in the People's Democracy, and second-rate party politicians were appointed to the post. (Among the more important joint conferences, the following may be cited: the June 1948 Warsaw Conference of the Foreign Ministers of the USSR, Poland, Czechoslovakia, Yugoslavia, Hungary, Rumania, Bulgaria, and Albania, with respect to the creation of a West German state; the October 1950 Prague Conference of the Foreign Ministers of the above countries, without Yugoslavia but including East Germany, on the problem of West German rearmament. Cf. *Pravda*, October 22, 1950.)

The decline in the importance of what formal ties there were was particularly reflected in the waning of the Cominform's position. It was originally designed to coordinate the most important Communist parties and to arrange for the mutual "exchange" of their experiences. By 1950, however, the problem of exchange had become a matter of one-way traffic, while the failure of the anti-Tito campaign had discredited the Cominform, a primary agent in the campaign. A further factor minimizing the significance of the Cominform as a binding organization was the fact that the recently victorious Chinese party was not included in its membership. (It is not known whether it was kept out by Stalin or whether the Chinese refrained from joining, which they might have done on the easy pretext that the Cominform was essentially a European organization.) The absence of China, the loss of Yugoslavia, and the direct Soviet involvement in East European affairs meant that the Cominform lost much of its original purpose and vitality. Its formal meetings became increasingly rare (the fourth, and last, plenary session took place in Hungary on November 27, 1949[9]), although its publication continued to appear. In fact, its function became increasingly informational and propagandistic. In its declining years the Cominform was used primarily against the Yugoslavs, and its lessened political instrumentality was symbolic of the predominant Stalinist reliance on informal and indirect devices for keeping the Soviet bloc together.*

THE INFORMAL DEVICES

Stalin himself constituted the most important informal instrument of control. Strange as it may seem in a situation in which socioeconomic processes played such an important role, a single individual was able to exert such influence in the shaping of societies and political systems. Thus it is quite impossible to discuss the pattern of Communist interstate relations at this particular juncture without specifically referring to Stalin's role. Stalin as a symbol, Stalin as a victorious leader, Stalin as the builder of socialism in the USSR, contributed to these relations an intangible yet crucial psychological dimension which introduced devotion, fear, and hatred into the policy-making process and made him present in any important discussion. To the Communist fanatic, love and devotion to Stalin were essential ingredients of one's beliefs. To the practitioner, fear made him act like

---

* In this an old tsarist domestic practice was perpetuated. This is discussed in my paper, "The Patterns of Autocracy," *The Transformation of Russian Society Since 1861*, C. E. Black, ed. (Cambridge, 1960).

the fanatic even as it induced hatred. And for most Communists, all these elements together created a certain ambivalence, even if not a complete charismatic commitment.

While it would be easy to exaggerate the devotion to Stalin and underestimate the ingredient of fear and hatred (as in the case of the dissolution of the Polish Communist Party), it still would be difficult to explain the impact on many Communists of Khrushchev's revelations of Stalin's crimes unless in fact they entertained this idealized image of him and through him of the system in general. Stalin somehow personalized the conviction that the ends justify the means, and it was not really so much the contents of Khrushchev's revelations that were so shocking but the realization that the "means" had not been really necessary. Yet it is no exaggeration to say, and this has been confirmed by many former East European Communists, that between 1949 and 1953 many (but certainly not all) of the most radical decisions were made not on the basis of direct orders from Stalin but through the application of the principle of "anticipated reaction" — by attempting to do what Stalin might wish done.*

This situation was further intensified by the fact that by this time all the East European leaders had been approved by Stalin personally, and, in his later years particularly, he was not known for approving those blessed with an independent character. As a result, the leaders of the area were usually people who had successfully demonstrated their commitment to Stalinism either early in the Comintern days — Ulbricht, Rakosi, or Dimitrov — through loyal service in the Comintern-NKVD *apparat* — Berman or Bierut — or through demonstrable employment of Stalinist methods in the handling of one's party — Gottwald or Gheorghiu-Dej. While the essence of Stalinism was always the maintenance of a degree of insecurity among local leaders, there was no doubt that to them the sole, albeit by no means certain, avenue of salvation was the intense practice of Stalinism. Stalin's lieutenants in East Europe knew this, and their knowledge constituted a basic factor in the shaping of Soviet-satellite relations.

Stalin's personal prestige was closely associated with the prestige of the CPSU as the original revolutionary party. To outsiders this may appear odd, but to those who were actually committed to the move-

---

* Rakosi was certainly one such leader, as brought out not only by Nagy but even by Kadar. Another example is Bierut of Poland, whose devotion even Stalin sometimes had to restrain. On one occasion, for instance, Bierut suggested that the Polish national anthem be replaced by a less nationalistic song. Stalin balked at this innovation with a remark, "It's a good song. Leave it for a while." Testimony of J. Swiatlo, a Polish Secret Police defector.

ment the CPSU had a special place by virtue of its unique position and historical role. In time Stalin tended to overshadow it, but even many of those who disagreed with Stalin still had a special, personalized commitment to the Soviet party which they felt could not ultimately err even if it should occasionally stray from the right path. Dedijer's descriptions of Tito's and his associates' reactions to Soviet threats is a case in point.[10] It brings out once again that, because for so many years the CPSU had been the only party actually building socialism, many Communists were unwilling to pit their views against those of the CPSU. The determination of policy on the basis of ideological assessments was thus conceded to be a Soviet prerogative because the CPSU had gained Communist virtue through the baptism of power.*

A pattern of autonomous controls resulted from the factors outlined above. In some respects the controls operated automatically, without continual communication and direction; or they operated merely through indirect hints, such as the aforementioned *Pravda* article condemning the Balkan Union or the January 24, 1955, article by Shepilov praising heavy industrialization (see Chapters 8 and 10). However, neither the East European leaders nor presumably Stalin seemed satisfied to limit these autonomous controls to an inner sanctum of the top-level leadership. Ultimately, as in the Soviet Union itself, the entire society should have a similar orientation.[11] For this reason, the adulation of Stalin and the USSR as a whole became a matter of purposeful policy designed to induce this broader orientation. The worship of Stalin became part of the daily routine of almost anyone engaged in factory or office work: the pictures on the walls, the incantations at exhortation meetings, the posters, the statues. In

---

* S. Bialer, until 1956 on the staff of the Polish Central Committee, in his testimony (*Wybralem prawde*, p. 7) states that even as late as 1955 the standard reply of Berman or Ochab to any doubts raised by their associates was: "We must have full confidence in the Presidium of the Soviet Party." Probably the best summary of the type of reasoning which typifies a self-imposed system of control was given by a high-ranking Yugoslav leader, S. Zhujovich, who opposed Tito's intransigence vis-à-vis Moscow: "The Soviet Union as the offspring of the October Revolution, a country of socialism, the homeland of the proletariat of the whole world, was a state with an administrative organization, with a leadership in the organization of the economy and production that corresponded to the teachings of classic socialism and the postulates of Leninism, theoretically formulated and elaborated by Stalin. Therefore, there was or could be no comment or explanation — only silence . . . the Soviet Party was the parent Party, the only complete and correct interpreter of Marxism-Leninism . . . above all: Stalin, the Leader, the Teacher" (Dedijer, p. 398). This type of orientation when operative *within a Stalinist system,* can easily result in the most orthodox Stalinist pattern of behavior, divorced from all reality.

every field of human endeavor reference to Stalin was made,* and with streets, parks, factories, and even cities named after him, Stalin personified the close relationship being forged between the USSR and the People's Democracies.

On a more general plane, similar efforts were made with respect to the USSR. In every People's Democracy a society for the propagation of friendship with the Soviet Union was established, both on an elitist and mass basis. Leading intellectuals were enjoined to enroll as members, and recruitment drives were held throughout the countries. In Poland, the membership amounted in 1956 to 7.1 million;[12] in Bulgaria 1.7 million;[13] in Rumania about 5 million;[14] in Czechoslovakia about 2 million in 1953. The societies, usually with branch offices in every town, sponsored Soviet exhibits, featured Soviet movies, held appropriate celebrations on Soviet anniversaries, published their own papers and magazines, arranged for translations of Soviet books, and organized Russian-language classes for adults (compulsory for school children).† Their task, in brief, was to eliminate negative conceptions of Soviet life and instill a positive emotional commitment to the USSR.‡

* Some sample press citations: "The teaching of Stalin embraces all the universal principles of nature in its smallest details. He solves all the practical problems of understanding natural science" (*Elet es Tudomany*, December 24, 1952). "Without the special care of Stalin, the present advanced techniques in meat-combines, preserve and sugar plants, fish, and everything else done in the field of food industry would not exist" (*Rabotnichesko Delo*, January 7, 1950). "It is only Stalin . . . who is able to analyze clearly and find with mathematical precision the exact way toward solution of present day problems" (*Rude Pravo*, December 21, 1952). *News from Behind the Iron Curtain*, March 1953, pp. 36–37.

† The teaching of Russian was also used as a medium for instilling devotion to the USSR and to Stalin. For example, the following is an account from a Rumanian newspaper of such a language class held for workers of the Bucharest Post Office: "From the first bench, Comrade Dumitrescu rises and goes shyly to the blackboard. He is now in front of it — he takes the chalk from Comrade Medelcovici and, following the word 'Mir' [Russian for peace], he writes, full of emotion, 'Slava Stalinu' — Glory to Stalin — " (*Viata Sindicala*, January 10, 1952). The scope of the activities of the friendship societies is suggested by the following figures: In Czechoslovakia, before 1947, Soviet publications constituted only 4 per cent of the books published; by 1952, the figure had risen to 50 per cent (*News from Behind the Iron Curtain*, December 1952, p. 40), and the total number of books printed was 21 million. In Poland, the society arranged, during ten years of its existence, for the translation of 5000 Soviet titles with a printing of 100 million copies, and also sponsored 1300 competitions on various Soviet themes (*Trybuna Ludu*, October 6, 1955). In 1954, of all the translations printed, more than 90 per cent were from Russian (Halecki, p. 146).

‡ Combating negative stereotypes took various forms. An interesting instance of typically totalitarian practice was prohibition of the use of certain words carrying a subconsciously negative connotation. In Poland, the most frequent translation of the word *Soviet* was *sowiecki* (Soviet Union: *Zwiazek Sowiecki*). Since this word had

The policy of stimulating a sense of commitment to the USSR was, of course, most seriously applied in the schools and youth organizations. The hope was that ultimately a new spirit of genuine and voluntary identification would emerge as "class hostility" to the USSR was undermined by the socialist transformation. Organized national adulation, and the beginnings of a form of cultural Russification, would in the meantime paralyze any independent responses through the creation of a surface unanimity which very few individuals would ever dare challenge. That day would finally come when diversity would no longer be desired or even conceived of. "If the mind is obligated to obey a word of command, it can at any rate feel that it is not free. But if it has been so manipulated beforehand that it obeys without even waiting for the word of command, it loses even the consciousness of enslavement." [15]

The application in East Europe of radical political and economic measures increased the dependence of the ruling Communist parties on Stalin's support. Without his support, by 1952, it is doubtful that any regime (even including the Czech) could have successfully maintained itself in power. This, of course, gave the autonomously operative controls an additional quality of self-interest insofar as the ruling stratum was concerned. The Soviet rulers, however, were unwilling, and indeed probably unable, to rely entirely on support derived from motivations of conviction and self-interest. For this reason they had elaborated at home a complex system of controls designed to maintain loyalty and to prevent societal and political relations from acquiring excessive rigidity. This system, presumably for similar reasons, was exported to and imposed on East Europe.

The first link in the informal chain of imposed political control was direct consultation between the Soviet leadership and that of the countries concerned. The second was the permanent supervision of domestic events through reliance on the Soviet ambassadors. The third link was a close contact with various party organs, particularly those dealing with ideological matters, through frequent exchange of

been used during the twenty years of Polish pre-World War II statehood and had acquired a certain value content which was rather anti-Soviet, the word was replaced by another derived from the literal Polish translation of the word *Soviet*, which means a Council, in Polish *rada*. The Soviet Union hence became *Zwiazek Radziecki* (Councillar Union). Another more frequent form of combating anti-Soviet sentiments was the prohibition of the sale of anything which might even indirectly lead to anti-Soviet views. For instance, after October 1956, it was revealed in the legal organ, *Prawo i Zycie* (no. 5, 1957), that a bookseller in Poznan had been sentenced in 1953 to three years' imprisonment for the sale of the official memoirs of a cavalry regiment which had fought against the Soviet forces in 1920.

experts and visits of Soviet "advisers." The fourth tie was the direct penetration of those governmental institutions particularly important as the instruments of power and force. And the fifth was the isolation of the various Communist states from the rest of the world and from one another. All of this was buttressed by Soviet military might, both in the potential and the actual sense. These controls, unlike the autonomously operative ones, were subject to purposeful Moscow direction.

The direct consultations with Moscow almost always occurred on a bilateral basis, with a given party leadership invited to a conference with Stalin and his associates. No multilateral top-level Communist consultations were held from 1949 until the Nineteenth Party Congress in October 1952. Accordingly, in each instance a party leadership was facing Moscow alone and Stalin was able to assure his visitors that the other parties had already endorsed and were enthusiastically backing the suggested policy. Under such circumstances a visiting delegation had no choice but to endorse whatever was suggested and to do so with enthusiasm and alacrity. The usual procedure was for the Soviet leadership to invite for "consultations" the trusted head of a party and some of his associates who were in charge of matters pertinent to the planned discussions.[16] A visit to Moscow was viewed by those selected as an opportunity to re-establish personal connections and to strengthen individual positions. The delegation would return home with a keen appreciation of the latest Soviet assessments and programs. This in turn would give its members an advantage in any power competition over those who had been left behind. That the range of Soviet intervention reached the most important personnel decisions as well was openly admitted by Imre Nagy in his memorandum prepared in 1955–1956 for the use of Hungarian leaders, and not meant for publication. He revealed that, even after the death of Stalin, the Soviet leaders considered it their prerogative to discuss and decide who ought to head the Hungarian government and what its policies ought to be.*

* In May 1953, following the Soviet decisions to establish "collective leadership," Rakosi traveled to Moscow for a major policy discussion. According to Nagy (*On Communism*), Comrade Malenkov pointed out that the Soviets had discussed with Rakosi the personal questions that concerned the separation of party and state leadership. "We asked, 'whom do you recommend as your deputy?' He could name no one. He had objections to everyone whose name was mentioned; he had something against everyone. Everyone was suspect except he alone. This appalled us very much, said Comrade Malenkov" (pp. 250–251). Describing a later Moscow conference, in May 1954, Nagy cites various criticisms of the Hungarian party leadership voiced by Khrushchev, and adds, "Comrade Malenkov, too, found that we were slow in cor-

The second lever of control was the Soviet ambassador. Direct intervention and interference were not always used in this sphere. Given the whole Stalinist complex — the fear of secret police, the internal competitions in loyalty, the genuine desire of some to be true Stalinists — the ambassador's very presence on the scene constituted an important lever of control. Every high party functionary knew that the Soviet ambassador continually reported his assessments of the situation, his evaluations of the "construction of socialism," his estimates of the attitudes and behavior of various important public figures back to Moscow. This is a normal, almost routine, aspect of ambassadorial activity. But in the existing context, considering the *personal* implications that might follow from such reports, all the leaders naturally wanted the ambassador's reports to give the "proper" evaluation of their activity and to correspond to their own reports to the Soviet leaders.[17] An unavoidable consequence was that the less secure a leader, the more anxious he would be to make certain that the Soviet envoy got *his* views of the situation, *his* estimate of the other party colleagues. Such a relationship could not help but develop a certain dynamic which in time established as a matter of regular practice the extreme importance of being on good and very close terms with the Soviet ambassador. The fact that the local leaders normally would not see his dispatches merely increased their uncertainty and diligence. Hence, even without actual meddling, the Soviet ambassador became a central lever of Soviet supervision.

Not all Soviet ambassadors, however, relied merely on the implications of their presence. Some are known to have intervened actively in the domestic affairs of the People's Democracies. The official Soviet position on the role of the Soviet ambassador was explicitly stated in the correspondence between Stalin and Tito prior to the break. A Soviet envoy in a People's Democracy was held to possess the right to gather information on all domestic matters, including the most confidential, and from anyone he pleased. He could do this either through his secret agents or by requesting such information from the most highly placed Communists without having to go through official channels. While reciprocity was not granted in this respect to the

recting our mistakes in Party leadership and that Rakosi, as Party First Secretary, was not doing the job well." He then cites what might have been the minutes of the meeting and quotes the Soviet leaders as stating, "Comrade Rakosi must take the lead in the fight to correct previous mistakes and to implement the resolutions of the Central Committee . . . The Party leadership needs Comrade Rakosi, but he must know and realize that he will have to merge into the collective leadership because that is the only way in which he can do his work well" (pp. 280–281). A certain "paternal" relationship is suggested by these comments.

envoys of the People's Democracies in the USSR, the privileged position of the Soviet ambassador was claimed on the basis of a true Communist-to-Communist relationship. In Yugoslavia, the Soviet ambassador thus felt justified in intriguing with those Politburo members who opposed Tito. In Poland, according to the testimony of a party defector who had read the transcripts of the July 1955 CPSU Central Committee Plenum, the Soviet ambassadors (V. Z. Lebedev, 1946–1953; G. M. Popov, 1953–1954) were said in this document to have sponsored intraparty intrigues, occasionally abusing the Polish party leaders, treating them as inferiors who could be summoned to the Soviet Embassy whenever the ambassador desired.[18] Lebedev's behavior apparently became so intolerable that after Stalin's death the Polish Politburo prevailed on the Soviet leadership to have him recalled.[19]

The Soviet envoy also acted as a transmitter of important policy decisions when no direct consultations were deemed necessary. At least two significant coincidences seem to suggest this: the arrival in Prague of V. Zorin just prior to the coup of the Czech Communist Party, and the flight of V. S. Semenov from East Berlin to Moscow and the announcement of the New Course in East Germany a few days after his return. The role that the Soviet ambassador played during the era characterized by Stalinism doubtlessly varied depending on the local circumstances, on the degree of actual implementation of Stalinist policies by the local leadership, on the indigenous strength of the regime, and on the personal ties of the leaders with Moscow. Nonetheless, his functions, both passive and active, went far beyond the realm usually prescribed by diplomatic protocol.

The third type of informal controls operated through the maintenance of close contacts between the CPSU Central Committee *apparat* and the party *apparats* in the People's Democracies. In the first instance, this involved the appointment of Communists with an extensive Soviet or Comintern background, frequently with experience in the NKVD networks, to head the various sections of the Central Committees. According to one source, the Inspectorate of Party Cadres in the Bulgarian Central Committee was staffed with former functionaries of the Soviet secret police, as was also the case with the Commission of State Control and the Commission of Science, Art, and Culture.[20] In Poland, apart from the two most prominent leaders themselves, Bierut and Berman, who had worked for the NKVD and the Comintern, respectively, even as late as 1956 a member of the Politburo, F. Mazur, was considered to be in the service of the MVD.

The same was said to be the case with the Polish ambassadors in Moscow and Peking.[21]

Beyond these glaring, but not infrequent, cases, control was exercised through visits of Soviet party functionaries whose task was to advise the East European Communists concerning the latest Soviet views on matters of interest to them, particularly on matters of ideological thinking. S. Bialer, a defector from the agit-prop section of the Polish Central Committee, reports that he consulted with Professor Alexandrov whose task was the ideological supervision of the party academies in Poland; other Soviet experts would occasionally be dispatched to consult with Polish philosophers or to discuss and guide the work of the Polish economists, and so on.[22] As a further assurance, the most promising young party activists were sent to study (usually for one year) in the Soviet Party Academy, attached to the Central Committee of the CPSU, where they could drink from the fountains of wisdom, acquire dialectical skills, and master the arcana of politics.

The most institutionalized informal control system involved the direct Soviet penetration of those governmental institutions which were particularly important as instruments of power: usually the secret police and the armed forces. The purpose was essentially twofold: to ensure their absolute loyalty to the USSR and to prevent their control by some local leaders who might then be tempted to oppose the Soviet Union. For this reason, the Soviet leadership felt it desirable to establish the most intimate links between its own secret police, under Beria, and the networks set up in East Europe, as well as between its armed forces and those being created in the People's Democracies. This association became particularly important in the later stages of Stalinism, when the intensity of the party purges all but liberated the police from party control and made it a semiautonomous agency subject, in the final analysis, only to Moscow itself.

According to Colonel Swiatlo of the Polish Security Forces, the Polish Security Ministry only occasionally reported to the Polish Politburo. Swiatlo's assertions were confirmed in 1956 by Berman, the head of the Politburo Committee on Security.[23] The organization of the secret police from the very beginning was carried on with the personal assistance of important Soviet officers. In Poland, General I. Serov assisted in the initial organization, and particularly in the liquidation of the Home Army.[24] The head of the Polish Security Ministry, S. Radkiewicz, had Soviet officers as his personal guards and was advised by General Lalin of the Soviet Ministry of State Security.[25] In the Polish ministry itself, of the twenty departments eight were headed by Soviet officers directly, three had Soviet "advisers," and of the eleven identified as Poles or Polish Jews at least four were former employees of the NKVD and one a former officer in the Soviet armed forces.[26] That seems to have been the pattern elsewhere as well.* In Bulgaria, for instance, already in 1948 — according to Yugoslav allegations — the Ministry of the Interior was under complete Soviet control,[27] and the Minister of the Interior, Georgi Tzankov, was a product of MVD training.[28]

The Soviet secret police, apart from penetrating and apparently subordinating these agencies, also maintained its own autonomous structure in East Europe and was empowered, whenever Soviet security was threatened, to arrest nationals of the People's Democracies in a People's Democracy. That certainly was the case in East Germany and the former enemy states, and there were also instances of this having happened in Poland. Furthermore, during the purges, the MVD headquarters and even Stalin himself would occasionally dispatch to a national party leadership materials incriminating some party official and would demand that the local security people deal with the situation.[29] In this manner, the Soviet leaders were directly involved in the problem of loyalty and security right up to the top levels of Communist leadership in the People's Democracies.

The armed forces were given similar attention. At the end of the war only Yugoslavia and Poland had sizable military establishments. The Yugoslav Army was highly politicized and fiercely loyal to Tito. The Polish Army was split into two parts, symbolizing the fate of the country. The armed forces in the west were demobilized and about one half of the soldiers returned home (many were subsequently arrested), the others having chosen exile. The army at home had been expanded from the units organized in 1943 in the USSR through mobilization and occasional incorporation of Home Army units which had escaped deportation to the USSR. After the war most of these forces were demobilized. In the initial period, the Soviet Union did not encourage the development of large-scale military forces in any of the other People's Democracies and, on the whole, those existing were badly equipped and inadequately supplied. After 1948, particularly because of the mounting international tensions, energetic efforts

---

* Czechoslovakia is a notable exception, although the evidence available is scanty. But studies of the Czech Communist regime do not point to intense Soviet penetration of the main organs of power, and apparently the Czech Communists, with considerable organizational experience behind them, had the situation well in hand. According to reliable Hungarian data, the AVH was advised by twelve to forty Soviet officers (depending on the period).

were launched to build up these forces into more modern military organizations. The problem of loyalty, both to the existing governments and to the USSR on whose side these forces would be expected to fight, thus became even more important.

The concern with loyalty was expressed through the appointment of trusted Communists to head the armed forces: in August 1948, M. Farkas, later to gain notoriety in connection with purge brutalities, was appointed Minister of Defense in Hungary; in April 1950, Gottwald's son-in-law, A. Cepicka, Minister of Defense in Czechoslovakia; in Poland, in a most striking case of direct Soviet control, the post was given in November 1949 to Marshal K. Rokossovsky, a Soviet officer. Rokossovsky, also to become a Politburo member, was virtually independent of any party control insofar as military matters were involved and conducted himself on the basis of direct Soviet commands.[30] He was assisted by numerous Soviet officers, who commanded all the major branches of the armed forces[31] and initiated a large-scale purge of the officer corps.[32]

The general pattern of Soviet controls, with some variation, was imposed in the following sequence: During the early stage the armed forces were deemphasized. The demobilization paved the way to a removal of any prewar officers whose politics were likely to be anti-Communist. In Czechoslovakia, for instance, former officers of the Czech Legion were particularly suspect; in Poland, those who had served with Pilsudski. In the former enemy states, "anti-Fascist" measures included the ferreting out of prewar officers on the grounds of having supported the war against the USSR. Only in Yugoslavia did the army retain its strength, primarily because of the tensions over Trieste and because it was firmly in the hands of the regime. The widespread elimination of many high-ranking professionals made possible the rapid promotion of a number of junior-ranking men whose new status was dependent on the existing political situation and who therefore had a vested interest in its maintenance. The most important posts, however, were filled with Communist officers who either had a Spanish Civil War background, or had served with Communist partisans, or had fought in the Red Army. A system of political and police controls on the Soviet model was established, and intensive political training was made a large part of each prospective officer's curriculum.

In addition, in all the armies, save Czechoslovakia's apparently and Yugoslavia's, Soviet officers served in command or advisory capacities. In Poland, they arrived as early as 1945, and helped to organize the army. After an interlude of about three years, a second wave came with Rokossovsky, paralleling similar developments elsewhere.* In Hungary, Soviet military advisers also came in two waves: first, in 1948, to train the army in the handling of new weapons; and then, much more openly, in the fall of 1949 when the modernization of the Hungarian Army was accelerated. The Soviet officers in Hungary were headed by a chief of the military delegation and by a political adviser to the Hungarian Army. They set up a system of controls very much like that in Poland and supervised the activities of their Hungarian fellow officers.† [33] The Soviet table of organization was adopted in all the armies, as were the Soviet drill and system of ranks. Only Poland retained its traditional insignia, although it too made modifications in the military uniform to conform with the general pattern. Through these devices, as in the case of the police, loyalty to the Soviet Union was to be ensured by the penetration of Soviet personnel and prevention of direct domestic control.

The Soviet levers of control made certain that purpose, policy, and performance in each People's Democracy were in keeping with the over-all Soviet objectives for the camp of socialism. An additional peculiarity of Stalinism as an interstate system was the isolation of each People's Democracy from the others. In terms of relations between parties this expressed itself, as already noted, in Soviet insistence on bilateral dealings between the CPSU and the other parties rather than on multilateral consultations. Until 1948 some of the parties had been very active in establishing and maintaining close contacts and frequent conferences. They terminated abruptly, and, even for some years after Stalin's death, contact between neighboring Communist regimes was at a minimum.‡ Nor did the various Central Committees and their sections exchange views or experiences. [34]

---

* Approximately 17,000 Soviet officers held command posts in the "Polish" Army during this time. (*Zycie i Mysl*, Warsaw, October 1964.)

† According to General Kiraly, by 1951 Soviet "advisory" staffs were operating even on the regimental level; in the General Staff College which he commanded there were fourteen Soviet "advisers," headed by a general, to a total of two hundred officers (from his interview with Professor Ferenc Vali).

‡ In the words of Imre Nagy: "A peculiar People's Democratic provincialism, an intensified estrangement in those efforts that are raising a veritable Chinese Wall, not only between our homeland and the Western capitalist countries but between the Hungarian People's Democracy and other countries in the democratic and socialist camp, is now developing. We have come to the point where Party members, even members of the Central Committee, cannot obtain the newspapers of sister Parties; the statements by Party and state leaders of other People's Democratic countries; the speeches or articles of Comrade Bierut or Siroky, or the resolutions of sister Parties. The same applies to numerous manifestations in culture, art, and literature, to the

The only times that East European leaders met were at various functions in Moscow on the occasion of some Soviet anniversary, such as May Day or Stalin's seventieth birthday. Moscow was thus the communications center for the Soviet bloc. Otherwise, contact was strictly curtailed and usually limited either to some important propaganda undertaking, such as the joint East German-Polish announcement that the Oder-Neisse line was the "frontier of peace," or to an occasional exchange of delegations. On a more general level, strict travel restrictions were applied, and procedures involving interstate travel were just as complicated as those pertaining to travel to a "hostile capitalist" country. Between Czechoslovakia and Poland a frontier zone existed, and citizens of the respective People's Democracies had to obtain special passes to be able to work in the proximity of a neighboring People's Democracy. (These particular restrictions were lifted only in 1956–1957.)

Soviet domestic experience again seems to pertain. In the effort to create the new society, all traditional bonds had to be dissolved since they constituted impediments to both policy and power. The consequence of these efforts has often been described, with some exaggeration, as "totalitarian atomization." An essentially similar procedure was followed with respect to the People's Democracies. Their traditional associations, as well as new ones formed by local Communists (such as the Balkan Union project), were a hindrance to the central leadership. Therefore, they had to be dissolved and, ideally, each party, much like every citizen in the USSR, was to face the center alone. Its isolation would thus become a source of unity and purposeful cohesion.*

---

debates in People's Democratic countries, to the exchanges of ideas, etc. Indeed, we have come to such a point that members of the Central Committee cannot even obtain certain publications of the Communist Party of the Soviet Union. Thus, for example, the agricultural resolution of the Central Committee of the Polish Party is banned in Hungary, and so is the evaluation of this resolution by the official paper of the Party, *Trybuna Ludu*, and so is a study concerning relationships of Polish and Western literature and art, etc. In numerous areas of Hungarian economic, political, and cultural life there is a hermetic seal isolating the problems that friendly countries share in the same areas; this indicates a fear of criticism, and at the same time — and this is more serious — it furthers the intensification of nationalism and of attitudes opposed to the teachings of Lenin on the subject of proletarian internationalism." *On Communism*, p. 240.

* But for this reason also the USSR could not go to the other extreme: *divide et impera*. It could not sponsor traditional conflicts between People's Democracies as a method of furthering its rule because these conflicts would become a source of strain and divisive tendencies. Probably only in the early stage could this have been possible, and in some cases appears to have been so used (as with the Rumanians and the Hungarians over Transylvania).

ECONOMIC ASPECTS

Isolation as a basis for unity was not only a political feature of the Stalinist pattern but was also vigorously applied on the economic plane. Political bilateralism and isolation were matched by economic bilateralism and autarky. Just as political bilateralism meant in practice Soviet domination, economic bilateralism involved a good deal of exploitation of the area by the USSR in the name of the over-all interests of the Communist bloc. At the same time, however, a further objective in the economic field was the integration of the entire "socialist bloc" into an interdependent unit, although the implementation of this goal was not very actively pursued during the Stalinist period and seems to have been subordinated to more immediate Soviet economic interests and to autarkic features of the Five-Year Plans. Integration would have meant foregoing certain profits for the USSR, and, with the prevailing scale of priorities, the economic welfare of the Soviet Union was viewed as more important. As a result, some measure of tension entered into the economic pattern of relations.

The formal foundations for a policy of economic exploitation — a policy which, in the Marxist point of view, could not exist between socialist states — were based on the war settlements imposed by the USSR after the conclusion of hostilities. The Soviet Union required both Hungary and Rumania to make reparations payments, for a period of six and eight years, respectively, to the amount of $200 and $300 million, respectively, *at 1938 prices.* That this represented a sizable portion of the annual expenditures of these two small states is attested by the fact that reparations commitments absorbed 26.4 per cent of the 1946–1947 Hungarian budget and 37.5 per cent of the Rumanian. In the following year the figures were 17.8 per cent and 46.6 per cent.[35] In the case of Poland, an allied country, the problem of reparations again served as a useful point of departure. German reparations to Poland were to be handled by the USSR and were to amount to 15 per cent of the total German reparations to the USSR. In its turn, Poland, according to the agreement of August 16, 1945, "undertakes, beginning with 1946, to deliver to the Soviet Union once a year throughout the entire period of the occupation of Germany, *at the special price* agreed upon, eight million tons of coal during the first year of deliveries, thirteen million tons annually in the next four years, and twelve million tons in each of the subsequent years of the occupation of Germany" (italics added). Subsequently the delivery quotas were lowered, but the "special price" meant that by 1956 Polish losses in coal exports to the USSR alone amounted to about two billion rubles or half a billion dollars.[36]

The reparations from Hungary and Rumania were reduced, but not abolished, in 1948 in the spirit of "socialist cooperation." The balance was halved, although the Soviet Union still insisted on receiving payments of the debts incurred by these states toward Germany. The seizure of former German property and the dismantling carried on in the entire area when it was still a war zone represented still more profit to the USSR. The creation of a number of joint companies, co-owned with Rumania, Hungary, and Bulgaria, was a further feature of the Soviet-satellite economic relationship. (In Yugoslavia it had been terminated by the rupture, while Poland was unwilling from the start to agree to such arrangements and the USSR apparently decided not to force the issue.) The joint companies were set up in the petroleum industry, quartz mining, shipping, and air transport, usually on a fifty-fifty basis. Moreover, much of the Soviet capital came from German assets seized locally, thereby giving the USSR a rather convenient means of financing these undertakings.[37] All in all, sixteen such companies were created in Rumania (Sovromtransport, for instance, controlled most of the larger Rumanian vessels and about one third of the entire tonnage[38]), six in Hungary (40 per cent of the bauxite output was subject to one company[39]), and seven in Bulgaria. Special secret agreements were made with Czechoslovakia and Hungary concerning uranium exploration. The least hesitation was shown in exploiting East Germany, and until 1954, even after the setting up of the GDR, the Soviet Military Administration continued to operate two hundred formerly German-owned enterprises.

A complete evaluation of Soviet-People's Democracies economic relations is rendered difficult by the secrecy which was maintained with respect to the content of economic agreements. Full and detailed arrangements were rarely published during the Stalinist period and even earlier, beyond the general statistical statements of the over-all turnover and warm affirmations of the mutual benefit to be derived from the specific treaty.* The secrecy became particularly marked as war tensions increased and the People's Democracies were required to develop armaments industries. Nonetheless, the November 1956 Polish-Soviet agreement explicitly admitted that "inequalities"

---

* For instance, *Nowe Drogi*, no. 7 (1953), p. 32, speaks of the "priceless treasure of Soviet experience" in the area of metallurgy which has been made accessible to Poland, and describes it as a "real spiritual wealth." See also *Nowe Drogi*, no. 1 (1953), article by S. Jedrychowski, "The Significance of Soviet Economic-Technical Aid for the Construction of the Foundations of Socialism in Poland."

in the relationship had existed and were in the process of being corrected. Earlier, these inequalities had been subject to strong Yugoslav criticisms, and the Yugoslav *White Book* cited numerous examples of the joint companies' being used to Soviet advantage. A general estimate of the amount extracted by the USSR from East Europe in the period 1945–1956 would put the total at about twenty billion United States dollars (see Chapter 12, p. 286, note).

A combination of economic and political motives resulted in a marked shift in the direction of trade relations of these states: from the West toward the USSR and one another. As the industrialization of East Europe, including East Germany, proceeded apace, the economic importance of the area to the Soviet camp grew accordingly. By 1953–1954, the combined steel production of the People's Democracies was about 31 per cent of that of the Soviet Union; pig iron, 27 per cent; electricity, 44 per cent; crude oil, 18 per cent; and coal, 103 per cent.

A closely integrated political bloc had to stress, therefore, closer economic ties, especially as the economies of the Communist states were moving forward into the industrial age. For this reason, beginning in 1948, foreign-trade agreements were drafted with reference to the long-range plans of these states, thereby becoming part of the general process of transformation and integration even though national plans were still not integrated.[40] In a short time, the former trading directions of the People's Democracies were reversed and their trade relations with non-Communist states became negligible (see table).

Trade with the USSR and other People's Democracies
(imports and exports in per cent of total)

	1937	1948	1949	1950	1951
Bulgaria	12	74	82	88	92
Hungary	13	34	46	61	67
Poland	7	34	43	59	58
Rumania	18	71	82	83	79
Czechoslovakia	11	30	45	52	60

Source: N. Ivanov, "The Foreign Trade of the European People's Democracies," *Vneshnaia Torgovlia*, no. 10, 1952.

Direct trade with the USSR amounted in 1951 to 29 per cent in the case of Hungary (which had practically no trade with the USSR before the war); 58 per cent in the case of Bulgaria; 25 per cent in the case of Poland; 51 per cent in the case of Rumania; and 28 per cent in the case of Czechoslovakia. In turn, about 80 per cent of all Soviet trade in 1951 was with the People's Democracies.[41] The table suggests that in Bulgaria and Rumania a major shift in the trading pattern preceded the Stalinist phase and was merely accentuated by it. In Hungary, Poland, and Czechoslovakia the Stalinist period sharply affected the trading patterns of these states.

The official economic equivalent to the Cominform was the Council of Economic Mutual Assistance, formed in Moscow in January 1949 as a response to the challenge of the Marshall Plan. Its organization was initially limited to six functional departments (this was expanded in 1955–1956 — see Chapter 12), and its stated purpose was to assist the economic development of its members: USSR, Poland, Czechoslovakia, Hungary, Rumania, and Bulgaria.* Its main emphasis, however, was on coordinating trade within the Soviet bloc, although there is reason to believe that the Council was also concerned during that time with stimulating the development of the armaments industry, which grew under Soviet pressure during the Korean War. (It is to be noted that such an industry is particularly unprofitable to underdeveloped but industrializing nations.) While the initial sessions of the Council did lay stress on pooling resources, no over-all plan for division of labor or specialization emerged, and industrial development continued on a more or less autarkic pattern.† [42] Probably its major accomplishment during this time was the introduction, in 1950, of the ruble as the standard currency for international transactions within

* In 1950 these states were joined by East Germany and Albania; North Korea and North Vietnam subsequently sent observers.

† In the cautious words of the Communist premier of Hungary between 1953 and 1955: "It must be pointed out that, although economic cooperation and mutual assistance between the socialist states brought significant results, the activity of CEMA [the Council] from the point of view of industrial production and development was extremely limited during the period of the First Five-Year Plan. This also contributed to the rise of inequities in work distribution among friendly countries. Despite the fact that agreements were made with some of the democratic countries with a view to assigning work in a way that would promote economic production and work distribution, parallel manufacturing, especially in the field of machine industry, had an increasingly detrimental effect on our export opportunities and consequently on our foreign trade balance. Parallel manufacturing affected not only trade among the friendly countries themselves but led to an unhealthy competition among them in the capitalist markets as well. The exaggerated trend toward autarky, which manifested itself in the machine industry in the other friendly countries too, was most apparent also in the fields of precision instruments and telecommunications. This was a serious blow to our most developed and most favorably producing export industries." Nagy, *On Communism*, p. 189.

the bloc, which made the USSR the ultimate arbiter of the rates of exchange.[43] Related to this was the systematically lower average of unit-value indices of goods sold to the USSR by the People's Democracies as part of the long-term (usually five-year) bilateral trade agreements initiated by the Council.[44]

Other than these measures, the Council apparently did not assume during Stalin's lifetime a major role in the direct management or planning of the economic life of the area. Like the Cominform, which declined into a mere anti-Tito organ, the Council was quite active in sponsoring the economic boycott of Yugoslavia. It thus appears that, as in politics, the pattern of economic relations was characterized by an absence of over-all formal arrangements and depended on direct relationships which were usually favorable to the USSR. In large measure these one-sided arrangements conflicted with the domestic aims of the socioeconomic transformation and made it a much more expensive proposition. However, the important dimension in this situation was the strengthening of the USSR in the face of alleged external danger — and Stalinism never hesitated to choose the political gain over the purely economic.

CHINA: THE FIRST ALLY

Stalinism as an interstate and international system did not have to cope with the specter of a powerful Communist Chinese regime. The problem of crystallizing the relation of the Chinese Communist Party to Stalinism was felicitously delayed throughout Stalin's life. Until the formation of a victorious regime in the fall of 1949, the Chinese Communist Party was embroiled in a bitter civil war and primarily involved with domestic problems. Foreign policy, particularly in terms of the American position, was a function of the civil war in which the USSR played the role of a benevolent, even if formally neutral, spectator. Hence, even in this case relations were dominated by the domestic conflict; the Chinese Communist perspective on international Communist problems was of necessity a narrow one and in essentials reflected the Soviet position. Following the conclusion of the struggle on the mainland, Chinese freedom of action continued to be limited by the Taiwan conflict and, within a very short period, by the Korean War which lasted until the end of Stalin's days. As a result, Communist China restricted its foreign liaison primarily to the USSR and largely abstained from participation in the expanding formal links binding the Communist camp. It was not until April 3, 1951, that a cultural agreement (but not a political one) was signed with Poland, followed by others in subsequent years (May 2, 1952, with Rumania; October 25, 1952, with Bulgaria, and so on). No formal treaties of alliance were concluded with the People's Democracies.

The absorbing Chinese international military undertakings put off an adjustment of the hierarchic and disciplined Stalinist system to the new situation. But the Communist Chinese victory in itself contained the need for somehow defining the status of China in the socialist bloc. Unlike all of the People's Democracies, but very much like the expelled Yugoslav party, the Chinese regime was, in the final analysis, an indigenous one and its victory, even more than in the Yugoslav case, was the achievement primarily of the party itself. Second, again unlike the People's Democracies but like Yugoslavia, the revolutionary tactics pursued by the party in the course of its struggle had raised some ideological issues on which the local leadership did not see eye to eye with Moscow. The Maoist concept of revolution, through reliance on an organized army based on a revolutionary peasantry, had not won the endorsement of the Soviet theoreticians, who tended to underestimate the strength and the potential of the Chinese party.[45] In spite of the Soviet reluctance to give the Chinese revolution its due credit, the Chinese quite explicitly asserted that Mao Tse-tung had developed — and the Chinese Communist Party had successfully applied — a revolutionary theory of special relevance to the backward regions of the world.

The emergence of Communist China, a great historical event in its own right, thus raised a basic problem for the Stalinist system: can a bloc of states bound together by the power of a central state and by common ideological purposes retain its cohesive, hierarchical organization when one of its members ceases to be dependent on the political power of the central state and in fact is able to enjoy a considerable scope of ideological autonomy? To respond effectively, both the Chinese and the Soviet leaderships had to develop a mutual understanding of the character of the international Communist state system, the role of the USSR in it, and China's new relationship to it. As in the case of the People's Democracies, this involved formal and informal aspects. Insofar as the formal measures were concerned, superficially the relations resembled those between the USSR and the European bloc. Mao Tse-tung, committed to the dichotomic world view, repeatedly stressed his belief that Chinese Communists, given their experience and existing historical situation, must pursue a "lean-to-one-side policy," which he defined in June 1949 as follows:

To lean to one side is the lesson taught us by the forty years of experience of Sun Yat-sen and the twenty-eight years of experience of the Communist Party. We firmly believe that, in order to attain and consolidate victory, we must lean to one side . . . Not only in China, but in the whole world, one leans without exception either to the side of imperialism or to the side of socialism. Neutrality is a hoax.[46]

His orientation clearly called for the closest links with the USSR, and shortly after the Chinese Communists had formally constituted themselves as the government of China, a delegation headed by Mao Tse-tung himself proceeded to Moscow. There they negotiated a treaty of "Friendship, Alliance, and Mutual Assistance" (February 14, 1950), as well as two subsidiary agreements concerning the disposition of the Changchun railroad, the ports of Dairen and Port Arthur, and a long-term loan to China. The clauses and affirmations of the political treaty resembled the agreements concluded between the USSR and the European bloc, with Japan taking the place of Germany as the potential aggressor and the United States more or less understood as the sponsor of such potential aggression.[47] The subsidiary agreements contained a number of provisions which could be interpreted as favorable to China, such as the transfer of the Changchun railroad in 1952 rather than in 1975 as envisaged in the Sino-Soviet treaty of 1945, an earlier withdrawal from Port Arthur, and a more generous compensation for property seized by the Soviets from the Japanese in China.[48] Of course, Soviet interests were not neglected, and the Chinese delegation also agreed to somewhat less favorable provisions concerning Dairen and compensation for Soviet "improvements" in Port Arthur.[49] Furthermore, the potentially divisive issues of Mongolia and Sinkiang were left in abeyance. While the treaty and the affirmations of friendship generally conformed to the pattern already traced, probably the most striking indication of the somewhat more complex relationship involved was the fact that the treaty negotiations in Moscow lasted over two months, from November 1949 until February 1950.

Any hidden complications notwithstanding, after the treaty relations between the two states seemed to take a familiar course. Soviet military experts arrived to assist in the training of the Chinese Army, which was modernized with Soviet equipment.[50] Economic advisers came to help organize and run the metallurgical, coal, oil, chemical, machine-building, and transport enterprises, as well as trade and cooperatives.[51] Chinese trade with the USSR and the People's Democracies, which in 1931 amounted to only 8 per cent of total Chinese trade, increased fourfold between 1950 and 1953 to about 75 per cent of the total.[52] As early as October 1949, a Sino-Soviet Friendship Society was established. By 1951, it counted some seventeen million members and engaged in various cultural-political activities designed to strengthen popular affection for the USSR. As in East Europe, ties with the USSR were explicitly stressed in the preamble to the constitution of 1954 ("indestructible friendship with the great Union of Soviet Socialist Republics") and in the first basic law passed after the 1949 victory, the Common Program.

Chinese leaders also repeatedly asserted that "the path already traversed by the Soviet people is exactly the path we should follow," [53] although they refrained from pronouncing their state to be a dictatorship of the proletariat. Hailing the People's China as a "new democracy," the Chinese leadership adopted the position that this was their version of the People's Democracy, a line in keeping with general Soviet notions. However, the stress on a domestic alliance of the peasantry and bourgeoisie under the leadership, or "the hegemony," of the proletariat clearly implied that China had not yet reached the stage of the dictatorship of the proletariat. After Stalin's death, the Chinese extolled this as a new and creative contribution to the theories of socialist transition, but as long as he was alive this apparent innovation was deemphasized.[54] Furthermore, on closer examination, one is struck not so much by the obvious differences in the official concepts of the People's Democracy as seen in Moscow and as proclaimed in Peking, but by the startling similarity between the Chinese position and that adopted by the East Germans, with obvious Soviet blessing.* It would, therefore, appear that in both China and Germany it was more a matter of concessions to international pressures and the great domestic problems than of pointed divergence from the Soviet-sponsored pattern.

These surface relations, and even the apparent subservience, shielded a reality much more complex than the simple Stalinist pattern would suggest. The Soviet military advisers in China could hardly be compared to the overlords in charge of the Polish and Hungarian Armies built from scratch by Communist regimes dependent on Soviet support. In China the revolution had been won by a poorly equipped

---

* Ulbricht, speaking at the Second Party Conference in July 1952, described the East German system as a new order based on an alliance of "the working class and the working peasant element" in cooperation with the intelligentsia. The leadership in the order was said to belong to the "most progressive" proletarians led by the SED (*Einheit*, no. 8, August 1952, pp. 739–740.) The Germans, however, were evasive on the crucial question of whether they could enter the stage of socialism directly.

primitive army, but still by a Chinese Army which, by 1949, represented a numerically impressive military establishment, led by men with a revolutionary consciousness and, presumably, a justified sense of achievement. In these circumstances, whatever Soviet aspirations might have been, the role played by the Soviet advisers was inevitably circumscribed. In addition, and this applies to economic advisers also, the Soviet and Chinese leaderships both were probably aware of the dangerous parallels between their relationship and that formerly existing between Moscow and Belgrade and, duly forewarned, strove to minimize unnecessary tensions.[55]

By 1949, in spite of Stalin's rigidities, the Soviet leadership must have realized that it had grossly miscalculated in the Yugoslav case and that an indigenous revolutionary movement develops a certain inherent capacity for resistance, even against as hallowed a shrine as Moscow. This is especially true if, in addition to the armed forces, the revolutionary movement controls firmly the security apparatus — as both the Chinese and the Yugoslavs did. Accordingly, the patterns for states like the People's Democracies could not be enforced in China. Indeed, an attempt in that direction would be detrimental since it would tend to obscure the natural community of interests dictated by the presence of the alleged capitalist threat. This was the period of the Formosa conflict, to be followed shortly by a war with the leading capitalist power. Given the international situation, particularly since the summer of 1950 (the Korean War), the lesser degree of actual Soviet control was compensated by the fact that the USSR was more necessary to the survival of the Chinese Communist regime than that regime was to the USSR.

On the eve of the war in Korea, China had just completed a period of almost fifteen years of uninterrupted warfare which had left its economy devastated, its communications disrupted, its administration disorganized and subjected to a revolutionary change. Soviet assistance, in the form of economic aid, was desperately needed if the Chinese Communist regime was to restore a semblance of normalcy domestically and pursue its internal and external objectives. Variations in ideological perspectives or even potential conflicts of interests, either territorial or involving leadership among Asian Communists, could not transcend the fact that common Leninist organizational experience and ideological orientation gave the Chinese leadership no choice but to maintain their association with the leading Communist power. A necessary concomitant of this association, considering the world situation and possibly even Stalin's foibles, was the acceptance of certain

informal obligations which, unlike the pattern in East Europe, operated entirely autonomously through the motivating force of self-interest. Thus Soviet leadership was recognized, imitation of the USSR
proclaimed, even if not fully practiced, and endorsement of Soviet
policies elsewhere unhesitatingly given.

China, faced by the external war and the violence of internal
changes, particularly in the countryside where a Stalin-like collectivization was forcefully pushed, could not afford, and indeed had
no reason to desire, to become a Yugoslavia. Its relations with the
USSR (and the absence of such relations with the People's Democracies) were dictated by a combination of a common ideological outlook and an overwhelming external pressure for unity, which was
not marred by crude Soviet requirements for subordination. Formal
equality was thus not accompanied by informal control but by informal recognition of relative scales of mutual interest, aspirations,
and power. On the Soviet side, even during Stalin's lifetime, the USSR
had no choice but to tolerate what it had not tolerated with Tito: a
fundamentally Stalinist regime which operated autonomously within
the framework of international Stalinism.

In the long run inherent in this relationship was the gradual diffu-
sion of Soviet authority. No matter how often the Chinese proclaimed
Soviet leadership or insisted on the obedience of others to Moscow,
the very presence in the camp of a power which was *de facto* independent and which pursued its own domestic policies was a denial of
the monolithic and hierarchical character of the international Communist system. No empire or church has ever maintained itself with
two capitals. Moscow and Peking had to ponder the fate of Rome and
Byzantium.

INTERACTION OF DOMESTIC AND INTERNAL PRESSURES

The external factors, so pre-eminent in the case of China, were
also important in shaping the pattern of events in the Communist
states of East Europe. The split with the West, which by 1949 and
the Berlin blockade had reached the proportions of a war scare, was
intensified by the Stalinist insistence on the dichotomy between the
forces that are for socialism and all others that are therefore "objectively" against it. Suspicion and hostility toward any state outside
the Stalinist system became particularly marked after the successful
Yugoslav stand against the Cominform onslaught. Fear of internal
diversion, either strictly "counterrevolutionary" or of a Titoist variety (and to Stalin the difference between the two was purely one of

orm), accompanied the hostile stance adopted against the external
world; it found reflection domestically in a growing stress on the class
struggle within the nation and the party, on a more intensive transformation of society, on a greater reliance on the instruments of violence
or the pursuit of domestic objectives. In this, all of the Communist-
uled states shared, from the USSR down.

With the outbreak of the Korean War came an even greater in-
ensification of the monolithic pressures inherent in Stalinism. The
threat of a total war, which to an East European Communist implied
more dire consequences than to his Soviet colleagues, obscured internal differences and created a unity born of fear. The conflict, no
matter who began it, seemed to bear out the Stalinist position that
America had been preparing for war against the Soviet camp. If it had
not, then why should it intervene in an area which it had previously
disclaimed as being of no political or strategic significance? The
United States' reaction clearly implied, to someone viewing reality
from the Communist perspective, that America was seizing an opportunity to engage in active military operation against the "bloc of
peace." Malenkov, in the political report addressed to the Nineteenth
Party Congress, expressed this point of view in the following words:
The U.S. attack on the Korean People's Democratic Republic marked
the transition of the American-British bloc from preparation of ag-
ressive war to direct acts of aggression." [56] Domestic Stalinism frequently resorted to an image of the "enemy" to justify its more violent
policies; Stalinism as an international system similarly relied on this
technique.

The application of this device was facilitated by the Soviet monopoly of any evaluation of the world situation. This evaluation then
served as a basis for the policies of the various People's Democracies,
intensifying those tendencies which make for greater reliance exter-
ally on the USSR and on repressive measures at home. In the cautious
but revealing words of Imre Nagy, writing to a central committee of
party still firmly committed to the USSR:

We never examined the international situation thoroughly in the light
: our own country's interests nor from the viewpoint of its effects on
ır country . . . This was the reason why changes in the international
situation often clashed sharply with internal politics. In the years 1949 to
)52, incorrect evaluations of the international situation, *overemphasis of
•e war danger*, and *the actions resulting from these assumptions,* played
very serious part in those grave mistakes that were made by our Party
adership with regard to the economic activities of the people . . . The

events in June, 1953, in East Germany, Czechoslovakia and Hungary, and elsewhere clearly show how an incorrect evaluation of the international situation and a resulting unsound foreign policy brought about grave crises in the internal life of the countries mentioned.[57]

It would be erroneous, however, to ascribe primary importance to external factors in the process of shaping the Stalinist international system. Soviet domestic Stalinism, with the expansion of Soviet power, could not help but become the form and content of relations between the new Soviet-dependent Communist states. It is very difficult for any state to conduct its relations with lesser powers in a fashion which drastically differs from its own internal politics. For a while, such divergence can be justified by real or alleged overriding national interest, but in time there must be coalescence in the forms of domestic and external politics.*

However, it is much more difficult for a totalitarian state to conduct anything else than a policy of domination against its weaker neighbors or associates. Not to do so would be to adopt restraints on its behavior wholly out of keeping with the image of the world which guides its domestic conduct and the aspirations which give shape to the sacrifices exacted from the population. Furthermore, a belief in environmental influence tends to exaggerate the importance of a community of views between the various leaders and the identity of institutions and socioeconomic systems. Similarity of material conditions becomes one of the vital guarantees of unity of action, and such similarity can best be established through the duplication elsewhere of the institutions of the dominant power. With *Zhdanovshchina* in full bloom on the fertile soil of Stalinism, with the Soviet dictator apprehensive about a possible decline in the pace of revolutionary change, the application in the People's Democracies of patterns other than the Soviet would have constituted a danger to the structure of Soviet power itself and a deviation from the clear-cut "we versus they" image of the world.

This pattern of institutional and ideological uniformity did much to eliminate divisive tendencies, such as those rooted in the domesticism of some leaders. Nonetheless, under the monolithic surface, some important differences among the various People's Democracies con

---

* In democratic states, the divergence, when it takes place, can only be away from the "democratic" pattern in external relations, but, after a while, internal pressure develop for adjustment. Some recognition of the principles which guide domestic life then follows in the sphere of international affairs. One example of this is the United States' policy toward its Latin neighbors.

tinued to exist even during the height of Stalinism, which could not effectively control *all* aspects of life and foil *all* forms of evasion. Some parties went quite far in imitating Stalinism in all its facets; others did not. The purges in Czechoslovakia, Hungary, and Bulgaria differed sharply from the pattern in Poland, East Germany, and Rumania. Similarly, not all states pushed collectivization forward at an even pace. However, procrastination and even evasion were not enough to constitute a significant deviation from the common pattern.

To conclude, the Stalinist interstate system was characterized by: (1) The worship of politics. In practice, this meant reliance on identical political "superstructures" and attaching primary significance to political controls and bilateral political contacts as the most reliable means of ensuring unity. (2) The leadership of Stalin and the USSR was openly acknowledged and a special bond of personal allegiance cultivated between Stalin and his chosen leaders for the People's Democracies (except China). Stalin's relationship with the satellite leaders could in effect be described as one of *feudal* subordination and obligation. Within the strict hierarchical pattern some concession was made to the particular position of China, which was usually assigned the second and special place of mention, and with which Soviet relations were only crystallizing. (3) Ideology served as an important source of self-imposed controls, although gradually declining in the course of this phase. No systematic ideological justification for Soviet supremacy was developed. Rather, a series of didactic assertions related to a rejection of alternative ways to socialism were postulated with the ideology providing a means of identifying the enemy. Ideology thus performed the broad function of pointing out the nature of the given international phase — the period of capitalist aggression — while in internal policies it relied on tried Stalinist practices. (4) A superficial framework of state independence, guaranteed by treaties, formal recognition of sovereignty and national equality, masked an informal though effective system of subordination of these states to the center. Soviet intervention in domestic affairs of the People's Democracies operated, however, in most day-to-day instances on the basis of local anticipation of Soviet *desiderata* according to the guidelines of Stalinist ideology and practice. Direct Soviet control was applied mainly through the secret police and the armed forces. The emphasis on indirect controls distinguished the Stalinist system from the Nazi domination. The Stalinist pattern involved a far more extensive reliance on indigenous participation and, unlike the Nazi destructiveness, also stressed social transformation with some positive attri-

butes. Soviet Armies, after the initial phase, played a secondary role
staying in the background, it was sufficient for everyone to realize
that they would be used when necessary. (5) Primacy of Soviet de
velopment justified the economic exploitation of the area even whi
its rapid industrial development was encouraged. This introduced fu
ther economic strains which increased the political dependence of th
regimes on the USSR.

Stalinism as a pattern for Communist interstate relations was
system noticeably untouched by innovation and experimentation. I
the final analysis, it merely relied on the Stalinist domestic experienc
and applied it to those areas which were within the purview of Sta
lin's power. Ironically, but precisely because of that, Malenkov w
probably right when he stated in 1952 that "the USSR's relations wit
these countries set an example of entirely new relations among state
relations never yet encountered in history." [58]

7 / THE STALINIST LEGACY

> If we cut down the time in which changes have to take place, especially in the sphere of social consciousness — such as ideology and culture, and in the forms of society, we may fall victim to the idealistic view that we can bring about changes in these phenomena independently of the material conditions which influence their formation. — Wladyslaw Bienkowski, "Socialism versus Mythology."

THE Stalinist legacy, in the terminology of the initiated, was the mounting contradiction between the imperatives of the political superstructure and the dictates of the material and social base. The priority assigned to narrowly defined political considerations meant that socioeconomic factors which politics were supposed to reflect were subordinated to the over-all political interests of the bloc as defined by its center. This subordination, in turn, had a restrictive impact on creative ideological development by divorcing ideology from precisely those elements which were said to stimulate its growth and refine its content. Ideology divorced from reality and rigidly dictating the established practice of one particular power degenerated into dogma and lost its dynamic component — its ability to relate itself to changing society. Even totalitarian ideologies, dogmatic almost by definition, must respond in some measure to domestic aspirations and must somehow reflect the existing reality, even while striving to change it altogether. This certainly was the case initially with the Nazi doctrine and with the Bolshevik appeal. A static ideology which reflects an actual and alien model tends to become corrupted, to lose its vitality, to become a mere rationalization for power. Tito discovered this shortly after the break, and after 1950 the Yugoslavs frantically sought new ideological formulations to take cognizance of the present and to shape the future (see Chapter 9). The East European Communists were not as fortunate and rapidly came face to face with a situation in which politics had few links with reality and in which their ideology had become a sterile guidebook for dubiously relevant socioeconomic practices.

139

COMMUNIST TESTIMONY

During the later stages of the Stalinist period an increasing number of Communists became aware of the dangers inherent in the established practices. This is evident from a number of statements made after Stalin's death, not designed for "hostile capitalist propaganda" but addressed to the local ruling parties and often favorably received by many party members. The difficulties and shortcomings discussed were clearly the products of the Stalinist era even if the suggested remedies already reflected the post-Stalin atmosphere. Nonetheless, we can get a relatively extensive picture of the Stalinist legacy as seen at least by a portion of the Communist elite from the following: the situations discussed in the summer of 1953 by the plenums of the Hungarian Central Committee and of the East German SED's Central Committee (see Chapter 8); the resolution of the Polish Central Committee's Third Plenum in January 1955; the elaborate statement written by Imre Nagy in 1955 and addressed to both the Hungarian and Soviet leaderships;[1] and a short volume of essays by Wladyslaw Bienkowski, until 1957 a close associate of Gomulka,* entitled *Rewolucja Ciag Dalszy* (The Revolution Continued), published largely before October 1956. Very similar themes run through the depositions of some former Hungarian Communists, interviewed by the Columbia University Research Project on Hungary.[2] One might also consider pertinent the speech delivered by Gomulka to the Eighth Plenum in 1956 upon his restoration to the post of First Secretary. These assessments of leading Communists are more relevant to the problem of Soviet-satellite relations than a general critique of the Stalinist legacy would be, for it was the Communists' perception of the situation that was reflected in the policies first adopted after Stalin's death.

The implicit and explicit themes of such assessments may be broken down into these three categories: political problems, related ideological and ethical issues, and economic difficulties. From the standpoint of the party, the critical issue was the party's increasing subordination to the secret police. Discussing this trend, Imre Nagy, writing during Rakosi's hegemony (see Chapter 10), stated that the secret police, with the "far-reaching aid" of Stalin, was raised "above society and Party and made . . . the principal organ of power." This resulted in a "degeneration of Party life" and the partial ex

* Bienkowski, appointed Minister of Education after Gomulka's return to power shared Gomulka's political eclipse after 1949. In 1957 he became identified with revisionism (Chapter 13) and gradually lost his political influence.

termination of the leading cadres of the party.[4] The net result was "Bonapartism," a term used by Leninists to denote a betrayal of the revolutionary ideals once power had been seized, and even "Fuehrerism," a manifestation of distrust for the party rank and file and for the masses.[5] Nagy was ably seconded by Bienkowski. Stating that "responsibility is an institutional matter" which cannot be ignored by merely asserting that one social order is free from contradictions,[6] he charged the Stalinist epoch with having created an abyss between the political leadership and society at large: "The working class and all other social forces were placed in the position of being a potential enemy of the socialist order, the true exemplar and devoted defender of which was the bureaucratized apparatus of power."[7] This fear of the masses in turn led to a fear of individuals, Bienkowski asserted. "Stalin, in a suspiciousness typical of dictators, persecuted first morally, and then physically, not only those who had the courage of their opinion but also those whom he suspected of being able to have it."[8]

A political system structured on suspicion and with a predilection toward personal violence could not develop organizational techniques such as those characteristic of the Weberian notions of a rational bureaucracy. Political controls within the bureaucracy, controls to check the controls, and general bureaucratic hostility toward the masses resulted in a system in which an expanding and rather inefficient bureaucracy lost all concern with human values and showed only occasional spurts of vitality whenever "a class enemy" was spotted.[9] The decline and eventual disappearance of revolutionary fervor within some of the ruling elites is therefore not surprising.[10] Both Nagy and Bienkowski vented their concern with the decline of morale within the ruling circles, a decline which could not be blamed on the vestiges of the pre-Communist past. Servility and corruption were to be encountered everywhere, and the legion of careerists "tends to increase because, instead of denouncing them, the leaders tolerate and quite frequently even pamper them, since their kowtowing flatters the vanity of the leaders, as they will do anything or carry out any orders for them without reservation."[11] Bienkowski, citing Lenin, warned that beyond the corruptive tendencies noted above, bureaucratization breeds a dangerous conservative impediment to social progress by creating a "closed class" of professionals who are professional only in the defense of their vested interests.[12] This development is again inherent in the mistrust of the masses and in the usurpation of the sole right to express the popular will.

A conservative inclination of this kind could not be limited to the administrative apparatus alone. In general, Bienkowski asserted, the socialist revolution was not able to rise above the historical tendency of revolutionary forces to become rigidified and brittle after their victory.[13] The revolutionary ideology becomes (as in the case of Stalinism) a defense of the status quo, too often defined in the narrow terms of self-interest of the new ruling elite. The revolutionary ideals degenerate into a series of pat institutional recommendations, and those in power forget "about living society, about man with his manifold, complicated, individual and social relations, at the crux of which are ethical and moral problems." [14] Certainly not all, in fact probably only a few, Communists were as perceptive as Nagy or Bienkowski. It was largely because of this that the gap between ideology and reality, between aspirations and practice, became so marked in a system in which power was worshiped and its exercise was considered to be the most hallowed ritual.

The Stalinist legacy in economics, as perceived by some Communists, came under equally scathing indictment. Describing it as "lunar economics," Bienkowski charged that the general tendency was to divorce theory from economic practice and to make the former a matter of dogma unaffected by any existential conditions.[15] The consequence was "idealistic voluntarism," which stressed political criteria with a reckless disregard for the complexity of economic processes. The frequent and triumphant citing of advances in specific production fields entirely ignored the simple fact that an economic organism, much like a human being, can have a healthy heart, lungs or stomach and yet be critically ill. Bienkowski's view was seconded by Nagy, who was particularly disturbed by serious disproportions which developed in planning due to the primacy assigned to industrial development. The situation was made worse by the outbreak of the Korean War; the Polish regime, for instance, according to its erstwhile party First Secretary, "spent millions for the defense industry and transferred its best workers and machines to it." [16]

The impact of the Stalinist notions was nowhere more disastrously felt than in agriculture. Even Communists acknowledged that collectivization was pushed forward without ensuring adequate food supplies for the urban population, while actual food production did not increase and even declined. The introduction of class struggle into the countryside was based on the principle "the worse the agricultural situation, the better it is" since it will lead to more rapid socialization.[17] Established methods of good farming suffered accordingly. Ideologically this move was justified as denying "accumulation to the private owner, who was considered an enemy of the new system. This policy was based on an artificial division of the peasantry into three categories: the poor, the medium, and the rich; the "socialist transformation" was to be effected through an alliance of the first two groups against the rich peasant. The liquidation of the kulak was to be the actual expression of the class struggle in the countryside, and was to facilitate a real workers-peasants alliance. But no one really knew how to determine who was a kulak. Prosperity might be one criterion, but what was the basis for that prosperity? If it was land holding alone, then some objective standard might be maintained. But that criterion was explicitly rejected,[18] and all too often the prosperous peasant was the good peasant, the efficient farmer. The frequent consequence was that the able farmers were made the butt of the "class struggle," that party posts in the countryside were filled with the worst rural elements whose only conception of action was to destroy the better farmer.[19] The existing political atmosphere merely intensified these tendencies. Agricultural productivity suffered, especially in the public sector,[20] while the myth of Stalinist infallibility was undermined.

The Stalinist legacy, which became a matter of open political dispute within a short period after the dictator's death, involved many additional factors which even the Communist critics were loath to acknowledge publicly. The most serious of these was the widespread impoverishment of the working class, to a great extent due to the rapid "socialist construction." According to data available, the low point was reached between 1951 and 1953. The forced social sacrifice, depressing the standard of living, intensified popular resentment and strengthened the widely prevailing suspicion that the USSR was also responsible for the decline. The rights and wrongs of this assumption notwithstanding, the political consequence was the mounting resentment of the working class and growing uneasiness among party planners.[21] At the same time, the rapid pace of the industrialization resulted in the introduction into posts of responsibility of managerial and technical cadres with relatively low training standards. This was particularly true in Hungary and Poland, which lacked an engineering intelligentsia, and applied, to a much lesser degree, in Czechoslovakia and East Germany.* Cohesion necessary to keep the system going was in-

---

* In Hungary, for instance, 30 per cent of the directors in the Ministry of Metallurgy and Machine Industry, 26 per cent of the directors in the Ministry of Heavy Industry, 50 per cent of the directors in the Ministry of Light Industry, and per cent of the directors in the Ministry of Building Industry had only eight years

creasingly provided by a resort to administrative pressures, including severe labor laws.

The cumulative effect of the application of Soviet experience resulted in a growing sense of apprehension among the more thoughtful Communists in East Europe. The open soul-searching typical later of the post-Stalin period was at this time limited to gnawing doubt. Personal fear, the sense of commitment, the impact of the Korean War, all tended to push into the deepest recesses of the mind the increasingly important question: is the Soviet model, developed in response to the alleged requirements of the Russian society as it existed in the first decades of the twentieth century, really relevant to the relatively more advanced societies of East Europe in the middle of that century?

At the same time the presence of often undiplomatic Soviet advisers, the suspicions concerning the nature of economic relations with the USSR, the mounting hostility toward the rulers and their Soviet sponsors stored up explosive popular forces which an open party airing of policy dilemmas could only too easily spark. A resolution of these dilemmas could be postponed only as long as Stalin lived, but the delay required a continued and mounting dose of Stalinist procedures to suppress the domestic pressures. The parties themselves were caught by the Stalinist technique of the "dilemma of the one alternative."

The excessive personalization of interstate relations by Stalin himself, his practices and ideas, was a strength only as long as he lived His legacy would unavoidably involve a political vacuum, a consideration which during his lifetime could not be publicly considered. A: a result, Soviet relations with the other Communist states remainec perched on a potentially unstable limb. Stalin limited the frequency of direct consultations with the other Communist leaders. These lead ers utilized the principles and methods of Stalinism as a guide to thei domestic action and as a vehicle of internal party struggles. As note in the preceding chapter, the indirect and informal structure of So viet controls was not formalized by treaties or fully legitimized b ideology. With respect to China, the formal alliance was reinforce

---

of secondary school education or even less (*Figyelo*, May 27, 1958). In Poland, i 1956, of the factory directors only 16 per cent had higher education and 45 per cer medium. Of the individuals occupying the ten top factory posts, 16 per cent ha higher education and 48 per cent medium. 59 per cent of factory directors held the posts less than five years and 15 per cent less than one year, with the percentage a preciably higher in the responsible technical posts (*Życie gospodarcze*, Februar 23, 1958).

by overriding international pressures, while the autonomous internal position of the Chinese leadership avoided some of the tensions inherent in the Stalinist legacy elsewhere. In East Europe some of the difficulties in Soviet-satellite relations might have been avoided had the Soviet Union been prepared to take a drastic step: to incorporate the People's Democracies into the USSR as Soviet Republics. In 1952 there was little to prevent such a step and, symptomatically, it was predicted in the East European capitals. However, the relatively effective functioning of the indirect controls made such a step seem unnecessary and bound to intensify short-range difficulties. In addition, it might involve international complications, including the loss of badly needed United Nations votes. Forms of independent statehood were accordingly preserved. Yet new circumstances could infuse them with new meaning.

Of course, it would be a distortion of the then-existing state of affairs to picture the Stalinist system as tottering on the brink of disaster and as being kept from toppling over only by the providential power of the aging dictator. The system, while facing difficulties which even some of the ruling elite could no longer ignore, was also characterized by elements of cohesion and strength that Stalin's death per se could not undermine. The first, most self-evident, and decisive was the factor of Soviet power, derived from the USSR's central position in world affairs and from its willingness to use that force for the preservation of its established interests. Efforts to loosen Soviet control, therefore, had to stop short of a provocation likely to induce a violent Soviet reaction. The chain of command and the solidarity of purpose derived from common outlook ensured unity of action, while the reliance on indirect controls freed the Soviet Union from an excessive commitment of its energies to keeping the bloc together. Furthermore, by 1950 the process of internal factional struggles, encouraged personally by Stalin,[22] had weeded out of power those whom the Kremlin did not consider to be trusted and experienced Stalinists.

The degree of that trust, as well as the margin of local autonomy enjoyed by respective Communist leaders, varied from country to country. Since the former involved the matter of personal relationship and the latter was a matter of occasional initiative rather than formal delineation of autonomy, one can only hypothesize about their actual scope. In general, it would seem that by 1950 Stalin could be quite certain that in all of the satellite capitals the heads of the parties were capable of operating on a day-to-day basis without continuing instructions from the center. Beyond this, however, he probably differentiated the Polish and Rumanian leaderships from the others. Stalir might have suspected that the reason for the relative Polish and Ru- manian tardiness in implementing the Stalinist programs (collectiviza tion, violent purges, and so forth) was their excessive concern witl their internal lack of support and their exaggerated consciousness o: anti-Soviet, or traditional anti-Russian, popular attitudes. Stalin migh have felt that Gheorghiu-Dej or even Bierut lacked the revolutionar) fervor of Rakosi or the more orderly zeal of Gottwald. Polish Com munists have repeatedly claimed after 1956 that on the eve of Stalin' death the Polish leadership was coming under increased pressure t intensify the domestic class struggle and that Moscow was showin; signs of impatience with Polish suggestions that there were special ex tenuating circumstances at work in Poland.

By far the most extreme regime was the Bulgarian, which showe its mettle in large-scale violent purges. In some respects during Stalin life, and afterwards also (see Chapters 12–13), the Bulgarians seeme to enjoy a limited form of inverted autonomy — being more Stalini: than the general norm. In part this was related to the relatively estat lished domestic position of the regime and in part to the fact th; Yugoslavia's hostility meant that Bulgaria, fearful of Yugoslav amb tions, had to rely on the USSR. However, no cause-and-effect equ; tion between domestic stability and domestic violence, or conversel between domestic instability and domestic moderation, can be posite The situation varied considerably from country to country. The rel; tively consolidated Czech and Bulgarian regimes engaged in conside: able internal violence and radical policies. The relatively unconsol dated Polish and Rumanian regimes did so to a far lesser extent. Tl case of East Germany, while falling by and large into the Polisl Rumanian category, must be considered outside this pattern becau of the overriding external factors. Hungary, on the other hand, pu sued an extreme domestic policy in spite of the regime's relative lac of domestic support. In this instance, personal, subjective factors, suc as the nature of the leadership, its morale, the relatively high inciden of Jewish membership in the Politburo (and the related problem anti-Semitism), the antiquated social structure — all these factors i fluenced the situation. However, the point is that East Europe seem pretty well Stalinized. The system appeared entrenched, too much to be wholly undermined by Stalin's death.

Stalin could also derive some comfort from the thought that t dispersal of society effected by the twin impact of political violen and rapid social transformation, applied to societies demoralized by war and postwar depravities and largely in a state of social flux,* meant that no cohesive groupings, political or social, remained. Effective opposition to a government which is prepared to suppress all opposition can be organized only if some common bonds remain, preferably of an institutional variety. After 1949–1950 the revolutionary social change and the sustained violence precluded any such resistance; the church as the sole surviving institution could remain simply a sanctuary of alternative philosophical and moral values, not a source of active opposition. It must also be noted that initially, probably until about 1951–1952, the Communist emphasis on the future, contrasted with a reality still bearing the marks of the German occupation, appealed to many, particularly among the younger generation. Even the emphasis on rapid industrialization, albeit destructive in some of its social consequences, was not without its appeal. Communism seemed to offer a key to the understanding of a complex and often brutally unpleasant past and a straight causeway to a socially controllable future. The era of uncertainty bred many who craved such certainty. The Communists seemed to enjoy a monopoly on the tomorrow to which those who opposed them were no longer able to provide any alternative. Thus even the unbelieving were brought face to face with the dilemma of the one alternative — to oppose Communism was to be against everything and for nothing.

STALIN'S TESTAMENT

Even if Stalin did not fully appreciate the decaying processes within his still smoothly operating system of controls, he was too perceptive a leader to be blinded by surface appearances of monolithic unity. Power and success usually breed a layer of insensitivity to inadequacies, errors, and distortions; in a totalitarian system the power of the leader produces a vacuum around the dictator, making it difficult for him to perceive fully the extent of any developing shortcomings. Considering this, it is indeed a testimonial to Stalin's

* For an excellent theoretical treatment of this problem by a leading Polish sociologist, written in Poland after October 1956, see J. Szczepanski, "An Attempt at Diagnosis," *Przeglad Kulturalny*, November 5–11, 1957; see also his *Inteligencja i Spoleczenstwo* (Warsaw, 1957). Szczepanski argues that the "informal ties integrating society" decayed during this period. The situation was most marked in Poland where, in addition to the factors mentioned, over 33 per cent of the population lived after the war in different places than in 1939. (It is to be remembered that this applied to a society still largely rural, and hence not mobile.)

perspicacity that in 1952 he was able to display an awareness of certain potential difficulties in the system he had built and that he attempted to establish a general framework for coping with them.

Stalin's political "testament" appeared late in 1952 in the form of a statement on "Economic Problems of Socialism in the USSR." Most of it pertained to domestic Soviet issues although some aspects were also relevant to the People's Democracies directly or, indirectly, through his analysis of the world situation. The statement reflected Stalin's continued preoccupation with political techniques, but it also showed some concern over their possible abuse. In a tedious, pedantic, and often didactic manner, Stalin appeared to be warning the Soviet Communists, and by definition therefore the other Communist parties, against excessive overconfidence in the capability of centralized planning to "create new laws of economic development." At the same time he also admonished them not to neglect that sense of purpose which is derived from the "basic economic law of socialism" — that is, from the efforts "to assure maximum satisfaction of the constantly growing material and cultural requirements of all of society through the constant growth and improvement of socialist production on the basis of the highest technology." [23] Stalin thus seemed to be reminding his fellow Communists that it would be dangerous to overestimate the capacity of the Soviet state, even "in view of the special role allotted by history" to it, and to assume that it had reached that historical stage of development in which it could satisfy the popular cravings inherent in socialist aspirations. Presumably with Voznesensky in mind,* Stalin condemned "rational planners" who had forgotten that the way to socialism is a long one and that it involved continued emphasis on heavy industrial development. To those Communists in East Europe concerned over excessive industrialization, this mush have seemed a particularly relevant admonition.

What was needed, Stalin seemed to be saying, was a sense of perspective and a common core of doctrine which could be derived only from a keen appreciation of the dynamic quality of Marxism-Leninism. He reflected:

The point is that we, as the leading core, are joined each year by thousands of new young cadres fired with the desire to help us, eager to prove

* N. A. Voznesensky, member of the Politburo and planning chief, disappeared suddenly early in 1949 and was shot in 1950. Subsequently he was charged with overemphasizing the "law of value" in economics and with creating the impression that economic laws can be created by willful action. See M. A. Suslov in *Pravda*, December 24, 1952.

themselves, but lacking an adequate Marxist education, uninformed of many truths well known to us, and thus obliged to wander in the dark. They are amazed by the colossal achievements of the Soviet regime, their heads are turned by the extraordinary successes of the Soviet system and they begin to imagine that the Soviet regime "can do anything," that "everything is child's play" to it, that it can negate scientific laws and fashion new ones. What is to be done with these comrades? I think that systematic repetition and patient explanation of so-called "commonly known" truths is one of the best means of Marxist education of these comrades.[24]

The relevance of these remarks was not restricted to the USSR. In fact, Stalin hinted strongly that the situation was even worse in the other ruling Communist parties. To cope with this, the essentials of Marxism-Leninism-Stalinism would again have to be restated, in a single-volume form, especially because "of the inadequate level of Marxist development of the majority of the Communist parties in foreign countries, such a textbook could be of great benefit also to the veteran Communists in those countries who are no longer young." [25] In brief, Stalin was openly fearful that Stalinist political "voluntarism" would be used to justify modifying economic Stalinism. By demonstratively rescuing old-fashioned determinism he was hoping to perpetuate his own Stalinist voluntarism in both economics and politics.

Turning to the world situation and its bearing on the socialist camp, Stalin repeated with firm finality his belief that the capitalist world was torn by internal contradictions which in themselves constituted a threat of war. Noting that the power of the USSR discouraged a direct attack on the Soviet Union (a reassurance needed by the war-weary Soviet people), Stalin warned that international conflicts were inherent in the market competition of the capitalist world and that such conflicts could not avoid generating political warfare among the capitalist states. By drawing analogies with the Second World War, Stalin hinted that in such an event even the USSR could again find itself enmeshed in an international conflict and that the only ultimate protection was the destruction of imperialism. Indeed, the emergence of a common socialist camp inevitably involves a shrinking of the area subject to capitalist exploitation and leads to "the aggravation of the general crisis in the world capitalist system due to disintegration of the world market." However, at the Nineteenth Party Congress in October 1952, Stalin was careful to remind the other parties that "it would be a mistake to think that our party, having become a mighty force, is no longer in need of support. That is untrue. Our party and our country always have been and always will be in need of the trust, sympathy and support of fraternal peoples abroad . . . As for the Soviet Union, its interests are altogether indivisible from the cause of world peace." [26]

Stalin's exposition, hinting that "errors" in action and thought were again cropping up in the Communist movement, implied that the aging dictator was not merely concerned with matters of ideological purity but also with behavior which was both deviant and harmful. Not since the mid-thirties had such an ominous warning been issued, and the earlier consequences of similar Stalinist admonitions were still fresh in Communist memories. The *Zhdanovshchina*, by way of comparison, involved issues more narrowly prescribed both in their ideological content and human scope. Stalin's 1952 observations could hardly be considered idle musings: they were preceded and followed by events which suggested a cause-and-effect relationship between his assessments of the situation and the fate of some individuals. The execution of Voznesensky, doubtless linked with internal party intrigues, appeared highly relevant to the views postulated by Stalin in "Economic Problems of Socialism in the USSR." The intensification of domestic vigilance campaigns in the USSR, culminating in the Doctors' Plot,[27] implied that Stalin was seriously contemplating the need to follow up his diagnosis with action. In other words, increasingly suspicious that somehow his system was becoming brittle and static, Stalin was preparing to deal with it the only way he knew how.

Stalin's death in March 1953, however, left no one able to perform the task, while the protracted search for a successor brought to the surface the internal doubts and difficulties. Whether a recourse to extreme violence could have sealed the gap between the "superstructure" and the "base," between political imperatives and socioeconomic realities, is doubtful. A violent purge might have revitalized the Communist movements and further obscured their internal dilemmas. Such a purge probably would have involved the final liquidation of Gomulka and his associates in Poland; it probably would have included the Jewish Communists in the Hungarian and Rumanian Politburos; it very likely would have embraced the top echelons of the CPSU, including the Politburo itself. Its surface consequence would have been an even more intensified dedication to Stalinism, a more rapid imitation of Soviet experience in the other Communist states, and an even further extension of secret police power. But this could only be achieved if the dictator lived for a few more years. Only he could supply the inner drive for the execution of a policy less and less related to reality even as seen by many Communists themselves. This was amply demonstrated by the policies adopted within a few months of his death. Stalin's last-minute effort to infuse Stalinism with a new purpose merely served to intensify the reaction against it.

The Third Phase: 1953-1956

*FROM THAW TO DELUGE — INSTITUTIONAL AND
    IDEOLOGICAL DIVERSITY*

The roads and conditions of socialist development are different in different countries . . . any tendency to impose one's own views in determining the roads and forms of socialist development are alien to both sides. — Soviet-Yugoslav Declaration, Moscow, June 20, 1956

8 / THE NEW COURSE:

STALINISM DISSIPATED

STALIN'S death did not lead to the immediate disintegration of the Stalinist system. It did deprive it of the crucial psychological ingredient of personal fear — a fear shared by the subdued populations of East Europe, to whom Stalin was symbol of the Soviet might, and by their Communist leaders trained in the stiff Stalinist school of the Comintern and promoted through the rigorous competitions of the Great Purges. For the time being, however, the institutions of power remained, particularly the links between the Soviet secret police and the satellite networks, and the Stalinist conception of the relations between the USSR and the Communist bloc as well. The new Soviet leadership groped carefully in the initial stages, seeking to maintain continuity with the past while attempting to develop its own solutions to a variety of domestic and external problems left by the Stalinist legacy. The surgical solution which Stalin might have been contemplating in the closing days of his life now had to give way to a prolonged cure.

Soon both the institutions of Soviet power in the Communist-ruled states as well as the theoretical framework governing their relations to the USSR were subjected to the pressures of changed conditions and new requirements. As the ingredient of power, so dependent on the personal impact of Stalin, gradually, almost imperceptibly, shrank, the Stalinist monopoly of ideology and power in Soviet-satellite relations slowly gave way to a greater reliance on ideology. The dilemma was that Stalinism as an ideology was so dependent on power that by itself it could not cope with the post-Stalin situation in the Communist camp. Under the circumstances, the ideological framework linking the Communist states had to be made more elastic to permit greater variation in domestic policies within the context of over-all unity. By 1956 and 1957 the search for new solutions was taking the form of a widespread dialogue between various Communist parties, leaders, newspapers, and intellectuals.* In effect, the Stalinist unity of ideology and power was dissipated within less than four years of his death. What led to this diversity? What were the new problems in the relations among the Communist states? The next four chapters (8–11) will attempt to provide the answers.

PROBLEMS OF SOVIET SUCCESSION

Stalin was not merely the Soviet dictator but also the leader of international Communism. Yet, in view of the central position of the USSR, it was only fitting that the succession be resolved, initially at least, within the framework of Soviet domestic considerations. The competition for power produced immediate and broad disagreements on policy, even if only as a function of the succession crisis. In addition, Stalin's death brought to the surface certain dilemmas which had long been obscured by the single-minded purposefulness of Stalinism as long as the dictator was at the helm. Dormant political and economic issues now demanded immediate attention and resolution. Unavoidably, such Soviet domestic preoccupations tended to leave the Communist leaderships in the neighboring states somewhat to their own resources.

Among the most important items on the agenda of the new "collective" leadership were the creation of some stable leadership arrangement which would safeguard the dominant interests of the upper levels of the political elite and prevent a violent and disruptive conflict; a reorganization of the party and administrative structure which had grown too large and unwieldy under Stalin; a diminution in world tensions which were imposing a heavy strain on Soviet and Communist development; and, finally, a review of the Stalinist economic formula which favored heavy capital development at the expense of consumption and agriculture.

---

* Admittedly, it is difficult to distinguish between ideological conflict which is politically motivated and that which primarily involves pure doctrine, especially when doctrinal positions form a basis for eventual political action. Nonetheless, one can point to certain ideological disputes in which problems of power are so involved that it is not unreasonable to suspect that the dialogue on theory is a mere sham for a brutal power struggle. The least one can say is that ideology and power have become inseparable at such a juncture. This would appear to have been the case with many of the disputes which developed after Stalin's death among various Communist leaders and parties in East Europe, including the USSR, and also in the case of the positions taken by the Chinese and French Communist parties. There is also, however, the more genuine conflict of ideas in which power plays only a secondary role. This seems to have been the situation with much of the ideological disputes which went on inside Poland, conducted by intellectuals not tied to specific posts of authority.

Now, it is highly unlikely that, following a devout wake for Stalin, his successors actually sat down and enumerated point by point the problems that they faced and the methods required for solving them. Some of the above issues were spontaneous products of the struggle for power which itself altered the relationships among the various institutions of Soviet power. Other issues arose as the new leaders proceeded to formulate policy and think independently, almost for the first time in their mature lives. Genuine conflict of opinion certainly might have arisen on the controversial issue of heavy capital development versus consumer-goods programs and agricultural growth.[1] Finally, it is quite likely that a review of foreign policy aiming at the reduction of tensions followed logically from Stalin's testament which had posited the intensification of conflicts within the capitalist camp. This testament, therefore, implied that the USSR should not allow the capitalists to obscure their internal contradictions by channeling their aggression against the Communist world. But here again a conflict of interpretation on scope and method was bound to arise and be exacerbated by the absence of a final arbiter. And ambivalence in Moscow, thanks to Stalinism, meant ambivalence in Prague or Warsaw.

The first year and a half following Stalin's death was dominated, within the limits of an uneasy "collective" leadership, by Georgi Malenkov. The initial succession problem which the new regime faced was that of the secret police which had grown powerful under Stalin and which now seemed to be reaching out for total power.* The echoes of the July 1953 announcement of Lavrenti Beria's arrest and the Christmas Eve 1953 execution of the former secret police chief and six of his top associates had particular significance for the East European Communist parties smarting for the preceding few years under police surveillance. The subsequent stress on "socialist legality," though still largely verbal, in itself represented a factor potentially limiting the formerly unchecked interference of the police in party matters. Tackling another of the problems it considered basic, the regime in 1954 took a first tentative step toward decentralization of the Soviet administrative structure,[2] although Malenkov continued the Stalinist practice of a multiministerial Council of Ministers, ruled internally by an inner cabinet of First Deputy Prime Ministers. The measure of duality of party and state administration

---

* At the time many observers were inclined to feel that the secret police was the actual ruler of the USSR. See the remarks by G. Kennan and H. Arendt in C. J. Friedrich, ed., *Totalitarianism* (Cambridge, 1954), pp. 76–77, 82–83.

which had developed under Stalin remained largely unchanged, and, indeed, the effort to avoid a concentration of power in one man's hands resulted in the appointment of different individuals to head the party and the administration.

It was in the sphere of economic policy that the Malenkov period was marked by the greatest innovation. Of course, here again, the position adopted by Malenkov — namely, that of stressing an improvement in the standard of living — in some measure may have reflected a commonly felt need among the post-Stalin leaders to court the people. However, soon it did become an issue in the struggle for power, with the government organ, *Izvestia*, and the party organ, *Pravda*, publicly disagreeing at one point on the policies that ought to be followed,[3] and with Khrushchev finally warning that abandoning the heavy industry priority is "nothing but slander of our Party . . . a belching of the rightist deviation, a regurgitation of views hostile to Leninism." [4] Khrushchev's violent outburst, accompanied as it was by Malenkov's dismissal as Premier, was nothing short of a complete repudiation of the Malenkov policy, which had been expounded in a major address to the Supreme Soviet as far back as August 1953. That policy had emphasized a shift in investment toward light industry and trade, as well as increased incomes for collective farmers and a greater availability of consumer goods. To underscore the importance of this program, the issue of *Pravda* which carried the full text of Malenkov's August 1953 address also ran special inside stories which emphasized only those portions of the speech pertaining to an improvement in the standard of living.

In foreign policy, the Malenkov period coincided with a reduction in world tensions, the most outstanding feature of which was the Korean armistice of July 27, 1953. In his August speech Malenkov took credit for a "normalization" in relations with Turkey, Iran, and Afghanistan, and for an exchange of envoys with Yugoslavia. As far as East Europe was concerned, Malenkov stood fast on the position that the People's Democracies were firmly tied to the USSR; much like Stalin earlier, he did not feel compelled to devote more than a passing phrase to them. One might well speculate, on rereading Stalin's "Economic Problems of Socialism in the USSR" that had the old dictator remained alive, Soviet foreign policy would not have been very much different. The Malenkov policy, too, seemed to take the permanence of the Soviet bloc much for granted and to count on growing tensions within the capitalist bloc to undermine the cohesion which had developed in the face of the earlier Soviet threat. In broad terms, the Malenkov policy may be characterized as a general continuation of Stalinism politically, possibly from sheer momentum, balanced by an attempt to reduce the harshness of the Stalinist economic policies. It was an attempt, in brief, to pursue a new course in economics without basically altering the framework of essentially Stalinist politics.

THE MALENKOV NEW COURSE

The Malenkov New Course struck a responsive chord among some of the leaders of the People's Democracies. Without yielding the most important Stalinist positions, it seemed to permit them to reduce somewhat the accumulated economic tensions. Political concessions, such as the introduction of collective leadership, were essentially procedural and, unlike the USSR, did not involve a substantive change in the East European power picture. In formal imitation, the leaders relinquished some of their posts to their associates, but this was of political significance only in Hungary. In some states which had lagged behind the others in Stalinist terror, such as Poland and Rumania, police violence mounted during this period.*

The first state to initiate a new course was East Germany. The mounting internal difficulties of this probably most Soviet-dependent regime forced the German Politburo to turn to Moscow, in April 1953, with an urgent request for assistance and to begin a reconsideration of the Stalinist capital-development policy. This was a particularly bad moment for approaching Moscow with such a request. The Soviet leadership was deeply divided, with Beria apparently favoring a radical political reform program for East Germany. On June 9, four days after the return from Moscow of the Soviet High Commissioner, V. S. Semenov, the SED Politburo made a public statement of self-criticism, admitting "aberrations in the past," and announcing a three-point program for alleviating the most acute hardships. Delivery quotas and taxes were reduced, state loans were made available to private business, and material allocations were increased. The radical socialization begun in 1952 was halted. The timing of the High Commissioner's presence in Moscow was particularly interesting because it was precisely at this time that the CPSU Presidium was holding talks with Rakosi as the preliminary to a new course in Hungary. This

* For example, in Poland, Cardinal Wyszynski was arrested in September 1953, and in May nineteen high army officers with distinguished war records were executed; in Rumania, Patrascanu, purged earlier from the party leadership, was executed in April 1953.

certainly seems to confirm the notion that the Malenkov New Course was a purposeful program of action not for the USSR alone but for the People's Democracies also. Because of this larger perspective, the New Course was not sidetracked by the East Berlin uprising which followed within a week of the SED announcement.[5] Indeed, the outbreak, followed shortly by Beria's arrest, even seemed to confirm the wisdom of the new policy: of political concessions there must be few, while economic concessions are warranted to relieve the political tensions. Following the suppression of the revolt by a show of Soviet strength, another SED Central Committee plenum convened on July 24–26, 1953. The Fifteenth Plenum rejected general criticisms of the party line, branding them as "defeatist and capitulationist," although it did admit that accelerated efforts to construct the socialist foundations had erred in ignoring practical internal and external considerations. The party pleaded guilty to disregarding the fact that a large portion of German public opinion lived under capitalist influence and that its views had to be considered when policy is framed. For this reason East Germany ought to strive for a standard of living higher than in West Germany. This would sound the death-knell for the Adenauer line by making East Germany an irresistibly appealing force.[6]

The main burden of the Fifteenth Plenum's resolutions was accordingly in the economic realm. The previous political line was judged essentially correct, the Ulbricht-Grotewohl leadership was absolved and even hailed, and those party officials who had wavered in the face of the crisis were dismissed.* At the same time, further economic concessions were made. The distribution of investments was altered, with the 1953 sum for heavy industry cut by 1.7 billion East German marks. Wage taxes and prices were reduced in October, and minor offenders were granted a partial amnesty. Simultaneously, however, the party reiterated its commitment to socialization in agriculture, and the percentage of collective and state-farm holdings grew (see table in Chapter 5, p. 98). In general, the easing of the economic situation — further aided by the return, on January 1, 1954, to East German control of German enterprises managed by the USSR and the termination of reparations to the USSR — did result in a marked improvement in the standard of living and relieved some of the politi-

---

* After the uprising, Wilhelm Zaisser, Minister of State Security, Max Fechner, Minister of Justice, and R. Herrnstadt, editor of the party daily, were dismissed and in 1954 expelled from the party.

cal tensions in the country. The Malenkov formula seemed to pass this test of experience.

The next state to adopt a new course was Hungary. The situation there, however, differed substantially from East Germany's. The Hungarian regime had been considerably more violent than the East German (see Chapter 5), and the economic changes adopted by it had been forced on a country with a much more primitive economic structure. Consequently, the impact of Stalinism had been felt a good deal more sharply. The violence of the purge trials and the executions of many non-Communist leaders were matched by an industrial-development drive which envisaged during the Five Year Plan a 380 per cent increase in the production of consumer goods.[7] Extricating the regime from the existing situation, therefore, was bound to be a far more complicated and dangerous task. Soviet initiative again was the decisive factor. In June 1953, a conference convened in Moscow between the heads of the CPSU and a delegation from the Hungarian Politburo, headed by Rakosi. The Soviet leaders apparently spared no words in castigating the Hungarians for *economic* excesses which "had driven the country to the verge of catastrophe."[8] At the conference Mikoyan, Malenkov, and Khrushchev took the lead in insisting on immediate economic reform to prevent unrest, while politically they appeared satisfied with an imitation of the limited Soviet amnesty and of the collective-leadership principle.[9]

In the Hungarian circumstances, the Malenkov adaptation of Stalinism could not avoid having profound political overtones. The critical economic situation, added to a long-term resentment of Rakosi's political practices, produced within the party an alternative to Rakosi strong enough to justify, in Moscow's eyes, Rakosi's resignation from the Premiership. The new Premier, appointed as a formal concession to the principle of collective leadership, actually happened to be an individual who was personally committed to the principles of the New Course — just as Rakosi was personally against it. Imre Nagy's appointment was thus politically significant for it pitted the combined prestige of a new policy and a new Premier against the entrenched power of the First Secretary of the party. The new Premier was supported by a minority faction within the Central Committee but, for the first time, this minority controlled an important state post and pursued an official policy blessed by Moscow. The First Secretary could not, therefore, oppose the New Course openly — he had to bide his time and make certain, in the meantime, that his position within the party *apparat*, made loyal to him through the purges and by a common vested interest, was not undermined. The economic part of the New Course in this manner created an ambivalent political situation: Rakosi retained party control and hence the power, but Nagy shaped the program and hence interpreted the ideology.

Nagy's program was officially inaugurated by a major parliamentary address delivered on July 4, 1953. The initial impact of the New Course was largely economic even though it did involve measures which sharply reduced the class-struggle atmosphere which dominated the preceding phase. But the economic ills which the New Course was to correct were so deep-seated in the system that efforts to remedy them involved profound criticisms of past policies and implicitly of the entire system. The new Premier promised that his economic policy would be guided by the principle of "cut your coat according to your cloth," * and he noted that "the development of a Socialist heavy industry cannot be an end in itself." [10] Nagy then promised to reduce the rate of development and to modify its direction "in conformity with the capacity of the country." He explicitly promised to reduce investments allotted to heavy industry, an act which would have the effect of raising the standard of living. He was particularly scornful of the agricultural policies pursued by his predecessors:

Agricultural production has been stagnating and during the past few years its pace has been determined by meager investments, the lack of support offered to individual farmers, the far too rapid development of producers' cooperatives, which is neither economically nor politically justifiable and has made the peasantry's work insecure.

During the land collectivization program too much bullying was practiced. This not only offended the peasant's sense of justice but also caused serious harm to our economy, and played an important part in bringing about the present state of affairs.[11]

Nagy then postulated "the consolidation of legality" as one of the most urgent tasks of his government and promised to abolish the internment camps and to separate the judiciary from the secret police. His program of action may be summarized under the following head-

* It is interesting to note that at this time there was considerable uncertainty concerning Nagy's position. In the *News from Behind the Iron Curtain*, August 1953, p. 8, he was even described as "a trusted friend of Rakosi." A Communist of many years standing, he had lived in the USSR since 1929 and returned to Hungary only in 1945. After serving in several ministerial posts, in 1951 he was promoted to the party Secretariat. According to the literal use of labels, he could have been identified as a "Muscovite."

ings: (1) price reductions, wage increases, reduced compulsory obligations; (2) cancellation of some agricultural deliveries and a 15 per cent reduction in taxes on the peasantry, as well as sanctioned withdrawal from collective farms; (3) greater religious tolerance, abolition of internment camps, and partial amnesty. The program thus closely resembled the Malenkov formula, even though distasteful to the more radical party faction headed by Rakosi. However, unlike the USSR, in Hungary the past policies, applied over a shorter time span and in different circumstances, produced far greater strains, while the division in Hungarian leadership immediately translated such tensions into a political conflict of major proportions. The New Course could not stay within the limits set by the Soviet example and presumably intended by its framers. Soviet-Hungarian relations could not remain unaffected (for further developments, see Chapter 10).

The next three countries to follow suit, but without the resultant political and international strains, were Rumania, Bulgaria, and Czechoslovakia, in that order. In none of them did the imitative application of the collective-leadership principle materially affect the substance of political power.* All of them had suffered the stresses of rapid industrialization but none to the extent of Hungary. In addition, in Czechoslovakia and Bulgaria the economic difficulties were not matched by a violent national hatred of Russia, while in Rumania, with a similar anti-Russian national tradition, economic Sovietization had lagged behind the other states.† Furthermore, in Bulgaria and Czechoslovakia, the Communist parties were much more solidly entrenched than in Hungary and therefore better able to withstand the tensions involved. The Rumanian New Course was initiated by Gheorghiu-Dej's address of August 25; in Bulgaria, by a similar speech delivered by Chervenkov on September 8. In both cases almost entirely economic measures were stressed (but notably with continued collectivization), and these were initiated by known and trusted Stalinists.

---

* It is interesting, however, to note that the pattern of choice of posts varied, with the "strong man" choosing in one case the post of Premier, in another that of First Secretary. In Poland, Bierut chose the party post; in Czechoslovakia, A. Novotny did likewise, and so did Rakosi in Hungary, Enver Hoxha in Albania, and Walter Ulbricht in the GDR; in Rumania, however, Gheorghiu-Dej chose the Premiership as did Chervenkov in Bulgaria.

† In the more industrially advanced Czechoslovakia and East Germany, industrial production by late 1955 was, respectively, 2.4 and 2 times higher than before the war. In the relatively non-industrial Poland and Hungary, the ratios were 4 and 3.5 times respectively. Yet in the case of Rumania, only 2 times (*Trud*, April 3, 1956).

The most enthusiastic response to the series of reforms which began in Hungary came from Czechoslovakia. There was good reason for this. Somewhat like East Germany, but without the wartime devastation and postwar reparations, Czechoslovakia suffered least from economic dislocation and social disintegration as a result of the rapid development envisaged in the Five-Year Plans. Thus a policy reversal was possible without serious political consequences, while a reduction in economic pressures was bound to strike a responsive chord in the population. The summer 1953 riots in Pilsen (prompted by a currency reform) were a warning to the regime of the potential dangers involved in maintaining economic Stalinism, and the regime welcomed the timely, and still relatively safe, opportunity for withdrawal. Accordingly, the Czech response to the Hungarian program was much more openly favorable than in any other East European state; there was greater press coverage of the new Hungarian policy — a sure indication in a Communist-ruled country of official approbation, when not accompanied by derogatory references. Finally, on September 15, 1953, the Czech Premier, Siroky, delivered an address in which he stressed the need for "proportionate growth" in Czechoslovak economy and announced a series of reforms in the existing plans. Apart from the usual decreases in taxes, wage increases, and reductions in delivery quotas, a slowdown in the rate growth in industrial production was promised and limited permission granted to withdraw from collective farms. The last provision was rescinded within a year and collectivization was renewed (see table in Chapter 5).*

In retrospect, it seems that the economic version of the New Course worked well in Czechoslovakia. The reforms reversed any existing trends toward an appreciable lowering of the standard of living without, however, capitulating on the essentials of socialist construction. The continuation of the collectivization policy (after a short halt) indicated the regime's determination to liquidate the last remnants of private ownership in the economy while politically and ideologically maintaining tight control over the country. The economic reforms appear to have stymied the opposition undercurrents within the party, while the finality of the earlier purges removed some of the potential leaders of such an opposition. Indeed, the Czech

---

* Between June 30, 1953, and November 1954, the number of collective farms declined from 7038 to 6530, and the percentage of socialized arable land from 44 per cent to 30 per cent (*Lidova Demokracie*, November 5, 1954). This presumably alarmed the leadership.

Communist leadership, partially because of the country's relative prosperity and advanced economy, partially because of the party's strength and greater experience, and partially because of a relatively pliant population, displayed the greatest skill in applying the modified policy and thereby in maintaining ideological and institutional unity with the USSR.

The last to adopt formally the New Course was Poland. It did so on October 29, 1953, at the Ninth Plenum of the Central Committee of the United Polish Workers' Party. The reforms adopted were minor. In his speech to the plenum, Bierut, whose power at this time was at its height, stressed the need to improve the standard of living but conceded nothing in the political field. He still called for a struggle against the kulak, although it was admitted that an error had been made in lumping together the rich with the medium peasant. From now on, it was promised, a distinction would be made between the two, and the party was to make a concerted effort to wean the latter away from the former. Only this would assure the final victory of socialism in the countryside.[12] Economic concessions were limited to some price reductions and to tax and compulsory-deliveries relief. The party also promised to reduce the share of accumulation in national income from 25.1 per cent in 1953 to 19.8 per cent in 1955 and to increase the turnover in socialized retail trade by 20 per cent.[13] The chief of Polish economic planning himself admitted that these changes were much more modest than elsewhere, particularly when compared to Czechoslovakia and East Germany.[14]

The political atmosphere remained basically unchanged. Indeed, as noted, some of the most extreme acts of violence took place around this time. Nonetheless, the very fact that Poland lagged in following the example of others and displayed considerable reticence when finally adopting the plan was significant. To some extent this could be explained by the previous policy of caution. Stalinism had been gingerly and timidly distilled in Poland. As has been observed in previous chapters, it involved a little less violence within the party itself, less collectivization and fewer compulsory deliveries for the farmers, and a little more circumspection in outright imitation and adulation of all things Soviet. Furthermore, the general instability of the economy, widespread poverty, and weakness of the party might have convinced the leadership, firmly in the hands of old Stalinists like Bierut or Berman, that a point of no return had been reached and that a sharp reversal would be dangerous. This was especially the case since they had not liquidated all the political alternatives. An admission of fundamental error would have been an implicit recognition that Gomulka, still living and not forgotten, had been right. Caution and restraint in moving away from a domestic policy of economic and political radicalism seemed the soundest political course to follow. The program was presumably cleared with Moscow, and the Polish leaders asserted with specific reference to Malenkov's August 1953 address that "the countries of People's Democracy and their leading force — the Communist and Workers' Parties — get their example and inspiration from the achievements and policy of the peoples of the Soviet Union and the leading force of mankind — the Communist Party of the Soviet Union." [15] Nonetheless, the primacy of domestic considerations seemed inherent in the new policy. This was not without its hidden significance.

During the Malenkov period the People's Democracies, with the Soviet Union leading the way, concentrated their efforts on coping with the economic legacy of Stalinism. However, the reaction of the various parties to Malenkov's New Course, while substantially uniform and hence in keeping with the Stalinist formula of unity, already involved varying shades of enthusiasm, timing, and degree of personal commitment. The broad pattern of Soviet controls was still not affected and the habit of obedience was still deeply ingrained, but it was certainly easier for the post-Stalin Soviet leadership to recommend policies which made the domestic tasks of the various party leaderships less difficult. The response of the satellite leaders on the whole was a reflection of their approval, with some qualifications, of the new line. But what would they have done if they had concluded that Moscow's policies would make their job harder or go counter to their personal interests or views?

The very fact that the New Course did take into consideration the peculiar domestic facts existing in each case is a reflection of the change that had taken place in relations in the Soviet world since Stalin's death. The disappearance of Stalin, the destruction of Beria, the signing of the Korean armistice and the resolution of the Indo-Chinese conflict, the Soviet acknowledgment that the February 1954 Berlin conference of Foreign Ministers of the major world powers had led to "better understanding" of the international situation[16] — all tended almost imperceptibly, but significantly, to alter the existing relationships. With the decrease in external pressures, the excessive personalization of Communist interstate relations, which had been a source of strength as long as Stalin lived, became a source of weakness when he died.

Malenkov's efforts not to disrupt the political structure, while remedying some of the underlying economic grievances,* did in fact achieve certain desirable results in the more economically advanced states and also in the least-developed states. However, in Poland and Hungary the Malenkov formula was insufficient to resolve the dilemmas bequeathed by Stalinism without a clear and sustained Soviet involvement. In the Hungarian and Polish reactions to the new pattern there were harbingers, very faint ones, of future diversity. In Poland, the New Course was applied more slowly because of existing internal tensions and earlier caution, as well as potential dangers involved in it; in Hungary, the New Course was applied quickly and extensively precisely because of existing tensions but also because of earlier excesses. In Poland, the presence of a political alternative which had inhibited the leadership and the sense of popular disappointment with the leadership's conservatism in applying the New Course gradually transformed it into a political phenomenon (see Chapter 11). In Hungary, the creation of such a political alternative through Nagy's appointment and the rear-guard struggle waged against the New Course by the Stalinist First Secretary of the party immediately made the policy a crucial domestic dilemma (see Chapter 10).

In the Soviet Union itself there was developing a marked ambivalence toward the policies to be pursued. The uncertainties in the Soviet line, which burst into the open through the unprecedented cleavage between *Pravda* and *Izvestia* in December 1954 and which had been a matter of earlier party discussions, could not leave the People's Democracies, and particularly Poland and Hungary, unaffected. The resulting disorientation and lesser Soviet involvement meant that a consideration of alternatives was gradually replacing the single-minded purposefulness of Stalinism as the basis for policy formation. Even if not participating actively in Soviet policy dilemmas, the East European Communists could not avoid taking sides emotionally, intellectually, or politically,† especially as long as the Soviet leaders continued to assert the relevance of the Soviet experience for

---

* Symptomatic of this approach were the announcements of the transfer of the Soviet share in the jointly owned companies to Rumanian ownership (*Izvestia*, September 25, 1954); to Bulgaria (*ibid.*, October 12, 1954); to Hungary (*ibid.*, November 10, 1954). In each instance, the recipient was to pay off the Soviet share on otherwise unspecified "favorable terms."

† Bialer (*Wybralem Wolnosc*, p. 12), in the report of his activities while on the staff of the Polish Central Committee, refers specifically to frequently heated discussions among Polish *apparatchiki* on the meaning and implications of various Soviet policy shifts during this period.

the People's Democracies.* But even distant and relatively passive participation in Soviet policy dilemmas meant a break with the mechanical acceptance of Moscow programs as "revealed truth."

KHRUSHCHEV'S CONCEPTION OF THE COMMUNIST CAMP

During 1954, the Soviet political scene was dominated by the rapid growth in the stature of the First Secretary of the party and by the increasingly peremptory tone of his pronouncements. As one authoritative observer has noted, "the step-by-step ascent of Khrushchev to a position of undisputed leadership represents a striking recapitulation of the Stalinist experience," [17] and it was accomplished primarily in terms of domestic issues and through the manipulation of domestic forces. By skillfully seizing the initiative in pressing for new and dynamic schemes of internal reconstruction, Khrushchev assumed the role of the Leninist revolutionary struggling against the vested interests of the bureaucrats, and he succeeded in mobilizing the party around him. His insistence, in Febraury 1954, on a new agricultural policy, his shuffles of the party *apparat*, as well as his active interest in the parties of the People's Democracies (demonstrated through personal visits to Poland, Czechoslovakia, and China), made him appear as the dynamic innovator so necessary to keeping a totalitarian system from stagnating. Naturally, this produced resentment from those sections of society interested in stability, but in late 1954 and early 1955, Khrushchev succeeded in gaining the support of the Central Committee of the party on the critical issue of the methods of industrialization and of the rate of development of heavy industry.[18]

In retrospect, it appears that the Soviet leadership was at the time divided into three groups: some Soviet leaders favored relatively "softer" methods on the international front and some domestic economic concessions; others, accepting the proposition that Soviet interests would be best served by a foreign policy somewhat less Stalinist in form though not in content, differed fundamentally on the domestic economic line and insisted on heavy industrial development; still others supported domestic and external policies essentially Stalinist both in form and content. To the degree that it is possible to generalize about as complex an issue as the policy outlook of specific Soviet leaders, it would appear that the first attitude was held by

---

* For instance, at the November 1954 anniversary of the Bolshevik revolution. M. Z. Saburov, the Moscow keynoter, stated that "Socialist construction in the USSR is the source of a wealth of experience for all the people who have now taken the path blazed by the Great October socialist revolution." *Pravda*, November 7, 1954.

Malenkov, the second by Khrushchev,* and the third by Molotov. It was a combination of the last two that united to remove Malenkov on the issue of domestic policy, although Molotov was apparently unable to carry the day on the international issue. Thus, in international politics, the new Khrushchev-Bulganin team continued the efforts to present the USSR as genuinely striving to settle all international issues, reflecting the reassessments made late in 1952. The Geneva Conference held in the summer of 1955 between the heads of governments of the United States, the United Kingdom, France, and the USSR (and with the First Secretary of the CPSU participating) was the culmination of this policy. It is likely that the Soviet leaders hoped that a measure of relaxation would allow the contradictions in the capitalist camp to mature while permitting the USSR and the People's Democracies to press their domestic industrialization unhindered by threats of war. Furthermore, the Soviet and other Communist leaders might have reasoned that such diminution of international tensions, symbolized by the Geneva handshakes with the leaders of the West, implicitly meant the West's acceptance of the status quo in East Central Europe.

In some respects it could be argued that the Communist calculations were well founded. However, the 1955 spell of international good will had a further and unexpected consequence. While possibly extinguishing any lingering hopes of Western "liberation" of East Europe, it also reduced the fears of the Communist ruling elites and undermined the feeling that they must "sink or swim" with the USSR. The internal Soviet ambivalence in policy and the reduction in international tensions produced the belief that the People's Democracies could now afford to frame their policies to fit their domestic requirements. The Stalinist "dilemma of the one alternative" was upset with the fading of the external enemy, while the Soviet return to heavy industrial development immediately put to the test the willingness of the parties — as well as their ability — to emulate the USSR under these new circumstances, even when such imitation imposed domestic strains. The situation was now quite different from the Malenkov New Course period.

That Khrushchev expected the People's Democracies to follow the new Soviet economic policy seems clear. Admitting that some "disproportions" had existed in the past, the Soviet leadership adopted the

---

* Khrushchev, however, already in mid-1954 dissociated himself from Malenkov's willingness to concede that an all-out nuclear war would spell the end of humanity and firmly contended that such a conflict would mean the final destruction of capitalism.

position that such errors had now been corrected and that correction of errors is not a substitute for policy. *Pravda*, commenting six weeks after the CPSU plenum which had repudiated the Malenkov line, stated:

It would be incorrect to think that the creation of the material basis for socialism is proceeding without difficulties. Reorganizing the entire technical base of a national economy requires large capital investments, new cadres and great experience. The difficulties experienced by the economies of the people's democracies were manifested first of all by a number of economic disproportions. The decisions of the administrative bodies of the Communist and Workers' Parties of the people's democracies point out the fact that the rate of growth of agriculture is insufficient to meet the working people's growing requirements. The development of the raw material and power base is lagging behind industry's needs.

In certain of the people's democracies the regrouping of capital investments carried out in order to eliminate these disproportions was interpreted by some as a renunciation of the preponderant development of heavy industry. The Party press in these countries writes that *these views,* which are *basically incorrect* and *harmful* to the cause of socialism, are being severely criticized.[19]

Pravda then commented approvingly on a recent resolution of the Hungarian Central Committee which had condemned such "anti-Marxist, anti-Party, opportunist views." [20] (See Chapters 10 and 11 for Hungarian and Polish developments.)

The Khrushchev formula for the USSR and for the Soviet bloc involved no basic change in the foreign-policy approach of the preceding two years, but domestically it stressed a return to an economic policy of maintaining heavy capital development while at the same time striving to improve agricultural productivity and to revitalize the economy. A by-product was to be an improvement in the standard of living, but without loss in heavy industrial development. However, because of the moderately relaxing effect of the two years' post-Stalin New Course, such an economic reshuffle could not be accompanied by a continuation of political Stalinism, and Khrushchev accordingly attempted to weave together some new fabric of unity and cohesion. By allowing an economic relaxation, Malenkov was able to ignore for the time being the political problem. By insisting on an economic "neo-Stalinism," Khrushchev had to face the political problem squarely. The formula which he apparently developed in the course of the following year involved increasing emphasis on common economic practices while tolerating an undefined and limited measure of political autonomy, unthinkable during Stalinism. Its further concomitant was to be the elevation of those Communist leaders who seemed more acceptable to the people, and Khrushchev made it painfully clear that Jewish Communists like Rakosi or Berman or Ana Pauker were in his judgment handicapping their parties. These efforts to develop some indigenous support for the various Communist regimes were to be matched by closer, formal institutional ties which would fill the vacuum left by the disappearance of the personal Stalinist ingredient, and by greater emphasis on common ideological bonds which would result from similar economic undertakings.

Indeed, allowing for the differences in scale, the Soviet-Chinese relations in the years following Stalin's death might have served as a basic model for Khrushchev's thinking. In October 1954 a top level Soviet delegation composed of Khrushchev, Mikoyan, Bulganin, and Shvernik, visited Peking and reached an agreement with the Chinese largely designed to transform the Soviet-Chinese relationship into a more mutually advantageous one. The Soviet Union agreed to withdraw from Port Arthur, to abolish the joint-stock companies, and to abandon Soviet-Chinese uranium exploitation in Sinkiang, all representing Soviet advantages asserted under Stalin. Military and economic assistance to China was stepped up and in the years 1953–1957 China obtained loans from the Soviet Union totaling 8.5 billion rubles.[21] This, however, did not resolve all outstanding issues. The Chinese remained resentful of the fact that the Soviets continued to expect repayment of the aid extended during the Korean War, and they also raised (but did not press) the politically sensitive question of Mongolia's status. As Mao revealed in 1964 (see Chapter 16), "In 1954 when Khrushchev and Bulganin were in China we took up the question but they refused to talk to us." [22]

These differences notwithstanding, the Khrushchev mission did create a more stable basis for Sino-Soviet relations. The Chinese Communists found it much easier to profess strict adherence to the Soviet model of socialism in the absence of the Soviet dictator, and the resulting Soviet search for a successor and a new program relieved them of any fear of actual subordination.* International pressures on China were also lightened, while the Soviet Union acted as China's "honest broker" in the international arena. Internally, the Chinese forcefully pursued a policy of rapid industrialization on, as they asserted, the Soviet model.[23] However, beyond these somewhat ritualistic formulas, the Chinese did insist during this period on "adapting" all of this to

* In February 1955, the Chinese were even described by Molotov as sharing in the leadership of the socialist camp, and following Khrushchev's visit the joint-stock Sino-Soviet companies were abolished.

specific Chinese conditions, and they even laid claims to having made creative and original contributions to Marxism-Leninism, particularly in the area of the "eradication of capitalism by peaceful methods of Socialist transformation." [24] They were careful, however, to restrict the applicability of this to the unique Chinese experience. The rather different techniques applied to cope with the domestic bourgeoisie, as well as the redefinition of the notion of the dictatorship of the proletariat in the Chinese context,[25] still did not weigh heavily on Soviet-Chinese relations and did not undermine what Khrushchev apparently considered the essentials of ideological unity: the leading role of the CPSU in the Communist camp, the Communist Party's supremacy in the domestic transformation of the various states, rapid industrialization and collectivization as essential components of that transformation.

Observing Sino-Soviet relations and bearing in mind the great dependence of the East European regimes on the USSR, Khrushchev could feel justified in altering the Stalinist formula in the direction of greater reliance on a community of economic patterns and emphasis on ideological uniformity. Such a framework could effectively contain the inherent pressures for diversity, but without the need for continuous Soviet involvement which Stalinism had demanded. In the words of Khrushchev's *Pravda:* "The historical experience of the Soviet Union and of the People's Democracies shows that, given unity in the chief fundamental matter of ensuring the victory of socialism, various ways and means may be used in different countries to solve the specific problems of socialist construction, depending on historical and national features." [26] In keeping with this, the return of the various states to a policy of rapid industrialization was a qualified one. Everywhere lip-service was paid to the pre-eminence of heavy industry. Nowhere did a full return to the Stalinist rate of industrialization take place.* [27]

* These figures have been adapted from Taborsky, cited in note 27:

Percentage increases in the gross industrial output
(previous year: 100)

	1951	1952	1953	1954	1955
Bulgaria	119	118	112	109	110
Czechoslovakia	115	118	110	104	111
East Germany	122	116	112	110	108
Hungary	130	124	111	103	108
Poland	124	120	118	111	111
Rumania	129	123	114	107	114

With Stalin gone, and the post-Stalin circumstances producing greater diversity, the Stalinist method of informal political ties had to be buttressed through formalization. Khrushchev, even though somewhat of a "vulgar Marxist" in his notions concerning the sources of cohesion between socialist states, was still sufficiently steeped in Leninism-Stalinism to recognize the importance of political bonds. This awareness was no doubt sharpened by certain international factors (such as the inclusion of West Germany into NATO), which made a more formal arrangement desirable. During Stalin's lifetime the independent state forms of the Communist-ruled nations had been emptied of most of their political content, but now there was the danger that such forms could become impediments to real international Soviet unity as the local regimes gradually began to emphasize a more domestic point of view. Since the formal abolition of these states as independent entities was no longer feasible — and, on the contrary, in some cases it was even desirable to increase their number, as was done with East Germany — it was necessary to adopt a solution based on their continued existence and probability of growing importance. The answer to this and to NATO was the creation of the Warsaw Pact and the invigoration of the dormant Council of Economic Mutual Assistance (CEMA).

The creation of the Warsaw Pact was presaged by a conference held in Moscow in November 1954 between the Soviet government, represented by Molotov, and the heads of the Communist governments. The conference took a firm stand against the Western policy of West German remilitarization and warned that the Communist states would be forced to act jointly if this should come about.[28] The Warsaw Pact was, accordingly, partially an answer to the German development. The Pact, entitled "On Friendship, Cooperation, and Mutual Aid," was signed in Warsaw on May 14, 1955, by all the European Communist states and the USSR. It contained a general political agreement and a military convention.[29] The states reaffirmed their unity of purpose and, in the vaguely phrased fifth clause of the agreement, allowed for the disposition of troops under a joint command as deemed appropriate by them and the command for purposes of mutual defense. No further agreements for the stationing of foreign troops on the soil of any one of the signatories was made (a matter regularized only after the Hungarian and Polish events in 1956), but the Pact itself represented a formal "legalizing" of the stationing of Soviet troops, especially since the military convention assigned the joint command to a Soviet officer and stipulated that troop disposition would be made according to mutual arrangements of the governments concerned (that is, between the USSR and the country concerned). The official Chinese observer, P'eng Teh-huai, the former Korean War commander, associated himself with the Pact and promised Chinese support in the case of foreign aggression.

The preponderance of Soviet power in East Europe should not obscure the political significance of the Warsaw Pact. It represented the single most important formal commitment binding the states to the USSR, officially limiting their scope of independent action, and legalizing the presence (and hence the political influence) of the Soviet troops stationed in some of them. The gradual return of "content" to the forms of state independence was in this fashion balanced by a treaty structure which provided for joint consultation on all major issues and Soviet command of all troops, and which did not provide any procedures for withdrawal from such treaty arrangement or for the removal of the Soviet forces.* Finally, since the sharp point of the Pact was directed against Germany, which some of the treaty members deeply feared, an element of mutual self-interest was also present.

These formal political ties were to be further buttressed by an increased reliance on CEMA. After several years of relative inactivity, during which it occupied itself primarily with channeling trade between the Communist states, CEMA became more vigorous after 1954. Meetings of the Council were held at least annually; the Council's organization was developed and its objectives defined. Its basic goal was to facilitate mutual exchange of experience and techniques; to promote a division of labor and specialization in industrial production; to coordinate investment and the subsequent Five-Year Plans.[30] The division of labor was a departure from the Stalinist notions of an essentially autarkic construction of socialist industrialization,† while the political significance of the economic co-

---

* The Political Consultative Committee created by the Warsaw Pact met in Prague in January 1956 and decided to meet regularly not less than twice a year and to create a standing commission for foreign-policy coordination and a standing Secretariat. In a sense this meant the abandonment of the Stalinist technique of bilateralism (*Zasedaniia Politicheskovo Konsultativnovo Komiteta*, Moscow, 1956, p. 53). The international military command, however, was not set up; the satellites did not appoint liaison officers to it; and control remained in Soviet hands. This underscored the primary political purpose of the treaty.

† Under the plan, East Germany was to specialize in the production of precision instruments and electrical equipment; Poland: rolling stock, ships, mining equipment, chemicals; Czechoslovakia: machine building, automobiles, engines; Hungary: diesel engines, motor trains, buses; Rumania: oil pipes, drilling equipment. Standing committees, functional in nature and distributed among the various capitals, were also

operation was openly stated. "Intensification of the coordination of the national economic plans of the USSR and the People's Democracies is needed to strengthen socialism," *Pravda* observed commenting on the activities of the Council.[31]

Hand in hand with this stress on economic integration went a growing emphasis on the benefits to be derived from cooperation with the USSR. "The mighty socialist industry of the USSR plays the decisive role in strengthening the great socialist camp. Relying on its economic capacity, the Soviet Union extends to the countries of People's Democracy fraternal assistance in the development of their economies,"[32] the Soviets asserted. They were correct in the sense that, by 1954, the industries of some of the states were highly dependent on Soviet supplies. About 70 per cent of Czech iron-ore imports in 1954–1955, 68 per cent of the Polish, and 100 per cent of the Rumanian and Hungarian came from the USSR, as did all manganese, a large part of cotton, and so on.[33] After 1955, the Soviet Union also became a more active source of credit for the People's Democracies,[34] although Khrushchev's boast to the Twentieth Party Congress that the total amounted to 21 billion rubles presumably included very large, secret military credits extended at unknown rates of interest during the Stalinist period. In March of 1956, in a further gesture of close cooperation, all the Communist states banded together in organizing a Joint Nuclear Research Institute to be headed by a Soviet scientist and to be situated in the USSR. The member nations were to make proportional contributions to its establishment.[35]

In this fashion the slightly greater measure of political flexibility in the bloc would be balanced by common economic interests and ideological commitment. Indeed, Khrushchev might well have hoped that the last two would more than compensate for any retreat from the rigid Stalinist insistence on political subordination which, in some cases, impeded the development of even "objective" ties. It is symptomatic that, unlike Malenkov's, the burden of Khrushchev's informal criticisms of Stalinist policies in East Europe involved political aberrations rather than economic ones (which in some measure had helped to produce the political).[36] Paralleling Soviet domestic re-emphasis of the party, the excessive Stalinist reliance on controls was giving way to an emphasis on close party links among the Communist regimes

---

t up. Reflecting the importance of these committees was the fact that the various member states were normally represented by the respective ministers or vice-ministers.
 Fidelski, *Wspolpraca Gospodarcza Polski z Krajami Socjalistycznymi* (Warsaw, 59), pp. 81–83.

in the hope that closer party relations would also revitalize the common ideological bonds.* While Soviet power remained a crucial background factor, ideology based on economy was to replace power masked by ideology.

THE ISSUE OF YUGOSLAVIA

Within this revised framework the conflict with Yugoslavia lost most of its meaning and, indeed, could only impede the implementation of Khrushchev's vision. On *this* score, Khrushchev might have been supported by some members of the displaced Malenkov group. In any case, given the changes in East Europe and recalling Tito's loyalty to the USSR prior to 1948, a portion of the Soviet leadership apparently concluded late in 1954 that the Soviet-Yugoslav rift was ideologically barren and largely a product of the late dictator's pathological hatreds and phobias. Noting that, domestically, Tito had been a forceful Communist, the Soviet leadership appears to have assumed that an arrangement stressing common party bonds while accepting Tito's domestic autonomy would establish a pattern for similarly firm Communist regimes elsewhere. They would be bound together through the rigorous party dictatorships run on similar doctrinal assumptions, reinforced by integrated economic processes. Khrushchev realized he could not wipe out Tito's national Communism, but he hoped to harness it.

The decision to improve relations was made sometime in the fall of 1954, but the limits of the projected improvement were left undefined and, in the summer of 1955, caused a sharp exchange of views within the Soviet leadership, particularly between Khrushchev and Mikoyan on one side and Molotov on the other. Initially, however even Molotov might have approved a "normalization" in relations for during 1954 the Soviet peace campaign directed against the Western European Defense Community (EDC) went into high gear and the Yugoslav position of "positive neutrality" also involved a rejection of the Western scheme. In the fall of 1954, Soviet newspapers carried several articles citing the Yugoslav views[37] but without the usual derogatory references to Tito, and even quoting verbatim lengthy passages of Tito's criticisms of the EDC and the Atlantic Pact.[38] Following a series of friendly gestures (such as the CPSU Presidium

* Characteristically, high CPSU officials were appointed as ambassadors to the various Communist states: for instance, in Poland, the appointment in May 1955 of P. K. Ponomarenko, former First Secretary in Kazakhstan, and in October 1957 P. A. Abrasimov, former party Secretary of Belorussia.

attendance at the Yugoslav Embassy celebration of the Yugoslav national holiday and laudatory press articles on the anniversary,[39] increased cultural contacts,[40] a limited trade agreement[41]), it was announced that direct talks between the Yugoslav and Soviet leaderships would be held in May 1955. The Soviet press emphasized that the Belgrade talks would end a situation which "had been only to the advantage of the enemies of peace." [42]

Khrushchev strove from the very outset of the talks, which began on May 27, to stress common ideological party issues and to put them on a Communist-to-Communist plane. Even in his apologetic airport speech Khrushchev adhered to this intention, while also revealing the basic assumptions of his thinking:

> The strongest ties are established between the peoples of both countries which have as their guiding force Parties that base all their activities on the teaching of Marxism-Leninism. The Parties that take the Marxist-Leninist teaching as their guide achieve complete mutual understanding because they have a common aim — struggle for the interests of the working class and the working peasants, for the interests of the working people.[43]

The agreement, however, that was signed on June 2 was purely a joint declaration of the two states and did not cover party or ideological matters as Khrushchev had wished.* Nonetheless, it explicitly acknowledged that Yugoslavia was a state building socialism and it did contain some implicit ideological concessions to the Yugoslavs. Reference was made to "mutual respect for . . . different forms of Socialist development" and, at the end of the eight-point agreement involving state matters (to which the Yugoslavs wished to restrict the conference), provision was made for "the exchange of Socialist experience." [44]

The Yugoslav reserve was understandable. Having gradually merged with an ideological position and certain institutional arrangements which they considered as their own creative contribution to Marxism-Leninism (see Chapter 9), they feared the new Soviet policy of minimizing ideological and party differences before a clear-cut, un-Stalinist principle of diversity was acknowledged. They might well have been disturbed also by the equivocation of the Soviet leaders on the subject of the 1948 resolution which had expelled Yugoslavia from the Cominform. Even though the Yugoslavs were formally act-

---

* A Yugoslav ambassador stated to this writer that the agreement was based on a Yugoslav draft.

ing as if it had been renounced, the Soviet leaders pointedly rejected only the November 1949 Cominform resolution which had so violently condemned the Yugoslavs as Gestapo spies and such; little was said about the 1948 declaration which had charged them with a variety of ideological sins.* To Khrushchev, however, allowing the Yugoslavs to place a somewhat wider interpretation on the revision of the past, and even having to acknowledge indirectly a tolerance of diversity implied by the agreement, represented a small price to be paid for drawing Yugoslavia back into the fold. Such a step would minimize ideological differences and strengthen the bonds between the Soviet Union and the other People's Democracies in this post-Stalin period. Past Yugoslav experience could even serve to reinforce the argument for the imitation of Soviet experience.

However, the Yugoslav reserve was apparently shared, for other reasons of course, by some of Khrushchev's colleagues, most notably Molotov (for East European reactions, see next chapter). The matter was raised at the July 1955 plenum of the CPSU Central Committee and led to a thorough airing of the entire problem of Soviet-satellite relations.[45] Opposition to Khrushchev's policy was voiced by Molotov who already, in February of 1955, had expressed misgivings concerning excessive fraternization with Tito.† Subsequently Molotov indicated that he approved normalization of diplomatic relations (presumably for reasons of international grand strategy) but still opposed Khrushchev's ideological initiatives. At the July plenum, Molotov charged that Tito could no longer be considered a Communist, that he was anti-Soviet, and that accepting him back on a party-ideological basis would be extremely dangerous. Molotov conceded that the 1948 break was unfortunate, but only in the sense that all avenues of resolving the then-existing differences had not been exhausted. H

---

* In 1958, both the organ of the SED and Khrushchev himself asserted, with no direct Yugoslav rebuttals, that the Yugoslav leadership had been told that it was the 1949 resolution only which was being denounced. See *Pravda*, July 12, 1958; *Einhei* no. 5, 1958. The November 1949 declaration, entitled "The Communist Party of Yugoslavia in the Hands of Murderers and Spies," in effect urged Tito's liquidation

† This also explains the strange exchange between Molotov, speaking to the Supreme Soviet in February, and Tito, addressing the Skupshtina in March. In his speech, Molotov alleged Yugoslavia's partial responsibility for the abyss existing between the two states, explaining it in terms of Yugoslav deviation from their initial postwar position. Tito indignantly rejected this allegation, and *Pravda* (March 1, without discrediting the Foreign Minister, attempted to smooth over the issue by suggesting that the matter was not really important. It seems, in retrospect, to have been a conscious effort by Molotov to torpedo the rapprochement or, at least, place it in its proper ideological perspective.

maintained, however, that although the break had subsequently caused complications, it nonetheless had been fundamentally justified since an absence of firm and decisive Soviet action might have caused Poland to follow in Tito's anti-Soviet, "provocative" footsteps. Thus, in a sense, it had been a matter of choosing the lesser of two evils, and Molotov warned against a policy which he felt would again create disruptive tendencies.

He was answered by Khrushchev, Kaganovich, Mikoyan, and Shepilov. Like Molotov's, their answers reflected a concern with holding the Soviet bloc together, but they interpreted the disruptive tendencies differently. Their replies in effect involved a general evaluation of Stalinism as a system of state relations. Kaganovich charged that, during Stalin's life, the Soviet ambassadors appointed by Molotov behaved in a manner calculated to provoke hostility to the USSR, while Mikoyan, in a severe critique of the joint companies and the role of Soviet economic experts, characterized Stalinist economic relations with East Europe as "economic nationalism" which played into the hands of Soviet enemies. He conceded Molotov's allegation that Tito and his associates, particularly Kardelj, were veering in some respects toward a Western kind of socialism. But he reminded his listeners that many of the East European Communist leaders were former Social Democrats — they too may have looser concepts of socialism — and thus it would be particularly important to bind Tito to the Soviet bloc and to influence him ideologically. Khrushchev, while admitting that the 1948 resolution had been fundamentally correct in its evaluation, claimed that unless the Soviet Union adopted a policy of drawing Yugoslavia back into the political and ideological fold, the other Communist states in the post-Stalin phase might be tempted to emulate the Yugoslav example, thereby causing the USSR unnecessary difficulties. That his view carried the day was duly recorded in *Pravda* which reported that "the Communist Party's Central Committee, which personifies the collective wisdom of our Party, resolved: 'To approve the results of the talks between the government delegations of the Union of Soviet Socialist Republics and the Federal People's Republic of Yugoslavia.' " [46] The paper then added significantly:

The Communist Party of the Soviet Union considers it desirable *to establish contact* and a rapprochement *between the CPSU and the Union of Communists of Yugoslavia on the basis of Marxist-Leninist principles*. The first results have now been achieved and the prerequisites have been established for this contact and rapprochement. It is hoped that rapprochement with the Union of Communists of Yugoslavia will continue and develop on the basis of Marxist-Leninist principles.[47]

The last few months of 1955 were accordingly marked by the gradual falling into line of the other Communist states on the Yugoslav question, although with markedly less enthusiasm (see next chapter). Khrushchev continued to apply pressure on the neighbors of Yugoslavia, and one by one they withdrew from their anti-Titoist positions.

THE TWENTIETH PARTY CONGRESS

Domestically, Khrushchev was busy consolidating his position. The CPSU's Twentieth Party Congress had been scheduled for February 1956, at which time the official party program was to be expounded and top party posts filled. Domestic issues accordingly occupied the Soviet leadership a good deal. The earlier July session had also discussed current problems of industrialization; in September an amnesty for certain political offenders had been decreed, a press campaign for more effective struggle against illegality developed, and the Stalinist architectural style repudiated. In consolidating his position, Khrushchev was raising the Leninist banner, calling for more revolutionary zeal, and appealing to the antibureaucratic prejudices of the masses. It was not the heavy capital development which was denying them the fruits of Soviet industrialization but the privileged and inefficient bureaucrats who were to blame, he argued, subtly linking his opponents with the bureaucrats. However, his domestic preoccupation did not lead him to neglect foreign policy. The agreement with Tito was followed by the Geneva Conference and later in the fall, by the triumphant tour of Asia by Khrushchev and Bulganin. The new leadership, by word and deed, was demonstrating to its adherents its determination to cope in an imaginative way with the legacy of Stalinism.

In ideological matters, continued stress was laid on the significance of doctrine in the relations among Communist states. A curious episode, probably linked with the July plenum, gave the party's theoretical journal, *Kommunist*, an opportunity to expound on this subject more fully. In September, Molotov, in a published letter, retracted a statement made by him earlier in the year to the effect that the foundations of a socialist society had already been built in the USSR. The statement could have implied that a complete socialist society had not yet been constructed in the USSR. In withdrawing the statement as "theoretically erroneous and politically harmful,

Molotov did not see fit to repudiate a further part of his original sentence, in which he had asserted that the People's Democracies "have made only the first, though highly important, steps in the direction of socialism." [48] A major disproportion in levels between the USSR and the other states was thus implicitly asserted. *Kommunist's* editorial, commenting on the issue, stated that Molotov's original formulation was harmful because it underestimated the ideological and socio-economic importance of the Soviet system, particularly in view of the "present-day struggle for Communism." The editorial went on to stress the vital need of the party to struggle against the "cult of the personality" which is part "of the struggle of the new with the old," and to stress pointedly the party's intolerance "of the complacency and conceit of certain leaders and cases of isolation from the masses." [49]

Having used the ideological issue as a point of departure for an attack on the domestic conservatives, *Kommunist* shifted to the international problem. Restating once again the thesis that the crisis within capitalism was deepening, the editorial charged that those responsible for foreign policy had been neglectful of the Marxist-Leninist orientation. It then noted that domestic construction of socialism in the USSR is inherently linked with the general problem of the socialist camp, or "commonwealth," as the editorial called it, "headed by the Soviet Union," since it involves a continuous search for theoretical formulations to guide the patterns of development, to decide what is general and what is particular, and to bind the socialist states in true proletarian internationalism. Soviet primacy is derived from its advanced historical stage and is accordingly justified ideologically. The Khrushchev formulation of the relations between Communist states was then explicitly stated:

A new, socialist type of international relations arose with the formation of the commonwealth of socialist states. These are relations of fully equal rights, genuine friendship, fraternal cooperation in the sphere of politics, economics and culture, and mutual assistance in the construction of a new life. These relations are determined by the nature of the social-economic system of the countries of the socialist camp; by the unity of their fundamental interests and ultimate great aim, the building of communism; and by the single Marxist-Leninist world view of the Communist and Workers' parties . . .[50]

Khrushchev's notion hence did not abandon Soviet primacy, but attempted to place it on a new and, as he hoped, firmer basis. He thus found himself agreeing with Tito that Stalinism — more as a form of consciousness which lags behind the new reality than as an actual force — was becoming an impediment to the achievement of Soviet domestic and external objectives.

In this light, Khrushchev's performance at the Twentieth Party Congress becomes even more meaningful. His speech on Stalin, a stunning surprise in the vigor of its condemnation, was designed to shake the Stalinist orientation prevailing among many party members at home and abroad. Khrushchev may have been carried away in his delivery, but there is little doubt that the speech was designed to destroy the myth of Stalin's infallibility, which would in turn permit Khrushchev to be more selective in deciding which portions of the legacy could be retained and which portions already represented a moribund past. Notably, the speech contained no references to Stalin's treatment of the People's Democracies — precisely suggesting that Khrushchev was leaving to himself the opportunity to select subsequently those aspects of Stalinism he might still want to retain. The verbalized rejection, however, of Stalin's view that the class struggle intensifies after the Communist seizure of power certainly had immediate relevance for the relatively new People's Democracies. The shattering effect of the speech on the delegates, despite the fact that they had been prepared by an earlier and also violently anti-Stalin speech by Mikoyan, is a matter of historical record. But a proper perspective on the speech should take into consideration that its primary design — to shake the rigid Stalinist attitudes which were impeding the task of adapting the Stalinist legacy — was meant to apply to the entire bloc.

More positive conceptions emerged from Khrushchev's formal public address[51] and were echoed by some of the other leaders. However, with the exception of the admission that under certain favorable circumstances socialism may be established by nonviolent parliamentary devices and the assertion that war was no longer inevitable due to the power of the Communist bloc, no startling changes in the existing trends were foreseen. Rather, these trends were given formal, explicit, and coherent form. The disintegration of the "imperialist colonial system" was analyzed and the development of "the zone of peace" noted as contributing to the decline of aggressive imperialism. With respect to relations with Communist states, Khrushchev now verbalized what he had been tacitly conceding since the summer of 1955: (1) ways to socialism may indeed differ and may in the future become "more and more varied" although socialism will presumably be the same; (2) "alongside the Soviet form of reorganiing society on socialist foundations, we have the form of People's Democracy," Khrushchev stated. Hence the two do differ (although his references to substantive differences were limited to the Chinese handling of private industry and trade and to the Yugoslav "unique specific forms of economic management"). There was still a paucity of detail in Khrushchev's speech on what is tolerable and what is not in the construction of socialism. But he did concede that, unlike the USSR, the construction may proceed by peaceful change if the working class shows sufficient strength and with the further stipulation that "in all the forms of transition to socialism, an absolute and decisive requirement is political leadership of the working class, headed by its vanguard. The transition to Socialism is impossible without this."

The restrictive clauses notwithstanding, Khrushchev's statement clearly suggested an ideological justification for institutional diversity which Stalin had not been willing to tolerate, and it was so interpreted in at least some of the other Communist states.[52] It must be remembered, however, that in the September 1955 Molotov affair it had been emphasized that the USSR had already constructed a socialist society, a goal toward which the other states were striving. This inherently imposed limits on the degrees of diversity that the other Communist states could adopt, since the ultimate objective was personalized by the Soviet system with the experience of socialist construction behind it. That seems to have been the nuance introduced in the Twentieth Congress deliberations by Suslov's speech, when he cited Lenin's "inspired prediction that while the path to socialism would *essentially be one and the same for all*, the transition of different countries to socialism would not be entirely identical." [53] In citing those parts of Soviet experience which are relevant to other states, Suslov gently implied that intensive class warfare after the seizure of power might be necessary:

> Political leadership of the state by the working class is necessary in order that over a shorter or longer period, depending upon the specific conditions, the capitalist class be deprived of ownership of the means of production and that the means of production be made public property, that *all attempts* by the overthrown exploiting classes to restore their rule be repulsed and that socialist construction be organized.[54]

Whether this represented a reasoned difference in view from Khrushchev's position or a new purposeful limitation on the initiative of other Communist leaders is difficult to tell. Nonetheless, the very ambivalence in Moscow meant more room for independent action and interpretation abroad, and a resulting tendency toward more diverse perspectives.

A restoration of uniformity would have required Soviet resources for the subordination and maintenance of Communist regimes, but this was made almost permanently unpopular because of the domestic rigidities it imposed. Such a policy would also have conflicted with the broad international stance adopted by the USSR after Stalin's death and, indeed, with some of the domestic reforms. Limited diversity opened a vista for the emergence of self-supporting Communist regimes but at the price of cohesion of the bloc. Khrushchev's somewhat ambiguous formula attempted to straddle this dilemma by superimposing ideological party unity on an acceptance of some domestic institutional diversity, which in turn he hoped would be balanced by growing economic ties. But this involved a rejection of Stalin the man and Stalinism the dogma, and these had been part of the power element which had buttressed and long since merged with ideology. Dissipating it, Khrushchev placed a tremendous burden on the ideology. At the same time the ideology had to cope with the domestic problems left behind by Stalinism and with the pressures emanating from the independent, but now legitimately Communist, Yugoslav position as well as from developing domestic events in Hungary and Poland. Their effect on relations among Communist states was to prove of critical importance, and the Khrushchev formula was yet to face its test.

9 / THE IMPACT OF YUGOSLAVIA

KHRUSHCHEV had restored Yugoslavia to the position of an active agent in the politics of the Communist camp. While Stalin lived, the appeal of Yugoslavia's independent position to the other Communist states was mitigated by the prevailing international situation and by the domestic weaknesses of the regimes, while their Stalinist systems required continued manifestations of hatred and doctrinal condemnation of the Yugoslav policy. Tito's regime was equated with the most despised "capitalist imperialists," and any indication of laxness toward him was considered sheer treason.* This dichotomic relationship was abandoned late in 1954, and Khrushchev's subsequent moves restored to the Yugoslav government the stamp of political legitimacy and, after some reluctance, even doctrinal purity. An authentic socialist state was recognized to exist in Yugoslavia, and its independent position was no longer considered an *ipso facto* source of deviationism. As noted in the previous chapter, in rejecting Stalin's earlier conception of the Yugoslav role Khrushchev might well have been drawing on the experience of Sino-Soviet relations in his efforts to eliminate needless sources of ideological conflict.

Faithful to his general concepts, Khrushchev moved rapidly after the Twentieth Party Congress to eliminate any remaining obstacles to the "true" Marxist-Leninist relationship that ought to prevail between the USSR and Yugoslavia. Khrushchev undoubtedly felt that once these obstacles were removed and a unity re-established which recognized Yugoslav autonomy, the central position of the CPSU, its prestige and its Marxist-Leninist experience, as well as Soviet might, would automatically assert Soviet primacy and discourage divisive trends. This would be especially true once the Yugoslav way to so-

---

* A by no means extreme illustration of the prevailing attitude are the following excerpts from a 1952 Czech book on Yugoslavia: "Thrown out by the worker parties, thrown out by the people . . . thus one day Rajk, Kostov and Slansky were found on the carcass heap of history. There one day Tito will be found. Their names will figure in history as prototypes of the most filthy treason . . ." (p. 25); "Who are the rulers of the country? It is Tito, a bloody maniac, it is Rankovic who only yesterday was an agent of the Gestapo, it is Moshe Pijade the professional demagogue. In a word a handful of political gangsters who are ruling the Yugoslav nations by Fascist terror" (p. 47). From L. Tarantova, *Zrada sidli v Belehrade* (Prague, 1952).

cialism no longer implied the glittering, but of course illusory, image of distinctiveness and independence. In April 1956 the Cominform was disbanded — a rather empty gesture since it had passed into obscurity some years earlier, but still a move greeted with approbation in Belgrade[1] — and in June 1956 Khrushchev again met Tito, this time in Moscow. The atmosphere of the meeting, quite unlike the previous one, was characterized by ebullient cordiality. To Khrushchev it meant the culmination of a policy pursued, despite obstacles and opposition, for a year and a half.

Tito's doubts and reservations of June 1955 no longer barred the way to an ideological agreement a year later. The Twentieth Party Congress had dispelled any lingering Yugoslav fears that Stalinism might still be the norm for relations among Communist states, while Khrushchev's formal address had clearly accepted what the Yugoslavs considered to be their own position on the problems of building socialism. Thus the Yugoslav press reacted with particular enthusiasm to the congress speeches of Khrushchev and Mikoyan, both of which made warm references to Yugoslavia. Indeed, the Yugoslavs felt that both the Twentieth Congress and history in general had vindicated their 1948 stance. Partly from vanity and partly from their desire to assist Khrushchev in the struggle against the remnants of Stalinism, the Yugoslavs were willing to ignore the Soviet equivocation on the 1948 Cominform resolution. It was probably in this spirit, and not merely as a vindictive and spiteful gesture, that on March 20 *Borba* published a condensed but accurate version of Khrushchev's secret speech on Stalin, thereby lifting the veil of secrecy surrounding it. By destroying Stalin, the Yugoslavs felt, a service was being performed both to international Communism and to those Soviet leaders who were struggling against the distortive remnants of the Stalinist myth. The Yugoslavs made no secret of this view, even though no official Soviet admission of the authenticity of Khrushchev's speech was made. Prefacing its account of Khrushchev's remarks with a laudatory comment on the achievements of the Twentieth Congress, and particularly noting the importance "of Lenin's principles that transition to socialism be effected in various forms and manners," *Borba* added:

The whole course of the Congress and everything that happened after it confirms that not only certain theoretical principles are involved but *an entirely new orientation*, which indeed from the point of view of theory and practice quite differs from the Stalinist one. The reality confirms that these theoretical principles are *the expression of a sincere wish and reso-*

lution of the Communist Party of the Soviet Union, headed by Khrushchev, Bulganin and Mikoyan, to realize them in all fields.

This resolution is eloquently proved by the fact that the Communist Party of the Soviet Union has not concentrated its efforts only upon theoretical disclosure of the cult of personality but also upon *concrete unmasking* of its supporter, Stalin.[2]

Khrushchev's public speech denounced the dogma while his secret speech, publicized for the first time by Belgrade, repudiated the man. The abolition of the Cominform removed the last institutional remnant of the past, while Soviet economic offers helped to heal the memories of the former boycott.[3] Convinced of Khrushchev's sincerity and of the depth of the changes effected by the congress, the Yugoslavs were fully in favor of an interparty-ideological embrace.

It was consummated by the June 20 agreement in Moscow. Its key provision was the joint affirmation "that the roads and conditions of socialist development are different in different countries, that the wealth of the forms of socialist development contributes to their strengthening, and . . . that any tendency to impose one's own views in determining the roads and forms of socialist development are alien to both sides." [4] It seemed that Stalinism was giving way to Titoism. And yet, curiously, Khrushchev and others (with the exception of Molotov) appeared to be guilty of an offense which no Marxist should ever commit: allowing their consciousness of reality to lag behind reality itself. For the Soviet bloc which Khrushchev was trying to repair was no longer the bloc it had been before the revelations of the congress. Tito was no longer the Tito of old, and Yugoslavia had also changed — and the changes were both institutional and ideological. Finally, Titoism was no longer predicated on the desire to be an autonomous Soviet-like regime within the Soviet system.

THE YUGOSLAV ROAD TO SOCIALISM

A retrospective glance seems appropriate here. Initially, even after the expulsion from the Cominform, Yugoslavia continued to profess its devotion to a model of socialism which essentially reflected the Soviet, and hence the Stalinist, experience. That, of course, was the most natural response of a leadership whose perspective had been molded in the rigid frames of Stalinist dogma and practice, although its personal allegiance to the center had been shaken. But even on that score, the Yugoslav leaders could not quite bring themselves to believe that Stalin could entertain views about them which the Yugoslavs knew to be incorrect. With their conscience clear of any deviationist notions, proud of their orthodox behavior, their normal reaction was to assume that what had happened had been a most tragic error — and that, therefore, it was merely a matter of time before the reality would win out and amicable relations be restored.

At the party congress in July 1948, which approved Tito's position vis-à-vis the Cominform, the assembled delegates hailed "Tito-Stalin," and the Yugoslav press continued to paint a dichotomic image of international affairs, with the USSR and its allies pictured as the "democratic and peaceloving" states threatened with aggression by the Western imperialists.[5] Speaking plaintively to the Third Congress of the People's Front of Yugoslavia on April 9, 1949, Tito cited press statistics to show that even then the Yugoslav press was "continuing to acquaint our masses with the successes of the workers of the countries of People's Democracy and the Soviet Union," and characterized as "slander" the possibility of United States aid to Yugoslavia.[6] As Adam Ulam, writing in 1951, put it: "One of the outstanding features of the continuing crisis between Yugoslavia and Russia has been the remarkable difficulty the Yugoslav Communists have experienced in reorienting some of their ideas and habits of thought."[7] In comparison to the intellectual debates, to the philosophical dialogue, to the preoccupation with the relation between ethics and politics that engulfed the Polish and Hungarian Communists during the dissipation of Stalinism, the emergence of a Yugoslav road to socialism was markedly unencumbered by intellectual soul-searching. Despite the violence of the break with Stalin and the abuse heaped on the Yugoslavs, men like Djilas and Dedijer were lonely figures. It was the party leadership, retaining dictatorial control over the society, which gradually manufactured the distinctive Yugoslav features and modified the Stalinist model. But they did so gradually, and for about two years after the break Yugoslavia continued to consider itself a dictatorship of the proletariat, with all its concomitants: the primacy of the party, the intensified class struggle, collectivization, the dichotomic vision of the world.

The Yugoslav road to socialism developed as it became apparent that a reconciliation with the USSR was not feasible and that a policy based on this expectation would demoralize the party while preventing Yugoslavia from accepting Western aid, desperately necessary in view of the Communist boycott.[8] This necessarily involved, first of all, a modification of the rigid Stalinist image of the two irreconcilable world blocs. Since it could not maintain indefinitely the stance of a rejected ally, and since Tito could hardly afford suddenly to announce his conversion to capitalism, a redefinition of international affairs was dictated by the imperatives of survival. Positive neutralism was the answer. It was to be based on the principle of coexistence between countries of differing socioeconomic orders, and it explicitly rejected Stalin's view that coexistence was a tactical adjustment not vitiating the fundamental inevitability of war. However, presumably because of the weakness of the Communist regimes in the People's Democracies, the Yugoslavs, while condemning their forcible subordination to the USSR, were rather reticent in suggesting alternative solutions to the Soviet domination of East Europe.

In large measure, the changes in Yugoslav thinking were shaped by the political requirements of the unenviable international position of the Yugoslav regime. In addition, however, Tito, Kardelj, and others, as Marxists, still felt compelled to take cognizance of facts which they could no longer ignore in the name of devotion to orthodoxy. The USSR was not modifying its position; the "aggressive" capitalist world was willing to come to Yugoslavia's assistance even while hostile to its system; Yugoslavia led by a Communist regime was being ostracized by states also led by Communist regimes. All of this did not fit the basic assumptions, and, after a suitable period of time had elapsed during which they had hoped against hope that reality would again reflect their orthodox views, the Yugoslavs found themselves with no alternative but to redefine orthodoxy to fit reality. And, in time, their new conceptions, involving a reasoned rethinking of their beliefs as well as a rationalization of Yugoslavia's position, acquired the rigidity of a new dogma which was again to restrict their freedom of policy (see below and Chapter 13).

A rejection of Soviet premises on international affairs could not avoid impinging on the domestic premises as well. It is a basic contention of Marxist-Leninist thought that the two are inseparable, and Tito and the others still thought of themselves as good Marxist-Leninists. Therefore, in dissociating themselves from Stalin's intransigent foreign policy, they inevitably became involved, willy-nilly, in mounting criticisms of the Soviet system itself. Marxism-Leninism was still their point of departure, but since neither Marx nor Lenin were noted for rigid consistency and since both had been voluminous writers, the Yugoslavs were not hard pressed to find numerous quotations to indict the Soviet system. Stalin was accordingly charged with having reduced the "creative" substance of the theory to a sterile rationalization for his personal dictatorship. This was superimposed on a socioeconomic system which had little in fact to do with socialism. The Soviet party was no longer the vanguard of the proletariat but a bureaucratized clique with a vested interest in its privileged position and periodically subjected to murderous purges by its bosses. The state ownership of the means of production, operative within this context, had lost its progressive social function and had degenerated into state capitalism with all its oppressive and conservative connotations.[9] After 1950, a number of Yugoslav leaders, particularly Kardelj, Djilas, and Dedijer, developed these notions into a vigorous and extensive condemnation of almost every aspect of Soviet domestic policy, ranging from Great Russian chauvinism and the introduction of large-scale social inequality and stratification, to a destruction of the solidarity of the international labor movement and a betrayal of Marxism-Leninism.[10]

Such criticisms in turn had to bear on past Yugoslav domestic reality. To criticize the Soviet system was implicitly to criticize what had happened in Yugoslavia itself, since for a number of years imitation of the USSR was considered the highest virtue. Historical periodization, however, provided the escape-hatch. The development of the Soviet system was broken down into favorable and unfavorable periods, with positive phenomena acquiring at a certain point rigidity and losing their dynamism, thereby being transformed into negative manifestations of bureaucratism and stagnancy. Revolution became reaction. Yugoslavia, however, was said to have avoided this dialectical pitfall of history through the adoption of timely reforms, before positive manifestations were transformed into negative ones. To demonstrate this, the Yugoslav leaders had to abandon some of the old Stalinist policies and adopt new variants and solutions. Theory and practice were again contingent. By the fifties some of the existing policies were clearly leading nowhere and to pursue them was to court disaster. True to their training, the Yugoslav leadership was loath to admit that this was the case, and preferred to pitch their justification for a change on the ideological level. Nonetheless, by 1950 it was apparent that the Yugoslav policy of heavy industrial development within the framework of a highly centralized and overbureaucratized administrative structure, handicapped by the Soviet boycott, had produced an inflationary spiral made more acute by shortages of essential goods and abandoned construction projects.

The turning point came in June 1950 with the passing of legislation handing "the ownership" of industrial enterprises to the workers themselves, who were to exercise this ownership through the Workers' Councils. This reform, which became the keystone of Yugoslav assertions of ideological originality, was followed by decentralization of the economy and the administration, revisions in the criminal code, and finally in 1953 by a new constitution which broke with the earlier Stalinist model.[11] Even the party did not come out unscathed and, as if trying to live up to his criticisms of the CPSU, Tito decreed that the Yugoslav Communists were no longer to enjoy special privileges.[12] The name of the party was changed to the League (Union) of Communists of Yugoslavia, symbolizing its alleged voluntary and democratic character.

The reforms, some of them important and novel, did not alter the substantive power situation in the country. The Workers' Councils were balanced internally by effective party controls, or League cells, by technical controls wielded by the plant director, and by the norms of the national economic plan. In subsequent years, the degree of the Councils' actual power varied and, on occasions, the regime felt compelled to move in so as to restore what competence remained.[13] But there is no doubt that, whatever the actual scope of the Councils has been, they played an important role internally in improving workers' morale and externally in emphasizing the Yugoslav claim to having established the true Marxist-Leninist method of constructing socialism.[14] The central role of the party was not undermined, and certainly Tito's power was not affected. But it was precisely a corollary of this undiminished importance of the Communist Party that agriculture, the orphan child of Marxist thinking, continued to suffer in the usual way even as the other reforms were being implemented. It was not until 1953 that collectivization was actually suspended, and only after the failure of a renewed drive. Apparently the regime had continued to feel that collectivization was inherent in a socialist society and, despite its 1950 assertions that the principle of volition would be respected, had expected to be able to pursue this line. The March 1953 Decree on Property Relationships and Reorganization of Peasant Working Cooperatives,[15] allowing the peasants to withdraw, sounded the end of the collectivization policy. From then on, the emphasis was on incentives and cooperative development.

Yugoslavia, isolated from the Communist bloc and lacking the self-sufficiency to shape reality in terms of doctrine, had thus to adapt to reality. The doctrine also had to adapt, and this meant still further criticisms of the Soviet model. For instance, the Yugoslav Workers' Councils were seen as proving that the oppressive functions of the state were "withering away" in Yugoslavia, which was said to contrast favorably with contrary trends in the USSR. Asserting that by definition the claim to universality of any one system was bound to lead to "reactionary results," the Yugoslavs insisted that true Leninists had to assert multiplicity of ways to socialism; they characterized their own way as that of "social democracy."

Probably the most explicit statement of the Yugoslav doctrine was made in an Oslo address, delivered in September 1954, by Kardelj. Using alternate paths to socialism as his basic motif, Kardelj elaborated the following propositions: the USSR has exaggerated the role of the state, which has assumed "a very special *economic position* within the system of social relations" (italics his); in Western Europe evolution toward socialism through the existing political structure is both feasible and is being realized; the Yugoslav revolution had been necessary due to the inability of the Yugoslav bourgeoisie to move forward with history; the first task of the new regime had been to change "the material ratio of social forces in favor of socialism" through industrialization, and hence a measure of internal discipline had been necessary; since then, unlike Stalinism, Yugoslavia had been able to avoid the danger of bureaucratism by initiating the gradual withering away of the state through the strengthening of socialism by means of social ownership, the Workers' Councils.[16] True socialism in Yugoslavia was thus sharply differentiated from the state capitalism said to prevail in the USSR.

Legitimate doubts may be raised concerning the theoretical soundness of the above propositions. Given the political context of the Workers' Councils, the old syndicalist view that "social ownership" through the Workers' Councils is the first step in the withering away of the state seemed to involve a rather artificial conception of the state as well as of the nature of ownership. The justification of initial terror in Yugoslavia, but with an arbitrary line drawn between desirable and undesirable terror, opens the door to claims that, because of alternate ways to socialism, conditions elsewhere might require a longer period of suppression (a position, incidentally, which the Yugoslavs found themselves forced to adopt after the 1956 rapprochement with the USSR). For our purposes, however, it is relevant to note that by 1955 the Yugoslavs had evolved a broad perspective on the nature of their own efforts and on the Soviet system. But experience wedded to doctrine can easily become an impediment to a perception of new phenomena which fit neither the realm of experience nor the framework of the doctrine. It certainly is easier to adapt the new into the categories of the old, thereby seeing the familiar rather than the strange in developing situations.

One sees evidence of this rigidity in the extremely suspicious Yugoslav responses to the first few changes in the USSR. Admittedly, caution and fear of duplicity were fully warranted, both in terms of past experience and in terms of what subsequently happened in the years 1957–1958. It is, however, interesting that because of their doctrinal position and their emphasis on broad social-institutional relationships the Yugoslavs initially dismissed Stalin's death as being of no consequence insofar as the Soviet system or its foreign policy was concerned. Denying that the essence had changed even though tactics admittedly had, the Yugoslavs felt justified in asserting that "it is completely irrelevant to us whether in such a USSR Stalin is or is not alive, and how much earth has been put on the grave of the deceased despot." [17]

The bitterness of the rejected devotee had also in time been sharpened by a reassuring doctrine of his own purity and of the fundamental depravity of the former idol. And since that depravity was said to be grounded in established political and economic institutions, the mere disappearance of an individual leader could hardly change the broad picture. Tito accordingly responded with the greatest caution to Khrushchev's overtures in 1955, and, while willing to accept normal diplomatic relations — a position clearly in keeping with Yugoslavia's policy of "coexistence" with the two blocs — he was unwilling to budge from his doctrinal stance which required a fundamental differentiation between the Yugoslav system, the capitalist system, and the state-capitalist system in the USSR. It was only after Khrushchev gave manifest proof of his desire and capability to deal with what the Yugoslavs considered to be the stagnant bureaucratization of the Soviet system — or Stalinism — that a sufficiently important "objective" change in the USSR was said to have begun to take place. A fundamental compatibility between the Yugoslav and the Soviet systems at that stage could again emerge and a doctrinal and party collaboration was warranted, indeed dictated, by the requirements of this new "objective" situation. The final proof came only with the Twentieth Congress and with the destruction of Stalin. From that moment on Tito considered himself as Khrushchev's first ally in the crusade against the remnants of Stalinism.

THE EMERGENCE OF THE ANTI-STALINIST AXIS

That the ultimate purposes of the two energetic leaders were not identical should be apparent from the preceding discussion. But the problem of the ultimate objective is always a complex one and liable to lead easily to misunderstandings. However, as long as the methods to achieve them are similar, an alliance can be maintained and the more concrete, immediate goal can obscure the long-range, ephemeral objective. Thus, for over a year, Tito and Khrushchev maintained an uneasy front against those forces which opposed the changes envisaged by Khrushchev and which bitterly despised and feared Tito. The burden of most of the combat fell on Khrushchev's broad shoulders — and reasonably so, since it involved conflicts within the Soviet party itself and in parties subject to the CPSU. Indeed, it was now for the first time since Khrushchev's ascendancy that the satellite Communist leaders were called upon to perform tasks manifestly displeasing to them (see Chapter 8). Their reaction, generally slow and hesitant, was mute testimony to the growing weakness of the Stalinist system without Stalin even before the fateful repudiation of the Twentieth Congress, and to a change in the pattern of relations.

The only party which could afford to emulate the CPSU at no risk to itself was the Chinese party. Its leadership did not feel threatened by the Tito episode and, since it was both powerful and indigenous, it could imitate with good grace the Soviet pattern in this particular instance. At the same time, no outstanding issues required settlement prior to a normalization of relations with Yugoslavia. Diplomatic relations were accordingly restored in December 1955, and trade missions were exchanged. The situation differed radically in the case of the East European Communist regimes. Albania, which as a consequence of the Soviet-Yugoslav rift had freed itself from Yugoslav tutelage, had everything to lose by an improvement in relations; Russian support against Yugoslavia and Greece would have been welcome to any Albanian regime. The Czechoslovak, Hungarian, and Bulgarian leaders, and to a much lesser extent the Rumanian, had consolidated their positions by bloody purges conducted in the name of anti-Titoism, and a shift in their attitude was bound to reawaken dormant issues and bitter memories within their respective parties. In Hungary the Nagy interlude of 1953–1955 had already created a political problem with which Rakosi, once again in command, was merely beginning to cope. In the case of Bulgaria, an added concern might have been a fear of a revival of the Balkan Union as a federative unit within a more loosely structured Communist commonwealth — a scheme which the ambitions of Tito and the unpredictability of Khrushchev might conjure up. The East Germans feared the new policy for the simple reason that any relaxation of bonds with the USSR and any efforts to promote more indigenous regimes immediately raised the question of the very survival of the Pankow rulers. In Warsaw, the domestic economic difficulties and the mounting intellectual ferment (see Chapter 11) were causing sufficient dilemmas without the regime's having to endorse Tito, since such endorsement indirectly reflected favorably on the "right-wing deviation" of Gomulka. The June 1955 and the later June 1956 Soviet-Yugoslav agreements could not have been viewed by the East European Communist leaders with favor.

The caution and patent discomfort of such leaders were thus understandable. With the exception of Czechoslovakia, and possibly Bulgaria, all of these regimes were still feeling the birthpangs of forced and rapid economic changes and of the consequent alienation of at least part of their party cadres and proletariat. Their position in this respect was quite different from Khrushchev's or Bulganin's. The Soviet leaders might undermine their own positions if their Yugoslav policy failed; the East Europeans stood to lose their positions as soon as the policy was implemented. In addition, the USSR of 1955 or 1956 had a certain measure of internal stability, acquired through forty years and a victorious war. The retention of some forms of Stalinism, and therefore only a partial reconciliation with Yugoslavia, was a *sine qua non* of most of these regimes' political stability.

The regimes accordingly dragged their feet and moved only when under pressure. This pressure came from two sides. Speaking in Sofia immediately after signing the 1955 agreement, Khrushchev specifically linked the People's Democracies with the USSR insofar as Yugoslavia was concerned: "Today we can say that the road toward the development of friendly relations between the USSR and the People's Democracies on the one side and Yugoslavia on the other has been opened." In a secret speech to the Bulgarian leaders Khrushchev, in an apparent effort to undermine their hesitation, launched an extensive attack on Stalinist policies in general and on Stalinist policy toward Yugoslavia in particular.[18] He personally communicated a similar message to the satellite leaders on June 5, in a hastily convened conference in Bucharest.[19] The Yugoslavs, in the meantime, while cautiously maintaining their policy of independence from both blocs, interpreted the agreement to be a repudiation of the entire anti-Titoist phase of the preceding seven years. Speaking eight weeks after signing the agreement, Tito, reiterating his nonaffiliation "with any bloc," hailed the Soviet leaders as "men who wish to follow a new path" and specifically noted that "they saw that Stalin's path was a wrong one." He then charged "certain of our neighboring countries" with practicing terror against those in favor of normal relations with Yugoslavia, slyly suggesting that its victims were merely people wishing to follow a course already charted by the USSR. Finally dropping his reserve, Tito specifically singled out Hungary and Czechoslovakia as having regimes which spilled the blood of innocent Communists and which were lacking "the Communist courage to admit their errors." [20]

In pressing for amends, the Yugoslavs, consistent with their doctrinal position, were unwilling to accept the Soviet interpretation which placed all the blame for the past on Beria and which, therefore, absolved all others of any responsibility. Tito pointedly included Stalin as "the main man," while the juxtaposition of "new men" in the USSR with the leaders of East Europe explicitly suggested that the positive trends in the USSR still awaited duplication in East Europe. Paradoxically, Yugoslavia, as some eight years earlier, was again demanding that East Europe imitate the USSR even though this time Yugoslavia was doing so in the name of diversity and the many ways to socialism. The Yugoslav condemnation of the Cominform — reiterated on numerous occasions after the June 1955 declaration — stemmed from the same roots: it had now become a stagnant and conservative institution which impeded the successful and rapid imitation of the USSR in East Europe, and any efforts to create a single international Communist center were bound to provoke difficulties, given the existing circumstances in the bloc and particularly in view of Soviet-Yugoslav relations. [21]

The East European leaderships, essentially still Stalinist, found themselves in an unenviable position. On the one side, they were being pressed openly by Tito whom they could no longer attack and, on the other, the Soviets were giving Tito at least tacit support. [22] Their desire to maintain an anti-Titoist position — a stance justified by considerations of survival — could be maintained only through firm adherence to the old Stalinist precepts which included a condemnation of Titoism. But a crucial component of Stalinism was also the elevation of Soviet experience into a norm of behavior — and in this instance that behavior required an abandonment of a Stalinist position. For a while, of course, a delaying action could be staged. They could claim that the Yugoslav-Soviet rapprochement represented merely temporary tactical maneuver and hence need not be imitated because it would shortly be reversed. Apparently, according to Tito, [23] this was the interpretation voiced in Rakosi's Central Committee when the question came up. Another line was to pin all hope on the relatively unsettled conditions in the Soviet leadership and expect a r versal in the Soviet position through the displacement of some existing leaders.

In the fall of 1955 the situation was not wholly clear and the future easily might have appeared to be still in doubt. The defenders of Stalinism, given their calculations and interests, accordingly maintained their orthodox positions, even though this necessarily implied an unorthodox nonconformity in behavior. In a roundabout way domesticism — almost verging on a form of national Communism in the name of Stalinism — was being adopted by the anti-Titoist Stalinists. Their unwillingness to adjust in effect amounted to a denial of a universal norm. For example, in Poland, which originally had delayed even a normalization in diplomatic relations with Yugoslavia,[24] two former ministers, W. Lechowicz and A. Jaroszewicz, purged earlier in connection with the national Communist purges, were tried and sentenced in the summer of 1955. Their fate might have served as a discreet reminder of the regime's attitude. The Hungarian regime, with Tito conjuring Rajk's ghost, responded to the Soviet-Yugoslav agreement only in August through a speech delivered by Rakosi, Tito's chief opponent. Rakosi, absolving himself of responsibility, blamed the past deterioration in relations on Gabor Peter, a former head of the secret police, and promised an immediate improvement in relations.[25] He, and the other Communist regimes, refrained, however, from rehabilitating the Communists who had already been purged, and often executed, as Titoists. The gesture made, the Hungarians refused to go any further, and in a curiously "neutral" fashion, symbolic of the new uneasy diversity, *Pravda* reported on September 27 that the Hungarian-Yugoslav economic negotiations had been broken off, citing first the Hungarian version, which blamed "excessive" Yugoslav demands, and then citing the Yugoslav version, which placed "the reason for the failure of the talks" on Hungarian unwillingness to meet their obligations.

Thus, in the six months following the Belgrade declaration of June 1955, the Soviet efforts to establish binding ideological ties and intimate party relations were met first by Yugoslav suspicion, which was exacerbated by their doctrinal notions about the Soviet system, and then by Yugoslav demands that the past be fully repudiated, particularly as it pertained to the anti-Titoist phase in the history of Yugoslavia's Communist neighbors. The latter, on the other hand, were willing to take the 1955 Belgrade declaration only at its face value and restricted themselves to the formal aspects of the new policy: interstate cooperation, trade agreements, cultural and athletic exchanges, border crossing, and minorities arrangements.[26] Indeed, on numerous occasions during the fall of 1955, the leaders of the People's Democracies made plain their willingness to improve only the "quite abnormal relations" that existed between them and Yugoslavia,[27] usually coupling this perfunctory concession with pointedly complimentary references to Stalin and with insistence on the universality of the Soviet experience. At the November 1955 celebration commemorating the Bolshevik revolution, Istvan Kovacs, a member of the Hungarian Politburo, hailed Stalin as "Lenin's best disciple and the perpetuator of his work" and ended his speech with a resounding cry "Long live our ideal, the CPSU and its Central Committee." [28] Stalin was similarly praised in the Czech festivities,[29] while the Rumanians, ignoring both Stalin and their relations with Yugoslavia, merely noted the improvement in Soviet-Yugoslav affairs.[30] The East European leaders were in this devious manner attempting to bridge the developing gap between the maintenance of Stalinist positions and the new Soviet policy. But even on this restricted level, some of them, like Hungary and Albania, were demonstrably slower in adjusting and were thus practicing, for the first time, a limited foreign policy of their own.

TITOISM FOR EXPORT

The aftermath of the Twentieth Party Congress subjected the camp to its severest test. In the course of four months following the June 20, 1956, Khrushchev-Tito declaration, the full measure of Khrushchev's miscalculation concerning Tito, as well as the capacity of some of the East European regimes to operate beyond the Stalinist framework emerged in startling proportions. In the summer of 1956 Tito seemed to be cast in the role of Khrushchev's nemesis. He not only continued to press for his pound of flesh but, with Stalinism dissipated and a substitute for it absent in the confusion and demoralization that followed in the wake of Khrushchev's pronouncements, also made it eminently clear that Titoism was now a doctrine available for export. The June 20 declaration was based on a Yugoslav draft, and it was the Yugoslavs who took the initiative in formulating the new norms for relations among Communist states.[31] Yugoslav parochialism — their defensive insistence on national Communism — had ended sometime between February and June 1956. In this post-Twentieth Congress atmosphere, Yugoslavia's national Communism was nation-

only in the sense that Tito considered many of its forms applicable to every Communist state individually.

Indeed, the Yugoslavs carefully and logically refrained from describing their system as one of national Communism. To have done so would have meant to deny its potential validity elsewhere.[32] On the contrary, the Yugoslav leaders and newspapers repeatedly asserted the need for a sharing of experience among the various Communist parties. In the case of borrowing from Yugoslavia, this clearly meant the adoption of those forms which were distinct from the already existing and available Soviet model. This was coupled with an increasingly vigorous condemnation of those East European Communist leaders who were proving themselves unable to adjust to this post-Stalinist situation, with the operative criterion being their willingness to repudiate their past anti-Titoist activities. The Yugoslavs insisted on this with a firmness which, combined with the apparent willingness of Khrushchev to appease Belgrade, must have been discomforting to the other Communist regimes. Even the disbanding of the Cominform, executed with some face-saving remarks about its formerly positive role "in developing and strengthening fraternal ties and mutual exchange of experience," [33] a phrase repeated with glee by the East European Stalinists, provoked immediate Yugoslav ire. The very next day they responded with a flat assertion that the Cominform (the creation of which they had originally urged) had been an undesirable institution from the very beginning.[34] Under the circumstances no one was prepared to argue the point.

At the same time, Yugoslav pronouncements on the Communist bloc assumed an air of authoritativeness which must have been galling even to those who favored a reconciliation with Belgrade. The Yugoslavs, while somewhat patronizingly congratulating the CPSU on having "rejected the old concepts about obligatory uniformity of ways and forms of socialism," [35] never missed an opportunity to point out that they had been right all along, and had been so by remaining the only true Marxists-Leninists. As M. Stajakovic, a member of the Commission for Foreign Relations of the Socialist Alliance of Yugoslavia, pointed out: "It is frequently said that the 1948 conflict with Stalin's hegemony was a 'misunderstanding' which has now been happily surmounted . . . In this struggle there was no misunderstanding; it was clear that the Yugoslav Communists and the entire Yugoslav nation were defending the fundamental principles of socialist policy." [36]

Belgrade made no secret of the fact that it regarded the Twentieth

Congress as having hammered the last nail into the coffin of Stalinism. It welcomed the repudiation of Stalin's executions and arrests of some party leaders with the observation that "in rehabilitated persons, Stalinism has perhaps the most outspoken opponents . . . Rehabilitation of old Bolsheviks in the Soviet Union represents a very important stage in the reestablishment of the ethical principles of the revolution." In the Yugoslav view, "objective" forces against a revival of Stalinism were being unleashed by the revelations and their impact was not restricted to the USSR. To help these forces a press and radio campaign was launched against the East European anti-Titoists who, unlike some of their West European counterparts,* could not afford the luxury of defending both Stalin and their own anti-Titoist past.

The dissipation of Stalinism occurred at a most unfortunate phase of development in some of these states — in the immediate aftermath of the most difficult stage of industrialization and collectivization but before the new social institutions could take roots — and their capacity to resist the suddenly combined external and internal pressures was severely taxed. Being directly dependent on the USSR, they could no longer ignore the new Soviet policy toward Yugoslavia, nor could they remain insensitive to internal pressures which were gaining the ideological upper hand. While no single formula stands out, it is apparent that the ability of each regime to ride out the crisis depended on the depth of its internal socioeconomic crisis, the degree of alienation of the working class and the intelligentsia from the regime and Communism as well as their revolutionary morale, the extent to which the regime had been involved in anti-Titoist policies, and the availability of alternatives in policy and leadership.

One by one the Stalinist bastions were assaulted. The most disastrous consequences occurred in Hungary and Poland where disintegrative processes had been under way ever since the relaxing effects of the New Course had first been felt. The Twentieth Party Congress pushed these trends further while the sudden prestige of Titoism gave them a more positive sense of direction and legitimization. The implications of the Polish and Hungarian patterns of development are discussed more fully in the next two chapters. But even in the other states, where the socioeconomic tensions had not been sharpened by politically significant events or led by "providential"

---

* The most rigid position was adopted by the French Communist Party which not only openly defended and praised Stalin (as in "Quelques questions capitales posées au XX Congrès . . ." *Cahiers du Communisme,* no. 4, April 1956, pp. 391–392) but also openly proclaimed that the 1948 Cominform resolution had been correct (M. Thorez, as quoted in *Cahiers du Communisme,* no. 6, June 1956, p. 776).

individuals who transformed the thaw into a deluge, the joint impact of the dissolution of Stalinism and the restored orthodoxy of Yugoslavia was felt deeply.

Posthumous rehabilitations became the vogue. In Bulgaria, the regime at first limited itself to pious editorials in *Rabotnichesko Delo*, such as "For a New Upsurge in Party Work," which condemned the cult of the individual but which also contained a warning against carrying the criticisms too far. "We must resist and unmask all hostile encroachments and unsound and rotten anti-party misconceptions in connection with the eradication of the cult of the individual," the party paper admonished.[37] This, however, was coupled with references linking Vulko Chervenkov to Stalin and the news that the Central Committee of the Bulgarian Communist Party had convened, with a well-feted Yugoslav delegation in attendance.[38] Chervenkov's fate was sealed when the official announcement of April 14 rehabilitating the hanged Kostov also condemned the Premier for having "considered that his word was law." [39] Three days later, Chervenkov resigned and was replaced, in the midst of attacks on his "brutality," by Anton Yugov, a former Minister of the Interior, who in the past was attacked by Chervenkov for his "lack of vigilance."

The Yugoslav delegation, however, apparently was not too convinced that fundamental changes were involved (a matter of some importance, given their earlier reservations), and the Yugoslavs' displeasure was vented shortly afterwards in a purported newspaper report from Sofia, featured in a provincial Yugoslav newspaper.[40] The story alleged that indignation was rampant in Sofia among Bulgarian Communists because the High Party School was still named after Chervenkov and still headed by his wife. It also reported that Bulgarian Communists felt indignant because the April plenum did not go far enough in condemning Chervenkov and that "energetic" action had not been taken against the secret police.

Whatever the degree of fiction in this newspaper story, it did reflect an element of reality. The shift in the Bulgarian party leadership had not brought to power leaders genuinely well disposed toward Titoism; they were merely another essentially Stalinist faction which took advantage of the situation to unseat the incumbents. T. Zhivkov, for instance, who became First Secretary during the "collective leadership" period, retained his post. In fact, considering the energetic purges in the past as well as certain traditional enmity between Yugoslavia and Bulgaria, particularly over Macedonia, it is doubtful that a faction truly friendly to Belgrade existed, or could exist, on any large scale in Sofia. Dimitrov's earlier plans, after all, were closely associated with his international Communist experience and ambitions, and because of his stature he could afford to consider close ties with Belgrade. In 1956, a Yugov or a Chervenkov was no match for Tito, and the change of guard in the Bulgarian Central Committee did not, therefore, amount to any more than just a change of guard. The old policies went on as before: Yugov and Zhivkov continued the intensive collectivization drive and in July launched a new militant plan designed to expand the collective sector and to make it more attractive by decreasing some of the burdens of the collective farmers.[41]

Nonetheless, the timing of the change in leadership could not avoid having an impact on rank-and-file party members. Discipline inevitably slackened and criticisms of the leadership were heard and openly published.* The party leaders felt compelled to note that "such ideologically disoriented comrades under petit-bourgeois influence have proven themselves unprepared to understand the main problems. Interpreting the spread of internal party democracy as freedom to speak whatever they wished, some of them expressed wrong political opinions."[42] The Bulgarian party leadership was thus striving to impose strict limits on internal dissent while externally attempting to live up to the strenuous requirements of this trying phase. Its efforts, however, were typical of what the Soviet and Yugoslav moves had wrought in each regime: more flexibility in coping with domestic problems yet with the same obligation of living up to the external uniformity.†

The Central Committee of the Bulgarian party met again in early fall, and its September 19 communiqué (issued exactly a month before Gomulka's return to power in Warsaw and the outbreak of the Hungarian revolution) defined with greater clarity the relevance of anti-

---

* For instance, *Rabotnichesko Delo* complained on May 20, 1956, that a treatment of the recent events, "The Lesson," published by *Otechestven Front*, "is directed against the leaders and against the Party and state cadres. According to this article, the Party and particularly the Party leaders have broken off from the people; shortcomings and mistakes are criticized in such a manner that the successes so far achieved are minimized."

† Thus the Bulgarians, while paying lip service to friendship with Yugoslavia, went out of their way to continue stressing the relevance of the Soviet experience for the Bulgarian building of socialism. The second slogan on the Bulgarian Liberation Day (Radio Sofia, August 25, 1956) read as follows: "Eternal gratitude to our liberator — the Great Soviet Union, the invincible pillar of peace and progress throughout the world! Glory to the heroic Soviet Army — our liberator! Long live the life-giving Bulgarian-Soviet friendship! Glory to the Communist Party of the Soviet Union — organizer of the first in the world socialist state, the great, inspiring, and leading force of the Soviet people in their struggle for peace, democracy, and socialism!"

Stalinism to the Bulgarian situation. To all intents and purposes, the communiqué, while stressing Bulgarian appreciation for the "profound Marxist-Leninist analysis" supplied at the Twentieth Congress through the criticisms of the "cult of the individual and its consequences," spelled out the notion that domestic circumstances in Bulgaria did not permit the party to allow any substantial deviation from previous practices. Indeed, the burden of the resolution was devoted to pointing out that because of the Twentieth Congress and the subsequent endorsement of many ways to socialism, "attempts have been made to deny or reduce the importance of our great successes in socialist building, to strike at the prestige of the Central Committee, to shake the workers' faith in the party leadership and its *correct* policy." The resolution abounded in references to "alien," "careerist," "petit-bourgeois," "liberal," elements who criticize the party.[43] The party leadership left no doubt that domestically Stalinism would remain in force — which, in turn, of course, made the Yugoslav-Bulgarian reconciliation a mere formality.

Similarly, in Czechoslovakia the initial response to the Khrushchev-Tito flirtation and the Twentieth Congress was one of caution and suspicion. The Czech Central Committee met in late March, and party Secretary Novotny's report, devoted to a critique of Stalinism (or, euphemistically, "the cult of the personality"), warned against any minimization of the authority of the party. "We must reckon with the fact that the enemies will abuse the fight against the cult of personality and the disclosure of our mistakes and shortcomings." [44] Lest anyone lose trust in Communism as a result of Khrushchev's disclosures, the membership was at the same time exhorted to resolve all problems of conscience with the simple formula: "have faith in the Party!" [45] Two weeks later, A. Cepicka, a member of the Politburo and Defense Minister, was dropped from the leadership as a token in the struggle against the cult of the personality.* No further important changes in the leadership were made. In May, however, in response to continued Yugoslav promptings and possibly even to Moscow sug-

* At the National Party Conference in June 1956, Cepicka made a self-criticizing declaration, excerpts of which deserve quotation: "Certain interventions and measures which bore positive results strengthened in me the inclination to act authoritatively and to make authoritative decisions . . . All this led me to be impatient with people. I now realize that by gradually adopting Stalinist methods of work, I also developed more and more the characteristics of the cult of the personality. To these characteristics of cult of personality I must ascribe the exhibiting of my photographs, the shouting of various slogans at demonstrations, and the claiming of credit for various achievements through the press. There is no doubt that I became a typical example of the cult of personality." Radio Bratislava, June 15, 1956.

gestions, came the partial rehabilitation of some of the previously condemned party leaders. V. Siroky, addressing the Central Committee of the Slovak party, asserted that Slansky and Clementis had in fact been justly executed for serious crimes (Slansky for brutality, oppression, and illegal use of the secret police; Clementis for "incorrect attitude toward political problems") but that Slansky's alleged Titoist conspiracy had been a Beria fabrication.[46] But, again, this was accompanied by warnings that enemies might take advantage of such admissions to attack the party.

In this rather conditional fashion the Prague regime strove to adjust to the requirements imposed on it by the new situation. These were limited concessions avoiding any substantial leadership and policy changes. But, as in the case of Bulgaria, in the over-all context, they generated the very public reaction which the regime had feared. The Second Congress of Czechoslovak Writers, which convened late in April, featured critical discussions of the Czech political scene and was followed shortly by student demonstrations.* The party leadership for this reason continued its warnings against abuses of criticism, claiming that it could be used only within the framework of party discipline.[47] Efforts to keep the reactions down were coupled with measures to improve the standard of living by cutting prices and improving wages, as well as by official announcements of restraints imposed in the name of "socialist legality" on the operations of the secret police.[48] The economic measures, particularly, were designed to satisfy the working class, thereby isolating the intellectuals and making them politically powerless.

In the other Communist states, East Germany, Rumania, and Albania, a policy of similar caution was pursued after the initial shock had somewhat faded. In Albania, the past anti-Titoist violence was blamed on a purged Politburo member, Koci Xoxe,[49] much as the Soviets had made Beria shoulder the blame. This in turn provoked a Yugoslav attack on the Albanian party chief, Enver Hoxha, as the major source of all past difficulties.[50] Late in June, a joint Yugoslav-Rumanian declaration of solidarity and cooperation was issued,[51] al-

---

* A students' resolution, for instance, demanded "the democratization of public life," abandonment of excessive idolatry of the USSR (such as playing the Soviet anthem at the end of Czech radio transmissions), and raised the problem of the Soviet exploitation of the Czech uranium deposits (*News from Behind the Iron Curtain,* July 1956, pp. 42–43). At the Writers' Congress, according to published reports (*Literarni Noviny,* April 28–29, 1956), officially sponsored candidates for posts in the Writers' Union were rejected, clemency was demanded for imprisoned writers, and the freedom of conscience of each individual asserted.

though again no major domestic shifts were involved. The same was largely the case in East Germany where the party leadership made only formal acts of obeisance to the new situation, although the initial impact of the Twentieth Congress had prompted Ulbricht to declare that "Stalin cannot be counted among the classics of Marxism."[52] Once composure was restored in East Berlin, the only concession was the late July rehabilitation of Dahlem, Merker, and the other high SED officials previously purged.[53] Again, much as in Czechoslovakia, this produced some reverberations among Communist intellectuals, and the party was repeatedly called upon to issue warnings against excessive abuses of the enlarged range of discussion. As in all of these states, strict adherence to "socialist legality" was promised.

Efforts to contain the situation provoked by the dissipation of Stalinism and by the increased aggressiveness of the Yugoslavs were facilitated by the fact that of all these states only Poland and Hungary had most of the necessary preconditions for a far-reaching change. In Czechoslovakia, East Germany, and even Bulgaria and Albania the socioeconomic crisis had not been, as already noted, quite as acute as in Poland and Hungary. The first two were already fairly well-developed industrial societies while the second two had not yet approached the critical transitional stage of Poland and Hungary. While East Germany and Czechoslovakia had some circles of alienated intellectuals, each lacked the support of the urban working classes, which were politically neutralized by a combination of economic concessions and strict control. Without the support of the urban working class the intellectual ferment could not be translated into successful politics. This same condition vitiated the significance of any discontent in Bulgaria and Rumania, both rural societies without a strong proletariat. Only in Hungary and Poland did real personal alternatives to the party leaders exist, and for the existing leaders to follow a Titoist path might have been disastrous. In most cases domestic Stalinism, with some adjustments and concessions, seemed the wisest course. In addition, Czechoslovakia lacked the religious and national homogeneity necessary for successful resistance, while its former democratic elites were discredited by the twin failures of the Czech Republic (1938, 1948). Together with the Bulgarians, the Czechs were also traditionally friendly to the Russians and, therefore, did not harbor a deep-seated hatred for the "Muscovites." In the case of East Germany, the presence of a Soviet Army and the fresh memories of the failure of the 1953 rising precluded any violent change. Indeed, of the Communist states outside of Poland and Hungary,

only Rumania might have come close to meeting the necessary preconditions for an upheaval. That it did not take place probably was
due to the absence of a political alternative to the regime and the
weakness of the urban working class, so necessary to a successful
coup. Nonetheless, the other factors made themselves felt and, had
the USSR failed to intervene in Hungary, it is likely that Rumania
would have joined Hungary and Poland in experiencing a revolutionary outbreak.

With ideological unity dissipated, with the local power of the
regimes threatened, with direct Soviet intervention in the domestic
affairs of these states lessened, it was the negative sanction of Soviet
power — the fear of a military intervention — that provided the backbone for the operation of political containment carried out by the
entrenched Stalinists. But for the operation to be effective, a clearer
line from the center was necessary to restore a common sense of purpose.

SOVIET SECOND THOUGHTS

Khrushchev certainly was not interested in presiding over the dissolution of the Soviet camp. Indigenous, even autonomous, efforts to
contain internal anti-Stalinist pressures were encouraged in the summer of 1956 by certain indications that the Soviet leadership itself was
becoming concerned over the interpretations given the Twentieth
Congress and the second Tito-Khrushchev declaration. The endorsement of the Yugoslav position and the approval expressed for extensive Yugoslav contacts with Western socialists — which, it was hoped,
might "overcome the split in the international working class movement" [54] — had, as Khrushchev came to see it, the unfortunate effect
of blurring the clear line which was said to separate Communism from
capitalism. Khrushchev's task now was to define the limits of the anti-
Stalinist aftermath and posit some common foundations for unity. On
June 30 the Central Committee of the CPSU issued a declaration
which answered some of the anti-Stalinist criticisms of the Soviet system. It stressed that "Marxist parties of the working class, naturally,
must retain and strengthen their ideological unity and international
fraternal solidarity in the struggle against the threat of a new war, in
the struggle against the anti-people's forces of monopolistic capital
striving to suppress all revolutionary and progressive movements." [55]

To bring this about, the Soviet leaders gradually moved in the
direction of clarifying the extent to which "different ways to socialism" had to be subordinated to some common core of doctrine —

without, however, undermining the new Soviet-Yugoslav friendship which was so important to Khrushchev's image of the post-Stalin Soviet bloc. The urgency of this task was underlined by the Poznan outbreak at the end of June, signaling a merger between the restless proletariat and the disenchanted intellectuals, as well as by the growing political instability in Hungary. The Yugoslav condemnation of the Poznan strike probably served to reassure Khrushchev that bringing Yugoslavia back into the fold would be a positive contribution to the internal cohesion of the bloc;* but, at the same time, the Soviet leadership began steadily to minimize the importance of many ways to socialism and to stress instead the special peculiarities of a common core, worked out through the Soviet experience. Common aims, common outlook, and an available model were hence to be the conditions under which specific adaptations would be tolerated. Addressing the Eighth Congress of the Chinese Communist Party, Mikoyan bluntly observed, "Assuredly, each country has its distinctive features and brings its own specific elements to bear in making the transition to socialism. But, as Lenin pointed out, these features can relate only to what is not most important." [56] The emphasis was again on the fine print, on the reservations made in Suslov's Twentieth Congress speech, noted in the preceding chapter.

The Soviet leadership began to draft plans early in the fall of 1956 for common institutional links with the other ruling parties which could not carry the stigma of the Cominform but which nonetheless would bind them together. The method considered was a theoretical journal. Furthermore, the Soviet leaders felt quite justified in dispatching a circular letter some time in September (the precise date is not known) warning the ruling East European parties against a "mechanical" imitation of the Yugoslav experience in the name of the newly legitimized multiplicity of roads to socialism. The existence, but not the precise text, of such a circular letter was revealed officially by Belgrade,[57] and it apparently claimed that the League of Communists of Yugoslavia was not an entirely Marxist-Leninist organization. This warning, given the increased emphasis on Marxism-Leninism as a binding force, could only serve to discourage, indeed to disapprove, any

---

* The Yugoslav press spoke darkly about antidemocratic forces which had marked the armed clash in order to prevent further democratization of Poland. This emphasis on provocation was in line with the Soviet interpretation. In retrospect, however, when one reads these interpretations one is struck by the fact that they could have been equally well aimed at the Stalinists (hence the pro-Soviet elements) in Poland. What the actual intent was is difficult to assess. For a Yugoslav commentary, see *Borba,* July 1 and July 6, 1956.

excessive enthusiasm for domestic Yugoslav experiments or ideological views. Almost at the same time, two hasty conferences were held between Tito and Khrushchev, beginning with Khrushchev's unheralded arrival in Belgrade on September 11 and followed by Tito's flight to Sochi a week later. The sense of urgency involved in these consultations was understandable since both leaders still had a vested interest in preventing the axis from breaking in two. To Khrushchev, Tito was needed to calm down the Hungarians* and to demonstrate that Khrushchev's original gamble had been justified. An open break at this stage would be an admission of error dangerous to Khrushchev's position, certain to be exploited by Khrushchev's internal opponents. Tito, too, wanted to keep avenues of contact open because without them Yugoslavia was too weak to exert the influence that Tito craved. As a result, the matter of the circular letter was aired, and the Yugoslavs appeared satisfied that it would not happen again.[58]

The Sochi meeting, however, was not without its disappointments and mutual disenchantments. Khrushchev energetically insisted that Yugoslavia must join one of the two world camps, and that, given her social system, "her natural place" was within the Soviet camp.[59] Tito's persistent unwillingness to abandon the principle, if not quite the practice, of neutrality was interpreted by Khrushchev as an indication that the Yugoslav party had become corrupted during its years of alienation from the socialist camp, especially since Tito, interpreting the June 20 agreement rather more liberally than his cosignatory, was welcoming the growing pressures for change in Poland and Hungary while openly disapproving the measures taken by the other Communist states.†

* At Sochi, Tito, without prior warning, was confronted with E. Gero, Rakosi's successor (see Chapter 10), and enjoined to give him his blessing. This Tito refrained from doing until mid-October.

† For example, *Borba*, August 23, 1958, two months before the Budapest uprising, described Imre Nagy's return to the Hungarian Communist Party as an "inevitable" prospect and called for the "rehabilitation of that for which he fought." It is to be remembered that Nagy's 1955 fall seems to have been connected with Malenkov's fall in the USSR.

Symptomatic of the disapproval was the communiqué issued by *Jugopress* on October 9, following the visit to Belgrade, to re-establish party relations, of the head of the Bulgarian party, Zhivkov, which noted disagreements with the Bulgarians on "the substance and forms of cooperation of Communist parties" as well as evidence of continuing "distrust and doubt." Its tone left no doubt as to who should revise their conduct and views before the Yugoslavs were to feel that proper relations existed. On another occasion, *Politika* (October 19, 1956) noted that "the Czechs and Slovaks . . . are asking what happened to all those persons who were sentenced in the period of the anti-Yugoslav campaign only because they were friends of Yugoslavia."

The difference in the long-range objectives, temporarily obscured by a short-range communality of method, began to emerge in sharper focus. The Yugoslavs, construing Soviet accommodation as a thorough break with the past, were dreaming of a new ruling trinity: Moscow, Peking, and Belgrade. To Tito, Communism would spread more effectively if it could operate on the basis of heterogeneity, making it more appealing to the masses of the world. His new contacts with Moscow, which seemed to suggest that "polycentric" Communism was also being embraced by Khrushchev, made Tito unwilling to raise openly the banner of national Communism or to expound openly a doctrine fitting the new circumstances and filling the vacuum created by the denunciation of Stalinism.* The Soviets, conscious of their power position yet wishing to place their leadership on a more reliable basis, were not primarily interested in a division of power, but in a *voluntary* acceptance of their primacy. To Moscow, a common core and a center was a requirement dictated by the instability of the East European regimes and by the hostility of the non-Communist world. Soviet insistence on unity distressed the Yugoslavs, and Tito's unwillingness to accept it strengthened Khrushchev's conviction that, without precipitating a new break with Tito, the narrowest interpretation must now be placed on the relevance in the other states of his agreement with Tito. Alas, by September 1956, Soviet redefinitions could no longer contain the developments nurtured by the dissipation of Stalinism and crystallized by the reconciliation with Belgrade. The thaw was turning into a deluge.

* How seriously the Yugoslavs took themselves is suggested by the following dialogue between them and Khrushchev on the subject of relations among Communist states at one of the 1956 meetings. In Khrushchev's version (not denied by the Yugoslavs), it went like this: "I reminded them of the following well-known popular saying, 'The whole company marches in step and only one soldier is out of step,' and asked who must change, the company or the soldier? Koca Popovic [the Yugoslav Foreign Minister], who was present at the conversation, asked: 'And who is the company and who is the soldier?'" *Pravda*, June 4, 1958.

10 / HUNGARY: THE TEST CASE OF NATIONAL COMMUNISM

THE toppling of Stalin's statue at the height of Budapest's heroic bid for freedom in October–November 1956, while symbolic of Stalinism's end, did not mean the beginning of Hungary's freedom. The dialectic of events did not lead from Stalinism through anti-Stalinism to national Communism, but rather to a reimposition of a Soviet-dependent regime which at first attempted a policy of reconciliation but which gradually moved toward mounting coercion. A Tito-like national Communist regime was found both to be incompatible with the Soviet conception of their own interests and to be lacking in domestic sources of stability.

The tragedy of Hungary began its climactic phase with the ouster of Nagy from the Premiership in the spring of 1955. Had he retained power and been allowed to pursue the policies initiated in July 1953 (briefly sketched in Chapter 8), it is likely that no major catastrophe would have followed the Twentieth Congress, the Soviet-Yugoslav declaration, or even the accession to power in Poland of Gomulka. The latter event proved to be the spark that ignited the accumulated tensions in Hungary. Nagy's policy had been one of gradually disarming the buried bomb which Stalinism without Stalin had become in East Europe, and particularly in Hungary and Poland. It is also possible, though less likely, that had Nagy not come to power in 1953 Rakosi's regime might have been able, like its Stalinist counterparts elsewhere, to adapt gradually to the new circumstances and ride out the crisis. However, considering its particular complicity in the anti-Titoist phase and its intensive identification with all the worst features of Stalinism, the reverberations of the dissipation of Stalinism would in all probability have struck at the Hungarian regime directly and would have produced serious tensions. Whatever the course of history might have been, the early Nagy period was particularly significant for it created a conception of an alternative economic and political policy within the existing framework. Nagy's program was more acceptable than Rakosi's to at least a significant portion of the Communist Party and certainly to the majority of the population. Rakosi's return to power in 1955 reversed the policy but could not destroy the knowledge of the alternative.

POWER VERSUS IDEOLOGY

A segment of the party remained unalterably opposed to Nagy's policy from the very moment of its inauguration. A variety of factors shaped this attitude. Basically, it stemmed from a distrust of the masses — a suspicion and fear which was so characteristic of Stalin's notions and which he injected so effectively into his own apparatus. The masses were construed as fundamentally unable to perceive the social significance of the changes that were being effected in society, and they were therefore easy prey to hostile propaganda. It was vital in view of this, both for reasons of power — a consideration probably uppermost in Rakosi's thinking — as well as of ideology — a matter with which Rakosi's comrade, Revai, was most conversant — that the masses should be suppressed politically and exploited economically until socialism was secure and its enemies liquidated. It mattered little if in the process the masses were alienated from the party and opposition grew in numbers as long as the instruments of power were able to cope effectively with any impediments to the execution of the regime's policy.

Men like Rakosi or Revai were probably more or less aware of the various economic tensions, potential disasters, and even disillusionment among the faithful that their policies provoked. But in their perspective such factors lost their immediate significance and could safely be ignored or even construed as praiseworthy successes of the regime since they were part of an unfolding pattern of the march into the future. To slow down the pace, to make concessions, was to capitulate before the transitional impediments of today and thereby betray the tomorrow.

In such a perspective the very factors which made Nagy willing to engage in the New Course made the unreconciled Stalinists more determined not to concede one iota. The Nagy faction could note that the working class had grown rapidly since the war — by about 50 per cent[1] — and it would worry about the prospect of proletarian alienation from the system, given the rapidly changing conditions and existing deprivations.* Concessions, it was felt, would prevent the in-

* According to Nagy, "industrial development amounted to 158 per cent in Poland from 1949 to 1955, to 98 per cent in Czechoslovakia during the same period, to 92.3 per cent in the German Democratic Republic from 1950 to 1955, to 144 per

escapable alienation from developing into violent political hostility. To Rakosi this very same fact would be welcome proof that the exploiting class was disappearing, that the proletariat was becoming dominant, but that temporarily the class-conscious, militant minority must retain tight discipline precisely because of the political immaturity of the new proletariat. The Nagy faction could note that the party rank and file was, on the whole, demoralized, fearful, and shared in the popular antipathy toward the regime's past policies while welcoming the New Course. Rakosi's *apparat*, in reply, would point to the party's expanded membership, amounting to about 10 per cent of the population (865,000 in 1954[2]), as proof that increased ideological work and the maintenance of firm control were required since it was likely that the party was penetrated by "apolitical" and even hostile elements. Nagy could observe improved morale and productivity in agriculture as a consequence of his concessions and could claim that the rural hostility toward socialism would consequently wane. Rakosi could note that in just one year of Nagy's rule 51 per cent of collective farm members had quit the collectives, causing 12 per cent of the collective farms to be dissolved [3] and the "socialist transformation of the countryside" to be further delayed. To statements that the Stalinist industrialization had been unrealistic and based on erroneous assumptions, the Rakosi reply was that "this does not mean, however, that the mistakes are very significant" [4] when compared to the socialist achievements of industrialization. Finally, to the argument that the New Course was in keeping with the prevailing Soviet thinking, the answer of the Rakosi faction might well have been that (1) it did not represent unanimous Soviet thinking even for the USSR itself and (2) that the USSR had already passed through its critical stage of development, was not infested with enemies within and without the party, and that hence true application of the "creative" Soviet experience required Stalinism to go through its full historical phase in Hungary.

To these considerations, there doubtless was attached a variety of personal motivations and interests. From what little is known of Rakosi, he appears to have possessed all the earmarks of a sadist driven

cent in Rumania from 1951 to 1955, to 120 per cent in Bulgaria from 1949 to 1955 and to 210 per cent in Hungary from 1949 to 1953" (*On Communism*, p. 185). The impact of the social change is illustrated by the following figures: in a country of less than 9 million people, during the years 1949–1954 the number of wage earners increased by 1,550,000 and workers in the "cooperative sector" by 710,000. At the same time, individual farmers decreased by 1,300,000 and "capitalists" by 540,000 (*Nepszabadsag*, July 10, 1958).

by a strong urge for power and capable of harboring bitter hatreds. The rebuke he received from Soviet leaders in 1953 was probably a deep humiliation to him, and he might well have nurtured a profound dislike for Nagy who had been handpicked by the Soviet leaders to replace him.[5] Such factors, after all, go far in shaping the patterns of history. Rakosi and his associates, furthermore, might have felt genuinely concerned about their personal positions and consequently had a vested interest in Stalinism. Apparently this feeling was shared by the majority of the Politburo and Secretariat which remained loyal to Rakosi and shared his distaste for Nagy's New Course (as contrasted with the lower echelons*).

In this spirit Rakosi from the very beginning of Nagy's rule attempted to undermine both the ideological basis for and the specifics of the New Course. In August 1953 the Politburo under Rakosi diluted the earlier criticisms of the past and was criticized for it by the October plenum of the Central Committee.[6] Unwilling to give up, Rakosi apparently decided to make his next move before the party congress convened on April 18, 1954, since an endorsement of the New Course by the congress would be bound to strengthen Nagy's hand. In March, the Congress Theses were published as a preliminary step to the "debates" of the congress, spelling out the party line for the functionaries who would be attending. However, two weeks later, on March 28, it was suddenly announced that the congress would be postponed to May 24. The delay in the congress was apparently linked to the intense dissension within the party on policy matters. Nagy had fallen ill during the spring while the congress preparations were in full swing. Taking advantage of this felicitous event, Rakosi rammed through the Politburo a resolution condemning both the New Course and Nagy personally, and then proceeded to plan a trip to Moscow to lay his case before the Soviet leadership.[7]

The 1954 Hungarian machinations are interesting testimony to the changing pattern in relations between the USSR and the Communist states. Within a year of Stalin's death, and with all the ear-

---

* Trying to explain in 1956 why the "liquidation of mistakes" had bogged down, that is, why Rakosi was successful in stopping Nagy, Rakosi's successor and close associate, Gero, had this to say: "Finally, the uncertainty was also caused partly by the fact that for various reasons *the Politburo did not feel that it could rely on unanimous* support from the Central Committee. They felt that no unanimous views were held within the Central Committee as regards relations to the Politburo or to its individual members, and that on the other hand, there was no full unanimity between the members of the Central Committee as regards the policy to be pursued by the party" (Radio Budapest, July 18, 1956). According to Nagy, the party at this time was controlled by Gero, Farkas, and Revai, led by Rakosi (p. 278).

marks of respect for Moscow's leadership and its general line, Rakosi, a Stalinist par excellence, felt confident enough to attempt a *fait accompli*. Admittedly, he still required Moscow's endorsement, but the attempt itself is an indication of the enlarged area of local autonomy, especially if one considers the fact that Nagy's policy appeared to enjoy unqualified Soviet support and, indeed, matched the con- temporaneous Soviet line. Of course, Rakosi probably realized that there was division of opinion in Moscow itself on both foreign and domestic policy, and he might have expected that a *fait accompli* to- gether with the backing of some Soviet leaders (Molotov?) might carry the day. But this too is testimony to the greater scope of do- mestic initiative enjoyed by the satellite leaders.

As it turned out, Rakosi's initiative was premature — but only by one year. The Soviet leadership given its 1954 domestic and interna- tional policy and noting the ambivalent attitudes in the Hungarian party, rebuffed Rakosi's solo venture to Moscow. In 1954 this was still enough, despite the implications of his initiative, to turn the projected coup into a fiasco. A Hungarian delegation, including both Nagy and Rakosi, ultimately traveled to Moscow in May 1954, and both Khrushchev and Malenkov heaped generous abuse on Rakosi's head in the course of the conferences. Rakosi was blamed for past and present inadequacies and "he was obliged to admit both in Mos- cow and before the Political Committee that he had made the Political Committee accept a resolution containing unfounded and misleading statements concerning collective leadership, unity of principle, and Party democracy, and that he had informed the Soviet comrades in this vein." [8]

Although in 1954 the Soviet leadership decided to go along with Nagy, it did not create the circumstances for the complete eradication of Rakosi and his group. It apparently felt that Nagy's policies would tax the Soviet resources less and would create more favorable con- ditions for the fulfillment of ultimate goals, presumably shared in common with Nagy. At the same time, however, the Soviet leader- ship, cautiously feeling its way in the first year after Stalin's death and possibly even restrained by internal disagreements, was apparently unwilling to go the full distance in destroying the Rakosi wing — in- deed, it seemed to be pursuing a policy of not burning all its bridges. The principle of *divide et impera*, whether circumstantial or purpose- ful, made the USSR an arbiter between two opposing but still loyal factions, thereby making up for whatever might have been lost in direct Soviet control over Hungary through the gradual erosion of fear following Stalin's death.

As far as Hungary was concerned, the situation thus remained unsettled. Nagy retained control over shaping the program but was not given sufficient Moscow backing to displace Rakosi's control over the party. Rakosi's power, on the other hand, was paralyzed by his knowledge of Moscow's backing for Nagy's policy. Thus ideology and power, rather than being united in one system merging policy and purpose, were set against each other under a very thin crust of superficial unity. This was evident at the party congress finally held in May. The head of the Soviet delegation, Voroshilov, endorsed the congress program with the cryptic observation that "all of us know that the new tasks of the Hungarian Workers' Party are not easy." [9] Nagy's statements represented a further development of the policies to be pursued within the framework of the New Course: only general references to collectivization which, as a policy, was at a standstill; increase in allocated agricultural investment from 14 per cent in 1953 to 24 per cent of the total in 1954;[10] 16 per cent increase in investment for light industry and the food industry;[11] and a planned decentralization of economic administration to increase the role of local government, hitherto usually by-passed by central organs.* In keeping with this, Nagy also envisaged a shift from external party control of the institutions of local government to greater internal activity of its members as participants within local government.[12] This would overcome the old practice of ignoring the masses, he felt, and overcome the bureaucratic tendencies inherent in the prevailing practice.

One can sense in Nagy's remarks a desire to shake up the party *apparat*, the main impediment to the execution of the tasks designed to place Communism, corroded by a clumsy Stalinism, on firmer Hungarian foundations. In fact, it was revealed at the congress that whereas formerly the party cells had been very active in carrying out their instructions, they had recently grown lax and slow, often ignoring central directives. It was clear that the *apparat* was not for the New Course. Considering the tongue lashing to which Rakosi had

---

* Under the plan, local National Councils would no longer be subject to the Ministry of the Interior but to the Presidium of the National Assembly. The economic departments of the National Councils would direct the economic activity within the localities, and the various central ministries would be expected to deal with them rather than to have a direct chain of command down to the lowest production unit.

been subjected in Moscow, his endorsement of the New Course was not unexpected. He dutifully approved it, condemned past excesses, and outlined reforms for the future in keeping with the general program. Nonetheless, he and his close associates did succeed in introducing a series of observations which could only be construed as veiled criticisms of the year-old policy. Rakosi noted, for instance, an increase in kulak activity and a decline in compulsory deliveries, while secret policeman Farkas, in paying lip service to the notion that the party had not kept in close touch with the people, pointed out that the Hungarian proletariat entertained "backward views" and lacked a revolutionary consciousness.[13] Without being more specific, he seemed to be implying the continued need for class vigilance and presumably, therefore, for the institutional devices for the maintenance of that vigilance. The situation was a stalemate, which could be resolved only by the intervention of some extraneous factor.

THE MEANING OF THE RAKOSI PHASE

One very important consequence of this situation was the gradual reactivation of those social forces suppressed by unbridled Stalinism. The Nagy-Rakosi semiparalysis meant that something vaguely reminiscent of pluralism began to emerge on the Hungarian political scene, resulting in a conflict of interest groups. This in turn meant that domestic factors were again becoming more important in shaping Hungarian destiny. The party *apparat* and the weakening secret police, somewhat disarmed by Nagy's amnesties, were becoming isolated from the party rank and file, while Nagy's programmatic position was becoming a magnet for hitherto silent intellectual circles. Hungarian life was very gradually taking on the character of that social and political diversity which, by definition, is incompatible with totalitarian dictatorship.

These tendencies in one sense were cut short but, in another sense, given even more vitality by Rakosi's return to power in the spring of 1955. As in 1954, the change in Hungarian leadership appears to have been a domestic initiative on the part of the unreconciled Rakosi but with certain important differences. A major shift in the locus of power and direction of policy had just taken place in the USSR. The replacement of Malenkov as Premier and the abandonment of his policy, accompanied by a vigorous statement in *Pravda* by Shepilov on the necessity of maintaining the priority of heavy industrial investment (see Chapter 8), appeared to undercut the ideological basis as well as the practical source of support for Nagy's program. Shepi lov's article, reproduced after a few days of stunned delay in the East European press, had the impact of a bombshell which threw into panic those elements which favored a redressing of the balance in the old Stalinist economic program.[14]

It seems clear that in these circumstances Budapest was left to its own resources to resolve its party conflict. This in itself might well be a clue to Moscow's attitude, since the Soviet leaders were presumably aware of the relative strength of the Rakosi and Nagy factions. Moscow "neutrality," even if dictated in part by its own domestic complications, was thus a form of negative involvement and even implicit endorsement for Rakosi's harder line. Noninvolvement in Hungarian domestic affairs, since a super-loyal faction did exist, indeed fit in well with Khrushchev's conception of voluntarily pro-Soviet regimes. In these circumstances even indirect hints sufficed to tip the scales in Rakosi's favor. The circular letter sent out by the Soviet leadership to explain why Malenkov had been removed provided such guidance, for it blamed him for introducing certain harmful characteristics into the relations of the USSR with the People's Democracies and specifically cited Hungary as an example.[15] Nagy was hence by implication linked with Malenkov.

The favorable external conditions seized upon by Rakosi occurred simultaneously, as in 1954, with a recurrence in Nagy's illness sometime in February 1955. Using his unchallenged control of the party Secretariat (which in making intraparty decisions he had used to by-pass the Central Committee and even the Politburo of which Nagy was a member) Rakosi apparently succeeded in excluding Nagy from the inner party deliberations on the grounds of his illness and proceeded to hold meetings and pass resolutions without informing Nagy of them.* In March Rakosi was able to prevail on the Central Committee to condemn Nagy's policies as "right-wing deviation" and as causing the weakening of the party in favor of the state — a parallel to the Malenkov episode (but also a reversal of the old Stalinist relationship). Presumably out of deference to Moscow, which had originally charted the New Course, and presumably also as a reflection of the changed times which did not permit a full turn

---

* Nagy (*On Communism*, pp. 290–291) makes reference to "the illegal and irregular resolution of the Political Committee that attempted to isolate and silence me completely on the basis of the medical report composed by the Committee"; he protests against "exaggerated regulations" made "on the pretense of my illness." Rakosi's concern for Nagy's health is a curious parallel to the case of Frunze in the USSR who died under the surgical knife after having been compelled by the Politburo to undergo an operation.

of the wheel, the June 1953 resolution was not repudiated, but praised for its "courage." Instead, Nagy was accused of inept and un-Leninist execution of the said resolution. Moscow support for Rakosi became more evident at this stage with *Pravda's* approving quotation of Rakosi's condemnation of the "anti-Marxist, anti-Party, opportunistic views . . . under the influence of which industry's development was checked, socialist accumulation diminished, and state and civil discipline weakened." [16]

Encouraged, Rakosi moved ahead. On April 18 Nagy was expelled from the Politburo, from the Central Committee, and removed from the Premiership. Almost ironically, but possibly to soften the blow, Farkas was simultaneously condemned for past abuses of socialist legality and linked with Nagy, clearly to discredit the latter. Nagy himself was condemned, in a statement drafted with Suslov's personal assistance, for a variety of offenses, ranging from factionalism — a usual charge against those whose faction has failed — to undermining the party through right-wing deviation, entertaining "anti-Party, anti-Marxist, and anti-Leninist opinions," and forgetting "the most important and supreme prerequisite for the triumph of Socialism — the necessity of steadily increasing productivity." [17] In the foreign-affairs realm Nagy was charged with "overestimating the easing of tension in international affairs," a serious sin according to the Stalinist dichotomic perspective. The shift was followed by a reemphasis on collectivization,[18] arrests of some kulaks, and a renewed party purge. The most prominent victim of the purge was Nagy himself, who was expelled from the party in November 1955.

But times had changed. Apparently what neither Rakosi nor Khrushchev realized was that processes had been set in motion which now would be difficult to contain and which Moscow's Yugoslav policy, at this time in the early stage of development, was bound to exacerbate. Rakosi's return to power galvanized into bitter opposition those party members and intellectuals to whom the Nagy period had marked the beginning of a new type of Communism, more suited to Hungarian tastes. The abrupt interruption in its development intensified the opposition to the regime, especially as past Soviet support for Nagy and its new Yugoslav line created a certain ambivalence toward Soviet views. More and more Hungarian Communists began to feel that Rakosi was an impediment not only to Communism in Hungary but even to proper relations between a Communist Hungary and the USSR.

In brief, the Nagy interlude was of vital importance both to Hungarian Communists and to those non-Communists whose opposition to Rakosi was muted by fear of the USSR. It provided an answer to the Stalinist "dilemma of the one alternative." Watching Rakosi's attempt to return to secret-police terror late in 1955, they observed a growing abyss between the "what is" and the "what is feasible" of a Communist regime. Hitherto, opposing Stalinism had been tantamount to opposing Communism, and this many Communists were clearly not prepared to do. At the same time, the anti-Communists were paralyzed by fear of Soviet might. Nagy, for the first time, seemed to suggest the possibility of change that both groups, even if for different reasons, could welcome. Rakosi's return welded them together.

CRYSTALLIZATION OF AN ALTERNATIVE: NATIONAL COMMUNISM

Nagy's program in 1953 had been a product of expediency, Soviet pressure, and existing Hungarian misgivings, as well as of Nagy's own still vague notions on what the policy of a Hungarian Communist regime ought to be. Prior to 1953, he had written a series of articles and delivered a number of speeches dealing with Hungarian economics; consequently he came to power with a background of political practice and ideological reflection. Nonetheless, it was only after his removal in 1955 and his ultimate expulsion from the party that he found himself drafting a more explicit and systematic statement on the practices and norms of Hungarian Communism.* His thinking had been shaped by intraparty polemics, his firmness increased by sharp personal conflicts with Rakosi, and his creativity stimulated by a favorable intellectual climate which encouraged and facilitated the refinement of his own ideas.

Nagy soon found that any consideration of the method of building Communism in Hungary had to face squarely the issue of Communist Hungarian versus Soviet interests. This was the crucial question at the heart of every Communist move, and to it Stalin had given an explicit answer, backed both by ideological concepts of the need for centralized unity and by Soviet might. By 1955–1956, Soviet moves in respect to Yugoslavia, as well as Hungary's limited experience with the New Course, made it clear that Stalin's formula did not possess the finality that he had desired. To Nagy and many others like him, the dilemma again became very real: how to construct within the changing context a coherent and ideologically motivated

---

* He had hoped to present his writings, or theses as he called them, a rebuttal of Rakosi's charges, to the Central Committee. They were subsequently published in this country as *On Communism*.

policy for implementing Communism in Hungary in a manner suited to Hungary. In his effort to resolve this question, by January 1956[19] Nagy was transformed from a Communist whose practical perspectives were essentially domestic and on broad issues subordinated to general Soviet requirements, into a national Communist willing to put the purposes of Hungarian Communism above the imperatives of Soviet policy. Writing for Rakosi's Central Committee under circumstances of mounting tension, Nagy could not state his thesis explicitly, even though the change in Soviet-Yugoslav relations at least had taken the treasonable sting out of his views. Nonetheless, there can be no doubt as to the meaning of his words.

Nagy realized that the crucible of any policy designed to construct his non-Stalinist brand of Communism in Hungary was the problem of international relations. To a great extent, the policy of subordinating national interests to those of the Soviet bloc — which in practice meant to those of the Soviet Union — was a reflection of the old image of two hostile worlds. Under such circumstances, the need to defend the Communist bloc tended to transform the bloc into an armed camp in which the strongest "fraternal socialist country" naturally played the leading role, defining strategy and assigning tasks and obligations. A small and weak Communist country necessarily was called upon to make great sacrifices which, of course, hampered its own urgent tasks of economic transformation and prevented the emergence of true socialist consciousness among the masses. Nagy felt, however, that since about 1954 a major change in this outlook had occurred, symbolized particularly by the Bandung Conference and the 1955 Belgrade declaration. The first posited the five basic principles of international affairs, subsequently endorsed by the USSR: national independence, sovereignty, equality, noninterference in internal affairs, and self-determination. The contents of the second have already been noted (Chapter 8). Nagy was convinced that the Bandung principles should be applied to the Soviet camp, and he thought he noted signs that this was the attitude of the Soviet leaders also. In any case, their application would only help the cause of Communism, he thought, since they would promote true internationalism by eradicating national tensions. They would make possible the "Marxist-Leninist theory of locally characteristic socialism," a position apparently accepted by the USSR for Belgrade.[20]

Up to this point, Nagy was essentially reiterating the old position that Marxists must recognize domestic circumstances when shaping policy. He went on, however, to assert that the Bandung and Belgrade principles were being opposed by the "remnants of Stalinist autocratic rule" in Hungary,[21] and that such principles did not reflect reality insofar as relations between various Communist parties and the CPSU were concerned. This assertion, stated cautiously in the form of a hope that the implementation of the Bandung and Belgrade principles in East Europe was not too distant, was affirmed further by Nagy's insistence that it was impossible to build socialism without true national independence. Developing his argument, Nagy then stated that true independence, particularly for small states, would be impossible in a world split into hostile blocs. Quite remarkably, he did not discriminate between "good" and "bad" blocs. But how should Hungary extricate herself from existing commitments? His answer, which marks his break with the idea of a priority for international Communist obligations over Hungarian interests, deserves quotation:

> The most practicable plan, seemingly, is the *active* coexistence of progressive democratic socialist or similar countries with those other countries having a different system, through a coordinated foreign policy and through *cooperation against the policies of the power groups*, through neutrality or active coexistence.[22]

Nagy was in effect advocating that Hungary adopt a neutral position between the "power groups," since that would be most compatible with the domestic task of constructing Communism. He could now state with equanimity that "it is the sovereign right of the Hungarian people to decide in which form they believe the most advantageous international status will be assured, and in which form they think that national independence, sovereignty, equality, and peaceful development will be attained." [23]

Noting that the assertion of such a right by Hungary was still a matter for future implementation, thereby more than implying Soviet oppression, Nagy called for the liquidation of the legacy of Stalinist subordination, for the shaping of policy which would no longer ignore his country's interests. His national Communism involved him in a rejection of anything that restricted or violated his country's interests as defined in terms of building Communism, which in turn led him to adopt a position which was not only non-Stalinist but even non-Leninist, and much like Tito's: that of neutrality in the conflict between the two large powers and their blocs. He did so by rejecting the fundamental dichotomy which views the world as engaged in continued, dialectical conflicts with one side basically in the right and the other basically in error. Instead he posited the proposition that

"we must . . . recognize that we are members not only of the socialist camp but of the great community of nations, to the countries and
peoples of which we are bound with countless ties, which we cannot
and indeed must not sever, because we do not want to be disbarred
from the great community of nations, and also because we could not
then successfully progress toward socialism through social and economic improvement." [24]

THE FAILURE OF CONTROLLED TRANSITION

The intellectual ferment, the activity of the Petofi Clubs where
vigorous debates popularized Nagy's views, the growing contacts
between the alienated intellectuals* and the workers, all providing
the momentum for the October 23 revolution, are a matter of well-
publicized historical record.[25] Within the context of relations among
Communist states, it is interesting to note that even though by December 1955 Nagy was emerging not only with an alternative program
but was actually consolidating around him a dedicated group of Communists,[26] Rakosi still did not dare to suppress a man chosen by the
Kremlin in 1953 to set Hungary's house in order. Possibly Rakosi no
longer considered Nagy an active threat once he had been expelled
from the party, but that is rather doubtful, especially considering the
paranoiac predisposition of this Stalinist party chief. Possibly Soviet
efforts to improve relations with Yugoslavia temporarily stayed
Rakosi's hand. Whatever the reason, an alternative to Rakosi thus
persisted.

For the time being, Rakosi continued a policy of relying on external imitation of the USSR. Soon this proved impossible. The
Twentieth Congress, with its downgrading of Stalin, the rehabilitation
of Bela Kun, and the continued pressure for the repudiation of the
anti-Titoist trials made his situation, especially given his professed

---

* A large part of the Hungarian intelligentsia was still the product of the pre-
Communist period, but even those who had been elevated into the ranks of the intelligentsia by the Communist system had gradually become repelled by it. A Communist daily, analyzing the role of the Hungarian intelligentsia, has this interesting
comment to make: "70 per cent of our intellectuals gained their qualifications prior
to the liberation and did not only bring this along with them from the past but also
their ideological errors. The remaining 30 per cent, which in certain professions
like those of teachers and engineers, reaches 50 per cent, has been educated in our
schools and universities, yet cannot be entirely exempt from the controversial influence produced by the policy of the period preceding the revolution. There is
still a considerable gap separating the way of thinking of a number of intellectual
workers from that of the working class . . ." *Nepszava*, June 8, 1958.

ideological position of being the most loyal Soviet lieutenant, increasingly difficult. He was increasingly forced to adopt a policy of compromise which inescapably, in view of the existing alternative, tended to further undermine his position. Thus on March 27, 1956, Rakosi yielded on the Rajk issue and, with an obvious lack of enthusiasm, rehabilitated Rajk and his associates.[27] Other concessions followed: Archbishop J. Grosz was amnestied [28] (but not Cardinal Mindszenty); in early July a partial amnesty was announced (bringing the total released to 11,398 persons);[29] even Bela Kovacs, a prominent anti-Communist long presumed dead, reappeared from imprisonment.[30] A series of measures designed to invigorate local councils and increase their fiscal authority were announced;[31] calls were issued for better labor relations;[32] and "socialist legality" was to be strengthened by limiting the arbitrary power of the administration.[33] Some of the pressure on the kulaks was to be relaxed, and the regime magnanimously would allow their relatives to join collective farms.[34]

These concessions still represented an effort to effect a limited version of the New Course, but under Rakosi's aegis. However, Rakosi's belated moderation was faced by a new complication: the intensifying ferment among the youth and the intellectuals. His response to this was true to his Stalinist training: the economic concessions were balanced by parallel measures to restrain the "troublemakers." The party press began to attack violently the literary circles for "slandering" the party,[35] and the more outspoken, such as Sandor Lukacsi, were expelled. Some of the writers replied by calling for "an end . . . to this present regime of gendarmes and bureaucrats." [36] The situation was fast approaching the breaking point, while news from Poland (particularly the Poznan outbreak) encouraged the Hungarians to believe that Stalinism was being repudiated throughout the bloc. The structure of dictatorship appears impregnable only until the first brick begins to fall away.

Paradoxically, it was the June 20 Soviet-Yugoslav declaration which prompted Rakosi's last bid for supremacy. He construed it as releasing him from the horns of the dilemma on which he had been impaled since his return to power. The declaration proclaimed clearly and explicitly Soviet approval for many ways to socialism. Rakosi could now remain the most loyal Soviet lieutenant *and* a Stalinist without any longer being obliged to imitate Soviet concessions at home. His brand of Stalinism seemed compatible with the newly established principle of diversity. He accordingly moved swiftly to restore his full control of the situation. On June 30 a resolution of the Central Committee stated that:

Gaining courage from the patience of the Party and Communists, the anti-Party elements have launched an attack, which has been gradually increasing in strength, against the policy and leadership of our Party and against our people's democratic system. . . . The open stands against the Party and the People's Democracy are mainly organized by a certain group which has formed around Imre Nagy. The press failed to take a stand against the anti-Party views. Certain newspapers and periodicals . . . have published misleading and unprincipled laudatory reports and occasionally even given space to articles of provocative content . . .[37]

The party organ followed with an attack on the Petofi Clubs, noting that "it cannot be considered accidental that these opportunist, harmful and anti-Party views were voiced by those who still maintain a close and systematic contact with Imre Nagy, who has been expelled from the Party because of his anti-Marxist views, hostile to the Party and the People's Democracy, and his factionalism . . . These people turned the debates into scenes of attacks against the People's Democracy."[38] At the Central Committee session of July 12, Rakosi finally announced his decision to liquidate the "Nagy conspiracy" by arresting him and approximately four hundred associates and by closing three literary organs which had been in the forefront of the anti-Rakosi struggle.

He moved too late. The very fact that he had to seek Central Committee approval was evidence of his weakened position and there he encountered unexpectedly stiff opposition with some members appealing (still in the old tradition but in the name of the new Soviet line) to the Soviet Embassy. The June 20 declaration notwithstanding, the USSR had to intervene, and Tito could not but welcome this act. Rakosi's initiative, the Soviets presumably recognized, might not only spark a repetition of Poznan, but undo the wobbling structure of undefined diversity so recently erected by Khrushchev and backed by Tito. Khrushchev's ultimate program for sounder relations among Communist states could thus be harmed by Rakosi's zeal. Rakosi, whose struggle against internal opposition received sympathetic Soviet backing only a few months earlier[39] was obviously becoming a political liability for Soviet external relations, not to mention the prompting of an explosive situation in Hungary itself. The growing disaffection with his rule even reached the staff of the party daily, *Szabad Nep*, and the Soviet Embassy doubtless kept Moscow abreast of all such occurrences. On July 17, Mikoyan arrived in Budapest, and on the following day Rakosi, complaining of hypertension — a justifiable malaise under the circumstances — submitted his resignation for reasons of health.

The Soviet intervention was a halfway measure. It betrayed the Stalinists without satisfying their opponents or Tito. The new leadership did not mean a return of Nagy, although several formerly imprisoned Communists, most prominently Kadar, Kallai, and Marosan, were elected to party positions in an effort to mollify both Tito and the domestic anti-Rakosi groups. The important post of First Secretary went to Gero, a close associate of Rakosi and a bitter opponent of Nagy, who was entrusted with the task of somehow bridging the gap produced by the period between March 1955 and July 1956. His appointment appeared to be a reasoned effort to effect a transition from Rakosi's rule without a violent undermining of the Communist regime. A further factor preventing Nagy's return might well have been his identification with some of Malenkov's policies, making him quite distasteful to the CPSU First Secretary. In any case, the solution seemed to be a compromise designed to contain disintegrative trends while maintaining in power a regime fully committed to the Soviet Union. Gero's line, as stated in his speech to the Central Committee[40] and subsequently reiterated in the Central Committee's resolution,[41] can be best summarized as a promise to wage a struggle on "two fronts" — pledging improvements, admitting inadequacies, restating the party's determination to rehabilitate those unjustly treated, but also emphasizing the priority of heavy industry and the need to continue collectivization, warning against domestic subversion, and finally condemning the opposition elements within the party. Gero's line, not unexpectedly, was thus fully in tune with the Soviets' second thoughts about Titoism and anti-Stalinism, and compatible with their belated efforts to restrict somewhat the meaning of many ways to socialism.

In a revolutionary situation halfway measures are rarely successful. Gero's appointment could not satisfy the masses which were by then craving a *political* reform, an implementation of the alternative which seemed not only feasible but even blessed with a Soviet endorsement. To the uninitiated, the ostensible Soviet policy indeed appeared to call for something rather like Nagy's program. Anti-Stalinism and greater diversity — that seemed to be the meaning of the Twentieth Congress and the June declaration. Gero's appointment thus appeared more and more to be an attempt to hold back the clock, especially since he could hardly acknowledge publicly Mikoyan's sponsorship. Tito's unmistakable distaste for him further intensified this impression.* The new First Secretary, given the unenviable and possibly unpleasant task of reforming Rakosi's legacy, found himself operating without a clear-cut conception of what his policy or even its basic assumptions ought to be. Moscow itself at this stage apparently lacked such precise notions. In Hungary the practical consequence of such a state of affairs was that ideology, in the sense of a Communist program of action, was firmly in the hands of the opposition.

All of this left Gero to rely entirely on the institutions of power. But these too were rapidly slipping away. The Rakosi period had accumulated the hostility, had created an antithesis which linked the masses and a majority of the party in opposing anything short of Nagy's return. Gero was left with the secret police, the army, and, ultimately, the Soviet occupying forces. The opposition, lacking formal organization,† could counter with a popular program, the passionate loyalty of most party and nonparty intellectuals (a group traditionally important in Hungarian struggles for freedom), the students, increasing numbers of urban proletarians, and the passive support of the vast majority of the peasantry. The party was particularly demoralized by the return from imprisonment of a large number of party members, purged and mistreated by Rakosi.

The subsequent three months were spent in continued agitation by the opposition and in desperate efforts by Gero to consolidate his

* It was to overcome Tito's objections to Gero that Mikoyan flew from Budapest to Yugoslavia and held urgent consultations with Tito, Kardelj, and Rankovic. Tito, however, remained unconvinced and did not change his attitude until after his two meetings with Khrushchev in September. For references to the Mikoyan meetings, see *Borba,* July 23 and 24, 1956.

† According to Hungarian Interview No. 563 (a former well-informed Communist official), Nagy's supporters were divided on the issue of whether to organize some sort of an opposition nucleus. "One wing of the Imre Nagy camp, though not Imre Nagy himself, attempted to organize an illegal Party organization. But Losonczy, Donath, and Ujhelyi opposed this and said that they would not join any such organization. Thus the organization remained somewhat casual, an organization based on friendships, with a very well developed grapevine . . . There was a chain linked together by close friendships, the first with the second, the second with the third, etc., which functioned very well at all times except during the Revolution. During such stormy events stronger organization was needed; then the Imre Nagy group fell apart into its component elements, each of which went his own way. This was because Imre Nagy's friends were intellectual anarchists and were unable to organize because there was not one organizer in the whole group. There were only publicists, orators, and national Weltschmerz artists (*vilagfajdalmas*). They got along very well with Imre Nagy. Nagy likes to philosophize and these people liked to talk and talk . . ." (p. 74).

position. He was granted Soviet financial credit,[42] and, together with the Soviet leaders, actively campaigned for Tito's endorsement. A number of concessions were announced,* and even a macabre re-interment of Rajk's remains staged. This gesture, however, backfired since it gave the opposition an opportunity to emphasize dramatically in human terms the abyss which divided the regime from the people. The popular pressure continued to mount, and at this juncture Moscow apparently advised further concessions. Early in October Gero and Kadar visited the Kremlin and talked to the Soviet officials most directly involved in Hungarian matters, Suslov and Mikoyan.[43] Within a few days of their return, Nagy's reinstatement in the party was announced. Paralleling similar trends in Poland, this must have seemed, even to the most devoted Stalinists, as an indication of imminent triumph for Nagy, and in politics nothing is more likely to assure victory than the apparent inevitability of victory. Cries for his return to power came from all sides.

The army was in a growing state of demoralization. In July, Gero expelled from the party the discredited and hated former Minister of Defense, Farkas. In October Farkas was arrested, following the rehabilitation of several generals previously hanged. Political indoctrination, in all the confusion over the prevailing line, came to a standstill, while the release of imprisoned officers placed in an awkward position those incumbents who had been promoted to replace the arrested commanders. Increasingly, the officer corps and the military cadets identified themselves with the restless intellectuals, even going so far as to take part in the discussion clubs.[44]

The Hungarian revolution began when it appeared that the most important of the remaining two props for Gero's regime was no longer willing to support him. Gomulka's accession to power in Poland, reported in the Hungarian press and radio as an event of "historic significance," was widely interpreted to mean that the USSR was not willing to use force to prevent the removal of Stalinist, or neo-Stalinist, leaders and their replacement by known national Communists backed by the people. At this late stage the literally last-minute October 23 announcement that Tito had finally been per-

---

* The role of the National Assembly was to be increased, and interpellation and recall of deputies introduced, although the parliamentary model was explicitly rejected (*Szabad Nep*, July 28, 1956). Officials, including ministers, were obligated to give instant attention to matters raised by deputies and to receive them immediately (Radio Budapest, September 5, 1956). People forced to leave the frontier zone next to Yugoslavia were allowed to return (Radio Budapest, August 25, 1956), and terror generally abated.

suaded to give Gero his endorsement and that a Yugoslav delegation would visit Budapest to repay the visit which Gero paid to Belgrade on October 15 had lost all its meaning. What Khrushchev had pleaded for with Tito at Sochi (see preceding chapter) came too late. Infuriated by Gero's unwillingness to resign, the crowds started to move, and the shots fired by Gero's only remaining source of support, the secret police, sparked the accumulated tension into fury. Gero's new policy was not in time, offered too little, was burdened with too much bitterness, and appeared to lack not only Hungarian but also Soviet support. The controlled transition failed.

SOVIET RESPONSE

The violence in Budapest put some hard dilemmas before the Soviet leadership. Its acceptance of Gomulka's leadership in Poland, a consideration almost causally related to the Hungarian upheaval, was apparently made on the spur of the moment and with some misgivings, and probably without unanimity in the CPSU Presidium (see next chapter). In Budapest, during the night of October 23, Nagy had been selected by the Hungarian Central Committee, apparently acting without Soviet advice and in desperation, to be the new Premier, although Gero remained First Secretary. In the course of the same night a member of the Hungarian Politburo, G. Marosan, at that time considered to be an anti-Stalinist, a former Social Democrat and only recently released from Rakosi's prison, appealed on the Politburo's behalf for direct Soviet military aid. Clearly, he could have done so only in the name of defending the regime (which now included Nagy*) against the "counterrevolution." The Soviet authorities probably felt that they had no alternative but to intervene, and were probably so inclined in any case since nipping an outbreak in the bud was preferable to dealing with a widespread revolution.

But once the intervention began, it was not clear against whom it was directed. The government was nominally headed by Nagy, the party still by Gero. Nagy continued to appeal for order, promising to follow "a Hungarian road corresponding to our own national characteristics in the building of socialism," [45] while Kadar, more acceptable than Gero as a public spokesman for the party, appealed for vigilance against the "counterrevolutionaries." On October 25 he replaced Gero and joined Nagy in appealing for order, promising

---

* The appeal was formally made in Nagy's name. On October 31 he denied that he had made the request, and after the revolution's suppression Marosan publicly took credit for it.

magnanimity to the rebels and assuring the people that Hungarian-Soviet relations would be reviewed. Thus, strangely enough, a disavowed revolution was being suppressed by Soviet troops who were protecting a regime which the revolutionaries were striving to set up.

To the Soviets, the situation must have appeared perplexing but still not entirely out of hand. Most of the violence was concentrated in Budapest. The Hungarian Army, however, remained largely neutral and did not participate on a large-scale or in an organized fashion on either side.[46] Indeed, the Defense Ministry was still under the control of officers loyal to the Soviets, and the chief of staff was able to manipulate the disposition of the troops so as not to help the rebels.[47] The Communist Party leadership, despite the fall of the Rakosi clique and the return of Nagy, still contained people like Kadar or Marosan — the latter had called in the Soviet troops and the former had applauded the Soviet intervention on October 24. At the same time, however, the Soviet participation in the fighting had provoked a state of unrest in Poland, and Polish and Yugoslav messages of sympathy addressed to Nagy and Kadar on October 28 were urging a stop to the bloodshed. Both messages were clear-cut endorsements of the Nagy government which on October 27 was reconstituted to admit several prominent non-Communists, such as Bela Kovacs and Zoltan Tildy. In brief, the situation was too fluid to be viewed with equanimity; but was it sufficiently extreme to warrant an intervention?

The position adopted at this stage by the USSR was highly ambiguous and probably reflected deep-seated uncertainties and conflicts within the Soviet leadership. On October 28 Nagy negotiated a cease-fire, and Soviet troops began to pull out of Budapest on the following day. In the meantime, Suslov and Mikoyan flew to Budapest to reconnoiter the situation. The Soviet press adopted the line that a counterrevolutionary *putsch* in Hungary had been suppressed jointly by the Hungarian government and the Soviet Army, claiming that it had been a foreign provocation, and indicated that Nagy and Kadar were the legitimate government, supported by the USSR. According to one source, on October 29 Mikoyan promised Zoltan Tildy that all Soviet troops would be withdrawn shortly.[48]

It was probably in keeping with this hopeful assessment that the October 30 Soviet declaration, "On Friendship and Cooperation between the Soviet Union and Other Socialist States," was issued. The declaration was obviously designed to prevent a Hungarian defection from the Soviet bloc and to define the new conditions created by the events in Poland and Hungary. The declaration asserted that "the countries of the great commonwealth of socialist nations can build their relations only on the principle of full equality, respect for territorial integrity, state independence and sovereignty, and noninterference in the domestic affairs of one another." [49] Attempting to dissociate the USSR from Stalinism, it admitted that these principles had been violated, offered to re-examine economic relations prevailing between the USSR and the Communist states and to recall all Soviet economic and military advisers (always a source of major nationalist irritation). In effect, the declaration was no less than a belated equivalent of Khrushchev's earlier speech on Stalinism in domestic Soviet affairs.

The declaration then went on to state that the USSR was willing to consider withdrawing its troops from the territory of any member of the Warsaw Pact which so desired but with the following significant stipulation:

In this, the Soviet government proceeds from the principle that the stationing of troops of one member state of the Warsaw Treaty on the territory of another member state of the Warsaw Treaty takes place on the basis of an agreement between all its participants and not only with the agreement of that state, on the territory of which, at its request, these troops are stationed or are planned to be stationed. [50]

This was the last attempt to hold to the line developed in the June 1956 agreement with Tito. It was immediately followed by a Chinese statement, hailing the declaration, reasserting the "five principles," characterizing Polish and Hungarian demands as "entirely proper," and condemning "chauvinism by a big country." [51] (For fuller treatment of the Chinese approach, see Chapter 12.) Nagy's regime thus seemed to have won the endorsement of international Communism.

The tragedy of Nagy's government, however, was that the anti-Rakosi coalition could not stay together once the Rakosi clique had fallen. A great many of the rebels, recalling Rakosi's return to power in 1955 and emboldened by Soviet hesitations, wanted to make absolutely certain that definite institutional guarantees would prevent the return of a dictatorship. They called for a multiparty government. Others distrusted Nagy, especially because of the ambiguous position he was forced into by the events of October 23–28, the date of the announcement of the Soviet withdrawal. All were embittered by the Soviet intervention and called for the complete pull-out of Soviet troops. Nagy in this manner was pushed more and more toward a fundamental revision of the political order along the lines of social democracy.

To those Soviet leaders advocating forceful suppression, the October 30 declaration might have provided the necessary breathing space for deployment of Soviet troops and for taking stock of the situation. In fact, large-scale Soviet troop movements did begin on that day, thereby casting doubts on the sincerity of the declaration. However, events in Hungary itself were strengthening the position of those in Moscow who favored a policy of force. On October 30 a multiparty system was restored and a "revolutionary military council" set up to by-pass the still inactive army command. In addition, even while Mikoyan and Suslov were conferring in Budapest in an attempt to get a firsthand feel of the situation, Nagy stated (on October 31) that it was not he who had originally requested the Soviet intervention and revealed that he was beginning negotiations for Hungary's withdrawal from the Warsaw Pact.* A day later, Hungary's neutrality was officially proclaimed by Nagy's government. National Communism was openly rejecting allegiance to the Soviet camp.

The final Soviet decision to intervene, facilitated by the Anglo-French attack on Egypt,† was probably made after Suslov's and Mikoyan's return to Moscow, sometime on November 1 or 2. Judging from the hesitant military moves, from published Soviet statements, and from consideration of the highly relevant policy of expediency adopted toward Gomulka, it would appear that until the Suslov-Mikoyan mission, the Soviet leadership, even though increasingly fearful of the revolution's spreading elsewhere, was uncertain how to react and was preparing for several contingencies. Military moves laid the groundwork for an eventual suppression by force, while last-minute political consultations and declarations explored the possibility of accepting Nagy, at least temporarily, provided certain Soviet *desiderata* were met — namely, retention of the dichotomic world image and close political-military ties. As of November, the tone of the Soviet dispatches reporting the Hungarian situation changed sharply, and

---

* According to General Pal Maleter, Mikoyan was informed of this directly on October 31. In response to a question, Maleter stated: "Tildy has informed Mikoyan that we shall repudiate the Warsaw Treaty in any case, and our government demanded that negotiations in this respect begin as soon as possible." Radio Budapest, November 2, 1956.

† The Anglo-French ultimatum to Egypt was issued on October 30, the day of the Soviet statement on relations between Communist states.

emphasis was put on alleged outrages against Communists.* On November 4 Soviet artillery fire signaled the Soviet determination not to permit a neutral and democratic government to replace a Stalinist one. It also marked Nagy's failure to create a stable national Communist government; the bitter legacy of Stalinism made the Hungarian people insistent that their government be truly a national and a democratic one. Budapest, in its tragic hour, became the graveyard for Tito's hopes and Khrushchev's calculations.

The Soviet suppression of the Nagy government in Hungary meant that, in the final analysis, the Kremlin interpreted its agreement with Yugoslavia as not applicable elsewhere, but as something which grew unnaturally out of certain "aberrations" in past relations — particularly the militant 1949 Cominform resolution plotting energetic action against Yugoslavia — and which gradually would dissolve as conditions changed. The ideological agreements, which would pave the way to the fading away of the "objective conditions" for national Communism would in the meantime diminish the most attractive element of Yugoslavia's position: its independent distinctiveness in theory and practice. The latter might even persist, but without the former it would not amount to much more than the restricted conception of peculiarities which Moscow was willing to tolerate in the summer of 1956.

Needless to add, such premises excluded any toleration of national Communism in East Europe, since such tolerance would be unhistorical and reactionary: it would be going against the expected trend of events even in the case of Yugoslavia itself, since, ultimately, it was hoped, Yugoslavia too would shed its distinctive mantle. It follows that acceptance of Yugoslav individuality was not meant to imply a general principle. Major domestic shifts from a common, uniform institutional pattern could be allowed in the post-Stalin phase in order to strengthen the local regimes, but not at the price of their losing sight of the limitations to such diversity. The regimes would have to be extremely careful in maintaining ideological unity precisely because of the post-Stalin adaptations, and ideological unity, still given Moscow's pre-eminence, in itself more than implied a retention of the hierarchical pattern of authority within the camp.

* That these in fact were very few is shown by the indictment delivered against Nagy in 1958. The indictment, with two years' time to prepare it, charged that 239 Communists were killed during his second tenure of office. Considering the atmosphere generated by the Soviet intervention and the bitterness against Rakosi's regime, the number is surprisingly low. Text of indictment in *New York Times*, June 19, 1958.

TITO'S DILEMMA

To Tito, the events in Hungary raised a dilemma. In one sense, they represented the fulfillment of both his hopes and his theoretical notions. Stalinism, as a political and economic system, had decayed, even though at one time it had created some of the preconditions for socialism. Subsequently, it had become a brake to the social progress of the countries involved and was therefore doomed to give way to more "progressive" social forces, with the Yugoslav example being highly relevant. The events in Hungary, and in the USSR, seemed to have taken a course compatible with these notions, although the end result had not been the desirable one. But what attitude should Yugoslavia adopt toward the Hungarian upheaval?

Several alternatives were theoretically open. Tito could approve the Hungarian events *in toto,* condemning both Soviet interventions. This would pit him squarely against Stalinism, making him the open champion of national Communism, but it would have the disadvantage of provoking an immediate isolation from the Soviet bloc, cutting Tito's links with those Soviet leaders, like Khrushchev, whom Tito considered to be anti-Stalinist; he would then be forced to wage the anti-Stalinist struggle purely from the outside, which would be inexpedient tactically and doctrinally. Poland had just gained a measure of autonomy, and Tito was anxious to cultivate relations with it, which a sharp break might well prevent. To approve the first Soviet intervention of October 23 and to condemn the second would have made little sense, since it was on October 23 that Nagy came to power and set up a Communist regime basically compatible with Tito's aims. Once the first intervention was approved, there would be even more reason for approving the second. But Tito could not approve both Soviet interventions, since such approval would have meant that Titoism no longer existed and would have sanctioned similar moves against Poland. Tito might have considered intervening himself in order to stabilize Nagy and prevent a collapse of the Communist state,[52] but this he could hardly do without Soviet approval. And to intervene, in effect, on behalf of the USSR would obviously be pointless.

The alternative that was finally adopted, to disapprove of the first Soviet intervention and to approve the second, was worked out gradually as events developed and was clearly designed to promote the continued Yugoslav purposes insofar as the entire Soviet camp was concerned. It had been for the sake of these purposes that Tito finally agreed early in October, in response to Khrushchev's urgent pleas, to back Gero, with the subsequent tragic effect of emboldening Gero on his return from Belgrade on October 23 to take such an intransigent stand. On October 28 Yugoslavia voted in the UN Security Council against placing the Hungarian matter on the agenda; on October 30 Belgrade made its appeal to the Hungarians to stop the fighting and prevent "reactionaries" from exploiting the situation;[53] on November 4 Yugoslavia abstained twice from voting in the UN on the resolution calling for the withdrawal of Soviet troops from Hungary. In his actions Tito appeared to be motivated by a form of dialectical reasoning. The Hungarian events, even if the Soviet intervention had set the clock back somewhat and had encouraged the Stalinists, still represented a revolutionary advance in the direction of the disintegration of Stalinism. In the struggle against Stalinism, which was bound to be lengthy, the Leninist principle of one step back and two steps forward had to be applied. Even the program of the new Kadar regime, which seemed to accept many of the policies of Nagy,[54] appeared to be a step forward from the policies of Gero which the Yugoslavs had endorsed on October 23. To prevent the Stalinists from gaining the upper hand, Khrushchev in Russia and Kadar in Hungary ought to be encouraged.

In order to keep Yugoslavia operating within the bloc, Tito was thus prepared to take a small step back: to sacrifice Nagy's national Communism as premature and "reactionary," and to sacrifice Nagy personally as an inconvenient impediment to the higher goals of Yugoslavia's policy. On November 21 an agreement was reached with Kadar which paved the way for the end of Nagy's embarrassing — and symbolic — sanctuary in the Yugoslav Embassy. While his arrest on leaving the Embassy was violently protested,[55] it did not lead to any serious political consequences. One can even sense a certain feeling of relief in Belgrade that an incumbrance had been jettisoned. Nonetheless, since the Hungarian revolution had produced major misgivings among Yugoslav Communists and since subsequent conduct might have clouded the clarity of Yugoslavia's position, Tito felt compelled to define his policy in the face of the new circumstances and categorically to state again that Titoism was available for export precisely because of Yugoslavia's behavior. His major address delivered on November 11 at Pula revealed once more the cross-purposes involved in the Tito-Khrushchev cooperation. Tito reiterated the Yugoslav belief that the Belgrade and Moscow declarations had been meant for the relations of all Communist states, expressed regret that Moscow, particularly since Poznan, was unwilling to interpret them that way, and suggested that the Soviet unwillingness might be due to lack of confidence in the stability of the People's Democracies once autonomy is granted them. Tackling the Hungarian question, Tito condemned as "absolutely wrong" the first Soviet intervention but, maintaining the balance so necessary to his purposes, he gave qualified endorsement to the second Soviet intervention as a bad thing which might turn into something good. He quite bluntly criticized Nagy for not offering "decisive resistance to the reactionaries" instead of calling "the people to arms against the Soviet Army and [appealing] to the Western countries to intervene." [56] His condemnation of the fallen leader of Hungarian national Communism was coupled with unqualified praise for the new Soviet-imposed Kadar regime ("I know these people in the new Government and . . . they, in my opinion, represent that which is most honest in Hungary." [57]) Tito then noted that because Kadar's popularity had been undermined by the Soviet intervention, the Yugoslavs must give him backing.[58] To Tito, Kadar seemed to resemble Gomulka more than he did Rakosi.*

Tito's speech was a compromise designed to keep his influence in the Soviet bloc (most particularly with Khrushchev, Gomulka, and Kadar) while continuing the struggle against Stalinism and remaining the champion of new conceptions for relations among Communist states. Much of his position was based on the belief that within the Soviet leadership a split existed between Khrushchev and a Stalinist faction, and that a sharp break would undermine Khrushchev's position. However, at this point a compromise solution satisfied no one — for the issues were drawn much too sharply, and the USSR and especially the neighboring Communist regimes violently resented even Tito's qualified censure. What made matters worse, Tito was still acting as if he expected Titoism to be formally accepted as the basis for Soviet-satellite relations and as if he felt himself directly involved in the internal politics of Yugoslavia's neighbors. The June 1956

---

* Tito met Kadar while entertaining Gero and was much impressed by him. He apparently remained convinced that he would be able to influence Kadar's policies, despite the Soviet suppression of Nagy. Marosan, Kadar's close collaborator, states that after the suppression of the revolution the new regime was advised by Belgrade not to reorganize the Party but to put the ill-famed workers' councils . . . into power. They even supported this anti-Marxist and anti-Leninist advice with arguments . . ." (*Nepszabadsag*, July 20, 1958). The Yugoslavs remained hopeful that the new regime would resemble Gomulka's, and they might have also hoped that Nagy, once in Kadar's hands, would help it. It is interesting to note in this connection that some of Nehru's confusion concerning the Soviet intervention in Hungary is explainable in terms of the interpretations supplied him by the Yugoslavs. (See also Chapter 13.)

declaration, the obeisance paid to him, Khrushchev's praise — all had tended to give his views undue weight and, from the Soviet point of view, the time had come to cut Tito down to size. This undertaking was shouldered not only by Moscow itself but with apparent relish by those Communist leaders who had the best reasons for entertaining a strong distaste for him.

The Soviet reply came on November 23 in the form of a lengthy *Pravda* article, entitled "To Consolidate Further the Forces of Socialism on the Basis of Marxist-Leninist Principles." [59] Its tone, in view of the charges made by Tito, was relatively restrained, especially if one considers that the Soviet Union might well have felt that Tito had misled them in pressing for relaxation in East Europe. Without going into too much detail, we may note that the article justified the necessity of the Soviet intervention in Hungary while conceding past mistakes; it accused Nagy of having pursued a two-faced policy; it rejected with greater indignation Tito's allegations about the Soviet system and the cult of personality and finally it passed on to a critique of some Yugoslav aspects. *Pravda* noted critically that the Yugoslav model subsisted on capitalist aid and that such a model could hardly be cited as an example for other socialist states. The statement particularly objected to Tito's propensity to speak authoritatively on matters involving the policies of other Communist parties and suggested that many of the Yugoslav positions showed a marked deviation from "proletarian internationalism." To Belgrade this Soviet inclination to question the virtues of the Yugoslav experience signified, despite *Pravda*'s call for a friendly discussion, a backsliding to the prereconciliation atmosphere. Belgrade accordingly replied that the only way to undo the past was to grant to the socialist states full equality with the USSR, for "basically, there are only two roads: a return to Stalinism or the establishment of democratic relations of equality among socialist states." [60]

At this stage the fray was joined by the other Communist powers. Apart from any Soviet promptings, Tirana, Sofia, and the other satellite leaders had good reason for objecting to Tito. Unlike Gomulka, Tito had clearly demanded that personnel changes be made as a price for his friendship. The satellite leaders now felt themselves released from the restraints imposed on them by the earlier Belgrade-Moscow rapprochement. They sprang into an attack on Tito and, more than that, gradually but inevitably into a vigorous defense of Stalinism. In both, either by design or through personal initiative, they went much further than Moscow. Unlike the concurrent ideological criticisms of

Gomulka's Poland, the attacks on Tito involved an invective reminiscent of former days. Referring to Tito without the usual prefix of "comrade," the organ of the Albanian party accused the Marshal of spreading "anti-Soviet lies" for the benefit of the imperialists and "the bandit Imre Nagy." At the same time, the paper asserted categorically that the Soviet experience of building socialism had a universal applicability.[61] In December, *Pravda* returned to the argument to take issue with the views advanced by Kardelj, who had stated that in the transition stage of building socialism the bureaucratic features of the dictatorship of the proletariat represented a distinct danger to the eventual withering away of the state. Noting sarcastically that the trial of Djilas "does not indicate that the state is withering away in Yugoslavia," *Pravda* accused the Yugoslavs of opposing the two fundamental aspects of Leninism: the dictatorship of the proletariat and the leading role of the party.[62]

Tito's efforts to hold to a middle line and yet preserve his freedom of action thus largely failed, and anti-Titoist positions remained firm in the East European states, except in Poland and, to a much lesser extent, in Hungary, where the situation was still relatively unstable. Even with Khrushchev himself Tito did not re-establish as close a working relationship as that which had existed for a few short months in 1956. But more serious still was Tito's abdication from the appealing posture of a national Communist. His approval of the second Soviet intervention, his condemnation of Nagy, and the unclear circumstances of Nagy's betrayal to the Soviet secret police meant that national Communism ceased to be an absolute principle for Tito but rather a matter of political expediency. The justification of the second intervention opened the way to Moscow's insistence on its own conception of "unity" and deprived Tito of any ideological arguments against it, or even against the later execution of Nagy. An absolute standard is sometimes more effective in critical situations than relative, and hence ambiguous, conceptions.

Tito's original appeal could never be directed toward the majority of the party *apparatchiki* in East Europe since they feared any break with Moscow. His appeal to the intelligentsia, to the Communist intellectuals, even to the working class, was in the name of independent socialism — of national Communism. His ambiguity on the Hungarian issue took away this appeal; he had failed to recognize that in the immediate post-October–November 1956 situation Communism in Europe was ripe for a doctrine of diversity, of national independence, of sovereign socialism. Nagy was destroyed when he tried to raise that standard; Gomulka could not afford to do so; yet the disaffected and revolutionary-minded Communists were seeking such leadership and such an absolute standard. This was Tito's historical opportunity, but his perspectives had been too narrow and too limited by his own doctrines to seize upon it. A bold and uncompromising stand at that juncture might have made Tito a symbol of change, all the more powerful since the climate for such change had been matured by the Twentieth Congress, the June declaration, and the Polish and Hungarian Octobers. But by conceding values higher than freedom or national independence, namely the protection of socialism, Tito in effect justified the tyranny he professed to abhor. Now any Communist regime could declare the urgent need for its subordination to the USSR in the name of "the defense of socialism," and Tito could no longer call this an error in principle.

Hungary hence marked a defeat for true national Communism.[63] National Communism could now be sought by various states only in relative doses, depending on the circumstances, the place, and the timing. And under such conditions, there could be no doubt that the overwhelming interests and political considerations of the Soviet state would be the determining factor. The Soviet regime, even in the most acute anti-Stalinist phase, had made it quite plain that it would insist on the leadership of its party in Communist counsels, on the maintenance of the dichotomic image of the world with all its political consequences, on the necessity of militant "proletarian internationalism." However, the next few years were to show that what could not be won on the field of battle could be quietly gained by gradually expanding the scope of domestic autonomy and priority. If the Hungarian revolt contributed to the drawing of a sharp line between true independence and membership in the Soviet bloc, the events in Poland opened the doors to a redefinition of the meaning of that membership.

11 / THE POLISH OCTOBER:
THE CHALLENGE OF DOMESTICISM

THE most far-reaching change in relations among Communist states was caused by events in Poland. The change lacked the drama of Nagy's withdrawal from the Warsaw Pact or the trauma of the street fighting in Budapest. Yet its significance for the Communist states was, in many ways, greater than that of the Hungarian revolution abruptly crushed by Soviet arms. The Polish developments were the product of an evolving pattern which was difficult for the Soviets at any specific point to interrupt justifiably; because of this the foundations of Stalinist controls in Poland were gradually undermined. Indeed, in contrast to Tito's external expediency and internal dictatorship, it appeared, for a few short months after October 1956, that out of this evolutionary pattern a challenging, new form of Polish Communism, combining internal freedom with external independence, might emerge to raise the standard of national Communism. This eventuality did not come about. Instead, Poland remained a member of the Warsaw Pact and of the Soviet bloc, even though the new domestic practices and doctrines shattered the former institutional and ideological uniformity. How did this pattern develop? What were its implications for relations with Communist states, the USSR in particular?

THE CONTROLLED TRANSITION: A SUMMARY [1]

In Poland, as elsewhere in the bloc, a New Course had been initiated during the Malenkov period. However, the Polish leadership realized that any excessive departures from established policies would immediately bring up the dormant issue of the "right-wing nationalist deviation" of Gomulka, and for this reason its adoption of the New Course was both delayed and more restrained than elsewhere. The extremely cautious character of the initial reforms, while failing to create a much-needed popularity, did not have the immediate effect of stirring up passions and enflaming loyalties. Poland thus avoided the political difficulties which the New Course initiated in Hungary.

The initial reactions of the population, to the extent that they could be perceived, appear to have been a commingling of suspicion, apathy, and only slight relief. It is to be remembered that the New Course was essentially an economic measure, and that in some respects political terror even mounted in Poland after Stalin's death. To many, all this appeared to be merely an application of the old Stalinist technique of balancing political coercion with economic concessions,[2] and this impression was strengthened by the insistence of the party that the new policies were a reflection of its strength — and woe to those who would interpret it otherwise.[3]

Nonetheless, the leadership soon found it impossible to limit the New Course to economic phenomena. Of paramount importance to the expanding scope of the reform was the liquidation in the USSR of Beria and the consequent weakening of the secret police. The pattern of imitation, still applicable in principle, required emulation in Poland — and within the party there were many who felt that the secret police had grown too strong. This feeling was sharpened by one of those felicitous circumstances that shape history: the defection to the West, in December 1953, of one of the most brutal secret policemen, Colonel J. Swiatlo, whose revelations of police tortures, of depravity within the ruling circles, of Soviet control of the whole secret-police apparatus,[4] were broadcast and airdropped by the Free Europe Committee to Poland, much to the consternation of the upper echelons of the party. This brought home to the party itself the fundamental question of any revolution: at what point does the human cost begin to outweigh the revolutionary ideals? The question, answered easily when the cost is paid by "enemies," takes on a different light when party members themselves become victims.

The current diminution in world tensions also meant that the need for domestic vigilance declined, and the party began to feel that the maintenance of a war-Communism atmosphere was a distinct liability. Reflecting this feeling, an article published in the party journal appealed for a two-way dialogue between the party and the nation and criticized the Communist youth organization's concentration on the "unmasking" of anyone who expressed doubts rather than on the intelligent tackling of the more serious problem of "internal emigration" — the passive but hostile withdrawal of the individual from social and political activity.[5] Despite simultaneous warnings against exaggerated departures from the principle of party hegemony, a climate favorable to more outspoken reactions was gradually created, at least within the party. The Swiatlo affair sparked this latent sense of misgiving into an open expression of dissatisfaction at a meeting of the Warsaw central party *actif* in December 1954. In a two-day session, characterized by unprecedented criticisms of conditions within the party, the Politburo for the first time found itself faced by a majority of resentful *apparatchiki*. The existence of the Communist regime itself was not questioned, but the methods of the Politburo were violently condemned. Its leaders were accused of suppressing all initiative within the upper party echelons and of treating the Central Committee as a rubber stamp. The Politburo, taken aback and on the defensive, kept the meeting a secret.[6] Two years later, this episode was described by E. Ochab, Bierut's successor, as having placed the Politburo in actual "isolation." [7]

This isolation forced the leadership to act. On December 7, 1954, much on the Soviet pattern but distinctly more meaningful in the Polish situation, the Ministry of Public Security was replaced by a committee, and, significantly, the former head of the Ministry, S. Radkiewicz, was not appointed to head the committee. The party journal simultaneously took notice of "aberrations" in the work of the Ministry.[8] The matter did not rest there. The Central Committee session of January 21–24, 1955, the third plenum since the preceding party congress, went on record with a much stronger denunciation of the secret police, noting that "with bitterness, with burning pain and shame we learned about facts of brutal violation of people's legality . . . There were cases of arrests of innocent people . . . shameful, inadmissible methods of investigation." [9] The party leadership was condemned, although in more cautious terms, for inadequate control over the secret police, for allowing the "vulgarization" of the concept of the class struggle, and for lack of contact with the lower party organs. It was publicly announced that a high secret police official, Colonel Feigin, was expelled from the party and his chief investigating officer arrested. Much more important, but kept secret, was the quiet release from confinement of Gomulka in December 1954. This act, in effect, meant that the party leadership was implicitly shifting its ground on the interpretation of the Gomulka 1948–1949 heresy: while still an ideological deviation, it was no longer considered treasonous. The first major shift, at the time not perceived as such, thus occurred *within* the party apparatus and Central Committee at the end of 1954 and the beginning of 1955. Undisputed leadership of the Politburo was for the first time challenged and tenuous links established between the restless elements in the party and the discontented populace.

Why was this trend not reversed after Malenkov's fall, as was the case in the analogous Hungarian situation? There is no doubt that the circumstances of Malenkov's removal had shaken the central *actif* in Warsaw a great deal, and Shepilov's article on industrialization in January of 1955 (see Chapter 8) provoked a lively debate, with some advocating immediate implementation but with the majority adopting a somewhat independent, critical position.[10] The party leadership took a middle ground, adopting the new Moscow line but justifying the Polish concessions as temporary expedients. At the March Plenum it again adopted an equivocal stand, praising both collectivization and industrialization but not disowning its moderate New Course. This constituted an important step in the direction of restoring the primacy of domestic considerations, something unthinkable a year before.

However, under the circumstances, there was little else the leadership could have done unless it was willing, despite the misgivings of its own central *actif*, to reimpose violent Stalinist terror and a radical "leftist" policy. Such a program, in turn, would have forced the leaders to increase further their dependence on Moscow, which no one seemed to desire. From the standpoint of the Kremlin, the Polish regime under Bierut and Berman could not be more loyal, and the only real alternative to them was Gomulka. No repetition of the Hungarian case was hence involved. Active intervention to turn back the clock would not have been in keeping with the prevailing Soviet line on Yugoslavia, the international situation, or Khrushchev's emerging notions on voluntarily loyal regimes.

In this manner, the Polish leadership, not beset by internal splits, became gradually committed to a policy of relaxation which was welcomed by the party membership and the people as a whole. The party still recalled the 1938 fate of the Polish Communist Party, and for this reason many members welcomed any opportunity to diminish the party's dependence on the USSR, provided it did not threaten the regime's survival. Nonetheless, as the new policy developed momentum — more in terms of the general atmosphere than in concrete measures — the former Gomulka line appeared less and less heretical. The soul-searching which became so frequent during this period among party members was also prompted by the fact that the membership contained a high percentage of the "working intelligentsia," including officials. Between 1949 and 1956, they grew from 20.3 per cent of the membership (which remained much the same in total number) to 39.5 per cent, or two out of every five members.[11] By the end of 1956, in the crucial Warsaw area, where 28 per cent of the Polish intelligentsia (those with university education) was concentrated,[12] they accounted for 64.7 of the party membership.[13] While not all of them were dedicated to change, a sufficient number were and could make their influence felt. They pressed for a rejection of the former practice of subjecting all cultural and intellectual activity to strict control, and soon influential party leaders themselves were condemning the "vulgar commandeering" in cultural policy.[14]

In spring of 1955, in a small Warsaw apartment, the first spontaneous, still not illegal, organized activity was launched: an intellectuals' discussion club, given the striking name of the Club of the Crooked Circle.[15] The idea proved very popular: by the fall there were twenty such clubs in Poland; during the winter of 1955–56 about forty; by the spring of 1956 almost sixty; by the summer one hundred and twenty; and by the fall over two hundred. The clubs rapidly became the equivalent of what was still forbidden — namely, political assemblies in which the important issues were debated and attitudes crystallized. From their sessions emerged ideas which gradually reached the populace.*

The clubs and the press (even though the latter was still subject to censorship) in this fashion became the breeding ground for a political line which went appreciably beyond the restrained official adaptations of Stalinism. Already as far back as March 1955, some party stalwarts, like W. Mach, felt compelled to denounce various "cultural subversives" who were accused not only of rejecting socialist realism but also "People's Poland." [16] In spite of this, the same literary weekly which had published the denunciations soon published the sensational and bitter poem by Adam Wazyk, "An Ode to Adults," since translated into many languages, which represented a courageous attack on the hypocrisy of the system. By late 1955 and throughout 1956, the Polish writers were asserting with increasing vigor the priority of artistic criteria over political requirements and heaping scorn on the "socialist realists." † Even otherwise loyal party members went so far

* For the history of one such club, founded by the graduate students of Cracow University and given the "revolutionary" name of The Club of the Flaming Tomato, and particularly for its activities with respect to the Polish October, see the account in *Tygodnik Powszechny*, October 13, 1957, written by one of the participants. It gives an unusually good insight into the role of the club, the gradual expansion of the scope of its activities, the formation of a mass club, called "Spring 56," to organize broad activities, and finally the last-minute preparations on the eve of the dramatic change-over in October 1956. See also sources cited in note 15.

† In the spring of 1956, the Session of Culture and Science criticisms turned into a veritable flood. The statements uttered at the session were striking, especially if one considers that Poland was still under the control of a Soviet-anointed leadership headed by Bierut and Berman. A. Slonimski, a well-known literary figure, is on

as to reject the Leninist precepts of "partyness" in arts.[17]

After Khrushchev's speech on Stalin in February 1956, the discussions in Poland mounted in intensity and the balance of forces shifted rapidly. The party dogmatists were clearly on the defensive. The void created by the destruction of Stalinism and by violent Polish attacks on Stalin himself led many of those who had previously embraced Marxism to search for some sort of individual statement of beliefs, for a self-defined frame of reference. This was particularly true of the young Marxists who now felt deceived by the past. In their quest they frequently combined a residue of Marxist concepts with hitherto-rejected idealism, humanism, and Polish nationalism. Imitation of the USSR was condemned for having stifled "independence, creative thought and initiative," which could only flourish with a "Polish way to socialism." [18] National feelings were extolled as the highest expression of dedication to the people, and national sovereignty was held up as the only basis for the construction of socialism. The dogmas of the past were now to be replaced by a genuine search for the humanist values of socialism, and one writer went so far as to suggest that the slogan "proletarians of all lands" is meaningless and should give way to a statement of common human aspirations.[19] No wonder that the party ideologue in social sciences, A. Schaff, mused sadly:

> We have to admit that in the broad circles of the intellectuals, the authority of Marxist ideology has been undermined. It is not a question of some hostility of the intellectuals toward Marxism, but rather a matter of continuing and serious errors committed by the Marxist camp in the conduct of science and in the ideological struggle.[20]

In this evolutionary pattern, the theoretical basis for the old regime was being washed away. At the same time the working class was brought into the orbit of these discussions, especially in certain key Warsaw factories to which party activists with advanced training had been assigned to supervise party work. These activists, drawn into the activities of the clubs, frequently became the links between the ideological discussions and those who theoretically were the backbone

record in the proceedings of the meeting as declaring that the decline of art began with the 1936 Congress of Soviet Writers: "It was then that Zhdanov, basing himself on the lightheaded opinions of Gorky and utilizing his literary standing, created the theses of socialist realism and handed out this precise instrument for the destruction of the arts to the bureaucrats who with satisfaction and application sharpened the fear, carried on for twenty years this destructive process." For fuller treatment, see my "Communist Ideology and Power: From Unity to Diversity," *Journal of Politics*, November 1957.

of the socialist state. In the factories, where there were many workers with prewar socialist traditions to provide the necessary leadership, the newly recruited proletariat responded sympathetically to the intellectual currents which seemed to offer an explanation of why the Stalinist oppression had taken place, how it could be overcome, how the workers, alienated from the regime, could begin to feel themselves the owners of the state. Through ideology the movement for change began to create an underpinning of potential power.

THE PARALYSIS OF EVOLUTION

The international policy of the USSR and Soviet domestic developments provided precedents in favor of liberalization. Up to the time of the Twentieth Congress it might have seemed possible to the leaders in Warsaw that a policy of gradual adjustment would ultimately strengthen the regime by reducing accumulated tension. In late 1955, the party's theoretical journal, while still defending past policies against "nihilist criticisms" and asserting that the Poles could learn much from Soviet experience, stressed editorially the need for more attention to the particulars of the Polish situation in the construction of socialism. This bow to domesticism was a halfhearted effort to arm the regime with a doctrinal justification more in keeping with the new situation. At no point, however, was the full authority of the party thrown against the developing ferment. The Communist intellectuals were therefore not immediately brought face to face with the old Stalinist equation: either with us or against us. Had they been, it is conceivable that some would not have traveled the tortured journey to a rejection of the dogma. Instead, the party attempted a policy of gradual adjustment and occasional warnings. Events, however, outstripped the Warsaw leadership. The Twentieth Congress had undermined the ideological premises of the regime, and these difficulties were suddenly compounded by the unexpected death, on March 12, 1956, of the firmly implanted Stalinist head of the party, Boleslaw Bierut.

Bierut's death, unsettling as it must have been, served in a way further to reassure Moscow that the situation was relatively well in hand. Khrushchev personally flew to Warsaw, vetoed Roman Zambrowski, an *apparatchik* of essentially Stalinist orientation, who was the Politburo candidate for the post of First Secretary, on the grounds that his Jewish origin would alienate the Poles, and sponsored the candidacy of another reputed Stalinist, Edward Ochab, a leading figure in the anti-Gomulka drive.[21] Ochab's selection, on March 20, had the effect of assuring Moscow that, as in Czechoslovakia or East Germany, a loyal regime was established in Poland and that the newly legitimized theory of many ways to socialism would be interpreted by Ochab in keeping with the broad interests of the Soviet bloc. In late April this impression seemed to be confirmed by Ochab's article in the Soviet press branding critics of his regime as "petty bourgeois" elements guilty of "opportunism and nationalism." [22] A week earlier, in a sharp speech to the Warsaw *actif*, he had reiterated: "We can assure our Soviet brethren that no machinations of imperialist adventurers, remnants of reaction, will weaken the alliance and eternal friendship between People's Poland and the Soviet Union." [23] Ochab also asserted that Gomulka's condemnation for nationalism had been fully justified although, significantly, he conceded that the party leadership had gone too far in interpreting deviation as equivalent to treason.[24] Ochab's leadership and his avowed loyalty to the Soviet conceptions thus helped to allay the Kremlin's apprehensions concerning internal Polish developments.

Even so, events were moving rapidly toward eliminating the most objectionable aspects of the Stalinist legacy. Gomulka's earlier release was for the first time officially confirmed. In April an amnesty for some thirty thousand prisoners, including nine thousand political, was announced and, in early May, Berman was divested of his posts. His removal was the most important feature in a series of governmental shifts which had already resulted in the dismissal of the Minister of Justice, the Prosecutor General, and the Chairman of the State Security Committee. With Bierut dead and Berman discharged, only Minc was left of the old triumvirate which had implemented the Stalinist patterns in Poland.

"We must free the people from the fear of making decisions," declared the Prime Minister, Jozef Cyrankiewicz,[25] and to make this possible many of the functions formerly controlled by the secret police, such as prisons, border control, and internal police troops, were transferred to the Ministry of the Interior, while the state security staff was cut by 22 per cent, not counting those transferred.[26] Following a series of published attacks on the trade unions, it was announced that the Central Trade Union Council had decided to abolish the practice of confidential reports on employees and that all existing records would be destroyed.[27] The Sejm (the Polish Parliament) was publicly ridiculed in the party papers for voting unanimously on all issues,[28] and it was conceded that "socialist democracy can have certain aspects in common with parliamentary democ racy." [29] This intellectual and political relaxation could not avoid impinging on economic matters. The most important manifestation of the new spirit was the criticism to which the views on the primacy of producer-goods output, restated so firmly by Shepilov in 1955, were subjected at the Congress of Polish Economists in early June 1956. For the first time it was openly stated that the Polish standard of living had declined in preceding years. Reforms, departing from the established Soviet pattern, were demanded. In addition, even in the party journal, voices were raised against the rigid antikulak line of the regime, and a more elastic approach, which would ensure the level of productivity, was demanded. [30]

All of this, even if followed with growing apprehension in Moscow, did not seem to call for direct Soviet involvement. Unlike Hungary, the pattern of gradual change was not interrupted, nor did it develop a revolutionary character. Even in retrospect it is difficult to find that particular moment when the Soviet leadership might have felt that its active intervention was justified. True, the Twentieth Congress was followed by an extremely intense outburst in Poland. But the Polish leadership still appeared to be in control of the situation and, like Ulbricht in East Germany, was setting a sharp anti-Stalinist tone to the debates. [31] From a dialectical point of view, the developments could have easily been interpreted as a necessary stage which would eventually lead to a firmer political future of Communism in Poland. The absence of a top-level party split during this period, the moderation of the regime's reforms, and the slowly evolving character of the change thus obscured the growing contradictions within the regime and failed to create a clear-cut situation justifying, in Soviet eyes, a direct Soviet intervention. It was also at this point that Yugoslavia seemed to be on the brink of rejoining the Communist camp, and Khrushchev's relations with Tito appeared closer, on a personal as well as a political plane, than with any other foreign Communist leader.* On the Polish side, Ochab and his associates, while possibly uneasy, had no reason to desire Soviet interference, and it may be surmised that they assured Moscow that the situation was well in hand. The formal rehabilitation of the Polish Communist Party, announced after the Twentieth Congress, gave the Polish Communists a new sense of dignity, and direct Moscow involvement in the summer of 1956 seemed unnecessary and "unhistorical."

---

* From the perspective of later quarrels and mutual incriminations, it is hard to imagine the joyful 1956 scene of Tito, Mrs. Tito, and Khrushchev walking down the streets of Moscow, hand in hand, licking ice-cream cones.

GOMULKA AND POWER

The situation was changed by Poznan. The late June workers' uprising, suppressed only through the use of the army,* signaled that the ferment had reached the working classes, smarting under oppressive labor conditions. However, the initial reaction of the Polish regime, while panicky, was quite firm and did not appear to require direct Soviet backing. Cyrankiewicz characterized the events as a foreign counterrevolutionary plot, while both Tito and Togliatti praised the firmness of the regime's response.[32] Although possibly both of them were anxious at the time to prevent an active Soviet reversal of the Polish trends,[33] their statements and the initial official Warsaw reaction undercut whatever grounds a Soviet intervention might have had, not to speak of its likely consequences for Khrushchev's domestic position or his broader policies.

The Soviet Union, probably reflecting also the prevailing uncertainties in the CPSU leadership, accordingly adopted a policy of indirect pressure which under Stalin had usually proved effective. Such response was also much more in keeping with the prevailing Soviet-Yugoslav amity and the adjustments then being effected in Hungary. However, it is apparent that the Poznan events were viewed with gravity in Moscow and that the Soviet leaders became more apprehensive about divisive tendencies within the bloc. A lengthy *Pravda* statement was issued to warn against the intrigues of those who "think that if such international working class organizations as the Comintern or the Cominform have ended their activity, then international solidarity is weakening and contacts among fraternal revolutionary parties, adhering to positions of Marxism-Leninism, are being destroyed." While conceding that "transition to socialism in various countries would not be exactly the same," the paper reminded all Communists concerned that ultimately they "are moving *toward one* goal, toward Communism. It is impossible to move separately or haphazardly toward such a great goal." [34]

It was with this message that a Soviet delegation, headed by Bulganin and Zhukov, traveled to Poland a week later, ostensibly to

* The use of the army had disastrous consequences on the morale of the military This writer, visiting Poland one year after the Poznan events, had occasion to observe the deep sense of shame prevailing among the military that they had allowed themselves to be used against their own workers and countrymen. In a published discussion about the October 1956 events, held on its first anniversary, the weekly *Nowa Kultura* (October 20, 1957) cites a colonel of the Polish Army as saying that the use of the military against the workers prompted widespread discussions among the officers and men and brought them closer to the developing ferment.

commemorate the founding of the Communist regime but also to attend the Seventh Plenum of the Central Committee, summoned in the wake of the Poznan outbreak. The message, stressing unity and the need for vigilance, appeared particularly timely since the Poles, once Poznan ceased to be an immediate threat, had shifted their position somewhat and were inclined to replace the "conspiracy" interpretation with admissions that the workers had had justifiable grievances. Arriving in Poland at the time of Mikoyan's sudden flight to see Tito, presumably with a similar message, the leaders of the Soviet delegation stressed the need for unity in the face of hostile efforts to exploit the post-Twentieth Congress atmosphere. "Every country should go its own way to socialism, but we cannot permit this to be used to break up the solidarity of the peace camp, and certainly not under the pretext of respecting national peculiarities or extending democracy," the Soviet premier warned.[35] Simultaneously, in the old-fashioned carrot-and-stick pattern, Bulganin offered to provide Poland with $25 million of consumer goods to alleviate the most acute shortages.[36]

Bulganin's warnings and gifts were somewhat belated. The former solidarity of the Polish leadership, already strained by the period of relaxation and by Bierut's death, was split by the impact of the Poznan violence. The Seventh Plenum, held in late July, became the forum for heated debate. Its official transcript was never published, but the broad outlines of its proceedings leaked out.[37] On the basis of what has become known, the stereotyped division of the "softs" (or liberals), favoring the return of Gomulka, and the "hards," recommending Stalinism, does not appear justified. The picture was much more complex. Everyone involved realized that a crucial factor in the deliberations was Poland's relations with the USSR — that this was the source of the mass demand for democratization and change, as Polish independence euphemistically came to be known. But if Poland were to change its relationship with the USSR, what would happen to socialism in Poland, that is, what would happen to the Polish Communists?

The recommended solutions basically went along two lines, but both in effect skirted the problem of Polish-Soviet relations. The first, advocated by a wing which came to be known as the Stalinist or Natolin* faction, and after October 1956 labeled as "dogmatist," favored the following measures: (1) closest possible external identification with the USSR, a policy bound to intensify domestic tension; (2) restraints on the press to cut down the literary ferment; (3) no

* Natolin is a small palace near Warsaw where the faction held its conclaves.

major change in agrarian policy and the class struggle; (4) limitation of the number of Jews in posts which are much in the public eye; (5) release of Cardinal Wyszynski; (6) 50 per cent wage increase; and (7) inclusion of Gomulka in the Politburo. It is apparent that the last four were demagogic devices designed to win popular support. In a way, the whole program was an effort to pursue some of the essentials of Stalinism but without Stalinist methods. A corollary of this was the advocacy of rejecting such well-known Stalinists as Berman. Gomulka's inclusion, particularly, would give the regime a much-needed symbol, thereby making up for the unpopularity of the first recommendation. At the same time, Gomulka would not be able to chart the regime's course, since he would be merely appended to the existing leadership and would be expected to disown his past nationalism.

The opposing line was taken by those who stressed that changes in Poland must continue in the direction of institutional reform, both political and economic, designed to liberalize the system, particularly in terms of personal freedom and legality. They may be described as "evolutionists" or, as some of them became known, "revisionists." This group rejected all of the recommendations cited above, either as being demagogic in character (this applied particularly to numbers four and six), or as being devices to avoid substantive change. Paradoxically, it seems that some members of this more liberal wing hesitated about Gomulka's restoration since they apparently feared that such restoration, combined with domestic reform, might strain Polish-Soviet relations too much. They accordingly went to some pains at the Seventh Plenum to dissociate themselves from Gomulka's alleged 1948–1949 nationalism.* At this stage, the group appeared to lack a crystallized program of action. Favoring change, its main source of cohesion was opposition to the Natolin program. Internally, the evolutionists were themselves split into at least two broad orientations. Some of them, particularly the former socialists and some of the intellectuals, saw in the movement for change the harbinger of a fundamental step toward social democracy. Others, and this particularly applied to the *apparatchiki* in the Politburo, men like Zambrowski and Ochab (they came to be known as the Pulawska group, from the street where they held their meetings), recognized that a return

---

* This fear allowed the "dogmatists" to accuse their opponents, at the plenum which brought Gomulka to power, of anti-Gomulka attitudes and to demand that the record of the Seventh Plenum be published. Wiktor Klosiewicz, the Trade Union leader and a very effective demagogue, was particularly outspoken on this score.

to the past was out of the question but had no desire to yield the party's dictatorship. They acknowledged, however, that the party would have to adopt some bold measures if its domination was to be perpetuated. Both groups agreed that, whatever the future course of the party might be, Polish-Soviet relations and Gomulka's role in the party were the top issues on the leadership's agenda.*

The Seventh Plenum, which Gomulka was allowed to attend, issued a resolution on July 28 which was liberal in its interpretation of Poznan, promised democratization which would limit both the administrative role of the party and the excessive bureaucratization of society, embodied provisions for an emergency program to improve the standard of living, and foresaw increased opportunities for artisans and small private-service industries. Gomulka's status was left unclarified. Return to anything like the situation before Stalin's death was rejected, but the announced program hardly constituted a satisfactory response to the challenge of the situation.

---

* Gomulka, speaking to a national conference of party activists on November 4, 1956 (Radio Warsaw) after his return to power, confirmed that the divisions between the dogmatists and the evolutionists involved fundamentally the problem of relations with the USSR and that those favoring domestic reforms were not necessarily in favor of his restoration: "The political differences in the leadership of the Party, that is in the Politburo, during the period before the Eighth Plenum and in the Central Committee of the Party, can be reduced to two basic problems: (1) the conception of Poland's sovereignty; and (2) the conception of what should be included in what we call the democratization of our life within the framework of the socialist system.

"Some members of the Central Committee of the Party feared that settling our Party and state relations with the CPSU and the Soviet Union on the principles adopted by the Eighth Plenum would bring unfavorable consequences. While not questioning the need for carrying out certain changes, they were, however, in favor of preserving the previous state of affairs. *This was the main line of division in the leadership of the Party.*

"Differences in the understanding of the context of the democratization of our life were not clear. All the same, they did exist in the leadership of our Party. Irrespective of these basic political differences, there were other problems causing discord in the Party leadership. Among these was the problem of appointments to leading Party and state posts and the question of approaching this problem from the national point of view. Some comrades approached this problem in a very simplified way which could be taken for anti-Semitism.

"In addition to that, before the Eighth Plenum, *many comrades, irrespective of what views they held on problems discussed earlier, differed among themselves on the problem of my return to active Party life.* It was, in this case, a problem not only of my person but of the right evaluation of all phenomena which in the past had been described as right-wing, nationalist deviation from the Party line.

"We can say, comrades, that irrespective of the main line of differences within the Party, there existed in the Party leadership and the actif various other lines of division, which linked some men otherwise divided by the main line of differences." (Italics added.)

Immediately afterwards, Ochab, accompanied by two members of the Natolin group, Zenon Nowak and Franciszek Mazur, flew to Yalta for consultations with Khrushchev. Ochab's position at this stage was ambiguous. Considered a "hard" Stalinist, Ochab apparently adopted a position at the Seventh Plenum which can best be described as middle-of-the-road: refusing to identify himself with the growing demands for a dramatic change and yet unwilling to back the Natolinites. His position was actually closest to that adopted a few days earlier in Hungary and apparently endorsed by Khrushchev. The reasons for it are unclear but it may be surmised that Ochab, recalling his 1949 attacks on Gomulka, may have particularly objected to Gomulka's inclusion in the Politburo and thus found himself siding with the evolutionists who feared the disruptive implications inherent in Gomulka as a symbol of national independence. In any case, the fact that the most openly pro-Soviet faction, which heeded Bulganin's warnings about the Polish press and the need for close unity,* was recommending Gomulka's inclusion in the Polish regime had far-reaching consequences. It seemed to convince the Soviet leaders that Gomulka's return to public life was not a challenge to their position in Poland and could even serve the Soviet interests. Viewed from that perspective it even fit into Khrushchev's categories. This was presumably the message conveyed by Nowak and Mazur, and the result was that during the next crucial three months, the increasing likelihood of Gomulka's inclusion in the leadership did not provoke an immediate Soviet response.

THE REVOLUTIONARY DYNAMIC

The Seventh Plenum merely established a certain pattern; it failed to resolve the problem of Gomulka. Division within the leadership, demoralization within the party, particularly within its youth organization,† and gradual democratization of the system (effected at this stage more by stealth than by design), all contributed to a growing

---

* Its public slogan, repeated at rallies, was designed to appeal to the antiintellectual and anti-Semitic tendencies among the masses: "Two things are responsible for Poland's troubles," they would shout, "the press and the race" (which two words rhyme in Polish).

† A whole chapter could be devoted to the emergence of *Po Prostu* (Speaking Frankly), the journal which became the leading critic of the status quo, and to the disintegration of the party's youth organization. An amazing series of letters from disillusioned youth was published at the time in the various papers. After October 1956, some of the internal discussions, revealing the depth of the crisis within the youth organization, were published in a small volume, *Co sie dzieje w ZMP?* (Warsaw, 1956).

feeling that the Seventh Plenum had not solved the fundamental issues but had merely postponed them. It became plain that the regime had neither a defined sense of purpose nor the capacity to suppress the emerging social diversity. On the other hand, those favoring more profound changes realized that because of the ultimate Soviet backing for the regime, such changes could not be effected without the regime.

Pressures accordingly mounted for reform and, thereby, implicitly for a restatement of the regime's internal and external position. One of the new party Secretaries, Jerzy Morawski, raised the Leninist and timely slogan, "more bread and more freedom." [38] A former socialist who was active in the ruling UPWP after the absorption of the socialists, Julian Hochfeld, while appealing for a reactivation of the Sejm, also attacked the regime's policy of blaming individual secret policemen for past bestialities while not recognizing that a more "fundamental guilt" was involved.[39] (The Supreme Court actually moved to review the sentences against five of them as being too lenient.) [40] The workers, particularly those in the Zeran automobile works near Warsaw,* established links with the metropolitan discussion clubs and raised the slogan of workers' autonomy, demanding the institution of workers' councils.[41] In some places they were set up by *fiat*. Even the issue of the USSR began to come out. One statement called for more frank discussions of Soviet reality, asserting that true friendship cannot be based on sugar-coated paeans,[42] while the youth weekly *Po Prostu* published a sharp criticism of Soviet collectivization policies, making it plain that they could not be applicable to Poland.[43] One of the formerly most violent young Stalinists reminisced in print about his stay in Moscow during the years 1952–1953 and characterized the period with the words "Fascisization, demoralization, careerism." [44] The Warsaw Board of the ZMP (the Polish Young Communist League, literally, the Association of Polish Youth) even made public its demand "for the public release of the contents of the

* In a discussion forum held in 1957 to commemorate the October 1956 events, L. Gozdzik, the young party secretary at Zeran, who had mobilized the workers in favor of change, had this to say: "The Twentieth Congress came. A discussion began. First there was panic in the ranks of the Party . . . we discussed all day and all night . . . we began to reflect. We recalled the days of the October [Bolshevik] Revolution . . . We decided that it would not be bad if a Workers' Council was set up in the factory to administer the enterprise." He added that after the Seventh Plenum he and his colleagues visited Warsaw University and became convinced that everyone wished a change. It was then a simple matter to establish contacts with other plants around Warsaw and throughout Poland. *Nowa Kultura*, October 20, 1957.

talks initiated by the Party leadership with Gomulka after the Seventh Plenum of the Central Committee," [45] thereby confirming the rumored negotiations between the former leader and the present leadership. More and more, Gomulka, even though his current views were not known, was becoming the focal point of the aspirations both of the radical pro-Soviet faction and of the broad circles of intellectuals, youth, and workers backing the evolutionists. Under these circumstances, his attitude became crucial and both sides were soon conducting parallel negotiations with him.

It is still not clear what role was played in the negotiations by Ochab, the First Secretary. By the middle of September, after his return from a trip to Peking, he proceeded to identify himself more actively with the evolutionists and, according to various Warsaw informants, his stand was taken to indicate tacit Chinese encouragement. It is conceivable that at this stage the Chinese favored a quiet redressing of the balance in relations among Communists states and might have encouraged the Poles in that direction. But even without such encouragement, Ochab might well have concluded that Polish Communism had reached a dead-end street and desperately needed a fresh start.

The turning point came early in October. In the first few days of the month, it became known that Gomulka's ideas on collectivization, on the interpretation of the 1949–1954 phase of the Polish regime, and on relations with the USSR diverged so sharply from those of the Natolin dogmatists that no arrangement was feasible. The evolutionists, in the meantime, now including both Cyrankiewicz and Ochab, became convinced that a sharp break with the past was imperative. Realizing that the basic issue on which all reforms would either fall or succeed was the problem of Poland's relations with the USSR, they concluded that only Gomulka, because of his symbolic status, could effectively reshape the external relations without undermining Polish Communism. They reached this conclusion in spite of the fact that, as late as September, some of them, particularly Ochab, still entertained major reservations about Gomulka's past and approved the 1949 condemnation.[46] The arrangement reached with Gomulka prompted the resignation on October 9 of Hilary Minc, the architect of the Stalinist economy in Poland, marking the departure of the last prominent Stalinist. The only outstanding questions left concerned the contents of the new program and the composition of the new Politburo.

These final questions were resolved only as late as the weekend o

October 13–15. On Saturday, Gomulka attended a regular Politburo meeting and, on Monday, agreement on the composition of the new Politburo was reached, according to some reports, in a friendly atmosphere, with Marshal Rokossovsky, slated for removal, even proposing a toast. In the course of the weekend, however, some members of the Natolin group apparently became concerned with the direction of the proposed policy and personnel changes and, outnumbered in the Politburo, turned to Moscow with urgent warnings.[47] In their dispatches they seized on the proposed removal of Rokossovsky as symbolic of the dangerously anti-Soviet character of the developing situation. Clearly in response to their pleas, the Soviet ambassador issued on October 17 a formal invitation to the Poles to visit Moscow for consultations.

However, even at this late juncture, the situation hardly seemed to warrant forceful intervention. The Soviet leaders expected that political pressure would suffice to contain any negative manifestations and that an accommodation could be arranged. The July 1956 situation in Budapest (see Chapter 10), which was resolved by political pressure, still seemed a good guide. But in Poland the situation had suddenly reached a point of no return. The lengthy evolution had run its course and the breaking point was at hand. The Natolinites became convinced that unless they acted quickly they would be completely cut off from power. They accordingly moved forward to do what Rakosi had successfully done in 1955: to stage a coup in the name of greater loyalty to the USSR. They probably reasoned that in the final analysis Moscow would back them, or, at least, would certainly welcome their leadership once they had been successful. They counted on the presence of Soviet troops in Poland to inhibit resistance, while Rokossovsky's control of the Polish Army would assure them the necessary ingredient of power. Furthermore, the provincial party apparatus was firmly in their hands. Unlike Rakosi, however, they no longer controlled the Politburo or the Central Committee; the international situation in the Soviet camp was distinctly unfavorable to them; and, domestically, the masses were already actively ranged against them. Only speed, as well as some intimidation via Moscow, would give them the necessary margin for success.

The Politburo, sensing the implication of the invitation to Moscow, begged off by pleading that the beginning of the scheduled Central Committee plenum, called to implement the recently concluded agreement with Gomulka, precluded their departure. The pro-Soviet faction then decided to move. On the night of October 18, the eve of the historic Eighth Plenum, the Zeran factory workers, who had been mobilized to back the projected changes,[48] intercepted a list of seven hundred people whom the Natolinites wished to arrest. According to the only official information on these events to have come out of Poland, a radio report of the account given the Gdansk party activists by its provincial leaders:

> With the speed of lightning all comrades were warned and not one of them stayed at home. They also prepared pamphlets urging the Army to cooperate, and so forth. These events were followed by the dramatic days of the Eighth Plenum. The security office of Warsaw supported as one man the side of progress. (Applause.) The Internal Security Corps also took the side of progress. (Applause.) In these dramatic days, the Internal Security Corps not only protected the Central Committee but it also occupied the premises of the Polish radio and many other important buildings. Suspicious troop movements started. And again the Zeran workers, who have many cars at their disposal, distributed comrades practically throughout Poland so that our progressive forces in the Central Committee knew all about these troop movements.
>
> The attitude the troops adopted you all know. When orders were issued to staff and political officers, they answered simply that these orders would be ignored. They said that they were with the people and that they would defend the working class.[49]

The domestic resources of the Natolinites thus proved inadequate to the task.[50] What remained to be tested was the degree of Soviet involvement and the capacity of the Poles to resist it.

THE PROBLEMATICS OF INTERVENTION

On October 19 a powerful Soviet delegation, including Khrushchev, Kaganovich, Mikoyan, and Molotov, arrived uninvited in Warsaw, determined to hold the consultations which the Poles had two days earlier declined. Their decision to come was a last-minute one and was not cleared with the Poles beforehand.[51] Simultaneously, according to a member of the Polish Central Committee, Soviet armored troops began to move from their bases near Wroclaw in the direction of Warsaw.[52] The Central Committee's deliberations were suspended, despite some opposition from its more hotheaded members, to permit the Polish leaders to consult with their unexpected visitors. The adjournment was voted following the rapid cooptation to Central Committee membership of Gomulka and three of his associates (Spychalski, Loga-Sowinski, and Kliszko). In addition, Gomulka, whose candidacy for the post of First Secretary was announced by

Ochab himself, was included in the Politburo delegation to negotiate with the Russians.

The course of these negotiations was not made public, although anecdotes as to what actually transpired are plentiful.[53] But even judging from the sparse comments made by the Polish participants, it is clear that at the time the Soviet leaders were principally concerned not with Gomulka's domestic program as such but with its consequences for Polish-Soviet relations. This point is important in considering subsequent relations between Gomulka and Khrushchev because, in effect, the Soviets were *a priori* conceding the Poles' right to build socialism in their own way. This concession, however, came with the proviso that it should not conflict with the broader unity of the Communist camp. Admittedly, such a reservation opened the way to varying interpretations as to what does and does not conflict with such unity and hence, depending on the time and circumstance, might still permit Soviet interference in domestic Polish policies.

The task of the Poles was accordingly twofold: to convince the Russians that domestic concessions planned by the Eighth Plenum were designed to strengthen the construction of socialism in Poland, and that the envisaged policy and personnel changes were meant to improve Polish-Soviet relations. From the Polish point of view, much could be done on this score by the Soviets themselves in view of past "aberrations" imposed by Stalin. That the conversations were tense and sharp was openly admitted by the Polish participants. The atmosphere in which they were conducted was described to the Central Committee by Ochab, during an intermission in the talks on October 19, as "matter of fact." [54] Reporting to the plenum on October 21, after the departure of the Soviet delegation in the early hours of October 20, Ochab referred to the conversations as "sincere, difficult and bitter." [55] He mentioned in passing that never before in his life did he have so much "bitterness" to swallow as in recent days and that "unjustified, unheard-of accusations" were leveled against him by "our Soviet friends." [56] No doubt, the Soviets felt that Ochab's position represented a treasonable departure from what had been assumed to have been an ultraloyal standing. His own justification, however, was both audacious and self-critical. Describing post-Stalin domestic policies of the Soviet leadership merely as "probably correct," he categorically rejected them as "certainly . . . not fit to our situation." [57] He asserted that in Poland "the rejection of the past" can and must move forward more rapidly than in the USSR, and he admitted his and the Politburo's culpability in not shaking off sufficiently soon the "traditionally superficial methods" of analyzing events, particularly when dealing with such phenomena as the Poznan outbreak.

His remarks, as well as those of Aleksander Zawadzki, another Politburo member, formerly considered a Stalinist, who sided at this juncture with the anti-Natolinites,[58] shed considerable light on the specific issues raised by the Soviet delegation. Given Ochab's and Zawadzki's Stalinist backgrounds, their versions are all the more noteworthy. Zawadzki, speaking on the morning of October 20,[59] a mere few hours after the 6 A.M. departure of the Soviet leaders, made the following references: (1) the motive of the trip was "the deep anxiety of the Presidium of the CC, CPSU, regarding the development of the situation in Poland"; (2) the Soviet leaders expressed concern with anti-Soviet propaganda in Poland, noting that even in bourgeois Finland such articles could not appear, and lack of adequate party response to it;* (3) the Soviet leaders charged the Poles with not giving them authoritative information on the Polish domestic situation, such as, for instance, the planned personnel changes in the Politburo, and in general with not maintaining close contacts; (4) the tense international situation made the Soviet leaders even more apprehensive about the implications of the above accusations. Zawadzki added that the conduct of the discussions was marked by not infrequent manifestations of "temperament" from both sides.

Still, the situation was at least partially resolved. As Zawadzki stated it, "during our talks with the delegation of the Central Committee of the CPSU . . . we explained to our Soviet colleagues that their anxiety as to the path People's Poland would take were unfounded." [60] On October 20, the Soviet troop movements within Poland generally ceased, and after the departure of the Soviet guests a communiqué was issued to the effect that further talks would soon be held in Moscow. However, the usual statement about "complete agreement" was not included in the brief announcement. Following the resumption of the Central Committee session, Gomulka delivered a lengthy programmatic statement — his domestic policies are treated in Chapter 14[61] — and on the next day, October 21, the Politburo elections were held. At this point, however, one of the men unreconciled to the changes, B. Ruminski, possibly acting in the hope that a sharp posing of the issue of Polish-Soviet relations would bring

* Ochab, however, in expressing regret, took the opportunity to return the charge, noting that a *Pravda* report on "Anti-Socialist Pronouncements in the Polish Press," published a day earlier and which charged the Polish press with anti-Marxist slanders aimed at undermining socialism, was "unwise, harmful . . . drawing perverted, slanted conclusions." *Nowe Drogi*, no. 10 (1956), p. 114.

about a greater measure of Soviet interference, suddenly nominated Rokossovsky, not slated for renomination to the Politburo. (That he would not be nominated had been clearly conveyed to the Soviet delegation.) The justification for his move was plainly stated: "It is most important how the masses will interpret the meaning of comrade Rokossovsky's non-election. In the prevailing atmosphere the masses will understand that this has an anti-Soviet accent." [62] His arguments were not openly challenged,* and the Central Committee proceeded to a vote, with the Soviet Marshal included as a candidate. The official slate of nine candidates obtained a sizable majority (in a secret ballot): it ranged from 75 out of 75 for Ochab, 74 out of 75 for Gomulka, down to 56 for Zambrowski (bitterly opposed by the unreconcilables as a last-minute waverer). Rokossovsky, with only 23 votes, failed to be elected. Gomulka was then elected First Secretary by a show of hands, with none voting against him.

No conclusive judgment can be made concerning the reasons why the Soviets allowed Gomulka to prevail. However, a recapitulation of the inferences which can be drawn from the above material might suggest some explanations for the Soviet behavior. It would appear, first of all, that the Soviet leadership did not go to Warsaw with either a clear-cut understanding of the situation or a formulated program to be imposed on the Poles, but rather with a set of specific grievances. They did not have *a priori* objections to the inclusion of Gomulka in the new leadership — something which even the neo-Stalinists†

---

* Except for one illuminating incident. Ruminski asserted that this was a form of pressure against the USSR and that this was being frankly stated in the back rooms and corridors. The minutes then show shouts of "who said it, who?" Ruminski answered the interpellator as follows: ". . . comrade Starewicz, now that you are pressing me, I will state that it was you who said so. I spoke with you, I think, a day after the Seventh Plenum. You told me that Poland cannot be independent because Soviet comrades do not allow it and interfere in everything. You told me also that comrade Khrushchev raised the matter of comrade Zambrowski at the Sixth Plenum and raised the Jewish problem . . . Comrade Starewicz, do not provoke me as to who said so because these are your views." He then argued that if Rokossovsky must go, the people must be prepared gradually for it and that his removal now would be construed as a manifestation (*Nowe Drogi*, no. 10, 1956, pp. 147–148). Ruminski's reference to Khrushchev pertains to the selection of Bierut's successor in March 1956 and indirectly confirms the point made earlier.

† There is a continuing problem of labels in all of this. This group might simply be called Natolin, which, however, is a geographical and not a political or ideological term. In some ways they can be called Stalinist or neo-Stalinist, particularly as far as their domestic program was concerned. On the Rokossovsky issue they might be called more pro-Soviet, although it should not be inferred that the others were anti-Soviet. Rather, a different conception of what constitutes "friendly" relations was involved here, much as it was also in Moscow. Hereafter, since the Eighth Plenum

had advocated — but became disturbed by the implications of Rokossovsky's expected removal, probably, in part, under the influence of interpretations suggested by the neo-Stalinists. In the course of conversations they acquiesced to his removal from the Politburo although he was to remain head of the army. During the often heated discussions the Soviet delegation was acquainted with the general outlines of Gomulka's domestic program, but they apparently refrained from either endorsing or rejecting it.

Thus, matters were left open until further negotiations. Presumably, the Soviets felt that the next few days would test Gomulka's ability to take hold of the situation and that their passive posture did not involve an irrevocable commitment. Certainly, the official communiqué had a most tentative character. Finally, it seems that the Soviet leaders conceded that Polish-Soviet relations needed repairs on both sides: the Poles must restrain certain anti-Soviet tendencies, while the Soviets expressed willingness to undo some of the concrete Stalinist abuses of Polish national interest.

But would it not have been better for the USSR to intervene by force of arms? A decision to that effect could not have been made without immediate provocation or without the utmost certainty that it was necessary. Among the factors to be considered there was the danger of undermining by precipitate action the tenuous links with Tito, who only recently had consented to help stabilize the critical Hungarian situation, and there was also the "friendly advice" of the Chinese, urging restraint.* Direct action might have also given immediate comfort to those elements in the USSR opposing the de-Stalinization campaign. Thus an important domestic consideration was involved in Soviet thinking. With the situation in Warsaw unclear and with the Poles postponing the Soviet invitation for them to visit Moscow, the Soviet leaders had decided to fly to Warsaw. A decision to intervene with arms could hardly have been implemented while the Soviet delegation was in the restless Polish capital. Apparently, it was

marks a turning point, if it becomes necessary to use a collective term for the former group, I shall use either neo-Stalinist or dogmatists (the latter in keeping with the domestic Polish usage).

* After two visits to Warsaw in 1957 and 1958 and conversations with many high-placed Polish Communists, this writer is convinced that sometime between October 20 (the date of the Soviet delegation's departure from Warsaw) and October 22 (on the evening of which Khrushchev telephoned Gomulka, see below), the Chinese had actually approached Moscow urging patience. One informant even claims to have seen "documentary" proof. There seems to be little doubt that the critical period was after Khrushchev's return to Moscow and before the outbreak of the Hungarian events,

seriously contemplated, since Soviet troop movements began concurrently with the visit. But their stay in Warsaw revealed to them that the Polish leadership was clearly in control of the situation; that it was united in its commitment to Marxism-Leninism and to the desirability of close relations with the USSR, although on a less subordinate basis (with such reputed Stalinists as Ochab, Zawadzki, and Zambrowski backing Gomulka); that the opposing faction was weak; and, finally, that the Polish Army was restive and, in a critical situation, would not obey Rokossovsky.

This was an unprecedented situation for the Soviet leaders. The closest analogy was Yugoslavia in 1948. Yet only a year earlier the Soviet leaders, after much debate, had reached the conclusion that the policy adopted in 1948–1949 against Yugoslavia had been un-Marxist in its impatience, in its unwillingness to prevail upon the Yugoslavs to mend their ways, and in the "subjective" anger which had pushed the situation to a breaking point. Considerations such as these must have been uppermost in the minds of the Soviet leaders as they flew back to Moscow, uncertain of the real meaning of the Polish situation and faced with facts which did not make for simple solutions.* Intervention might have been called for to forestall an imminent catastrophe or if very favorable circumstances made it a relatively simple matter to execute. In the former case, ideology provided a further inducement: counterrevolution must be prevented. In the latter, a facile maximization of Soviet power is always justified. Neither of these two conditions existed, and the absence of a positive set of demands to be presented as an ultimatum to the Poles strongly suggests that an intervention would have had an essentially negative function. This writer is accordingly skeptical of those who suggest that some dramatic Chinese communiqué or the Polish threat to fight was central in staving off the Soviet Army. Rather, it was the factors enumerated above which translated the Soviet indecision and absence of program into a policy of wait-and-see.

* It is noteworthy that among the various accusations hurled by Khrushchev against Molotov after 1957 (including the charge that he opposed Khrushchev's Yugoslav policy), an accusation of having favored active intervention against Poland was not included. Such an accusation, from the perspective of Khrushchev's and Gomulka's friendly relations in 1957 or 1958, would have been quite effective. Its absence suggests that no major Soviet leader favored such a step, at least not immediately. (According to some indications, Marshal Zhukov might have been more sympathetic to such a course; after his demotion, Khrushchev accused him of "adventurism" in foreign policy.) And it is more than likely that Khrushchev's personal position demanded that he press for restraint so that a subsequent improvement in Polish-Soviet relations might vindicate his anti-Stalinist campaign.

It was upon Gomulka's triumph that the Polish situation took on a revolutionary flavor. Even as Khrushchev was telephoning Gomulka from Moscow on the night of October 22 to assure him that the Soviet leadership accepted Gomulka's domestic line and to promise him that all Soviet troops would return to their bases, anti-Soviet demonstrations were spreading throughout Poland. Most slogans called for Rokossovsky's complete removal, and there were occasional attacks on Polish-Soviet Friendship Society offices. The demonstrations became particularly intense as events in Hungary developed into a patriotic war against the Soviet Union, and the Poles, traditionally friendly to the Hungarians, openly manifested their sympathy. The Polish Central Committee, in an effort to stabilize the Hungarian situation before it resulted in the complete collapse of the People's Democracy,* publicly endorsed Nagy's government.[63] At the same time, however, the Soviet moves to suppress the Hungarians provided Gomulka with the necessary weapon which could be used to contain his inflammable countrymen. Hungary had thus a triple effect: it created a situation in Poland which could justify Soviet intervention; it gave Gomulka a basis for an appeal for calm and order which the bloodletting in Budapest made very meaningful to all; and, by keeping the USSR preoccupied, it prevented any immediate Soviet measures against Poland. By satisfying the popular demand for the removal of Rokossovsky (he was first given a leave of absence and, on November 13, was altogether dismissed and sent back to the USSR), an issue of rather symbolic significance, and by continuously pointing to the Hungarian tragedy, Gomulka thus succeeded in riding out the most immediate crisis.

In short, the October revolution triumphed because of five interacting conditions: (1) it had been preceded by a gradual and continuing dissolution of Stalinism in Poland in response to the anti-Communist sentiment of the vast majority of the people; (2) power in Poland was retained by the party, which initiated and executed the transfer of authority to Gomulka; (3) Gomulka's past, and the events connected with the Soviet arrival in Warsaw, invested the transfer of authority with a dramatic element of Polish national self-assertion which a mere change in party program would have lacked; (4) Gomulka's program was essentially one of domestic reform without

* According to one unconfirmed report, the Polish leadership dispatched two emissaries to Budapest, A. Starewicz (a Gomulka man) and M. Naszkowski (a follower of the Ochab-Zambrowski *apparatchiki*), to confer with Nagy. *Imre Nagy Un Communisme qui n'oublie pas L'Homme* (Paris, 1957), pp. 42–43.

direct challenge to areas of greatest Soviet sensitivity — membership in the bloc and the role of the party; and (5) the pattern of Polish events was such that the Soviet leadership, seeing some analogies to the Yugoslav 1948 break, was tempted to take the path of least resistance and reserve the always risky policy of armed force as a last alternative. Caution on both sides prevented an open conflict.

CONCLUSION: DOMESTICISM AND NATIONAL COMMUNISM

Ideological and institutional diversity thus came to characterize the once monolithic Soviet bloc. Poland joined Yugoslavia in following its own distinct domestic policies. The other People's Democracies practiced and voiced a line essentially Stalinist although tempered by the intervening period of the New Course. The USSR's position toward Hungary clearly evidenced a willingness to employ force when the ideologically viewed political situation created a revolutionary stage. By the same token, the Polish situation warranted manipulation and concessions, despite the reactions of the other Communist leaderships. On November 18, the Soviet leadership warmly received Gomulka in Moscow and signed an agreement with the Poles regularizing the new relationship of "mutual respect, noninterference and sovereignty." Despite Polish unwillingness to endorse Soviet policy in Hungary (and Gomulka could claim that to do so would weaken his party's rule in Poland), Poland was compensated for past economic iniquities by the cancellation of Polish debts to the USSR to the amount of 2.4 billion rubles. A later military convention, while allowing the USSR to retain its troops on Polish soil as part of the Warsaw Pact, at least gave the Poles formal control over their disposition and movement.[64] The Soviet response was clearly one of adjustment.

Soviet behavior, in retrospect, appears to have been justified. A sharp reaction against Gomulka, on the pattern apparently favored by some of the other parties (particularly the East German and the Czech), would have had the effect of forcing him to rally the people around a national standard and to join the ranks of national Communism. There is little doubt that as a last resort Gomulka would have been prepared to do so — in the name of saving Communism in Poland — and that domestic pressures were already pushing him in such a direction. The Soviet leadership, once it had gambled on waiting, certainly must have wished to avoid a situation which would leave the Polish party no alternative. Following his agreement with Khrushchev, Gomulka publicly admitted that he had been "nervous" that the Soviet leaders would not "evaluate correctly" the Polish situation and that he was relieved to see that they had.[65]

Gomulka, from the very instant of his assumption of power, coupled all references to independence with assurances of Polish friendship for, and need of, the Soviet Union. In his speeches he never deviated from the basic dichotomic image of world affairs, even if initially toning down the vigor of his attacks on "Western imperialism." In domestic matters his references to internal reform and de-Stalinization were qualified by attacks on those who expected that his policy would lead to a "second-stage": to the abandonment of Communism. Thus, from the very beginning, the national Communism of Poland, as it was often called by observers, was restricted by Gomulka to domestic affairs, to an insistence on internal autonomy, without translating it into an external ideological challenge or a fundamental revision of Poland's place in the world. The ideological problems that did develop were in part a result of the revolutionary situation, and in part stimulated by the high degree of sensitivity evidenced by the more rigid, essentially Stalinist, regimes surrounding Poland. Gomulka's attitude still indicated that he had not crossed the Rubicon even if some of his followers were in the process of wading across. Gomulka was neither a Nagy nor a Tito.*

Unlike Tito, Gomulka did not have the backing of a cohesive political movement capable of independently constructing Communism in Poland. In late 1956, the United Polish Workers' Party was at its low point in morale, with the rank and file identifying itself with the broad aims of Gomulka but not clearly differentiating between nationalist reactions against the past and the ideological precepts for the future. The lower-ranking party *apparatchiki* were especially fearful that Gomulka's regime would mean the end of their status and role in society. A complete break with Moscow, of his or Moscow's making, would have either placed Gomulka at the mercy of nationalist and revisionist elements, as Nagy was, or would have forced him into a Kadar-like position. A suspended Soviet threat in the background was thus a strange source of stability, beneficial not only to Soviet interests but also to Gomulka's survival. Moscow's problem was how to maintain the intricate balance of threat and adjustment without exaggerating the element of threat, which might intensify the tensions, and without diminishing it prematurely, which might encourage

---

* More will be said in Chapter 14 about Gomulka's ideological views and his relationship to the October events, particularly as relevant to domestic development in Poland.

those elements elsewhere anxious to imitate Gomulka. The pendulum movement between these two extremes accounted for much of the uncertainty evident late in 1956. It obscured the fact that most anti-Communist Poles were willing to concede that close alliance with the USSR was imperative for Poland's retention of the Oder-Neisse frontier. And no Communist regime in Poland, concerned as it had to be with economic planning, could overlook the degree of Polish economic dependence on the USSR.*

Gomulka's regime, therefore, oscillated from the very start between a very mild form of national Communism and the more restricted orientation of domesticism. With neither the capacity nor the will to become a full-blown national Communist regime, Gomulka increasingly reverted to the earlier pattern of domesticism (see Chapter 3) in which the policy outlook of his regime was characterized by an *inward perspective*, but without making a deliberate choice between the international and national interests. The clash between the two, so characteristic of national Communism in its Titoist and Nagy variety, gave way to a continuing effort to establish some sort of harmony between the demands of Communism as an international revolutionary movement and Communism as a constructive national undertaking. Domesticism was thus a much more complex operation, lacking the clear and absolute criteria inherent in national Communism. For this reason the position of Poland after 1956 required a difficult process of adjustment, though from the start there was no explicit external ideological and political Polish challenge, thereby differentiating Poland from Yugoslavia.

Yet the Polish events had a broader significance. The Soviet decision to tolerate Gomulka, and the even friendly relations eventually established between Moscow and Warsaw, meant that the USSR was gradually, hesitatingly, abandoning its own national Communism and moving toward a greater realization that its leadership in the camp required a more equitable adjustment between Soviet interests and those of the other members. This shift, not without its reversals and certainly not made willingly, meant a return to some of the limited diversity which characterized the bloc before 1947. At that time, the

---

* For detailed data, see *Trybuna Ludu*, May 21, 1956. The Soviet Union imported, in 1955, 95.6 per cent of Polish rolling-stock exports, 63.3 per cent of Polish machinery exports, 33.7 per cent of coal exports, and so on. On the other hand, 34.6 per cent of Polish grain imports came from the USSR, 73.8 per cent of unprocessed cotton, 74.2 per cent of oil, 68 per cent of iron ore, and so on. Given the relative strength of the two economies, there was no question as to which was the more dependent. (For 1957–1958 economic relations, see Chapter 12.)

diversity was one dictated by the weakness of the Communist regimes and by the uncertainties of the postwar situation. By 1956–1957, however, the new diversity was primarily a function of the diverging national interests of the various Communist regimes once the initial totalitarian revolution, common to all of them, had run its course. A recognition of this state of affairs necessarily dictated a more flexible approach than the old Stalinist formula that what is good for the USSR has to be good for all the members of the Communist camp.

Soviet interests were bound to remain of primary importance in the scale of decision making. Nonetheless, as long as they were not directly affected, some domestic diversity among the satellites could be accepted and not considered as proof per se of treasonable deviation. Even in Hungary things did not return to the former Stalinist pattern after November 1956, and the Kadar regime pursued a socioeconomic policy more liberal than that in Czechoslovakia or Bulgaria. Relations among the Communist states thus increasingly took on these features: the triumph of domesticism operating both in the name of proletarian internationalism (as in the case of regimes still essentially Stalinist) and local considerations (Poland and Hungary); the absence of common ideological norms for these relations; the decline of the active ingredient of Soviet power, except in emergency situations; a greater Soviet preoccupation with its domestic problems related to the Stalinist succession crisis; a growing reliance on top-level bilateral consultations of the various leaderships with Moscow; the increasing stature of China and Yugoslavia, and to a lesser extent Poland, as active agents within relations between Communist states.

In addition to these inherent factors of growth, this new situation was also the culmination of certain errors of analysis in Soviet policy, induced by Soviet ideological perspectives. These errors were essentially fourfold: (1) The underestimation of Tito's ambitions, affecting his attitude toward the USSR and the other states. (2) The overestimation of the influence of socioeconomic changes (such as the creation of "the foundation for the construction of socialism") on the political stability of the East European regimes and, as a result, the underestimation of the extent of alienation and hostility produced by this process, particularly in Hungary and Poland. (3) The failure to comprehend the inherent influence of a mass following on the top leadership, which in the East European circumstances took the form of pressure on the leaders to make domestic conditions paramount in the drafting of further programs. (4) The excessive application of purely Soviet standards in framing those aspects of Soviet policy which would directly affect Communist regimes elsewhere. The most glaring example of this was the attack on Stalinism which, in the Soviet Union, had largely a *shock* effect without undermining the firmly implanted institutions of the system. In the bloc, however, it had a *disintegrative* impact on Stalinist institutions just in the process of construction.[66] Connected with this lack of differentiation was the underestimation of the desirability of external tension for maintaining internal cohesion in the new Communist regimes. The impact of the Geneva Conference had little political significance in the CPSU, but in the People's Democracies it opened all sorts of avenues to doubts, to a questioning of the class struggle and even of the role of the USSR — all with fateful political consequences.

Khrushchev, however, in countering the above criticisms of Soviet policy, could at the same time point to certain hopeful signs which the crisis had revealed "dialectically." First of all, the majority of the regimes had successfully adjusted to the new situation, even as the most negative features of Stalinism were being dismantled, while the most dangerous trends in Poland and Hungary had been contained. Inherent in Gomulka's return to power was the likelihood that a more popularly endorsed Communist regime would ensue, even if some of its domestic policies were not to be condoned. Finally, Tito's ambivalence toward Hungary weakened appreciably the ideological impact of the Yugoslav position. In brief, the total picture was more hopeful if one considered the longer-range trends and not merely the crises of the recent past.

To the Soviet leaders of the Communist camp, the immediate problem for the future was how to prevent the new ideological and institutional diversity from exploding into irreconcilable splits. Could this be avoided without strictly limiting the independence of the new Polish regime or abandoning the leadership position of the USSR? Admittedly, the preceding two or three years had shown that the existing formulations and the reliance on past experience were adequate in coping with a challenge such as presented by Hungary but were not sufficiently elastic and perceptive to prevent the dilemma posed by Poland. The Soviet leaders discovered that their doctrine was rich in guidelines for coping with enemies but that it offered little for resolving conflicts and organizing relations among Communist states. Mere similarity of institutions and socioeconomic structures was not enough to guarantee unity. This was a lesson to be pondered by the Soviet leaders, for it revealed a dangerous weakness in a system of ideology and power which, by stressing dichotomic relationships and dialectical conflicts, showed itself too rigid to respond to important changes effected by evolutionary processes. But there could no longer be any question of a return to Stalinism. The Soviet leaders, including even Molotov, had too good a Marxist sense of change seriously to contemplate a return to a system so closely associated with a specific historical phase and a specific individual. The task after 1956 was to establish some commonly held ideological criteria and to forge new bonds of unity to prevent the diversity from becoming political disunity.

The Fourth Phase: 1957-1959

THE COMMUNIST "COMMONWEALTH" — INSTITUTIONAL DIVERSITY AND IDEOLOGICAL UNIFORMITY

What do we want? We want unity, closed ranks, and rallied forces. We acknowledge different paths, comrades. But among the different paths, there is one general path, and others are, as you know, like a big river with tributaries. In the same way there are specific peculiarities, but there is only one path, the Marxist-Leninist path. This is the path on which the task of the construction of Communist society must be tackled. — Nikita Khrushchev, Prague, July 11, 1957

12 / THE MAOIST EFFORT
TO RECONSTRUCT A CENTER

The experience of the USSR and other socialist countries has fully confirmed the correctness of the tenet of Marxist-Leninist theory that the processes of the socialist revolution and the building of socialism are governed by a number of basic laws applicable in all countries embarking on a socialist path. These laws are manifested everywhere alongside a great variety of historically formed national features and traditions which should be taken into account without fail. — Declaration of the ruling Communist parties, Moscow, November 1957

THE uncertainties produced in the Communist camp by Khrushchev's policy of undercutting the Stalinist myth were only partially dispelled by the Soviet readiness to suppress the Hungarian uprising. The use of force established the outer limits of tolerable diversity. Yet the Soviet willingness to gamble on Gomulka, as well as the continuing endorsement of Yugoslavia as a socialist state, clearly left some key questions unanswered. At what point do gradual quantitative changes become qualitative ones? At what point does a socialist state cease being one under the influence of excessive diversity in ideology and practice? Where is the borderline between the legitimate domestic concerns of a Communist leadership and its higher allegiance to the general interests of the Communist camp? These questions had been answered simply and directly by the Stalinist formula which maintained that only one standard was valid: Soviet experience as the yardstick for policy and as the source of theoretical evaluation. That this formula was no longer viable was clear to all but the most rigidly dogmatic elements. But what was to replace it? On that score, the Soviet leadership was vague, indecisive, and divided within itself.

Given the Soviet ambivalence, and presumably out of general concern for the future of Communism, the experienced and tested Chinese Communist leadership decided to assume for the first time a more active role in reconstructing Communist unity. It was spurred to undertaking that initiative by its feeling that Khrushchev had shown poor judgment in the manner in which he launched the anti-Stalin campaign,[1] and indecision during the fateful days of October.* Far from wishing to establish Soviet hegemony over the bloc but fearful of disintegrative tendencies, the Chinese sought to combine the new diversity with the collective recognition of Soviet leadership in the pursuit of policies that *the Chinese* favored.

THE INTER-COMMUNIST DIALOGUE

The doubts and the disagreements stimulated by the Twentieth Congress and Khrushchev's Yugoslav policy came to light in the aftermath of the Warsaw and Budapest crises. There was new ideological conflict and definite political diversity. But since none of the states was yet willing to dissociate itself from socialism, the ideological conflict became a method of expressing existing political diversity while maintaining the outlines of unity.

After the Polish and Hungarian events, the following issues seemed to need the most clarification: the definition of socialism and the number of roads leading to it; Stalin, Stalinism, and the Soviet system; the historical meaning of the Hungarian revolution and of the Polish October; the dictatorship of the proletariat and the problem of class struggle; proletarian internationalism or bilateralism Leninism and revisionism; the Communist camp and the principle of Soviet leadership. These were only some of the major items, but each one touched almost every aspect of the dogma.

The greatest outburst came from Poland. The October assertion of internal autonomy meant that political power, weak and dependent on popular support, had to be more responsive to local currents of thought, even if attempting to contain them. As a result, much of this debate was transferred into the political arena, thereby also becoming despite Gomulka's efforts to concentrate only on domestic issues, concern of the other Communist countries. In a sense, the opening

---

* Several years later the Chinese took credit both for the Soviet decision not to intervene against Poland and for the intervention against the Hungarians. According to the Chinese, the Soviets first wanted to intervene against Poland and then shifted to the opposite extreme with respect to both Poland and Hungary. The Soviets did not refute the Chinese version, which is to be found in "The Origin and Development of the Differences Between the Leadership of the CPSU and Ourselves," Comment on the Open Letter of the Central Committee of the CPSU by the Editorial Departments of *Jen-min Jih-pao* and *Hung Ch'i,* September 6, 1963, Foreign Languages Press (Peking, 1963), pp. 17–18 (cited below as "Origin and Development") In the same document the Chinese claimed that the important Soviet declaration October 30 attempting to regularize inter-Communist relationships (see Chapter p. 229) was issued at their suggestion.

shot was fired on October 20 by Gomulka himself, in his report to the Eighth Plenum of the United Polish Workers' Party. Addressing himself to the question of the Polish way to socialism,* Gomulka noted that:

This theory was created by the first classics of Marxism. They never imagined their theory to be complete . . . What is immutable in socialism can be reduced to the abolition of the exploitation of man by man. The roads of achieving this goal can be and are different. They are determined by various circumstances of time and place. The model of socialism can also vary. It can be such as that created in the Soviet Union; it can be shaped in a manner as we see it in Yugoslavia; it can be different still.[2]

But what of the Stalinist phase which had insisted on uniformity? Did it result solely from a degeneration in the leader's personality, or was it something more basic and related to the Soviet system? The latter proposition was advanced earlier by Togliatti but timidly withdrawn after the Soviet reply of June 30, 1956, which forcefully declared:

Our enemies assert that the personality cult of Stalin was not engendered by definite historical conditions which have already passed but by the Soviet system itself, by what they consider its lack of democracy, and so on. Such slanderous assertions are refuted by the entire history of the development of the Soviet state.[3]

Gomulka seems to have taken an intermediary position, but his remarks have a dangerous ambivalence to them:

The cult of personality cannot be confined solely to the person of Stalin. The cult of personality is a certain system which prevailed in the Soviet Union and which was grafted to probably all communist parties, as well as to a number of countries of the socialist camp, including Poland.[4]

The Polish position also deviated on the Hungarian issue. The Central Committee of the party characterized as "tragic" the Hungarian request for the first Soviet intervention and went on to add:

We are of the opinion that the problem of the defense and maintenance of the people's power and of the gains of socialism in Hungary can be

---

* One of the secretaries of the Polish Workers' Party, Wladyslaw Matwin, addressing the trade union plenum a month later, defined socialism as follows: "We still do not quite know what this new socialism will be like. We only know fairly well what cannot be like, what it ought not to be like; this we know from our own experience. We must do a great deal of work together in order to evolve a model, to lay its foundations, to make it — as a comrade of the Cegielski works said last week — to a kind of socialism one likes." Radio Warsaw, November 18, 1956.

solved by the inner forces of the Hungarian people, headed by the working class, and not by intervention from without.[5]

Even after the second Soviet attack had crushed the uprising and the USSR had explicitly assumed responsibility for what had transpired, the Poles refused to condemn the uprising as a counterrevolution, refrained from supporting the USSR in the UN, and in the November 18 agreement with the USSR limited themselves to endorsing the new Hungarian regime's efforts "toward the development of socialist democracy and the consolidation of fraternal cooperation with other socialist countries on the basis of *full equality* and regard for *state sovereignty*." [6] The last two points thus again reemphasized the Polish position that relations among the countries of the Soviet bloc have to be based on these principles. The Polish press, for a time free of censorship, went much further in expressing the feeling that what happened in Hungary was a genuine revolution produced by Rakosi's and Gero's crimes. *Nowa Kultura* and *Po Prostu* ran a series of articles, describing with approval the executions of former AVH members, and even making somewhat unfriendly references to "soldiers with red stars on their helmets," who, according to the correspondents, seemed embarrassed and uncomfortable in their role, surrounded by the seething hatred of the Hungarians.[7]

The Polish position also veered from the established views on the nature of the dictatorship of the proletariat and of proletarian internationalism. The former was hardly mentioned at all, and the process of democratization, referred to so frequently by Polish speakers and writers, was interpreted to mean the broad participation of society and not just the proletariat in the process of building Polish socialism. This emphasis on the Polish aspect meant that the international character of the Communist movement would have to be reviewed critically, since in the past it had been subverted by excessive stress on Soviet interests. The Poles accordingly displayed considerable sensitivity to the developing Soviet-Yugoslav debate, prompted by mutual disenchantment and sparked by Tito's Pula speech (see Chapter 10 section on "Tito's Dilemma"). The weekly of the Polish party described Tito's statement as containing an essentially "correct" analysis of the relations in the Communist camp,[8] while the Soviet reaction to it, reflecting a "zigzagging lack of consistency" in the Soviet struggle against Stalinism, was said to have been caused by the CPSU's historical association with the emergence of Stalinism.[9] More concretely, references to proletarian internationalism, which to Moscow mean the principle of unity over any national interest, were coupled with insistence on full sovereignty and with a marked preference for bilateral party dealings. Thus, paradoxically, in order to avoid being isolated among more rigidly inclined party leaderships, the Poles were rejecting multilateral party contacts in favor of directly bilateral party negotiations, a method previously used by Stalin to maintain his hegemony.

The disappearance of Stalinism as a guide to Soviet-satellite relations meant that a new line had to be established to take into account the radically changed conditions prevailing as of early November 1956. It came on November 6 in the form of an authoritative statement by Suslov. Reflecting the failure of the Soviet declaration of October 30 to contain disintegrative developments in the bloc, and conceding the importance of specific national methods, forms, and rates of development, Suslov attempted to set down what the universal laws of building socialism are for all the socialist states:

> First, the establishment of political rule by the working class led by its vanguard; second, the thorough strengthening of the alliance of the working class with the peasantry and other strata of the working people; third, the liquidation of capitalist ownership of industrial enterprises, banks, transport, and communications, the establishment of public ownership; ownership of the basic means of production and the consequent planned nature of the economy; fourth, the resolute defense of the gains of the socialist revolution from the encroachments of the former ruling exploiting classes.[10]

These factors, according to Suslov, suggested that certain features of the Russian revolution had an international, universal significance. The road to socialism was not a matter, as the Poles seemed to suggest, of mere goodwill and a generous dose of experimentation, but also of pursuit of known and established laws.

More explicit criticisms of the Poles appeared in the December 23 issue of *Pravda*, in a long article entitled "On Proletarian Internationalism" by A. Azizian. The *Pravda* writer took issue with a Polish article on Yugoslavia which criticized the former practice of making loyalty to the USSR the focal point of proletarian internationalism. The Polish writer had suggested a new concept of proletarian internationalism, one based on "coexistence" among socialist states and on elimination of national hegemony and the struggle with Stalinism.[11] The *Pravda* article rejected with scorn the idea that a significant aspect of the present meaning of proletarian internationalism was the struggle with Stalinism and suggested that this was a mere mask devised by reaction to fight against Marxism-Leninism. Implying that the Polish writer was falling victim to nationalist tendencies, *Pravda* noted significantly:

The German Socialist Unity Party and the Czechoslovak Communist Party vigorously reject any attempt to form any other platform for the communist movement. All talk about the mythical "National communism," their statement reads, is contrary to Marxism-Leninism. Both parties stress the necessity of unity . . . of a joint struggle . . .[12]

Pravda was quite correct. Either goaded by Moscow or fearful for their own security, the satellite leaderships of East Germany and Czechoslovakia responded to the anti-Stalinist challenge from Warsaw with far less delicacy and restraint. In Czechoslovakia the regime launched a mass agitation campaign, under the sycophantic slogan, "With the USSR forever," and German and Czech delegations promptly appeared in Moscow to cement the bonds of proletarian internationalism and to reemphasize the primacy of the USSR in the camp of socialist states. In the latter effort they were joined by Thorez and the French Communist Party. The East Germans were particularly alarmed by Polish claims that a real "October revolution" had taken place in Poland. A revolution against Stalinism could not be a Marxist revolution, Hermann Axen violently proclaimed in *Neues Deutschland*, and he who says so joins the enemies of socialism.[13] Polish talk of "humanistic socialism" was thus admittedly most unsettling to the East German leadership, relying precariously on the support of Soviet arms. For the East Germans, their assertion of loyalty to the USSR and condemnation of the Poles as revisionists was therefore a matter of political survival.

The implications of Polish insubordination were not so immediately dangerous to the Czechs. There the party had succeeded in wielding power without the presence of Soviet troops, and the consideration presumably uppermost in the minds of the Czech leadership was the longer-range implication of the Polish position. For this reason, rather than attacking directly the Polish October, the Czechs, in the words of Novotny, "took a reserved view in evaluating the situation in Poland." [14] However, in emphasizing the need for close cooperation among socialist states, and rejecting bilateralism as a method of interparty relations, *Rude Pravo* strongly condemned those generalizations which have as their intent a desire "to weaken confidence in the Soviet Communist Party," adding:

it is worth noting that some foreign quarters are expressing doubts as to whether conferences in which more than two communist parties participate are correct and expedient. Views have been expressed that such multilateral talks are inopportune; they carry with them, so it is said, the danger of isolation of communist parties from other organizations of the labor movement, particularly from the socialist parties of the West.

Such conclusions must be flatly rejected. No events of the recent past have altered the need for an expediency of conferences between communist parties, which holds good also for meetings between more than two parties . . .

With socialist parties it is indeed possible, or rather necessary, to seek an understanding, particularly in questions of unity of action on the basis of working class unity. Yet it is no use blinding oneself to several serious facts. A number of socialist parties have completely abandoned Marxism. In a number of questions, they have adopted the attitude of the bourgeoisie, as was again shown recently during the events in Hungary . . .[15]

Having thus rebuked the Polish insistence on bilateral dealings, an insistence dramatized by Polish absence from the early January meeting held in Budapest between the Soviet, Bulgarian, Czech, Hungarian, and Rumanian parties (Khrushchev and Malenkov attending), the Czechs proceeded to strengthen their ties with similarly oriented parties. On January 22 they issued the joint French-Czech Party declaration,* and a week later signed a broad economic agreement with the USSR in which the above ideological points were reasserted. Ironically, it was through these bilateral declarations that the Poles were being ideologically isolated for their insistence on bilateralism. But, as was not the case with the Yugoslavs, the Polish leaders, and particularly Gomulka, were never singled out for attack, and all specific references were directed at individual Polish spokesmen, who were clearly differentiated from the leadership. This was Gomulka's trial period, and Moscow's caution still restrained the extremists in Prague and Pankow.

The Soviets on the whole avoided taking public issue with the Poles in an official way. Indeed, it may be surmised that the outbursts from the local satellite leaders, combined as they were with attacks on Tito, stemmed from their sense of domestic insecurity, which the Kremlin leadership certainly did not share. Grand strategy for these leaders was hence very much a case of making their own immediate interests the basis for the policies of international Communism. The

---

* *L'Humanité*, January 22, 1957. Part of the declaration may be cited here: "All attempts to divide the Communist movement into so-called 'Stalinist' and 'non-Stalinist' or 'old' and 'new' camps, as well as the idea that there can be several centers of the international Communist movement, serve only to question Marxist-Leninist principles and proletarian internationalism to which the two parties are attached."

Soviet leadership was doubtless fully aware of the need to crystallize an ideological conception to fit the situation and to evolve new bonds to replace some of the Stalinist controls. Suslov's November 1956 speech was an initial effort in this direction, and in December 1956 the CPSU's Central Committee further deliberated the matter. Some members of the Committee, particularly Molotov, apparently assumed an "I told you so" attitude, while others, especially those charged with economic matters, expressed profound concern with the impact of the political developments on economic planning within the USSR and the camp in general.[16] But in December 1956 a return to the old Stalinist formula seemed to involve too many risks. Most particularly, it would have required an armed intervention in Poland without even the warrant of a clear-cut provocation from Gomulka. A return to Stalinism, furthermore, could not be restricted to the matter of inter-state relations in view of the close interaction between Soviet ties with the other Communist regimes and Soviet domestic developments. Khrushchev, who had a personal interest in his gamble on Gomulka paying off, thus succeeded in maintaining his position in large measure precisely because the situation was so unprecedented.

With Moscow wavering, Peking stepped forward to resolve the dilemma. It is to be recalled that in welcoming the Soviet October 30 declaration, the Chinese suggested that they shared the Polish feeling that Soviet-satellite relations must be critically re-examined:

> Because of the unanimity of ideology and aim of struggle, it often happens that certain personnel of socialist countries neglect the principle of equality among nations in their mutual relations. Such a mistake, particularly the mistake of chauvinism by a big country, inevitably results in serious damage to the solidarity and common cause of the socialist countries.[17]

Even after endorsing the suppression of Nagy, the Chinese still seemed to fear that the major problem in Soviet-satellite relations was the danger of a return to Stalinism, and in hailing the November 18 Polish-Soviet agreement the Chinese press* made the interesting observation that the treaty would correct also "whatever was wrong

---

* For an interesting commentary, see the November 13, 1956, editorial in *Ta Kung Pao*, "What are the similarities and differences between Polish and Hungarian Incidents?" The article suggested that in both cases there were legitimate grievances and errors but that in Hungary a mass reform movement was penetrated by the enemy and was poorly led, and hence had become reactionary. At this time, the Chinese press featured many sympathetic articles concerning Poland, including pictures of Gomulka, a sign of tacit approval.

with relations between the Soviet Union and Hungary." [18] By December, however, one could detect signs that the Chinese regime was becoming increasingly concerned over disintegrative trends in the bloc and with the absence of an effective Soviet response. Given its international isolation and its acute hostility to "Western imperialism," Peking had a special interest in restoring Communist unity. Domestically the country was in a state of transition reminiscent of the violent transformation of Russia in the thirties while the Polish and Hungarian events had the undesirable consequence of suggesting to some Chinese intellectuals that less radical methods of building socialism existed within the framework of Communism. In their attitude these intellectuals had been encouraged by the initial semiofficial endorsement given by Peking to the Poles. The Chinese party leadership could hardly tolerate either such internal views or its external sources. In the fall of 1956 the focus had been on a change in the pattern of relations in the Communist camp for the sake of unity. By winter 1956 the emphasis was on unity to improve relations.

DIVERSITY IN UNITY: THE CHINESE SOLUTION

The Chinese leadership stepped forward late in December with a programmatic statement concerning relations between Communist states. The declaration, published on December 29 in *Jen-min Jih-pao*, was accompanied by a note that it was a summary of discussions held by the Chinese Politburo. The contents of the declaration were presumably cleared beforehand with Moscow and were immediately reproduced in full by the Soviet press.* However, the fact that the statement originated from Peking instead of Moscow symbolized the degree to which Stalinism had inhibited the Soviet leadership from coping with a new situation. The Chinese statement involved concessions to what the Chinese must have considered to be the imperatives of unity as well as an attempt to define certain areas of inde-

---

* It has been suggested that the Chinese declaration was merely a trick sponsored by Moscow and designed to utilize Chinese prestige in resolving the existing problems. This in itself, of course, would mean a much greater role for China and an admission of China's position in East Europe. However, given internal disagreements in Moscow, it is more likely that the initiative came from Peking, and was endorsed by Moscow.

The increased role of China was acknowledged at the time by a Soviet international-affairs publication which stated: "The Soviet Union with the Chinese People's Republic head the united family of the countries of socialism." S. Sanakov and V. Zniazhinsky, "The Leninist Policy of Peace and Friendship among Nations," *Mezhdunarodnaia zhizn*, no. 12 (1956), p. 31.

pendence previously prohibited by Stalinism. In this manner the Chinese hoped to contain the strains of diversity, without, however, making the error of striving to turn the clock back. Their statement accordingly conceded that contradictions between Communist parties were indeed possible although these were "not the result of a fundamental clash of interests between classes but of conflict between right or wrong opinions or of a partial contradiction of interests." It urged patience for the efforts of the CPSU to correct Stalin's mistakes and rejected the thesis linking Stalinism with the Soviet system. Furthermore: "In our opinion Stalin's mistakes take second place to his achievements," the Chinese Politburo decided.[19]

The Peking statement was categorical in stressing two points concerning the reservations which had been raised by the Poles and the Yugoslavs: the issue of the dictatorship of the proletariat and the question of Soviet leadership. Since the former was related to the general problem of the role of the Communist Party, so recently challenged in Hungary, and also relevant to domestic Chinese problems, the statement minced no words in asserting the importance of the dictatorship of the proletariat for the construction of socialism:

> Those "Socialists" who depart from the dictatorship of the proletariat to prate about "democracy" actually stand with the bourgeoisie in opposition to the proletariat . . . they are, in effect, asking for capitalism and opposing socialism, though many among them may themselves be unaware of that fact . . .

On the subject of Soviet leadership, which was of less vital domestic importance, the Chinese were primarily guided by external considerations. Given their position of mediator, the Chinese could stress Soviet leadership in the camp with little fear that its assertion would substantially reduce Chinese freedom of action. Consequently, their Politburo unequivocally described the USSR as the "center of international proletarian solidarity," and Chou En-lai, dispatched suddenly to East Europe in January 1957 on a fence-mending trip, repeatedly made unqualified references to "the socialist countries headed by the USSR." To sweeten the bitter pill, the December statement did reiterate the earlier warning against "big power chauvinism."

In brief, the Chinese seemed determined to set up a pattern of ideological and political unity while recognizing the possibility of limited local diversity. The Chinese statement approved of Poland's new position while Chou En-lai repeatedly, but without success, at tempted to obtain official Polish assent to a statement of Soviet primacy in the camp.* Despite their inflexibility on this issue, the Poles apparently did agree in the course of their discussions with the Chinese Premier not to air their ideological differences with the USSR, not to attempt to export their views, and to accept the notion that proletarian internationalism and not just coexistence should characterize relations among Communist states. The first implied much closer, supranational, bonds, whereas the second suggested a more formal, distinct relationship. The Polish position was thus markedly different from the Yugoslav insistence on the practical and ideological implementation of many ways to socialism, and it was essentially on this ground that Peking made its move against Tito:

> It is understandable that the Yugoslav comrades bear a particular resentment against Stalin's mistakes. In the past, they made worthy efforts to stick to socialism under difficult conditions. We also agree with some of the points in comrade Tito's speech, but we are amazed that, in his speech, he attacked almost all the socialist countries and many of the communist parties . . . This can only lead to a split in the communist movement . . .
>
> Clearly, the Yugoslav comrades are going too far. *Even if some part of their criticism of brother parties is reasonable*, the basic stand and method they adopt infringe the principles of comradely discussion.[20]

Following this implied accusation of political disloyalty, the campaign against Yugoslavia snowballed. The satellite newspapers, guided for the first time since June 1956 by a more or less common ideological standard, were filled with articles critical of the Yugoslav position and with indirect warnings to Poland against falling into the "revisionist" pitfall. Like the Chinese, these statements all re-emphasized the ideological verities: dictatorship of the proletariat, proletarian internationalism, primacy of the USSR. The Bulgarian party launched a vigorous campaign against efforts designed to undermine Communist unity by appeals to nationalist feelings,[21] and went explicitly on record as staunchly upholding the principle that "the attitude toward

---

* Polish press reports of Chou En-lai's visit to Poland in early January 1957 loyally transmitted the texts of his speeches with the invariable ending, "Long live the unity of the socialist countries with the USSR at their head!" And just as loyally, next to these speeches, would appear remarks by Gomulka, Cyrankiewicz, or Rapacki, stressing variable roads to socialism, sovereignty, equality of rights, and friendship with all socialist countries. See also the text of Chou's speech in Moscow in which he explains his mission as having been of utmost importance in forging new unity in the socialist camp (*Pravda*, January 18, 1957). In an interview in India, Chou openly stated that his trip had "helped to consolidate relations between the Soviet Union and the Eastern European countries." *New York Times*, January 25, 1957.

the Soviet Union and the CPSU is the touchstone and the cornerstone of proletarian internationalism." Condemning the Yugoslavs for questioning this, the Bulgarians asserted that the CPSU is "the tactical and theoretical example for all other parties of the proletariat." [22] The least refined attack was launched, as might have been expected, by Tito's old enemies, the Albanians. On February 13, speaking before the plenum of the Central Committee, Enver Hoxha delivered a blistering critique of the Yugoslav line, spelling out in detail the issues on which the Yugoslavs were said to be erring. Hoxha concluded his indictment, which neatly summarized some of the major ideological issues, by calling on all parties to defend Marxism-Leninism against revisionism, expressing his conviction that "with great confidence in the final victory of socialism, our countries, led by the glorious Soviet Union, are marching always forward." [23]

The crux of the matter, however, was clearly the question of Soviet primacy. This was finally stated bluntly by Popovic, the Yugoslav Foreign Minister, who, explaining the deterioration in Soviet-Yugoslav relations, stated:

ideological differences, in the narrow sense of the term, have not played a decisive role this time. The attitude toward the socialist camp is not an ideological question in the true sense of the word. However, ideological arguments have again served, regardless of whether or not this has been done consciously, as a suitable means for establishment of such interstate relations as the Soviet government considered correct, that is, *convenient* to it.[24]

Although the arguments and disagreements certainly did not end here,[25] enough has been said to illustrate the general pattern of disintegration of the ideological arrangement reached in the June 1956 Moscow agreement. However, since the Poles were in the meantime quietly practicing much of what the Yugoslavs were being loudly accused of, many of the charges against Belgrade were also aimed indirectly at Warsaw.

With the gradual settling of the dust following the explosion prompted by the dissipation of the Stalinist formula, the East European situation began to emerge in clearer focus in early 1957. The Chinese statement of December 29 provided an ideological framework which could accommodate the newly emerged diversified environment. As a result, throughout the early months of 1957 the torn fabric of East European Communism was being mended by weaving together a new formula for Soviet-satellite relations, based largely on the Chinese statement, through a series of bilateral party agreements or declarations* which served to reemphasize certain common principles: (1) Soviet primacy in proletarian internationalism; (2) the struggle against imperialism internally and externally; and (3) the ubiquity of the concept of the dictatorship of the proletariat. Soviet statements generally relied heavily on quotations from the Chinese declaration, and, while chastising Tito for his open challenge to Communist unity, they seemed satisfied with the absence of direct external defiance by Gomulka.

That Chinese insistence on Soviet leadership was not unqualified, however, was highlighted by the subdued and private, but still rather unprecedented Chinese rebuke to the Soviet leadership for highhandedness and lack of balance in denouncing Stalin. As revealed some years later, Chou En-lai, during his January 1957 East European trip, reproached the Kremlin leaders for their failure "to consult with the fraternal parties in advance," and criticized the "total lack of an overall analysis" and "self-criticism" in the anti-Stalin statements made at the Twentieth Congress.[26] The Chinese leaders were thus serving notice to the Kremlin that henceforth its leadership required at the very minimum advance coordination with other parties, and with the Chinese in particular.

The picture was thus radically different from the black-and-white dichotomies which so characterized Stalinism in East Europe. Unlike the "monolithic unity" of the past, as of early spring 1957 reluctant lip service was being paid in Poland to the last two principles of the three cited above, although neither of the two was being fully reflected in actual policy or action.[27] The first was simply ignored.†
In the other satellites, official statements were stressing all three principles but with most emphasis on the first, while domestic policies

---

* To list a few: Albanian-Bulgarian (January 29), Soviet-Hungarian (March 28), Bulgarian-Rumanian (March 27), Soviet-Rumanian, Soviet-East German (January 7), Czech-East German, Czech-Soviet (January 29), Czech-French (January 22), Czech-Chinese (March 27), Czech-Italian (April 3), Bulgarian-French (April 15), Soviet-Albanian (April 17), Soviet-Bulgarian (February 21).

† The Polish position, and Chinese acceptance of it, was again shown in the declaration signed in Peking on April 11, 1957, by Premier Chou En-lai and Premier Cyrankiewicz. The declaration speaks of socialist solidarity based on "the Marxist-Leninist principles of proletarian internationalism and equality among nations." Soviet primacy is not mentioned. It goes on to state that the Chinese party welcomes the changes in Poland since the Eighth Party Plenum (October 1956). Yet, even while Cyrankiewicz was still on his way home, the Chinese were greeting Marshal Voroshilov with statements about the camp of socialism and proletarian internationalism, headed by the USSR. This is a good example of the new flexibility in interstate relations.

changed little from the past. The Yugoslavs were stressing the need
of adjusting dogma to new situations and, without major departures
from past internal policies, were rejecting the stress laid on the above
principles as doctrinaire rigidity, replying to charges of revisionism
with countercharges of dogmatism. However, in keeping with this
greater elasticity, even the anti-Yugoslav campaign declined by early
spring 1957. The neighboring and still basically Stalinist leaderships
began gradually to realize the new pattern of relations and to perceive
the implications of the new ideological conception.* Accordingly,
they adopted Moscow's more subdued tone. Chou En-lai touched on
the crux of the matter when, reporting on his East European trip, he
stated: "Even if no unanimity can be reached for the time being, it
would also be normal to reserve the differences while upholding our
solidarity." [28]

THE ECONOMICS AND POLITICS OF UNITY

The Chinese formula was primarily a stopgap measure, as Chou's
remark revealed. It was meant to contain disintegrative trends by
focusing on common objectives, allowing time for the repair of more
tangible bonds of unity. At this stage ideology was particularly important — especially in the case of Poland, where it buttressed a
relationship which only recently had jettisoned the Stalinist controls
and was delicately balancing potential external Soviet threats with
certain common interests (such as the Oder-Neisse line). A commitment to similar social objectives and a sharing of certain perspectives
for viewing reality established a common bond between Gomulka
and Khrushchev which, under the circumstances, was important to
cultivate. By stressing again and again the points of unity, the divisive
tendencies inherent in a situation of diversity might be kept in the
background. The Chinese formula also left room for hope that Yugoslavia, despite the tensions and the arguments, might be willing to
shift the emphasis of its outlook toward those aspects of Marxism-
Leninism which it shared in common with the other regimes. Tito's
reaction to Hungary, as we have observed, did not rule out such ex-

---

* The outward change took place over a period of about one month. On March 3
Scinteia published a relatively restrained reply to Popovic's address and it was subsequently reprinted in *Pravda* on March 6, thereby gaining central endorsement, and
two days later in *Rude Pravo*. In early April both Khrushchev and Bulganin, on
greeting an Albanian delegation in Moscow, went to some pains to indicate that despite ideological differences, Yugoslavia was to be considered on a much friendlier
plane than capitalist countries and that fundamentally it too was engaged in socialist
construction although not directly part of the socialist camp.

pectations since it indicated again that the institutions of socialism, even if subject to aberrations, were more important to the Yugoslavs than any other principle. It is to be noted, however, that already at this time the Chinese were categorical in drawing a line between legitimate Communist dialogue and treasonable discourse.

While the Chinese were coping with the ideological dilemma and securing the East Europeans' adherence to the new formulations, the Soviet leaders were busily turning to more familiar and less ephemeral remedies: tightening the economic bonds and reestablishing political-institutional ties. The December 1956 CPSU plenum accordingly included a discussion of the economic problems raised by the political changes.[29] The Hungarian and Polish events had many roots in the economic conditions prevailing in the bloc and the Soviet leaders were not unaware of this. In addition, some of them, like Khrushchev, realized that an important substitute for Stalinist coercion was to create such economic interdependence that any separatist temptations would be tantamount to courting national disaster. The fact that Poland's economic dependence on the USSR had helped, among other things, to inhibit Polish aspirations had not been lost on the Soviet leaders, and they accordingly strove throughout 1957 to create an economic equivalent to Stalin's political technique of "the dilemma of the one alternative."

The political events of 1956 had a sharp impact on Soviet economic relations with East Europe. Until then the area had been a source of appreciable economic advantage to the USSR, with an estimated annual Soviet net extract of at least one billion United States dollars.[30] The Soviet admission that past economic policies of the area, largely Soviet-imposed, had courted disaster,[31] the need to bolster the East German regime, to promote the recuperation of Kadar's Hungary, and to stave off a calamitous nation-wide repetition of Poznan in Poland, all forced the USSR late in 1956 and in 1957 to extend credit to these regimes. As a result, Poland, Hungary, and East Germany briefly became economic liabilities.[32] Since, ironically, this meant that less reliable regions were being rewarded, pressure unavoidably arose also to reward the more loyal regimes elsewhere, thereby increasing Soviet economic commitments.* No wonder then

---

* The February 21, 1957, Soviet decision to suspend the promised $250 million credit to finance aluminum plants in Yugoslavia has to be viewed in the light of these pressures. Soviet credits to East Europe since early 1956 included: 370 million rubles to Bulgaria in February 1956; 1.2 billion rubles to East Germany in July 1956 and January 1957; 200 million gold rubles to Hungary in December 1956; 400 million gold rubles to Poland in September 1956 and 700 million in November 1956; 270 million

that such economically oriented party leaders as Saburov or Pervukhin became increasingly concerned with the implications of Khrushchev's policies and gradually became attracted to those CPSU circles which opposed him on ideological and political grounds.

The loan policy had been adopted to deal with an emergency situation. A broader task, however, was to be performed by the Council of Economic Mutual Assistance (CEMA), so neglected in the past by Stalin. Indeed, it is remarkable that the Soviet leadership had ignored this potentially most promising method of binding the Communist states together. It was again mute testimony to Stalin's dependence on political solutions, and CEMA's reactivation was a compliment to Khrushchev's perceptiveness. Only after Stalin's death did the Council begin to meet regularly, and the year 1957 was especially marked by a series of moves designed to give it new life and energy. In June 1957 permanent secretariats to the various specialized CEMA committees were set up and were empowered to draw preliminary development plans for some ten to fifteen years ahead.[33] A multilateral-payments scheme, with the state bank of the USSR as the clearing agent, was scheduled for 1958.[34] It was also agreed that "broad coordination of the plans of the socialist countries' national economies" was desirable and would be pursued. In December 1957 a meeting of the economists of the participating countries was held in Prague to evaluate their foreign trade with "capitalist trade markets" [35] and was followed in January 1958 by a plenary meeting of CEMA in Moscow, with the heads of government leading the delegations.

The Moscow conference marked a determined bid to integrate

---

rubles to Rumania in December 1956. The November agreement also provided for a cancellation of Polish indebtedness to the amount of 2.3 billion rubles.

According to the most thorough study available (J. Wszelaki's *Communist Economic Strategy: The Role of East Central Europe*, Washington, 1959), the sum total of Soviet credits granted to the European Communist-ruled states in 1956–1957 was $1.3 billion. To this ought to be added $1.8 billion in Soviet credit cancellations, or a total of $3.1 billion. However, these figures must be compared with the actual net Soviet gains derived during the 1945–1956 period. Wszelaki's estimates are: $15 billion from East Germany, $2 billion from Rumania, $1 billion from Hungary, $2 billion from Poland — or *a total of $20 billion gained through exploitation* (see Wszelaki, pp. 68–77). There is also striking evidence that despite the Soviet loan policy, price discrimination in exports from the area to the USSR and imports from the USSR continued to favor the USSR during 1957 and in fact increased in comparison to preceding years, thereby offsetting the Soviet loans. See H. Mendershausen, *Terms of Trade between the Soviet Union and Smaller Communist Countries 1955–1957* (Rand Corporation, January 1959), published in *The Review of Economics*, May 1959 and "The Terms of Soviet Satellite Trade: A Broader Analysis," *The Review of Economics* (May 1960), pp. 152–163; and a rejoinder by F. P. Holzman, "Soviet Foreign Trade Pricing and the Question of Discrimination," *The Review of Economics* (May 1962), pp. 134–147.

economically that which was proving ideologically and politically divisive. Poland was still interested in foreign, particularly American, loans and was attempting to shift some of its trade Westward, especially coal, its major export item. The conference produced a comprehensive plan of cooperation covering the years 1959–1975, divided into two parts: 1959–1965 and 1965–1975. The first part was worked out in detail while the second part set the broad outlines. Specific tasks for each member were also established, aiming at increased productive specialization of CEMA members. Such specialization, despite its immediate economic merits, in the long run would be bound to restrict the range of economic activity of any one partner, and place all the specializing countries in a relationship of dependence vis-à-vis their major supplier of raw materials and the only member not subject to effective specialization, the USSR. At the same time, the development of such an intimate relationship, particularly given the industrial development of the states, would further increase their economic significance to the USSR's own development plans. For instance, already by 1956 imports of machinery and equipment from East Europe exceeded by about $100 million annually the Soviet exports of similar commodities to the area.[36] Economic ties were indeed outstripping political unity.

In some respects the integration, preceded by intensive industrialization, did open new vistas to East Europe, so long plagued by splinter national economies and so long used merely as a market for Western industrial exports and predatory investments. The transition from a raw material and nonindustrial goods export area into an important source of machinery, particularly for the underdeveloped countries, without doubt represented a major advance for East Europe.* Inte-

---

* Noteworthy is the shift in the role of finished industrial items, particularly machinery, in the export trade of these states:

	Prewar	*1948*	*1953*	*1956*
Bulgaria	—	0.1%	3.0%	2.7%[a]
Czechoslovakia	6.4%	20.3	42.4	40.3
East Germany	—	31.9[b]	62.6	57.0
Poland	0.7	2.2[c]	12.9	15.6
Rumania	0.1	0.8	8.3	10.1
Hungary	11.4	17.4[c]	38.2	30.3

[a] 1955
[b] 1950
[c] 1949

Source: *Probleme Economice*, no. 5, 1958 (this issue contains a detailed treatment of changes in the structure of foreign trade of the European Communist states).

For a useful summary of economic development in the bloc, emphasizing the positive aspects only, see *Razvitie ekonomiki stran narodnoi demokratii*, N. I. Ivanova et al., eds. (Moscow, 1958).

gration, involving greater technical specialization, offered opportunities for more rapid development of technological skills and for promotion of goods for competition in the world market. However, whatever the long-range material benefits might be, the immediate political consequences were to create more binding ties to the USSR and China. Indeed, the converse result was also of political significance: with Western markets closed, China, absorbing more than half of East European machine exports, became dependent on economic stability in the bloc for the promotion of its own development. Within the pattern of specialization a particular role was to be played by East Germany and Czechoslovakia, the most industrialized and politically loyal states. They were to serve as the key suppliers of industrial equipment within the bloc and particularly to the USSR.[37] In 1957 Czechoslovakia even adjusted upwards her Five Year Plan in order to fulfill the industrial-export obligations imposed upon her, as was frankly admitted by Communist planners.[38] Also in 1957, partly for sound economic and partly for political reasons, the USSR negotiated far-ranging agreements with Czechoslovakia, integrating Soviet-Czech industrial plans,[39] and with East Germany, providing for trade and industrial cooperation, especially in the development of the chemical industry, planned jointly until 1965.[40] According to the plan,[41] Czech export trade was to undergo by 1956 the following structural change:

	Capitalist states	USSR	Other Communist states
1957	32.6%	33.8%	33.6%
1965	26.0	41.8	32.2

Soviet economic ties with Czechoslovakia, combining the desirabl characteristics of an advanced, highly skilled industrial base and hyperloyal regime, went beyond any arrangement concluded with other states.[42]

Of the most immediate political significance were the increase economic ties developed between Poland and the USSR. The Amer can loan of $94 million granted in mid-1957 was negligible compare to the total turnover in Polish-Soviet economic relations, which i 1956 amounted to 2,562 million rubles and which grew in 1957 t 2,747 million rubles. According to an itemized breakdown of goo imported and exported,[43] published in detail in order to dissipate pu lic suspicions stimulated by past secrecy, in 1957 Poland was d pendent on Soviet supplies for 100 per cent of its oil supplies, 70 per cent of its iron ore, 78 per cent of its nickel, and 67 per cent of its cotton. Particularly important, but advantageous to Poland, was the fact that almost half the Polish exports to the USSR in 1957 (of the total 1,023,600 rubles) involved Polish machinery and industrial goods, representing about one half of total Polish machine exports. By way of contrast, only about a fifth of the imports from the USSR constituted industrial goods and machinery, most of it raw materials necessary for Polish industry. Polish leaders could not afford to ignore the potential implications of this economic relationship.

Beyond these purely economic aspects, there was a further consideration involved in the increased zeal of CEMA activities. Since the organization antedated the October 1956 events and, unlike the Cominform, was not branded by Stalinism, the Poles could hardly claim that CEMA was being revived in order to limit their independence. Even during the relatively open anti-Soviet season in the Polish press no significant charges were raised against the Council, and all complaints had been aimed directly at Soviet-Polish economic relations. At the same time, however, CEMA's existence presented the Soviet leaders a most opportune and institutionalized forum for *multilateral* consultations where the Poles were bound to be isolated and unable, given their weak economic situation, to wield a veto power. It is no wonder then that, from 1957 on, most of the Communist press, with the significant exception of Poland, sang praises to the role played by CEMA.

The economic measures provided a general underpinning to the more pressing political problems. True, common economic ties and a common economic organization would create centripetal forces so sorely needed. But the Soviet leadership was too steeped in the Leninist-Stalinist tradition to rely merely on gradual economic processes. Its political efforts took three approaches. The first, as already noted, involved bilateral agreements between the most loyal parties reasserting proletarian internationalism, hailing Soviet leadership, and proclaiming certain universal prerequisites for the construction of socialism. The purpose of these bilateral agreements was to underscore those principles which in themselves created pressures for unity. It was hoped that emphasis on recognition of Soviet leadership would effectively undercut the divisive tendencies inherent in "many ways o socialism" and, in a roundabout fashion, restore the old Stalinist prerogative of evaluating and guiding the domestic experience of other Communist states. The declarations, coming as they were from all sides, created pressures on Poland and, to a lesser extent, on Yugoslavia to identify themselves with the stated principles lest their silence be interpreted as negation. They also provided ammunition to the unreconciled neo-Stalinists in Poland who, without fear of being charged with "subversion," could innocently keep prodding Gomulka to identify himself with such praiseworthy principles.

The second method for which the Soviet leadership developed a sudden predisposition was the multilateral conference of Communist leaders in which all disagreements could be ironed out in comradely discussions. The Soviet leaders were obviously not unmindful of the numerical voting strengths that would prevail in such conferences, and they were only too willing to apply the Leninist notion of democratic centralism to them. The application of this principle to international Communism would, they felt, unavoidably strengthen unity and supply a justification for Soviet leadership. With this in mind, the Soviet leaders decided to take advantage of the forthcoming fortieth anniversary of the 1917 Revolution to stage an international Communist celebration in Moscow. No true Communist, not even Tito, could refuse to attend.

The third approach aimed at reviving something like the Cominform, an interparty organization which would translate the multilateral conference into a continuing multilateral consultation and guidance. Such an arrangement was in keeping with the former Soviet reliance on the Comintern and the Cominform and thus had the added advantage of being rooted in familiar experience. While ostensibly not clashing with the Chinese formula of unity in diversity, it would grant the Soviet leaders their sorely needed organizational control. But it was precisely the Comintern and the Cominform experience which was calculated to raise the most impassioned Polish and Yugoslav opposition. To the former, the Comintern was a reminder that the Polish Communist Party had been dissolved as a "Fascist conspiracy" with most of its leaders shot by the NKVD. To the latter, the Cominform symbolized the very worst features of Stalinism. Unity could hardly be restored by reference to this particular ancestry of international Communism, and even initial Soviet efforts to promote a common interparty theoretical journal were opposed as a portentous revival of the past. These fears in Warsaw and Belgrade were hardly allayed by the clumsy efforts of the Czech party's weekly, *Tvorba*, which while conceding that a revival of some form of Cominform would not be favorable "under present conditions," still seemed to suggest the general desirability of common organizational links: "

would seem that for the sake of firm unity of international Communism roughly the same contacts should be promoted as existed when the Cominform was in existence." [44] During this period, Prague and East Berlin consistently took a more rigid stand than even Moscow.

Yet in the new situation the Soviet regime had to be more responsive to the dominant views prevailing in the Communist world. Soviet power had not declined; in fact, it had grown in every respect. But the new element in the situation was that the power of Communist regimes elsewhere had also grown. The Politburos in Prague and Sofia were no longer staffed by cowed *apparatchiki* intently detecting the significance of the latest Soviet pronouncement, convinced that the center knows best. After the unmasking of Stalin and the October 1956 events, the center's infallibility no longer appeared above question and, indeed, the neo-Stalinist centralists* in the Communist regimes could easily claim that they had perceived much earlier the dangers of the flirtation with Tito or of the tolerance for the Poles. In doing so, they could confidently tell Moscow that after ten-odd years in power they knew best which policies would promote and which policies would undermine Communism in their respective countries. Centralist domesticism thus became a source of pressure on Moscow for more energetic measures to ensure disciplined unity.

Internal considerations also affected the mood of the CPSU Presidium. The record shows that Molotov from the start opposed Khrushchev's experimental approach and favored sticking to established processes. Suslov's formulations at the Twentieth Congress had shown greater caution in endorsing the "many ways to socialism" thesis. And even Khrushchev himself by late 1956 was toasting Stalin as a great leader of Communism. By early 1957 it had become clear that continued maintenance of Soviet leadership would require a greater degree of organizationally structured discipline within the bloc and a common center for defining ideological prerequisites and universals. The year 1956 had taught Khrushchev a priceless lesson in the vagaries of political diversity and in the dangerous ambiguities of Marxism-Leninism as the sole bond for unity.

* It would be misleading to use the Stalinist and anti-Stalinist categories in this post-October period. The issue of a return to Stalinism as such was no longer really meaningful. Rather, it was mostly a question of the degree of unity and subordination within the bloc necessary for the construction of socialism. By "neo-Stalinist centralists" I mean those leaders who favored the closest links with the USSR even if practicing at home policies not based on the Stalinist principle of abject imitation all that is Soviet. Khrushchev, for instance, could not be described as a Stalinist although in 1957, as we shall see below, he was a centralist.

POLAND AND THE PRINCIPLE OF SOVIET LEADERSHIP

The problem of unity in East Europe meant coping with two recalcitrant Communist regimes: Poland within the bloc and Yugoslavia on its fringes. The maximum objective, drawing Yugoslavia back into the bloc, was bound to prove the more difficult task, as will be shown in Chapter 13. The establishment of political and ideological ties between Poland and the rest of the camp was the objective for 1957 and, given Poland's ambiguous position, had the greater chance of success.

The Soviet position on Poland remained uncrystallized until sometime in February or March 1957. Soviet fears about the direction of Poland's future course were exacerbated by the rapid collapse of the collective-farm system after October 1956, by the strange alliance between Gomulka and the Roman Catholic Cardinal, by the continuing ideological ferment, and by the unclear situation within Gomulka's party. The neo-Stalinists, highly critical of Gomulka's agricultural concessions and dubious of the consequences for Polish Communism of Gomulka's line on "national sovereignty," were still sufficiently active to warrant the thought in Moscow that a more suitable alternative might still be available. At the same time, however, the Soviet leadership could derive some comfort from a series of reassuring signs. In the course of the January 1957 electoral campaign for the Sejm, which in substance was a plebiscite for Gomulka, some of the more outspoken anti-Soviet candidates were dropped and a Catholic youth organization, with nationalist leanings, suppressed. The elections demonstrated that Poland was willing to support Gomulka's Communist regime as a preferable alternative to the neo-Stalinists who, to rule, would require a more active Soviet support. In the government formed after the elections, Zenon Nowak, a leading member of the Natolin group, was retained as Deputy Premier. Then in mid-March the regime condemned as one-sided a resolution of the Warsaw committee which singled out for attack only Stalinism, reminding the committee that the revisionists were also a major danger. To their remarks about national equality the Poles began to add the meaningful phrase "proletarian internationalism." Finally, also in mid-March, Gomulka conceded that the Hungarian revolution ultimately had become a counterrevolution, thereby essentially endorsing the Soviet position.

While it is impossible to pinpoint the date of the Soviet decision to abandon their temporizing attitude and actually to buttress Gomulka's position in Poland, something approaching such a policy decision must have been made prior to the March 25, 1957, agreement granting Gomulka's request for the complete release of many hundreds of thousands of Poles (including many anti-Nazi underground fighters) still under detention in the USSR. Since no previous Communist ruler of Poland had been able to obtain Soviet agreement — and even Bierut had tried after Stalin's death* — Gomulka's success could not fail to increase his standing at home. A few weeks earlier, Khrushchev, speaking of Soviet-Bulgarian friendship, significantly chose that occasion to praise publicly Gomulka's leadership.[45] Gomulka shortly afterwards began to display, for the first time, some vigor in dealing with the Natolin group which had continued its agitation against him. At the Ninth Party Plenum in May, provoked by their criticisms and demands for a formal acknowledgment of Soviet leadership, Gomulka moved sharply against his critics, bluntly rejecting their contentions that his position was weakening socialism. Symptomatic of the Soviet attitude (and certainly not lost on the Polish *apparatchiki*) was the fact that a Soviet Embassy attaché, V. Maslenikov, who had criticized the post-October regime, was recalled to Moscow a few days after the plenum, in response to an unprecedented request by the Communist Warsaw government for his removal.[46]

The Ninth Plenum gave Gomulka an opportunity to restate the meaning of his position in the light of his improving relations with Moscow. Referring to the "Polish (or national) way to socialism," he noted explicitly that Poland's differing conditions required a different way than the Soviet. According to Gomulka only diversity can do justice to proletarian internationalism, and he rejected the view held by "comrades here and in other parties" that Communists must agree on every detail. While stressing the imperative significance of Polish-Soviet ties, Gomulka reiterated his belief that proletarian internationalism would flourish if it tolerated a continuing discussion, based on *common principles*, and with history being the sole judge of who had been right.[47] (For a fuller development of Gomulka's internal policies, see Chapter 14.)

His reference to common principles was significant. It revealed an underlying area of agreement with the Soviets which had been

---

* The most that Bierut could do was to obtain in 1955 the release of 6000 individual Poles held in the USSR, many of them veteran Communists arrested during the purges. *Po Prostu*, December 23–30, 1956.

obscured by the openly aired differences and the uncertain political situation. Gomulka listed four such common principles for building socialism:

(1) The organization of a Marxist-Leninist Party of the workers' class and the laboring masses, which governs itself according to the principles of democratic centralism, conducts a policy of alliance of the workers' class with the laboring peasantry;

(2) After the overthrow of the authority of the bourgeoisie — the creation of the dictatorship of the proletariat over the exploiting classes and suppressors of the laboring masses;

(3) The socialization of capitalist means of production, a gradual reconstruction of productive relationships in the countryside, absorbing the entirety of the national economy into specific frames of central planning and direction;

(4) Conduct of policy in accordance with the Leninist principles of proletarian internationalism, the observance of equality and sovereignty of all states and nations, the uniting of countries and socialist powers to oppose imperialist aggression and to defend peace.[48]

It is noteworthy that Gomulka's first three points embraced all but one of Suslov's "universal laws" as stated in November 1956. The part omitted involved Suslov's justification for resolute class struggle after power had been seized — a position identified in Poland with Stalinism — but the sharpness of this divergence was dulled by Gomulka's inclusion of the dictatorship of the proletariat concept, which could imply much of Suslov's point.

Gomulka's ideological effort also served to underline the areas of recalcitrance, the defense of which he considered vital to his efforts to build socialism in Poland. His "laws" made explicit reference to gradualism in dealing with the peasants (a point further developed in his remarks) and elevated his insistence on national independence and equality to a binding law for socialist construction. This had been a cardinal tenet in his beliefs all along, since he well realized that without it the Soviet Union would have the right to judge his internal policies. Throughout the spring and summer of 1957 Gomulka therefore refused, even when signing joint declarations with the most subservient parties (such as the East German on June 20), to employ any of the standard formulas used to acknowledge Soviet leadership.

Indeed, it was largely to defend his stand on this issue that Gomulka displayed such reluctance to engage in multilateral conferences and, especially, in multilateral organizations. The frequent Polish praise for bilateralism in relations between Communist parties was designed to provide the procedural substructure for the principle of national independence.* In September 1957, following an improvement in Soviet-Yugoslav relations, Gomulka journeyed to Belgrade and the joint Polish-Yugoslav declaration asserted that "both parties consider that today bilateral relations between Communist and workers' parties should particularly be developed." [49] Such an assertion, issued only two months before the scheduled Moscow multiparty conference, even if accompanied by Tito's concessions to Gomulka's desire not to enflame Moscow,† still reflected Gomulka's continued intransigence on a semantic point pregnant with political significance. The CPSU and the other parties recognized it as such. It was no accident that the May 1957 issue of *Voprosy istorii* singled out the parties of China, France, Germany, Czechoslovakia, and Rumania as the "vivid examples of the consistent and steadfast struggle for the purity of Marxism-Leninism." These were the parties which stressed the desirability of closer ties, with the Czech party's plenum in July calling again for a common interparty journal and even a common commission for political-economic problems.[50]

By the late summer of 1957 two basic formulations of Soviet rule had emerged. The more extreme, espoused by the Czechs, East Germans, Bulgarians, and Albanians, spoke of the "leading or directing role" of the USSR in the Communist camp. The Soviet role was a special one, involving leadership in ideological and political matters and implying in turn its authority even in the domestic matters of other Communist states. These parties also occasionally used the phrase "the socialist camp headed by the Soviet Union," preferred by the Hungarians and the Rumanians and which in January 1957 the Chinese had desired the Poles to adopt. The Soviets tended to use the latter version in their own statements,[51] although also quoting with apparent approval the more "centralist" formulations.

It would be an oversimplification to maintain that the Soviet insistence on this special role was merely a matter of self-interest or power. It was hard for the Soviet leaders not to feel that the October Revolution had blazed a path for all "progressive" humanity and had initiated a new historical phase. This very fact in turn had endowed the USSR with a compelling mission, and all Communists had to real-

---

* On one occasion, when the French Communist Party refused to endorse bilateral-m in a joint French-Polish declaration and reference to it was accordingly omitted om their joint statement, the Poles editorially, with tongue in cheek, declared that e Polish-French Communist negotiations had once again proved the profitability of lateral relations between parties.
† See Chapter 13, p. 318.

ize that their fate was inextricably linked with the Soviet Union. The Soviet experience in building socialism established it as the most advanced socialist state, and a Communist would be guilty of a harsh distortion of reality if unwilling to recognize this. The traditions of the CPSU, and its experience, inescapably established its right to comment authoritatively on ideological matters, and the scope of such comment could not be limited by such formalistic considerations as national frontiers. Finally, the very fact of Soviet power placed the Communist states in debt to the USSR, because it was Soviet might which made the construction of socialism possible, protecting these states from the imperialists. Did not all this establish objectively the unique position of the Soviet Union? the Soviet leaders felt entitled to ask. On what grounds, other than crude nationalism, could any Communist question Soviet leadership? [52]

Gomulka accordingly was careful not to go on record as denying the principle of Soviet leadership. He either ignored it or would employ his own formulation which inevitably had the merit of being as vague as it was true. When hailing the Soviet Union he would normally refer to it as "the first and mightiest socialist power," historically and factually correct but without the strong overtones of hierarchy contained in the centralist formulations.* Even at the November 1957 multiparty conference in Moscow, amid repeated incantations to Soviet leadership, Gomulka spoke of "the first socialist state in history, the Union of Soviet Socialist Republics. It takes first place in the democratic family of socialist countries." [53]

But as Gomulka personally discovered in Moscow in November 1957, the pressures for unity within the camp became increasingly difficult to resist. Much of the original Polish confidence, so evident in the summer of 1957,[54] had been rooted in an erroneous analysis of pertinent external phenomena. Two such cases stand out: the meaning of Soviet leadership changes and the attitude of China. In the case of the former, the late June 1957 expulsion of Molotov, Kaganovich, Malenkov, and Shepilov from the CPSU Presidium was interpreted in Poland as indicating the victory of a conception of the Communist camp which would allow considerable latitude for independent action. Gomulka, for ideological as well as geopolitical reasons (especially the Oder-Neisse frontier problem), did not desire to leave th

---

* It may not be too farfetched to suggest that an analogy to the Polish formulation would be if some archbishop in the Catholic Church insisted on referring to the Papacy simply as the "first and oldest bishopric in the Church." Indeed, that formula came to be used in the Catholic Church in the mid-sixties, when the ecumenical spirit overcame the old Curia doctrines!

camp, but he did hope that ultimately the camp would be transformed into a commonwealth of essentially equal states. The expulsion of a faction which, at least in part, was held together by past objections to Khrushchev's bloc policies, seemed an encouraging sign, especially as it was followed shortly by renewed Soviet-Yugoslav contacts. Possibly in this interpretation the Poles were right. Khrushchev was certainly preferable to Molotov. But their optimism made them forget that there was still a considerable gap between their views and Khrushchev's. They did not realize that Khrushchev, by not attempting to move the clock all the way back, ultimately might be much more effective. Finally, they did not know that inter-Communist relations were only indirectly involved in the expulsions.[55] The fact is that Khrushchev's consolidation of power served to free him to respond with greater energy to the problems of unity.

An even more glaring case of exaggerated optimism was involved in the Polish calculations concerning China. Despite Chou's visit to Poland, despite his insistence on Soviet leadership, despite the clear lines drawn between internal autonomy and external obeisance in the Chinese December 29 statement, and, finally, despite the sharpness of the Chinese condemnation of the Yugoslavs, the Poles continued to picture the Chinese as their allies in the struggle against centralist tendencies, particularly against a reassertion of effective Soviet leadership. Mao's secret speech on "Contradictions within a Socialist Society" provoked unfounded hopes in Poland that it signified a major shift toward a greater toleration of diversity, excluding, almost by definition, a center for international Communism and the hegemony of any one party. His speech was interpreted as relevant "for all countries which are building socialism"; it was compared to the Polish October upheaval and was construed as endorsing the Polish position:

We in Poland speak about our "October." The Chinese speak in their own manner about "a hundred flowers." It appears, however, that between these two expressions there is a great similarity. It appears that the statesmen heading the Chinese Communist Party favor those changes which took place in Poland half a year ago. And, what is more, *they are ready to support our efforts* aimed in the direction outlined in October.[56]

Carried away by their blind enthusiasm, the Poles failed to note that by the summer the Chinese were stressing that the major danger to socialism was revisionism, not the dogmatism which the Poles identified with the neo-Stalinist, centralist positions. Even more important, had the Poles re-examined closely the Chinese statements since October 1956, they would have noted that their major theme was unity and that Soviet leadership, particularly since Chou En-lai's visit to Moscow and East Europe in December–January, was clearly considered to be an integral part of that unity. Mao's hundred-flowers speech, it seems, was essentially designed for internal Chinese consumption; the Polish efforts to represent it as an oblique Chinese redefinition of the character of the camp even might have served to provoke Peking into adopting a more unequivocal position.

THE DIALECTICS OF UNANIMITY

The November 1957 Moscow celebration became a testing ground for the Poles' ability to maintain their position and for the Chinese capacity to impose their conceptions on the bloc as a whole. The major business of the conference was conducted at a special closed meeting of the governing Communist parties, held at the end of the celebrations. It was dominated by two major lines of debate. One concerned the broad direction of further Communist development, particularly in regard to foreign policy and doctrine. Here, the protagonists were primarily the Soviets and the Chinese. The second involved the reconstruction of camp unity. Here, the Poles and the Chinese stood at opposite ends, with the Soviets under crossfire from both.

The months prior to the November conference were marked by a striking divergence in Chinese and Soviet domestic trends. This divergence doubtless contributed a psychological climate to the differences that emerged between the Soviet and the Chinese leaders. In Russia, Khrushchev's triumph over the Stalinist faction in the Presidium, a considerable domestic relaxation, and the launching of the first ICBM created a sense of more relaxed optimism. To the Soviets, the period of crisis had passed, while to Khrushchev personally his improved relations with Gomulka and correct relations with Tito were a useful reassurance against neo-Stalinist hostility elsewhere.

The Chinese, on the other hand, during this period increasingly became convinced that a repetition of the 1956 crisis, the domestic dangers of which their own "Hundred Flowers" campaign had amply demonstrated,[57] could only be avoided by a unity of all Communist states based on militant action against all bloc deviants. The belated discovery that revisionism had found a fertile soil among Chinese intellectuals created profound misgivings in Peking. The Hundred Flowers campaign that began in 1956 was brought to an abrupt end in mid-1957, and it was followed by a vigorous "rectification."[58] The

National People's Congress in July 1957 was highlighted by a series of abject confessions by "rightists" who had gone too far in criticizing the regime. These confessions set the mood for an assertion within the ruling elite of a tougher, more radical line. For some years subtle alignments of a "conservative" and "radical" character (but not in the form of factions) apparently had existed within the top party echelons, and the radicals succeeded in placing their stamp on domestic policy in mid-1957 and on foreign policy subsequently. This became more evident in 1958 with the launching of the People's Communes; but already in late 1957 extravagant, radical statements concerning the agricultural policy, the class struggle, and the transition to Communism began to dominate the party press, while the party cadres were urged to undertake manual labor. But it was characteristic of the internal stability and cohesion of the Chinese Communist leadership that the shift did not involve any purges at the top; Chou En-lai, who has often been considered as leaning toward moderate policies, remained in a key position, and the "rightist" alignment could still represent a potential future alternative.[59]

These internal developments provided the underpinning for the dissenting Chinese views on world affairs, on Communist ideology, and on the Communist camp. Although Soviet nuclear and especially rocket development had made the Soviet leaders more confident of their capacity to deter a first-strike attack by the United States and of their own ability to pursue a more assertive policy, the Kremlin was far from exaggerating the importance of the change. In somewhat nuanced terms, it stressed (and for public consumption perhaps even consciously overemphasized) the change in favor of Soviet power, but without asserting that a qualitative shift in the world balance of power had occurred: "It is a question of a change in the balance of forces between socialism and capitalism, of the strengthening of the former and the weakening of the latter." [60]

The Chinese were not so subtle: ". . . the socialist forces are overwhelmingly superior to the imperialist forces," boldly declared Mao to the Communist leaders assembled in the Kremlin, noting that the "international situation has now reached a new turning point . . . the characteristic of the situation today is the East wind prevailing over the West wind." [61] On that basis, Mao urged a more militant general line, designed to exploit the camp's alleged strategic superiority, now capable of deterring the "imperialists" from resistance in local wars. And, should the "imperialists" either miscalculate or just overreact, the resulting nuclear war would at worst cause the death of half of mankind, but "the other half would remain while imperialism would be razed to the ground and the whole world would become socialist." [62]

It may be surmised that these reflections on the historical blessings of a nuclear holocaust cooled the ardor of many a hardened revolutionary. In some it may have even prompted greater sympathy for the "peaceful coexistence" line advocated by Khrushchev. However, at the same time, many of the old-time East European Stalinists — Gheorghiu-Dej, Hoxha, Ulbricht, Novotny — were unattracted by Khrushchev's semi-public denunciations of Stalin, by his evident inclination to seek a stable modus vivendi with Tito and increasingly also with Gomulka, by his related tendency to revise the ideology in order to make room in it for a somewhat wider variety of Communisms, and by his attempt to link the "non-inevitability of war" thesis with the notion of "peaceful transition to socialism." Thus, if the Chinese on the whole tended to isolate themselves with their advocacy of Communist nuclear brinkmanship, Khrushchev somewhat exposed himself on the doctrinal front.

That front witnessed some lively action. In a document submitted to the meeting (but made public only in 1963), the Chinese proposed that the Twentieth Congress thesis on peaceful transition to socialism be substantially diluted, warning the parties that its adoption by the meeting would result in weakening Communist revolutionary morale. It is noteworthy that the declaration issued by the meeting did meet this Chinese objection by stressing the continued relevance of violent revolutionary forms of transition whenever the "reaction" refuses to yield. Moreover, the Chinese later claimed that they succeeded in adding to the declaration an explicit denunciation of "U.S. imperialism [as] the center of world reaction" and that they prevented the declaration from reiterating "the erroneous views of the Twentieth Congress on many important questions of principle." [63]

From a historical perspective, notwithstanding the likelihood that in subsequent years the Chinese may have found it convenient to exaggerate both the intensity of their criticisms and the degree of their success in imposing their views on the meeting, the ideological discussion was of very great importance. It was probably even more significant for the subsequent evolution of the bloc than the simultaneous war and peace debate. In the latter case, the Chinese were still acting as deviants who are "more holy than the holy," sinning by an excess of zeal. While bothersome and potentially even dangerous, that posture within a still ideologically militant movement was less noxious than the effort to portray the leader of the movement as doctrinally in error.[64] To the extent that Khrushchev must have sensed immediately that some of the Chinese charges had, at least, the silent sympathy of many East European Stalinists, and, indeed, certainly also of some Soviet opponents of Khrushchev, the discussion with Mao sharply posed the question of Khrushchev's own personal power and gave the Sino-Soviet divergence an additional and very critical dimension.

Yet, in the midst of all these dialectics, the Soviet Union undertook an important and portentous commitment to China: on October 15, 1957, an agreement "on new technology for national defense" was reached by the two countries, providing for Soviet assistance to Chinese weapons developments, including as the Chinese later claimed, nuclear development. (A high-level Chinese military mission was also present in Moscow at the time.) Although in subsequent negotiations the Chinese did not succeed in obtaining directly Soviet nuclear weapons,* the military convention did have the effect of pledging the Soviet Union to help in the modernization of the Chinese armed forces, thus facilitating China's quest for strategic stature.[65] The agreement obviously reflected the weakened Soviet position in the bloc as well as the then still ambivalent nature of the Sino-Soviet relationship. Perhaps the Soviet leadership did not take at face value the new militancy of the Chinese, so much in contrast with their international posture of the mid-fifties. In any case, the Kremlin did need Chinese support in restoring some order to the Communist camp and in reasserting the Soviet leadership in it. The military arrangement was thus presumably part of a larger bargain. In 1957 the Chinese concern with Communist unity must have seemed reassuring to the Soviet leaders, and it should be remembered that Sino-Soviet relations at the time were on the whole still relatively close, and that the alliance was still a reality in spite of a number of outstanding differences.

To be sure, in pleading for the public recognition of Soviet leadership, the Chinese clearly had mixed motives. In addition to strengthening their own capacity to pressure the Soviets in the direction of greater militancy, the effort might have been designed to force Tito to bow explicitly before the concept of a united anti-revisionist camp, or to drive a wedge between Khrushchev and his new Belgrade friend. However, to the extent that Mao's insistence on Soviet leader-

---

* "The Chinese leaders . . . strenuously tried — this is not a secret — to get the Soviet Union to give them the atomic bomb. The CPSU and the Soviet government naturally could not consider this, as it might have led to the most serious consequences." Radio Moscow, July 10, 1964.

ship also could force the Poles into line and even perhaps help to set a standard for Peking itself, the Chinese attitude also served some immediate Soviet needs. The Poles went to the meeting believing that they would not be required to acknowledge Soviet leadership, and their hopes were raised by the absence of any mention of it in the draft of a resolution to be issued at the end of the conference and circulated beforehand.[66] In keeping with this policy, Gomulka pleaded the "special sensitivity of the Polish people to questions of their country's independence and sovereignty" and warned that to ignore it would be "nihilistic dogmatism." [67] His was a lonely stand. (In public speeches only Kadar took a more moderate position, but his domestic weakness made him a doubtful source of support.) From all sides came repeated demands that Soviet leadership be acknowledged publicly in the resolution which would be issued *jointly* at the conclusion of this multilateral conference. To the surprise of the Poles and the delight of the centralists, much of the pressure came from the Chinese. In his speech to the gathering, Mao used the formula "socialist camp headed by the Soviet Union" four times[68] and was quoted as explaining to the Chinese students at Moscow University that "in the socialist camp there must be a head and that head is the Soviet Union. Among the Communist and Workers' Parties of all countries there must be a head, and that head is the CPSU." [69] The open recognition of Soviet leadership by the only party which was in a position to dispute it placed Gomulka in an extremely difficult position. Under these circumstances, his refusal to join in acknowledging Soviet primacy would amount to arrogant defiance which he could ill afford and which, for ideological reasons, he did not cherish. While disagreeing on the nature of the socialist camp, he did not share Tito's more extreme position that the camp itself was expendable (see next chapter).

Gomulka was also faced with two other difficult demands. One was to systematize multilateral party contacts through a joint theoretical journal, reminiscent of the one published by the Cominform, and the other was openly to condemn revisionism as the major danger to international Communism, with its "excessive emphasis . . . on the peculiarities of individual countries." [70] Thus, in a curious case of history repeating itself, Gomulka was replaying the role he had played at the founding of the Cominform (see Chapter 3): opposing the almost unanimous pressure for monolithic international unity which would inevitably limit the domestic freedom of the smaller Communist states. But even though isolated, under pressure from all sides, lacking the support he had expected, even though faced by a conflict between his loyalty to Communism as an international system and his conception of a Polish way to Communism, his situation in 1957 in Moscow was more favorable than in 1947, at Szklarska Poreba. Stalin was gone and the Soviet claim to infallibility went with him. Gomulka was in control of his party and secure in the knowledge that his party's rule in Poland was being strengthened by his stand. The party was no longer entirely dependent on Soviet support, and he realized that, while he could not afford a complete break with the camp, the Soviet leadership preferred to avoid one also. And, finally, he must have felt that despite the unanimity of the views ranged against him he still symbolized a strong current within the Communist movement, a current of change which could be channeled, maybe dammed, but no longer reversed.

The outcome was a partial capitulation by Gomulka and a partial compromise by the others. The planned periodical was not mentioned in the declaration issued at the end of the conference, although the East Germans promptly revealed the conference's decision "in principle" to issue it.[71] (It did come out after some further delays in the fall of 1958, entitled "Problems of Peace and Socialism," published in Prague and edited by A. M. Rumyantsev, a specialist in ideological matters and former editor-in-chief of *Kommunist*.) As far as the major ideological issues were involved, the declaration as signed by Gomulka did use the formula "the socialist camp headed by the Soviet Union" *once;* elsewhere it employed Gomulka's version, "the first and mightiest state." On other issues, it is worthwhile to compare some of the points of the theses adopted by the CPSU on the occasion of its fortieth anniversary, which served as the basis for the Soviet position at the conference, with the declaration as issued following the discussions (with Yugoslavia abstaining):

CPSU theses	*Declaration of the ruling Communist parties*
The views of those who stress the national peculiarities of each country marching toward socialism, and who forget the general basic, fundamental principles of socialist revolution, are profoundly alien to Marxism-Leninism.	Disregard of national peculiarities by the proletarian party inevitably leads to its divorce from reality . . . is bound to prejudice the cause of socialism and, conversely, exaggeration of the role of these peculiarities or departure, under the pretext of national peculiarities, from the universal Marxist-Leninist truth . . . *is*

just as harmful to the socialist cause . . . both these tendencies should be combatted simultaneously (italics added).

The ideological subversive activities of the forces of reaction against the Communist movement have lately been reflected in the spread of the pernicious ideas of so-called "national communism," in the spread of all kinds of revisionist attacks within the Communist Parties . . . The Communist and Workers' Parties are waging a struggle against the harmful influence of present-day revisionism and giving it a fitting rebuff.[72]

The meeting underlines the necessity of resolutely overcoming revisionism *and dogmatism* . . . In condemning dogmatism, the Communist Parties believe that the *main danger at present* is revisionism . . . However, dogmatism and sectarianism *can also be the main danger* . . . It is for *each* Communist Party to decide what danger threatens it more at a given time (italics added).[73]

The above suggests that the declaration did not fully assert the centralist position even though Gomulka did join in acknowledging Soviet leadership. The declaration, however, while reflecting the pressures for unity and stressing again and again the areas of common interest and the universal laws of socialist development, left sufficient areas of ambiguity to allow Gomulka room for domestic maneuvering. Indeed, on his return home, Gomulka promptly reasserted his autonomous position by pointedly using his old formula for describing the USSR. In a speech addressed to several thousand Warsaw activists he attempted to balance the need for unity with his insistence on independence for Poland. He left no doubt that, unlike the Yugoslavs, he favored a community of Communist states since such liaison was needed for both ideological and power considerations in the age of imperialism. He thus still displayed a strong predilection toward the Leninist dichotomic vision of the world, even if qualified by his observations that trends in favor of coexistence were also noticeable in the West.[74] At the same time, however, he went out of his way to reassure his listeners that the declaration would not limit the Polish party's internal autonomy and that it was compatible with strict Polish interests.

In the same speech, Gomulka particularly emphasized that multilateral conferences could not dictate the internal affairs of any one party and, while conceding that such conferences were useful in addition to bilateral contacts (which he pointedly praised), he made the curious observation that they ought to be conducted on the basis of an agenda known beforehand to all its participants. Apparently Gomulka desired to protect himself against a repetition of the Moscow situation where demands for an acknowledgment of Soviet leadership and for a common journal were sprung on him without warning and contrary to the original draft resolution examined in Warsaw.

The persistence of some irritants notwithstanding, from the centralist point of view the conference was not without positive consequences. Above all else, it combined the notion of the "Communist commonwealth" with the recognition that such a commonwealth was headed by the USSR. Even Gomulka's insistence on returning to his old formula could not undo the precedent established in Moscow, namely that for the sake of unity he too was willing to concede a principle which had the potential for becoming an operational limitation on his own autonomy. The Soviet commentators clearly suggested that the acknowledgment of Soviet leadership implied the general applicability of Soviet experience elsewhere.[75] Gomulka's grudging concession would make it doubly difficult for him to resist pressures exerted in the name of the camp and buttressed by the authority of the recognized leader. In case of conflict, is not the leader best qualified to decide whether a party is exaggerating national peculiarities? Gomulka's concession thus represented the achievement of the minimum objective: retention of Poland within the camp with at least implied recognition that there were higher considerations than the peculiar requirements of the construction of socialism in Poland. Already the first tangible expression of this was the splitting of the Poles from the abstaining Yugoslavs. The conference helped to clarify — and with Gomulka's assent — the borderline which he could not cross without branding himself a traitor to Communism.

The challenge of evolution was thus met by a clearer proclamation of certain common features which must characterize a state building socialism,* and by the effort to reconstruct a center which could

* The declaration's statement of these "laws" was in effect a combination of the points made by Suslov and Gomulka's assertions, with the word "gradual" making the reference to agricultural socialization palatable to Gomulka: "These general laws are: leadership of the masses of the working people by the working class, the core of which is the Marxist-Leninist party, in bringing about a proletarian revolution in one form or another and establishing one form or another of the dictatorship of the proletariat; alliance of the working class with the bulk of the peasantry and other strata of the working people; the abolition of capitalist ownership and the establishment of public ownership of the basic means of production; gradual socialist reorganization of agriculture; planned development of the national economy with the aim of build-

authoritatively interpret the common standard. However, neither of these measures, even if satisfying the postulates of the centralists, meant a return to Stalinism. Stalinism did not require objective standards or acknowledgments of leadership as a basis for leadership. Stalinism was based on an enforced claim to infallibility and on the rigid transplantation of its own experience. The centralists merely adopted one of its facets, disciplined unity, but they were otherwise prepared to recognize that blind imposition of Soviet experience was in fact an impediment to that unity. This in itself represented a significant change in the internal relations of the bloc. The issue henceforth was between varying images of the camp and not a return, externally or internally, to the practices and theories of Stalinism.

The method employed to reconstruct the center testified to the new times. Unlike the period of Stalinism, Soviet leadership in the bloc was no longer an autonomous fact due entirely to Soviet power and monopoly of ideological experience. Soviet leadership in November 1957 was contingent in considerable measure on the backing that it received from Communist regimes much weaker than itself but strong enough to be needed if that leadership were to be asserted. China did play a crucial role, but it would be an error to underestimate the importance of centralist support from East Europe. Their vehemence and unanimity had the gradual effect of making Moscow appear Warsaw's best friend, thereby making Warsaw more responsive to Moscow. But, because of that, the Soviet leaders henceforth would have to take into account the more radical attitudes of their supporters in East Berlin or Prague or Sofia. This meant, in turn, that the internal insecurities of the more Stalinist-inclined Czech or Bulgarian leaderships would have to be reflected in the policies framed for the bloc by the Soviet leaders. Although the elevation of Soviet leadership to a matter of principle made a farce of the claim that the Communist camp had become a true commonwealth, the camp thus did differ significantly from the old Stalinist bloc. The latter could be compared to a military phalanx in which no one would

---

ing socialism and communism, raising the working people's standard of living; the accomplishment of a socialist revolution in the sphere of ideology and culture and the creation of a numerous intelligentsia devoted to the working class, the working people and the cause of socialism; the elimination of national oppression and the establishment of equality and fraternal friendship among peoples; defense of the achievements of socialism against encroachments by external and internal enemies; solidarity of the working class of a given country with the working class of other countries – proletarian internationalism."

even conceive of questioning Stalin's leadership and in which everyone acted with monolithic unity. The "socialist commonwealth" of November 1957 was much more like a political organization headed by a "boss" who, to be effective, always had to manipulate his forces in order to ensure himself the continued support of a powerful majority.

A good example of the new pattern was Soviet behavior at the November conference. The burden of the attack against the Poles was carried by the Chinese and the other parties, with the Soviets remaining "neutral." At the end, Khrushchev proposed a "compromise" involving the points already cited.[76] To some extent this may have been merely a maneuver designed to make the Soviet position seem most reasonable, but even so it did mark a new method of leadership in the camp. Moreover, the Soviet concessions to the Chinese and the self-confidence of Mao's criticisms of some Soviet doctrinal positions augured Peking's rising challenge to Moscow, even if at the time no one in the Kremlin could have anticipated the acrimony that subsequently came to characterize the relations between the two leaderships. At the same time, the partially successful Chinese effort to foist on the bloc a more militant line under the guise of unanimous acceptance of Soviet leadership had the effect of narrowing the gap dividing Khrushchev from Gomulka (and later even from Tito), thereby marking the beginning of what subsequently became an anti-Chinese coalition. Thus forcing Gomulka to bow to the principle of Soviet leadership was somewhat of a pyrrhic victory for the Chinese, and it certainly did not restore the former bloc unity.

The Stalinist bloc of Communist states had been in effect one totalitarian system with one undisputed head. The socialist commonwealth emerged as a number of totalitarian states (or, as in the case of Poland, a state ruled by a totalitarian party),[77] linked together by common goals and political pressures but still containing the dangerous seeds of pluralism.

A more general lesson taught by this brief phase in Communist relations was that in a system of states in which considerations of power are very closely linked with ideological goals, pressures inherently arise either for intense conflict or for ever-tightening bonds of solidarity and subordination. A loose federation of Communist states certainly is not precluded by Marxist-Leninist thought, although it would be difficult to conceive of it in practice. Power when combined with a conception of national interest can result in a loose association of states for the promotion of certain vague objectives or for the protection of certain interests. Such states, as in the British Commonwealth, can enjoy a variety of institutional arrangements and subscribe to a variety of basic outlooks. But power which is cultivated for the execution of tasks determined by ideological perspectives raises issues which inevitably produce conflict. Matters pertaining to the domestic development of any one state become critically relevant to the purposes of the international association of such states and generate polemic issues of doctrinal purity. (By analogy, the Catholic Church would find it difficult to embrace national churches not recognizing papal infallibility, for example, or tolerating polygamy.) Belief in one correct path stimulates rigorous condemnation of error. Fear of contamination is then translated into fear that the power of the state will be sidetracked from the correct purposes and historically ordained directions. To avoid this, there must be explicit and binding universal laws. But how can such laws be established, how can they be applied, and how can they be interpreted without creating pressures for discipline and an authoritative center to answer such questions?

Unless there is subordination, the "universal" laws can become a mere disguise for unlimited diversity (as in the case, for instance, of the Protestant movement). Diversity in turn is bound to create weakness and diffuse common purposes. The only way to establish unanimity in purpose and unity in action is to impose a common center and to maintain sharp distinctions between membership and nonmembership, between correct views and treasonable error. The effort to reconstruct the center and to obtain Poland's grudging subordination to it was meant to fulfill the former requirement. The struggle against Yugoslav revisionism, which followed shortly, was designed to establish the latter.

13 / UNITY THROUGH THE STRUGGLE AGAINST REVISIONISM

Let a hundred flowers bloom, let a hundred schools contend! — Mao Tse-tung, February 1957

Weed them out and use them as fertilizer . . . this is . . . the way in which we should beat revisionism. — Lu Ting-yi (Agitprop Chief, Kianghi), March 1958

WITH the issue of Soviet leadership seemingly and at least temporarily resolved, the other major problem facing the Communist camp was that of revisionism. If it can be said that China and Poland, in different ways, questioned the meaning of Soviet primacy, Yugoslavia introduced into the relations among Communist states the vexing problem of revisionism.

Revisionism has had a long history in the Communist movement. Conflicts of interpretation, tensions between "spontaneity" and "conciousness," reformism and class violence, have plagued the Communists at almost every turn in their quest for power. Bitter controversies and lasting splits were their usual by-products. The distinctive feature, however, of the new outlook which developed in some Communist parties following the dissipation of Stalinism and which was labeled revisionism was that it arose within ruling parties which had already effected the primary revolutionary break-through[1] and had created the structural outlines of a "socialist" society. The argument, even when involving doctrinal issues, revolved around the problem of reforming or improving a going concern, a People's Democracy, and not the methods to be adopted to promote the socialist revolution.

NONINSTITUTIONALIZED REVISIONISM

Revisionism following the dissipation of Stalinism and the October 1956 events was most pronounced within the Polish party, although all the ruling parties had been infected by it. The loosening of internal party discipline and the initial lack of a sense of direction in Gomulka's Poland led to a lively exchange of views in the course of which many of the tenets of Marxism-Leninism as applied in the USSR were questioned. According to B. Ponomarev, head of the CPSU Central Committee's department dealing with other Communist parties, the seven cardinal sins of revisionism were: (1) minimization of imperialist aggression; (2) denial of CPSU leadership; (3) rejection of class struggle and collaborationism between classes; (4) Social Democratism; (5) denial of Leninist dictatorship of the proletariat; (6) rejection of a centralized, disciplined party; and (7) adoption of national Communism.[2] In many respects, revisionism could be thus identified with the policies of the Polish and certainly the Yugoslav regimes. But revisionism was not merely a matter of political policy. Much of revisionist thought revolved around basic philosophical assumptions which, if adopted, would threaten the entire edifice of Marxism-Leninism.

Among the revisionist writers, the most coherent exposition, and therefore politically the most dangerous, was developed by Leszek Kolakowski, a former Stalinist ideologue and a gifted young scholar in philosophy. His views provoked a violent stir among the more orthodox Communists not only in Poland but particularly among the neo-Stalinists throughout the bloc. Kolakowski's views, not entirely original, were developed in a series of articles which appeared in the Communist literary journal, *Nowa Kultura*. The first of these "The Permanent and the Transitory Meaning of Marxism," [3] attacked the dogmatization of Marxism. It charged that Marxism had ceased being an intellectual concept and had become an institutional dogma. "Similarly, the word 'Marxist' no longer means a person who recognizes a definite, meaningful view of the world, but a person of a definite intellectual make-up who is distinguished by his readiness to recognize the views established institutionally." Maintaining that Marxism had made creative contributions to social and historical analysis, Kolakowski advocated that its "apparatus of concepts" be revised to keep up with more recent phenomena and warned against excessive commitment to any particular historical interpretation since the very "objectivity" of historical fact is open to question. History is usually politics looking backward, he warned, protesting against historical determinism as scientifically untenable. From these positions, Kolakowski moved against any party interference in scientific and intellectual pursuits, since any such interference is bound to be by definition, un-Marxist, for Marxism above all else is a continuing rational effort to understand the processes of change in material re-

ity. True Marxists do not need any special camp to protect the monolithic unity of their views.

His philosophical position was expounded later in the same year
in four successive weekly issues of *Nowa Kultura*,[4] in essays entitled
"Responsibility and History" and subdivided into four parts: "The
Conspiracy of Aesthetes," "The Opiate of the Great Demiurge,"
"Consciences and Social Progress," and "Hope and the Fabric of
History." To summarize Kolakowski's position, developed skillfully
and with great passion, is not an easy task. In the first essay, constructed as a dialogue between the intellectual and the revolutionary
(or, as it is hinted, the *apparatchik*), Kolakowski defends individual
judgment as superior morally and more reliable than dependence on
history and the social and economic forces that help to shape it. In
the other essays, Kolakowski maintains that historical determinism
not only fails as a source of moral criteria but is in itself merely a
political tool, invested with faith, and not a scientific doctrine. He
concludes by calling for an insistent commitment to a program based
on *moral* considerations, even if such a program is not immediately
feasible, and for an enduring suspicion toward any action commitment lest it become irrevocable while founded on error or ig-
norance.*

* The following three citations touch upon some of Kolakowski's central points:
"If we are forced to take some immediate attitude to current changes, then we
cannot, of course, wait for the uncertain results of historico-philosophical discussions
which may remain unresolved for a hundred years. Therefore, our choice will always
be best if it is detemined by that small particle of certainty which we possess. Lasting
moral values, elaborated in the long development of man up to this moment, are the
surest support we have if reality demands from us a choice which, ultimately, is also
of moral character. In any case, they are more worthy of confidence than any historical science. And this is the reason why, ultimately, I stick to my opinion.
    Whatever happens?
    Whatever happens . . ."
                                    ("The Conspiracy of Aesthetes" — the dialogue)
"I repeat that it was possible, in the difficult moments during the last war, to expect the laurel of victory to fall to the Nazis. This supposition is, in itself, not subject to moral judgment, but the practical conclusions drawn from it, and the attitude
adopted as a result of such a world view, are subject to such judgment. Nobody is
free of the moral responsibility for supporting a crime merely because he was intellectually convinced of its inevitable victory. Nobody is exempted from the moral
duty to fight against a system of rule, a doctrine, or social conditions which he considers to be vile and inhuman by resorting to the argument that he considers them
historically necessary. We protest against such forms of moral relativism in which
it is assumed that the criteria or moral judgment of human action can be deduced
from knowledge of the *Weltgeist* . . ."
                                    ("The Opiate of the Great Demiurge")
"A philosophy of history worthy of consideration describes only what has existed,
the past, and not the creative future of the historical process. For this reason, those

Not surprisingly, Kolakowski was extensively criticized with
and without Poland. His views, it must be admitted, would unde
mine the very basis of a Communist's subordination to the party ar
the subordination of the party to any one ideological center. As a r
sult, they could hardly pass unchallenged. The Soviet philosophic
journal devoted a full article to him, mixing its refutations with stror
doses of invective: "a pitiful compilation of already nauseating attac]
on Marxism," "hysterical defamation," "naive," and so forth.[5] Oth
Soviet journals, as well as the satellite press, followed suit, both
form and content.[6] The brunt of the attack was on the "objective
consequences of such views: "What Imre Nagy did in Hungary
practical politics, the Kolakowskis are doing in theory," *Pravda* coi
cluded.[7]

Polish revisionism, by provoking reaction elsewhere, became
matter of interparty relations. In the case of the Polish revisionis
however, an important extenuating circumstance tended to conta
the centrifugal implications of the revisionist dialogue. Even thoug
Kolakowski spoke as a party member, and even though in the la
summer of 1957 he became editor of an important philosophical jou
nal, he did not speak for the party, his views were not endorsed k
its leadership, and Gomulka even singled him out for criticism.
Polish revisionism, through its universalist intellectual position, a
peared to be on the market for export, it was definitely not sponsor
by the party, the leadership of which was just in the process of ma
ing its accommodation with the rest of the camp. More and more,
the Polish party consolidated its position (see next chapter), the Poli
revisionists became the spokesmen for alienated intellectuals,[8] c
vorced from power.

The Harich case in Germany was another important case of no
institutionalized revisionism. Wolfgang Harich, like Kolakowski,
philosopher with one-time strong Stalinist leanings, became concern
after Stalin's death with the inability of Communism to adjust to p
culiar national conditions[9] and, together with several other East Ge
man Communist intellectuals, began holding discussions to crystalli

---

who wish to subordinate their own engagement in future processes to the pronoun
ments of the philosophy of history are only tourists who write their names on t
walls of dead cities. Everybody can, if he wishes, interpret himself historically a
discover the determinisms to which he was subject in the past. But he cannot do
with respect to the self he has not yet become. He cannot deduce his own futu
development from the pronouncements of the philosophy of history in which
trusts. To work such a miracle would mean to become the irrevocable past ones
that is, to cross the river of death which, the poet says, no one ever sees twice."
("Hope and the Fabric of History

a Communist program of action more in keeping with German traditions. In this he was encouraged by the Soviet policy toward Yugoslavia and particularly toward Poland after October 19, 1956. By November 1956 he and his associates drafted an extensive program, based in some respects on the Polish pattern, and Harich proceeded to make contacts in Poland and with the SPD in West Germany. The latter step proved to be his undoing, for it gave the East German regime an easy opportunity for an accusation of treason. Harich was accordingly arrested and sentenced in March 1957 to ten years' imprisonment.

However, unlike those Polish revisionists, who before October 1956 made common cause with the party leaders anxious to restore Gomulka to power, Harich's group had no influential support in the party *apparat* and failed to join with a group of party leaders who were surreptitiously opposing Ulbricht's leadership. This group, crushed by Ulbricht early in February 1958, and composed of K. Schirdewan, E. Wollweber, and F. Oelssner, had already in late 1956 considered the necessity of large-scale concessions and thus leaned in a direction toward which Harich was headed. Harich's program, despite his Leninist protestations, however, went too far in calling for common SPD-SED action and free elections, the consequence of which would be the collapse of East Germany.[10] This was too much for even the anti-Ulbricht elements in the party, just as Kolakowski's views were unpalatable to the practitioners of power in Poland. Noninstitutionalized revisionism could not effectively challenge the institutions of power. Primarily a long-run threat to the party's sway over the intellectuals, its essentially utopian bent made it ineffective as an action program.

THE QUEST FOR UNITY: TITO OUTMANEUVERED

The Yugoslav practitioners of power did not permit an ideological dialogue outside the party's direction. To Moscow, this was a reassuring sign. Like Harich, the chief Yugoslav revisionist, Djilas, was rotting in jail. The Yugoslav party tolerated within itself no views other than those endorsed by its leadership, and the latter's firmness against Djilas underscored its determination to crush anyone who undermines the party's ideology and discipline. The ambivalent position taken by Tito on the Hungarian uprising, and the sacrificing of Nagy on the spurious guarantee of Kadar, indicated a fundamental commitment to a common outlook and to common practices which made Khrushchev unwilling to write Tito off as already on the other side of the barricade. Admittedly, the very fact of Yugoslav discipline made the portent of any Yugoslav revisionist views more serious since such expressions could not be differentiated, as in Poland, from the leadership. Nonetheless, Tito, in Soviet eyes, had not burned all his bridges, and the Chinese formula could be utilized transitionally to minimize areas of disagreement, to stress the common outlook and fundamental aspirations, and to promote the maximum objective of the Communist camp for the year 1957: drawing Yugoslavia back into the bloc.

For their part, the Yugoslavs still clung desperately to the views crystallized during their "painful reappraisal" between the two Junes of 1955–1956, in spite of the violent attacks directed at them early in 1957 (Chapters 11 and 12). Just as their own doctrinal perspectives had made them leery of Soviet overtures in 1955, their new outlook made them basically hopeful about relations with the Communist states, the Hungarian events and anti-Tito invective notwithstanding. They dismissed all of these manifestations as hangovers from the past, all the more violent since their Stalinist "socioeconomic" basis was said by them to be slipping away. Convinced that Stalinism, and therefore also centralism, was dead — and unable to perceive that the latter was possible without the former — they looked almost benignly on the frothings of Hoxha or the Bulgarians, firm in their belief that such vituperation stemmed from weakness. They were particularly optimistic in their evaluation of the Soviet scene. Here two factors were central. Tito and his associates apparently believed that in the Soviet leadership a continuing struggle was being waged between Stalinists and Khrushchev, the latter dedicated to a more moderate version of Communist relations; and that this power struggle was merely obscuring the fact that Soviet society by 1956 had largely shaken the dominant characteristics of Stalinism. In the long run, the base was bound to affect the superstructure, even if Khrushchev were to lose in the meantime.

However, since they considered themselves to be a socialist (Communist) society and since their actions were bound to affect the Communist camp, the Yugoslavs thought it unwise to do anything which might prejudice Khrushchev's chances. They felt that his collapse would in turn minimize their role in that camp. Their stand on the Hungarian revolution and their support for Kadar, whom they identified with Khrushchev and, above all else, their support for Gomulka were rooted in this orientation. Khrushchev's consolidation of power following the expulsion of his opponents in June of 1957 was greeted by great enthusiasm in Belgrade, where the Soviet opposition to him was categorized under the all-embracing term of Stalinism. His victory was held to be a vindication of the Yugoslav trust that change in Moscow would have to come.

Undoubtedly, personal and domestic factors played a role in framing this Yugoslav stand. While very little is known about disagreements within the Yugoslav leadership, it appears that, as in Moscow, there were conflicts of interpretation of Soviet-Yugoslav relations. Judging from the public record, it is evident that Kardelj had been most explicit in stressing those aspects of the Yugoslav doctrine which were irritating to the Soviets. Rankovic, Tito's likely successor, on the other hand, was reported to have become concerned over the potential demoralization within the party ranks as a result of protracted Yugoslav isolation, and he therefore favored closer links with the camp. To Tito, an isolated Communist leader on capitalist dole, a return to the status of 1956 would have meant a repetition of his triumph and his restoration as one of the leaders of international Communism. Not surprisingly, after the June Kremlin purge Tito immediately moved in the direction of a rapprochement with Khrushchev who, for reasons noted earlier, was also not inclined to interpret current Yugoslav doctrines as an insurmountable barrier to a stress of common ideological and political commitment. Hoping to restore unity, Moscow accordingly encouraged the Yugoslav attitude:

> Our views are identical in the majority [of cases]. Both the USSR and Yugoslavia consider the main task of all peace-loving people to be the struggle for relaxation of international tension, for a general reduction of armaments and for the unconditional prohibition of atomic and hydrogen weapons . . . Every possibility exists for even broader and more fruitful cooperation between our countries, particularly since the June plenary meeting of the CPSU condemning the anti-Party group of Malenkov, Kaganovich and Molotov, who attempted to destroy the unity of our country and to attack its general line — the historical decisions of the Twentieth CPSU Congress.[11]

Within days of the Moscow shake-up, Tito requested a meeting with Khrushchev.* Such direct contact with Moscow was not only the logical consequence of the Yugoslav position but also fitted in

---

* On July 11, while in Prague, Khrushchev referred to a forthcoming meeting with Tito (*Le Monde*, July 12, 1957) and in 1958 explicitly stated that it had been Tito who requested it (*Pravda*, June 4, 1958). Thus Tito must have made his move almost immediately after the expulsion of the anti-Khrushchev elements.

with the Yugoslav procedural emphasis on bilateralism "which includes in itself the struggle against hegemony and centralism." [12] In their enthusiasm, the Yugoslavs apparently were even prepared to ignore those pronouncements of Khrushchev which seemed to run counter to the Yugoslav notion of his *real* views. Within days of a speech by Tito on June 25, in which he had referred to the Workers' Councils as "one of the greatest, indeed it may be said one of the historic acts in the development of Yugoslavia's socialist order," Khrushchev was sneeringly referring to the Councils as having been constructed with American funds and warning that there was only one kind of socialism good for all nations.[13] He then laid down in the same speech his conditions for an improvement in relations: "We won't criticize you, and you must not interfere in our affairs . . . But if you want to criticize us, comrades, we know how to pay back." [14] This would be the message he would give Tito, Khrushchev boasted, promising to point out to him that Western support for Yugoslavia was based on a desire to split the international Communist movement. "What do we want?" he asked rhetorically. "We want unity, closed ranks, and rallied forces. We acknowledge different paths, comrades. But among the different paths, there is one general path, and the others are, as you know, like a big river with tributaries." [15]

Despite the uncompromising tone of these assertions, Tito apparently persisted in his belief that Khrushchev represented a "progressive force," that he deserved all the support he could get, and that his statements still left room for diversity and cooperation. Believing that the phase of upheavals in East Europe had ceased and that the Stalinist faction in the USSR had been routed, Belgrade felt optimistic about a gradual return to the June 1956 principles. However, this time the Yugoslav sights were more limited. No longer interested in precipitating rapid changes in East Europe lest they provoke a repetition of the Hungarian situation, Tito hoped instead to obtain Khrushchev's assent to greater diversity among the existing Communist regimes, an endorsement of Yugoslavia's independent position, a halt in satellite censure of Yugoslavia,[16] and renewed economic cooperation. Indeed, a renewal of Soviet aid, suspended in February, was announced on June 30 after an exploratory trip to the USSR by Rankovic and Kardelj. It was within this conflicting framework of cross-purposes and expectations, a curious repetition in reverse of the 1955 and 1956 pattern, that Tito hastened to meet Khrushchev on August 1 and 2 in Bucharest.

According to the limited information available,[17] the conversations resulted in a limited agreement which both sides hoped would pave the way for the fulfillment of their longer-range objectives. Khrushchev apparently reiterated his warning against open Yugoslav attacks on the Communist camp, although agreeing to promote a cease-fire in the camp's anti-Yugoslav campaign. Playing on the "I need you against the Stalinists" theme, Khrushchev skillfully obtained the Yugoslav endorsement of Soviet foreign policy in Europe, particularly in terms of Yugoslav recognition of East Germany and support for the Soviet position in the Middle East — steps calculated to result in Western resentment against Yugoslavia. The Yugoslavs, furthermore, agreed to participate formally in the forthcoming November 1957 Moscow conference and to help draft the resolution, thereby implicitly signaling their membership in the international Communist movement.[18] To the Yugoslavs, these concessions appeared to be worth the price. The declaration that was issued after the meeting pointedly did not establish proletarian internationalism as one of the key characteristics of Soviet-Yugoslav relations, a point which the Poles had by then conceded, and it reaffirmed the validity of the 1955 and 1956 Soviet-Yugoslav declarations. The stage thus appeared to be set for a return, on a modified basis, to the diversity which the Yugoslavs so desired, and Tito was preparing for his triumphant appearance at the Moscow celebrations as one of the chief leaders of Communism, on a par with Khrushchev and Mao Tse-tung, not to mention Gomulka.

The August conference was the last attempt to bridge the gap between the Soviet efforts to establish a unity based on *belonging* and Tito's insistence, by then limited primarily to Yugoslavia, on unity through association. The solution appeared on surface to have been a substantive agreement on external issues and ideology, but without formal Yugoslav membership and with the Soviet recognition of their independence. The compromise, however, did not bridge the disagreement in basic perspectives. The conflict between the traditional Soviet dichotomic image of the world and the Yugoslav version of an interrelated, world-wide, and largely organic development toward socialism was not resolved. The latter viewpoint necessarily made a more diffuse Communist camp the only intelligible method of operation. The former demanded unity and a center.

The Yugoslavs, much like the Poles, underestimated the pressures for such unity and placed false hopes on the person of Khrushchev. His elasticity in tactics and a willingness to experiment apparently made it possible for him to convince Tito that his desire to shake off the inexpedient remnants of Stalinism also involved a departure from the dichotomic vision. But it was only on this tactical level that Khrushchev was willing to adopt occasionally more flexible positions than his more rigid colleagues in the camp. His determination to launch Communism on a new dynamic phase, unencumbered by those features of Stalinism which were only necessary in the "revolutionary" period, did not involve junking the Leninist notions of a cohesive, monolithic movement. The forced wedding of August 1957 could not be consummated.

Tito tried his utmost. Even though Belgrade acknowledged after the meeting that "an abyss" still divided the CPSU from the Yugoslav Communists,[19] in mid-October Tito recognized East Germany, thereby undermining his ties with the West and causing the Western press to proclaim his return to the Soviet camp. He intensified his contacts with Kadar. In mid-September, at Gomulka's urging, possibly in an effort to improve the Pole's position as the "honest broker" between Belgrade and Khrushchev, Tito accepted proletarian internationalism as one of the principles guiding relations among Communist states. "Coexistence of socialist states" was not mentioned, while the usefulness of multilateral contacts, in addition to bilateralism, was endorsed.[20] While not going so far as to accept the Soviet line on unity of Communist states, Tito did endorse the notion that a "strengthening" of relations between Communist states was desirable. Tito basically lived up to his part of the bargain.*

To have expected Khrushchev to live up to his commitment to implement the pledges of 1956 involved a thorough misreading of Khrushchev's position. While it might be an exaggeration to maintain that this entire episode had been a cunning plot to isolate Yugoslavia from the West and then to confront it with demands it could no longer afford to refuse, thereby forcing it into the camp, Khrushchev's maneuver was clearly designed to stimulate external pressures on Yugoslavia which would limit its freedom of action. In keeping with this, the draft resolution of the November conference, submitted in advance to Belgrade, did not contain any reference to Soviet leadership, a point which would have been displeasing to Gomulka and absolutely intolerable to Tito. At the same time, however, the

---

* The full measure of the Yugoslav concessions can be better appreciated by comparison with a later article in *Politika* (December 26, 1957) which restated the original Yugoslav position after a worsening in Soviet-Yugoslav relations and which described proletarian internationalism as "nothing but a nice idea" which, however, was used to impose discipline on socialist states.

draft reiterated the fundamental Communist dichotomic position on world affairs, thereby not only making shambles of the Yugoslav claim to neutrality but also implicitly establishing the binding principle of unity, a mere hair's breadth away from the unarticulated premise of Soviet leadership. The accompanying attacks on revisionism (only subsequently balanced by attacks on dogmatism), while not singling Yugoslavia out, were in effect condemning the very basis for Yugoslav domestic policies. These points Khrushchev had to include. Not to have done so, given the parallel Polish problem (Chapter 12), would have meant the discarding of the principal doctrinal tenets and the destruction of almost the last remaining ideological bonds among Communist states since the dissipation of Stalinism and the resurgence of domesticism.[21] No Soviet leader could do that, least of all when faced with pressure from centralist elements at home and abroad. November, after all, was to be a triumphant celebration of forty years of expansion, hardly the occasion for the public abandonment of the basic concepts of the struggle.

Tito accordingly refrained from making the trip to Moscow and was represented by Kardelj and Rankovic. The fact that a Yugoslav delegation attended in full knowledge that a declaration would be issued suggests that the Yugoslavs still hoped to be able to reach some accommodation to justify their signature on the declaration. Possibly, in addition, they preferred not to leave Gomulka, and even Kadar, prematurely isolated. Nonetheless, at the conference, like the Poles, they were suddenly confronted with demands which went considerably beyond the draft and surprised by Mao's insistence on an unequivocal statement of Soviet leadership. Less surprisingly, Mao also was the most adamant in insisting on a severe condemnation of the West with which, of all the Communist states, China was on the worst footing.

Outmaneuvered by Khrushchev and misled by their own evaluations, and with their concessions already implemented, the Yugoslav delegation had only two choices left. They could either capitulate or refuse to sign: the latter move would place them outside the international Communist movement. But even at this critical juncture the Yugoslavs strove to equivocate. They refused to sign the declaration but, so as not to burn all their bridges, then endorsed the Peace Manifesto proposed by Gomulka and signed by all parties. Curiously, however, even though the manifesto was more temperate in its formulation, it still implicitly endorsed the Soviet line and strongly hinted at a world divided into imperialists and anti-imperialists. Disappointed by Khrushchev, outraged by the Chinese, and placed outside the pale, the Yugoslavs still sought to save face. Yet it was precisely their compromising policy and their attendance which strengthened the universal legitimacy of the November conference and which gave Khrushchev a firm basis for warning the Yugoslavs that their actions were inimical to international Communism. A deserter usually provokes greater indignation than an enemy.

INSTITUTIONAL AND INTERNATIONAL REVISIONISM

The Yugoslav abstinence, following directly on the heels of a series of gestures suggesting that common areas of agreement would finally prevail over points of disagreement, meant that a mere return to the pre-August situation was no longer feasible. Yugoslavia had come so close to the camp that drawing back emphasized all the differences which previously had kept them apart. To the Communist camp, the Yugoslav position translated revisionism from an internal affair of a party into an institutional system with international overtones. The consequence of November was hence to push both sides further apart and to render explicit the underlying disagreement.

Of the two sides, it was the Yugoslavs who, in their disappointment and embarrassment, were the more aggressive. In order to justify to their own party the strange zigzags of their relations with the USSR, they were increasingly driven into articulating their position and indicating why the "strengthening" of relations among Communist states, so recently endorsed by Tito, resulted three months later in open defiance of the entire camp. It is to be recalled that the Yugoslav public was not informed by its press of the arrangements made by Tito at Bucharest, which resulted in a certain disorientation. The most reliable way of minimizing it was to raise again the banner of independence and to revive Yugoslav claims to an original and universally valid development of Marxism-Leninism.

It appears further that the November events shook the Yugoslav leaders to the point of their undertaking a broad revision of the perspective developed between 1955 and 1956. The reappraisal led them gradually to the conclusion that they had not only underestimated centralist pressures within the bloc but had mistakenly assigned Khrushchev the label of an anticentralist reformer. They belatedly moved, therefore, to systematize an ideological alternative to the November resolution in order to sum up, in one self-contained message, the scattered and often contradictory Yugoslav ideological pronouncements. Such a document was needed since their earlier statements, while perhaps useful to scholars or analysts, could not be construed by Communists abroad and in Yugoslavia as a sufficiently cogent answer to the dichotomic, centralist argument.* Abandoning any hope of working from within as a bona fide socialist ally, they proceeded to lay the ground for an external ideological challenge. They did so with Khrushchev's warning not to criticize the Soviets openly still ringing in their ears. This in itself is evidence to support the proposition that the Yugoslav position shifted radically after November 1957. In the spring of 1958 the Yugoslavs finally moved to create what they had lacked in 1956: a coherent ideological alternative to the prevailing framework. Unfortunately for them, the political situation was much less in their favor than in October 1956.

The Yugoslav theoreticians accordingly proceeded to cement their claims to being the true Leninists by broadly hinting that Lenin's major contribution to Marxism involved *revisions* of previous thinking (especially on revolution and imperialism) and by asserting that it was Lenin who first recognized the fatal dangers of dogmatism, the antithesis of revisionism. "Once dogmatism nestles within a proletarian party . . . such a party can no longer do anything sensible; life passes such a party by, and the party cannot influence life," they warned, reminding the Communist states that it is idle to assume that all their internal difficulties spring only from "imperialist machinations." [22] In keeping with the revived emphasis on originality, the Workers' Councils, politely ignored even by Tito in his joint declaration with Gomulka, again became fashionable. Writing in the theoretical weekly, a Yugoslav sociologist, M. Hadzi-Vasilev, critically compared the Yugoslav Workers' Councils with the newly instituted Soviet production conferences and reached the not unexpected conclusion that only the Councils are capable of resolving the "antagonistic contradictions" which arise as a consequence of "the danger of the bureaucratic usurpation by the state" of all control.[23] Hadzi-Vasilev rejected as merely propagandistic the Soviet contention that their workers, working in a socialist state, were therefore working for themselves, and pointed out the need for each worker to realize that his individual interests are represented in his

---

* It was also needed because of the prevailing ideological confusion in the Yugoslav party ranks, caused by the policies of the preceding two years. See the "Circular Letter of the Executive Committee, Central Committee, Union of Communists, to all Organizations and Leading Organs of the UCJ, about Future Tasks of UC in the Struggle for the Elimination of Negative Manifestations in the Political, Economic, and Social Life as Well as Elimination of Shortcomings in the Work of UC," Belrade, February 28, 1958.

work. This the Workers' Councils were said to do, while their absence in the USSR, he implied, allowed for the arbitrary identification of "individual interest with the collective and then on that basis building up all economic relationships in the name of a great future." [24] Other Yugoslavs pointed out that by stressing primarily the struggle against capitalism, the dogmatic Communists created a "one-sided" identification of socialism with the state and all its regulations. This was said to be a more primitive version of socialist development than the "higher and complicated" Yugoslav pattern, a statement which more than hinted at Yugoslav ideological primacy.[25] The stage was thus set for the unveiling of the Yugoslav program which would mark the final break with the hopes and calculations of the two preceding years.

Following the November conference the Soviet leadership maintained a restrained position. The Soviet attitude of August 1957 was not incompatible with Khrushchev's public warnings in Prague, and had been premised on the primary goal of forging close unity which would, only if possible and not at any price, also include Yugoslavia. The outcome of the conference, therefore, gave no cause for sudden shifts, even with the Yugoslav abstinence and increasing articulateness. The Soviet illusions concerning Yugoslavia had been gradually fading since October 1956 and, while the Soviet leader was prepared to make one last try in August 1957, he was already coy and waited for the Yugoslavs to come forth. As far as Khrushchev was concerned, Tito was no longer to be treated as a great leader or as a threat. Rather, the policy was to treat Yugoslavia as an unimportant small country, in the meantime consolidating the political unity of the bloc.

Accordingly, the Soviets proceeded in the spring of 1958 to buttress the position won in the November meeting. On March 14, a Prague conference, attended by representatives of the leading European Communist parties, including Gomulka's, made a preliminary decision to publish a common theoretical journal. Poland, increasingly isolated because of the Chinese position and the Yugoslav withdrawal bowed to these demands, made in the midst of a mounting campaign against revisionism within Communist ranks. What is more, throughout the bloc revisionism was identified with increasing frequency a treason, and "the merciless suppression and liquidation of revisionis views as an important precondition of the triumph of socialism" wa postulated.[26] Dogmatism was no longer mentioned, except in Poland and prominent "dogmatists," such as Vulko Chervenkov, Tito's *bêt noir,* were again coming to the fore.[27] The authoritative theoretical journal of the CPSU led the campaign by warning that it had to be expected that the revisionists would intensify their efforts and refine their methods following their rebuff at the November conference.[28]

From the antirevisionist point of view this warning was vindicated by the publication on March 13, 1958, of the draft program for the forthcoming congress of the League (Union) of Communists of Yugoslavia. The contents of the lengthy 100,000-word document signaled both to Moscow and to Peking that revisionism, not just anti-Stalinism, had become formally linked with the power of the Yugoslav party and that it was being formulated as the latest and most important refinement of Marxist-Leninist doctrine. The program, while emphasizing its particular relevance to the Yugoslav party, reiterated that it "represents the analysis of the contemporary differences in the world . . . expressing the principled views on some of the most essential problems of the contemporary international workers' movement and the development of socialism in the world." [29] Such claims of universality, following in the footsteps of Yugoslavia's November stand, would have caused major irritation, even if the contents of the document had not been objectionable.

But the document was also bound to be irritating. Had the Yugoslav leaders limited themselves in their comprehensive statement to matters clearly within Yugoslav practical purview, they conceivably might have avoided provoking the ire of the Communist parties elsewhere. Since Marxist-Leninist perspectives, however, necessarily involve evaluation of broad international trends, the Yugoslavs could hardly have done so without renouncing their implicit claim to being the true Marxists-Leninists. Indeed, to limit their concepts to Yugoslavia alone would have been a roundabout way of admitting that which the Yugoslavs always reject, namely national Communism. As a result, they felt justified in commenting authoritatively from the Marxist-Leninist perspective on world affairs, on the problematics of the march toward socialism, and on relations among Communist states. Not unexpectedly, these proved to be the most offending passages.

Aware of the charges of revisionism leveled against them, the Yugoslavs' statement went to some pains to define the prevailing deviations from the "true" doctrine and discovered them in "two ideological tendencies": dogmatic revisionism and bourgeois revisionism. The former springs from bureaucratism and etatism, leads toward "pseudo-revolutionary sectarianism and . . . the loss of confi-

dence in the strength of the working class," toward internal violence
and terroristic rule, and expresses itself by branding as "revisionism
every true effort aimed at really developing the Marxist idea in the
contemporary social conditions." The Yugoslavs also rejected bourgeois revisionism, which was said to be based on outmoded "bourgeois-democratic illusions" and which, in effect, provides the dogmatic
revisionists with their ammunition. Thus Western social democracy
was also explicitly rejected. The Yugoslavs were calling upon all
Communists to wage a struggle "on two fronts" in order to preserve
and promote socialism, once again establishing themselves as the only
legitimate standard-bearers of the Marxist-Leninist ideology.

The Yugoslavs then proceeded to pass judgment on the most vital
issues in the Communist world view. Declaring themselves to be simultaneously an integral part of both "the socialist world" and of
"the European and world community," the Yugoslavs ascribed most
of the prevailing international tension to the existence of "two blocs"
which were fathered by the wartime creation of spheres of influence
between the major allied powers. Without differentiating between
the two blocs, the declaration flatly asserted that "the division of the
world into blocs impedes the realization of the idea of coexistence,
and is at odds with full independence and sovereignty of peoples and
states." The statement, made in the name of Marxism-Leninism, pitted
not only capitalism but the Communist camp itself directly against the
best interests of mankind.

In addition, the Yugoslavs, taking a broad look at the socioeconomic processes of the contemporary age, rejected the notion that,
in the progression toward socialism, the Communist parties were indispensable tools of historical change. Doctrines to that effect were
denounced as "theoretically wrong and practically very damaging."
The Yugoslavs asserted that even under conditions of capitalism the
state, because of the complexity of modern economy and technology,
is increasingly limiting the role of private capital and that, while the
danger of Fascism is incipient in that development, the overwhelming
pressures of the increasingly articulate working class are pushing society into the epoch of socialism. "Socialism is more and more becoming the matter of the practice of all nations, it is ever more becoming
a universal process and system," the Yugoslavs postulated.

With socialism expanding, the question of relations among the
Communist states was all the more pressing. Commenting on it, the
Yugoslavs pointed to the pernicious consequences for the interna-
tional Communist movement of the "bureaucratic-etatistic tendencies"

which arose in the USSR because of its retarded prerevolutionary condition and which were encouraged "subjectively" by Stalin. These tendencies were said to have resulted in dogmatism. However, the Yugoslavs noted hopefully, the consequent deformation in the Soviet socialist system had not been fundamental and had been basically shaken by the Twentieth Congress. In the new circumstances produced by it, the various Communist states were able to give more adequate attention to their domestic conditions. But the Communist parties must at all times be conscious of their own national peculiarities, and no party can be allowed to acquire a monopoly of ideological evaluation in the Communist world, even if a specific party, because of its special power, can at some time become the standard-bearer in the struggle for Communism. "Proclamation of the road and form of development of socialism of any country as being the only correct one is nothing else but dogma, which impedes the process of socialist transformation in the world." Accordingly proletarian internationalism could no longer be defined in terms of one's attitude toward the USSR but in terms of respect and noninterference among all socialist forces. Its true application would not allow a situation in which "it has been possible for a socialist country to maintain in various forms unequal relations with one or several other socialist countries."

It would be inconceivable to assume that the Yugoslavs did not expect a violent reaction to the above theses from the Communist camp. The draft program involved a denial of the dichotomic image so crucial to the existence of the Communist camp and the Communist Party, a denial of Soviet leadership, and a theoretical statement which, by attempting to establish a general perspective for the prevailing historical phase, could be construed as the latest and most authoritative alternative to the views crystallized by the November Moscow declaration. Even if the Yugoslav condemnations of the USSR were somewhat more veiled than at their preceding congress and even if the program did make some concessions, such as abandonment of "coexistence" as the basis for relations among Communist states, it still postulated concepts profoundly alien to Soviet thinking and, what is more, the Yugoslavs must have known it. Past Yugoslav criticisms could have been discounted as essentially reactions to the "aberrations" of Stalinism. But, in Soviet eyes, there could be no excuse for such an ideologically divisive move in 1958. The violent reaction from Moscow and the other Communist capitals was not long in forthcoming.

In a transparent effort to appear conciliatory once the damage had been done, and possibly in response to Polish pleas for moderation, the Yugoslavs, almost on the very day that a lengthy denunciation of their program was published in the CPSU's *Kommunist*,[30] made certain revisions in their text. Most particularly, they rephrased the part pertaining to the two blocs to differentiate between NATO and the "defensive" Warsaw Pact, omitting the discussion of the ancestry of "spheres of influence." The fundamental theses, however, were not amended — and hardly could be, once the Yugoslavs had re-evaluated the internal conditions in the Communist camp and had decided that a crystallization of an ideological alternative, and not secretive Tito-Khrushchev arrangements, was the best method of influencing the pattern of Communist development.[31]

The conflict with the Communist camp, semidormant since November, at once came to life. Speeches by Yugoslav leaders to their congress, boycotted demonstratively by the Communist parties, further sharpened the disagreement by replying to external criticisms. The underlying theme of the speeches, starting with Tito's, was emphasis on Yugoslav independence and a labeling of all criticisms as interference in Yugoslav affairs.[32] At the same time, stress was laid on two superficially contradictory propositions: the program's universality was emphasized together with pointed assertions of precisely those points on which the Yugoslav position differed from the Communist camp. Indeed, as if determined to destroy the Chinese-Soviet diversity-in-unity formula, the Yugoslavs ignored the points of agreement.

Yet there seems to have been a method in this apparent contradiction. By simultaneously stressing disagreement and suggesting that their program had universal relevance,* the Yugoslavs were establishing their doctrine as an alternative to the established views and were making up for the errors of 1956 when they had allowed themselves to overstress the points of agreement with the camp. In 1958, frustrated in their efforts to work from within and resentful of being ignored, the Yugoslavs were determined to bring existing ideological conflicts into the open. Belgrade remained convinced that underlying

---

* Yugoslav commentators left no doubt that Tito's horizon did not end on the Rumanian or Bulgarian frontiers. For instance, N. Pasic in "Socialism as a World Process" flatly asserts the following: "The Program elaborates and solves the fateful dilemma between war and peace in this atomic century within the framework of a well-developed and scientifically validated conception of active coexistence . . . The conception of socialism as a world process is the basic view from which the UCJ Program considers and appraises the situation in the international workers' movement . . . Conscious socialist forces will be much more successful in their struggle if they realize more clearly the world proportion of the process of growth of socialism and the great wealth of is forms." *Nasa Stvarnost*, May 1958.

social forces working for more heterogeneity within the camp would ultimately prevail and that open exposure would give a sense of direction to and facilitate such processes. In his address to the congress, Tito professed to see signs of this already, as for instance in the greater reliance on bilateralism within the camp[33] (even if, for the time being, not used for the right ends), and the Yugoslavs hoped that ultimately Communist unity would be restored by unanimous acceptance of the principle of diversity.

THE DYNAMICS OF LEADERSHIP

The struggle against revisionism was acquiring concreteness. The vagueness of "the many ways to socialism" period and the difficulties of making a qualitative judgment when faced with evolutionary changes gave way to a concretization of the enemy, to the unmasking of revisionism as not merely an act of revising a sacred tenet but as its actual betrayal. On that score, particularly in view of the possible consequences of revisionism for the less stable Communist regimes, there was essential agreement among the other ruling Communist parties, save that of Poland. There was uncertainty, however, in how best to react against it, particularly the Yugoslav form.

Following November 1957, Khrushchev's apparent remedy was to ignore Tito, thereby denying him status through mutual dialogue and debate. It would appear that the Soviet leaders felt that the Yugoslav initiative in the fall of 1957 had sufficiently compromised Tito and that restraint in reaction would implicitly deny the relevance of Yugoslav views outside of Yugoslavia, while maintaining the formula of not stressing differences.* The publication of the draft program, however, must have raised questions about the wisdom of such tactics and presumably placed the Soviet leader under pressure from the centralist elements neighboring on Yugoslavia and most hostile to Tito. The Soviet position accordingly shifted. Until the publication of the program, and despite the November disagreement, all the Communist parties planned to send official delegations to the Yugoslav congress, thereby tacitly confirming Yugoslav status as a regime guided by Marxism-Leninism. On April 5 Belgrade was confidentially informed of the Soviet decision to boycott the congress,[34] but the

* There is reason to believe that until then the Soviets were toying halfheartedly with the possibility of limited reconciliation. Kadar held an exploratory meeting with Tito on Yugoslav soil on March 27–28, and there are some grounds for suspecting that another Tito-Khrushchev meeting was being considered. Khrushchev arrived in Budapest on April 2 but, with neither side yielding, the meeting with Tito (as far as is known) was not held.

matter was not made public, presumably in the hope of still effecting some Yugoslav concessions. At the same time, the preparation of an official rebuttal to the Yugoslav program was initiated, and the issue of *Kommunist* containing it was set into print on April 15. Two days later the Yugoslav *Komunist* printed the minor Yugoslav revisions, which presumably had been communicated to the other parties. On April 19 the Soviet critique was made public, and its text suggests that the Yugoslav revisions had come too late to be considered in the Moscow statement. The estrangement of the preceding few months had become a public matter.

Quite naturally, the *Kommunist* critique attempted to refute particularly those parts of the Yugoslav statement which appeared to undermine the general Bolshevik perspective and which criticized the pattern of relations within the Communist camp.[35] It involved essentially a restatement of familiar Soviet theses. However, considering the importance of some of the Soviet notions that the Yugoslavs were rejecting, the Soviet reply still seemed relatively restrained and designed to preserve some common basis. While occasionally lapsing into harsh language, the article nevertheless expressed the hope that its "comradely comment on a number of questions of principle . . . will be favorably received and considered by the authors of the draft." The *Kommunist* refutation displayed a particular sensitivity to Yugoslav charges that in the past unequal relations had prevailed between socialist countries and rejected the notion that the essence of relations between Communist states is defined by the principles of equality and noninterference said to be the content of proletarian internationalism. "The draft actually defends national communism," *Kommunist* charged. If the Yugoslav line were to be adopted, it could only lead to disunity among Communist states. The statement ended by categorically warning that improvement in relations with Yugoslavia will never be made "by means of concessions at the expense of Marxist-Leninist principles."

Kommunist was both a first shot in the new conflict and a last warning. It reiterated what Khrushchev had been saying in 1957 but which the Yugoslavs, joyfully remembering the June 1956 declaraation, were unwilling to understand: that henceforth no ideological ambiguities which might give cause to disunity would be tolerated. However, the Soviet statement was to no avail; the Yugoslavs had passed the point of no return. Their draft program reflected a reasoned reconsideration of their previous views, and in such matters Communists, despite tactical elasticity, do not shift easily from week to week. The congress which convened on April 22 reaffirmed the revised theses.

At this stage, the dynamics of leadership within the Communist camp came into play. Soviet primacy within it, despite the setbacks of 1956, was a matter of sheer fact, given the USSR's military strength and industrial development. But the acceptance of its leadership as a proposition and the actual exercise of that leadership, as differentiated from the *potential* capacity to lead, depended now to an unprecedented degree on the support of centralists in the leaderships of the other states, and particularly in China. Moreover, China was in a better position than ever before to exercise pressure and to set a tone which the other centralists could endorse, thereby placing the USSR in the not unfamiliar position of a leader being forced to lead by his following. At the same time, a certain amount of restraint seemed warranted by the gradually improving Soviet-Polish relations.

The problem which faced the camp was essentially a tactical one. There was basic agreement that the Yugoslav program was revisionist, that ideological concessions were out of the question, and that open attacks must not go unanswered. But the degree of condemnation and the sharpness of reply to the gauntlet cast by Belgrade was a matter on which differences of judgment apparently arose. The differences were to a great extent the product of the varying experience of the leadership involved. Khrushchev, determined not to repeat Stalin's error, appeared anxious to avoid a repetition of the 1948 break or, if such a break were unavoidable, to let the Yugoslavs effect it. In addition, to return to 1948 would have meant a repudiation of Khrushchev's policies of the preceding three years. Accordingly, he appeared to favor a return to approximately the 1955 situation: maintenance of the normalized state relations but rigidity in party matters. An added advantage of such a policy would be that Yugoslavia would not be pushed headlong into "the imperialist camp." The East European centralists naturally favored more extreme measures. The entire Tito episode had been a threat to them, and a sharp line against him would also restrict Gomulka, for whom the centralists entertained intense distaste.

The Chinese, in all probability, had more complex motives. To them Tito was not a threat but a symptom of a potentially growing malaise within the camp as a whole and in the Soviet Union in particular. Yugoslav revisionism, the Chinese feared, could become infectious unless quarantined, while an explicit denunciation of Tito's foreign policy views would be likely to inhibit any tendencies on the part of Khrushchev to seek a reduction in tensions with the West. Moreover, the Chinese were certainly outraged by Belgrade's open airing of Communist disagreements and feared that persistent tolerance for Yugoslavia would cause the degeneration of the Communist camp into a loose confederation. Accordingly, Peking identified itself with the East European centralists in their harsh attitudes toward the Yugoslavs, and pressured Moscow to act accordingly. The time when Moscow could set unilaterally a new line for the camp was past.

The Chinese inclination toward severity was transplanted into policy with the publication on May 5 in *Jen-min Jih-pao* of a scathing critique of the Yugoslav program. Moscow immediately associated itself with it but, at the same time, seemed to suggest that a Yugoslav recantation would be met with a merciful response from the Kremlin. Two days after the Chinese statement, as if to underscore the Soviet attitude, *Pravda* reprinted the text of a Khrushchev telegram to Tito wishing him success in office and expressing hope for a "strengthening of friendship between our countries." The telegram made it clear that Khrushchev was sending it as Soviet Premier and addressing it to the Yugoslav President.[36] He thus was still maintaining the distinction between party relations and state relations. But the line adopted by the Chinese made the maintenance of that distinction increasingly difficult. The Chinese statement, phrased vituperatively without once referring to Tito or the Yugoslavs as "comrades," made four basic points: the Yugoslav program meant the abandonment of socialism; it fit the subversive plans of American imperialists; the 1948 Cominform condemnation of Yugoslavia had never been reversed by the Communist parties concerned; and the Yugoslav behavior during the Hungarian uprising had abetted counterrevolution. Their statement went appreciably beyond the Soviet line, while the waving of the 1948 resolution, immediately and gleefully imitated by the East European centralists,[37] was calculated to drive the Yugoslav leaders to white fury, especially since they had long been implying to their own party that the 1955 and 1956 agreements had involved a repudiation of the Cominform resolutions.

It is to be recalled that at this point these events were occurring within the framework of growing international tensions. The situation was particularly acute in the Middle East. To the Communists, the Western reactions were the confirmation of the old thesis that, when faced with collapse, the imperialists might resort to war. Unity seemed imperative, as did a return to "revolutionary vigilance," to the sharpest demarcation between friend and foe. Given the warm centralist response to the Chinese statement which, as expected, provoked a sharp Yugoslav reply charging the Chinese with returning to "the notorious Cominform declaration," engaging in "filthy insinuations," and interfering in Yugoslav affairs,[38] Khrushchev moved to abandon the distinction between state and party relations. On May 9 *Pravda* published a sharp statement warning Belgrade that such a distinction would be untenable in view of the developing ideological dispute. An official secret message to that effect from the Central Committee of the CPSU was delivered to the Yugoslav party on May 11 by the Soviet ambassador.

Once the Chinese succeeded in reviving the issue of the 1948 Cominform resolution, any fleeting chance of a Yugoslav accommodation faded. The Soviet message was therefore merely an empty gesture and might have reflected the persistent Soviet determination to place the onus for any break squarely on Tito's shoulders. With the Yugoslav stance unchanged and with the Yugoslavs still sputtering with rage at the revival of the 1948 Cominform declaration,[39] the Soviet press adopted a more belligerent tone. The Yugoslav position was compared to the "treachery" of Imre Nagy,[40] even though the Soviet leader still expressed the hope that existing Soviet-Yugoslav misunderstandings would be overcome for the sake of "further strengthening the unity of the Socialist forces in the world."[41] That this, however, was considered at best only a remote probability was strongly hinted by Soviet action two days later, forcefully linking the problem of party relations to state relations: the Soviet credit of about $285 million for an important aluminum project was unilaterally "suspended."

The suspension of the credit was followed by two speeches of Khrushchev, in Sofia on June 3 and in East Berlin on July 11, which bridged the discrepancies between the Soviet and Chinese analyses of the Yugoslav problem.* In Sofia, in a bitter but not entirely consistent outburst (Khrushchev, for instance, occasionally referred to the Yugoslavs as "comrades"), the Soviet leader for the first time openly stated that the CPSU had never retracted its adherence to the

---

* In addition to the differences in emphasis already noted, the following remark by *Jen Min Jih Pao* (June 4, 1958) suggests tactical differences between Peking and Moscow on how best to handle the Yugoslavs: "Perhaps some people feel that even though the Yugoslav Communist League program is revisionist and advantageous to imperialism, it would be best not to point this out in order not to push the ruling group of the Yugoslav Communist League to the side of imperialism . . . to fail to say that they are playing today to imperialism could elicit nothing but a malicious smirk from the Dulleses."

1948 Cominform excommunication of Tito and, secondly, charged the Yugoslavs, just as the Chinese had done, with abetting the Hungarian uprising. While still not accusing the Yugoslavs of acting as United States agents or of betraying socialism, Khrushchev characterized the Yugoslav program as outright revisionism which, in turn, he defined as the Trojan Horse of imperialism. By refusing to subordinate themselves to the unanimous judgment of the other parties, Khrushchev stressed, the Yugoslavs were no longer marching in the company of those who guide themselves by Marxism-Leninism.

Khrushchev amplified his views a few weeks later in an address to the East German SED Fifth Congress.[42] In the intervening period, the Yugoslav-Chinese dialogue had become even more violent, with Tito charging the Chinese with aggressive designs in Asia and with courting war. In the course of his defense of Russia's chief ally, the CPSU First Secretary moved even closer to the Chinese position. The two charges made at Sofia, and reiterated in East Berlin, were amplified by ridicule of the Yugoslav system as a kind of socialism which is built on American alms and by a charge that the Yugoslavs, with their revisionist program, were "concurring" in the imperialist attacks on Communism. Khrushchev in this fashion adopted basically the Chinese four-point condemnation of Tito.

The Soviet leader did, however, go to some pains to point out that everything had been done to improve relations with Yugoslavia and that no Communist could feel that he, Khrushchev, had not done his share in this regard. Revealing the Soviet leadership's acute sense of outrage that anyone who considers himself Marxist-Leninist could differ and could refuse to identify himself with the Communist camp, Khrushchev warned that efforts to improve relations must cease "when Yugoslav leaders say that they are Marxists-Leninists, but use Marxism-Leninism only as cover for misleading trusting people and to turn them from the road of revolutionary class struggle . . . they are then trying to rip out of the proletariat's hands the sharpest class weapon." [43] Both his Sofia and his East Berlin speeches made it clear that it was not the offensive content of the program per se which precipitated the reaction (similar views had been expressed by Belgrade before), but the fact that the program posed a "systematized" ideological alternative, that it was timed to pose a challenge, and that Yugoslav "neutrality" through its revisionism was directed against the camp.

By adopting in essence the Chinese charges, presumably because of sustained Chinese pressure, Khrushchev abandoned his previous distinction between state and party relations — which, in practice, could have meant a return to the summer 1955 situation. In his East Berlin speech he still reiterated the proposition that the Yugoslavs were the only ones to gain status by an argument with the camp and that, therefore, the CPSU was not inclined to promote Yugoslav megalomania by a continuous dialogue. Minimizing the issue, Khrushchev was avoiding Stalin's mistake of making it a critical concern for the ruling Communist parties, and he was striking home at one of Tito's chief weaknesses, his vanity. The Chinese line of simply identifying Tito as a "Judas and renegade," or, in other words, Stalin's 1948–1953 position, was not adopted. Instead, there was to be a return roughly to the mid- and late-1954 relationship, involving a firmly, even violently, stated ideological condemnation and a certain chilly correctness in state relations. It would be as if the preceding four years had never happened. In many ways, that was the most effective way of coping with Yugoslavia.

To cement the new policy there was a need to create a firm landmark which would serve as a lasting reminder to all Communists that the absence of a continuous barrage does not mean that revisionism was no longer tantamount to subversion. Furthermore, there was the need to puncture any lingering Yugoslav hopes of influencing their neighboring Communist states. This requirement was to be met by a human sacrifice. The final act in the restoration of the dichotomy so necessary to unity was to personalize its enemy and then, by destroying him, demonstrate dramatically the line between neutrality which leads to treason and commitment which is the basis of unity. With Tito not available, on June 17, 1958, the execution of Imre Nagy was announced.*

Nagy's execution had the added function of serving as a test case of Gomulkaist Poland's loyalty to the higher interests of the bloc. Despite basic Polish sympathy for the Yugoslav efforts to transform

---

* Executed with him was General Pal Maleter, the hero of the uprising, arrested while negotiating with the Russian command. Nagy's execution was preceded by a concerted campaign, linking his "revisionism" with treasonable plans to undermine the Communist camp. For a brief period after his arrest in November 1956, a distinction was made between his motives (not treasonable) and their consequences (objectively treasonable). That distinction was subsequently dropped with the campaign against revisionism mounting. Nagy was identified directly as a traitor. See "The 'Conceptions' of Imre Nagy and the Ideological Preparation of the Betrayal," *Tarsadalmi Szemle*, November–December 1957; "From the History of the Ideological Preparations for the Counter-Revolutionary Rising in Hungary," *Voprosy istorii*, no. 12, 1957. The frequent linking of Tito with Nagy in these statements made it clear that Nagy's execution was not meant to be merely a footnote to the Hungarian tragedy.

the camp into a looser confederation and a common anti-Stalinist orientation, in several important instances Gomulka was himself inclined to view Tito's opinions with suspicion and to feel that his Yugoslav friend was embracing deviant revisionist positions. Most particularly, Gomulka still basically subscribed to the notion that, given the alternative of belonging to the Communist camp or rejecting it, a true Communist must choose the former, especially in view of the general conflict with imperialism. Gomulka also found it difficult to accept Tito's views on "socialism as a world process" which minimized the imperative role of the Communist parties in effecting the socialist revolution. In brief, while anti-Stalinist, Gomulka remained basically a modified, Polish-style Leninist (see next chapter), whereas many portions of Tito's program recalled Bernsteinian and Bukharinite positions.[44]

For this reason, Gomulka himself probably disapproved of many portions of the Yugoslav program. But, mindful of the past and not wishing to establish any new precedents for Soviet interference, he was cautious and restrained in his reactions. On April 5, his weekly theoretical journal, *Polityka*, reproduced the substance of the Yugoslav program without any comment whatsoever, while Polish Politburo members, Ochab and Morawski, were quietly but vainly pleading with Tito for exclusion of the most offensive portions of his draft.[45] Ten days later, with the Soviet boycott common knowledge, his party's daily printed a lengthy editorial which criticized the Yugoslav views on state capitalism, the program's excessive concern with bureaucratic tendencies in Communist states, and the incorrect assessments of the process of the withering away of the state.[46] However, the paper gave the Yugoslavs credit for their efforts to promote peace, specifically referred to the "errors of 1948" in the camp's relations with Yugoslavia,* expressed the hope for a friendly, comradely dialogue, and, most important, equivocated on the Yugoslav critique of past relations between Communist states. The Polish reaction during April–May represented most closely the actual Polish position: some ideological disapproval but not ideological disavowal.

Gradually, however, Gomulka's grudging acceptance of Soviet leadership and his commitment to the bloc, intensified by Polish dependence on Soviet protection of the Oder-Neisse frontier and by

---

* Gomulka's position in 1948, however, was not unambiguous. Although under considerable pressure, he still at the time defended his views on other matters while being quite critical of the Yugoslav position on the grounds that its "narrow nationalism," leading to a break with the camp, would lead to the collapse of Communist power. See *Nowe Drogi*, no. 11 (1948), p. 42.

Poland's economic isolation, forced him to elaborate his basic critique into a more extensive condemnation. Nagy's execution meant that sides had to be taken, and to be silent in the general chorus of approval was also to take sides. Having already conceded for the sake of Communist solidarity the principle of Soviet leadership, a point potentially impinging on his own autonomy, Gomulka must have felt that to rupture his relations with the bloc for the sake of Yugoslav views, some of which he disapproved, or for the principles of a man already dead, even though the Polish leaders privately expressed their abhorrence of the execution, would be to engage in an idealism which he as a Polish Communist could ill afford. Accordingly, on June 28, he finally sided with the camp. In a speech delivered at Gdansk,[47] he stressed the need for unity and emphasized that Yugoslavia could build socialism only because the presence of a united Communist camp prevented capitalist aggression against it. Hence, "objectively" speaking, the Yugoslav abstinence from that unity, so favored by the West, was actually aiding imperialism. The same principle he applied to Imre Nagy, whose execution he described as "severe" (the centralists called it "deserved") and whom he characterized as a revisionist who "step by step moved to capitulation before the counterrevolution, performed its assignments, was destroying the socialist order in Hungary." Gomulka's only equivocations were not to refer approvingly to the 1948 Cominform resolution or to argue that revisionism leads to treason, unlike the centralists who equated revisionism with treason.

Gomulka's speech, immediately picked up by the Soviet anti-revisionist theorists,[48] was an important element in the restoration of unity within the camp. It marked Gomulka's second most important concession since October 1956. The principle of Soviet leadership was now solidly coupled with the sanctity of the camp's unity, and the ideological argument for any future Soviet interference was accordingly immeasurably strengthened. Any effort to resist it could be condemned as an act against socialism which, in Gomulka's own words, could only be built through unity. In this connection Gomulka could hardly ignore the fact that already in the anti-Nagy campaign emphasis was put on Nagy's agricultural compromises as proof of his revisionism. However, for the time being, the campaign against revisionism did not mean a return to internal institutional uniformity, although it did establish the ideological basis for such a step.

The appeal of Yugoslavia was thus being contained. Many of the Communist intellectuals elsewhere, who had previously attached great hopes to Yugoslavia's separate path, became disillusioned by Tito's external Machiavellianism, while the East European *apparatchiki* realized that the adoption of the Yugoslav position would be tantamount to breaking the unity of the camp. To be able to do so, a Communist regime would have to have an indigenous base to maintain itself in power without Soviet support and presumably in spite of the USSR. Most Communists felt that the Yugoslav position represented an extreme alternative which no Communist regime in East Europe could at this time emulate. This was the significant difference between Yugoslav national Communism or revisionism, and the quiet practice of domesticism.

Nonetheless, the Yugoslav program did articulate a conception of the world and of relations among Communist states that in the years to come became increasingly acceptable even to the Soviet leaders themselves. In politics, however, being too far ahead of the times is usually tantamount to being wrong. For the time being, Yugoslav theoreticians could only derive an intellectual — but not a political — satisfaction from their concepts. The Soviet leaders, primarily concerned with rebuilding the camp, for which task they still needed Chinese support, and anxious to reassure the loyal Stalinists in East Europe that Gomulka was a special case and not the norm of the future, felt they had to draw a sharp line between tolerable internal institutional diversity and ideological uniformity. To them, Yugoslavia's position was a useful example of what was considered to be outside the pale.

By 1957–58, Khrushchev had come to feel that Marxism-Leninism would be drained of any universal content if specific national particularities were permitted to dictate the programs of individual Communist parties. Stalinism as an international dogma relied on subordinating the particular to the general (although "erring" by identifying the latter always with Soviet experience). But without a common power center jealously to protect certain universal ideological imperatives, Marxism, even Marxism-Leninism, was shown to be inadequate in providing unity for international Communism. Diversity of thought, emerging once the center's controls lapsed, immediately brought to the surface the divisive forces which survived even the heyday of Stalinist unity. National animosities, cultural affinities, territorial claims, specific ideological traditions, all gradually came to the front. All of them could be fit within the framework of the ideology once it became responsive to domestic conditions. Disunity inevitably followed, revealing the ultimate failing of Mao Tse-tung injunction to "let a hundred flowers bloom, let a hundred schools contend!"

Ideology could thus divide rather than unite. That precisely was why Khrushchev warned that to allow the Communist parties to be fully independent "would lead the Communist and Workers' Parties to contradictory action and, in the final count, to disagreement." [49] The weeding out of revisionism, so necessary to forge unity, was an affirmation of the need for ideological monopoly and a belated expression of distrust in the capacity of ideology alone to promote common action.

14 / THE POLISH WAY TO SOCIALISM

VICTORY rarely re-establishes the *status quo ante*. The conflict generated by a direct challenge to existing arrangements is merely a more accentuated manifestation of continuous and often almost imperceptible change. A successful defense of an established order creates an illusory impression of the past's having been recaptured by the present. Yet on closer examination that past turns out to be rather different, maybe not quite as profoundly different as the challenger had desired but certainly unlike what might have been expected if the challenge had never arisen. The restoration of unity and the recognition of Soviet leadership were, in a sense, acts of successful defense of an established order. The Polish way to socialism tolerated within the order was an important new element, highly relevant to the problem of relations among Communist states.

GOMULKA AND THE OCTOBER UPHEAVAL

Gomulka was the symbol, but not the architect, of the Polish October. The distinction is important to an understanding of Polish developments after October 1956, the internal trends of which this chapter will attempt to synthesize. An architect is the source of much of the form and content of his design. A symbol is shaped to a far greater degree by the events and purposes it is said to represent though it need not be powerless. If in time, however, the force which promoted the symbol find it indispensable, it may then acquir an independent position and become a directing force. This was exactly the case with Gomulka.

Gomulka was the indispensable ingredient in the brew concocted by those who made the October Revolution. The intellectuals could create the atmosphere, stimulate the desires, crystallize the general purposes. The students could produce the ferment, the sense of urgency, the passionate commitment. The workers, restive after Poznan could dramatize the corruption of the ruling party, which ironicall bore the name of the United Polish Workers' Party, and at a crucial juncture provide the necessary physical backing to an upheaval. Th party activists, even *apparatchiki* like First Secretary Ochab, could hand over the sinews of power, could immobilize the secret police and arouse the army. But none of these groups could simultaneously effect a change profound enough to satisfy the most embittered while not driving away the most indifferent, produce a sense of *real* change and yet not overthrow the system. As a symbol, Gomulka offered something to everyone. He was a former victim of Stalinism and its recognized opponent. His "right-wing" deviation appealed to nationalist outrage at Soviet domination. He was a dedicated Communist who never wavered in his commitment and who presumably could be trusted not to initiate the dissolution of Communist rule. To the anti-Communists, he was the leader of a movement toward independence; to the revisionists, toward a democratic socialism. To the concerned Communists, he was the saviour of the crumbling Communist rule. His ability to personalize conflicting aspirations, and subsequently to channel them, was another demonstration of the role of the individual in history.

The diverse aspirations of October and the conflicting hopes of the various partisans obscured for a while a factor crucial to an understanding of Gomulka. He was above all a Marxist-Leninist. The son of a disaffected peasant who had emigrated to America only to return disappointed to Poland, Gomulka (b. 1905) was active from his youth in Communist movements.[1] They were to him both a school and a profession. A self-taught Communist whose formal education ended at the age of fourteen, Marxism-Leninism became his only perspective from which to view and eventually shape reality. This did not mean that in every instance a doctrinal precept was the basis for his actions. Gomulka repeatedly showed a keen sense of political realism and undogmatic elasticity. Marxism-Leninism, however, provided him with all his conceptual tools and his sense of commitment. It gave him a broad doctrinal outlook which dictated the ultimate direction, which served as a key to understanding the unfolding course of history, and which justified and necessitated certain actions as both good and inevitable. A sense of self-righteousness tied to historical inevitability can have an enduring attraction, particularly to the self-educated. (It is interesting to note the strong parallels between Gomulka and Khrushchev in this respect.)

Gomulka became the party leader during the highpoint of Moscow's wartime policy of favoring moderate changes in East Europe, expressed through the allegedly distinctive character of the People's

Democracy (Chapters 1–3). Unlike some of his more radically doctrinaire colleagues, Gomulka welcomed the wartime policy since it fit well into both his basic Communist commitment and his specific evaluation of the Polish scene. It would be incorrect, however, to conclude from this that Gomulka was characterized by a special sense of liberalism or that he was not fanatically committed to Communism. Indeed, the political opponents of the Communist regime in the immediate postwar period recall that he stood out as one of the most violent and energetic Communist leaders, ruthlessly suppressing the political activity of the opposition and unsparing in his condemnations of the non-Communist Polish underground or of the Polish Army which had fought in the west.[2] Generous in his praise of the secret police, anxious to consolidate his power, he stood solidly with his Moscow-trained comrades in the leadership. But sharing a common purpose is not the same as agreeing on policy. Building Communism is a complex problem involving not only methods, but stages, timing, and coordination of domestic policy with the external interests of Communism as a world movement — or, more specifically, with the interests of the USSR as Communism's center. It is on this level that conflicts are generated, that ambiguities ensue and ideological disputes arise. This was the case in Poland once the primary task of crushing the anti-Communists opposition had been achieved. Gomulka had to comment on many of these issues, and it is testimony to the depth of this man's inner convictions as well as to his intellectual rigidity that in 1956 he reemerged from obscurity very much the same Communist that he was before 1949.

In studying Gomulka's ideas one finds several themes which appear to be at the core of his thinking and which he has reiterated frequently. To bring out their striking continuity, it might be useful therefore to compare his pre-1949 formulations of certain key issues with his post-October 1956 statements.[3] There is first of all the firm belief that Communism can be built only if there is a monolithically united labor class:

1947	1957
the working class can perform its historical mission of reconstructing of societal relations . . . only when it is monolithic, when in its struggle it utilizes the unconquerable weapon of Marxism . . .[4]	The indispensable condition for the overthrow of bourgeois power and for the construction of socialism is the direction of these processes by the Marxist-Leninist Party of the working class.[5]

This theme Gomulka verbalized repeatedly after October 1956, even at a time when Soviet pressure was not yet involved.[6] Similarly, before and after his own incarceration he expressed the view that internal violence was necessary and that the secret-police organs therefore perform a positive function:

1946	1956
The Security Organs as a whole are healthy and very dedicated in their work. And as such we will defend them against all unjustified and false accusations. For the Security [Organs] are a sharp weapon in the hands of the Polish democracy in the struggle against reaction. We will not allow this tool to be wrenched from us.[7]	The public security employees have proven that, together with the whole Party and all the progressive forces in our country, they stand unflinchingly on guard over the interests of the nation, that they wholeheartedly support changes in our life, and that they are ready to prevent any attempts aimed against the political line mapped out by the leadership of the Party.[8]

Gomulka, however, did concede that there is a point at which violence becomes a negative manifestation and that it is no longer a major requirement following the defeat of "reaction." Its use to defend the party's monopoly of power was a right still to be reserved, however.

Turning to the central issue of the role of labor in a socialist state, Gomulka's approach, while proclaiming the rule of the working class, has been characterized by a firm insistence that labor's real role in building socialism is to remain disciplined and to increase production. In 1945 he took a firm stand against those workers' demands which took a too literal conception of "the workers' state":

The Plenum [of the Central Committee] has been sharply against the relaxation of labor discipline among the working class and against all sorts of harmful tendencies to limit the scope of the authority of factory directors.[9]

Without raising labor productivity, no one can improve the welfare of the working class.[10]

After October 1956 his attitude toward the spontaneously formed Workers' Councils, which had backed him during the critical period, was one of suspicion and caution — the attitude of a Leninist who jealously protects the political monopoly of the party. He accordingly warned that "the workers' councils are not organs of the political power of the labor class . . . are not links in the administrative apparatus of the people's state," [11] and in outlining the scope of their legitimate activity he pointedly stressed socioeconomic productive goals only.[12]

The post-October Gomulka accordingly still held to his belief in the key role of the party, in the desirability of its monopoly of power, in the justified necessity of occasional violence, and was suspicious of any reforms which might weaken the party's hold. At the same time, however, this orthodoxy was balanced by his unchanged adherence to views which earlier had prevented him from pliantly adjusting to Stalinism. These views, which he firmly restated after 1956, concerned above all his position on the agrarian question, the specifics of the Polish situation, and, especially, Polish-Russian relations. Gomulka seems to have long entertained the opinion that socialist construction is a complicated and involved process requiring not only Stalinist determination but also simple human patience. In 1945 he warned: "The way to socialism is neither short nor can it be shortened . . . It would be a gross oversimplification to claim that a turn of such fundamental importance to Poland can be immediately, from today to tomorrow, fully and well understood and accepted by the totality of all classes . . ." [13] His advice applied with particular relevance to the problem of the Polish peasantry, steeped in tradition and religion, land-hungry, and fearful of socialism which to them meant collectivization. In the immediate postwar period Gomulka therefore stressed, as we have seen, that the peasant must be convinced that socialism was a good thing, that it meant land and freedom. Only afterwards, once the peasant suspicions have collapsed, could they be encouraged to undertake cooperative and collective development. Although Gomulka never explicitly rejected collectivization as such, he went far in stressing those peculiarities of Poland which made its adoption in the phase of People's Democracy unacceptable:

1946	1956
We have not the slightest need to follow in the footsteps of Soviet agrarian policy. *We have rejected collectivization, because in the Polish condition it would be harmful economically and politically.*[14]	The road to setting up a vast network of cooperative farms in Poland's countryside is a long one. A quantitative development of producer cooperation cannot be planned because, on the basis of voluntary entry in a cooperative, this would amount to planning the growth in human consciousness, and that cannot be planned.[15]

Gomulka grounded his objections to an accelerated collectivization program on the general differences between the Polish and Russian revolutionary conditions, a position not acceptable after 1948 and only rather halfheartedly endorsed by Soviet leaders after 1956. He stressed that one of the specific "objective" factors of the Polish scene which had to be considered by any leader was intense Polish nationalism. As a Communist, he felt that to ignore it was to commit an error in evaluation of reality unworthy of a true Marxist-Leninist. To recognize nationalism, he believed, was not to become a national Communist, even if temporarily this might appear to be the case to those who saw only the surface of things. Gomulka argued that a true Marxist-Leninist policy for the construction of socialism had to recognize such domestic specifics, and in recognizing them it must respect the autonomy of a given Communist Party to choose the best methods of overcoming them. Equality and independence were thus indispensable to overcoming nationalism.

In 1946, Gomulka pointed to three crucial characteristics of the Russian revolution which he felt were absent in Poland: tsarist oppression, the strength of capitalism in 1917–1920, and foreign intervention.[16] The very same considerations were mentioned eleven years later, in his address to the Ninth Party Plenum.[17] Again, in 1946 he was quite blunt in criticizing his party for underestimating the nationalist element in the Polish scene: "*The basic error of Communists was that in fully appreciating the problem of struggle for the social liberation of the working class they underestimated the matter of* [national] *independence . . .*"[18] And eleven years later, writing in *Pravda*, Gomulka repeated the same theme: "a particular trait formed [in the Polish people] in the course of their historical development as a result of age-long foreign oppression and deprivation of freedom . . . is the special sensitivity of the Polish people to questions of their country's independence and sovereignty. The underestimation or denial of national traits and peculiarities in the building of socialism is nihilistic dogmatism . . ."[19] A proper policy must always strive to balance universal requisites with these profound national specifics.[20] Independence and diversity therefore are not ends in themselves in Gomulka's thinking. They are the necessary, enduring preconditions for true international unity and for the domestic construction of socialism. Domestic autonomy and mutual respect must be protected not in order to enshrine independence and nationalism but to create the climate for their eventual transition into a higher Communist brotherhood.

The pattern of post-October political development in Poland becomes more meaningful when considered within the framework of these continuities in Gomulka's thinking, as well as when related to the external factors traced in preceding chapters. Indeed, the only important new element in Gomulka's thinking, but one clearly derived from his general position that in order to change popular consciousness in Poland the factors shaping that consciousness must be appraised properly, was his articulate admission of the importance of the Polish Catholic tradition. In his judgment, the Stalinist period resulted in the unfortunate intensification of religious feelings: "the Party . . . cannot ignore the fact that the former conflict with the Church set millions of believers against the People's Government." [21] An adjustment was thus a necessary concession which would ultimately facilitate the march toward socialism.

Such, in brief, were Gomulka's basic patterns of thought when he came to power. They were, to be sure, tactically elastic, but in substance they had little in common with social democracy or with revisionism. But before they could be translated into the Polish way to socialism they had to survive a confrontation with the post-October political realities.

THE PERIOD OF RESTRAINED SPONTANEITY

There was no blueprint for the changes that occurred after October 1956. Gomulka's speech to the Eighth Plenum, elaborated in several public addresses, came the closest to charting a path for "Polish socialism," but it did so only in broad generalities. Indeed, guides for action had to be inferred from the more specific criticism that he made of the Stalinist system previously prevailing in Poland. But such negative instruction was not very helpful in drawing the precise limits to the anti-Stalinist measures that were bound to follow in post-October Poland. As a consequence, the period immediately following Gomulka's accession to power was characterized by a series of spontaneous developments, expressive of a variety of hitherto suppressed aspirations.

In politics, Gomulka's break with the past was interpreted by a large segment of the population to mean a conscious departure from the former totalitarianism, even if not going quite as far as to formally introduce a multiparty system. From the start, therefore, developments in politics were limited by the necessity of recognizing Communist one-party monopoly of power. Still, considerable areas for spontaneous change remained. It can be said that until some time after the January 1957 elections to the Sejm, the Gomulka regime did not actively shape the pattern of Polish life but merely responded whenever a direct challenge to its rule arose. The regime's primary objective at this stage was to win a resounding popular endorsement which would serve to convince the bloc that, in the interests of international Communism, Gomulka ought to be accepted. Abdication of domestic initiative was the consequence of the need to mobilize nation-wide support in the January elections. Given the simultaneous disorientation and demoralization of the Party membership[22] — symptomatically, party members had stopped wearing party emblems in their lapels — and the complete disintegration of the party's youth organization (ZMP), it was not surprising that rapid reactivization of formerly suppressed political elements took place. The two non-Communist members of the National Front, the United Peasant Party (ZSL) and the Democratic Party (SD), emaciated remnants of once-active political organizations,* were revitalized by the release from confinement of many former activists. In the Peasant Party the return to public life of many former pro-Mikolajczyk elements resulted in considerable upheaval. The new party Chairman, S. Ignar, elected following a purge of those leaders who had become too identified with Stalinism, by mid-1957 was forced to wage a regular campaign against efforts from below to transform the party into a genuine spokesman for peasant interests.[23] The Communist Party cells in the countryside, with only 125,000 members as against the ZSL's 202,000, remained passive.†

While in the countryside the dissipation of Communist power essentially led to a return to the traditional passive independence of the Polish peasant, the party *apparat* on the district levels initially remained largely untouched by the new political situation. Thus in the medium-sized towns the "spirit of October," either as an intellectual

---

* The ZSL was built by combining the original Communist front organization, the Peasant Party, with the remnants of Mikolajczyk's anti-Communist Polish Peasant Party (PSL), after the latter's suppression. Almost entirely inactive during Stalinism, it served to transmit the regime's instructions to the peasantry. The Democratic Party was a haven primarily for those intellectuals and scholars who felt that they had to show some political interest but who could not bring themselves to be card-carrying Communists. Of its members, 68 per cent were from the intelligentsia. *Tygodnik Demokratyczny*, January 23–29, 1958.

† January 1, 1958, ZSL total membership stood at 261,314 members; the Communist membership on September 30, 1958, was 1,023,577. *Zielony Sztandar*, March 30, 1958; *Trybuna Ludu*, December 28, 1958.

challenge or in the form of new organizations and clubs, was successfully kept out. The change was more profound in the large urban
centers like Warsaw, Cracow, Lodz, Poznan, and so on, where the
spirit of rebellion had originally been kindled. The war, the Nazi and
Soviet exterminations of the Polish elite, the rapid social transformation produced by the industrialization drives, and the emphasis placed
on mass education had radically changed the sociology of Polish
urban politics. The postwar Communist dictatorship made a determined effort to prevent the formation of social pluralism and rejected any conception of politics based on the interaction of plural-
istic groups. In practice, however, the very process of stressing the
role of conscious, planned political activity designed to reconstruct
society put a premium on the role of intellectuals* in society and
created the basis for their gradual emergence as a politically oriented
group. The moment the totalitarian party began to loosen its grip on
society, the moment that doubt about the correctness of the regime's
program began to be tolerated, the intellectuals were able to assume
the leadership in the emerging dialogue to an extent which would
have been difficult in prewar Poland, where so much more was left
to unchanneled spontaneous action outside of politics. The intellectuals' influence was all the greater because the premium placed on
"rational" planned social action meant that the party had to encourage them to join,[24] and after October they again identified themselves as intellectuals first and party members second. Grand designs
and programs became the vogue. The "problematics" of development was the theme of post-October discussions. In effect, they involved a search for some measure of politically significant social
cohesion after years of Stalinist social atomization.[25] If achieved, this
would be bound to become an impediment to the party's rule.

Such efforts were facilitated by the postwar spread of higher education among the masses, which resulted in a large-scale intermediary
stratum of so-called working intelligentsia, acting as a link between
intellectuals and workers.† The industrial workers, led by prewar

* This term is used loosely to denote writers, journalists, academicians, "ideologues," economists, but not professionals such as doctors, lawyers, engineers.
† Between 1949–1950 and 1955–1956 about 700,000 young people, mostly peasants
and workers, received higher education. For comparison, we may note that the so-
called "mental" workers in all of Poland in 1931, with a population that was larger
by a third, totaled 664,000. Among Polish sociologists there is a lively dispute as to
whether this new stratum has developed its own character or whether it is essentially
adopting the values of its prewar predecessors.

socialist activists as well as by their own intelligentsia, responded favorably to the search and expressed, through workers' self-government, their own quest for something more than centralized political authority. It was to these Workers' Councils that the intellectuals directed their attention. The so-called intellectuals' clubs, modeled in some respects on the revolutionary Jacobin clubs, were eager to link hands with the Workers' Councils, which seemed to bear some resemblance to the early soviets or even the Paris Commune. With the party vacillating, what stopped the formation of a common front of the restless proletariat and iconoclastic intellectuals?

Three reasons might be advanced. The first, and most important, was self-imposed restraint; the second, absence of a common purpose; and the third, Gomulka. The restraint, evoked by the tragic consequences of the Hungarian revolution, meant that no responsible individual was willing to undermine the precarious structure of post-October Poland, to engage in any activity which might set in motion an irreversible revolutionary chain of events. The example was set by the Catholic Church itself, even though its hostility to the ruling ideology could not be doubted. Indeed, those anti-Communists who were willing to take advantage of the regime's passivity and of the new pluralism to organize some independent political activity did not find much backing anywhere — neither among workers nor the intellectuals nor the Church. The short-lived Union of Democratic Youth, a non-Communist, nationalist youth organization, was suppressed by the regime without provoking popular indignation. The experience of this particular organization showed that while the vast majority of the population remained anti-Communist the circumstances were such that most were prepared to act only as non-Communists.* In the words of a prominent Catholic leader, "it is demagogy to raise slogans which ignore the real conditions and the objective necessity. It would be demagogy to launch now in Poland a program of parliamentary democracy. The problem of a system cannot be resolved abstractly." [26]

The absence of a common purpose was also a powerful factor. Despite the popular rejection of Stalinism and the continuing hatred of Russia, a re-evaluation of the meaning of independence had taken

---

* This, however, did not exclude individual or collective acts of retribution. Gomulka felt compelled to call upon the miners to stop attacking particularly hated administrators, while the militia complained that any intervention by a militiaman immediately earned him the label of a Stalinist and even physical assault. Radio Warsaw, December 3 and 28, 1956.

place among many Poles. The futile Warsaw uprising of 1944 had a shattering impact on the Polish belief in the capacity of Poland to shape its destiny alone. Nationalist romanticism gave way to political "positivism." More and more, the Poles were inclined to concede what they had opposed only a decade before: the necessity of close alliance with Russia, especially in view of the Soviet support for the Oder-Neisse line. A change in outlook on this point had occurred, and it was, indeed, a profound one. Peasant opposition was disarmed by the collapse of collectivization, openly tolerated by the regime. The support given Gomulka by the Church eliminated, for the time being, religion as a basis of cohesion for a common purpose. The workers gloried in their Workers' Councils and the more active even thought of organizing a nation-wide Workers' Council publication.[27] At the same time, they were handicapped by the presence of many thousands of first-generation proletarians, recruited from the poorer rural elements, lacking in trade-union traditions, demoralized by the new environment, and unable to adjust in a mature fashion to the new responsibilities. As a result, some of them attempted to use the Workers' Councils for short-range gratification, thereby undermining their political significance. The remnants of the middle class, as the fate of the Union of Democratic Youth showed, lacked the cohesion and the economic power to shape an alternative political program.

The past anti-Communist alliance could not be resuscitated. The society, disintegrated by war and by profound socioeconomic changes, rejecting monolithic bonds in a spontaneous and leaderless process, could not create within itself a unified sense of direction. Intellectuals almost by definition are incapable of forging a monistic program of action, but merely can help to crystallize through continuing dialogue a general sense of the desirable, with many specific points left in doubt or subject to conflicting interpretations. Rejecting orthodoxy, they would be the last to adopt a new doctrine. Views such as Kolakowski's (Chapter 13) could not be a concrete program of action. It was only Gomulka who could skillfully fill this vacuum. He never tired of warning the Poles of the dire international consequences of undermining the party's rule, and yet, by avoiding a specific commitment to the future, he remained in the initial post-October period the embodiment of many conflicting hopes. Since any action against the ruling party was also action against its First Secretary, his unique position as the object of mass adulation (which, however, did not long endure) effectively contained the opponents of the regime at the time of the regime's greatest weakness. In January 1957 Gomulka was given a resounding popular endorsement.*

It was in this context of political stalemate that Polish life moved away from the ideological and institutional uniformity of the Communist camp but without destroying the Communist rule. Some of these changes may be briefly enumerated under the general headings of political, economic, social, and intellectual. In politics, the specific changes were negative ones, that is, reactions to the rejected past: release of prisoners,[28] absorption of the secret police into the Ministry of the Interior and dismissals of parts of the staff, removal of Soviet military advisers, rehabilitation of some formerly dismissed judges, end to the jamming of foreign broadcasts, introduction of some limited debate in the Sejm, and the like. Finally, above all, there was a general popular feeling that the government in Warsaw was a Polish one, despite its ideological views and continued dependence on Soviet backing.

In economic life the most striking change was the collapse of collectivization.† Within a few short weeks, only about 1,700 of the 10,600 collective farms were left.[29] Reform was promised in industry, although the nature of large-scale industrial organization precluded any significant alterations. The first step in the direction of change was the demotion of the powerful Central Planning Commission from a super-ministry responsible only to the top leaders to an organ of the Council of Ministers,[30] and the setting up of a competing institution, the Economic Council, charged with drafting a "model" for the Polish economy. Its thinking was well reflected by the following observations of its chairman, Oskar Lange: "The Stalinist scheme of

* The elections were, in effect, a plebiscite for national independence, and no contest was involved since a National Front slate was presented and Gomulka urged the voters to vote only for it. However, in voting for the slate, a voter could rank his preferences, and in that limited way express his inclinations. It is interesting to note that the slate's "nonparty" candidates (usually leading intellectuals) had the highest median, followed by the SD, ZSL, and United Polish Workers' Party in that order, although the differences were slight. In terms of the nineteen provinces, the "nonparty" candidates had the highest average in fifteen, the SD in three, the ZSL in one, the ruling party in none. Based on J. Wiatr, "Sejm Elections — A Preliminary Analysis," *Studia Socjologiczno — Polityczne*, no. 1, 1958.

† S. Jedrychowski, Gomulka's planner, made this revealing admission: "Some people, especially bourgeois commentators, believe that the retreat in developing the cooperatives and dissolving of many of them were the result of Party policy. The truth that the retreat was caused by the pressure of anti-socialist elements at a time when the Party was not strong enough to counter this pressure." "Socialism on the March," *World Marxist Review* ("Problems of Peace and Socialism"), II, no. 5 (May 1959).

industrialization . . . was not suited to a mechanical transfer to Poland, a country of entirely different economic-geographical conditions . . . A miniature of Soviet-type industrialization was forced. This miniature also imitated the autarky of the Soviet Union." [31] The Council, in addition to favoring decentralization of the economic structure, also leaned toward a limited reintroduction of private enterprise in retail trade, handicrafts, services, and small-scale production.[32] On the factory level, the mushrooming Workers' Councils were regularized through an official decree, although the range of their activities was pointedly restricted to the socioeconomic sphere, and efforts to organize nation-wide links among the Workers' Councils were prohibited.[33] The right to strike was for the time being tolerated and was used by the workers in a number of instances, with success. Probably the most significant act of the regime was the announcement that Western credits would be sought to help Poland through the difficult period of readjustment.

To the average citizen of the Polish People's Democracy, the changes effected during this period of restrained spontaneity were in the less tangible social and intellectual sphere. The restraint and unanimity of the preceding period gave way to a sudden outburst of intellectual vivacity, to the mushrooming of clubs, newspapers, and discussion circles, to large-scale contacts with the West and relatively unrestrained travel abroad. For a short while, the press was virtually in the hands of the "revisionist" intellectuals, and the official censors, bereft of official guidance, in effect stopped functioning. Even articles critical of the USSR were published.* The formerly vilified Home Army was publicly lauded, resulting in the large-scale publication of memoirs by non- and even anti-Communist underground fighters, many of whom joined the official veterans' organization (ZBWiD) with some even claiming veterans' status for antiregime activity! Public-opinion polls appeared in many newspapers, often revealing a high degree of hostility to Communism.[34] In the universities banned subjects and ousted professors reappeared, while on the lower levels official textbooks were withdrawn. Religious instruction within the schools was reintroduced, following the arrangement made between the state and the Church, and Catholic newspapers and magazines

---

* By no means untypical was an enthusiastic account of a trip to France by a *Przeglad Kulturalny* correspondent, who then described by way of contrast a visit to the USSR, involving the companionship of a boring guide, life in an atrociou hotel, huge profits for the Intourist, and compulsory visits to the "workshops" of Soviet literary "realists" (December 6–12, 1956).

reappeared. Such, in summary form, was post-October Poland. But was it a Gomulkaist Poland?

RESTORATION OF CONTROL

A Gomulkaist Poland began to emerge only with the restoration of political control. Constructing socialism, and eventually Communism, was Gomulka's goal. The most obvious problem facing him was that of the party. Without the party the ideological goals could not be pursued. For the time being, Gomulka could maintain himself in power by relying on his popularity as well as on his control of the army, ensured by the appointment of his close associate, Marian Spychalski, to the post of Minister of Defense, and on his control of the police network, headed by S. Moczar. This might have been enough if Gomulka were satisfied to become a traditional dictator, ruling a status quo society by balancing instruments of power and interest groups. However, the state of Polish society urgently required action, while Gomulka's own views and the views of those on whom he depended for support dictated a specific kind of action. His primary task was thus to revitalize the party and to assert his control of it before the self-restraint of the non-Communists gave way to greater political appetite and before the Natolin dogmatists, favoring a radical policy, attempted more violent solutions.

Gomulka could not rely on the "revisionists," who had helped to bring him to power but to whose views he was clearly unsympathetic. To Gomulka, a hard-bitten party leader, the revisionist intellectuals and their socialist labor friends must have appeared as an argumentative, overintellectualized lot, who could discuss but never construct socialism. Yet within the party, which would be his primary instrument of action, he could not count on unqualified support. In the Central Committee, the anti-Gomulka Natolinites could rely on about twenty to twenty-five votes of the total seventy-seven, with the rest primarily in the hands of the professional party apparatus, headed by Zambrowski and Ochab, whose associates also controlled the key party organs. Gomulka could count on the personal loyalty of only a handful of members, as well as on the support of the four-odd revisionists who would always back him against the Natolinites.[35] Thus from the start Gomulka had to associate himself with the dominant group within the upper party echelons. This group eschewed a return to the past but also viewed with the profoundest disfavor the revisionist declarations, which even called for the acceptance of an opposition within the party.[36] Gomulka, who became the

First Secretary of the party not to preside over its dissolution but to make its goals compatible with Poland's, accordingly identified himself with a position and an outlook which, for lack of a better label, might be called centrist.

In March 1957 the Gomulka leadership made its first move against the revisionists by stigmatizing their activity as undermining the very foundations of the party and drawing it toward the bourgeoisie.[37] Gomulka's move was well-timed, for it reassured the party *apparat* and undercut the whispering and pamphleteering campaign being waged against him by some of the unreconciled dogmatists. The position of the latter had become weakened in the meantime by rapid changes effected on the provincial party levels, some spontaneously and some by central direction, which resulted in the removal of ten of the seventeen provincial party Secretaries and changes in all seventeen committees,[38] as well as a rapid reduction in party staffs.* Gomulka's retention of Zenon Nowak as Deputy Prime Minister also had the effect of conciliating some of the Natolinites. It was around this time that Moscow began more actively to endorse Gomulka (see Chapter 12).

Gomulka's ability increasingly to make himself appear as the chief bulwark of the *apparat*'s interests forced the dogmatists to put all their hopes in a frontal attack on Gomulka's policies at the Ninth Plenum in mid-May 1957. Their move was ill conceived. As First Secretary, Gomulka opened the proceedings and placed considerable emphasis on the revisionist threat. The sharpness of his attack, combined with his massive popular support (still strong in mid-1957), convinced the party professionals that without him a serious conflict was almost inevitable. Even at this point the danger of Hungary was not to be excluded, and only with Gomulka at the helm did the party's rule appear more or less secure. Consequently, when some of the dogmatists proceeded to charge the Politburo with failing to recognize Soviet leadership (see Chapter 12), with having betrayed Communism through its policies on agriculture and toward the Church,† their indictment fell on deaf ears and provoked a bitter

* Radio Warsaw, August 7, 1957, reported the transfer of 8,669 party officials to other work. This reduced the party administration from about 13,000 to 5,000 and, carried out rapidly during the height of Gomulka's popularity, strengthened his internal position.

† The leading spokesmen were K. Mijal, W. Klosiewicz, and S. Lapot, members of the Central Committee but not front-rank leaders. It is noteworthy that the former leaders of the Natolin group, such as Nowak and Mazur, were cautious and restrained.

outburst both from Gomulka and his predecessor Ochab, now in charge of agriculture. Gomulka followed up his two-front offensive by prevailing upon the Central Committee to elect two of his supporters, Zenon Kliszko and Jerzy Morawski, to the party Secretariat. Kliszko, purged in 1949 during the anti-Gomulka campaign, was given the important task of directing the party's organization section, balancing Zambrowski's influence. Morawski, responsible for the section dealing with relations with the other Communist parties, could be relied upon to uphold Gomulka's views on relations within the bloc, and subsequently represented him at the East German, Italian, and Yugoslav party congresses.

The May plenum, unlike October's, was truly Gomulka's personal victory. Although neither the revisionists nor the dogmatists, to use the standard Polish terminology, were fully dispersed, the plenum materially strengthened Gomulka in his "struggle on two fronts." Happily for him, the ideological differences dividing the dogmatists and the revisionists were so profound, and their hostility so intense, that Gomulka could always count on the support of the one group against the other, with the revisionist weakness in the party counsels being compensated by their strong position in the press and among the intellectuals.

The Ninth Plenum was followed by more purposeful moves to unify the party and to isolate the "deviants." Not surprisingly, most of the concrete steps were directed more often against the revisionists than the dogmatists. The latter had been isolated from the people since October and during the period of spontaneity were unable to exercise much influence. The realities of Polish life with which Gomulka was faced in mid-1957 were primarily of the revisionists' doing. For this reason, Gomulka's two-front war was directed more frequently at his former allies than at his current foes.

By the time of the Tenth Plenum, held late in October 1957 on the eve of the Moscow conclave, Gomulka's control was well consolidated. The first revisionist strongholds to fall were those in the press. Between March and May changes were effected in the editorial staffs of party dailies (including a new editor-in-chief for *Trybuna Ludu*[39]), and a warning was issued that freedom of the press did not mean the freedom of party members to agitate against the party. In September press censorship was restored, despite vigorous resistance,[40] and its logical extension was the closing on October 2 of the crusading party youth paper, *Po Prostu*. While the party was formally within its rights in suspending a party paper that was at variance with the regime's policies, the suspension of *Po Prostu,* which had become a symbol of October, provoked a strong reaction in the population, quite unlike the passive acceptance earlier of the dissolution of the Democratic Youth Organization.[41] A majority of the editorial staff was expelled from the party,[42] while some prominent revisionist writers demonstratively resigned from the party.[43]

Gomulka's struggle against revisionism within his party, described by him as a "grippe," did not make him forget dogmatism, which he analyzed as tuberculosis intensified by the grippe.[44] In mid-June, shortly after the Ninth Plenum, some of the dogmatists used the Warsaw party conference as a forum for attacks on two of Gomulka's associates, Zambrowski and Cyrankiewicz. They did so on the grounds that a recent Central Committee decision to expel Berman and Radkiewicz from the party as those responsible for past terror should have also included Gomulka's above-named friends, who held high posts during Stalinism. This demagogic attempt to discredit his regime was accompanied by efforts to seize control of the Warsaw organization. Their efforts were repulsed,[45] and Gomulka quickly followed this up by purging the party *apparat* of the Warsaw-center district, an important party organization in view of its location.[46] Accordingly, when the Tenth Party Plenum convened in October 1957, an exact year after his coming to power, Gomulka could speak with the authoritative firmness of a party leader and not merely as a revolutionary symbol. Declaring flatly that "the Party must be monolithic," Gomulka condemned both revisionism and dogmatism and, warning that there is no room in his party for either, ordered a party purge.[47] His speech was a firm assertion of his determination not to allow any political diversity within the system and marked the effective restoration of one-party rule.

The emergence of a Gomulkaist Poland through the consolidation of political authority also made possible the elimination of those nonpolitical gains of October which did not enjoy Gomulka's favor. Indeed, it was only after the political consolidation that Gomulkaism — or the directed Polish way to socialism — began to appear in sharper focus. While its character was obviously determined to a large extent by the encirclement of Poland by the Communist camp, it should be apparent from the preceding that its roots were also in large measure domestic. Sometimes described as Leninism applied to Polish conditions, Gomulkaism involved an attempt to water down the impatient Stalinist reliance on pure political force and establish a balance between purposeful coercion and gradual change in social consciousness

The nature of such a balance could not be spelled out with any degree of precision, and only practice could determine its content.

The January 1958 issue of the party journal stated: "The Party can and ought to lead everything." [48] During 1957–1958, censorship was especially intensified in the ideological sector, with the regime suppressing about 50 per cent of the articles in such discussion weeklies as *Nowa Kultura* and *Przeglad Kulturalny*.[49] In October 1957 the party announced that permanent commissions of the Central Committee for control of science, culture, and education, abolished a year earlier, were to be recreated,[50] while a party spokesman explicitly asserted that Poland must have a "cultural policy that promotes the objectives of its system and its ideology." [51] Presumably not irrelevant to these measures were the anti-intellectual suspicions frequently voiced by Gomulka (paralleling similar utterances by Khrushchev). Ideological alternatives would no longer be tolerated even if Gomulka's regime was tardy in stepping forth with its own program.

The reactivation of party rule also meant the gradual limitation of the politically significant right of free association and the quiet reconstruction of the secret police apparatus. The intellectuals' clubs, survived only in the largest urban centers,[52] and these were forbidden to organize a formal nation-wide assembly. The sixty-odd nonparty members of the Sejm were not allowed to form a parliamentary club, and early in 1958 political control was reimposed on the resuscitated Boy Scouts movement and on the veterans' association. The secret police, incorporated earlier into the Ministry of the Interior, was reorganized into nine departments (to watch the intellectuals, to supervise former underground fighters, and so on) within the ministry, and dismissals from it were halted. By the summer of 1957 its size was reliably estimated at 21,000 men.[53] In November 1957, Gomulka's Minister of the Interior issued a statement stressing the need for security operations against "the reactivation of groups which can be traced to forbidden political parties or reactionary organizations." [54]

In the economy the problem from the very beginning was how to readjust the former Stalinist model without causing widespread dislocation and large-scale decline in production. Furthermore, the low standard of living exerted strong pressures for increased wages which, in turn, threatened to create an inflationary spiral. The economists themselves were split, with two dominant groups evident: those favoring a rather large-scale decentralization, indeed a new Polish economic model," and those who advocated moderate reforms in the existing structure. The former were in the advisory Economic Council and propagated their views through the economic journal *Zycie gospo-darcze;* the latter were headed by the party economists of the State Economic Planning Commission and of the newly created Economic Committee of Council Ministers, given the special task of evaluating alternative models. It soon became a haven for the more rigid dogmatic planners and was headed by E. Szyr, essentially a dogmatist. On the margins of this dispute was the radical faction which, without an active role in the drafting of economic plans, utilized party plenums to press in general for an intensification of socioeconomic changes in Poland.

The group favoring decentralization submitted its plans in May 1957. In February 1958 a party commission rejected the key recommendations of the Economic Council, namely, the transfer of direct authority (to fix annual plans, to approve investments, and to make decisions on new productions) to the factory or enterprise.[55] However, it did not move back to the rigid Stalinist pattern and urged instead that such authority be entrusted to intermediary complexes or trusts, with provisions for the sharing of a certain percentage of the profit (in the shipping trust, for instance, it was fixed at 17 per cent) with the personnel. More extensive decentralization, on the Yugoslav model, was rejected as unsuitable for the "more advanced" Polish economy.[56] A further consideration, political reasoning apart, might have been the extremely low level of training among industrial cadres (due to rapid industrialization) and hence the dangers of granting them extensive autonomy.* Limitations were also imposed on the right to strike,[57] while the authority of the Workers' Councils, by late 1957 established in the majority of the industrial establishments,[58] was severely circumscribed in April 1958 by the superimposition over them of a so-called Workers' Self-Government Conference. In this, the representatives of a council were outnumbered by delegates of the trade union and the party cell, with the party Secretary acting as chairman.[59] The Workers' Councils became essentially grievance boards, although they were still of some importance in articulating the views of the working class.

A special problem which Gomulka had to face in 1957 and 1958 was the question of state-Church relations. The modus vivendi of

---

* See education and training statistics in Chapter 7, p. 143, n. That this condition persisted was confirmed by the statistics published by *Polityka,* September 11, 1965 Particularly disturbing was the fact that many directors and chief engineers who had absolutely no training were retrained at their posts for political reasons, while new university graduates were going unemployed.

October 1956 was clearly an emergency solution which could not endure once the party regained initiative. The top party leaders had little desire to return at this time to Stalinist violence which Gomulka had so explicitly condemned. There was, however, growing fear that the increasing scope of the Church's social activity (organized professional pilgrimages, chaplains assigned by the Church to scouting units, worker-priests, Catholic clubs in the universities) represented an institutional challenge which the political leadership under no circumstances could long tolerate. By early 1958 the regime felt strong enough to launch a press campaign against alleged Church infractions of the existing agreements, and this was followed by occasional trials of priests accused of violating the "tolerance" clause of the Polish constitution (such as a priest's refusal to bury an active Communist in a Catholic cemetery), by an increase in state control of clerics assigned to teach religion in the schools, and by fiscal measures against the Church. However, there was also a special, unpublicized motivation behind the increased vigor of the party's attacks on the Church. The party leadership had become concerned over the general decline of "revolutionary zeal" in the party and decided to use the anti-Church campaign as a method of unifying the membership and, also, to undercut the radical dogmatists. This was quite openly admitted in party circles.[60]

The foregoing discussion points to the conclusion that the retrogression which took place in Poland in 1957–1959, and which continued into the sixties, with periodic acts of repression directed particularly at the intellectuals and at the Church,* did not take place merely as a function of external Soviet pressure. Such pressure doubtless existed, and was even manifested by open Soviet criticisms of many aspects of the Polish scene in contrast to its praise for the more orthodox practices of the other Communist states, and by approval of the retrogressive measures described above. However, both the dynamics of one-party rule and of Gomulka's specific views on the construction of socialism would have required such limitation of the freedoms won in October.

The question really is not whether the domestic policies pursued during this time were a response to external pressure but rather the extent to which they were aided or handicapped by it. To this ques-

* These acts ranged from occasional arrests of the more outspoken intellectuals, and even imprisonment in 1965 of several brilliant young sociologists, to persistent harassment of the Church's activities and institutions.

tion a clear-cut answer cannot be given. In one sense, external pressure was indispensable because without the USSR Gomulka could not have carried on. But once that proposition is granted, Soviet pressure could also be construed as a handicap to Gomulka's domestic policy insofar as the very presence of an all-powerful Soviet partner so near to Poland continually forced Gomulka to pay greater heed to domestic aspirations in order to gain and maintain national backing. Thus curiously, the same external pressures for unity and hierarchy which Gomulka was fearfully opposing to protect his autonomy (see Chapter 12) were making it possible for him to translate his own Communist ideals into domestic policy.

However, just as retrogression fundamentally reflected Gomulka's growing power and not simply Soviet interference, so did the consolidation of certain tangible achievements of October reflect a new political approach within Poland. Despite pointed Soviet praise for those states which collectivize their agriculture, collectivization appears to be postponed in Poland until such time as it becomes economically attractive, with the number of collective farms stabilized at about seventeen to eighteen hundred[61] and the state obligation shouldered by the peasants substantially reduced.[62] Local government was reformed to encourage greater popular participation, which necessarily meant a partial limit on direct party control and active participation on the local level of the two subordinate parties in the National Front.* In the Sejm, where the outcome of the vote still remained predetermined by the artificial Communist majority, the practice of unanimous vote was abandoned, committee work became of some importance in the discussion of issues, and the practice of interpellation was introduced.[63] The press, despite increased censorship, remained lively and undogmatic, occasionally rebutting Soviet criticisms of the Polish scene and carrying stories about the West. The universities, which were freed of practically all political control after October 1956, retained some of their internal freedom, though with growing restrictions on publications, particularly in the sensitive area of social sciences.[64] Leading revisionists were not imprisoned, even under pressure to desist in their "deviation." Finally, the retrogression that did take place did not involve a full return to the Stalini-

---

* For example, before October the Peasant Party had only two provincial executive chairmanships (roughly a provincial prefect); in 1957 the number was 5 out of 17. The number of district chairmen grew from 35 out of 321 to 69. This, of course, is not decisive within the framework of a one-party political dictatorship, but it can mean a certain slight decline in the monolithic control of all posts by that party. *Zielony Sztandar*, March 30, 1958.

past, and it did not undo, even if it did restrict, the relative sense of emancipation evoked by the October outburst.

THE LIMITS OF POLISH AUTONOMY

Gomulkaism involved an accommodation of the requirements of the Polish reality to the demands of the party, as well as to the interests of the bloc. It was not an easy adjustment, and certainly not one which would permit a static solution. It meant that the Gomulka regime would be faced with a continuing problem of reconciling external concessions with domestic recalcitrance and, vice versa, domestic Communist aspirations with external Communist aid. To do that successfully, Gomulka had to go out of his way to indicate that the Polish peculiarities were just peculiarities and that it would be an error for any other party to attempt to duplicate the Polish experience.[65]

In explicitly rejecting any claims to universality Gomulka was also mollifying Soviet fears. At the same time, the conclusion of a successful trip in late 1958 to the USSR, marked by repeated Soviet endorsement of Gomulka, allowed the Polish leader to turn with added confidence to the task of liquidating the remnants of the neo-Stalinist, excessively pro-Soviet faction. This was well demonstrated by the Twelfth Party Plenum in October 1958 during which the remnants of the old Natolin faction, led by second-stringers like the economist Szyr and the *apparatchik* Ruminski, attempted to attack the party's economic plan for 1959–1965 on the ground that it envisaged an insufficiently rapid development of socialism in Poland. The plan, stipulating an increase of 49 per cent in industrial production between 1961–1965 (considerably below the 1950–1957 period, when it grew two and a half times), was described by its proponents as "the plan of economic stabilization." [66] According to a stenographic report designed strictly for internal party use, much of the argument against the plan and for the extremist point of view was based on the Chinese experience, and Gomulka and his associates could easily dispel it precisely on the grounds of irrelevancy. S. Jedrychowski, a prominent party planner and Politburo member, firmly concluded the official rebuttal by stating: "Our pace of economic development we should define ourselves, on the basis of our own, most conscientious appraisal of our conditions, needs and possibilities . . ." [67] Another Politburo member, A. Zawadzki, even allowed himself to voice the thought that the radical Chinese example not only does not prove (as Szyr argued) that changes in social consciousness can outpace changes in social conditions but that "the example of China is not entirely convincing" and that it is very doubtful that the Chinese masses had been won over to Communism.[68]

The plenum itself was an interesting reflection of the growing consolidation of Gomulka's power. He was solidly supported by the party's provincial Secretaries who simply ignored the ideological arguments of Szyr and Ruminski; no revisionist issues arose; his Politburo associates spoke out as forcefully as he against the critics; and, finally, it was apparent that the critics had no hopes of displacing Gomulka but were merely striving to push him into a more radical path. This was the last outburst of collective opposition to Gomulka. By way of contrast, the Third Congress in March 1959 was almost dull in its endorsements of Gomulka; the Soviet delegation, including as many as three CPSU Presidium members, was unstinting in its support of the First Secretary; and the new Central Committee was rigorously purged of the remaining neo-Stalinist deviants.* In a symbolic gesture the 1949 condemnation of Gomulka was stricken from the party records. Gomulkaism was now registered in the sacred rolls of orthodoxy.[69]

Partly for reasons of personal inclination but primarily because of the continuous fear that Polish domesticism could be construed as a threat elsewhere, Gomulka continued to avoid ideological formulations for the Polish way to socialism. The Third Congress, while a personal triumph for Gomulka, contributed nothing in the way of an ideological definition of Gomulkaism. Yet the dangers which continued to face it domestically were to some extent rooted in the absence of a crystallized program of action for this Polish way. The outstanding problems confronting Gomulka, such as the Church issue, the social anarchy, the alienation and frustration of the intellectuals, the loss of the allegiance of the youth (a particularly serious problem for a regime led by aging products of Stalinism),† the weakness of

---

* Judging by the membership list published in *Nowe Drogi*, no. 4 (April 1959) pp. 761–763, at most only five former Natolinites survived the purge. Mazur was dropped altogether (a former Politburo member and Khrushchev's candidate in 1956 for Bierut's job).

† For instance, the reactivated party youth movement numbered by the end 1957 only 90,000 members, including "several thousand" students. In the Warsaw Polytechnic, for instance, there were only 12 members out of a student body 14,000 (*Sztandar Mlodych*, October 23, December 10, 1957). Furthermore, even rapid increase in their numbers would not be a resolution of the profound problem of ideological skepticism and rejection of Marxism, strikingly revealed by public opinion polls (in this writer's possession). Especially distressing was the sharp

the collective movement in the countryside, all these in the end raised ideological issues which could not be delayed indefinitely, unless the party was willing to adopt the proposition of "spontaneity," of "automatism" in social change, which it clearly feared.*

In agriculture, for instance, the gradual process of splintering of land holdings was bound to produce eventual pressures for some radical change, especially when it began to affect agricultural productivity.[70] The nationwide demographic upsurge was posing with increasing urgency the prospect of large-scale unemployment both in the country and in the cities. At the same time, the striking improvement in the standard of living of the peasants raised an acute ideological issue. It must be disconcerting for Communists to note that the only class in the socialist society to enjoy appreciably better living conditions are private landowners, not subject to state planning and operating on an individual basis. No wonder that the Third Congress sounded muted warnings that the party would sometimes have to reconsider its present policy. To mobilize support, to produce revolutionary élan, to build socialism, a sense of purpose is vital and must be stated. Muddling-through, with the silent understanding that it was necessary to avoid foreign interference, could not be a long-range response to the problem. Both Gomulka and his opponents knew it, and this awareness lurked in the background of the Twelfth Plenum discussions and in the dull unanimity of the Third Congress in March 1959.

The Polish way to socialism was thus based on Gomulka's recognition of Polish national peculiarities, including widespread hostility toward Communism, on the specifics of the Polish agrarian scene and the rugged political and social individualism of the Polish peasant, on the more advanced state of industrialization in Poland than at the comparable stage of socialist development in Russia, on a close alliance with the USSR but not on domestic subordination to it, on domestic autonomy without external ideological ambitions. It was hence not comparable to Tito's national Communism or even to China's indigenous Communist regime. At the same time, the efforts of the

---

ne in the number of party members of 25 years of age and less. In 1955, 15.9 per nt of the party's membership was in that category; in 1956, 13 per cent; 1957, 10 per cent; 1958, 6.8 per cent (*Nowe Drogi*, December 1958).

* It was this that Andrzej Werblan, speaking for the "impatients" in the party, who want action but not necessarily a return to Stalinism (which it might well require in some aspects), attacked in his secret speech to the party Press Commission May 1958.

regime to maintain a measure of independence from the USSR, despite domestic weakness, resulted in a degree of moderation which did not characterize either Mao Tse-tung or Tito in their revolutionary periods. But these considerations should not obscure the fact that Gomulkaist Poland was a Communist state which could not be maintained without the support of the USSR, the interference of which Gomulka rejected. Therein lay the paradox and the inherent long-range weakness of the Gomulkaist solution.

The problem was hardly solved by Gomulka's assertions of unity or by his reluctant acceptance of Soviet leadership. While laying the groundwork for possible Soviet interference in Polish domestic affairs, such assertions served in the first instance as mere ritualistic requirements to prevent stigmatization as traitor. They granted Gomulka a certain amount of immunity from external attack, in spite of the fact that his very existence was considered a threat by the more rigid Communist states. The Polish pattern seemed to offer a less violent alternative to the established method of building socialism, and hence is was a living refutation of the Stalinist "dilemma of the one alternative." It was no accident that after 1956 Polish newspapers were much in demand, even in the USSR,[71] and that Polish events stirred up lively discussions in neighboring countries, and "not always the right way either," as a critical Czech paper put it.[72] The special appeal of the Polish solution to intellectuals elsewhere meant that, despite Gomulka's immunity, the problem could not be ignored — advocacy of the Polish pattern could well become a sanctuary for revisionists hiding behind the "socialist legitimacy" of Poland.

To cope with the demoralizing implications of Gomulkaism, a twofold approach was pursued on the basis of the Soviet example, even after November 1957. Gomulka himself, his immediate "entourage," and "Polish socialism" in general were not to be attacked, but those specifics of Polish life not clearly identified with a program personally articulated by Gomulka were to be singled out for continuing criticism. This was undoubtedly designed to prevent Gomulka's regime from officially sanctioning them. Furthermore, the Polish leaders were to be subjected to unrelenting but informal and indirect pressure in conferences and meetings, through bilateral declarations of other parties, and the like; this was intended to make Polish Communists deeply aware of their isolation and eventually induce in them a certain amount of Communist soul-searching. A typical example of this was Khrushchev's speech in Sofia on June 1958, in which he stressed collectivization as an important attribute building socialism and then pointedly praised those states actively engaged in collectivization. In the same speech he attacked Yugoslavia for accepting United States loans; not once did he mention Poland, but the inference was clear. Furthermore, by occasionally forcing the Poles through such indirect means, or even by economic or political pressure, into *declarative* unity, as was the case with Gomulka in November 1957 or with the more violent Polish condemnation of the Hungarian revolution issued finally in April 1958,[73] it was hoped that Poland would be ultimately forced into complete uniformity in action. A good example of the effectiveness of declarative unity was the undermining of Polish resistance to an interparty ideological journal. Once unity and Soviet leadership had been conceded by Gomulka, the ideological arguments against such a publication, based on equality and independence, lost most of their meaning, and the Poles had no choice but to participate in it.

In this fashion, the Polish autonomy was gradually to be whittled down. The press of the neighboring states, partially to immunize its own intelligentsia and partially for the Poles' benefit, tended to concentrate most of their fire on the intellectual and cultural aspects of the Polish scene. Polish revisionists were pictured as wielding considerable influence in the party: "The majority of them do public work and thus have great possibilities to influence the theoretical, political and scientific thinking as well as the preparation of cadres at school," a Czechoslovak journal complained.[74] Polish legal writings advocating the development of the Sejm into a truly legislative organ were interpreted to signify the abandonment of the dictatorship of the proletariat and the return to "bourgeois democracy." [75] The organ of the Czech Central Committee went so far as to publish a black list of Polish journals guilty of propagating revisionism, and suggested that Polish revisionism was a weapon in the imperialist arsenal.[76] It was no mere coincidence that by 1959 Prague was the only important Communist capital, with the exception of the distant Peking, not visited by Gomulka.

The year 1958 marked a distinct turn for the better in Polish-Soviet relations. Gomulka's domestic policies, as well as his position on revisionism, seemed to vindicate Khrushchev's "confidence" in him and presumably were gratifying to the Soviet leader's self-esteem. At the same time, the greater rigidity demonstrated by the other Communist leaders, including the Chinese, helped to create a feeling in Warsaw that within the Communist camp Khrushchev was the only leader with whom the Poles could bargain. That certainly seemed to be the case during Gomulka's prolonged trip to the USSR in October–November 1958. He was received with demonstrable cordiality by Khrushchev, and then, accompanied by the entire Polish delegation, including Cyrankiewicz and Zawadzki, traveled to the major urban centers of the USSR. Gomulka's trip could be interpreted as a coordinated effort, presumably backed by Khrushchev, to "sell" the Polish leadership to the Soviet *apparatchiki* who had always been wary of the Polish experiment.[77] Gomulka accordingly went out of his way to convince the various republican leaders, members of the Central Committee, of his fundamental commitment to the common cause, while also pleading the need for them to understand the special characteristics of the Polish situation. Apparently, as a price, he shifted toward greater uniformity on the still vital issue of Soviet leadership, although just a few months earlier he had rigidly applied his own formula, "first and mightiest," even when visiting the centralist leaderships of Bulgaria, Rumania, and Hungary. In the course of his Soviet trip Gomulka devised a new formulation, more submissive but still somewhat vague. He now described the Soviet Union as the "foremost" (*czolowe*) socialist state. The Soviet press at first translated this incorrectly as "leading" or "directing" (*vedushcheie*) but then quickly shifted to the more ambiguous Polish meaning.

In return for these concessions, Gomulka obtained, in the joint Polish-Soviet declaration, a condemnation of dogmatism as well as revisionism and a firm restatement of Soviet support for the Oder-Neisse frontier. It was clear that the Poles had to pay the higher price for the rapprochement that was achieved, but at the same time, however, it served to consolidate Gomulka's position both at home and within the camp. At the Twenty-first CPSU Congress in February 1959 Gomulka was recognized as one of the foremost international Communist leaders and assigned the second place of honor. His attacks on revisionism and his support of the Soviet policy on Germany were a welcome proof to the other Communist leaders of Gomulka's loyalty. Possibly also for Gomulka's benefit, Khrushchev emphasized at length that CPSU's "headship" of the camp was essentially a recognition of its historical role and of its strength, and had no other implications. Following the Polish party's Third Congress, in March 1959, in which Gomulka so firmly established his position, the Tass report on the congress decisions even implicitly approved Gomulka's deviant agricultural policy by stating that the Polish party "has secured a faster growth of agricultural production, improved the situation of the village and, liquidating the perversion in the relations between the state and the village, has strengthened the union of the workers and peasants." * [78] Indeed, something even remotely resembling the old Khrushchev-Tito axis seemed to be emerging out of Gomulka's relations with Khrushchev.† [79]

The gradual improvement in Polish-Soviet relations and the domestic consolidation of Gomulkaism made a return to the pre-October relationship rather unlikely. Indeed, it could be argued that a certain amount of domestic autonomy for Poland was desirable even from the standpoint of the camp. By its very presence and power it absorbed internal pressures and prevented the mobilization of domestic national resistance. In foreign affairs, it could take an occasional initiative such as the Rapacki plan for the "denuclearization" of Central Europe, which felicitously combined Soviet and Polish interests and a general emphasis on the conduct of operations on the international arena in a more "Western" style. Poland also could be used to restrain Tito and could serve as a model for the Yugoslavs after Tito's death, even while encouraging other East European states to emulate its "domesticism." [80]

But the limits to the autonomy were firm, and no Pole could seriously contemplate the likelihood of Polish autonomy's becoming true independence in the near future. The Warsaw Pact, the geographical isolation, the economic integration, the question of the Oder-Neisse frontier, were formidable barriers. Observers in the West, noting Polish hostility toward Communism and Russia, ought not to lose sight of the fact that more and more Poles were beginning to reason along the lines of this argument:

What would Poland mean in the Western alliance? . . . It would occupy a lowly place, after England, Germany, France, Italy in Europe and

---

* The shift in the Soviet position becomes clear when the above statement is contrasted to the remarks made in 1958 by K. Voroshilov, Chairman of the Presidium of the Supreme Soviet of the USSR, after his visit to Poland. Voroshilov bluntly stated: "Of course here we must say frankly that there is much to be done by the Polish people and first, not so much by the State authorities as by the Communist Party, the UPWP. In this respect Polish agriculture has not yet placed itself completely on socialist rails." Radio Moscow, April 26, 1958; omitted in *Pravda*, April 27, 1958.

† Khrushchev also visited Poland in July 1959 and roundly condemned the "dogmatists" for opposing "our friend . . . our dear friend and comrade," Gomulka. Khrushchev rejected the claims of the dogmatists that their views coincided more closely to those of the CPSU and advised them to support Gomulka "firmly." Gomulka, in turn, did not hide his feeling that he considered Khrushchev as the Communist leader most friendly toward the present Warsaw regime. *Trybuna Ludu*, July 22, 1959.

dozens of other states on a world scale . . . In view of the primary importance to America of Germany it would be the losing party in any Polish-German conflict . . .

In the socialist camp the proportions are reversed: Poland as the largest People's Democracy is third on the list of socialist states after the Soviet Union and China, and second in Europe.[81]

The limits of the Polish autonomy were thus also defined by Western policies and attitudes.

15 / DIVERGENT UNITY

IT SEEMS in retrospect that the Soviet leadership, usually so attentive to the meaning of history, did not fully grasp the historical significance of the 1957 Chinese intervention in East European matters. While the Chinese strove to restore unity within the bloc, they also conclusively broke their ages-long political confinement to the Asian continent. In 1957 China intervened decisively in Eastern Europe, and the Peking leaders no longer saw China merely as a regional power. Having helped the Soviets in their internal bloc difficulties (see Chapter 12), they were quite willing to assist in the formulation of the bloc's global strategy, thus laying claim to the status of a world power. Khrushchev's formula for bloc unity had made no provision for more than one center of political and ideological guidance, and even less for the eventuality of major disagreements between any plurality of such centers.

The great significance of this development was initially obscured by the simultaneous process of abatement of tensions in Eastern Europe. The revolutionary wave, which had reached its crest in 1956, had receded. Soviet hopes were again high, stimulated by Soviet space achievements and by a growing Soviet conviction that the West was gradually adjusting to the notion of the peaceful emergence of global Communist supremacy. Khrushchev's domestic popularity had never been higher, benefiting also from marked improvements in the Soviet standard of living.

This outward stability — as well as the intense efforts to promote close economic, political, and cultural integration of the bloc, which moved apace after 1957 shielded a number of grave problems. Marxism-Leninism as a vital ideology was badly shaken by the post-Stalin crisis, and it had not recovered. Revisionism failed as a political substitute,[1] but at the same time many of its assumptions had penetrated, informally and "by the back door," some of the ruling political elites, not as a formal ideology but rather as part of the prevailing climate of political opinion. As an amorphous force, revisionist views became more difficult to uproot and began to merge with the decaying structure of the official Marxist-Leninist doctrine. The approaching crisis of generations — the wartime gap between the ruling elite of men in their fifties and the rising careerists in their thirties — accentuated the problem, since revisionist thinking seemed to reflect more closely the aspirations of the more youthful East European pretenders to the mantle of leadership. At the same time, the majority of the young people were becoming increasingly "privatized" and avoiding all political entanglements.[2] This development, related closely to the general influence of West European traditions and culture on Eastern Europe, threatened to increase further the gap between the East European Communist states and their zealous, revolutionary Asian counterparts, still experiencing the initial impact of the confrontation of their retarded but restless social environment with an all-embracing ideology of change, modernization, and dichotomic hostility to the rest of the world. Dying in Eastern Europe, feverishly oscillating in Russia, the ideology was being resuscitated in Asia.[3]

China accordingly raised two long-range problems for the Communist camp. Both of them involved China's future potential as a great power (and in our age, our consciousness of the future affects the present to an unprecedented degree) as well as the specific internal changes launched in China in 1958, following the 1957 "rectification campaign" designed to subdue restless intellectuals. The first of these was the old problem faced by Stalin in 1947: can the bloc remain homogeneous if its uniformity is *only* ideological? Can there be a centralized bloc in which domestic practices vary appreciably from state to state, particularly if the two leading powers differ substantially in their practice even while professing ideological unity? Secondly, how long would the Soviet leadership, based in part on the voluntary consent of its dependents, endure if it leaned too heavily on the endorsement of another large power which might eventually differ with it on major issues?

THE SILENT SPLIT

Khrushchev, in his effort to construct a Communist commonwealth, had to cope during the late fifties with the mounting crisis posed by a silent split with the Chinese. Destined to break out into the open in 1960, the increasingly acrimonious Russo-Chinese dialogue was at this time conducted surreptitiously, at closed meetings only echoed in subtly diverging public pronouncements.[4]

It is difficult, probably impossible, to pinpoint precisely the beginning of the Sino-Soviet dispute. In some respects, it can be dated back to the 1920's, when Moscow directives led the Chinese Communists into the jaws of destruction.[5] In terms of more contemporary issues, there is reason to believe that the Chinese Communist victory in 1949 was neither expected in Moscow nor achieved by methods advocated by Stalin.[6] Following the victory, there were hints that the Peking-Moscow relationship was not the warmest, and it was only after Stalin's death that the Soviet leadership began to cultivate more affirmatively its Chinese allies. The Kremlin probably felt that its efforts were rewarded by the energetic support given it by the Chinese in the aftermath of the Polish and Hungarian revolts. At the same time, it was precisely this engagement that produced in the Chinese an acute crisis of confidence in Khrushchev's leadership of the bloc, encouraging them to take a more active part in shaping the bloc's over-all line.

In 1960, when the disagreements between the two parties became public knowledge, they exchanged strong mutual criticisms and, in so doing, attempted to date the beginning of their conscious and actively expressed disagreements.[7] It is revealing to note that Khrushchev adopted the position that it was only after the November 1957 meeting that the Chinese began to deviate from the common line. In effect, Khrushchev was claiming that the Chinese started to strain the unity of the bloc just after it had been reconsolidated and that it involved a conscious, "subjective" Chinese act. The Chinese, however, went to some pains in stressing that the Sino-Soviet divergence began with the reckless and unilateral launching by Khrushchev of the anti-Stalin campaign in 1956 and that it was subsequently reinforced by the indecision of the Soviet leadership during the October–November 1956 crisis. They also harped on earlier differences, dating back even to 1926. The Chinese, in effect, were saying that the dispute was rooted, "objectively," in the transformation experienced by the bloc after Stalin's death and that it was an inevitable consequence of the failures of Soviet leadership.[8]

There is truth in both versions, although it would seem that neither party had "creatively utilized" its Marxism-Leninism in analyzing the origins of the silent split in their world outlook that developed between 1956 and 1959, erupting into an open dialogue in 1960. Both "subjective" and "objective" factors played a role, and it would be useless to attempt to separate them. Basically, the Sino-Soviet divergence can be said to have been rooted in the interaction within the Soviet and Chinese contexts of three elements: domestic developments, their relationship to bloc affairs, the interaction of the two with world affairs — all as perceived within the jointly shared Marxist-Leninist outlook of the two parties.

The Chinese domestic scene during the years 1957–1961 was dominated by the following characteristics: (1) an apparent shift to the left in the Communist leadership; (2) a revolution on an unprecedented human scale in agriculture, carrying with it significant ideological implications for the Communist bloc and a challenge to Soviet ideological primacy; (3) a general "Great Leap Forward" in all economic sectors, but one accompanied by mounting economic difficulties, especially an agricultural crisis in 1959–1960, as well as by natural disasters (floods, etc.); (4) the awakening of an intense sense of national pride and energy among 650 million Chinese, hitherto politically pliant but now fascinated with industrialization. In effect, the domestic scene involved the simultaneous merging of Communist, industrial, and nationalist revolutions — a combination hitherto not experienced anywhere.

The Great Leap Forward was initiated by Liu Shao-chi's speech to the Party Congress on May 5, 1958 (published on May 31), in which he related the change on the international scene — now said to favor decisively the forces of "socialism" — to domestic Chinese affairs and explained the necessity of proceeding with "the uninterrupted Chinese revolution." Mass enthusiasm and total mobilization of human energy were to be substituted for material-technical development, thereby paving the way for rapid advance into the stage of Communism.[9]

Accordingly, on September 10, 1958, a nationwide program of people's communes was launched. The announcement marked a turning point of fundamental ideological significance. In the words of the resolution, "Concerning the Creation of People's Communes in the Village":

It seems that the realization of communism in our country is already not something far away. We must actively use the form of the people's commune and through it find the concrete road of transition to Communism.[10]

In two brief sentences the Chinese leadership established itself on the threshold of Communism — something which no other Communist state had yet done.

The new communes laid the ideological basis for Chinese preeminence. The Soviet position of leadership, apart from the admittedly vital consideration of power, rested on the claim that it was i

Russia that the socialist revolution had first taken place and that it was there that socialism had first been constructed. Just as the Molotov recantations of 1955 had underscored the more advanced stage of Soviet socialist construction, so the Chinese statement suggested that China might be the first state to realize Communism. In view of this, whether the Chinese leadership wished it or not, its claim meant that China was placing itself on a more elevated historical plane, an indispensable ingredient to ideological primacy.

No wonder then that a measure of Soviet chagrin was evident under the cloak of official approbation. Soviet press coverage of this important event was remarkably sparse, and, in one instance, the reference originally cited on "the realization of communism" was translated as "the realization of the communes." [11] The Soviet press referred to the people's communes as a "new low-level form of organisation of socialist society in China," [12] while the Soviet ambassador to Peking, in a speech commemorating the October Revolution, pointedly reminded his audience that the USSR is "now entering on the stage of communist construction on a tremendous scale" and referred to China as marching "along the road of building socialism." [13] Indeed, in the course of his visit to Peking in July 1958, Khrushchev told Mao directly about the Soviet "doubts" concerning the Chinese innovations and claims, and earned in return the epithet of "conservative." [14]

The Soviets were presumably concerned that the Chinese emphasis on the rapidity of their changes, so out of tune with the general vagueness of Soviet references to a *gradual* transition to Communism, was emphatically linked with Mao Tse-tung's ideological direction, thereby establishing him as the only Communist leader since Stalin's "Economic Problems of Socialism in the USSR" to be tackling the problem of the transition to Communism. "It is obvious that under the direction of Mao Tse-tung's thought, under the banner of Comrade Mao Tse-tung, and at a time when the national economy and culture are developed at such a rate that 'twenty years are concentrated in one day,' one can visualize the gradual transition of our country from socialism to communism," proclaimed one Chinese statement, blandly linking the standard formula of "gradual transition" with "twenty years in one day." [15]

Furthermore, the Chinese transition to Communism apparently was to be characterized by features unique to China. The scheme of people's communes involved a socioeconomic and political transformation which was to combine, within a few years, all administrative

Comparison of selected economic statistics during the "big push"
in the USSR and Communist China

Steel (million metric tons)				Coal (million metric tons)			
USSR		China		USSR		China	
1928	5.0	1954	2.0	1928	38	1954	80
1929	5.2	1955	3.0	1929	44	1955	95
1930	5.6	1956	4.5	1930	50	1956	150
1931	5.5	1957	6.0	1931	57	1957	200
1932	5.6	1958	8.0	1932	64	1958	275
1933	7.0	1959	13.0	1933	82	1959	347.8

Electricity (billion kilowatt-hours)				Cement (million metric tons)			
USSR		China		USSR		China	
1928	5.0	1954	12.0	Average		Average	
1929	7.0	1955	13.0	annual rate		annual rate	
1934	21.0	1956	18.0	of increase		of increase	
1940	48.3	1957	22.0	1928/29–		1954–1959	
		1958	28.0	1937		25%	
		1959	41.5	11.5%			

and economic functions within a commune, thereby marking the
withering away of the state. "The function of the state will be only
to deal with aggression from external enemies and will not operate
inside," Mao explained.[16] In addition, the new societal framework
and production relations were expected to stimulate the growth of
productive forces and create the conditions of plenty, or the conditions of Communism. This indeed was straying away from the prevailing Soviet emphasis on increasing productivity as the necessary
precondition for entering into Communism. The Chinese could not
hope to outstrip the Soviets in industrial production in the foreseeable
future, and as long as that was the basis for entering Communism, the
Soviets could confidently expect that the foundations of Communism
would be constructed first in the USSR. But the Chinese method
neatly disposed of the economic aspects and represented a convenient
shortcut for China.

    The many-roads-to-socialism concept had caused the Communist
camp considerable discomfort. The Chinese, preaching unity and hailing Soviet leadership, seemed to be implicitly confirming the validity

of the many-roads principle, and it was noteworthy that the Poles quickly pointed to this as again validating their stress on autonomous domestic patterns. A potential ideological challenge to Soviet leadership as well as the implicit reassertion of the varieties of domestic Communist construction were thus posed by the presence of China in the "commonwealth."

The preceding considerations were closely related to the divergence in the assessments made after 1957 of the international scene, and particularly of the existing opportunities for further expansion of Communism. To the Soviets, a certain balance of terror seemed to make indirect expansion possible (through economic aid and political intercourse with potentially pro-Communist elements), while to the Chinese the missile gap seemed to be the basis for more explicit linkage of political and military tactics. Thus, here as elsewhere, ideology and national interests were interacting. The Chinese concern over Formosa and Ladakh provided the underpinnings of national frustration, but the Chinese involvement in Algeria and Cuba could hardly be interpreted purely in terms of national interest. Inescapably differing Soviet and Chinese domestic experiences and interests affected their worldwide Communist aspirations and perspectives. The interaction of these elements created a dilemma: "How the existing differences in ideology and in material situation can be transmuted into ideological and material uniformity. What are the dialectical processes through which uniformities may be developed from dissimilarities?" [17]

A temporary abatement of tensions occurred late in 1958 and early in February 1959, after the Twenty-first CPSU Congress. It may be assumed that the sudden opening by Khrushchev of the Berlin crisis (fall of 1958) made the Chinese hopeful that the Soviet Union would henceforth pursue a more forceful policy. This may have made the Chinese less inclined to press their challenge. In any case, in December 1958, the Chinese leadership issued a further declaration, 'On Some Questions Concerning the People's Communes," warning against the danger of becoming "dizzy with success." A gradual transition to Communism was referred to no less than 211 times in the 10,000-word document,[18] making it quite clear that China had to complete the construction of socialism before any realization of Communism might be contemplated. At the same time, however, the specificity of the Chinese road was maintained, even though the processes of socialist construction were to take another fifteen to twenty years.[19] This retreat was followed by explicit Chinese acknowledgment at the Twenty-first CPSU Congress in February 1959 that the USSR was entering the stage of the construction of Communism and by praise of Khrushchev's contribution to the "treasure house" of Marxism-Leninism. Since the Soviet leader's ideological elaborations concerned the problems of transition to Communism, the Chinese recognition placed him at least on a par with Mao Tse-tung as the only living leaders who have made contributions on that matter. In return, the Soviet Union undertook to loan China further technical and industrial aid, officially estimated at five billion rubles, although it was clear from the agreement that a loan and not assistance was involved.[20]

However, the basic differences were not bridged and the accommodation proved to be very short-lived indeed. The launching of the first Soviet ICBM in the fall of 1957, followed by the Sputnik, and then by the 1958 recession in the United States, had firmly convinced the Chinese, in the words of *Jen-min Jih-pao*, that "U.S. imperialism already has one foot in the grave and can with as much justice be described as a 'rotting bone in a graveyard.'"[21] It is quite evident that in the course of this period the Chinese were acting on the assumption that there had been a fundamental and decisive turning point in international affairs in favor of the Soviet bloc and that the West no longer has any choice but to compromise, either willingly or by being forced.[22] Having challenged the Soviets on the pace of the domestic march to Communism, the Chinese were also pressing them with respect to external efforts for the attainment of a worldwide Communist victory. The policy implications that they drew from their assessment were, in turn, closely related to their more general interpretation of our era as "an epoch of imperialism, wars, and revolutions."[23] Given that, as well as their appraisal of imperialist strength, their policy prescriptions naturally followed.

In effect, the Sino-Soviet "war and peace debate" of 1959–196 (more open in the latter year) can be reduced to the following exchanges. The Soviets to the Chinese: "You overestimate the ability of the imperialists to initiate a war, hence war is not inevitable; you underestimate the destructiveness of war and our deterrent capabilities; you underestimate the danger of a total war developing out of local conflicts; you underestimate the worldwide appeal of socialism as a powerful force and the global significance of the economic power of the world socialist system." The Chinese to the Soviet "You overestimate the destructiveness of war; you overestimate the willingness of the imperialists to make peaceful concessions; you un derestimate the militant revolutionary opportunities and the dangers of coexistence to the revolutionary zeal of the international Communist movement; you underestimate the ability of the socialist camp to win local wars or to force the imperialists to desist when they start one. Finally, you underestimate the possibility of the imperialists plunging the world into war, either out of despair or duplicity, and hence, there is a continuing danger of war." [24] The Chinese never argued for war as such; they believed that greater activism and even local wars need not lead to a real war. Thus Peking continued to place primary stress on the necessity of developing "the imperialist rear into an active anti-imperialist front," [25] and in so doing the Chinese asserted the general relevance of their revolutionary experience.

At the same time, the Chinese were intent also on pursuing their narrower national interests, even while perhaps identifying them with broader revolutionary goals. Hence to the Soviets, the Chinese predisposition, for example, to sacrifice Indian good will (and perhaps the chances of Communism in South Asia) because of the desire to gain full control over Tibet and, even more so, because of the Chinese determination to insist on a minor frontier change in the dispute with India seemed hardly compatible with an internationalist revolutionary spirit. Similarly, Peking's desire to subordinate the collective security interests of the Communist camp to the Chinese quest for the off-shore islands appeared to the Soviets to contain a greater dose of pure nationalism than the Chinese leaders were prepared to admit.

Grievances accordingly multiplied. From the Chinese point of view, Soviet support for China's position during the Taiwan Straits crisis of August–September 1958 must have appeared disproportionately trifling in comparison with American assistance to the Nationalists and, doubtless, the point was bitterly made to the Kremlin.* Even more outrageous to the Chinese was the openly proclaimed Soviet "neutrality" in regard to the Sino-Indian border incidents of the fall of 1959.[26] To the Chinese, the public statement of Soviet neutrality, a statement issued on the eve of Khrushchev's visit to America, an event not particularly welcomed by the Chinese, was proof of Khrushchev's blatant disregard for the principle of proletarian internationalism. Moreover, approximately at this time, a number of minor incidents had occurred on the Sino-Soviet border of

---

* Several years later, the Chinese pointedly noted that verbal Soviet support for the Chinese came only *after* the Soviet side convinced itself that there was no longer any danger of nuclear involvement (Chinese statement of September 1, 1963).

Sinkiang, with some Kazakhs rising against Chinese suppression and fleeing, apparently with Soviet assistance, into the Soviet Union.[27] Although both sides retained silence on these events until the violent and public polemics of 1963, they doubtless contributed to a further chilling of Sino-Soviet relations.

There can be little doubt that the Chinese attitude and behavior was becoming more and more an impediment to the effective prosecution of the grand strategy on which Khrushchev had embarked in the late fifties. With the newly acquired ICBMs serving primarily as psychological leverage, Khrushchev hoped to pressure the West into substantial concessions in Europe (especially via the Berlin crisis), while obtaining at the same time for the Soviet Union the co-status with America of a world power. To that end, Khrushchev was eager to have a summit meeting with President Eisenhower, and it was held in early fall 1959, despite Chinese reservations. For the developing nations, the Soviet Union was inclined to favor "a Bandung spirit" policy, and the Soviet leadership was chagrined to see China abandon it in regard to India, possibly the most vulnerable and certainly the most important long-range target of that policy.

Accordingly, the Soviet leadership began to disengage itself from its still baffling 1957 commitment to aid in the development of China's strategic weaponry (see p. 301). Apparently, that aid was not only promised but delivered during 1958–1959, thereby substantially facilitating China's entry into the world's nuclear club in October of 1964. Why such Soviet aid was forthcoming is still a matter for conjecture. It certainly involved a departure from the long-standing Soviet inclination to maintain a monopoly in the Communist camp on the latest weapons technology and it was hardly compatible with the various Sino-Soviet disagreements that had been mounting in acerbity since at least 1957. Perhaps even in 1958 the Chinese challenge still appeared to be a "nonantagonistic contradiction" among friends; perhaps Chinese political aid was so badly needed that it had to be purchased almost at any price; perhaps the Soviet leaders felt that some aid to China's military would help to build a real Communist "commonwealth" and overcome Chinese fear of Soviet "big-power chauvinism"; perhaps there was the though that by modernizing the Chinese Army, thereby making it more de pendent on Soviet aid, China would become more closely tied to th Soviet Union; perhaps Khrushchev thought that it would be easie to enlist Chinese support for a test-ban agreement with the Unite States if he avoided creating the impression that the agreement wa directed at China. Whatever the motives and calculations, by mid-1958 and early 1959 the Soviet leaders began to have second thoughts.

Their first impulse was to search for an intermediary arrangement, combining continued assistance to China with increased Soviet control over China's military potential. (Noteworthy here is the parallel with the almost simultaneous appearance of a similar problem for the United States with regard to France.) It may be presumed that the Soviet concern with the possibility of unilateral Chinese ventures mounted during 1958, in view of China's attitude on international affairs. At the same time, it was far from the Soviet intention to precipitate a headlong clash with the second most important ruling party, a party that enjoyed very high prestige throughout the Communist movement. In any case, Khrushchev and Mao (and their military aides) met in July 1958, and the two leaders reached an agreement concerning Soviet economic and military aid to China. According to some reports, it provided for missiles as well as help in the construction of nuclear reactors. Simultaneously, however, the Soviet leaders proposed to the Chinese a command arrangement that the Chinese were later to characterize as having been "designed to bring China under Soviet military control." [28] It was therefore rejected.

The Soviet response to the Chinese refusal of the Soviet proposal was to move in the direction of public pressure on the Chinese on behalf of "an atom-free zone . . . in the Far East and the entire Pacific Basin," [29] a proposal in turn simply ignored by China. The next step, presumably influenced by the crescendo of Chinese denunciations of revisionism (a charge that Khrushchev could decipher with little difficulty), by the accumulating grievances, and by growing Soviet expectations of accommodation with the United States, was to disengage the Soviet Union altogether from its previous commitments. In Peking's aggrieved words: "Not long afterwards, in June 1959, the Soviet government unilaterally tore up the agreement on new technology for national defense concluded between China and the Soviet Union in October 1957, and refused to provide China with a sample of an atomic bomb and technical data concerning its manufacture." [30] *

* The Soviets did not deny the substance of the Chinese version when it was revealed in 1963, but charged in return that Mao Tse-tung had become a security risk who revealed Communist defense secrets to the "imperialists."! Moscow added that henceforth "hardly anyone . . . will . . . trust [Peking] with information of defensive importance." Statement of the Soviet government of August 20, 1963.

This step probably was of fundamental importance in jelling the Chinese leadership in a posture of unmitigated hostility to Khrushchev. And if that did not, then Khrushchev's subsequent visit to Peking in October 1959 (the tenth anniversary of the Chinese revolutionary victory) certainly must have had that effect. The Soviet leader, fresh from a cordial visit to America, proposed to the Chinese that their interests would be best served by an acceptance of the "two-Chinas" formula, that is, in effect the abandonment of their claim to Formosa.[31] Coming in the wake of a severe blow to their nuclear ambitions, the Soviet proposal, made only weeks after an "unfriendly" comment on the Indian-Chinese frontier dispute, must have been interpreted as part of a deliberate and elaborate effort to reach an accommodation with the West at China's expense.* The reception that Khrushchev got in Peking was somewhat less than cordial.

All of this strengthened the Chinese determination for "going-it-alone." Already from the late summer and early fall of 1958 the Chinese had been stressing that China would develop its own weapons and that it would rely primarily on its own people in the great worldwide struggle. Warnings were issued against dependence on outside aid, while the theme that "the atomic bomb is a paper tiger" was elevated to the rank of a classic and universally valid formula.

This defiant mood crystallized into policy at the Lushan Plenum of the Chinese leadership, held in July–August 1959. In retrospect, it appears more clearly that it was then that the Chinese leaders reached the important decision to escalate the struggle against "Khrushchev revisionism," while also crushing any internal opposition to Mao's general line. The Defense Minister, Marshal P'eng Teh-huai, and four Vice-Ministers, allegedly involved with an "anti-party group," were summarily dismissed.[32] Apparently, concerned with the further modernization of the Chinese Army, the Marshal opposed policies that could result in China's isolation and had even taken the unprecedented step of communicating on this matter with Khrushchev. The Lushan Plenum was followed by stepped-up and increasingly undisguised denunciations of certain "modern revisionists"; by the announcement that China would not be bound by any interna-

---

* As the Chinese later put it (reflecting, it may be presumed, their original feelings): "The tearing up of the agreement on new technology for national defense by the leadership of the CPSU and its issuance of the statement on the Sino-Indian border clash on the eve of Khrushchev's visit to the United States were presentation gifts to Eisenhower so as to curry favor with the U.S. imperialists and create the so-called 'spirit of Camp David.' " "Origin and Development . . ."

tional agreements concerning disarmament unless it was a direct party to them, even if the Soviet Union should reach a suitable agreement with the United States; by the Chinese refusal to endorse the planned May 1960 summit meeting; and by increasingly shrill polemics against those who preach "peaceful coexistence," "peaceful revolution," and the "non-inevitability of war." [33]

The culmination was the publication of a series of articles under the general slogan "Long Live Leninism" released in conjunction with the ninetieth anniversary of Lenin's birth in April 1960. Their unmistakable thrust was that China, and not the Soviet Union, was now the true standard-bearer of the revolutionary Leninist tradition. An article by Yu Chao-li, "On Imperialism as the Source of War in Modern Times, and on the Way for All Peoples to Struggle for Peace," [34] warned against mistaking tactical changes in imperialism "for changes in the nature of imperialism" and quoted Mao Tse-tung as saying, "If the imperialists insist on unleashing another war, we should not be afraid of it . . . if the imperialists should insist on launching a third world war, it is certain that several hundred million more [people] will turn to socialism." The article asserted that only by actively pressing "imperialism" and isolating it could a war be averted, and only then could local wars started by it be ended at a disadvantage to the imperialists. Using Lenin as his authority, Yu Chao-li emphasized that national liberation wars are "inevitable" and that it is dangerous to conclude "that imperialism will no longer make war." Speaking to a mass rally in Peking on April 22, Lu Ting-yi warned against those "revisionists" who "develop from fear of war to fear of revolution, and proceed from not wanting revolution to opposing other people's carrying out revolution . . ."

Although the stage was thus set for a head-on confrontation, the formal Soviet position throughout the period was that there was no disagreement. This was a proper and tactically wise stance for the acknowledged leader and most powerful state in the bloc to adopt. Ignoring the Chinese assertions seemed far more effective than responding to them and thereby being drawn into a debate.[35] The Chinese, on the other hand, seemed to rely on their domestic techniques for handling problems: they seemed convinced that "non-antagonistic contradictions" with Moscow would ultimately lead to unity, through their internally tested process of "unity-criticism-unity." However, by early 1960 it became clear that China's national ambitions, as well as the general world outlook of its highly ideologically oriented Communist leaders, were incompatible with the insistence of the Soviets on playing the game of international affairs purely in terms of their own estimates and interests.

The Chinese, the weaker partner, brought the dispute out into the open. By forcing the issue — in effect, by practicing brinkmanship (that is, letting the situation get somewhat out of their control) — they could hope to put the Soviets on the defensive, to force them to respond. At the same time, being more radical, they actually increased their leverage within international Communism since their radicalism inevitably served to reassure all Communists of their honest revolutionary intentions. Finally, by openly straining their unity with the Soviets and acting as if they were willing to risk this unity, they put the burden of protecting the unity on the Kremlin, thereby compensating for their economic-military weakness and equalizing the Sino-Soviet bargaining situation. Unity thus became a hostage in the relationship.

By mid-1960 the increasingly open dispute assumed grave proportions and the "hostage" was in some danger. The Chinese apparently abandoned any lingering hope that Khrushchev might be displaced, and rather than wait for a change in the Soviet line, they decided to force one. Furthermore, the Chinese must have felt that in the course of the year 1959 they had been reasonably successful in gaining support among the Communist and revolutionary movements and that, no longer alone, they could more effectively pressure Moscow into changing its policies. Peking was probably especially gratified by the increasingly intimate contacts with the Algerian rebels and by closer relations with the leftists in many of the Latin American countries. Furthermore, at the Tenth Chinese Anniversary in October 1959, visiting East German, Czech, and Albanian delegations spoke in such warm terms of the Chinese party that the Chinese leadership could have construed their remarks as indicating support.[36] Last, but certainly not least, the Chinese probably feared that the forthcoming May 1960 summit meeting in Paris would lead to the international isolation of China. For domestic, for bloc, and for external reasons, the Chinese felt that the issue had to be joined.

THE NEO-STALINIST LOYALISTS

China, Poland, and Yugoslavia were not the only items on Khrushchev's agenda of "commonwealth" problems. The very existence of a challenge on the left and on the right created hitherto unprecedented opportunities even for the most loyal satellite leaders to deviate, if only through an excess of loyalty. Indeed, one can surmise that, in view of the unfortunate 1956 consequences of Khrushchev's Yugoslav policy, the advocates of the more rigid program might have felt that they knew better than Khrushchev how to construct socialism in their own countries, and they were certainly encouraged by the Chinese pressure on the Kremlin. Despite their proclamations of loyalty, even to them Soviet infallibility was a thing of the past. As Ulbricht put it, while ostensibly pleading for general acceptance of Soviet leadership: "Who is the one who determines what is truth, and what complies with the principles of the Marxist-Leninist doctrine?"

The new sense of domestic self-confidence of these regimes was masked by persistent assertions that the path they were pursuing was the universal, Soviet-tested way, and that their domestic efforts were based on the generally binding concepts of Marxism-Leninism. Realizing that their security depended on the closest links with the USSR, they returned to the pre-Twentieth Congress stress on the importance of the Soviet experience. One Hungarian enthusiast even claimed that past difficulties were due not to "the fact that we took over too many experiences from the Soviet Union; on the contrary, these are far too few in number. And if there were mistakes, it was not because we used these experiences but that we applied them superficially." [37] Similar themes were stressed elsewhere.

The verbal emphasis on uniformity was reflected in some important areas of action. High among these was the domestic response to the challenge of revisionism through the full reassertion of the party's control over the intellectual sphere. Throughout East Europe the antirevisionist campaign involved a reversion to ideological orthodoxy,[38] buttressed by terror. As was to be expected, the most extreme repression took place in Hungary, where the regime boasted that "we not only liquidated the Writers' Association which turned counterrevolutionary but also managed to put an end to the organized hostile activity of certain writers' groups which, even as late as summer 1957, reaction inside and outside the country tried to utilize." [39] In Bulgaria, the return of Vulko Chervenkov to the Politburo, after serving as Minister of Culture, was closely related to the intensified campaign against "hostile views" which were said to have penetrated the cultural front and even the Karl Marx Institute.[40] The theoretical monthly of the Czech Central Committee warned that "the experience of the international Communist movement shows that the slogan 'freedom of criticism,' unlimited freedom, has always been the watchword of anti-Party elements and of the enemies of socialism." [41] In

March 1959, a national conference of the Union of Czechoslovak Writers condemned the "harmful opinions" expressed by Czechoslovak writers in 1956 and elected a new Presidium composed of more orthodox and politically minded Communist writers (including Ladislav Stoll, former Minister of Culture, who was attacked by the more liberal writers in 1956 for his dogmatism).

The policy of enforced ideological orthodoxy was accompanied by a partial return to economic Stalinism. Heavy industrial development was again given the highest priority, and the post-Stalin criticisms of overconcentration on capital investment were no longer mentioned. At the Eleventh Czech Party Congress, the party leadership announced its 1965 economic goals (closely linked to CEMA obligations), and their meaning was unmistakable: industrial production was to increase by 90–95 per cent, electric consumption by 115 per cent, steel production by 77–87 per cent, chemical production 150 per cent, machinery 130 per cent, while consumers' purchases by a mere 45 per cent and agricultural output by 40 per cent (compare with parallel Polish plans, Chapter 14).[42] Similar trends could be observed in the Hungarian Three-Year Plan announced in May 1958,[43] and in the East German "Economic Tasks up to 1960."[44] An interesting change, however, took place in Bulgaria where the 1958 plan was suddenly revised upward in the agricultural sector, with the announced purpose of tripling production by 1961. At the same time, however, the regime reiterated that in the effort "to reach rapidly a period of gradual transition to Communism," heavy industrial development remained all important, and assigned to it was 61.7 per cent of total investment, a ratio higher than during 1953–1956.[45] (The Bulgarians significantly described their efforts as a "great leap.")

The verbal insistence on unity and uniformity did reflect a considerable measure of underlying reality. It was also designed, however, to mask a growing diversity among even the relatively Stalinist states. This diversity their leaders were unwilling to acknowledge even while practicing it. Yet the increased scope of their initiative forced them to recognize problems which previously they could ignore. For example, the Czech and the East German industrial administrative reorganizations, announced in February and March 195? respectively, even though outwardly based on the Soviet pattern,[4?] were much more conservative than the Soviet in scope and retained hierarchical pyramids of industrial control cutting across territoria lines. Nonetheless, it was claimed that "our approach is identical with that of the Soviet Union." [47]

The inclination even of the orthodox leaderships to give priority to domestic considerations ("domesticism") at this time went the furthest in Rumania. Its leadership was firmly consolidated in the hands of Gheorghiu-Dej, who in July 1957 succeeded in eliminating his last rivals to power. During the Hungarian revolution the Rumanians stood with Moscow, and subsequently even provided the facilities in which Imre Nagy and his associates were held (after their kidnaping by the Soviet secret police from Budapest). At the same time, however, the Hungarian revolution, as well as the Soviet vacillation and finally the intervention, convinced the Rumanian leadership of the urgent desirability of standing on their own feet. It is interesting to note that the Rumanian party, which had purged its membership down to a mere 3 per cent of the population, undertook in the late fifties an intensive membership drive, which had the effect of widening its national base even if diluting its ideological purity. (By 1965, party membership had increased by 230 per cent!) At the same time, the Rumanians resumed their traditional policy of suppressing the Hungarian minority in Transylvania on the excuse that it had displayed "counterrevolutionary tendencies" in 1956. The denial of various concessions granted earlier to the Hungarian minority in the name of "proletarian internationalism" certainly appealed to Rumanian chauvinist traditions.

The Rumanian leadership also took steps to expand its own "sovereignty." In July 1958 Bucharest announced the departure of all Soviet troops, a concession presumably won from Moscow because of Rumania's "good behavior" in 1956 and in return for Rumania's support in the continuing post-1956 bloc political maneuvers. That event, however, permitted further Rumanian self-assertion. Late in 1958, during the November Plenum of the Rumanian Central Committee, the Rumanians apparently decided to expand their trade relations with the West, and in the succeeding years the percentage of their trade with the Soviet Union began to drop sharply. In the summer of 1959 a Rumanian governmental delegation toured Western Europe in search of trade and credits. The new Six-Year Plan, finally adopted in the summer of 1960 but discussed during 1959, provided for a sharp increase in Rumania's rate of industrialization, thereby implicitly putting a question mark behind the Soviet-inspired public discussions concerning the desirability of a "socialist division of labor" among the East European states. To a relatively backward country, but one rich in natural resources, the prospect of rapid industrialization was certainly more appealing than the proposed "division of labor" which seemed to imply the perpetuation of Rumania's backwardness. By pursuing an orthodox economic line, the Rumanian leadership was thereby gaining increasing domestic stability, which it could eventually use in resisting external pressures.[48]

Another important manifestation of diversity was the response to the revisionist challenge in its Polish or Yugoslav shape. The East Germans, the Czechs, and the Bulgarians, not to mention the distant Albanians, reacted much more forcefully than either the Hungarians or the Rumanians. On the Yugoslav issue, the Czechs pointedly remarked that they had correctly drawn "basic conclusions" about Yugoslav deviationism back in December 1956,[49] and the Czech, East German, and Bulgarian responses were closer to the Chinese than to the Soviet tone (compare Chapter 13).[50] The Hungarians, echoing some of the violent anti-Yugoslav attacks, were much more restrained in their references to Poland. The Rumanians, who had gone the furthest in improving relations with Tito, were the slowest in working themselves to a fever pitch of hatred, and their initial reaction to the Yugoslav draft program was relatively mild.[51] Similarly, Rumanian reporting of the Polish scene avoided the sharp criticisms so typical of the other states.[52] *

Perhaps of even greater concern to the Kremlin was the ambivalent response of the other Communist states to China's domestic and external policies. China's appeal to East Europe varied. In the more industrial states, particularly Czechoslovakia and East Germany, Chinese domestic practice, derived from a primitive economy, could hardly be applicable. However, the Czechs and the East Germans saw in the Chinese communes further proof of the desirability of "voluntaristic" and radical social change, even if the specific Chinese institution was not relevant domestically to them. Moreover, they welcomed Chinese antirevisionism and may have speculated that it may be useful in restraining Khrushchev's occasional outbursts of

---

* The Polish press made strikingly frank references to this. A Gomulkaist weekly noted: "In the Rumanian press, in contrast with that of other countries, we do not find the slightest critical reference to the current political trend of events in Poland. A similar independence — since silence can also be a sign of independence — is also evident in the attitude to the Yugoslavs, although there is not such a noticeable sympathy for Tito as for Gomulka. 'We believe that you can take care of yourselves, but for God's sake keep your nerves; do not let your imagination run away with you; and carefully calculate your strength. Our fate depends on how you will succeed.' Various people told me this . . ." *Polityka*, July 24–31, 1957.

reformist exuberance.* The Albanians and the Bulgarians initially went much further in stating that the people's communes may be pertinent to them, and the Bulgarians even proceded in one case to label some of their newly amalgamated collective farms as a people's commune. They also both welcomed with enthusiasm Chinese anti-Yugoslav polemics and saw in them a potential bulwark against any dangerous (to them) Soviet-Yugoslav reconciliation. The Poles and the Rumanians approved the Chinese self-assertion only to the extent that it confirmed once more the general proposition of a variety of methods in the march toward Communism. The North Koreans and the North Vietnamese were steadily moving toward the Chinese position, hailing the Chinese domestic developments and echoing the Chinese line on war, imperialism, and revisionism, even while still repeating the Soviet formula on peaceful coexistence.

The prospect of increasing Chinese influence in East Europe, probably to an even greater extent than the mounting volume of Chinese polemics, forced the Soviet leadership to abandon its preferred stance of aggrieved restraint. The Chinese criticisms were too pointed to pass unanswered and continued silence was only creating ambiguity and perhaps even causing a gravitation in the Chinese direction. Moreover, quiet anti-Chinese persuasion could be effective only in regard to the most supine satellites: thus late in 1958 the Bulgarians were successfully persuaded to contradict themselves by announcing that "it is incorrect to think that the Chinese experience is being transferred to our country," and they reaffirmed their loyalty to the Soviet pattern.[53] But by late 1959 and early 1960 the line had to be drawn more sharply and the whip cracked more publicly.

The February 1960 Warsaw Treaty meeting provided a convenient setting for lining up East European support. Using peace as his central theme and the forthcoming Paris summit meeting as a test, Khrushchev strove to force the others to choose, in effect, between peace and war, and thereby also between the Soviet Union and China. The Poles were already firmly pledged to Moscow, so the occasion was used to obtain the open commitment of the other leaders to a posture that the Chinese could not favor.† Although the Chinese

* For extravagant East German praise of the Chinese communes, see Paul Wander the GDR Ambassador to Peking) in his "A New Decisive Step in the Socialist Revolution in China," *Einheit*, December 1958. Prior to the summer of 1960, East German spokesmen were also generous in their praise of Mao's ideological contributions.

† Symptomatically, in the February 1960 meeting of the International Union of Students, held in Tunis, Chinese attacks on the Yugoslavs were not supported by either the Poles or the Bulgarians.

observer opposed the summit, violently attacked "imperialism," and warned of the likelihood of a major war,[54] his speech was ignored by the Soviet and East European mass media and the expected summit meeting approved. By the summer, praise of the Chinese, which had been a prominent feature in the East German, Czech, and Hungarian press, ceased almost completely.

The problem was more complex in the case of the Asian ruling parties, not to speak of those outside the bloc. The continuing tension in Laos, as well as the division of Vietnam, made the Vietnamese party especially fearful of Chinese absorption, but at the same time it was attracted to policies urging the rapid expulsion of the "imperialists" from Southeast Asia. In July 1959 Ho Chi Minh visited Khrushchev (and on his way back through China did not meet with Mao Tse-tung), but the Vietnamese press, by and large, continued to avoid siding with either Moscow or Peking. In August the Soviet leader was visited by Tsedenbal, the Mongolian leader who also paid a state visit to India, with whom Peking was badly at odds. The Mongolians, who might have been incorporated into the USSR if first World War II and then the Chinese Communist victory had not intervened,* had received sizable Soviet credits in 1958 (Soviet generosity seemed to increase in direct proportion to analogous Chinese efforts) and, still thoroughly under Soviet control, were unlikely to side with the Chinese.[55] The outside parties were a more difficult matter since overt pressure could easily become public knowledge; the Soviets thus preferred to keep them out of internal bloc affairs.

However, the somewhat reticent reaction from one hitherto very orthodox East European party must have perplexed the Soviet leader. Although at the February meeting the Albanians, perhaps because they were isolated or not yet certain of Chinese support, seemed to go along with the others, there was no mistaking their growing hostility to Khrushchev's general line, and his policy toward Yugoslavia in particular. The Albanian party developed during the war

---

* A revealing observation was made in this connection by I. G. Yur'yev "Laws and Characteristics of the Transition to Socialism in Socially and Economically Retarded Countries," *Vestnik Moskovskogo Universiteta*, no. 1, 1959), who, after arguing that aid "given within the framework of a single multinational socialist state is more effective and speeds up the rate of the transition from feudalism to socialism," hastily added that "from the analysis from the economic side of the question, however, we must not conclude that it is necessary for the Mongolian People's Republic to become part of the Soviet Union or the People's Republic of China, because *in the complex international situation*, political factors play a far from minor role." (Italics added.)

under Yugoslav tutelage, and between 1945 and 1948 Albania had been a Yugoslav satellite.[56] On at least one occasion Stalin encouraged the Yugoslavs to incorporate the country,[57] and the Stalin-Tito break may have actually saved Albania from that fate. A series of violent purges directed at pro-Yugoslav Albanian leaders followed, with no less than fourteen out of thirty-one Central Committee members and thirty-two of the 109 Assembly deputies liquidated, including the most outstanding pro-Yugoslav leader, Koci Xoxe. With Xoxe liquidated, the leadership was firmly consolidated in the hands of Enver Hoxha and his lieutenant, M. Shehu.* In many respects it resembled a clan: in the 1960 Central Committee of forty-three members, there were said to be ten married couples and fifteen other relatives.[58]

The post-1955 Soviet-Yugoslav relations gave rise to strong misgivings on the part of the Albanian leaders, and they strongly opposed any efforts on behalf of Xoxe's rehabilitation. Apparently in May 1956 Suslov had urged Hoxha to take that step,[59] but the Albanian leader, sensitive to its implications, wisely demurred. However, opposition to him became quite outspoken during 1956, reflecting presumably a feeling that Hoxha's position had weakened. He was saved by the Hungarian revolution and the immediate worsening in Soviet-Yugoslav relations that followed. His opponents were quickly arrested and several were executed in November 1956. (Khrushchev later charged that one opponent, Liri Gega, had been pregnant at the time of her execution.)

The 1958 Soviet-Yugoslav polemics, and especially the violence of the Chinese attacks on Tito, were enthusiastically welcomed in Tirana. They seemed to provide a guarantee against a recurrence of the Belgrade-Moscow flirtation, so directly dangerous to the Albanians. In June 1959 Khrushchev was greeted in Tirana with unprecedented deference, and it may be assumed that the Albanians were hoping that the newly opened Berlin crisis and the gradually developing Chinese involvement in East European affairs would protect their position. That is why the emergence of the Sino-Soviet rift presented them with a very difficult choice. The other East European leaders basically risked little in bowing to Khrushchev, and would risk a great deal in opposing him. The Albanians likewise risked much in opposing Moscow, but potentially they even risked

* It is interesting to note that Hoxha and many of his associates were of middle-class origin, educated in western Europe, and of intensely nationalistic orientation. The principal pro-Yugoslav leader, Xoxe, was a proletarian, and the two groups were ready feuding in 1944 (see Griffith, *Albania and the Sino-Soviet Rift*, p. 17). Xoxe and some of his associates were executed in 1949.

more by bowing before Khrushchev. By turning against China, as Khrushchev demanded, they would become totally dependent on Soviet good will, and they probably could predict that the dynamics of the Sino-Soviet dispute would eventually lead to a rapprochement between Moscow and Belgrade. Rather than having to opt for Peking, they preferred a Sino-Soviet dialogue that gave Tirana unity with options, but under no circumstances could they afford to divorce themselves from China. If a Sino-Soviet showdown came, and China did not bow before Soviet pressure, the Albanians would have an ally.[60] In the spring of 1960 all eyes in Tirana were directed at Peking.

THE PRICE OF PRIMACY

The exercise of leadership in the bloc was thus becoming increasingly onerous and complicated. There is little reason to doubt that the expansion of the Soviet sphere of influence following World War II met with the general approval of the Soviet people. The creation of new Communist states, formally friendly and in fact subordinate to the USSR, gave the average Russian a greater sense of security in a world portrayed as dominated by anti-Soviet imperialist forces. To those motivated by nationalist feelings there was the additional element of pride involved in the expansion of Russia. To the "faithful," the new situation gave cause for deeper ideological satisfactions. The emergence of a camp of Communist states was tangible proof that their doctrine was well founded, that their historical perspectives were in tune with the pattern of historical change. The growing number of Communist states, as well as the increasing ferment in Asia, the Middle East, and Africa, irrefutably bore out the most optimistic expectations voiced by the Soviet leaders. Beyond all this, there were even material blessings in the new relationships. "To the victor belong the spoils" was the operational principle of the millions of Red Army men pouring through East Europe or Manchuria in 1945. Victory and primacy were expressed in tangible personal ways. The official Soviet policy of dismantling and reparations was another very tangible manifestation of the new, economically beneficial relationship.

Gradually, however, a change took place. After Stalin's death, the allied Communist states began to appear less and less as tributaries and more and more as claimants to Soviet resources. The Soviet regime, anxious for reasons of international prestige to appear as benefactor, was unable to reveal openly to its own population the fact that economic relations with the People's Democracies had been to the Soviet advantage. On the contrary, even during the Stalinist phase of acute exploitation of the neighboring states, the Soviet population was led to believe that the USSR was selflessly aiding the other Communist states. After 1956 the Soviet government was compelled to revise its economic relations with the bloc, and Soviet credits were granted to obtain political benefits. Indeed, thereafter the Soviet regime was constantly pressed for credits. The Poles demanded and obtained them as compensation for past iniquities. The Hungarians got them to help Kadar restore control. The Chinese got them to push forward their economic planning. The East Germans received them partially to alleviate the dislocation caused by Polish export readjustments and partially to make it appear that the Poles were not being rewarded for their recalcitrance. Even the Albanians obtained substantial Soviet aid in 1957, presumably in part in order to balance growing Chinese influence. And the North Vietnamese and the North Koreans were also beginning to learn how to play this game. To the average Soviet citizen this appeared to be merely a further extension of the policy of economic generosity. With the Soviet regime still unwilling to state that relations in the past had benefited the USSR, many Soviet citizens, as noted by some visitors, began to resent such generosity, especially as the people were being called upon to make sacrifices. Primacy, in this respect, became a burden. Admittedly, such sentiments could have little direct consequence for Soviet policy. They do, however, become part of the amorphous climate of opinion which even a totalitarian leadership must weigh.

Primacy also had its political price. The Soviet leadership was said to reflect the advanced stage of the Soviet Union's transition to Communism as well as of its industrial and military might. To protect its ideological claim, the USSR had to be wary of excessive innovation elsewhere lest it render Soviet experience inapplicable. The Soviet social and economic institutions had to reflect the pioneering role of the USSR in the construction of socialism. They could not therefore allow themselves to become historically dated or outpaced by any other Communist society. Social and institutional changes and industrial primacy were among the essential prerequisites for the retention of leadership. Yet Soviet society no longer benefited from the advantages of "backwardness" — it was no longer in a state of flexibility. As a result, social and political changes were becoming more difficult to carry out than, for instance, in Bulgaria or China. It was becoming increasingly harder for the Soviet leaders to announce transitions to new, higher historical phases through dramatic reforms or revolutionary undertakings. The new Communist states could now do what the USSR in the past was able to do economically: borrow foreign experience, telescope it, and change faster than the original model. Leap-frogging need not be merely the prerogative of delayed industrialization; it may also be a characteristic of ideological emulation.

The Twenty-first CPSU Congress in February 1959 gave the Soviet leadership an opportunity to state once again the grounds for claiming its primacy and to clarify the problem of building Communism. Primacy was claimed through the gigantic development schemes and industrial advances envisaged in the Seven-Year Plan which, according to the Soviet leadership, meant that the Soviet Union had already entered the stage of accelerated construction of Communism. The other states were said to be only completing their construction of socialism. Turning to the problem of "passing to Communism," Khrushchev developed a new thesis, one for which he was hailed even by the Chinese and which combined the virtue of compromise with its implicit claim for continued Soviet primacy. It is to be recalled that the September 1958 Chinese Plenum had raised what amounted to an ideological challenge by suggesting that China might enter soon into Communism. The first Soviet response was to hint that European Communist states, because of their more advanced economies integrated by CEMA, would be the first to enter jointly into Communism, followed subsequently by the Asiatic Communist states.[61] However, the Chinese ideological concession made in December 1958 (see p. 373) made it possible for the Soviet leaders to postulate a new formula, namely that all the Communist-ruled states will be able to enter Communism simultaneously. This eliminated the possibility of any one Communist state again raising the claim that it would be the first to enter into Communism; and Khrushchev's justification for the simultaneous transition — that the more advanced Communist-ruled states would assist the less advanced ones — meant that Soviet economic advances remained the chief guarantee of Soviet supremacy. Khrushchev could confidently expect that Soviet economic leadership in the camp was not likely to be challenged in the foreseeable future. Soviet industrial indexes were Khrushchev's most potent instrument for laying this ideological issue to rest.[62]

According to Soviet theorists, the first stage of the building of Communism will presently involve the following measures: (1) the elimination of the existing differences between town and village life through the absorption of socialist property into state property, through the liquidation of private plots in the collective farms, and through the absorption of collective-farm property into state ownership; (2) the abolition of classes through the elimination of differences between a rural and an urban worker, and by decreasing the differences in rewards for physical and mental work (this process has already begun); (3) the creation of a new "Communist personality" by reducing national distinctions within the USSR and by an intensified educational-ideological campaign; (4) an increase in the directing role of the party as the internal functions of the state are passed over to so-called public organizations. A precondition for all of this was the surpassing of the United States in per capita production. Soviet society was thus being forewarned that changes do not cease with the construction of socialism.[63]

Khrushchev's remarks to the Congress, cited widely by the Communist press, established his claim to the position of the leading theorist on a question which seemed to be of increasing importance to the Communist camp. But to the extent that this was a personal claim, Khrushchev's new stature pointed to a potential problem peculiar to dictatorial systems: that of succession. It took Khrushchev several years to establish his own standing, and it is to be recalled that, at first, he was viewed with considerable contempt among international Communist leaders. His eventual successes notwithstanding, his relationship with a Novotny or an Ulbricht, not to speak of Gomulka, could never be compared to the relationship between these same men and Stalin. The longer it should take for a new Soviet leader to emerge, the worse for Soviet primacy and the higher the price the internally competing Soviet factions will have to pay to their external allies. Soviet domestic politics will thus gradually become increasingly responsive to pressures from without.

All of these problems reflected the growing pains of the still relatively young Communist empire. Its outwardly monolithic organization merely shielded from prying eyes a continuing process of inward change and adjustment. A comparison between the Communist camp at the time of Stalin's Nineteenth Party Congress in October 1952 and at the time of Khrushchev's Twenty-first Congress in February 1959 might suffice to illustrate that persistent evolution. Toward the end of Chapter 6, five broad characteristics of the camp were noted. Six years later the same camp was characterized by (1) a continued reliance on political ties, but with multilateral conferences becoming a frequently used method for seeking unity between political regimes alike in the sense that they were all Communist but increasingly subject to growing differences in domestic methods and outlooks. Indeed, unlike Stalinist uniformity, the bloc in 1959 contained regimes such as the Polish and even Hungarian, which were pursuing domestic policies somewhat "rightist" in character (some compromise and concession), and more "leftist" radical regimes in East Germany, Czechoslovakia, Bulgaria, and Rumania, with the Soviet and Rumanian regimes displaying rather greater tolerance for the Polish pattern, and China taking the most radical line, increasingly echoed by North Korea and North Vietnam. (2) The former feudal relationship had given way to a curiously hierarchical structure, with the USSR occupying the first place* but coming under growing chal-

---

* It is interesting to note that in the "socialist commonwealth of equal states" there is a very definite and revealing hierarchy. It is strikingly illustrated by the order in which the heads of the delegations from the ruling Communist parties have addressed important Soviet party gatherings, as shown below:

Nineteenth CPSU Congress *October 1952*	*Twentieth CPSU Congress* *February 1956*
1. B. Bierut, Poland	Chu Teh, China
2. Liu Shao-chi, China	B. Bierut, Poland
3. K. Gottwald, Czechoslovakia	A. Novotny, Czechoslovakia
4. M. Rakosi, Hungary	W. Ulbricht, East Germany
5. Pak Chon-ae, Korea	G. Gheorghiu-Dej, Rumania
6. V. Chervenkov, Bulgaria	V. Chervenkov, Bulgaria
7. G. Gheorghiu-Dej, Rumania	M. Rakosi, Hungary
8. E. Hoxha, Albania	E. Hoxha, Albania
9. D. Damba, Mongolia	Choe Yong-kun, Korea
10. W. Pieck, East Germany	Tru'o'ng Chinh, Vietnam
11.	U. Tsedenbal, Mongolia

Fortieth anniversary *November 1957*	*Twenty-first CPSU Congress* *February 1959*
1. Mao Tse-tung, China	Chou En-lai, China
2. W. Gomulka, Poland	W. Gomulka, Poland
3. A. Novotny, Czechoslovakia	A. Novotny, Czechoslovakia
4. W. Ulbricht, East Germany	W. Ulbricht, East Germany
5. C. Stoica, Rumania	G. Gheorghiu-Dej, Rumania
6. T. Zhivkov, Bulgaria	J. Kadar, Hungary
7. J. Kadar, Hungary	T. Zhivkov, Bulgaria
8. Ho Chi Minh, Vietnam	Kim Il-song, Korea
9. Kim Il-song, Korea	Ho Chi Minh, Vietnam
10. E. Hoxha, Albania	E. Hoxha, Albania
11. D. Damba, Mongolia	U. Tsedenbal, Mongolia

(In 1957, Kardelj, speaking for Yugoslavia, followed immediately after Zhivkov and preceded Kadar.) There is too much regularity to this whole pattern for it to be a matter of chance. Indeed, at the Twenty-second CPSU Congress, held in October 1961, the 1959 "protocol" was followed, except for Albania which was omitted. A sequence reflecting population would have been the following order: 1. China; 2. Poland; 3. East Germany; 4. (Yugoslavia); 5. Rumania; 6. Czechoslovakia; 7. Vietnam; 8. Hungary; 9. Bulgaria; 10. Korea; 11. Mongolia; 12. Albania.

lenge from the often conflicting aspirations of the other states, particularly China. (3) A concerted effort was made to revitalize ideological bonds by greater clarity in defining the universals of building socialism and Communism, by an effort to legitimize ideologically the special Soviet position, and by limited concessions to the impact of domestic conditions on these ideological prerequisites. (4) Soviet controls, while still relying on the potential threat of military intervention, largely gave way to combined political, economic, and ideological pressures and to a greater dependence on a balancing of conflicting interests of the various regimes, most of which had a continued interest in maintaining Soviet leadership, being dependent on its support. (5) Economic relations, a matter of considerable long-range importance, were developed in the direction of increasing interdependence and specialization, with only the USSR and China free to pursue an autarkic policy. Economic unity was to be the foundation-stone of political uniformity. Direct Soviet exploitation declined, although individual states were still called upon to make sacrifices for the "common weal." [64]

The evolution in the Communist camp progressed more rapidly than possibly even its own leaders fully realized. Most of them still tended to speak with the single-minded unity of old. Nonetheless, a gradual change had taken place in the direction of greater diversity, especially as the individual Communist regimes became more concerned with the complex task of building the future and less with simply destroying the past. In that novel setting, the Communist leaders, even though accustomed to viewing the non-Communist world from a perspective which stressed change, were finding it difficult to adjust to the notion that relations among Communist states were also in a state of flux. Pretending that their ideology created insoluble bonds, they simply drifted toward an intensification of tensions. In 1960 the accumulating grievances came out into the open, and the Sino-Soviet dispute became the dominant concern of the Communist world. If the year 1958 had been one of shadow-boxing and 1959 one of steady testing of grip and muscle, the stage was set at the beginning of 1960 for open grappling. The Communist commonwealth could hardly prosper in that context.

The Fifth Phase: 1960-1965

COMMUNIST PLURALISM — INSTITUTIONAL AND IDEOLOGICAL DIVERSITY

Soviet Communists, like Marxist-Leninists throughout the world, cannot restrict themselves to the criticism and political evaluation of the erroneous, anti-Leninist view of the CCP leadership. Everyone inevitably asks himself the question: How could it have happened that the leaders of such a party as the CCP, which has behind it considerable experience in revolutionary struggle and building a new society, took the road of struggle against the worldwide Communist movement? Who are we facing in the shape of the CCP leaders? . . . Yes, comrades, one must say openly that the theoretical and political views of the leaders of the CCP largely represent a rehash of Trotsky-sm, cast away long ago by the international revolutionary movement. — Report by M. Suslov to the Central Committee, CPSU, February 14, 1964

Following in Khrushchev's footsteps, the new leaders of the CPSU are bringing about the further degeneration of the Soviet Union toward capitalism . . . Taking advantage of the state power they wield, the new leaders of the CPSU have centered their efforts on undermining the economic base of socialism, socialist ownership by the whole people and socialist collective ownership, and on setting up and developing a new system of exploitation and fostering and supporting the new bourgeoisie, thus accelerating the restoration of capitalism. — "The Refutation of the New Leaders of the CPSU on 'United Action,'" by the Editorial Departments of *Jen-min Jih-pao* and *Hung Ch'i, Peking Review*, no. 46, November 12, 1965, p. 19

16 / THE SINO-SOVIET CONFLICT

IT IS difficult to exaggerate the historical significance of the Sino-Soviet conflict. It has influenced every facet of international life, not to speak of the Soviet bloc itself. No analysis of the relationship between Washington and Moscow, of the problem of nuclear proliferation, of the orientation of Indian nationalism, of the thrust of revolutionary movements in the Third World would be complete without taking into account the impact of the increasingly bitter dispute between the two onetime seemingly close allies. For the international Communist movement, it has been a tragic disaster, comparable in some respects to the split in Christianity several centuries ago. The Communist and Christian experience both showed that in theologically or ideologically oriented movements disagreements even only about means and immediate tactical concerns can escalate into basic organizational and doctrinal, indeed, even into national conflicts, fundamentally destructive of the movement's unity.

For Moscow and Peking the dispute has meant the end of an illusion that each for a while had entertained about the Communist world. Khrushchev had hoped to create a new international Communist system to replace Stalin's crude, non-institutionalized and highly informal supranational autocracy. Tolerating domestic diversity but bound by a common ideology, the new system would be a self-regulating one, with the Soviet Union recognized as its head because the other ruling parties perceived the advantage of an arbiter and not because the Soviet Union had imposed its leadership. While honoring the right to domestic autonomy of its constituent units, the system in its foreign policy would be guided by the assessments (and therefore indirectly also by the interests) of its leading and most powerful state which had the special responsibility of providing a general military shield for the Communist world.

The Chinese shared some of these illusions but with one vital exception. They wanted unity, and hence pressed for general recognition of Soviet leadership; but they wanted only militant unity, actively directed against the enemy. In order to obtain that militancy they did not hesitate to apply pressure on Moscow for the sake of harsher ideological formulae (as during the 1957 meeting) and of sterner policies toward the "imperialist" powers. Yet in doing so they inevitably undermined Soviet leadership, thereby weakening the Communist unity that in all probability they were sincere in seeking, and they set in motion a dynamic escalation of the Moscow-Peking dialogue into a dispute, then a conflict, and finally a rift.[1]

ISSUES AND ORIGINS

The dispute climaxed in the Chinese accusation, for the first time spelled out most fully in 1965, that the Soviet Union, the birthplace of the first Communist revolution, was actively engaged in the restoration of capitalism and was eagerly seeking an alliance with the chief "imperialist" power, the United States. No graver charge could possibly be made against a state professing Marxism-Leninism. By then both states were also unabashedly pursuing foreign policies designed to thwart each other's international objectives, and not merely competing for support within the Communist international movement. The relationship of "non-antagonistic contradiction," to use a term the Chinese popularized, had become one of antagonistic conflict.

During the preceding years, every conceivable issue capable of dividing two Communist parties and two neighboring states had been dragged out into the open and had become often the object of not only bitter disputes but even of abusive polemics.* It may be useful

* Their flavor is well rendered by the following Chinese commentary on Khrushchev's critique of Stalin:

"Khrushchev has abused Stalin as a 'murderer,' a 'criminal,' a 'bandit,' a 'gambler,' a 'despot of the type of Ivan the Terrible,' 'the greatest dictator in Russian history,' a 'fool,' an 'idiot,' and the like. When we are compelled to cite all this filthy, vulgar and malicious language, we are afraid it may soil our pen and paper . . .

"Khrushchev has maligned Stalin as a 'bandit.' Does this not mean that the first socialist state in the world was for a long period headed by a 'bandit'? The great Soviet people and the revolutionary people of the whole world completely disagree with this slander!

"Khrushchev has maligned Stalin as a 'fool.' Does this not mean that the CPSU which waged heroic revolutionary struggles over the past decades had a 'fool' as its leader? The Soviet Communists and Marxist-Leninists of the whole world completely disagree with this slander!

"Khrushchev has maligned Stalin as an 'idiot.' Does this not mean that the great Soviet Army which triumphed in the antifascist war had an 'idiot' as its supreme commander? The glorious Soviet commanders and fighters and all antifascist fighters of the world completely disagree with this slander!

"Khrushchev has maligned Stalin as a 'murderer.' Does this not mean that the international Communist movement had a 'murderer' as its teacher for decades? Communists of the whole world, including the Soviet Communists, completely disagree with this slander!"

— "On the Question of Stalin," *Jen-min Jih-pao*, September 13, 1963.

to summarize these issues, including some discussed already in Chapters 12 and 15, under three general headings of party issues, foreign policy issues, and state issues. As may be expected in the case of polemics conducted largely at party conferences or through party journals, ideological issues were most numerous, although not necessarily most important. They did, however, provide the general cast for the dispute, especially its highly doctrinaire flavor.

The party — or ideological — issues included:[2]

1. *The role of the CPSU.* While ostensibly pleading for the recognition of Soviet leadership and insisting both in 1957 and in 1960 on the acceptance by all parties of the CPSU as leader, the Chinese were really striving to create a militant international phalanx, pursuing policies advocated by themselves. The Soviets, although increasingly inclined to abjure any claim to Soviet leadership, were at the same time seeking to obtain the support of other parties for policies most convenient to the Soviet Union. Thus the issue was primarily a screen for the broader question: which party shall formulate the general line for world Communism? When finally the Chinese reached the reluctant conclusion that they could not get the Soviets to accept the Chinese formulation of the general line, they simply declared that the CPSU, because of its revisionism, had "automatically forfeited the position of 'head' " in the international Communist movement.[3]

2. *Revisionism or dogmatism.* The Chinese argued that revisionism was the major threat to Communist purity, and they identified it publicly first with Tito and, from approximately 1963 on, openly with the Soviet leadership. The Soviets, after an initial antirevisionist spurt in 1957–58, maintained that "both" revisionism and dogmatism were a threat to Marxism-Leninism, but after 1963 moved toward an emphasis on dogmatism as the basic threat, and began to identify the Chinese leaders as its exponents.

3. *Nature of our epoch.* This issue provided the broad theoretical underpinning for some of the foreign policy debates. In a nutshell, the Chinese argued that our era is dominated by the conflict between "socialism" and "imperialism," with the tide already turned in favor of "socialism." The Soviets argued that the appearance on the world scene of the "world socialist system" was the decisive event of our time, and that its combined economic-political-military strength would effect a further — and even accelerating — expansion of Communism.

4. *War or peace.* The preceding led the Soviets to conclude that

peaceful expansion of Communism is possible, since war by the "imperialists" could be deterred. Accordingly, war was no longer inevitable, while the appearance of highly destructive nuclear weapons made its avoidance desirable. The Chinese argued that the alleged military superiority of "socialism" made a more forceful policy feasible, and that the "imperialists" could be forced to yield. If they did not, war would spell the doom of "imperialism," even if a third or a half of humanity perished.

5. *Peaceful transition to socialism.* The Soviets were inclined to argue that peaceful transition to socialism was possible, and that in the more advanced Western states power could be attained by Communists by following the parliamentary road. The Chinese held this to be nothing short of Bernsteinian revisionism and a betrayal of the Leninist revolutionary tradition.

6. *Dictatorship of the proletariat and the class struggle.* Insofar as their own society is concerned, the Soviets argued that the class struggle had been completed victoriously, and that the dictatorship of the proletariat had been transformed into a state of all the people. This in turn had permitted a relaxation in some of the repressive policies "necessary" during the preceding "historical stage." The Chinese rejected this as sheer sophistry, designed to mask "the lush growth of bourgeois elements inside the Soviet Union,"[4] which were said to be threatening the Leninist concept of the dictatorship of the proletariat and the class struggle.

7. *Nature of a Communist society.* The latest Soviet version was formulated by the program of the Twenty-second Congress in October 1961. In effect, it was an attempt to picture a state of collectivist affluence, in contrast to the earlier Chinese experimentation with a Communist society based on social equality in a condition of material deprivation morally elevated by a militant Communist consciousness. The Chinese could rightly point out that the standard that Khrushchev was setting for his Communist society was that of the capitalist United States.

8. *Stalin.* Although ostensibly a historical problem, the evaluation of Stalin's role implicitly raised the question of the contemporary relevance of Stalinism. The Chinese not only rejected the Soviet accusations that Stalin was a tyrant but explicitly asserted the continuing relevance of Stalin's external and internal policies (having, however, occasionally in the past ignored both). They hoped thereby to gain the support of external militants and of those bloc leaders who personally feared the consequences of de-Stalinization.

9. *Albania and the bloc*. The question of Albania was perhaps primarily a foreign policy issue, but initially at least it involved a party matter. Does the CPSU have the right to determine which ruling parties belong to the Communist camp and what is a true socialist country? This problem illustrated the paradox raised by the first issue (the role of the CPSU): the CPSU, denying that it was exercising leadership, unilaterally asserted the right to expel Albania from the bloc because the Albanian leadership had defied Moscow; the Chinese, still insisting as late as the end of 1961 that the CPSU is the leader, violently condemned the Soviets for their unilateral initiative in excommunicating Albania.

10. *Interparty polemics*. Although both parties repeatedly noted the impropriety of public polemics within the Communist movement and, largely at the behest of other parties, occasionally even muted them (for example, in the spring of 1962), each consistently blamed the other for the invariable reappearance of open attacks and criticisms. The Chinese (not to speak of the vulgarly vociferous Albanians), being the weaker partner in the debate, were more inclined than the Soviets to stress the benefits of public airing of interparty differences. As Peking smugly observed in the fall of 1965: "Khrushchev revisionism has been refuted down to the last point, and this poisonous weed has been converted into good fertilizer on the fields of world revolution. Truth becomes clearer through debate; the more the polemics, the higher the level of revolutionary consciousness and the greater the degree of revolutionary vigor."[5]

Although more specific in character, the foreign policy issues dividing Moscow and Peking were clearly interrelated with the divergent ideological assessments. Five principal issues stand out:

1. *Grand strategy*. This argument largely duplicated items 3, 4, and 5 in the list of ideological issues, but was applied to the specifics of foreign policy. Should the Communist camp concentrate its effort on fomenting world revolution, especially in the backward countries, or should it (as the Soviets argued) stress the further development of the Communist camp's economic potential — especially that of the Soviet Union — in order to defeat "capitalism" on the critical front of economic competition, which would automatically give Communists a decisive military advantage? The adoption of the former strategy would inevitably establish China as the key model and source of leadership; adoption of the latter would reinforce the Soviet position.

2. *"National liberation" struggle*. Although the Soviets committed

themselves in Khrushchev's famous January 1961 speech to the support of such struggles, the Soviet Union remained conscious — indeed, in subsequent years even became quite sensitive — of the dangers that such a war could transform itself into a local war between the major powers and hence could pose the threat of nuclear escalation. The Chinese considered these fears to be highly exaggerated and to reflect a basically revisionist attitude. In their view, such struggles would isolate and eventually undermine world "imperialism." From approximately 1965 on, the Vietnamese war became the test case for this issue, with each side charging the other with conduct inimical to the best interests of international Communism.

3. *Detente with the United States.* To the Soviets the detente prior to the Cuban confrontation of November 1962 seemed to offer a relatively painless way for the expansion of Soviet influence, with the West gradually accommodating itself to the notion of its "historical decline." After the confrontation, which so strikingly and unexpectedly revealed both the superiority of American power and American willingness to use it, the detente offered an opportunity to buy time, to concentrate on Soviet domestic development, to establish trade relations, and generally to reduce international tensions, which had proven more dangerous than even the Soviet leaders had calculated. To the Chinese, the initial Soviet flirtation seemed misguided; the second, cowardly; and both inimical to the interests of world revolution. They were seen as the external reflection of the domestic tendencies expressed in item 6 of the party dialogue.

4. *The Test Ban Agreement.* Although closely connected with the preceding issue, the Test Ban Agreement to the Chinese represented a qualitatively new step by the Khrushchev leadership toward *an alliance* with the principal "imperialist" power directed *against* China's interests, and not merely a humanitarian arrangement, as the Soviets represented it.

5. *Neutrality on the Indian frontier issue and economic aid to India.* Given the steadily worsening relations between China and India, and Indian intransigence on the Sino-Indian territorial dispute, Soviet aid to India naturally appeared to Peking as a hostile act, while Soviet neutrality on the frontier issue was viewed as a betrayal of proletarian internationalism. To Moscow, Chinese policy toward India appeared shortsighted and excessively motivated by Chinese nationalism, with the undesirable effect of driving India into the hands of America.

Many other conflicting foreign policy issues and interests served to drive Moscow and Peking further apart between the late fifties and mid-sixties, but the items listed above were the key ones. In addition, at least three basic conflicts of interest arose on the national (state) level, filling the dispute with much deeper emotional content:

1. *The question of military assistance.* The Chinese felt deeply outraged by the Soviet abnegation of previously made commitments (see earlier discussion, pp. 301, and 377) which, when evaluated in conjunction with other issues already outlined, appeared to Peking to reflect a deliberate Soviet effort to shed its revolutionary obligations. To the Soviets, traditionally jealous of their military technology, any further strengthening of China seemed simply destined to increase China's capacity to exert pressure on the Soviet Union.

2. *Economic assistance.* The Chinese, it appears, were never fully satisfied with the extent of aid received from the Soviet Union and resented the obligation to repay the Soviet loans received for the conduct of the "common" struggle in Korea. The suspension of Soviet aid to China was interpreted by Peking as evidence of an inadmissible Soviet inclination to use economic pressure as a means of conducting a dialogue between two Communist parties. The Soviet Union, finding itself under mounting demands for aid from many Communist states as well as from some neutralist ones, and with its own resources rather strained, was increasingly inclined to the conclusion that economic aid to China would have the same undesirable effect as military assistance, and would therefore be counter to Soviet interests.

3. *Territorial claims.* Although already in 1954 the Chinese had raised — but apparently not pursued — the question of Mongolia's relationship to China, the open airing in the sixties of Chinese grievances against Russia's earlier territorial expansion at China's expense introduced into the dispute the extremely volatile issue of just borders, historical claims, and national security. Even though the issue at the time was not pressed, the very fact of its appearance broke the essentially ideological cast of the dispute and gave it also the more traditional character of territorial irredenta and national enmity.

Many of these divisive issues have had a long history in the Sino-Soviet relationship, and there certainly was a legacy of mutual suspicion dating back not only to the immediate post-World War II period but even to the mid-twenties,[6] but the Sino-Soviet dispute cannot simply be attributed to any one single and decisive cause. On occasion it has been suggested that the dispute was essentially a matter of pure and simple nationalism; ideology merely provided a screen for profoundly different national traditions, goals, and feelings.[7] It would be idle to deny the importance of these factors. Varying Russian and Chinese national styles and ambitions inescapably created a setting in which an unbalanced alliance was more difficult to maintain than a relationship of competitive antagonism. Specific national grievances doubtless intensified the significance of other issues about which the two leaderships did not see eye to eye.

But nationalism alone does not provide an explanation of why from 1956 on the conflict began to intrude so heavily on Sino-Soviet relations nor why it surfaced and became so bitter in the early sixties. It does not explain why certain issues divided the two parties in the late fifties but united them half a decade earlier. It does not explain the change in the leaderships' interpretation of what was their specific national interest in a given place or time. For that matter, nationalism does not explain why the Communist leaderships of Poland and Hungary, probably the two most anti-Russian nations in Eastern Europe, could cooperate so well with Khrushchev whereas the Chinese could not. Accordingly, nationalism may be seen as a constant source of strain but not as the cause for specific sources of conflict, especially in the case of states led by nationalists who subscribe overtly to a common ideological doctrine that ostensibly overrides their nationalism and creates a common sense of historical destiny.

Another explanation concentrates on the stages of growth of the two countries. The Soviets are said to have gone through their industrial revolution, have become more bureaucratic and even "bourgeois," and hence more inclined to settle for the status quo. The Chinese, barely at the subsistence level, still dreaming of an industrial society, imbued with a relatively youthful sense of revolutionary commitment, simply could not tolerate the patience and the gradualism increasingly favored by the Russians. Differences were hence inevitable. The Chinese themselves have somewhat favored this explanation. On the basis of economic factors it makes the Soviets appear as the deviants; the Chinese as the dedicated revolutionaries. It is thus Marxist in form and flattering in content.

Doubtless, that explanation, as in the case of nationalism, is helpful in defining the general setting of the conflict and in pinpointing the importance of the particular issues at stake. In addition, Chinese dissatisfaction with the extent of Soviet economic assistance was certainly a major factor in the dispute, and one closely related to China's desire to overcome rapidly its backwardness. However, the levels-of-economic-development theory is also not fully satisfactory as an explanation of the conflict. How is one to fit into that interpretation the Chinese behavior prior to 1957, a behavior far more moderate than the Soviet, yet coming at a time when the Chinese were at an even earlier stage of their development? It is now often forgotten how widespread at the time was the view that the Chinese were the true moderates in the international Communist movement; that this was due to their special blend of Communism and Confucianism; that the other parties should learn moderation and restraint from the Chinese. (Apart from various Western advocates of this view, the Indians were especially articulate in disseminating it.) Moreover, the economic-levels theory does not explain why East Germany and Czechoslovakia, the most industrialized Communist states, were for a while quite sympathetic to the more militant Chinese point of view, nor does it provide an explanation for the reckless Soviet behavior in 1962, culminating in the Cuban missile crisis.

A variant of the "historical levels" theory is the generations explanation. The two party leaderships are composed of men of essentially different generations. The Soviet revolutionary generation has faded from the scene; it has given way to a bureaucratic leadership to whom bypassing a bureaucratic channel is in itself almost a revolutionary act! This leadership finds it hard to relate to a revolutionary Chinese elite that personally participated in the Long March, victoriously led the civil war, and even directly challenged the United States in the Korean War. These differences in background inescapably produce different perspectives on the world and inhibit mutual understanding.

Again, although undoubtedly containing a great deal of truth, the above explanation suffers from some major flaws. For one thing, Tito was more similar in these respects to Mao than to Khrushchev, not to speak of the bureaucrat Brezhnev. Yet Soviet-Yugoslav relations have been steadily improving. Perhaps personal antipathy between Khrushchev and Mao, concerning which there have been many reports, was an aggravating factor but it is doubtful that it could have been much more than that. The history of Sino-Soviet relations after Khrushchev's fall testifies to the fact that personal factors were at most only one of many contributory causes to the dispute.

Last but not least, the dispute is often seen as an ideological or as

an organizational struggle for supremacy in the Communist movement. In that sense, it is seen as part of the old story of doctrinal
splits in once united and militantly doctrinal movements. And certainly both factors, as already seen, have been of crucial importance.
The very fact that the dispute has an ideological cast shows that at
least the participants in it thought in ideological categories. The borderline between thought-patterns and belief-patterns is quite thin,
and hence there must have been an element of conviction of intellectual (doctrinal) intensity that otherwise would be lacking in a
dispute between two major allied powers (say, the United States
and France). To the extent that the dispute took place also within
an international movement, scoring ideological points was tantamount to improving one's organizational posture in the movement; a
stronger organizational posture in turn made it easier to score ideological points. Hence the ideological and the organizational struggles
were interwoven.

Yet the ideological and organizational conflict was hardly the
whole story, for it blended with the national, economic, and personal
interpretations already mentioned, all of which contained a partial
truth concerning the inherent instability of an intimate and enduring
Sino-Soviet national alliance and Soviet-Chinese Communist revolutionary unity. But insofar as the actual character, intensity, and
thrust of the Sino-Soviet conflict was concerned, the causes have to
be sought in more specific contexts, involving tactical moves by each
side, often made at the cost of longer-range interest. Causes must be
sought further in frequently inept responses which in turn introduced new issues and widened the breach; in simple errors of human
judgment and of political intelligence; in the impact of personal impatience, lack of tact or diplomatic skill; in the mutual absence of the
tradition of agreeing to disagree; and finally, in the inherent tendency
of the ideological perspective to absolutize conflicts into dichotomies
and to abjure compromise as equivalent to opportunism. Cumula-
tively these factors worked to spiral specific divergencies into an
ever-widening split, in a pattern which can be meaningfully understood only if viewed in a perspective of dynamic escalation.

DYNAMIC ESCALATION

The dynamic pattern of this escalation can be seen through a
tightly compressed historical view of selected highlights of the Sino-
Soviet conflict during the years 1960–65.[8] The eventual victims of
that escalation were both Communist unity and Communist ideology.

By 1960, as noted in Chapter 15, the dispute had reached the point that one side was prepared to push the dispute out into the open, and the other was determined to respond with increasingly severe sanctions. Neither thought of a break and each expected to force the other to yield. Thus the mutual assumption of unity still acted as a restraint. But within that framework the Chinese had concluded that purely internal debates were not likely to budge the Soviets and that more public pressure had to be brought to bear upon them. Although not explicitly naming Khrushchev and still relying on the expedient of implicit condemnation, the Chinese outburst in April 1960 (see p. 379) took issue unmistakably with Khrushchev's ideological innovations articulated at the Twentieth Congress and with Soviet views on war and peace. The Chinese followed this up at the June World Federation of Trade Unions (WFTU) meeting held in Peking. Their attacks on the Soviet position were all the more offensive to Moscow since they were delivered before an assembled international Communist audience. In doing so the Chinese may have become emboldened by the May U-2 crisis and the subsequent collapse of Khrushchev's renewed venture in summitry. The effect was that the Soviets could no longer pretend that Peking was arguing merely with Belgrade.

The Soviet response, apart from a public reassertion on April 22nd of the Soviet position by O. Kuusinen, in which the Soviet spokesman went as far as to assert that nuclear weapons could in effect interfere with the Marxist law of the "inevitable" progression of humanity toward Communism, came at the Rumanian Party Congress in June. What originally was meant to have been a festive occasion was suddenly transformed into a violent confrontation between Khrushchev, who personally led the Soviet delegation, and the Chinese participants, headed by Politburo member P'eng Chen. The Soviet delegation in effect demanded no less than a condemnation of the Chinese position by all the other participating Communist parties. Without warning, the Soviet delegation distributed a circular letter itemizing Chinese offenses, while in his speech Khrushchev hinted that economic sanctions might follow unless the Chinese desisted from their criticism. For good measure, Khrushchev included the Albanians in his indictment.[9]

The Bucharest meeting was the first entirely hostile head-on collision between the two parties. It therefore had the effect of forcing the other parties to take sides. But though forced to choose, not all parties chose with the same degree of commitment, intensity and zeal. Some identified themselves fully with the Soviet position; some did likewise but in a more lukewarm spirit; some did not; and some objected violently. Moreover, some parties still hoped that a split between China and Russia could be averted and hence preferred not to cast their lot completely with one or the other side. Doubtless, too, some saw in the emerging divergence an opportunity to assert greater autonomy for themselves and were not eager to transform a formerly monolithic bloc into two monolithic blocs.

The most stalwart support for the Soviet position came from those East European leaders who had broken the least with Stalinism: Gheorghiu-Dej, Zhivkov, Ulbricht, and Novotny. One may infer that their endorsement was in part an old reflex and in part a reflection of a preference for a centralized bloc, but not a deliberate endorsement of Khrushchev's Twentieth Congress doctrines. Indeed, one may suspect that the intensity of their support was designed to compensate for their past (and in some cases even lingering) support for some of the Chinese positions. More restrained backing was forthcoming from Ochab, Kadar, and the Mongolian party delegate (presumably anxious not to arouse his Chinese neighbors). The Korean and Vietnamese delegates avoided most controversial issues, concentrating on one only: the U.S. threat. They leaned in favor of China approximately as much as the Poles and Hungarians did in favor of Russia. Finally, the Albanian delegate fully identified his position with that of Peking.

The Soviet behavior at the Bucharest meeting was typical of a political warfare operation. It was not an exercise in compromise but in conflict. To be sure, the Soviets had been badly provoked. Moreover, as later years were to show, an international setback for either Russia or China tended almost immediately to rebound against the Sino-Soviet relationship, prompting mutual recriminations. In this case, Khrushchev was still smarting from the embarrassing conjunction of the U-2 incident with the collapse of the summit meeting that he had so eagerly sought, and he was in no mood to tolerate Chinese crowing. He thus came determined to rebuff the Chinese charges against himself, to isolate the Chinese in the bloc, and even to humiliate and punish them. It is difficult to assume that he expected the Chinese to capitulate — but it is also important to make room for irrationality in any analysis of political behavior, and in Khrushchev's case this room should not be too narrow.

The effect, of course, was an immediate intensification of the conflict. The Chinese furiously and contemptuously rejected Khrushchev's charges and, seeking support, they encouraged the Albanians to do likewise. This in turn outraged the Soviets even further, for they now saw the Chinese openly intriguing in what the Soviets considered to be their own secure East European backyard. In that setting, Moscow proceeded to make good on the threats made by Khrushchev in Bucharest: in July–August the Soviet Union began a drastic cut in its economic and technical assistance to China. Approximately 2,000–3,000 Soviet specialists were suddenly recalled, apparently either removing or destroying the blueprints of whatever Soviet-sponsored projects they were constructing.*

The adoption of economic sanctions against China was probably interpreted by Peking as an even more hostile act than the bitterly resented Soviet violation of the 1957 military agreement (see p. 377). The refusal to provide military aid denied something to China; the economic sanctions directly hurt China. The former action protected Soviet monopoly; the Chinese certainly resented it but probably also understood it in terms of power politics. The economic sanctions were not defensive but offensive; they could only be meant to subdue China and they came at a time when China was struggling with the consequences of several natural calamities and with the failures of its own economic "big leap forward." Thus the Chinese were probably venting their true feelings when they charged that Moscow's "perfidious actions disrupted China's national economic plan and inflicted enormous losses upon China's socialist construction." [10] Ironically, the only precedent in Communist history for such blatant pressure was the policy adopted against Yugoslavia by Stalin, a policy now condemned by Moscow but defended by Peking.

At the Bucharest meeting the only real point of agreement was the decision to take advantage of the forthcoming anniversary of the Bolshevik Revolution to hold another major interparty conference. It may be assumed that conflicting Soviet and Chinese estimates were at the root of the joint decision. The Soviets may have calculated that continued pressure on the West would eventually give the Soviet Union an international success and they probably wished to capital-

* Subsequently, and apparently somewhat embarrassed by their own actions, the Kremlin leaders attempted to argue that Soviet economic assistance was discontinued because the Chinese did not wish it and because the Soviet technicians were occasionally even humiliated by the Chinese. (For example, in one factory, while the Chinese engineers were awarded a red banner for their efforts, the Soviet team was ostentatiously handed a white one, allegedly for its lack of revolutionary determination.) However, it appears quite clear that the initiative in curtailing the aid was Soviet and so was the abrupt form of the action.

ize on the atmosphere generated by a series of Soviet space successes. Perhaps they also hoped that the combined effect of their
new prestige and of the pressure applied on China would be a
change in the Chinese posture, reestablishing Communist unity on
the basis of the Soviet ideological postures. The Chinese, as became
evident later, still were hopeful that Khrushchev would be repudiated by his own party, and they counted on the presence in Moscow
of the delegates from the more activist parties of the Third World to
induce a change of heart at least among some of the "contemporary
revisionists." However, the conjunction of the ideological dispute
with the direct military and economic grievances on the state level
had had a profoundly embittering effect on Sino-Soviet relation,
and hence the conference convened in a somewhat unpropitious
climate.

The Moscow meeting of eighty-one Communist parties was perhaps the last international Communist gathering with a pretense to
unity. In the years that followed the cleavage between the principal
participants widened, while some of the non-ruling parties even split
into pro-Soviet and pro-Chinese factions. Though the conference still
made an effort at maintaining a common front externally, its deliberations were dominated by the Sino-Soviet struggle. For many assembled Communists from outside the bloc, the open display of Sino-
Soviet hostility was an unexpected, profoundly disturbing, and even
disillusioning development.[11] Whatever their feelings about it — and
many resented the unyielding attitude displayed by both Moscow
and Peking — they could not avoid being drawn into the struggle,
and henceforth the Sino-Soviet dispute was an issue for the entire
international Communist movement, with hardly a party unaffected.

Before the start of the conference, the CPSU had prepared a
programmatic draft to be submitted to the participants. (Suslov,
Kuusinen, and Ponomarev apparently constituted the drafting commission.) Probably as a result of the protracted dialectics with the
Chinese, Soviet ideological formulations were a little more precise
than heretofore. We may suspect that the vagueness that characterized earlier Soviet pronouncements on such matters as the nature of
our times, which wars were or were not inevitable, and so forth, was
the result in part of Khrushchev's own temperamental predisposition
to sweeping assertions and in part of a Soviet tactical preference not
to be tied to precisely defined general and strategic concepts. During
the fall a series of articles appeared which more systematically developed the Soviet line, clearly in preparation for the forthcoming

debate.[12] It is interesting to observe how Khrushchev's ideological views became more and more precise under the Chinese hammering. From a purely academic point of view, Khrushchev's intellectual development made impressive progress during this period.

By the time the leaders and delegates of the eighty-one Communist parties began their deliberations in Moscow in early November,* some preliminary redrafting of the statement prepared by the CPSU had taken place. In October a commission representing twenty-six parties (including the twelve bloc parties) had reviewed the Soviet draft but unanimity had not been achieved.[13] The debates lasted into early December, and even official Communist sources made it clear that there were major differences among the parties.[14] The Soviet-Chinese divergence was the basic line of division, but not the only one. Some of the Latin American and Asian parties objected to parts of the projected declaration dealing with the anti-colonial struggle; some of the East European neo-Stalinists were sympathetic to a more violent anti-Yugoslav statement; the Albanians strongly supported the Chinese on most issues and even urged that a Yugoslav Communist Party "in exile" be set up.

During the conference the Soviet delegation opposed both the setting up of a new form of the Comintern and the formal labeling of the CPSU as its head. In adopting this position the Soviets might have been anticipating the opposition of others. It may also be surmised that in both cases the Soviets felt that the Chinese pressure, as well as the Chinese efforts to formalize party relations, were designed to enchain the CPSU, and they now preferred the more informal device of irregular party consultations and the vaguer label of "vanguard." As Khrushchev quaintly put it to the Chinese: "What do you want a head for — so you can chop it off?" [15]

After acrimonious debates, in which French, Italian, and Polish Communists also took an active part, a declaration was issued on December 6th. Since neither party was prepared to yield on the gut issues, the declaration was "a collation" of the Soviet and Chinese views, although still with a preponderance of Soviet formulations.[16] Consequently, in the words of a frustrated Belgian Communist, the declaration could be used "to support the settlement, the defence, and the application of political views diametrically opposed, and often outrageously divergent . . ." [17]

The 1960 meeting was accordingly an important watershed in

* Mao Tse-tung did not go, and the Chinese delegation was headed by Liu Shao-chi. Togliatti also did not attend.

the history of the Communist camp. Before an international audience the hitherto sacrosanct Soviet leadership was defiled and defied by the Chinese. Perhaps even more symbolic of the diminished Soviet stature was the vilification to which the Soviet leadership was subjected by the Albanians. The behavior of both was a startling break with almost forty years of Soviet domination in the councils of international Communism. Moreover, no delegate could return home without having become aware that a gauntlet had been cast before Moscow. The Soviet leadership was confronting a basic challenge to its ideological and political primacy. Finally, the extensive and important participation in the discussion by such leaders as Thorez of France and Longo of Italy meant the internationalization of the Sino-Soviet issue. Implicit in their participation was the notion that henceforth Moscow had an obligation at least to consult with the other parties on major issues, with the concomitant effect of somewhat restricting Moscow's freedom of action. The meeting thus marked the end of the muted dialogue and the beginning of public — even though still somewhat veiled — polemics. The form and the content of the dispute was accordingly set for the next three years. It was not until 1963, after the Cuban crisis, that the Sino-Soviet conflict again took a qualitatively new turn.

Since in 1960 neither party was prepared to push the other to the breaking point, even if determined at the same time not to accept the other's point of view, mutual self-restraint was still the order of the day. Indeed, in order to deny to the outside world the satisfaction of observing the disintegration of Communist solidarity, the two parties collaborated in preserving an external appearance of unity. Accordingly, the meeting was followed by some abatement in Sino-Soviet polemics, and the principal (and most unyielding) Chinese delegate, Liu Shao-chi undertook a goodwill tour to various Soviet cities, with Communist unity as his major theme.

But that was only a façade. Although both parties came out of the Moscow meeting with mixed feelings, nothing had happened to induce either one to change its posture or tactics. The Chinese, on the one hand, found themselves surrounded by a large majority of pro-Soviet parties and they clearly failed to change the Soviet attitude with regard to the principal issues. On the other hand, they must have noted with satisfaction that approximately a dozen parties showed themselves sympathetic to China,[18] and that in itself was a net gain. They could calculate that persistent — even perhaps intensified — semipublic pressure might gradually cause other parties to reevaluate the relative merits of the Chinese and Soviet positions and, together with the expected failures of the Soviet "revisionist" line, cause a gradual accretion of strength in favor of China. Thus the Chinese saw no need for a drastic alteration in their "conflict management." *

The Soviet leaders similarly could calculate that major changes in the Soviet posture were, at least for the time, not necessary. They perhaps still felt that the combined political-economic pressure they were exerting on China might cause a change in China's attitude. Even more, they might have calculated that the Chinese challenge would fade if in the meantime Soviet foreign policy was strikingly successful elsewhere, thereby *objectively* establishing the validity of the Soviet-favored "general line."

It is to be remembered that the years 1960–1962 marked perhaps the very high point in Soviet global optimism. The United States seemed to be declining in political and economic vigor; it appeared hopelessly behind in the space race, and to be falling behind even in weapons technology. The Soviet leaders were hoping that the new American administration would resign itself to "the laws of history" and gracefully yield the mantle of world leadership. Never before had the Soviet Union shown such international involvement and thrust. From a regionally dominant state it seemed to have become a globally involved power. Its military and technical personnel carried Soviet influence into the farflung corners of the world, where no direct Soviet presence had ever been felt before: Laos and Cuba, Guinea and Congo (where a pro-Soviet government almost succeeded in gaining power). At the same time, America was fumbling in the Bay of Pigs and the Wall was going up in Berlin. To Moscow, this contrast seemed to reflect historical laws. Within two years this bubble was to burst during the Cuban missile confrontation, and the Soviet Union to withdraw again into its more traditional domains; but in the early sixties Soviet policy seemed to possess a momentum and a direction that could only have filled the Kremlin with headstrong optimism.

As a consequence the Soviet leaders were still inclined not to meet

* Moreover they enjoyed an important debating advantage: "The Chinese argued their case mainly on ideological grounds. It had at least a virtue of being logical and consistent, however unpalatable its implications. Besides, China, in attacking the leader of the socialist world, could only do so on doctrinal grounds . . . The Soviet Union, on the other hand, found her basically 'revisionist' policies less easy to justify in terms of doctrine. It was necessary for her to discredit China's case and to insinuate ulterior motives." As a result, "other parties were to some extent alienated by the tone of the Soviet attacks on China." (John Gittings, "Co-operation and Conflict in Sino-Soviet Relations," *International Affairs*, January 1965, p. 74.)

the Chinese challenge head-on, except at the points of direct friction. If attacked, the Soviets would respond, but for the time being the indictment presented at Bucharest was not pressed. It had served its purpose in forcing the East European parties to make their choice, and it effectively ended any lingering Chinese-East European dalliances, except for one: the Peking-Tirana axis. Lest it prompt any reconsideration in the fealty given Moscow by Sofia, Bucharest, or East Berlin, the seats of the neo-Stalinist regimes, further action against the Albanians thus seemed called for. At the very best, it could result in the elimination of that particular irritant; at the very worst, it would be an indirect signal to China not to meddle in Soviet-East European affairs and a lesson to the other East European states. It seemed to have the advantage of striking at China without hitting her directly.

Accordingly, the year 1961 saw a dramatic deterioration in Soviet-Albanian relations.[19] The Soviets began to boycott the Albanian leadership; no personal messages, no "comrade" prefix, no references by name to the Albanian leaders. The Albanians responded with a campaign designed to rally the Albanian party around Hoxha, and they effusively praised the Chinese. At the February 1961 Congress the Albanians proclaimed their fidelity to the Soviet Union (much as Tito had immediately after the break in 1948), religiously repeated the many points of agreement with Moscow, and then restated the familiar Chinese arguments concerning imperialism, war, and particularly the Yugoslav revisionism. Hoxha put it quite bluntly: "It is a crime against world peace; it is a crime against the socialist camp; it is a crime against the socialist countries of the Balkans, and, in particular, it is a crime against Albania not to denounce publicly the aggressive plans of the Titoists." The Congress cheered Stalin and heaped praise on Hoxha, ignored Khrushchev, explicitly approved the conduct of the Albanian delegation during the Moscow conference, emphasized both unity with the camp and "the correct" Albanian interpretation of Marxism-Leninism, and stressed that no summits were possible without Chinese participation.[20]

The Albanian Congress revealed a great deal about the attitude of the various parties. The Soviet delegation, headed by Pospelov, warned against any "arbitrary interpretations" of the common line and condemned "opportunists," "renegades," and "people who have betrayed Marxism-Leninism" and who criticize the CPSU. Even more direct criticism was delivered by the Polish delegate, who laid great stress on the general relevance for the bloc of the anti-Stalin Twentieth CPSU Congress. Both parties also warned against dogmatism, and neither stressed the Yugoslav deviation; they were supported by the other East European parties. By way of contrast, the Chinese delegation — which, unlike the Soviet one, received a standing ovation — praised Hoxha, extolled the "correct" leadership of the Albanian party, attacked the Yugoslavs, and stressed activism against the "imperialists." Particularly revealing was the fact that these views were echoed by the Vietnamese and the North Koreans, as well as by the Malayan and Indonesian parties (see table on p. 416).

With the liquidation in Tirana during the summer and early fall of 1960 of a pro-Khrushchev faction (which the Soviets had apparently encouraged to displace Hoxha), the Kremlin had no choice but to react on the plane of external relations. During the spring of 1961 the Soviet Union peremptorily (but not publicly) suspended its economic assistance and withdrew its personnel. The Albanians, uncowed and encouraged by Chinese help, simply stepped up their vitriolic attacks on all manifestations of "revisionism" while deriving personal gratification from harassing and humiliating Soviet officials stationed in Albania. Moscow's official silence gave Tirana added immunity, so much so that the Yugoslavs, naturally interested in widening the Sino-Soviet breach, launched a press campaign designed to convince Moscow that Soviet and East European silence on this question merely played into the hands of the radicals.[21] In a special report to the Yugoslav Central Committee, the Yugoslav leadership stated that Soviet and East European efforts to minimize their differences with the more radical Chinese and Albanians were actually harmful to the international Communist fraternity. "The question being posed today more and more insistently is whether it is necessary, in the interest of the cause of socialism and the ideological education of the working class, to conceal these differences at all," an authoritative Yugoslav statement asserted,[22] launching a campaign designed to force the Soviets and the East Europeans to clarify their positions.

Eventually Khrushchev reached the same conclusion but still sought to avoid a direct attack on the Chinese. As a result, the Twenty-second CPSU Congress, scheduled primarily to discuss the new Communist program for the future, held in October 1961, was suddenly jarred by a direct, public, and extraordinarily sharp Soviet attack on Stalin and on the current Albanian party leadership. Immediately afterwards the Soviet Union broke diplomatic relations with Albania, a step curiously reminiscent of the traditional pattern of "capitalist" international relations that Communist theoreticians had been so fond of criticizing. Tying this action to the struggle against

Some of the major issues disputed at the Albanian Congress	War can be and should be averted	Imperialism and war threat emphasized	Revisionism in general attacked	Yugoslav revisionism singled out	Dogmatism attacked	The Twentieth CPSU "anti-Stalin" Congress endorsed	Positive references to Khrushchev	Positive references to Hoxha	Praise of the "correct" leadership of the Albanian Party
Hungarian Party: Ilku	O	O	F	O	O	O	1	O	O
Malayan Party: Greeting	O	O	ER	ER	O	O	O	2	S
Japanese Party: Yonehara	O	F	F	F	O	O	O	O	O
Indonesian Party: Supit	O	O	ER	F	O	O	3	3	S
China: Li Hsien-nien	F	S	S	S	F	O	O	2	ER
Poland: Nowak	ER	O	F	O	F	ER	2	O	O
Czechoslovakia: Barak	S	O	F	F	S	S	1	O	O
Vietnam: Duy Trinh	O	O	O	S	O	O	O	1	ER
East Germany: Axen	S	O	F	F	F	S	2	O	O
North Korea: Kum-chol	O	S	O	S	O	O	O	1	ER
Rumania: Voicu	S	O	F	O	F	O	2	O	O
Bulgaria: Velchev	F	O	F	F	F	S	O	O	O
USSR: Pospelov	ER	F	S	F	S	S	4	O	O
French Party: Ansart	ER	F	F	F	S	O	6	O	O
Italian Party: Roasio	S	O	F	O	F	O	1	O	O

Code: ER—emphatic, repeated assertions; S—strong assertion; F—formal assertion; O—no mention.

Source: The original version of this chart appeared in the paperback edition of *The Soviet Bloc* (New York, 1961), p. 433; this revised version is based on Griffith, *Albania and the Sino-Soviet Rift*, p. 73, with information based on *Zeri i Popullit*, February 15–19, 1961.

Stalinism was a convenient catch-all designed to paralyze ideologically all those who might be sympathetic to the Albanian position. Furthermore, the overt character of the attack on the Albanians reversed the Soviet relationship with the Chinese. It now gave the Chinese the option of either protecting Communist unity or of splitting the camp, thereby putting them on the defensive. Knowing of their economic weakness, their radicalism, and of their emphasis on Communist unity, Khrushchev perhaps expected that they would adjust to the situation. The fact that a Chinese delegation had come to Moscow knowing that the Albanians had not been invited to the Soviet congress, may have been a source of further reassurance to him. Nonetheless, it is apparent from subsequent events that Khrushchev was determined to push his offensive, and within days of the Moscow congress, the Soviet ambassador to Peking publicly, and in the presence of high Chinese dignitaries, repeated the charges against the Albanians.

Another reason for the move made at the Twenty-second Party Congress was Khrushchev's apparent conclusion that sham unity was providing a bargaining advantage to the more radical parties, which were thus able to exercise covert pressure on Moscow and covertly sabotage Soviet moves. An open airing of the dispute through the device of the attack on Albania was hence preferable. Last, there were presumably domestic causes for his initiative; these related to the persisting neo-Stalinist opposition to some of Khrushchev's recent initiatives. By linking all opposition with Stalinism, and, in effect, also with the external Communist radicals who allegedly wished to embroil the Soviet Union in a war, Khrushchev was undermining whatever social base such an opposition may have had at home. His attack, furthermore, may have been sparked by Molotov's critical letter, submitted to the Soviet leadership on the eve of the congress, which sharply disputed Khrushchev's program. This may have been a signal to Khrushchev that his external opponents were attempting to take advantage of his internal difficulties.

The real importance of the Soviet-Albanian break, however, is to be sought in its impact on Soviet-Chinese relations. The Chinese quite accurately interpreted it as an effort to humiliate China, and Chou En-lai ostentatiously withdrew from the Soviet congress. Within days the Chinese republished a vitriolic and highly personal Albanian attack on Khrushchev, and in January 1962 both the Soviet and the Chinese parties moved to the point of warning their members that a split was possible.[23] The Sino-Soviet dispute in that manner became more direct and openly hostile, with neither party able to control the spiral of the dispute, irrespective of their Communist interest in avoiding a split. To the Chinese, the Soviet action was nothing less than a brutal act of big-power chauvinism, designed to dictate to the Communist camp the standard of membership — namely, acceptance of the Soviet line. The severance of Soviet-Albanian diplomatic relations and the abrupt termination of economic assistance stood in sharp contrast to Soviet behavior toward the "imperialist" world, and reinforced Peking's suspicions concerning Khrushchev's long-range goals and his loyalty to the Communist cause.

Soviet conduct during both the Cuban missile confrontation of October 1962 and the simultaneous Indian-Chinese border conflict provided the Chinese leadership with final confirmation of its worst suspicions. And if that had not, the American-Soviet Test Ban Treaty concluded in the summer of 1963 certainly would have dispelled any lingering Chinese hopes for Khrushchev's ideological redemption. The polemics that erupted almost immediately after the termination of these two crises marked the beginning of a new phase in the Sino-Soviet rift: that of direct, overt, and explicit exchange of abuse between the two governments and the two party leaderships. The new phase also involved the surfacing of several key issues that had remained latent, most particularly territorial questions and the alleged *internal* deviation of the respective party leaderships from Marxism-Leninism. Of course, all the other divisive issues were also aired in an extraordinarily acrimonious manner.

The territorial dispute erupted into the open in the course of an almost comical pattern of name-calling. Khrushchev, personally offended by public Chinese charges that he had behaved cowardly during the Cuban crisis and presumably under enormous pressure from his disillusioned supporters at home, taunted the Chinese for their lack of courage in dealing with the "imperialist colonialists" in Hong Kong and Macao. Stung, the Chinese promptly responded by listing in an editorial statement in *Jen-min Jih-pao* all the "unequal treaties" imposed on China, including three that resulted in Russian territorial acquisitions at China's expense, adding: "We know very well, and you know too, that you are, to put it plainly, bringing up the questions of Hong Kong and Macao merely as a fig leaf to hide your disgraceful performance in the Caribbean crisis." [24] The Chinese went on to warn their ally that picking up "a stone from a cesspool, with which they believe they can fell the Chinese" can backfire, for China may choose to demand the reexamination of all its territorial losses. A year later the Chinese formally stated that eventually they would insist on "a reasonable settlement" of the border dispute, and their ostensibly reasonable observation that "pending such settlement, the status quo on the border should be maintained" made it clear that revisions in China's favor were expected.[26] *

Once the territorial issue broke out into the open, other pertinent revelations followed. There were accounts of border clashes, of defections across the frontiers, broadcasts from refugees, detailed descriptions of alleged Soviet subversion in Sinkiang, and of Chinese persecution of helpless Kazakhs.[27] A year later, on July 10, 1964, in an extraordinary interview granted to a group of visiting Japanese, Mao himself expanded the scope of the territorial dispute by charging his fellow-Communist allies with having taken "everything they could" in the aftermath of World War II; he specifically listed Mongolia, a part of Rumania, a portion of East Germany (from which "they chased away the local inhabitants"), a part of Poland, of Finland, and he added that "some people have declared that the Sinkiang area and the territories north of the Amur must be included in the Soviet Union. The USSR is concentrating troops along its borders."

It is difficult to conceive of an issue more suited to prompt an explosive Soviet reaction or to stimulate widespread nationalist antipathy between the Russians and the Chinese. In an emotionally charged statement, Khrushchev accused the Chinese Communists of "all but proposing the division" of the Soviet Union and of practicing the theory of the *Lebensraum*, in addition to having been guilty of subjugating smaller nations.[28] Clearly not unrelated to all this, and certainly reflecting Soviet growing concern with the long-range dangers involved in awakened Chinese territorial ambitions, was the startling Soviet initiative of January 4, 1964, addressed to all the states, and proposing that all states renounce the use of force in resolving territorial disputes and refrain from making territory "the object of any kind of encroachment." The proposal contained a remarkably un-Marxist analysis of the causes of war, seeking them largely in territorial-national ambitions. The analysis doubtless reflected the Soviet national interest, but it also showed vividly the destructive impact of the Sino-Soviet dispute on Marxist-Leninist ideology.

The territorial issue erupted in the context of steadily escalating

* In its late 1965 secret letter to CPSU members and to all fraternal Communist parties on the subject of the Sino-Soviet dispute, the Soviet leaders charged that "the official Chinese representative to bilateral consultations on border questions directly threatened that the CPR authorities would consider 'other ways' of settling the territorial question and stated: 'It is not out of the question that we will try to restore historical rights.'" (As cited by *Die Welt*, March 21, 1966.)

ideological charges and widening differences in foreign policy. Together, these made the Kremlin more inclined to seek a showdown.
Khrushchev thus moved toward the adoption of tactics previously
pursued by the Chinese, namely, pressing (as of the early fall of 1963)
for a multilateral conference of Communist parties at which he hoped
to effect (through what W. E. Griffith has felicitously labeled "collective mobilization") the condemnation of the deviant, whom the
Soviets now publicly charged with seeking to seize the leadership of
the international movement.[29]

The Chinese, on the other hand, sensing that the Soviets were
opting for a split in order to forestall rising Chinese influence among
the potentially revolutionary parties, began to shift from their previous insistence on a multilateral discussion of the divisive issues (at
which they hoped to expose the Soviets to ideological embarrassment)
to a demand for a slow bilateral process of Sino-Soviet consultations.
They hence resisted the Soviet call for a multilateral conference —
and, much to Khrushchev's annoyance, his initiative was also viewed
skeptically by a number of Communist parties (notably the Rumanian, Italian, and even the Cuban and Polish), which, although not
sympathetic to the Chinese, did not desire a final consummation of
the Sino-Soviet rift. Since the whole notion of collective mobilization
depended on the massive support of other parties, it soon became clear
that this particular Soviet venture would not prove overly effective.
Indeed, it even provided grist for the Chinese mill by allowing them
to charge, with some justification, that "the leaders of the CPSU
are the greatest splitters of our times," and to announce, in grand style,
the formal demotion of the CPSU:

At the 1957 Moscow meeting of fraternal parties . . . our proposal
that the socialist camp should have the Soviet Union at its head was written into the declaration . . .
By embarking on the path of revisionism and splittism, the leaders of
the CPSU automatically forfeited the position of "head" in the international Communist movement. If the word "head" is now to be applied to
them, it can only mean that they are at the head of the revisionists and
splitters.[30]

The dethroning of the Soviet Union was accompanied by the
formulation of the ideological underpinnings for Chinese primacy in
the international Communist movement. Its most explicit statement
came in a lecture delivered in September 1963 by a Chinese ideologue,
Chou Yang, and published at the end of 1963.[31] Chou Yang not only
stressed that "China is one of the oldest countries in the world" but

he developed a novel and important concept which may be described as *the theory of the changing geographical vortex of the revolution.* In Chou Yang's words:

> There is inevitably a realignment in the forces of revolution, in the course of the struggle between the proletariat and the revolutionary people on the one hand and the forces of reaction on the other and in the course of the struggle between Marxism on the one hand and opportunism and revisionism on the other.
>
> Marx and Engels once mentioned that the center of gravity of the European working-class movement had temporarily shifted from France to Germany after the defeat of the Paris Commune . . .
>
> At the beginning of the twentieth century, Russia became the focal point of the various contradictions in the era of imperialism . . .
>
> Then the storm of revolution reached the East.

Chou Yang contrasted this development with the spread of revisionism among formerly revolutionary parties, thus pointing to one conclusion: that today China was the leader of the revolution.

Indeed, emboldened by Khrushchev's humiliation in Cuba, enraged by the Soviet sympathy for India during the Indian-Chinese clash, convinced by the Test Ban Treaty that the Soviet leadership was seeking a Soviet-American alliance, the Chinese went so far as to appeal publicly to the Soviet Army, hailing it as a "great force" and warning the Soviet military that "to follow his [Khrushchev's] wrong theories would necessarily involve disintegrating the army." [32] The Chinese also stepped up their efforts to exclude the Soviets from various Afro-Asian bodies and their attacks on Soviet proposals for closer economic participation among Communist states,* and began to promote an alternative concept of international relations, designed to offset the threatening American-Soviet constellation. Labeled "the second intermediate zone," the notion rested on the idea of a new grouping in world affairs, to include in one front China with France, Great Britain, West Germany, and Japan and to be aimed against the alleged American-Soviet attempt at establishing global hegemony.[33] Implicit in it — as already noted in the case of the Soviet analysis of the role of frontiers in causing wars — was a sharp break with an ideological approach to world affairs, since it pitted against each other

---

* In a transparent effort to gain Rumanian sympathy, the Chinese charged the Soviets: "You bully those fraternal countries whose economies are less advanced, oppose their policy of industrialization and try to force them to remain agricultural countries and serve as your sources of raw materials and as outlets for your goods." Letter of the CC of the CCP of February 29, 1964, to the CC of the CPSU.

two mixed sets of Communist and capitalist states. Thus, in the course of a debate conducted in ideological terms, ideology was being progressively undermined.

Once the Soviet leadership had concluded that a break was inevitable, the flow of abuse from Moscow was also stepped up. The Soviet government announced that two successive statements concerning the Test Ban Treaty made by the Chinese government, once the most important ally of the USSR, were not accepted and were returned "to the sender," justifying this serious act by "their slanderous and hostile nature toward the Soviet Union." [34] In its own formal and public statement, the Soviet government mocked the Chinese as warmongers "who have only a hearsay acquaintance with nuclear weapons . . . whose [pronouncements] sound like mere prattle"; it condemned the alleged Chinese desire "to build a higher civilization on corpses and ruins," adding "we are against this savage concept"; finally it described as "fraudulent rantings" the Chinese argument that the Test Ban Treaty would interfere with the development of the "national-liberation struggle." [35]

More important than this unusual abuse, as well as some related incidents,* was the systematization by both sides of reciprocal doctrinal excommunications. On the Soviet side, the effort to formulate a systematic theoretical indictment coincided with the resumption in the spring of 1964 of the effort to organize a multilateral meeting, an effort temporarily suspended in view of the reticence displayed by some parties and in deference to a somewhat embarrassing and unsolicited Rumanian effort to mediate the dispute. Once the Rumanian effort failed, the Soviet leadership felt itself free to press on. But this time, unlike 1960 and 1961, the Soviets were determined to present a reasoned ideological condemnation of the Chinese, thereby offsetting some of the gains scored by the Chinese in the course of the earlier polemics in which the Chinese had enjoyed the ideological initiative.[36]

A systematic Soviet ideological response was elaborated by Mihail Suslov, in a report on Communist unity delivered to the Central Committee on February 14, 1964, but only released, because of the tactical

---

* Perhaps the most ridiculous of these was the Naushki Station incident on the Soviet Far Eastern frontier, where, in addition to political charges, some Chinese were accused by a female Soviet official of shockingly unprincipled behavior: "As a woman, I find it difficult to describe what I saw. They unbuttoned their trousers and started to urinate. We were surprised. Only animals could behave in such a way. This is how low they sank. Shame on them . . ." For an account, see Griffith, *The Sino-Soviet Rift*, pp. 174–76.

considerations mentioned, on April 3. Its principal charges were as follows: all Soviet efforts at reconciliation have been rebuffed and the Chinese have pushed the various divergencies to the point of transforming them into a fundamental disagreement; Chinese attacks on the Soviet Union were no longer restricted to foreign affairs but involved also Soviet internal affairs; the Chinese in their splitting activities in the various Communist parties were relying on the help of anarchists and Trotskyites; the Chinese were making use of racial prejudices in their appeals to Africans and Asians; the Chinese concept of war was inhuman, and the Chinese spoke with equanimity about sacrificing for the sake of victory the complete populations of such countries as Italy or Czechoslovakia; the Chinese concept of "national-liberation struggle" was undifferentiated and simply ignored the enormous differences between continents and nations; the CCP was seeking to create its own bloc "with its center in Peking," and Peking was hoping to cause the CPSU to remove Khrushchev from power: "an empty, hopeless adventure . . . doomed to a complete and shameful failure." (Record shows stormy applause.)

More significant than the indictment was the analysis: the Chinese were behaving in such outrageous fashion because the CCP had fallen victim to a "petty-bourgeois, nationalist, neo-Trotskyite deviation" within its leadership. This could happen whenever a Communist revolution took place in a country with a weak industrial proletariat, susceptible to bourgeois nationalist ideology, and where the party was led by leaders of low "theoretical maturity." That is why, Suslov triumphantly pointed out, the Chinese theses and behavior not only corresponded to Trotskyite prescriptions but the Chinese had won the enthusiastic support of the Trotskyite movement. The pursuit of the Trotskyite line, Suslov added, caused the Chinese not only to embark on a reckless foreign policy but to undertake a calamitous domestic program that has yielded only havoc.* The spring 1964 Soviet analysis and indictment represented the most severe and bitter condemnation to date of the Chinese leadership. Together with specific moves

---

* Suslov's analysis was followed by the publication of a series of supporting accusations, all adding up to a monumental indictment of a party that a mere few years earlier had been held up as a model of revolutionary virtue. The Chinese party was accused of not observing its own statutes and of being led, in effect, by an illegal leadership. Chinese domestic disasters were described in detail to a Soviet audience that for years had been told only of Chinese accomplishments. The racist charge was duly elaborated in a series of comments, and the Chinese theoreticians were condemned for attempting the "Sinification of Marxism-Leninism." Mao's writings were described as oversimplified popular expositions.

on the economic and military levels, the charge of "petty-bourgeois nationalist and neo-Trotskyite deviation" made of the Chinese leadership by a Secretary of the CPSU, addressing the Soviet Central Committee, created the basis for a formal rupture in party and state relations, should the Soviet side decide to embark on such a drastic course.

Suslov's indictment, however, never came to serve its original function, for the condemnatory multilateral meeting was not held. Persistent opposition from other parties forced the Soviet Union by the summer of 1964 to redefine its purpose to that of seeking to "enrich" the 1957 and 1960 platforms and even to make the humiliating pledge to the invited parties (letter of July 30, 1964) that it would not "excommunicate anybody . . . or cast irresponsible charges." Scheduled for December 1964, the meeting had to be postponed after Khrushchev's fall in October. Finally held in Moscow in March 1965, and attended by only 19 of the 29 parties invited (the same parties as those that drafted the 1960 statement),[37] * it was later relabeled by Moscow as a "consultative meeting," reflecting its meager accomplishments. On the Sino-Soviet conflict it had little to say and even less impact. The Chinese were able to mock it as offering further proof of the declining Soviet capacity to lead the international Communist movement.

Almost simultaneously, the Chinese also publicly elaborated and systematized their own view of the Soviet Union and its leadership. In seeking an explanation for the Test Ban Treaty and particularly for the alleged Soviet desire to establish an amicable Soviet-American relationship, the Chinese focused on the phenomenon of revisionism. At first, they only hinted that the CPSU was being seduced by it; they focused their attacks on the Titoist infection by which, they alleged, the Soviets were getting contaminated, and which was sapping Soviet revolutionary morale. In 1964, however, the Chinese expanded their critique to Soviet *internal* affairs and they made it much more explicit and elaborate. On the eve of Suslov's speech, the Chinese related the shortcomings of Soviet foreign policy to the already cited

---

* Suslov's analysis was followed by the publication of a series of supporting accusations, all adding up to a monumental indictment of a party that a mere few years earlier had been held up as a model of revolutionary virtue. The Chinese party was accused of not observing its own statutes and of being led, in effect, by an illegal leadership. Chinese domestic disasters were described in detail to a Soviet audience that for years had been told only of Chinese accomplishments. The racist charge was duly elaborated in a series of comments, and the Chinese theoretician were condemned for attempting the "sinification of Marxism-Leninism." Mao writings were described as oversimplified popular expositions.

"lush growth of the bourgeois element inside the Soviet Union . . . to the widespread capitalist forces at home," [38] and made the restoration of Communist unity dependent on a complete Soviet capitulation, including Khrushchev's removal (see supra for Suslov's quick rejoinder).

They followed this shortly by an extensive attack on the domestic principles of the recently adopted Soviet party program, flatly declaring the Soviet claim of building Communism to be "a lie." On the contrary, according to the Chinese, "as a result of Khrushchev's revisionist rule . . . the capitalist forces in Soviet society have become a deluge sweeping over all fields of life in the USSR, including the political, economical, cultural, and ideological fields," and the Chinese warned that this alleged development "is opening the floodgates for the restoration of capitalism." Peking's basic political message was succinct:

Now is the time — now is high time — to repudiate and liquidate Khrushchev's revisionism! Here, we would give the leading comrades of the CPSU a piece of advice: since so many opportunists and revisionists have been thrown into the rubbish heap of history, why must you obdurately follow in their wake?[39]

During the summer of 1964, the Chinese continued to elaborate on this theme, notably in their July 13 statement "On Khrushchev's Phony Communism and Its Historical Lesson for the World," which developed the theme that the Soviet Union was ruled by "a privileged bourgeois stratum," and contrasted this degeneration with Mao's determination to struggle even for several centuries in order to construct Communism. Soviet passivity in the face of the Tonkin Bay incident, and even the Kremlin's inclination to view it as a Chinese provocation, provided the fuel for the fire.[40]

Khrushchev's sudden fall in October 1964 was initially misconstrued by the Chinese as involving the acceptance by some presumably uninfected Soviet comrades of the advice so explicitly offered above. Chinese polemics were suspended — as were also the Soviet — and a Chinese delegation hurried to Moscow, hoping to attend the burial of the capitalist and bourgeois forces nipped in the bud. The Chinese misconception was fortified by the initial inclination of the new Soviet leadership to tone down Khrushchev's polemical style and perhaps even to abandon some of the more extreme measures that he may have been planning against China. However, what the Soviet leaders were essentially seeking in Sino-Soviet relations was to freeze the ideological discord while improving state relations. They were not prepared to change either their line or their policies.*

The full measure of the Chinese disappointment was well documented by the bitterness of the 1965 Chinese comments on the post-Khrushchev leadership. All the basic postulates were repeated and some new ones were added in regard to the alleged Soviet lack of support for the North Vietnamese in their conflict with the United States. Admitting frankly that "we had hopes regarding the new leaders of the CPSU, and watched and waited for several months," the Chinese leaders bitterly concluded that "compared with Khrushchev, his successors are practicing a more covert, cunning, and dangerous revisionism." Their revisionism, in Peking's view, reflected a historical process at work in the Soviet Union, repeating the disagreeable experience of the Second International, the Mensheviks, and the Titoists, all of whom put up a revolutionary façade in order to conceal their revisionist degeneration.[41] This Soviet degeneration led the Kremlin, the Chinese charged, into actual collusion with the United States in the Vietnamese conflict, with the Soviet leaders allegedly providing Washington with advance information concerning Soviet military activity in North Vietnam.[42] †

Of more lasting significance were the continuing Chinese elaborations on their argument that the Soviet Union was restoring capitalism and the political conclusions drawn from this analysis. The September 1965 Soviet economic reform was interpreted in Peking as having "marked a big step along the road of the restoration of capitalism in the Soviet economy . . . substituting free competition for socialist planned economy." The new Soviet leaders were said to be "using a variety of economic and administrative measures to encourage and foster the growth of a new kulak economy, sabotaging and disintegrating all aspects of the socialist collective economy." The assertion of this historically fundamental reversal in Soviet domestic developments provided the ideological underpinning for the Chinese conclusion that a complete split would be desirable: "At present, the

---

* After Khrushchev's fall, particularly during Kosygin's visit to Peking in February 1965, the Soviet side tried to "normalize" relations by proposing bilateral meetings at the highest level, a mutual discontinuation of polemics, the expansion of Sino-Soviet trade, scientific-technical and cultural cooperation, and consultation on foreign policy.

† As a result of the bitter exchanges over Vietnam, Moscow witnessed in March 1965 the unusual spectacle of Chinese and Vietnamese students, who attempted to demonstrate in front of the United States Embassy, being dispersed by charging Soviet soldiers. Injured Chinese students, expelled from the Soviet Union, were welcomed as heroes in Peking.

task facing all the Marxist-Leninist parties is to draw a clear line of demarcation *both politically and organizationally* between themselves and the revisionists . . ." [43] The stress on the need to draw *organizationally* a line of demarcation was especially significant. It provided publicly an ideological legitimation for the eventuality of a formal split.[44] *

The Sino-Soviet dispute in that manner escalated from an implicit and indirect argument primarily over external issues, which it had been during the years 1957–1960 (see Chapters 12 and 15), into a still implicit but increasingly direct dispute over external issues during 1960–1963, and after that into an explicit and direct confrontation over both external and internal matters. The escalation combined increasingly hostile actions on state and diplomatic levels with growing gravity of doctrinal charges. The ideological escalation was thus both a reflection of the embittering effects of other actions (such as economic sanctions) and in itself an intensifying factor, rigidifying mutual misconceptions, legitimizing reciprocal feelings of hostility, and systematizing hostile interpretations of each other's motives, behavior, and social development. The violence of the polemic inherently prompted in both sides the adoption of more extreme ideological postures. Thus the Chinese, who in 1960 did make a better Leninist case than the Soviets, by 1965 were indeed talking like Trotskyites; the Soviets, who in 1958 were condemning the Yugoslav program (Chapter 13), by 1965 seemed to be largely parroting the views of Kardelj and the Yugoslav revisionists. For Marxist-Leninists at large all this offered the curious and presumably saddening spectacle of the first country of socialism being charged with actively pursuing the restoration of capitalism and of the most triumphantly revolutionary party with falling prey to petty-bourgeois Trotskyism.

THE FATE OF THE ALLIANCE

The pattern of escalation was not without its occasional downward dips, and there were periodic lulls in the dispute: after the 1960 meeting; during the spring of 1962; in the beginning of 1964; and for a brief while after Khrushchev's fall. At no point, however, was there a real detente. More often than not, the lulls were either induced by the

* The Chinese refusal to attend the proceedings of the Twenty-third CPSU Congress, held in March 1966, was a decision clearly in keeping with the desire to draw this "organizational line of demarcation" on the level of party relations. At the same time, according to the charges contained in the secret Soviet letter of 1965, the Chinese stepped up their "subversive activities" against the Soviet government, particularly by radio and written appeals to non-Soviet nationalities, directed at the Great Russians, and to Soviet party cadres, directed at the Soviet leadership.

pressure of other parties or were tactical efforts by one side to make the other appear more responsible for the destruction of Communist unity.

More important perhaps in terms of the dispute's over-all global significance was the tendency for the Sino-Soviet rift to widen as a consequence of international crises. The Quemoy-Matsu crisis of 1958, the U-2 crisis of 1960, the Cuban confrontation of 1962, and the American bombing of North Vietnam in 1965, all were followed by intensified polemics, mutual accusations, and, it may be presumed, by accentuated suspicions concerning each other's motives and good faith. This sequence of events seemed to suggest that conditions of stress tended to drive further apart the Chinese and Soviet national interests and ideological assessments; while in a setting in which either or both could pursue their goals without endangering or negatively affecting each other's interests, the latent Communist interest in preventing a total split tended to be reawakened. However, precisely because international tension further divided the two allies and embittered their relationship, it made a mockery of their alliance which was presumably designed to ensure mutual action and defense in the face of some international threat.

Formally, as of the beginning of 1966, the Sino-Soviet alliance was still binding. However, it had been largely drained of any significant political and military content. To all intents and purposes, after 1963 China was no longer receiving any Soviet military aid, while Soviet neutrality with regard to Indian-Chinese armed clashes and Soviet passivity in the face of mounting Chinese-American tension made the alliance appear rather hollow. Moreover, in the course of the polemics the Soviet leadership had gone on record as not considering itself bound to provide military support for Chinese offensive aspirations.[45] * The Chinese in response laid emphasis on national self reliance in the military sphere, and they clearly regarded their success in developing a nuclear weapon (October 1964) as providing at least a partial justification for their stand. Nonetheless, even the most optimistic Chinese leader could not fail to note that the modernization of the Chinese military establishment had badly suffered because of the absence of Soviet military deliveries and the withdrawal of Soviet

---

* As early as August 1960 a Soviet commentator warned that China, because of its policies might find itself "in an isolated position" in the face of "an economic blockade" and "military blows from without," launched by the "capitalist powers" (See Zagoria, *The Sino-Soviet Conflict*, p. 335.) It may be safely assumed that similar statements were made privately and more forcefully by Khrushchev, especially after 1963.

technicians. Chinese dependence on the politically unreliable availability of Soviet petroleum also negatively affected the Chinese capacity to sustain a large-scale military effort.* All of this stood in sharp contrast to Soviet deliveries of relatively modern weapons to both India and Indonesia (where, in the former case, they could be used against China and where, in the latter case, they were employed to crush an important pro-Chinese Communist party!).[46]

More generally, it is undeniable that the Chinese economy had been badly hurt by the withdrawal of Soviet assistance. In the course of the polemics, the Chinese noted that Soviet assistance had not been very large, that it was "rendered mainly in the form of trade and that it was certainly not a one-way affair . . . It is necessary to add that the prices of many of the goods we imported from the Soviet Union were much higher than those on the world market." [47] Moreover, the Chinese stated, even the assistance received from the Soviet Union during the Korean War, in which "the Chinese people, too, made great sacrifices and incurred vast military expenses . . . has not been given gratis." [48]

The Soviets, of course, stressed the selfless character of the aid and its importance to Chinese development. "Thanks to the aid of the Soviet Union, a preliminary basis for modern industry and technology have been created in China," claimed Suslov, listing in detail the dimensions of Soviet aid and blaming the Chinese for disrupting Soviet-Chinese economic relations.[49] That this aid in fact was not negligible was inadvertently admitted by the Chinese themselves when they charged that Soviet economic aid was "an instrument for exerting political pressure on fraternal countries" and complained — as already quoted — that its withdrawal "inflicted enormous losses upon China's socialist construction." [50] †

These economic and military indicators testified to the mori-

---

* The scale of Soviet petroleum deliveries provides a good quantitative illustration for the three principal stages of the dispute: in 1959 (just prior to the 1960 confrontation), the Soviet Union delivered to China 187.1 million rubles' worth of petroleum; by 1962 (on the eve of the 1963 polemics) the figure shrank to 72.5 million rubles; in 1964 the sum was 19.4 million rubles. (As per *Vneshnaia Torgovlia* trade summaries.)

† Soviet-Chinese trade declined accordingly. Total turnover in 1959 stood at 1,848.4 million rubles; in 1962 at 674.8 million rubles; in 1964 at 404.5 million rubles. Even more striking is the decline in deliveries of Soviet machinery and equipment: from 537.9 million rubles in 1959 to a mere 51.8 million rubles in 1964. In 1959 China outranked all the East European countries in volume of trade with the Soviet Union; in 1964 it was behind all of them, save Albania, and its trade with the Soviet Union was only one sixth of that with East Germany.

bund state of the Sino-Soviet alliance. The pursuit by the two nations of divergent — and sometimes even sharply colliding — foreign
policies,[51] and their mutually damaging ideological condemnations
strongly confirmed that diagnosis. Did this mean that a reconciliation was altogether impossible? And if not, then on what terms? Presumably both Moscow and Peking have pondered these questions. In
the case of the Chinese leaders, despite their outward ideological composure, the thought that the Sino-Soviet reconciliation could someday
take place without a prior Soviet capitulation had given rise to a striking confession of concern. Mao Tse-tung has been publicly quoted as
having "often said to comrades from fraternal parties that if China's
leadership is usurped by revisionists in the future, the Marxist-Leninists of all countries should likewise resolutely expose and fight
them . . ."[52] The Chinese leadership was in this manner raising the
possibility of a dramatic reversal of China's general line as well as
reaffirming its determination to wage indefinitely the struggle against
Soviet revisionism. It was clearly striving to make a commitment so
clear and so binding that no future generation of Chinese leaders
could reverse the Maoist line without threatening their own power.

In thinking about the foreseeable future of the Chinese-Soviet relationship (that is, the next decade), at least six alternatives come to
mind: (1) a total break between the two parties and the two states,
the intensification of territorial disputes, all eventually pointing even
to a confrontation between them; (2) continuing bitter hostility, ideological and organizational conflict within the international Communist movement, much on the pattern and the level of the years
1963–1965; (3) the same as above, but on a less intense basis, involving perhaps a measured deescalation to the levels prevailing prior to
1963 (or for a while in 1964 after Khrushchev's fall); (4) a working
state-to-state alliance, involving international cooperation against the
West, determined largely on national interest grounds, with agreement to silence ideological polemics; (5) a return to Soviet leadership,
with the Chinese leadership accepting the Soviet line and foreign
policy; (6) the acceptance by the Soviets of the Chinese line, including the Chinese concept of revolutionary struggle.

In weighing the various alternatives, it should be noted that in
many respects the Sino-Soviet conflict has been the product of factors
beyond the control of either the Soviet or Chinese leaders. Domestic
developments in the two countries as well as events on the international scene also helped to shape the conflict. They are likely there-

fore to continue shaping its future. Speculating in most tentative and general terms, the first alternative could materialize if both Russia and China were stymied internationally and were inclined to blame each other for their failures (the destruction of the Indonesian Communist Party after its abortive 1965 coup would make an excellent topic for such an exchange). However, given the enormous Soviet economic and military preponderance, it is extremely unlikely that the Chinese could — or would — mount more than protracted border skirmishes and agitate extensively in Soviet Central Asia, hoping perhaps to capitalize politically by representing the Soviet Union as a colonial power.

The second and third alternatives are basically extensions of the situation prevailing in the first half of the sixties. Perhaps a post-Mao leadership might be inclined to reduce the level of the dispute, much as the post-Khrushchev Soviet leaders tried. Without resolving any of the divisive issues, that would nonetheless somewhat normalize the relations between the two parties, but it would not end the dispute and it could hardly contain the factional conflicts stimulated by it in other parties. These factional conflicts would serve to create new tensions, and perhaps prompt an escalation again in the dispute, eventually pointing to the emergence of two more formally demarcated camps, each with some organizational and ideological expression, but with neither able to halt the general trend toward a polycentric Communism.[53] Barring drastic changes in the international scene and in the domestic affairs of the two states, this fluid combination of the second and third alternatives seems likely, especially given the environmental differences affecting the perspectives of any Soviet and Chinese leaders. Unlike the Soviets, the Chinese find their basic national ambitions unfulfilled, and their intense sense of national awakening is bound to color for some time to come also their perspectives of international affairs.

The fourth alternative probably would require as a precondition the death of Mao and the emergence in China of a more pragmatic and less ideologically militant leadership. It may also be dependent on some Western appeasement of China's expansionist inclinations, for Sino-Soviet tensions — and the rupture of an effective Sino-Soviet alliance relationship — has been very much the product of Western resistance and the consequent Soviet fear of becoming embroiled in rash Chinese undertakings. Therefore, rather than contributing to an intensification of Sino-Soviet tensions, successful Chinese expansion southward could have the effect of making a stabler relationship more likely. Since Soviet caution, and Chinese bitterness, were stimulated also by the Western stance in Berlin and in the Cuban confrontation, the effectiveness of Western responses to offensive Soviet initiatives likewise will have a rather direct bearing on the Sino-Soviet relationship.

The fifth and sixth alternatives, at the present less likely, presuppose drastic domestic upheavals and calamities. The fifth, probably more likely than the sixth, would be dependent on a widespread disintegration of the Chinese political system and economy, and perhaps even a major Chinese defeat in a war.* The sixth would require a basic reversal in Soviet political, economic, and social trends, probably the reimposition on the Soviet people of policies reminiscent of Stalinism, and a rather basic change in the essentially bureaucratic character of the present Soviet elite, all preceded by Soviet domestic disintegration and ineffective Western responses to Chinese revolutionary strategy, thus completely refuting the Soviet emphasis on caution. The acceptance by the Soviets of the Chinese position probably would require a major Soviet underwriting of the Chinese economic development.

Whatever the future pattern of the Sino-Soviet dispute, its impact on the Communist camp has been disintegrative. The dispute stands out as the most monumental failure of the capacity of the Communist ideology to create a stable international order, thereby refuting one of the most cherished utopias of committed Communists. Moreover, the specific conduct of the two principal Communist parties did not provide the other ruling Communist leaderships with an edifying example of how to overcome their own national prejudices for the sake of proletarian internationalism.

* The Soviet attitude in the event of military hostilities between the United States and China is likely to be ambivalent. Khrushchev might very well have been tempted to abandon China altogether. His successors perhaps could be also. However, given their somewhat more orthodox and cautious behavior, it seems more likely that they might see in such a war an opportunity for the Soviet Union to gain a political advantage over both the United States and China. They could thus decide to provide military assistance to China in sufficient quantities to prevent a speedy defeat of China but without giving China any strategic means for striking at the United States and hence provoking an American reaction against the Soviet Union; to embroil the United States in a costly and prolonged conflict; and to make the Chinese leadership increasingly dependent on the Soviet Union for its survival and hence more responsive to Soviet desires.

17 / SATELLITES INTO JUNIOR ALLIES

"IT IS obvious that the conductor's baton is becoming less and less effective and the centrifugal forces are increasing. The Soviet leaders' policy of great state chauvinism has resulted in a policy of local nationalism among revisionists of other countries, particularly among those of other socialist countries. Each is trying to defend its own economic, political and military interests and oppose them to other interests. *The laws of capitalist mutual relations are working with ever-increasing force among the revisionists.* Contradictions within CEMA and the Warsaw Pact are corroding from within these two organizations which were set up to strengthen economic cooperation and increase the socialist countries' defense power. The situation within these organizations is much like that of the 'Common Market' and NATO." [1] This description of Soviet-East European relations came from a Communist regime, and it was certainly not far off the mark. By the mid-sixties, not only the Stalinist uniformity of the early fifties but even the more recent Khrushchevite dreams of genuine unity based on ideological commitment and close economic integration seemed like mere relics of a remote past. "The laws of capitalist mutual relations," that is, the traditional patterns of interstate relations, were indeed becoming dominant in the Soviet bloc. Communist ambassadors were delivering notes to Communist Foreign Ministries and the notes were being indignantly returned; economic sanctions were being applied because of political differences; territorial issues were reviving; the mistreatment of national minorities was becoming widespread. In the revealing words of a Foreign Minister of one of the Communist states: "Proletarian internationalism means promoting our own welfare, not anybody else's." [2]

The restoration of the primacy of the interstate relations, and the consequent decline in the relative importance of the formerly paramount party channels were prompted by the disruptive impact of the Sino-Soviet rift on Communist ideology and unity, and by the increasing self-assurance of the East European Communist elites that the political status quo was basically here to stay. The Sino-Soviet dispute discredited both the ideology and the two disputants and ideologically demoralized the true believers. The feeling that the East

European status quo was no longer directly threatened gave the East European rulers greater proprietary sense toward their states and stimulated in them a keener awareness of their own state interests.[3]

DE-SATELLITIZATION, DE-STALINIZATION, AND IDEOLOGICAL NATIONALIZATION

Even though for Communism in general the Sino-Soviet dispute was a disaster reminiscent of the great splits in Christianity, for the East European Communist rulers there were some concrete advantages resulting from it. Precisely because the dispute did not lead to a precipitous Sino-Soviet break and to the immediate formation of two hostile international organizations, the East European margin of autonomy increased greatly. Greater East European autonomy forced the East European leaders to face more directly their own domestic problems; these particular domestic problems, in turn, to complete the triangle, affected the East European leaders' responsiveness to Moscow's wishes.

One may surmise that much of the evident East European antipathy for Khrushchev's determination to condemn and expel the Chinese — a step evidently planned for late 1964 — stemmed from East European awareness of their self-interest and not from abstract devotion to the cause of ideological unity. Strikingly, the party leadership most favorably inclined to Khrushchev's scheme was that of Yugoslavia, a country that already had successfully and fully asserted its independence, and that now hoped that the final consummation of the Sino-Soviet split would encourage further revisionism domestically in the Soviet Union, a desire not necessarily shared by the East European Communist leaders who wanted more autonomy but not necessarily more domestic evolution. For most of them, de-satellitization and de-Stalinization were two separate processes, and they preferred to keep them apart, so that one would not reinforce the other, eventually causing the situation to get out of hand, as happened in Hungary in 1956.

Moreover, as long as the dispute was in progress, East European votes and voices were of greater importance to Moscow than otherwise would be the case, and this inevitably reduced the highly asymmetrical power relationship between the Soviet Union and Prague or Budapest or even East Berlin. It increased the East European bargaining power, with the effect that throughout East Europe by the sixties the most blatant and obnoxious signs of Soviet predominance had been quietly eliminated. Some East European leaders even developed a personal relationship of confidence and respect with the Kremlin, not altogether unlike that prevailing between some Western statesmen and Washington, in spite of the obvious disproportions in power. It appears certain that Gomulka achieved a particularly good working relationship with Khrushchev, and his counsel, as well as that of Kadar, was listened to with respect in the Soviet capital.* Khrushchev's fall from power further reduced — if not altogether eliminated — any lingering feelings of personal fealty among the East European leaders toward the Kremlin incumbent.†

Because of the over-all change in relations, some East European leaders could even adopt publicly a detached attitude toward the Moscow-Peking conflict. This was especially the case with Rumania. While Gomulka and others were quietly urging the Kremlin to exercise self-restraint and to explore the possibility of reconciliation, the Rumanians in early 1964 offered their services as mediators, thereby embarrassing Khrushchev's scheme of "collective mobilization," predicated as it was on the assumption of the irreconcilability of the Soviet and Chinese views. Moreover, in a striking departure from the posture of a satellite, the Rumanians repeatedly admonished both Moscow and Peking for their (mis)conduct during the public polemics, and urged both to exercise more mature self-restraint.‡

The Rumanians similarly opposed the Polish effort in early 1966 to organize a multilateral meeting ostensibly to discuss aid to North Vietnam but really designed to isolate China. The Polish initiative was in keeping with the Brezhnev-Kosygin leadership's decision to try again to mobilize the anti-Chinese forces, and it represented a change in the Polish posture, a change perhaps induced by Gomulka's fears of further disintegration in the camp unless the Chinese were exposed and by his concern that the Asian war might escalate into an American-Soviet confrontation. The Rumanians were apparently able to

---

* Without straining the analogy too far, one may say that Gomulka's views about Mao Tse-tung were as eagerly sought in the Kremlin as Spaak's were on de Gaulle in the White House.

† It is interesting to note that the East European leaders learned of Khrushchev's removal by telephone on the afternoon of October 14, 1964. Some were highly irritated and all were disturbed, as evidenced even by their public declarations. That advance notification, however, was itself an act of courtesy, acknowledging the Soviet feeling of contingent relations. There is no record of anything like this at the time of Malenkov's removal in 1955.

‡ This became a frequent theme in Rumanian editorials: thus the Russians and the Chinese were lectured that their unity may be restored if "first of all, the ending of accusations and invectives" is brought about by both sides. *Scinteia*, December 18, 1965.

obtain both Hungarian and Bulgarian backing,[4] thus providing further evidence of the return of international politics to East Europe.

In some respects even more indicative of the extent of the change were some remarkable Czechoslovak views on the subject of the Sino-Soviet dispute, published in late 1965 in a country which (unlike Rumania) did not make an issue of its independence of Moscow's control. Its Czech author, V. Kotyk, quite boldly asserted that "the interest of unity excludes any form of pressure, any subordination of the weaker party to the stronger one, and any creation of a mechanical and formal unity, as well as mutual isolation or elimination of mutual cooperation." [5] Given the Soviet handling of the Albanians, the Yugoslavs, and the Chinese, it would be difficult not to construe his views as constituting at least implicit criticism of Soviet efforts at "deviation control." That such opinions about the Soviet Union were published in a state hitherto known as the most pliant Soviet tool was vivid testimony of widespread Communist reassessment of the character of relations among Communist states.

Of great relevance to that reassessment was the reconciliation between Moscow and Belgrade stimulated in large measure by the widening Sino-Soviet rift. Although initially the Soviets had been quite outspoken in their condemnation of Yugoslav revisionism, the uninhibited Chinese excommunication of Khrushchev as a Yugoslav-type revisionist and the identification of Soviet domestic policies as involving Yugoslav-type revisionism gradually compelled the Soviets to undertake the defense of Yugoslavia as a bona fide socialist state, in spite of some Soviet reservations that were still registered, largely for the record. Moreover, Moscow found it useful to improve its relations with Belgrade because Yugoslavia offered an invaluable source of access to the new nations among whom the Kremlin wished to protect its influence from Chinese encroachments. Tito's close relations with Nasser, Ben Bella or Sékou Touré more than compensated for the likelihood of some unhappiness among Zhivkov and his associates.[6] Accordingly, there was a return to the warmth that prevailed in the Tito-Khrushchev relationship during the years 1955–56, with similar exchange of visits, upturn in trade, and emphasis on basic identity of views on major international issues (such as Germany Berlin, the Congo, and so on).

However, all of this was purchased at no inconsiderable cost. In their July 1963 open letter, responding to the Chinese, the Soviets decisively defended Yugoslavia as a socialist state, but in so doing they were forced also explicitly to accept the notion that the ex istence of some fourteen Communist states ruled out any common standard for evaluating their doctrinal orthodoxy. (It is to be recalled that Suslov tried to formulate such a standard in November 1956; see Chapter 12, p. 275.) Although still pleading for "unity and cohesion," it was clear that the Soviet leadership itself no longer knew what the source of that unity and cohesion ought to be. For East Europe, the Soviet action provided additional legitimation of Yugoslavia's independent course. It showed that the Soviet leaders, because of the changes wrought by time and by the pressures of the Sino-Soviet conflict, had now accepted Yugoslavia as a socialist state. This despite the fact that Yugoslavia had not conceded any error with respect to its 1958 program (see Chapter 13); had not become a member of the Warsaw Pact; had not fully become assimilated into the CEMA structure (although it had expressed an interest in limited participation); and domestically was pursuing policies far more moderate and pragmatic than even the most unorthodox East European leaders thought desirable. For the more orthodox, such as Zhivkov of Bulgaria, who in late 1965 had to toast in Sofia an ideologically triumphant Tito, Yugoslavia's reentry into Communist camp politics on its own terms certainly spelled even greater domestic danger.

The more varied East European attitude toward Moscow was not only a function of the disruptive consequences of the Sino-Soviet dispute, but it was also shaped by the almost simultaneous abatement among the East European Communist elites of a hitherto widespread fear of domestically or externally originated upheavals. The suppression of the Hungarian revolution in 1956 demonstrated vividly the predominance of Soviet power in the region. Paradoxically, however, it worked also to reduce it. By convincing the East European populations that no Western succor was to be expected and that any uprising would be ruthlessly crushed, the October–November 1956 experience reduced the likelihood of a repetition. By the same token, the crushing of the East European spirit of resistance markedly reduced also the sense of dependence of the East European rulers on Soviet bayonets. The psychological and political process was not unlike that which America experienced in West Europe; by effectively repelling the Soviet challenge and by reducing the felt likelihood of its repetition, America also proportionately reduced its own leverage on the West Europeans.

If the Hungarian experience can be said to have minimized the fears of the East European rulers of domestic upheavals, and consequently also their sense of dependence on Moscow, the erection of the Wall in Berlin in August 1961, and the 1963 American-Soviet detente, eliminated what was left of the once widespread East European conviction that the West was seriously striving to change the East European political status quo. This again worked to reduce direct Soviet leverage, while the steadily increasing importance of East Germany to Soviet economic growth — not to speak of the Soviet political and ideological stakes in it — reassured Prague and Warsaw that the Soviet interest in this buffer was too great to permit Moscow to alter drastically its commitment to the Central European status quo. International tension and instability helped Stalin to forge his monolithic system. Inter-Communist conflict and stability in Europe were loosening it.

On the external plane de-Stalinization meant automatically de-satellitization. But de-satellitization did not automatically mean domestic de-Stalinization. On the contrary, as each regime had to make its own adjustment, a variety of trends emerged. The Warsaw regime, which was largely de-satellitized and de-Stalinized in 1956, gradually restricted many of the domestic freedoms, presumably out of fear that the process of evolution would transform the political system itself. This, as well as the country's continuing economic difficulties, prompted widespread popular dissatisfaction. Hungary, without visibly striving to change its external relations with Moscow, after the early sixties moved rapidly forward in its domestic de-Stalinization, but by 1966 was attempting to slow down its pace, lest the regime be threatened by it. East Germany and Czechoslovakia, cautious not to strain their ties with Moscow nor to expose to challenge their systems of political rule, initially avoided any significant change in political styles, although Czech cultural life witnessed a remarkabe revival. However, both states undertook significant economic reforms, considerably ahead in scope and in degree of innovation of those attempted in the Soviet Union. By 1965 both had adopted, and the former even implemented, far-reaching schemes abandoning in large measure the Stalinist systems of command economy. At the same time, the Poles and the Bulgarians were experimenting with more timid adjustments,[7] while the Rumanians, after granting a major amnesty and establishing contacts with the West, were eliminating the more oppressive features of the system that endured largely unchanged from Stalinist days. However, unlike its neighbors, in the mid-sixties Rumania was enjoying rapid economic growth and was therefore not tinkering basically with its economic structure. Nonetheless, in Rumania, too, Stalinism as a generalized system of rule and a way of life was gradually being pushed aside by more particular domestic realities. The neo-Stalinist tightening, attempted by several East European states as a reaction to the events of 1956, simply could not be maintained in the looser international setting.

Throughout the area, the individual search of each regime for a more favorable balance between domestic support and external dependence on Soviet sponsorship was reflected in a widespread process of nationalization of governments that came to power almost entirely through foreign force. National achievements were glorified and national traditions extolled. This in itself need not be significant externally, except that in East Europe one nation's glory has been usually another's tragedy. Celebrating Slovak national traditions automatically meant reflecting on Hungarian oppression. Similarly with almost all the others. Moreover, in different ways each nation saw itself as a carrier of a special mission, not always quite compatible with the notion of membership in the Communist community. For example, the Rumanian Communists even unearthed the writings of Professor Nicolai Iorga, an eminent prewar Rumanian nationalist ideologue, who could not have won Rumanian Communist endorsement by his opposition to industrialization, but who clearly made a niche for himself by his stress on the special mission of Rumania, an isolated outpost of Latin civilization in a sea of Slavic barbarity, as a link between the Byzantine east and the Latin west.*

With the older, Stalin-trained generation of leaders everywhere on the wane, East Europe was gradually being taken over by new elites, which were only beginning to define their own indigenous relationship to their societies. It would be difficult to describe these elites with a single label, although their outlook can best be described with the term "domesticism" (see Chapter 3, p. 52). Few of them were Moscow-trained; many matured at a time when Stalinism was at its most decayed stage. Having witnessed the turmoil of de-Stalinization, to them Moscow could no longer appear as the center of infallibility. Largely of peasant and proletarian background, they mixed their Communist categories of thought, acquired in party training, with intense nationalism and a strong proclivity toward political and ideological intolerance. Trained as bureaucrats in a setting in

---

* The rehabilitation of Professor Iorga may have a special meaning for the Rumanian-Soviet relationship: doubtless, the Soviets recall that in June 1940 Professor Iorga urged the Rumanian king not to accept the Soviet ultimatum demanding Bessarabia but to resist, by force if necessary. (Gafencu, *Preliminaires de la Guerre à l'Est*, p. 292, as cited by H. Seton-Watson, *The East European Revolution*, New York, 1956, p. 61.)

which nothing but the state (or the party bureaucracy) mattered, they tended to accept statism as a way of life, while their social origins made them impatient of the revisionist liberalism of the intellectuals. In many respects, they were not unlike some of the prewar East European social-fascists: radical modernizers, statists, authoritarians, vague doctrinairians, nationalists, chauvinists, anti-intellectuals, even (whenever convenient) anti-Semites.[8] *

The increased national parochialism of the East European Communist elites made it easier for the traditional ethnic-national and territorial issues again to surface, and — as the Albanians correctly noted in the citation at the beginning of this chapter — this was bound to affect relations among the Communist states. The list of potentially disruptive and far from dormant territorial disputes capable of bitterly complicating the stability of the Soviet-East European bloc and certainly providing great opportunities for Chinese mischief-making, was quite impressive. At some critical juncture Bulgaria could have claims on Yugoslavia (Macedonia); Albania on Yugoslavia (Kosmet); Hungary on Rumania (Transylvania); Rumania on the Soviet Union (Bessarabia); Poland on Czechoslovakia (Teschen); Poland on the Soviet Union (Lvov, etc.); East Germany on Poland (Szczecin or Wroclaw). In the first four cases, the situation could be emotionally dramatized by the presence in the disputed territories of sizable minorities of the same nationality as the potential claimant and, generally, subjected to traditional discrimination. Already in 1964 murmurings about Bessarabia could be heard in official Rumanian circles. If the conflicting Chinese-Soviet claims and the Chinese-Mongolian aspirations were also listed, territorial irredenta in the Communist camp become quite impressive, indeed. (It would seem that of all the Communist countries, Cuba alone did not have a territorial claim to make on another Communist country!) Given the prevailing mood, Chinese endorsement of, say, the Bulgarian claim against Yugoslavia or of the Rumanian claim against the Soviet Union, could have a greater impact on the attitude of these countries toward the Peking-Moscow dispute than the fiercest ideological cannonades. Some day the temptation for Peking to play the territorial game may prove irresistible.[9]

As the Communist elites become more nationalized, their prevailing domesticism tends to become transformed into narrow national

---

* In Poland, for example, some of the younger Communist leaders tried to exploit the fact that during the Stalinist period several key officials of the secret police (tried after 1956 for their brutality) were Jewish.

ism. With Moscow's declining capacity to restrain these conflicts, the effect on Communist unity is bound to be disruptive. Moreover, the nationalization of the Communist elites in itself accentuates potentially explosive tensions in some of the multinational Communist states. In Czechoslovakia, according to mounting evidence, the problem of Slovak nationalism has been becoming more acute in the sixties. Stalinist efforts to suppress it merely multiplied Slovak grievances. In the post-Stalinist context, Prague has had little choice but to strive to pacify the Slovaks, so far through limited concessions but concessions nonetheless. This in turn has prompted Slovak Communist spokesmen to demand publicly "a situation of equality" with the Czechs, in effect a more federal arrangement.[10] Similarly, in Yugoslavia all indications point to intensified tensions among the constituent republics, with more developed Croatia and Slovenia resenting the burdens imposed on them for the sake of over-all national economic development. On November 9, 1965, Tito publicly warned of the possibility of "open national unrest," and it is certain that the struggle for succession in Yugoslavia will be dominated by the national question.

Elsewhere, the struggle for power may focus directly on the question of the degree to which a particular regime ought to identify its interests with Moscow and/or how rapidly it ought to tackle the task of its de-Stalinization. The Bulgarian military conspiracy of April 1965 may be regarded in that respect as symptomatic. According to the limited information available, the plotters were mainly former Communist underground fighters who wished to break with Zhivkov's supine submission to Moscow. Theirs was not an anti-Communist conspiracy and their success would have meant that even Bulgaria was embarking on the road followed by Rumania or perhaps Yugoslavia. Their failure was not as important as the fact that within the Bulgarian ruling elite such an initiative could have germinated and actually been attempted. Elsewhere, however, opposite tendencies may appear. It is likely that the Yugoslav struggle for succession will involve also the issue of Yugoslavia's relationship with Moscow, in addition to the national question mentioned above. There is considerable evidence to suggest that a faction basing itself on the party *apparat* will argue that the preservation of Communist rule in Yugoslavia requires a reversal in domestic democratization and a development of closer ties with Moscow.

De-satellitization and de-Stalinization were thus extremely volatile and contradictory processes. They did not point in a straight line in an evolutionary direction toward liberalism or social democracy. A more likely prospect for the immediate future was that of Communist bureaucratic and national dictatorships. Perhaps eventually in some cases these could give way to more democratic systems, but too many altogether unpredictable factors cloud the picture to permit a confident forecast. In post-Stalinist East Europe the element of historical contingency was all the more important because the political systems had not yet fully defined themselves nor had they established a firm social bond with their societies. Although the political elites felt more secure, they still feared their peoples and were unwilling to permit them political self-determination. (Large-scale arrests in Hungary, effected during late 1965 and early 1966, testified to the difficulty encountered by Kadar in finding the borderline between moderation and evolutionary threat to the stability of the Communist regime.) In such a setting, accidental elements played a greater role than otherwise might be the case. That is why behind the ruling elites' new sense of confidence there still lurked a gnawing realization of their lingering dependence on Moscow which tempered even their own nationalism.

THE RUMANIAN SELF-ASSERTION

The contradictions inherent in the processes of de-Stalinization and de-satellitization were best exemplified by the Rumanian self-assertion against Soviet dictation. That self-assertion involved neither a tragic rebellion on the Hungarian model nor a dramatic change in leadership as during the Polish October. Effected by the established party leadership, the Rumanian self-assertion nonetheless constituted a far-reaching defiance of Soviet plans by a geographically isolated Communist state, thus signifying the further transformation in relations among the Communist states.[11]

Because of all the changes that transpired in the Communist camp in the course of the last decade, a tendency has developed among some analysts to antedate all conflicts among Communist states, and certainly in the Rumanian-Soviet case much evidence could be produced to show that tensions had long existed in the Moscow-Bucharest relationship. Clearly, Gheorghiu-Dej and his Rumanian Communist underground fighters resented the assertion of leadership by the Moscow-trained Pauker-Luca factions, finally purged in 1952 (see p. 95). In the course of the November 1961 Central Committee Plenum, devoted largely to a rehashing of past infighting among the Rumanian party oligarchs, a great deal of light was thrown on the bitter factional conflicts between the two groups. The "Muscovites" were accused of having opposed the Rumanian party's initiative in staging the Bucharest coup of August 1944 and of having preferred the Red Army to occupy the country; of having decided "while still outside the country" (that is, in Moscow) to seize the party's leadership on their arrival in Bucharest and for that purpose of having created in the Soviet Union a so-called "buro"; of having instigated massive purges on the Soviet model; of having even tapped Gheorghiu-Dej's telephone; and generally of having pursued an antinational course.[12] Their elimination in 1952 was described by Gheorghiu-Dej, its chief beneficiary, as nothing less than "a turning point in the life of our Party." [13]

It is noteworthy, however, that Gheorghiu-Dej's leadership was thereafter secure and the composition of the Politburo remained remarkably homogeneous. After 1956 a party faction, in part supported by the former Muscovites, did attempt to use the Soviet de-Stalinization to embarrass the Gheorghiu-Dej leadership. It was, however, promptly crushed and in the November 1961 discussions it was conveniently bracketed with the Stalinists Pauker and Luca as opponents of Gheorghiu-Dej's "patriotic" line. There is no evidence — nor Rumanian hints — that in this latter instance Gheorghiu-Dej's opponents had Moscow's backing. Accordingly, by the sixties Gheorghiu-Dej's leadership was reasonably well established, and he could tackle the Rumanian-Soviet relationship from the position of a firmly entrenched Stalinist political system. Thus what Harold Lasswell called "restriction through partial incorporation" [14] applied particularly well to the Chinese and more recently to the Rumanians: By adopting basic Stalinist patterns, they used the earlier "Soviet national Communism" against the Soviet leaders. The achievement of true Communist internationalism under Soviet direction was thus paradoxically inhibited by the spread of earlier Soviet methods: "The specific process by which the universal was parochialized was that of partial adaptation and countersymbolization." [15]

Questions of economic policy involving the bloc as well as the general issue of the proper character of relations among the Communist leaderships seem to have been paramount in the appearance of the Soviet-Rumanian divergence. These questions emerged in the late fifties and gained urgency in the sixties, as the Soviet leadership groped for some new basis for unity. The Soviet-Rumanian divergence in turn brought to the surface the long-suppressed Rumanian national resentment of Soviet (Russian) exploitation and territorial expansion at Rumania's expense. The Rumanian leadership found it convenient to identify with this resentment and it, no doubt, also at least in part shared it. As a consequence, Rumanian domestic life became dominated by an intense revival of nationalism, including even an inclination to defend the behavior of the prewar Rumanian government against Soviet critics.[16]

Rumanian opposition to Khrushchev's schemes of closer economic integration manifested itself in the 1962 sessions of CEMA, and some reservations were shared by other member states, presumably fearful that Khrushchev's plans would encroach on their independence as well.[17] The Rumanians were probably also emboldened by the fiasco of Soviet policy during the Cuban missile crisis and by the relative success of both Chinese and Albanian defiance. They strongly opposed the Soviet argument, supported by the more industrially developed East Germany and Czechoslovakia, that the "division of labor" in the Communist world should be based on "the principle of efficiency," which could only mean that less industrialized nations, such as Rumania, should settle for slower industrial development and for providing the others with the raw material base and agricultural support for their further industrial expansion.*

The Rumanian response was explicit: "Just as on the domestic scene an absolutist criterion of efficiency cannot be countenanced, so in the field of specialization and cooperation between the socialist countries economic efficiency and profitability cannot be accepted as the one and only criterion for evaluating new economic steps." The Rumanian spokesman further asserted: "Building communism on a worldwide scale is incompatible with the notion of dividing countries into industrial states and agrarian states, into developed countries and underdeveloped countries."[18] East European economists who supported the Soviet proposal were even accused of repeating the views of capitalist economists.[19]

Moscow's capacity to respond effectively to the Rumanian challenge was limited. West Europe could step in and offer the Ru-

* A Polish-Russian social theorist and revolutionary, W. Machajski (1866–1926), developed the theory that the revolution would produce not a true proletarian democracy but merely the dictatorship of the more skilled workers and the disaffected intellectuals over the working masses. Thus continuous pressure from below would be necessary even after a successful revolution for the achievement of true social justice. The ruling parties of the less developed and more aggrieved states could begin to feel that Machajski's theory might apply to the bloc; its inclination to express the interests of the more developed states seems analogous to the danger of the revolution being managed purely in the interest of the intelligentsia, as Machajski warned.

manians alternative trade arrangements, thereby eliminating the threat of a Soviet economic boycott. Moreover, internal economic difficulties in the Soviet Union and in East Europe reduced the capacity and the willingness of these states to engage in a common effort to pressure the Rumanians into changing their posture. Finally, the Sino-Soviet crisis made the Soviets more wary in asserting their will lest an excessive display of power prejudice the support that Moscow was soliciting within the international Communist movement. The Kremlin was keenly aware that the Chinese were striving to exploit the Rumanian charges of discriminatory treatment, with Peking pointedly observing that "we hold that it is necessary to transform the present Council of Economic Mutual Assistance of socialist countries to accord with the principle of proletarian internationalism and to turn this organization, which is now solely controlled by the leaders of the CPSU, into one based on genuine equality and mutual benefit, which the fraternal countries in the socialist camp may join of their own free will." [20]

Moscow's reticence may have encouraged the Rumanians to issue the remarkably vehement public declaration of April 22, 1964, which arrogantly criticized both the Chinese and the Soviet behavior during the Sino-Soviet dispute, vigorously rejected the Soviet prescriptions for CEMA, and emphatically asserted the Rumanian right of independence in all policies. The comments on CEMA and Communist interstate relations were especially damaging to the Soviet effort to build its own community in Europe. Supranational management and planning bodies were bluntly described as "not in keeping with the principles which underlie relations among the socialist countries. The idea of a single planning body for all CEMA countries has the most serious economic and political implications . . . superstate or extrastate bodies would make of sovereignty an idea without any content." The Rumanians stressed their determination to "develop [Rumania's] economic links with all states irrespective of their social system" and noted, with a touch of irony probably meant for the East Germans and the Czechs, that "undoubtedly, if some socialist countries see fit to adopt forms of cooperation in direct relations different from those unanimously agreed upon within CEMA, that is a subject which exclusively concerns those countries and can be decided by them alone in a sovereign way."

The Rumanians also made important comments on the general subject of relations among Communist states. In a remark pointedly aimed at the Soviet inclination to equate their own good with the good of the Communist world, they noted that "no specific or individual interests can be presented as general interests, as objective requirements for the development of the socialist system." They openly criticized past Soviet practices which had gone "as far as the removal and replacement of leading cadres and even of entire central committees, as far as imposing leaders from without, the suppression of distinguished leading cadres of various parties, as far as censuring and even dissolving Communist parties." The Rumanian statement left no doubt that in its view both domestic and foreign policies were "each party's exclusive right" and that "no party has or can have a privileged place, or can impose its line or opinions on other parties."

The defiant tone of the Rumanian declaration was underscored by its issuance a mere three weeks after an eloquent personal plea by Khrushchev for greater interdependence in the Communist Euro-Asian community. Speaking on April 3 in the course of his visit to Hungary, the Soviet leader had urged more coordination among CEMA and Warsaw Treaty countries, not only on economic matters but also on foreign policy. The Rumanians instead advanced the proposition — almost the opposite of the Soviet view — that each nation must first prepare its own economic plan before engaging in bilateral and multilateral arrangements with others. It was ironic to think that the Soviet spokesmen in the past had frequently cited the principle of unanimity in CEMA's operations as proof that international Communism inherently respects national sovereignty. The Rumanians, by asserting their right to veto, demonstrated that national sovereignty can frustrate common Communist policies.

This stand, as well as the already noted Rumanian "neutrality" in the Sino-Soviet dispute, the Rumanian lack of enthusiasm for strengthening the Warsaw Treaty, and the open Rumanian interest in some sort of Balkan semi-neutrality, must have deeply disturbed the Kremlin leadership. Yet short of an invasion, there was little it could do. Economic sanctions had not worked in regard to poorer Communist states than Rumania. The threat of backing Hungarian claims on Rumanian-held Transylvania was a double-edged sword, for it could precipitate open Rumanian airing of the Bessarabian issue. While Rumanian irredenta in themselves need not worry Moscow, an open territorial crisis, given all the other complications prevailing in the Communist camp, certainly could not serve Soviet interests.

Gheorghiu-Dej died in March 1965, and the Soviet leadership took advantage of the change of government in Bucharest to seek a modus vivendi. The Rumanian leadership, headed by the new Party Secretary, Nicolae Ceausescu, typical of the "new men" gaining power throughout East Europe, was also apparently not prepared to push the existing divergencies to a showdown. Thus both Moscow and Bucharest agreed to disagree, which meant, in effect, that the Rumanian self-assertion had been successfully consummated. Whether it had been contained was another matter. The Rumanians began by emulating the Poles in the practice of "domesticism" but by the mid-sixties they were beginning to seek the status of Yugoslavia. Indeed, at one point even Tito urged the Rumanians to exercise self-restraint in the pursuit of their independence.[21] Nonetheless, to the Rumanians the warmth of the Moscow-Belgrade relationship was argument enough that they too could have normal relations with Moscow without necessarily being limited by membership in CEMA or even in the Warsaw Pact. Thus more subtly and hence more dangerously the Rumanians were reviving the challenge of nonaligned Communism for which Nagy had paid such a high price. Given the Soviet stake in good relations with Yugoslavia, the Rumanians posed an argument that Moscow could not easily refute and it pointed up the dilemma that the Soviet Union was increasingly likely to face as the East European states ceased being mere satellites.

EMANCIPATION AND INTERDEPENDENCE

In the mid-sixties the East European regimes were still residually dependent on Soviet support. But this alone did not resolve the question of how to find a basis for unity in the increasingly accepted condition of ideological and institutional diversity. Indeed, as Khrushchev already found, any single formula tended to create new tensions. The fading ideology, although alone incapable of assuring unity, gave all the elites at least a sense of shared historical identification which meant, however vaguely, that there was still something that they had in common. If a sense of general interest could somehow be added to it, thereby compensating for the declined factor of direct Soviet control, the process of disintegration could perhaps be halted or slowed.

The formula could no longer be the same for all the Communist states. Their elites tended to perceive the external world in rather more parochial perspectives than was the case with their predecessors. The great struggle as seen from Moscow, not to say from Peking, seemed less vital to a Lenart than to a Gottwald, to a Ceausescu than to a Gheorghiu-Dej. That is why de Gaulle's concept of a "European Europe" of nationalist states stirred such genuine interest among the East European rulers, irrespective of Moscow's obvious desire to exploit it tactically against the United States. To the East European rulers, it offered an image of the future in which they could continue to enjoy both the advantages of their bureaucratic national Communist leaderships and of eventual Soviet protection, while also meeting some of the domestic pressures for closer ties with Europe.[22] Most of them, if they could dare, would probably prefer to abstain from participation in the Sino-Soviet wrangles and emulate the Rumanians who simply refused to come to the March 1964 Moscow meeting. Even the East Germans defined their attitude to that dispute in part on the basis of their own special interest: fearful that a complete Sino-Soviet split would drive the Chinese into a Peking-Bonn axis, they occasionally displayed their lack of enthusiasm for the more bellicose Soviet anti-Chinese moves.[23]

The variety in external perspectives was matched by the diversity and the extent of East European dependence on Soviet support. For the East German regime, direct Soviet military presence (or, at the very least, popular conviction that Soviet troops would reenter in the event of any upheaval) was necessary for survival. For Gomulka or Novotny, Soviet presence in East Germany checkmated even the most hotheaded domestic rebel. It was thus useful in overcoming domestic opposition and (as noted) was also helpful in turn in making their independence of Soviet control more secure. Neither therefore needed or wanted Soviet occupation forces in his country, and only two Soviet divisions were stationed in Poland as of 1965. However, both Gomulka and Novotny found it convenient to stress the German danger, and continued West German ambiguity concerning the territorial ambitions of a reunited Germany made it easier for them to emphasize the vital importance of their alliances with Moscow. Indeed, on that issue there was remarkable unity of mind among Communists and non-Communists, and this feeling of dependence on Soviet protection contained much of the drive toward greater emancipation.*

It may be assumed that this relationship would retain some vitality even if ideological bonds were to erode altogether. On the Soviet side the Soviet interest in retaining a stable relationship of accepted predominance in Poland, Czechoslovakia, and East Germany was also reinforced by more traditional national considerations, in which se-

---

* That is why Gomulka in early 1966 launched a violent campaign against Cardinal Wyszynski, when the latter had pleaded for Polish-German reconciliation; Gomulka saw in this the danger of being deprived of his principal asset, the anti-German feelings of the masses.

curity factors played not the least role. Thus ideological erosion in Moscow would not necessarily eliminate the Soviet concern over the future political complexion of this key region. Even a more traditional-nationalist regime in Moscow would still strive to prevent qualitatively decisive political changes in the area immediately west of the Soviet Union, although conceivably someday a less self-consciously Communist regime in Moscow might prefer more popularly accepted regimes in Prague and Warsaw. In any case, Moscow, in its relations with Prague and Warsaw, also increasingly emphasized the binding elements of common national interest.

For Hungary, no consideration of national interest justified continued Soviet military occupation. Much of Nagy's appeal was derived from his plea for neutralism and still in the mid-sixties a great deal of Hungarian internal propaganda was devoted to discrediting the attractive power of this idea. Kadar's regime strove to develop domestic popularity and in many respects it succeeded, but primarily in terms of the Hungarian realization (often misunderstood by Western observers) that his regime was the best possible, *given* the fact of continued Soviet domination. Although in form that domination was no longer so visible and exploitative as under Rakosi — and hence less likely to offend national sensitivities — it was still a political reality. The absence of any underlying national bonds between Hungary and Russia inescapably meant that increased Hungarian autonomy would revive pressures in favor of Hungarian neutralism. This posed a danger both for the ruling Communist elite and for Moscow, given its still ideological interests in international Communism. Thus Budapest and the Kremlin had a joint stake in retaining a close relationship, although no longer one of blatant subservience.

Soviet influence in the Balkans receded dramatically during the twenty years after World War II. In 1945 the Soviet Union seemed firmly entrenched on the shores of the Adriatic and on the borders of Greece and Turkey. Twenty years later, Yugoslavia was a courted ally; Albania a hostile deviant, issuing the most vociferous denunciations of the Soviet leadership; Rumania at least as autonomous and domestically oriented as was Poland in 1957; while Bulgaria had just weathered a domestic upheaval, which was clearly focused on the question of the Soviet-Bulgarian relationship. Even the Zhivkov regime, normally a pliant satellite, was beginning to stir, presumably under the influence of the Soviet acceptance of Tito and the success of Rumania's policy. Improving relations with its neighbors, Bulgaria went on record in the joint Bulgarian-Rumanian declaration as believing that "every party, while creatively applying Marxist-Leninist teachings under the concrete conditions and under a different stage of development of its country, has the right itself to determine its own political life . . ." [24] As was aptly observed by a historian of Eastern Europe: "By 1965, Russian influence in the Balkans had declined almost to the level of eighty years before . . ." [25]

Differing intensities of commitment to the concept of Communist unity thus merged with different national priorities. The result was a diversity in approaches to the question of the preferred form of relations among Communist states. Some ruling leaderships, notably those of East Germany and Czechoslovakia, for a long time expressed a preference for multilateral arrangements for East Europe and the Soviet Union. They saw in them an obstacle to the spread of domestic revisionism and to the pursuit of narrower national goals. It was also evident, however, that both East Germany and Czechoslovakia had a specific economic interest in economic multilateralism, especially in the so-called "socialist division of labor." If accepted by all the Communist states, it would perpetuate the somewhat favored economic status of East Germany and Czechoslovakia, as the most industrially advanced Communist states, and it would mitigate against the likelihood of political changes in individual Communist states disrupting East German and Czechoslovak long-range industrial development.[26]

Bilateralism was preferred by the Poles and the Rumanians; by both in political matters but with the Rumanians expressing an unambiguous preference for it in economics as well.[27] While bilateralism offered both the Poles and the Rumanians greater opportunity for asserting and protecting their domestic autonomy, different Polish economic needs made the Poles apply a more flexible standard to the question of sovereignty than was the case with the Rumanians.* Short of investment funds and in need of greater flexibility in converting bloc funds, the Poles pressed for greater multilateral cooperation in investments and were instrumental in the promotion of the bloc clearing facilities and a CEMA bank.[28]

Regional arrangements, so feared by Stalin, were also gaining greater favor as a means of creating a framework for unity. In politics, it was reflected by persistent Yugoslav and Rumanian exploration of

---

* The different Czech, East German, Polish, and Rumanian interests in inter-Communist economic cooperation and particularly in CEMA were evident in the varying emphases placed on the desirability of such cooperation in the addresses delivered to the Twenty-third CPSU Congress in March 1966 by Ulbricht, Novotny, Gomulka, and Ceausescu. The last did not even mention CEMA.

an atom-free zone in the Balkans, a concept which by itself did not go counter to Soviet foreign policy interests but which did carry with it the germ of regional political solidarity. Poland, Czechoslovakia, and East Germany were the principal foci of proposals like the Rapacki Plan or the Gomulka Plan, both designed to create a special zone of security in Central Europe. Again, it would be a gross exaggeration even to imply that these proposals went counter to Soviet needs; the recognition by the West of East Germany, which was implicit in both proposals, was an objective long sought by Moscow. However, in some Central European minds there still lurked the notion that schemes such as the above would be the first, most timid step toward eventual regional cooperation, with perhaps the long-range effect of diminishing the extent of direct and potential Soviet sway over the area.

Regional economic undertakings were also gaining favor. Cooperative ventures to utilize the Danube moved apace, after having been stymied for years by Soviet anti-Titoism. Schemes such as Intermetall — a belated Communist approximation of the Coal and Steel Community — as well as joint Polish-Czech-East German investment ventures were meant to overcome, on a purely rational basis, the legacy of Stalinist and even pre-Stalinist East European autarky. Unlike CEMA, whose membership included even Mongolia and was clearly ideological-political in origin, the scope of these regional initiatives was determined by purely economic considerations. (For a more detailed discussion, see the next chapter.)

As a result of these varying interests and multiple initiatives, it was increasingly difficult to find a common unifying denominator for all the pro-Soviet Communist states. As late as 1959 the Soviet leaders still entertained some rather utopian conceptions concerning the long-range effects of intensified economic integration within CEMA. Speaking to the East Germans, Khrushchev painted a vision of such intimate economic cooperation among Communist states that "in these conditions the old concepts of borders as such will disappear. With the victory of Communism on a worldwide scale, state borders will disappear, as Marxism-Leninism teaches. In all likelihood only ethnic borders will survive for a time and even these will probably exist only as a convention. Naturally these frontiers, if they can be called frontiers at all, will have no border guards, customs officials, or incidents. They will simply demarcate the historically formed location of a given people or nationality in a given territory . . . The foundations for Communist relations among peoples have been laid in the Soviet Union and in the entire socialist camp . . . Extensive cooperation in all spheres of economic, social, political, and cultural life is developing among the sovereign countries of the socialist camp. Speaking of the future, it seems to me that the further development of the socialist countries will in all probability proceed along the lines of consolidation of the single-world socialist economic system. The economic barriers which divided our countries under capitalism will fall one after another. The common economic basis of world socialism will grow stronger, eventually making the question of borders a pointless one." [29] Again in 1964 Khrushchev urged the East Europeans to consider that "it would be expedient to think jointly about those organizational forms that would make it possible to improve the constant exchange of opinions and the coordination of foreign policy." [30]

Khrushchev's pleas notwithstanding, effective integration of Communist-type economies seemed unlikely unless a common objective, enunciated through a common plan, came to be accepted by all the Communist states concerned. This would require either an unprecedented identity of views or the presence of a paramount political authority.* Neither condition prevailed in the East Europe of the sixties, with the Rumanian unwillingness to subordinate its sovereignty being merely the most extreme example. Paradoxically, the economic reforms undertaken by several East European states away from the Soviet-type economy could eventually eliminate the structural impediments toward more effective economic cooperation inherent in the more rigid command-type economies. However, to the extent that these reforms also reflected genuine domestic pressures and needs, they reinforced the trend toward greater concern over domestic interests, and reduced the likelihood that national considerations would be sacrificed for the sake of more abstract conceptions of Communist unity.

---

* As Professor A. Zauberman noted in his analysis of Communist economic integration: "The process of integration will be fully consummated only if and when the orbit economies are directed as a single unit in accordance with a single plan drawn up and implemented from a single center of authority. This would practically make the forging of an *organic political entity* a necessary precondition for full-fledged economic integration . . . In this writer's view, the experience of CEMA lends strong support to the proposition — theoretically evolved by the well-known American economist, Professor Jacob Viner — that it is far more difficult to integrate centrally-planned socialist economies than market economies, without the suppression of national identities. Herein lies the fundamental dilemma of the Soviet planners" (italics in original). A. Zauberman, "Soviet Bloc Economic Integration," *Problems of Communism*, July–August 1959.

As a result, the Soviet Union itself was increasingly relying on long-term bilateral deals, especially with its key East European economic partners, East Germany and Czechoslovakia, with Soviet industrial development more dependent on these bilateral treaties than on multilateral arrangements. But even here, growing sensitivity of the East Europeans to their own economic needs was creating difficulties. In late 1965 there were persistent reports of Czechoslovak objections to the October 5 Soviet-Czech trade agreement,[31] and even some Czech press reports of minor friction in trade matters.[32] An even more dramatic example of growing East European unwillingness any longer to subordinate their needs to that of Moscow was the suicide on December 3, 1965, of the chief East German planner, Erich Apel, immediately after the signing of an East German-Soviet trade agreement on the same day.*

The difficulties in creating an economic framework for unity led the Soviet leaders to explore further the possibilities inherent in the Warsaw Treaty for developing a common political organ. In his 1964 remarks about the desirability of further institutionalization of relationships, Khrushchev explicitly mentioned both CEMA and the Warsaw Treaty. There was also considerable evidence that the once largely paper and dormant provisions of the Warsaw Treaty were being infused with life. "Specifically, Soviet policy served to elevate the importance of the military contributions of the other Pact countries in over-all Soviet planning; to extend the mission of the East European Pact forces from primary emphasis on air defense to a more active joint role in defensive and offensive theater operations; and to promote joint training and re-equipment of the Pact forces commensurate with their apparently enlarged responsibilities."[33]

Brezhnev has continued to place major emphasis on "the task of further perfecting the organization of the Warsaw Treaty,"[34] and the Soviet leadership revealed that talks were held with the East Europeans concerning establishing "within the framework of that pact a permanent and prompt mechanism for considering pressing problems."[35] In striving to stimulate a positive East European response, the Soviet leadership placed primary emphasis on the West German threat, including the allegedly growing probability of West German access to nuclear weapons. Moscow could quite sensibly calculate that this would evoke the greatest response from Poland, Czechoslovakia, and East Germany, which along with the Soviet

* As Richard Lowenthal aptly observed: "This shows what happens to an East German who imagines he could act like a Rumanian."

Union were described in some Communist commentaries as "the first strategic echelon" of the Communist military system.[36]

However, reliance on the popularly felt national interests and fears of the East European Communist states was a double-edged sword. Evoking the West German threat could mobilize some Polish, Czech, and East German support. By the same token, as it increased, say, the Polish interest in strengthening the Warsaw Treaty organization, it reduced the Hungarian, Bulgarian, and Rumanian interest none of whom particularly feared the Germans. There have been reports that the Rumanians refused to participate in 1965 in joint exercises held outside of Rumania,[37] and, at a time when the first "echelon" was stressing the growing German danger and the thickening war clouds because of the Vietnamese conflict, Bucharest announced a reduction in the duration of compulsory military service (thereby indirectly reducing its standing forces). In this way the effort to achieve unity both on a national and on an ideological basis was resulting in a highly differentiated condition of some cohesion, some compliance, and some conflict.

The developments since 1956 have thus changed the nature of direct Soviet power in the bloc. In most cases, that power today could be defined as "a last contingency power" — that is, the Soviets would be almost certain to intervene by force to keep a Communist state from defecting to the "imperialist" side, but they no longer have at their disposal the more intricate combinations of power, authority and consent, or the direct and indirect channels of control that Stalin wielded for the purpose of preventing most of the national elite from taking even a limited step that displeased him. Furthermore some of the rulers — especially those who in the past were more obedient to the Soviets — have already manifested a psychological condition of "ecstatic emancipation" from their former mentors which often turns to violent hostility.[38] This was very much the case with the Yugoslavs after 1958; with the Albanians in 1960; with the Rumanians in 1964. Tomorrow it could be the Bulgarians or the Czechs.

Moscow must therefore be very careful in how it handles its junior allies. Economic levers, political displeasure, and induced isolation are the means that Moscow can still apply, but in each case it must now weigh the possibility that pressure can be counterproductive and that a party can turn to the Chinese, or even to the West, for help (particularly if economic levers are used). The Kremlin can still intrigue within a ruling elite, taking advantage of factions but Gomulka's and, more recently, Hoxha's and Gheorghiu-Dej's experience suggests that this is not always an effective lever. Furthermore, such a maneuver puts a premium on united leadership in Moscow; a disunited Kremlin would find it hard to play the factional game.

In politics one change has a way of leading to another. At the November 1960 conference the Soviet Union still commanded the loyalty of the vast majority of the parties, and even those favoring the Chinese probably would have sided with the CPSU if the chips were down. Yet almost a third of the invited parties refused to attend the March 1965 Moscow meeting. At some future conference the CPSU may be faced with more opposition. It simply no longer follows that what is good for the Soviet Union is automatically accepted as good by the other Communist states.

18 / THE SOVIET ALLIANCE SYSTEM*

DURING Stalin's lifetime the Soviet bloc operated essentially through a relatively simple subordination of the various units to the dictator's will, generally expressed by indirect methods of police and party control. This rather informal organization reflected in part the old dictator's specific political style; in part it was a function of the relatively immature stage of the bloc's development after the war. But forms which sufficed during this early period rapidly became obsolete as the bloc matured. With crises in inter-Communist relations, the need for new and more complex interrelationships between these states became apparent.[1] Real efforts for the consolidation of the East European part of the camp began in the early 1960's.

MULTILATERAL INSTITUTIONAL TIES

The existing formal institutional ties among the Communist state became much more prominent after Stalin's death; however, the basis for the development of many of these ties was laid under the dictator. Such things as relatively uniform domestic systems of law of central planning, of bureaucratic institutions, and of legislation came into being in those states which were subject to Soviet control. This standardization of institutions within the Soviet bloc was introduced in some cases because of Soviet military presence, but more often because of the unity of doctrine and outlook held by their various leaders, many of whom had spent a significant part of their lives in the USSR. Attempting to build Communist systems in their countries from the foundations up, these leaders, usually with Soviet pressure or encouragement, imported en masse the institutions of their Soviet model. Some, such as those connected with economic autarky, were taken over without much discrimination or realization that they had developed out of the specific historical experience of the USSR and did not necessarily fit the environment and tradition of postwar Eastern Europe. Although this has been a significant cause of difficulties within the bloc ever since, the similarity of these

* Prepared by David L. Williams, in consultation with the author, on the basis of the author's "The Organization of the Communist Camp," *World Politics*, XI (January 1961). Mr. Williams' major contribution is gratefully acknowledged.

domestic social, economic, legal, and political institutions has provided an underlying unity which has undoubtedly facilitated the efforts to unify the bloc as a whole by means of various interstate ties.[2]

The two most important multilateral organs binding the European Communist states together are the Council of Economic Mutual Assistance (CEMA) and the Warsaw Treaty Organization (WTO). There is no organ officially including all Communist states. It is symptomatic of the post-Stalin diversity in the orbit that efforts to create a new supraparty bloc organ were resisted by some of the leadership in and out of the bloc, and that the unity of even the European part of the camp has had to be promoted through the utilization of institutions existing prior to 1956. With the increasing diversity and nationalism within the bloc in recent times, even CEMA and WTO have had a difficult time maintaining themselves as agencies for the articulation of common purposes and the promotion of cohesion and integration among the Communist states.

On May 14, 1955, under the Treaty of Friendship, Cooperation, and Mutual Assistance, WTO was established. It serves externally as a counter to NATO and internally as a formal device for the perpetuation of close ties between the Soviet Union and the European Communist countries. The WTO is thus both a political and military organization, the importance of which, as a unifying factor in the bloc, has increased as disunity has appeared in CEMA. Indeed, given the relative success of Rumania's opposition to CEMA, the WTO has become the most important multilateral organization binding the European Communist states together. Previous to its establishment, military policy for the bloc had been, for the most part, handled within the Soviet Army. However, the beginnings of organization can be seen in the August 1952 military conference in Prague. This conference, attended by representatives of the USSR, Bulgaria, Czechoslovakia, Hungary, Poland, Rumania, and China, was for the purpose of reorganizing the satellite armies — expanding and equipping them. The conference was reported to have established a military coordinating committee under Marshal N. A. Bulganin.[3] China was associated with WTO at the beginning, but only as an observer, never as a member. The same is true of North Korea, North Vietnam, and Mongolia (which joined in 1959). However, all the Asian Communist states (except for Mongolia) and Albania (which had been a formal member) withdrew from participation of any kind by the summer of 1962.

The founding meeting of the WTO provided for a Political Consultative Committee that was empowered to establish supplementary multilateral organs. The Committee exercised this power in the January 1956 Prague meeting when it set up a regular secretariat with representatives from member states and a standing commission for foreign policy coordination (the Committee for Foreign Policy).[4] The 1956 meeting also decided that the Committee was to meet not less than twice yearly. In fact, its subsequent meeting was more than two years later (May 27, 1958), and in the course of ten years there have been only seven meetings.* So far the meetings of the Political Consultative Committee have served primarily as forums for the articulation of a common stand on important international issues and, in effect, for implicitly delegating the USSR to be the spokesman of the bloc in dealing with the West.†

The meetings of the Political Consultative Committee have generally lasted only one or two days and have, for the most part, taken place in Moscow. Sometimes there have been follow-up meetings of bloc party leaders (for example, June 1962 and July 1963). The January 1965 meeting was an exception to this pattern. It took place in Warsaw, unlike the previous meetings, but like them it lasted only two days and echoed the Soviet position against Western plans for a multilateral nuclear force and for giving nuclear weapons to West Germany. (There is some speculation that there was more debate at this meeting than at previous ones because of the members' demand that the Soviet Union give them nuclear weapons. Soviet statements stress that their nuclear power is sufficient to protect the bloc and that ground forces are still essential).[5] It appears that the Political Consultative Committee does not serve as an active policy-making agency in any real sense.

The WTO has political importance because (1) it provides a formal framework binding the various Communist states together, (2) it supplies a juridical basis for limiting the exercise of the individual states' sovereignty by forbidding their participation in other alliances (article 7), and (3) it serves as a useful forum for the articulation of unanimity, expressing ritualistically the bloc's support o

---

* The seven meetings of the Political Consultative Committee took place in January 1956, May 1958, February 1960, March 1961, June 1962, July 1963, January 196; See R. Garthoff, "The Military Establishment," *East Europe* (September 1965), pp 2–16.

† This does not, however, exclude a certain division of labor in dealing with the outside world: for example, the Polish initiative in the form of the Rapacki Plan the East German scheme for a Baltic Peace Zone; the Rumanian-Bulgarian plan for a Balkan Treaty; and so forth.

Soviet foreign policy initiatives versus the West. It is significant that one of the charges most often cited against Imre Nagy was that he violated the unity of the bloc through his unilateral decision to leave the Warsaw Pact. The Albanians, who stopped participating in 1960–1961, are a different case since the Soviet Union had broken off relations with them.

At the Prague meeting of the WTO in January 1956 a United Command was also established, and its formation was soon announced. Soviet Marshal Konev (succeeded in June 1960 by Marshal Grechko) was appointed commander in chief; another Soviet officer became joint chief of staff, and it was announced that the command head-quarters was to be situated in Moscow.[6] The defense ministers of the participating countries were to be deputy commanders in chief and to attend the sessions of the Political Consultative Committee.

Until the fall of 1961 the role of the commander in chief of WTO forces seemed to be mainly that of commander of Soviet forces on the Western front (in GDR, Poland, Hungary) and of some of the troops of WTO members. However, on September 8–9, 1961, Marshal Grechko held a conference in Warsaw of the defense ministers and chiefs of staff of WTO members to discuss practical measures for the strengthening of WTO defense capacities. Following this meeting, joint military exercises began for the first time. These have continued at the rate of at least two per year.* Each exercise normally involves the forces of several countries and is attended by the defense ministers of most of the WTO members. By at least September 1963 non-Soviet generals were in charge of some of the exercises. Rumania, despite its stand in relation to CEMA and the issue of national sovereignty, took part in some of the exercises in 1962, 1963, and 1964. However, its decision to reduce unilaterally its term of conscription in October 1964, and its lack of participation in the 1965 exercises, may have indicated its desire to express its independence in the military area also.

* Joint Exercises:
Autumn 1961 — USSR, Poland, Czechoslovakia, GDR
April 1962 — USSR, Hungary, Rumania
Autumn 1962 — Hungary, Rumania, Czechoslovakia
   "   " — USSR, Poland, GDR
June 1963 — USSR, Rumania, Bulgaria
September 1963 — Czechoslovakia, Poland, GDR
Autumn 1964 — USSR, Czechoslovakia, GDR
September 1964 — USSR, Rumania, Bulgaria
April 1965 — USSR, GDR
October 1965 — USSR, GDR, Poland, Czechoslovakia

The second major multilateral organization uniting the East European states and the Soviet Union is the Council of Economic Mutual Assistance. Originally set up in January 1949, it was activated only after Stalin's death, and particularly after the disruptive events of October–November 1956. The founding members were the USSR, Poland, Hungary, Czechoslovakia, Rumania, and Bulgaria. Subsequently, they were joined by Albania (February 1949–1961), East Germany (September 1950), and finally Mongolia (June 1962). The member-states of CEMA have about 330 million inhabitants, or about 10 per cent of the world population.

In its initial stage, CEMA was mainly restrictive in purpose, since it was designed to keep the European Communist states out of the Marshall Plan.[7] Following its founding session, CEMA held only two more plenary sessions during Stalin's lifetime: one in August 1949 in Sofia to arrange for scientific and technical cooperation and one in November 1950 in Moscow on interregional trade. During this early period, the organization concentrated primarily on redirecting the trade of its members toward each other. It may be surmised that it coordinated the development of the members' armaments industries during the Korean War.

After Stalin's death, plenary sessions became more regular and increasingly more important. At first primarily formal gatherings, they gradually developed into working sessions at which common decisions were formulated. In May 1956 the Council set up twelve standing commissions (7th session in Berlin), and others were created later. In 1958 multilateral action under CEMA began with the joint construction of an oil pipeline from the USSR to several of the East European countries and an international electricity grid for the bloc.

It was only in December 1959 that CEMA members finally agreed on a formal charter for the organization, setting forth CEMA's purpose, functions, powers, organs, and so on.[8] The charter came into force on April 13, 1960. At the same time a convention on immunities was signed which allowed an international civil service to be set up. The Secretariat of the Council had been mentioned in the founding statement of 1949 but did not begin to become active until after the 7th session of the Council in May 1956. According to the charter of 1960 the job of the Secretary, his deputies and staff was to prepare proposals for the consideration of the Council's organs, to coordinate the work of the standing commissions and to draft multilateral agreements. The headquarters were to be in Moscow and a Russian, N. V

Fadeyev, a former USSR Minister of Finance, became the Secretary.*

It was not until December 1961, when the Council adopted the Basic Principles of International Socialist Division of Labor, and June 1962, when top party leaders of the member countries approved these Basic Principles in Moscow, that CEMA gained the potential to be truly effective as an international planning and coordinating body. Under the new arrangement, in June 1962, the 16th session of the Council set up an Executive Committee, composed of the deputy premiers of the member governments, which was intended to have real decision-making power at the highest levels. The Executive Committee meets far more frequently than did the Council, approximately every two or three months, and has taken on most of the planning and coordinating functions that the less flexible sessions of the Council previously performed.[9]

The potentialities of the Executive Committee of CEMA have not been fully realized, however, largely because of the provision in the Charter of 1960 which states that: "The Council of Economic Mutual Assistance is established on the basis of the principle of the sovereign equality of all member countries of the Council" (article I). In addition, article IV states that "All recommendations and decisions by the Council shall be adopted only with the consent of the interested member countries . . ." and that "they shall not extend to countries which have declared their lack of interest in the question concerned." When Rumania began to express its opposition to supranational planning at the June 1962 and July 1963 meetings of party leaders of CEMA countries, and especially in the Rumanian declaration of April 1964, the rapid movement toward long-term planning, specialization, and integration was drastically slowed. Emphasis once again returned to bilateral agreements, coordination of national plans over a shorter period (1966–1970, rather than to 1980 as earlier foreseen), and scientific cooperation.[10]

For instance, as an alternative to supranational planning, the Bureau of the Executive Committee on Joint Problems of Economic Planning was set up after the July 1963 meeting of party leaders.

* An indication of the institutional growth of CEMA is the construction, begun in 1965, of a modern 30-story glass building in Moscow. The building will house the permanent representatives of the member countries of the Council, the Secretariat and the International Institute of Standardization. Among other features the building will have auditoriums for conferences and its own printing plant. *Vneshnaia Torgovlia* (1964). For Fadeyev's views on CEMA, see his book, *Sovet Ekonomicheskoi Vzaimopomoshchi* (Moscow, 1964).

This bureau, which is composed of the deputy chairmen of the members' state planning commissions, is designed to provide information on economic development to the Executive Committee and to provide coordination among national planning commissions.[11] Those countries wishing to increase specialization and efficiency in the mutual utilization of resources had to create formal bilateral or multilateral organizations outside of the CEMA framework which would exclude those members who expressed a lack of interest.

Despite such setbacks as the Albanian absence in 1961 and the Rumanian declaration of 1964, CEMA remains the single most important institution for the economic integration of the bloc. Its bureaucratic machinery and the work of its 21 permanent specialized standing commissions,[12] each corresponding to a major branch of the economy and located in the capital of a particularly interested member state, have continued to grow. Even after non-CEMA Communist states have stopped attending sessions of the Council and the Executive Committee, they have continued to send representatives to the standing commissions as observers. Cuba, since March 1963, and Yugoslavia, since September 1964 (having also attended during 1956–1958) have been observers at meetings of certain standing commissions.*

Several multilateral organizations, which are connected with CEMA but have autonomous councils, have also been formed. One of these is the International Bank of Economic Cooperation, which was officially created during the 9th meeting of the Executive Committee in Moscow (October 22, 1963) and which began operation in January 1964 in Moscow under a Soviet chairman, K. I. Nazarkin, previously a deputy chairman of the USSR State Bank.[13] The purpose of the International Bank is to provide loans for reconstruction and industrial projects approved by the participating countries, each one

* China was an observer at Council sessions from 1956 to February 1961 and at the Executive Committee meeting of October 1963 only. North Korea observed from 1957 to December 1961 (Council) and October 1963 (Executive Committee). Vietnam observed from 1958 to December 1961 (Council) and October 1963 (Executive Committee). Mongolia observed from 1958 to June 1962 (Council) and became member.
    Cuba, Yugoslavia, Korea, Vietnam, and China all had representatives at the nineteenth session of the standing commission on agriculture (*Pravda*, May 20, 1965) They were also at the standing commission on foreign trade meeting in Moscow (*Pravda*, June 5, 1965). Yugoslavia on September 17, 1964, asked to join the following standing commissions: foreign trade, currency and finance, ferrous metals, nonferrous metals, chemical industry, and coordination of scientific and technical research.

having one vote in making decisions "arrived at on the principle of unanimity." The observers to CEMA can, and have, participated in these multilateral negotiations. Multilateral clearing operations in conversion rubles are also to be handled by the Bank, but by 1966 little progress had been made.[14] Another such multilateral organization is the Common Railway-Wagon Pool, which was approved at the 10th meeting of the Executive Committee in December 1963. This organization, which by 1965 had 93,000 railway cars in it, was initially rejected by Rumania; subsequently Rumania changed its mind and the Common Railway-Wagon Pool became an autonomous part of CEMA.[15]

This pattern was not followed in the case of the formation of a multilateral organization for cooperation in ferrous metallurgy. As a result of the Rumanian lack of interest in such a project, the organization Intermetall was formed completely outside CEMA. It was set up during the 13th meeting of the Executive Committee of CEMA, on July 15, 1964. Originally including only Hungary, Poland, and Czechoslovakia, it was joined by the USSR, GDR, and Bulgaria within the next three months; it began operation in January 1965. Intermetall acts as an authority for planning steel investment and programming current production of iron and steel. Its headquarters in Budapest are staffed by 30 specialists — five from each participating country — and is equipped with a computer.[16] The organization is headed by a council in which each member has a delegation of three men, but only one vote. Decisions can be made only with the consensus of the members.[17] It seems likely that Intermetall will be the prototype of any future multilateral organization which is set up in the bloc when one or more of the members of CEMA refuses to participate.[18]

There are several other multilateral bloc organizations which should be mentioned briefly. The first of these is the Danube Commission, set up in August 1948,[19] which includes the USSR, Bulgaria, Czechoslovakia, Hungary, Rumania, and Yugoslavia (Austria was admitted as an observer in 1955 and as a member in 1959; West Germany is an observer). The purpose of the Danube Commission is to ensure normal navigation on the Danube as an international waterway. The Paris Peace Conference of 1946 provided for such an organization, but the United States, the United Kingdom, and France refused to sign the August 1948 agreement on the grounds that it violated the provisions and intentions of the Paris agreement. The

Danube Commission held its first session in November 1949 and since then it has met twice a year (usually in June and December), failing however, to meet in December 1956.

Since the Commission from the outset contained a participant from outside the bloc, it cannot be viewed as primarily an institution for the promotion of the bloc's political unity. However, during the Stalinist phase it did serve, under Soviet directorship, as an agency for the promotion of Soviet bloc objectives in the campaign against Yugoslavia. (The May–June 1951 and December 1952 sessions were preoccupied with mutual recriminations.)

A major change took place shortly after Stalin's death: the Soviet manifested an increasing willingness to pass control over to the Danubian powers. Also, since June 1956 the European Economic Commission has been participating in the sessions as an observer and since June 1957 both Austria and West Germany have attended a experts. As a result, the Danube Commission has increasingly become an international technical agency, not restricted to the camp alone.

Furthermore, with the appearance of difficulties between Rumania and CEMA, the Commission took on the aspect of an alternativ organization to which members of both organizations could turn. For example, it was originally planned that the Iron Gates project for the utilization of the Danube to provide hydroelectric power and to regulate the flow of the Iron Gates and provide water for irrigation was to be handled under a CEMA subcommittee (it was argued that the Danube Commission should be restricted to navigational affairs and the project lingered on through the vicissitudes of Soviet-Yugoslav relations (Yugoslavia being an observer at CEMA's commission on this problem from 1956 until June 1958). However, in June 196 Rumania and Yugoslavia signed a protocol on the project which envisaged the Danube Commission rather than CEMA as the source of project funds.[20]

Another multilateral Communist organization that should be noted here is the Joint Institute for Nuclear Research, set up in March 1956. In part its establishment reflected pressures on the Soviet Union to share its nuclear monopoly with its allies. The original founding agreement was signed by all the Communist states, save North Vietnam, which joined in September of the same year. The agreement appears to have been the outgrowth of the Soviet decision of January 7, 1955,[21] to undertake collaborative research efforts with China, Poland, Czechoslovakia, Rumania, and East Germany — countries which supply the Soviet Union with uranium and which could be expected to entertain scientific ambitions. Curiously, however, Hungary did not appear on the list of members, even though it was known to be an extractor of uranium. The January 1955 decision was followed by a series of bilateral agreements concluded by the USSR and the aforementioned states in April 1955, providing for the supply to these states of limited quantities of fissionable material, experimental accelerators, atomic piles, relevant equipment, and documentation.[22] This series of agreements was followed in June 1955 by an identical agreement with Hungary. (Possibly Nagy's fall from power eliminated doubts that might have existed earlier in Moscow.)

The preceding agreements laid the basis for the March 1956 conference of eleven Communist states which finally resulted in the creation of the Institute. It was planned that the Institute be located at Dubno, just north of Moscow, and that it be headed by a director and two assistant directors. In practice, the former was always to be a Soviet scientist, while the latter was to represent the participating states. Dues for the maintenance of the Institute were apportioned among the participating states on a graduated basis. The Institute was subdivided into specialized laboratories, each apparently to be headed by a Soviet scientist.

Thus, though the Soviet Union did meet, in part, the desire of the other bloc members to share in nuclear development and to acquire the basis for training cadres of their own, effective Soviet control was maintained. Furthermore, the Institute long seemed to be exempt from the pressures of the Sino-Soviet dispute as was indicated by the fact that the Chinese were reported to have surpassed the Czechs as the most numerous non-Soviet contingent at the Institute in January 1965. This situation changed, however, in early July 1965 when the Chinese withdrew from all participation. In summary, the Institute, as a multilateral organization, can be seen as combining elements of control with some adjustment to the demands of the bloc.

Finally, there are two further multilateral organizations: the Organization for International Railway Cooperation and the Organization for Socialist Countries in Telecommunication and Posts.[23] Both organizations are basically technical in character and unite the European and the Asian Communist states. Handling the physical ties among the Communist countries, these organizations are essential to any plan for further integration. The Organization for International Railway Cooperation was decided upon at a conference in June 1956 but not formally set up until September 1957. It is made up of the representatives of member countries, who are usually ministers of railroads, and a Committee for Railway Traffic, which heads a bureau handling administrative problems and issuing an information bulletin. The headquarters of the organization are in Warsaw. In spite of the Sino-Soviet dispute the twelve ministers met in Hanoi in March 1965.[24]

The Organization for Socialist Countries in Telecommunication and Posts was established in December 1957 as a counterpart to the five other regional postal unions of the world within the Universal Postal Union. The organization began to function in June 1958 and is basically a conference of the various ministers of communications and posts of the member states; the conference meets once a year. There is also a secretary and a secretariat who are responsible for the minutes of the meetings and publication of documents. The conference of this organization has continued to meet despite the Sino-Soviet rift. For example, a meeting was held on July 16, 1965, in Peking.[25]

BILATERAL AGREEMENTS

This multilateral framework is buttressed by an increasing web of bilateral agreements. In the face of the division within the Communist camp, these treaties have become increasingly important in recent years. Of these the treaties on friendship, cooperation, and mutual aid are particularly significant. These treaties have been concluded, usually on the Soviet example, between most of the Communist states. Normally for twenty years, they are directed against a specific threat — usually Germany or Japan and their possible allies — and they contain pledges of mutual support. In this way an effort is made to relate the alliance to a concrete danger, activating the deeply felt anti-German or anti-Japanese popular feeling which exists within some of the Communist-ruled states. Whereas these treaties at first tended to be essentially a cloak for political subservience to the Soviet Union, while maintaining the juridical fiction of equality, in recent years they have become formalized statements of an alliance relationship with some imposition of meaningful obligations on both sides, and without implication of complete subservience to the Soviet Union.

These treaties were first concluded between the USSR and its wartime allies within the bloc (Czechoslovakia in 1943, Poland in 1945, and Mongolia in 1946), and with the ex-enemies in 1948 (Rumania, Bulgaria, and Hungary) about a year after the Paris peace treaty with them. The Chinese-Soviet treaty was signed on February

14, 1950. North Korea had to wait until July 6, 1961, when the pressures of the Sino-Soviet split seem to have overcome Soviet hesitance to sign such treaties with divided states. Even the GDR finally received its friendship and mutual assistance treaty on June 12, 1964.[26] Like the others, it was aimed at West German "revanchism" and emphasized the maintenance of the GDR's state borders. The significance of these treaties to the Soviet leaders in the present conditions is made apparent by the great publicity and ceremony that has attended the re-signing of the Polish-Soviet treaty in April 1965 when Brezhnev and Kosygin traveled to Warsaw,[27] and the re-signing of the Soviet-Mongolian treaty in January 1966 when Brezhnev traveled to Ulan-Bator.[28] Recent Soviet statements have emphasized that these treaties, together with WTO and CEMA, are "the reliable instruments of socialist solidarity." [29]

The original mutual aid treaties concluded under Stalin gave no juridical basis for the stationing of Soviet troops on the territory of the members of the camp, and although this was covered in the Warsaw Treaty, that agreement was very general in its wording. It was not until after the crisis in the fall of 1956 that the matter of the status of the Soviet forces stationed in Eastern Europe became part of the formal treaty system between the USSR and Poland, Hungary, Rumania, and GDR. These new treaties (Poland ratified in February 1957, Rumania in April 1957, Hungary in May 1957, GDR in March 1957) reflected the changed relationship of these states to the USSR, including the fact that East Germany was not yet quite equal to the others, though its sovereignty was asserted.[30]

Insofar as Poland and Hungary are concerned, the joint Polish-Soviet and Hungarian-Soviet government and party declarations of November 18, 1956, and March 28, 1957, respectively, represent the most important bilateral agreements concluded within the bloc. The first of these made it possible for the Polish Communist leadership to remain within the bloc while pursuing policies of relative domestic autonomy, some of which were at the time obviously displeasing to the Soviets. Nevertheless, the granting of compensation for past Soviet economic exploitation, the withdrawal of Soviet overseers from Poland, the acceptance by the Soviets of the Gomulka regime, and the restrictions imposed on the Soviet troops in Poland, were all substantive measures designed to normalize and improve Polish-Soviet Communist relations.

In the case of Hungary, the March 28 declaration was also designed to improve Soviet-Hungarian relations and involved economic concessions and promises of aid. However, unlike the Polish case, the declaration was much more a unilateral effort on the part of the Soviet government to improve the domestic position of a satellite regime, recently imposed on the population by the force of Soviet arms, than an agreement between two states. Nonetheless, it did involve a step forward for the Hungarians as well, especially when compared with the earlier period. Generally speaking, the agreements subsequent to October–November 1956 can be seen as reflecting a recognition on the part of Soviet leaders of the need to regularize the semicolonial pattern of relations prevailing between the Soviet Union and most of the other Communist states. An expression of this recognition was the declaration issued by the Soviet Union (prompted directly by the Hungarian revolution) on October 30, 1956, promising to liquidate the most obnoxious aspects of the Stalinist pattern of Soviet-satellite relations.[31] This policy was generally implemented in the other bloc countries subsequently.

With respect to the matter of diplomatic relations among the Communist states, considerable regularization is to be noted. In the course of 1957–1958, the Soviet Union concluded a whole series of consular conventions with the other members of the bloc, defining consular competence and clarifying such still outstanding issues as dual citizenship, problems of mutual legal aid, and civil, criminal, and familial legal issues.[32] However, the Soviet Union still retained its traditional reticence concerning the opening of foreign consulates on Soviet soil; the Poles, for instance, were unsuccessful in their efforts to increase their consular representation in the Soviet Union.

Bilateral trade treaties since about 1957 have been designed to express, in more detail and in a binding manner, the recommendations of CEMA. Since the failure of the creation of an over-all system of economic coordination and planning, they have again been stressed as one of the basic means of economic interaction among the European bloc members.

Although prior to 1956 and even to some extent presently, these treaties have been discriminatory in favor of the USSR, the extent of Soviet domination of trade has decreased, while remaining an important bond between the Communist states. Even in those states whose relations are at a low ebb with the Soviet Union, trade with the other bloc countries has remained a vital factor.[33] These treaties are normally long-term agreements, varying from two to seven years, depending on the plans of the respective countries. In 1965 the members of CEMA all concluded five-year trade treaties to cover

1966–1970, as a means of coordinating their plans. Within the long-term treaties there are usually protocols, valid for one year, which provide a detailed breakdown of the items to be traded. The protocols are usually renegotiated for subsequent single years; at that time any needed adjustments can be made. These treaties often include agreements on coordination of capital investment and cooperation in production as well as credits.

On the basis of these treaties and the "perspectives" for even longer periods which they often include within them, the contracting parties are able to plan several years in advance and remain relatively confident of both their supply and their external markets. At the same time the treaties tend to keep those countries which are more developed (Czechoslovakia and East Germany especially) dependent on the USSR for their supplies of machinery, and so on. Particularly for those countries which have, due to the economic autarky of the camp, developed industries that cannot compete with the open market, these long-range agreements have been a source of security.*

To facilitate this bilateral coordination of plans and investment, intergovernmental commissions on economics, and scientific and technical collaboration have been created.[34] These commissions were to provide contacts between corresponding technical and administrative organizations of the two countries concerned. They were initially formed between various East European countries, starting with one between Poland and Czechoslovakia in October 1957. Others followed soon after; 1958: Bulgaria-Czechoslovakia, Rumania-Czecho-

---

* It should be mentioned here that the exchange of scientific-technical achievements among the bloc countries is carried out on the basis of bilateral long-term treaties on scientific-technical cooperation and, to some degree, on a multilateral basis, through the standing commissions of CEMA.

The Soviet Union made these treaties with the other bloc countries during Stalin's regime (except for the treaties with China, North Korea, and Mongolia, which were signed in 1954, 1955, and 1961 respectively). Bulgaria and Mongolia also have such treaties with most of the other bloc countries. In 1961 the USSR signed protocols to the agreements with Bulgaria, Hungary, Poland, Rumania, and Czechoslovakia. By these protocols the area of collaboration was extended from industrial production to construction, transport, communications, agriculture, and other branches of the economy. These were to last for five-year periods. On June 19, 1961, the USSR also concluded a new agreement with China for a period of ten years. These agreements usually set up a joint commission that meets twice a year to discuss measures to be taken in the area of the agreement, such as the exchange of documents. For example, during 1960–1962, more than 38,000 sets of technical documents were exchanged among CEMA countries.

For more on this, as well as statistics on document exchanges, see S. D. Sergeev, *Ekonomicheskoe sotrudnichestvo i vzaimopomoshch' sotsialisticheskikh stran* (Moscow, 1965).

slovakia, Bulgaria-Poland, Hungary-Poland, Rumania-Poland, Hungary-Rumania; 1959: Czechoslovakia-GDR, Rumania-Bulgaria; 1960: Poland-GDR; 1961: Bulgaria-GDR, Czechoslovakia-Hungary; 1962: GDR-Hungary; 1963: GDR-Rumania. With the reverse to economic integration suffered at the July 1963 meeting of party leaders, the Soviet Union moved into this field with vigor. In 1963 it concluded such an agreement with Czechoslovakia and in the following year with Bulgaria, GDR, Hungary, and Poland. The Kremlin did not get Rumania to form such a joint commission until Ceausescu visited Moscow in September 1965. Recently such commissions have also been formed with Yugoslavia.

The formation of joint investment projects and enterprises is another form of bilateral action between bloc members. The Stalinist joint enterprises, formed between the USSR and several of the bloc countries, were clearly exploitative and were abolished in 1954. However, in recent years new forms of joint investment have been devised, such as the Hungarian-Polish Haldex Corporation to process coal slack, and the Hungarian-Bulgarian joint enterprise to develop engineering and consumer goods production in Bulgaria.[35] Poland has been particularly active in joint investment projects. Changes in the method of economic organization were officially approved at the September 1965 Plenum of the CPSU and adopted by other European bloc countries for greater future use of such joint projects.[36]

A final link in the web of ties that deserves brief mention is provided by the cultural agreements concluded between the Communist states. Since art, culture, and science are subject to state control under the Communist system, all cultural contacts between the various members of the camp must be regulated through official and formal channels. During Stalin's lifetime, however, such contacts were very limited and only began to develop with the gradual lifting of the internal iron curtains by which the old dictator had isolated each Communist state. Thus, although European Communist states concluded cultural collaboration treaties with one another and also with China quite early in the history of the bloc (1947–1948 — except for China and East Germany which concluded such treaties in 1951 and 1952 respectively), cultural contacts remained essentially dormant until the middle 1950's.

The Soviet Union displayed ostentatious contempt for such arrangements, and refrained (with the exception of Mongolia, February 27, 1946) from concluding such broad cultural collaboration agreements until the mid-1950's. This abstinence, however, did not prevent the USSR from concluding a whole series of limited agreements with the members of the bloc, providing for the training of their citizens in Soviet institutions of higher learning, for "cooperation" in radio programming and subsequently also in television, and finally for collaboration between their respective Academies of Sciences.

It was only in the wake of the attack on Stalin and within the context of very hurried efforts to improve and normalize Soviet relations that the Soviet Union concluded cultural collaboration agreements with all the Communist states. These agreements provided for expanded contacts in education, art, music, literature, the theatre, films, press, radio, television, sports, and even tourism. In effect, these agreements were meant to establish a broad social basis for contacts with the "first country of socialism" hitherto sealed off hermetically. In all but four cases, the agreements were to run for five years; in the case of Mongolia, half-absorbed by the USSR, and the then Soviet-controlled Korea and what was still Rakosi's Hungary, the agreements covered ten years; in the case of North Vietnam, only three years.

In an effort to remove obvious discrimination, in the course of 1956–1957 the Soviet Union set up friendship societies with China, Bulgaria, etc., to match analogous friendship societies with the USSR that had existed in the other states since the late 1940's. During 1957–1958 friendship societies also were established among all the Communist states.

INFORMAL ARRANGEMENTS AND DYNAMIC PATTERNS

At best the formal institutional aspects can only provide a broad framework for unity. In order for this framework to have any meaningful influence on attaining unity, there must be a continuous interaction of the members of the camp, the resolving of conflicts, engaging in exchanges and, to some extent, responding to the demands of the camp's most powerful state. These unifying processes take various forms within the camp, often revealing the degrees of existing cohesion. Such dynamic aspects of the relations among the Communist states also illustrate the processes by which the Soviet Union is attempting to maintain its position in the context of growing disunity and ideological diversity which has accompanied the Chinese challenge to the Soviet dominance.

The most important of the dynamic aspects of the camp's unity has been the increased frequency of contacts between top leaders of the various ruling parties. This practice involves an important change in the political style of the bloc. During Stalin's domination, when the primacy of the USSR was unchallenged, contacts between party leaders were rare and usually involved bilateral dealings with the Soviet leaders in Moscow. Since Stalin's death, and particularly since October–November 1956, relatively frequent bilateral and multi-lateral consultations between party leaders have taken place.

The desirability of multilateral meetings of party leaders was asserted at the twelve-party meeting in November 1957 (Moscow) at which the Polish objections to such gatherings were overcome. Thereafter, such gatherings of top party officials have taken place on the occasion of CPSU congresses as well as some of the other national party congresses, revolutionary anniversaries, and ceremonies. Other occasions on which top party leaders have gathered have been meetings connected with CEMA and WTO.

Initially, the calling of multilateral meetings was of direct benefit to the Soviet Union, because it could muster the overwhelming support of the other regimes. This allowed the Soviet leaders to use them as a useful forum for the articulation of common principles and for forcing recalcitrant parties (the Poles to start with, then the Chinese and the Rumanians) into declarations of unity. This technique could be useful only as long as the recalcitrant parties were willing to submit.[37] As the Sino-Soviet split deepened, compromises had to be made in the ideological declarations issued by the meetings. This has resulted in conglomerate statements embodying the varying points of view, such as occurred in the declaration of the 81-party conference that met in Moscow in December 1960.[38] The Twenty-second Congress of the CPSU in 1961 saw the Chinese delegation, led by Chou En-lai, walk out.[39] In the absence of the Chinese, subsequent gatherings of party leaders once again became forums for the expression of pro-Soviet views and calls for Chinese submission. This atmosphere prevailed through the June 1962 (Moscow) meeting of CEMA party leaders, which resulted in the statement of the Basic Principles of the International Socialist Division of Labor. However, the July 1963 meeting of first secretaries and heads of government (Moscow) saw a change in atmosphere once again, as the Rumanian objections dispelled the hope for the Soviet proposals for supranational planning among CEMA members. When the pro-Soviet leaders gathered on the occasion of Ulbricht's seventieth birthday, the Rumanians did not send a representative. Neither did they send a representative to the rather abortive March 1965 (Moscow) meeting, called for the purpose of unifying the camp.[40] The attendance of the Rumanians, like that of the Koreans and Vietnamese, at the Twenty-third Congress of the CPSU was in all likelihood predicated on an agreement that the Congress would not become a forum for attacks on the Chinese or for the forcing of a joint declaration.

The recognition of the value of meetings and conferences as a method for the maintenance of unity within the camp has been explicitly noted by Soviet leaders. As an editorial in the Soviet-dominated ideological journal of the bloc put it:

> The objective need to strengthen the world Communist movement engendered, during the almost half century of its history, different forms of unity, corresponding to the different stages of its development. One method that has emerged in recent times, a method most suited to the present conditions, is that of periodic meetings of the representatives of the parties, which enable them to exchange views on questions of mutual interest, to generalize the experience of struggle, enrich Marxist-Leninist theory by collective effort and jointly work out the political line for the future.[41]

The March 1965 meeting of the pro-Soviet parties emphasized this point of view, while stressing also the quality and independence of the various parties at such meetings. Khrushchev's desire to use this method of enforcement against the Chinese seems to have been a contributory factor in his removal from power, but his successors failed to find any alternative to it. They have vigorously adopted it as the only "scientific" way to maintain the bloc's unity.[42]

Beside these multilateral meetings, another important outcome of the events of 1956 is that Soviet leaders now journey frequently to other Communist states and necessarily have become more conscious of the problems that the other ruling parties face. Although not all of these bilateral meetings are of actual policy-making importance, they do help to keep the various party leaders better informed about current difficulties and they have invariably involved a measure of discussion.

It is impossible to say how much of this development was due to the specific political style of Khrushchev and how much of it was a necessity if the bloc was to be maintained in the period of reaction to de-Stalinization. Despite the fact that such discussions and meetings do seem to have been particularly adapted to Khrushchev's methods of leadership, the fact that his successors have continued to travel and hold meetings can be interpreted as an indication that it was probably a necessity in any case. In 1965 alone, Kosygin left the USSR to go to North Vietnam, China, North Korea, East Germany (twice), and Poland, while Brezhnev traveled to Hungary, Poland (twice), Rumania, Czechoslovakia, and East Germany. Mongolia and North Korea were visited by Shelepin, who early in 1966 went to North Vietnam while Brezhnev went to Mongolia. In 1965 Suslov went to Bulgaria and Podgorny to Czechoslovakia and Hungary. Other Soviet party leaders also traveled extensively. At the same time Moscow remained the most important center for bilateral discussions. In 1965 first secretaries from all CEMA members and top-level leaders from the rest of the camp visited Moscow at least once. Usually these meetings resulted in a joint ideological declaration. In the condition of diversity within the camp unofficial meetings, which require no such formal declaration, have been resorted to increasingly. The informal nature of these discussions (often without advance notice and sometimes in the form of hunting trips) encouraged close contact and frank discussion between the leaders.

It should also be noted that Moscow's geographical position between the European and Asian Communist states makes it a normal stopping point for delegations going in either direction. For example, two of the five times when Kadar met bilaterally with Brezhnev in 1965 Kadar was on the way to and from Mongolia. Each time the Asians sent party or state delegations to multilateral or other meetings in Eastern Europe, such as the Rumanian party congresses, they stopped in Moscow. Since these stopovers usually lasted for several days, they were convenient occasions for negotiation without being specifically designated as such.

Bilateral contacts have also been utilized increasingly between leaders of the other members of the camp. For example, in the four months after Ceausescu became Rumanian First Secretary, he met with Zhivkov on four occasions and with Kadar once. (Maurer met with Kadar on two later occasions.) During 1965 Tito met with all CEMA first secretaries except Ceausescu and Tsedenbal. The latter visited Novotny in June 1965 and Kadar in October. Novotny met Gomulka in Poland in January 1966 and so on.

Although Brezhnev in his report to the Twenty-third Party Congress claimed that these "businesslike contacts and political consultations between the leaders of fraternal parties of the socialist countries have become a system," they still operate on an ad hoc basis. At present, there is no multilateral party organization resembling the Comintern or the Cominform. These organizations, discredited by Stalinism, have not been resuscitated. The failure to develop any regular institutionalized form of top-level multilateral or bilateral contacts has led the Soviet leaders to look for other means of interparty coordination. In the conditions of the Sino-Soviet dispute the success of these Soviet efforts has not been impressive.

Following the November 1957 multilateral party meeting, an interparty political, ideological monthly magazine was founded in Prague. It was entitled *The World Marxist Review* in its English edition and "Problems of Peace and Socialism" in its Russian edition. (It was originally published in the twelve languages of the bloc and seven others: English, French, Spanish, Italian, Dutch, Swedish, and Japanese.) Soviet dominance on the magazine was ensured by the placing of A. M. Rumyantsev, editor-in-chief of the Soviet ideological magazine *Kommunist*, in the top editorial position. With the fall of Khrushchev in October 1964, Rumyantsev temporarily became the editor-in-chief of *Pravda*, and G. P. Frantsov took over in Prague.[43] The fact that Frantsov was the rector of the Academy of Social Sciences, on the CPSU Central Committee, and a member of the editorial board of *Kommunist*, indicated that the Soviet party leadership continued to value the role of *The World Marxist Review*.

Although distribution of the magazine was not limited to the bloc, it was clear from the time of the first issue in September 1958 that one of its tasks would be the consolidation of a common ideological-political line for the bloc. This was precisely why it was hailed by the East Germans[44] and met with silence in Warsaw.

However, in the first years it did not live up to expectations as a vital organ of the bloc. While the only interparty publication on ideological-political matters and in some ways the successor of the old Cominform newspaper *For a Lasting Peace, for a People's Democracy*, it soon became primarily an organ for the world pro-Soviet Communist movement, particularly for nonruling parties. This change was reflected in the fact that as the Sino-Soviet split developed, editions in Albanian (1962), Chinese, and Korean (1963) were halted. At the same time, new editions were added in Greek (Cyprus) and Portuguese (Brazil) in 1962 and in Singhalese (Ceylon) by 1965. Distributing centers in underdeveloped areas have increased.* Of

* In 1964 and 1965 there were no more defections. The Vietnamese and Rumanian editions continued. It is curious that there is not yet a Serbo-Croatian edition; this is probably due to the Yugoslav resentment of the earlier organ of the Cominform.
In these same years there has been an expansion of distributing centers to Austria, Switzerland, Uraguay, Mexico, Chile, and Argentina. It is curious to note that there is no specifically Cuban distributing point. There are now nineteen distributing points outside the bloc and only ten within the bloc.

those bloc countries which contributed to the journal, Soviet Russia, Czechoslovakia, and East Germany have continuously the highest level of participation. (This was true in 1958–1960[45] and in 1963–1965.) The Asian Communists have completely stopped writing for the magazine; and in 1964 and 1965 the Rumanians also stopped writing for it.

Another method for achieving continuous interparty coordination, developed by the Soviet leadership in the post-Stalin period, was the reliance on experienced party officials, many of them members of the CPSU Central Committee, as ambassadors to the other Communist countries. Some of the ambassadors were undoubtedly placed in these positions as a form of exile (Molotov in Mongolia, Pervukhin in GDR, and Ponomarenko in Poland). But as the interparty struggle subsided in the USSR after 1957 the ambassadorships were increasingly filled with specialists on bloc relations. Yu. V. Andropov, the present CPSU Secretary for bloc relations, was an ambassador to Hungary in 1954–1957. A number of party officials have served in more than one bloc country since 1957: P. A. Abrasimov in China (as Minister Counselor), Poland, and GDR; S. V. Chervonenko in China and Czechoslovakia; G. A. Denisov in Bulgaria and Hungary; A. M. Puzanov in Korea and Yugoslavia; and M. V. Zimyanin in Vietnam and Czechoslovakia. While the period of interparty struggle saw a rapid shifting of men in these positions, since 1957 the length of time served per country has grown to a norm of about three years.

Military collaboration and contacts have also increased along with greater party contacts. During the years since his appointment in June 1960 to the post of commander of WTO, Marshal Grechko has spent a major part of his time visiting the various party and state leaders of the member countries. For example, in 1965 he made publicized calls upon Ulbricht (in April and October),[46] Maurer (in May),[47] Ceausescu (in June),[48] and Gomulka (in November).[49] At the same time conferences of military leaders have been called, such as the one in May 1965 in the Transcaucasian military district of the USSR for a demonstration of new weapons, equipment, and tactics.[50] A similar conference took place in Warsaw in November 1965.[51] The frequent interaction of top military and political leaders has undoubtedly been designed to stimulate the feeling of an alliance relationship.

Since in the planned economies of the Communist countries, as their ideology states, economics and politics are inseparable, the economic interaction of the bloc countries may be seen also as an indicator of political relationships. This political-economic interrelationship is shown most clearly within the bloc in the cases of China and Albania. Starting in 1960 China's previously increasing trade with the Soviet Union began to decline steadily.* The other CEMA members followed the Soviet lead. Poland, Hungary, Bulgaria, Czechoslovakia, Rumania, and East Germany all began to reduce their trade with China. This trend was reversed in the cases of East Germany and Rumania in 1965, showing that the East Europeans were no longer following in Soviet footsteps.

The Albanian case was somewhat different. Its trade turnover with the USSR increased until 1961 when it was markedly reduced; by 1962, according to Soviet figures, it had completely disappeared.[52] In response to this, Albania's trade with China doubled in 1961 and by 1962 China's percentage of Albania's total trade turnover had reached 51 per cent.[53] (Thus, it almost reached the Soviet figure of 53.9 per cent in 1960.) However, the other bloc countries did not follow the Soviet lead in the case of Albania to the extent they had with respect to China. None of them ceased trading with Albania, and some even increased their trade with Albania. In fact, in 1963 Albania concluded long-term trade agreements (five years) with all the Communist states except the USSR.[54] This behavior can be seen as a demonstration of the increasing ability of the bloc members to ignore Soviet leadership in certain areas. This stands in sharp contrast to their behavior at the time of the Soviet-Yugoslav split under Stalin.

At the same time, the Soviet Union remains the dominant economic force within the bloc. This is reflected by the fact that all the CEMA countries still carry out the single largest percentage of their trade with the USSR, as the chart on p. 478 shows.

The bloc countries are also tied to the USSR by such things as the new oil pipeline and the electric power grid. The unifying effect of such enterprises should not be underestimated. Whole complexes of factories and refineries have been built in the various European countries. These sections of the economies of the serviced countries depend on a continued good relationship with the Soviet supplier. The Soviet Union is also a major market for East European machinery and equipment, which is often not competitive in the West. At the

---

* Percentages of Soviet trade turnover in China:

1958	1959	1960	1961	1962	196?	1964
17.5	19.5	14.9	7.8	5.5	4.2	2.9

Sources: *Vneshnaia Torgovlia SSSR za 1959–1963 Gody* (Moscow, 1965), pp. 10–11, absolute figures, and p. 22, percentages. *Vneshnaia Torgovlia*, November 1965, p. 9, percentages, and Supplement, absolute figures.

Percentage of annual trade with USSR

Country	1961	1962	1963
Bulgaria	52.1	53.3	—
GDR	44.2	48.9	48.6
Rumania	40.5	40.6	40.2
Czechoslovakia	33.6	37.8	38.9
Hungary	33.4	35.9	34.3
Poland	32.4	30.5	33.7

Source: UN, *Yearbook of International Trade Statistics* (New York, 1965).

same time, the USSR is a major supplier of raw materials, vitally needed in the bloc for which there is no readily available alternative source.* Rumania is the exception to this, being the only European bloc country that is endowed with substantial resources. Its attitude toward CEMA and its unwillingness to follow the lead of the more developed countries of the bloc, as well as its attitude toward trade and relations with China, Albania, and the West, is in part a reflection of this. However, its closest ties remain within the system.

Like trade in many respects, personal contacts and cultural ties between the various Communist states are subject to a large degree of party and state control. The flow of books, newspapers, radio and television programs as well as of artists, writers, scholars, and even tourists has been a matter of careful regulation. Such contacts have been therefore subject to curtailment or expansion depending on interparty and interstate relationships. This is clearly seen in the statistics of visitors from China to the Soviet Union as their ideological split widened:[55]

1956	1957	1958	1959	1960	1961	1962	1963
56,296	47,350	42,343	38,502	36,134	25,639	28,788	no figure given

* For example, some of the economic bonds which tie the bloc to the USSR are mentioned in an article by B. Szalai (Hungarian Deputy Minister of Trade), "On the Principles of Fraternal Collaboration," *Vneshnaia Torgovlia*, November 1965, pp. 25–28. The Soviet Union supplies the Hungarians with such raw materials as oil (80–90 per cent of Hungary's supply comes from the USSR), timber products, cotton (60 per cent of Hungary's supply comes from Uzbekistan) and the USSR takes machinery as payment. In trade with Western Europe there is very little market for Hungarian machinery and Hungary is forced to sell raw materials.

Poland sold about 90 per cent of its machines and equipment in 1964 to socialist countries, predominantly the USSR, Czechoslovakia, GDR, and Hungary. M. Dmokhovski, "The Foreign Trade of Poland in 1964," *Vneshnaia Torgovlia*, July 1965, pp. 7–9.

A similar disruption in contacts was visible as a result of the ideological disputes between the USSR and Albania and the USSR and Yugoslavia. However (with the possible exception of Yugoslavia), the contacts of peoples and ideas among the Communist states, even China and Albania, has generally been maintained at a level which is greater than that of any of these states with non-Communist countries.[56]

Much of the personal contact between the people of the bloc countries is arranged under various cultural and scientific agreements.[57] Under the agreements for cultural cooperation, during the early 1960's, up to 6,500 scientific and cultural workers of the various Communist-ruled countries annually went to the USSR, and an equal number of such persons went from the USSR to the other bloc countries. On the student exchange, in 1962 alone 2,000 students from the bloc graduated from Soviet higher educational institutions and 3,000 more entered them.[58] Under the technical-scientific agreements, between 1960 and 1962, 30,000 workers from various branches of the economy were exchanged among the CEMA countries in order to study production methods and increase their skills.[59]

Among the more important of the interpersonal contacts uniting the bloc countries are those on the academic level where ideas and points of view are exchanged. This part of the interpersonal contact is expressed not only in the numbers of participants on student and other scholarly exchanges, but also by the joint research projects and the pooling and borrowing of ideas and experience.[60] The Academies of Sciences of the various bloc countries are among the organizations engaged in these activities. Agreements have been signed between the various Academies about joint work and exchange of personnel. In 1964, for example, 1,107 scholars went to the Academies of Sciences of the other socialist countries and 1,888 came to the USSR.[61] In the same year the USSR Academy of Sciences carried out about 20 joint research projects or coordinated work with each of the Academies of the CEMA countries including a number of projects involving several Academies.[62]

Another form of contact at this level was initiated in March 1962, when the first conference of representatives of the Academies of Sciences of the Communist states met in Warsaw. These conferences have met annually thereafter in the capitals of the various bloc countries. They are intended to be a means for "strengthening of scientific collaboration between the Academies of Sciences of the socialist countries uniting the efforts of scholars of the world socialist system around the most important problems of science." [63]

These exchanges and interactions of scholars have been instrumental in the publication of a number of books and articles on various aspects of the development of the bloc as a whole, especially its economic aspects, over the last several years. This literature of unity includes a number of serious works of scholarship.[64] The interest in the economic aspects of the bloc's development is also reflected in the formation in 1961, within the USSR Academy of Sciences, of the Institute of Economics of the World Socialist System.

One of the areas where the interaction of scholars and of ideas within the bloc is influencing the thinking of the ruling elite is sociological research. This recently blossoming field of study, suppressed and attacked under Stalin, threatens to erode the ideology which still unites the bloc, since sociological findings, based to some extent on empirical data, are often hard to reconcile with the prescriptions of the Marxist-Leninist classics. While sociological research had been carried out in some of the bloc countries, especially Poland, during the 1950's,[65] it is only since 1960–1961 that it has spread to the other "fraternal" countries.[66] An instrumental role in this spread was undoubtedly played by the August 1961 conference of sociologists from Poland, Czechoslovakia, USSR, and Bulgaria, at the offices of the *World Marxist Review* in Prague.[67] Since that time the study of sociology has spread to most of the European bloc countries,[68] finally even reaching the domestically conservative regimes in Rumania and GDR.[69] Cooperation between the new and still weak sociological research institutes in the USSR and the Poles, Czechs, and Hungarians appears to be growing both by personal contacts and by exchange of information.[70]

One of the forms of interpersonal contact which has increased in recent years within the bloc is tourism. The number of visitors between the various East European countries began to increase gradually after the 1956 crisis and especially during the early 1960's. A major change occurred in 1964 and 1965, with the signing of a series of agreements between most of the socialist countries. These agreements abolished the need for visas and the need to have an invitation from the receiving country for those desiring to travel between fraternal states. One of the first of these agreements was between Hungary and Czechoslovakia (January 1964). In the year that followed this agreement, the number of persons traveling in and out of Hungary more than doubled as compared with the previous year. The

Czechs received two and a half times as many visitors as in previous years and four times as many of their own citizens went abroad.[71] At the same time the travel between Hungary and Czechoslovakia showed an increase of three and a half times as many Hungarians going to Czechoslovakia as previously had, and five and a half times as many Czechs went to Hungary as previously had.*

In July 1964 a similar agreement was made between Hungary and Poland. This undoubtedly helped to account for the doubling of Polish tourism in 1964. The Bulgarians were slow in following the others; they concluded a tourism agreement with Hungary in October 1964 and with Poland, Yugoslavia, and the USSR (to a limited extent) only in the spring of 1965. Despite this the number of visitors to Bulgaria in 1964 was twice that of 1963, and 1965 saw a further increase. Rumania and the USSR have been the slowest to allow changes in the handling of tourism. (In November 1965 they were the only members of CEMA with whom the Hungarians had not made agreements on the abolition of visas.) The Bulgarians (May 20, 1965), the Poles (July 15, 1965), and the Czechs (September 19, 1965) reached partial agreements with the USSR, but there is no evidence of Rumanian cooperation in this area to date.

While contacts with the Western tourists have increased in recent years, and favorable currency and visa policies have been instituted in a number of the East European countries to encourage Westerners to come, a dominant percentage of the travel within the bloc is between member states. Thus, in 1964, tourists from Communist states constituted five sixths of those tourists arriving in Hungary, well over three fourths of those arriving in Czechoslovakia, and approximately seven eighths of those arriving in Poland. On the other hand, it was reported that a little over half of Bulgaria's tourists in 1964 were from the West, as were an even greater proportion in 1965.†

* Number of Persons Traveling to Hungary:

1951	1960	1961	1962	1963	1964
99,000	224,000	337,000	464,000	585,000	1,302,000

Number of Hungarians Traveling Abroad:

1951	1960	1961	1962	1963	1964
99,000	301,000	374,000	456,000	572,000	1,486,000

The number of Hungarians traveling abroad in 1964 was 15 per cent of the total population, and five sixths of them went to socialist countries. (Laszlo Adam, "The Trend of Tourism.")

† The statistics on tourism within the CEMA countries over the last several years show that the Czechs and the East Germans provided by far the most tourists. In 1965 the foreign tourists coming to Czechoslovakia totaled 2,947,000, of whom the vast majority were from other Communist countries: 2,329,000. Thus, in spite of the general decline in tourism as compared to the record 3.6 million visitors in 1964, the

The foregoing discussion indicates that recent years have seen concrete efforts in the direction of (1) the regularization of relations among the pro-Soviet states; and (2) the intensification of such relations. Many of the earlier sources of tension were due to the essentially informal and indirect system of Stalinist controls, to the blurred lines between central authority and domestic autonomy, to the airtight compartmentalization of the camp's members, each surrounded by an iron curtain and beholden only to Moscow. The regularization of these relations and their concomitant intensification have been designed to reduce the number of tension points, and to liquidate the earlier ambiguities in the division of power between the center and the dependencies and/or allies.

However, in spite of all the efforts invested in recent years in building a framework of unity, the Soviet alliance system by the mid-sixties was still organizationally underdeveloped. Indeed, it was lagging considerably behind comparable West European organizational development. There were several reasons for this condition.

First, the economic development of East Europe under Soviet sponsorship was, from the early years, based on the Soviet model of economic autarky. This model was applied by the new Communist regimes in each case as the only appropriate method of economic de-

---

dominance of the bloc proportion remained approximately the same. Only 1,735,000 Czechs went abroad in 1965. (*East Europe*, March 1966, p. 46.)

The Czechs made up the greatest percentage of tourists in Hungary, Poland, and Rumania in 1963 while the East Germans were the highest in Bulgaria and Czechoslovakia, and second only to the Czechs in Poland and Rumania. At the same time the Rumanians, Hungarians, and Bulgarians traveled in the other bloc countries at a rather low rate. This divergence in the patterns of personal interaction closely parallels the divisions over questions of economic integration within CEMA. This may be no more than saying that people from countries with more developed economies tend to travel more than those from less developed countries. On the other hand, to the extent that tourism is subject to state regulation, these differences may be interpreted as another piece of evidence of the differences in attitude toward integration held by the various members of CEMA. The rather remarkable change in the Hungarian pattern in 1964–1965 may be an indication of its attitude toward integration.

It should be noted here that while interaction of this sort shows the political and even the economic cohesion of the parties and states of the Communist bloc, the statistics do not necessarily reflect the feelings toward one another at the mass level. It may safely be said that in spite of the high degree of interaction and personal contact which exists between the GDR and the other bloc countries (including the USSR), there is very little love lost by the Russians and other bloc nationalities for the Germans. Anyone visiting Eastern Europe cannot avoid the awareness of an antagonism on the part of the peoples of a number of these countries toward both the Russians and the Germans. This is true in Poland, for example, despite the fact that they send the highest bloc percentage of visitors to the USSR and receive large number of Germans each year.

velopment for a Communist state. The fact that CEMA was not really put into operation until after the 1956 crisis meant that each of the members had about ten years of autarkical development, during which time they had each built up many of the same basic industries, often on an uneconomic basis. The decision to develop an organization which would break down the barriers earlier established meant that a number of the new industries — as well as some older ones — would be threatened. The least developed countries within the bloc would suffer more in this respect than the more economically advanced ones. Opposition to integration was therefore bound to arise.

Second, the original CEMA agreement specified that each country was to remain sovereign and equal. The founding document did not set up a supranational common market commission but only a council for mutual aid. Thus when the attempt to change the powers of the council to that of an organization for common action was made, those who felt that they would not benefit by losing any of their sovereignty were legally in an advantageous position to object. With the Soviet Union needing as much support as it could muster from the other "fraternal" parties in order to counter the Chinese, the Kremlin was not in a position to impose sanctions against any recalcitrant member of CEMA. It is likely, therefore, that economic cooperation in East Europe will move in the direction of more restricted regional or purely functional ventures, without the broader integrative ambitions or the original ideological aspects of the Soviet CEMA concept.

Third, the Soviet Union is clearly economically dominant. It is hard to form a union of equals when one of the members of the union is by no means equal. Although in Western Europe there is no single power which is clearly dominant in resources, individual power, population, and military strength, the opposite is true in the Eastern case. Full economic integration in Eastern Europe inescapably tends to mean that the smaller countries become absorbed into the USSR. Given the national feelings which exist in these countries, it is not hard to understand why they would be reluctant to promote full-scale economic integration. This is all the more true at a time when it looks as though they may be able to enjoy the fruits of the military protection of the Soviet Union, as well as its markets, while trading with the West on conditions which do not require them to give up their sovereignty. This alternative is especially appealing to those countries that happen to possess raw materials and goods which the Western market needs, while not possessing many industries of the type which are already well developed in the West. Thus it is a far better alternative for Rumania with its oil than it is for Poland, whose industries are often inefficient by Western standards.

Finally, the effort to create political ties was hampered by the Stalinist legacy of an imperial relationship. As a result the East European leaderships had reason to fear that any multilateral political arrangement was essentially a design for the perpetuation of Soviet hegemony. Moreover, the Soviet effort to infuse collective political organs with a new life came at a time when the East Europeans were becoming more sensitive about their sovereignty, and when the Communist parties were preaching the principle of complete independence. All this put obstacles in the way of a vital Soviet alliance system.

19 / IDEOLOGY AND POWER IN RELATIONS AMONG COMMUNIST STATES

> Friendship is real and strong when people share the same views about events, about history, about life. If you do not share the philosophy of the Communist Party because you have your own principles and your own views, then it is possible to maintain good relations with Communists but it is difficult to achieve a deep friendship as we understand it. — Nikita Khrushchev, March 1958

NIKITA KHRUSHCHEV was speaking of the role of ideology in relations between individuals and among nations. His remarks make it clear that he was addressing himself essentially to the question of political friendship, to that state of affairs in which diverse parties have concluded that there exists among them a sufficient community of interests to justify political collaboration. To a Marxist-Leninist, however, politics requires not only purposeful action to achieve particular objectives but also the conscious awareness of how that action relates to existing reality. Hence we can understand Khrushchev's emphasis on history, on philosophy. In brief, he was suggesting that politics, the exercise of power, cannot be viewed independently of ideology, the source of political purpose.

The importance of the dynamic relationship between power and ideology to Communist practice has been stressed in the preceding chapters. On the basis of the foregoing analysis it now might be appropriate to attempt some tentative generalizations about the role of ideology and power in relations among Communist states, defining at the same time somewhat more precisely the nature of modern ideology. The discussion which follows, while perhaps wide-ranging, might help to bring out the underlying assumptions of what has preceded and provide the basis for evaluating some possible trends in the future.

The importance of ideology in contemporary politics is closely related to the spread of literacy, the increasing pace of socioeconomic change, and the growing political awareness of the populace, all of which have made politics a matter of much broader popular concern The mass character of modern politics typifies not only the demo cratic systems but also the contemporary totalitarian movement which engage in mass indoctrination and attempt to channel the growing political consciousness of people. Political power has accord ingly become much more dependent on the successful mobilization and manipulation of the masses. This development, in turn, has re sulted in a new kind of responsiveness between the ruler and the ruled. In democratic societies the emergence of party systems with certain programs of action has been in large part a response to this social development. In many parts of the world, however, intense so cial dissatisfaction with the status quo, a sense of political frustration the weakening of traditional bonds induced by economic change have resulted in the emergence of a new type of political action which is nondemocratic but which also requires the mobilization of popula support. The continued spread of literacy and industrial technolog has at the same time resulted in an optimistic expectation that soci engineering based on certain theories about the nature of society ca resolve the existing social, economic, and political dilemmas. Th bond between those wishing to reorganize society through politic action within the context of real or imagined deprivation and th masses whose support is necessary to such action has usually bee supplied in modern times by a revolutionary ideology embodied i a political movement. Unlike the more implicit and relatively ur articulated ideological outlook of the stable democratic societies, th ideology of a revolutionary movement is overt, its logic is expose and its relationship with political action not only evident but crucia

Modern revolutionary ideology is essentially an action progra derived from certain doctrinal assumptions about the nature of realit and expressed through certain stated, not overly complex, assertio about the inadequacy of the past or present state of societal affair These assertions include an explicit guide to action outlining metho for changing the situation, with some general, idealized notions abo the eventual state of affairs.

Modern revolutionary ideology thus combines five elements whic make it qualitatively different from social consensus and philosophic traditions which characterize, for instance, the American way of lif

1. Such ideology is based on certain *stated* assumptions. In oth

words, it is normally an explicit statement to which reference can be made for purposes of inspiration, guidance, or indoctrination.

2. Precisely because ideology serves in part as a link between the political leaders, their movement, and the masses, such statements cannot be excessively complex, and at least parts of the written doctrine must be available in the form of relatively simple, dogmatic tenets, often combining elements of myth with a certain rationality (the latter required by the spread of literacy and technology). Lenin's *Imperialism* or Marx's *Communist Manifesto* — as contrasted with other, essentially philosophical Marxist writings which play a greater role in influencing the more educated and intellectually oriented groups — would be typical examples.

3. Ideology attempts to place the blame for existing inadequacies on some identifiable object, be it a special class, state, or race, thereby concretizing to the masses the nature of their dissatisfaction.

4. It is a guide to action in that it offers specific methods for changing the existing situation, for destroying the identified enemies, and for satisfying mass cravings.

5. Finally, ideology defines generally the nature of the future society in which the existing dissatisfactions will be absent, although in this respect ideology usually tends to be imprecise insofar as specific, concrete, institutional aspects are concerned. The ultimate ideal state tends to be a myth and an aspiration, sufficiently general to satisfy most individual wants.

The preceding definition groups both Communism and Fascism or Nazism under the general heading of revolutionary ideology. The case is not so clear-cut with nationalism since, by definition, there is no universal nationalist ideology, except in the general sense that all nations are entitled to their political independence and sovereignty. Nationalism can be seen as the most basic, even the most primitive, modern ideology, the first to mobilize mass support for purely political purposes, namely to create or strengthen a nation-state. Nationalism planted the seed of political consciousness among the people without which contemporary ideologies would find it difficult to flourish; and the rise of modern revolutionary ideology is, accordingly, closely related to the emergence of the "politics of mass consciousness," that politics which are based on the assumption that all members of society should identify themselves with the political process (although not necessarily direct it), and that all members should consciously acquiesce in the officially stated purposes of that political activity.

The politics of mass consciousness rejects the notion that society is a spontaneously developing entity, but emphasizes the need to perceive the nature of social change and the feasibility of steering and even shaping such change. That change is said to lead to the victory of virtue over vice, both viewed in absolute terms.[1] Although future-oriented, a revolutionary ideology might become also the source of a defense of the status quo after the ideologically oriented movement has seized power. However, it is very doubtful that the leaders of the movement would then claim that the final stage of fulfillment has been reached. Even after power has been seized, the ideology would continue to serve for purposes of mobilizing support — claiming that Today's is the best possible world but that Tomorrow's will be better yet.

POLICY AND IDEOLOGY

The relationship between ideology and power, as some of the preceding thoughts suggest, involves several facets. Ideology in some respects is inherent in power, as when it serves to raise morale or to stimulate fanatical convictions. Ideology also shapes the purposes for which power may be used, helping to determine the direction in which power is applied; it often serves to rationalize power, to justify it, thereby in effect becoming part of it while implicitly transforming power into authority. For purposes of clarity, we might define power either in its substantive or relational meaning, as simply the ability to obtain a desired action from others, or to produce a desired event. Ideology might be considered under certain circumstances as a factor of power (just as wealth is), and generally its locus is likely to correspond to that of power. For instance, in the early stages of the Communist camp it was sufficient to know Soviet views or ideological assertions concerning a particular subject to predict the behavior of the other Communist leaderships. Since power, however, involves reciprocal, and usually asymmetrical relationship (that is, the power wielder is also influenced, but to a lesser extent, by the objects of the exercise of power), the role of ideology in affecting the reactions and shaping the expectations of both the subject and object, either as individuals or as states, becomes relevant. A widespread expectation of a mode of behavior might even help to induce such behavior and thereby become a factor of power relationship.[2] Power, however, is not necessarily equivalent to *authority*, which can attain results similar to those produced by the use of power by being accepted as legitimate or wise, and therefore obeyed even if the actual force impel compliance is lacking. In time, ideology, by justifying power and transforming it into authority, can diminish the amount of power which must be applied to achieve compliance or to produce the desired effect.

In brief, then, the relationship between ideology and power is viewed here not as causal but as contingent, with ideology being essentially a doctrine of political power which simultaneously defines the ends, outlines the methods for their fulfillment, and mobilizes support for them. Under certain conditions, the imperatives of power may affect the ideological concepts, but it could be argued that the tenets so affected were fundamentally operational ones — those outlining the methods of achieving the ultimate goal — and so may occasionally change without affecting the final ends.

The preceding comments might be clarified if a distinction is made between those aspects of the ideology which can be called its philosophical component, those which can be called its doctrinal component, and those which might be referred to as its action program. Although the three aspects cannot always be neatly compartmentalized and will often overlap, basically the philosophical parts involve the *a priori* assumptions which form the foundation stone of the ideology. In the case of Marxism-Leninism this involves dialectical materialism, the existence of matter independent of human consciousness, and so on. The philosophical parts are least subject to change and are essentially dogmatic. The doctrine pertains to such matters as historical laws and phases, the role of the dictatorship of the proletariat and of the Communist Party, the inevitability of the collapse of capitalism, contradictions within imperialism, and the like. These are historically contingent concepts of a strategic character. The action program, derived from the doctrinal principles which in turn are grounded on the philosophical assumptions, involves the purposeful process of fulfillment of that which is held to be immanent. It can change if need be, and the success of the change in itself establishes a new contingent truth. The question of socialism in one country, or of many versus one way to socialism, is of this variety. Without the doctrine, ideology would be equivalent to mere pragmatism; relying on doctrine alone, ideology would be just a static dogma. Doctrine linked with action program gives modern ideology its religious fervor, its sense of constant direction, as well as its freedom of maneuver in the use of political power to achieve that which must be, while the dogmatic philosophical basis gives the ideology the appearance of possessing the absolute truth. Doctrine is thus the politically crucial link between dogmatic assumptions and pragmatic action.[3]

Ideologically motivated power, while subject to occasional practical adjustments, also creates pressures for the fulfillment of the ideology. The maintenance of political power precludes static situations and continuously requires action and policy. The political power of an ideological movement stems from and then requires a response to a situation of stress, of social unrest, or of promised utopia. Since an important ingredient of the movement's power is the element of explicit and proclaimed purpose which furthers its seizure of political power, the fulfillment of major portions of the ideologically stated objectives becomes a necessity dictated by power, by the inner dynamic of the movement itself. It is therefore doubtful that Hitler could have survived without gradually increasing the scope of the National-Socialist revolution in Germany, or that Stalin and his regime could have maintained the New Economic Policy without ultimately losing power. But a mere "power analysis," postulating that the maximization of power is the basic political impulse of these regimes, would be inadequate to an understanding of German and Soviet developments. They only become meaningful when ideology, while considered an element of that power, is at the same time seen as a substantive and residual element in its own right. Purpose and policy thus constantly interact and are inseparable.

There is a further consideration to be taken into account. The exercise of power is in itself a matter of judgment, and ideology accordingly influences the choice of alternatives for action. Ideology as a method of organizing the perception of reality provides certain categories for determining the meaning of an era, the nature of the era's dominant forces — it distinguishes between broad trends and mere passing episodes. It helps to clarify the various observable contradictions and conflicts, and through this provides a sense of purpose and a clarity of direction which involve a long-range commitment transcending the short-range crises. In this respect it is a source of confidence, even blind confidence. As one commentator recently stated: "Our empiricism dooms us to an essentially reactive policy that improvises a counter to every Soviet move, while the Soviet emphasis on theory gives them the certainty to act, to maneuver and to run risks."[4] This too may have its shortcomings, but the question here is not its effectiveness but the matter of the nature of commitment and its relation to power.

To dismiss ideology as an irrelevant criterion to an understanding of the political conduct of Soviet or Nazi leaders[5] raises another problem. To do so would be to assume that it is possible to build up a large organization ostensibly dedicated to certain explicit objectives, in which individuals are promoted on the basis both of their professional ability and their demonstrable ideological dedication, but in which an inner sanctum operates, makes decisions with a complete disregard of the ideological principles of the movement, indeed remains immune to the constant pressures for ideological justification, and cynically disregards the official creed. However, it is a matter of historical record that many of the Soviet leaders suffered personal hardship in the name of their ideological commitment, were educated through the absorption of well-defined concepts, in turn contributed to their further elaboration, and subsequently educated others in the arcana of the ideological thinking. Once in power, they tended to view the world, particularly the outside world, in categories of thought shaped by that ideology and made political decisions on the basis of information forwarded to them by bureaucrats who were either indoctrinated with that ideology or who knew well that their leaders subscribed to it. As a result, the information flowing to the leaders in itself contained interpretations bound to reinforce the doctrine. These leaders, in turn, being intensely concerned with the use of power for the sake of pursuing their ends, made ideological faith a basic criterion of membership within the movement, and subsequently of advancement within it.

A skeptical leader would run a serious risk of undermining his power if he were to allow himself to question the ideology. It is very doubtful that even Stalin could have done it — although this is not to exclude appeals to other than ideological sentiments (such as his wartime nationalist appeals). So much of Stalin's power, however, involved his special position as the creative and sole interpreter of Marxism-Leninism that for him to denounce the ideology would have meant to deny himself an important source of strength. Of course, in shaping policy he might have dismissed it altogether, although the very implementation of that ideology through the re-creation of society made the concepts part of the conditioning environment. Indeed, it could be said that as ideology ceases to live in the hearts and minds of the revolutionary "ideologues," it is reborn in the institutions of the new society.

All this suggests that even if Stalin's chief criterion of action was "will this increase or limit my power?" he still had to phrase his policy ideologically; he still employed ideological categories which imperceptibly shaped his thoughts; and he consequently was acting as if committed to it. His operational language and concepts in their turn affected the processes of communications and of information. Given his power, this very fact forced his lieutenants to respond in keeping with the ideological categories, thereby creating a chain reaction downward, emphasizing to the lower minions the importance of ideology. They would accordingly strive to demonstrate *their* ideological fidelity. Echoes of this ideological orthodoxy within the institutions of power would subsequently be heard at the top, making it difficult for the leaders to act in open disregard of the ideology, or at least forcing them to justify their acts in terms of it. However, since the ideology, as observed previously, does not involve the same amount of doctrinal complexity for all the members of the movement, a considerable element of flexibility is retained at the top, especially since changing situations may be said to dictate new departures and solutions. In a way, such flexibility is reassuring evidence to the devotees that their ideology is living and is "creatively" linked with the changing reality.[6]

Still, could not one argue that the critical factor in relations among Communist states is their respective power and the interests of the various leaderships? But, again, both power and interest involve judgments, purposes, and assumptions. When Molotov was furiously attacked in 1955 (see Chapter 8) for underestimating the historical stage of socialist construction in the USSR (and hence undermining the exalted status of the USSR among the other Communist states), the Soviet regime was illustrating the close interconnection between domestic developments, ideology, and the USSR's paramount position in the Communist camp. Similarly, when the Chinese charged the Soviet leadership in 1965 with restoring capitalism in the Soviet Union, they were attempting to strike at the very foundation of Soviet authority in international Communism. The fact that so much importance was attached to the doctrinal issue not only suggests that actual conviction is involved but that the existing system is ideologically oriented and that ideological issues, since they have the capacity to lead people astray, are more than mere rationalizations. If neither Molotov nor his colleagues actually believed that there is an important difference between saying that "the foundations of a socialist society have already been built" in the USSR or that the USSR is now in the stage of "the gradual transition from socialism to communism," they must have at least thought that many others in the system did. And by acting on that assumption they were actually cementing the place of ideology as an aspect of the existing system, not only internally but also in terms of the Communist camp in general.*

The unwavering Soviet insistence on the radical internal reconstruction of states falling under Communist control is also in keeping with this interdependent relationship of ideology and power. Even if the reason for enforcing dramatic, indeed revolutionary, changes in East Europe was merely the desire to strengthen Soviet power over the area and not to construct Communism per se, the mere fact that the method of strengthening that power was conceived in terms of large-scale socioeconomic changes shows the underlying ideological basis. One could certainly argue that a more moderate program would have created much less resistance and hence would have favorably affected the Communist power situation. The standard Communist answer — that Communism is not safe without creating a social upheaval that uproots the existing interest groups — in itself reveals an approach to problems of political power that is strongly tinged with ideological assumptions. This approach then dictates Communist strategy and tactics.

The progressive channeling of ideology, from a general worldview down to everyday tactical actions, permits the Communist leadership to feel that Communist policy, even when forcibly stimulating change, is in keeping with a natural historical process. Khrushchev was most probably deeply sincere when he said to Adlai Stevenson: "You must understand, Mr. Stevenson, that we live in an epoch when one system is giving way to another. When you established your republican system in the eighteenth century the English did not like it. Now, too, a process is taking place in which the peoples want to live under a new system of society; and it is necessary that one agree and reconcile himself with this fact. *The process should take place without interference.*" [8] In such a view, the emergence of Communist-ruled states and the forcible transformation of their societies is part of the historical process. The realization of unity among such states is a necessary attribute of such a process and, in turn, a proof of ideological validity. Conversely, the appearance of disunity is a major threat to the vitality of the ideology. Maintaining a balance between ideological unity and a recognition of domestic diversity is an intricate operation and has shaped much of the history of the formation of the Communist camp and of the relations among its members.

* "The question of the construction of Communism in the USSR cannot now be considered in isolation from the problems connected with the existence and development of the growing camp of peace, democracy, and socialism," *Kommunist* commented critically on Molotov's statement (no. 14, September 1955).

PATTERNS OF INTER-COMMUNIST RELATIONS

In theory and for a long time in practice these relations could best be described as integral relations. The rulers of the Communist states subscribe to certain common ideological assumptions about the nature of social change; they have fundamentally similar utopian conceptions of social engineering; they have been exposed to similar operational and ideological training; and, finally, they share a self-righteous hostility toward a mutual enemy. In brief, even without assuming that their ideology always influences their policy, there is a common and explicit faith linking the rulers of these states. The lowest common denominator of that faith, joining such diverse leaders as those from Peking and from Prague, can be reduced to several core assumptions: (1) that capitalism is inevitably doomed to collapse and that socialism (Communism) as a form of political socioeconomic organization must prevail in its place; (2) that the social processes dooming capitalism must be promoted purposefully through disciplined organization, action, and class conflict; (3) that in societies ruled by Communists internal social change must be stimulated through rapid socialization and industrialization, the latter also of critical importance in altering the balance of force between capitalism and Communism; (4) that, because of domestic resistance and external threat, political power must be firmly held by the Communist Party and that Communist parties must make certain that their external unity is maintained through centralized leadership, common agreement on the ideological principles, and basic similarity in action. It can be readily seen from the foregoing that the sequence of these central assumptions leads from the general to the more specific. Taken together, they provide a unity of outlook which helps to bridge the great national and cultural gaps in the multinational, Euro-Asian Communist camp.

Relations among the ruling Communist parties were integral in the sense that the policies of any party were derived interdependently from its power purposes and ideological concepts, neither of which regards any aspect of society as outside its purview and both of which are related to a "universally" valid process of historical change. Since a Communist Party not merely struggling for power but already engaged in the construction of socialism comes under great pressure to adjust to domestic circumstances, only a continuous "consultation" between the various ruling parties can maintain the cohesion so essential to the universal victory. Any political decision related to the core assumptions said to originate from a single source, Marxism-Leninism, necessarily becomes relevant to the political decisions made by other

Communist regimes. As a consequence, a policy of a given regime either helps to validate the policy of another regime or, if at variance with it, constitutes a threat to its legitimacy and ideological orthodoxy. Accordingly, the traditional international-relations principle of noninterference in the domestic political affairs of one sovereign state by another became inapplicable to relations among Communist-ruled states. This consideration explains why it has been so difficult for the Communist states to adjust from the condition of unity to that of diversity. Diversity in action, especially in domestic practices of one state, automatically challenged the ideological validity of another state. Diversity in theory, of course, made things even worse.

The fading of Soviet predominance has accentuated this difficulty. For several decades the Soviet Union was the only state engaged in implementing policies said to be derived from Marxism-Leninism. Many of the tactical or strategic questions with which other Communists were faced after coming to power, even if under substantially different conditions, had been experienced by the Soviet party. Its leaders naturally felt qualified to comment authoritatively on the domestic policies of the new regimes. But more important still was the political dependence of the new regimes on the power of the USSR and the personal training of the new leaders by the CPSU. Most of the Communist leaders had been exposed to international Communist activity, either as Comintern agents or as revolutionary leaders, in an era dominated by Stalinism. As a result, among otherwise very diverse nations the ruling elites shared a similar schooling, similar patterns of experience in organizing and viewing reality, and, finally, similar operating and bureaucratic methods. Furthermore, faced in their respective countries by almost universal hostility, the newly installed leaders must have felt much like the Christian missionaries on pagan soil. How many concessions could they make before compromising the faith? How many should they make to promote its acceptance? The Jesuits, for instance, under the energetic leadership of Robert de Nobilibus, attempted to convert India during the seventeenth century through adapting to local conditions. Posing as Brahmans, adopting existing customs and rituals, although claiming that the latter were merely civil rites, they made thousands of converts, despite growing apprehension in the Vatican.[9]

However, to the East European Communists, directly dependent on Soviet power, the problem of adjustment was not merely one of ideology but also of power. Their weakness put Moscow in a position to maintain a continued and direct involvement in the political decisions of the new Communist regimes. The special role played by the USSR, even if resulting initially in nonreciprocal integral relations, helped to establish the principle that the political practice of one Communist state is materially relevant to another, and that each Communist state must continually refer its practice to the general practices of the camp. The unity of theory and practice should never be confined to narrow national frontiers. Over a prolonged period of time, however, that general principle could not be applied with regularity and uniformity. Many varying factors inevitably affected the actual application of the principle to relations among ruling Communist parties. The gradual decline of Soviet predominance and the need to base unity on the recognition of diversity led to the transformation of the integral relations into the more traditional international pattern.

In the course of this study, five basic phases in such relations were noted, each resulting in differing degrees of accepted involvement of one Communist Party (usually Soviet) in the affairs of another ruling party. An examination of these five phases strongly suggests that without some central power, or eventually authority, the unity rooted in ideology disintegrates under the impact of time, change, specific interests, and differing conditions. The fate of the Protestant churches, once they split from the recognized authority of the papacy, might be a case in point. Therefore, if ideology is to serve as the basis for unity, it must have an institutional source of sanctioned interpretation and a built-in ideological justification for the existence of that source. This goes considerably beyond a mere reliance on the similarity of socioeconomic conditions and institutions to guarantee identity of view and unity in action.

Within the five broad phases noted in the preceding chapters, it may be observed that during the first the element of Soviet political power provided the general protective shield under which action was undertaken by the various Communist parties to capture and consolidate their power. Relations among Communist parties during this period formally resembled the traditional pattern of interstate relations. The preliminary nature of their activity in itself allowed for greater diversity, which was also justified by the international situation and Soviet preoccupation with reconstruction and consolidation. Integral relations developed in the second phase, during Stalinism. This phase was characterized by the central power's insistence that its experience in building socialism be the slide rule for all domestic calculations of the ruling Communist parties. Ideology declined in importance as a unifying element and became essentially the translation of past Soviet history into current Communist practice. In the third phase, Soviet efforts to reintroduce the core assumptions of the ideology as an active unifying element, together with the actual decline in direct Soviet power and the unsettling consequences of the Soviet policy toward Yugoslavia, created a situation in which domestic developments in the various Communist states began to interact, leading to a dissipation of the uniformity. A divisive interparty dialogue developed out of the varying blends of specific national conditions and universal requisites. The fourth phase saw the continued reliance on common ideological commitment being buttressed by a concerted effort to rebuild and legitimize a common center within the camp. In this phase integral relations became more reciprocal, with the central power's domestic policies more responsive to the domestic policies of the other ruling parties. International relations of the more traditional type became dominant during the fifth phase, with the failure of the Soviet effort to create an accepted source of ideological unity, a failure precipitated by the disruptive consequences of the Sino-Soviet dispute which stimulated further self-assertiveness in East Europe.

The methods used to organize relations among the Communist regimes changed with each of the five phases. These methods can be divided into state treaties, both bilateral and multilateral, interstate economic relations, bilateral and multilateral party dealings, and finally supranational organizational ties, both on the state and party basis. During the first phase bilateral state treaties played a role in organizing and consolidating the politics of the bloc, with such agreements as the Soviet-Czech or the Polish-Soviet or the Yugoslav-Polish actually expressing and strengthening the political status quo. These were thus comparable to regular bilateral treaty relations elsewhere. Similarly, the Yugoslav-Bulgarian interstate ties were of considerable political significance, although essentially in the planning stage. At this juncture, no multilateral interstate ties existed, although some were planned — as, for instance, the possible accession of Rumania to the Yugoslav-Bulgarian federation, a scheme ultimately condemned by Moscow. Interstate economic relations were both bilateral, in the sense of trade treaties and reparations arrangements, and multilateral in that regional economic ties were planned, such as among Poland, Czechoslovakia, and Hungary. Party dealings moved from bilateral ties, existing initially between each party and the CPSU, in the direction of multilateral "consultation," institutionalized in the Cominform, through which the CPSU exploited the weakness of the parties to ensure unity in doctrine and practice.

In the second Stalinist phase, all state treaties declined in importance, and were only used to formalize a relationship of strict hierarchical, almost feudal, subordination. At the same time, the previously planned schemes of political collaboration on a regional basis were abandoned under Soviet direction, and each regime essentially dealt with the USSR only. Significantly, only the Chinese-Soviet political treaty could be regarded as of any consequence during this period, suggesting that Soviet-Chinese relations in 1949–1950 were in a stage similar to, for instance, Soviet-Yugoslav relations in 1945–1946; this also reflected, of course, the special relationship existing between Moscow and the strong and confident Peking regime. Economic relations among the states similarly involved bilateralism, with the central focus being the USSR, while autarky was the operational principle for each state. Interparty contacts became infrequent and involved primarily relations between individual parties and the CPSU.

The third phase, one of rapid change and crisis, saw an effort to revitalize the importance of formal interstate ties through the Warsaw Pact, a multilateral political-military treaty. However, more restricted regional political ties were not developed, partly because of the different internal trends within the Communist-ruled states and partly because such a development would certainly have been discouraged in Moscow. In economic relations, the new recognition of the desirability of formal multilateral political ties was matched by the creation of a standing economic organization. Interparty contacts grew in frequency, and interparty declarations of understanding were issued more often than before on a bilateral basis, primarily between the USSR and the respective parties.

The fourth phase, dominated by the effort to reconstruct the camp, involved a renewed importance of bilateral interstate relations. The Polish-Soviet agreements of November and December 1956 played such a role. In brief, interstate relations began to take on the shape of the more traditional patterns of international affairs. This development was paralleled by an effort to increase the importance of the permanent multilateral economic organ, ultimately shaping the *economic interdependence* of the bloc. Party ties during this phase were cultivated with unprecedented intensity, with more bilateral declarations of common understanding and purpose issued than during the preceding three phases together. The parties striving to pro

tect their autonomy favored bilateralism in view of the relative decline of Soviet power, while Moscow and the centralist parties used
bilateral declarations to promote multilateral contacts. Several multilateral conferences were actually staged and used by Moscow to subdue the recalcitrant parties through the combined pressure of the
camp's membership. However, the appearance of the Sino-Soviet dispute vitiated the utility of these multilateral conferences as a means
of promoting unity.

The fifth phase, marked by the appearance and eventually even
the acceptance of pluralism,[10] was marked by the Sino-Soviet conflict and by the search for a new framework of unity. Multilateral
party meetings were dominated by strife, while the attempt to transform CEMA into a supranational multilateral organization was successfully defied by Rumania. In that setting, increasing reliance was
placed by Moscow on developing bilateral party and state ties with
sympathetic regimes, hoping thereby to weave a fabric of unity and
to isolate the Chinese. Narrower regional political and economic relations were also being developed by some states, with Moscow
neither able nor perhaps inclined to oppose that. The Kremlin itself
began to stress more the Warsaw Treaty as a common bond. Nonetheless, the paramount feature of relations among Communist states
during this phase was the failure of Communist diplomacy to avert
bitter interstate and interparty breaks,[11] and the increasing similarity
of relations among Communist states with relations among non-Communist states.

Throughout the five phases there was a close connection between
external relations and internal factional conflict. In Stalin's time, the
conflict usually involved the elimination of those leaders who could
conceivably oppose his supremacy. Later, many of the conflicts involved efforts by dissatisfied Communist elements to redress the acute
imbalance in relations among Communist states. It is likely that in the
future internal factional conflicts will continue to focus on the question of relations with Moscow and/or Peking as well as on the over-
all issue of the degree of desired national independence. Instability
in Moscow is likely to pose these issues in sharper relief and to contribute to greater flux in relations among the Communist states.

In general, it is improbable that the existing condition of pluralism
can be statically maintained on the basis of two Communist con-
stellations, a more industrially advanced European-Soviet, and an industrially retarded but rapidly industrializing, violently anti-Western
Sino-Asian complex of Communist states. Pluralism tends to be a

dynamic condition, and it will either grow or be compressed. In spite of their professions of acceptance of diversity, and even their seeming resignation to pluralism, the Soviet leaders may be expected to try to contain the centrifugal pressures. The CPSU has tried several times to institutionalize multilateral party contacts and it may be expected that these efforts will be repeated. Moreover, the Soviet leaders may be presumed to entertain the hope that further economic integration, in spite of the obstacles encountered by CEMA, will also contribute to greater political unity. Thus efforts to develop additional economic bonds in order to create interdependent economic relations, in which the Soviet Union would remain as the only autarkic component, will continue in the future.

To rely on economic ties alone, however, would be the economic determinism long since thrown overboard by Marxist-Leninists. The growing consolidation of Communist regimes with their home-grown personnel raises with increasing urgency the question of nationalism and poses the threat that creeping domesticism can be transformed in the long run into national Communism. The fanatic, highly intelligent Stalinists of 1945, men like Dimitrov, Rakosi, or Bierut, have gradually given way to hierarchically trained, pseudo-intellectual party *apparatchiki*, primarily interested in their own power; these leaders in turn are coming under pressure from the younger generation of technically trained intelligentsia, concerned with the domestic development of their countries. There is a growing tendency therefore for a ruling Communist Party to view the Communist camp from the standpoint of domestic interests and to evaluate it in terms of the camp's capacity to satisfy these interests. In domesticism there is always the latent danger that the basic question of Soviet versus national interest will ultimately be raised, even if that national interest merely means the most efficacious methods for the domestic construction of Communism and even if for the time being the power interests of the ruling elites dictate close ties with the USSR. Rumania's defiance of Moscow, stimulated largely by Rumanian domestic economic conditions, is a case in point. Moscow may hence periodically seek some reassurance of the continued primacy of the universal perspective which economic integration alone cannot ensure. Only a situation of ideological stress and of hostility to the outside world be it to the United States or to China, can prevent such a process from materializing rapidly.

Developing tighter political bonds within the Warsaw Treaty turning it into a "Commonwealth Politburo," may be one answer

That could be justified either by the danger posed to Eastern Europe and Russia by West German acquisition of nuclear weapons and/or by the threat for the East raised by Chinese territorial claims on Russia. Since the second eventuality is not likely to elicit too much East European concern, the nuclear problem and the alleged threat from Germany will probably continue to provide the central arguments on behalf of close Soviet-East European political cooperation. This cooperation could take the form of some common nuclear security arrangements, designed to emphasize the common fate and the common stake of the region. Pressure on Moscow for the sharing of that monopoly is inevitable, and the arguments which may be advanced on behalf of this sharing will not be easily refuted. Starting from the formal premise of equality and true friendship among socialist states, the Czechs, pointing to their record of political and ideological orthodoxy, could request them to counterbalance the West Germans. The Poles, fearful of the Germans, could similarly claim them. Even the East Germans could request nuclear weapons on the grounds that they cannot effectively compete with West Germany if the West Germans appear to enjoy greater trust among their allies than the East Germans do in Moscow. The Soviet Union may thus find it politically convenient to "lease" nuclear weapons and Soviet technicians to its allies, thus satisfying their craving for nuclear status without undermining Soviet know-how and employment monopoly. The Soviet military command of the Warsaw Pact would be a further guarantee of effective Soviet control within such allied "sharing," while a common political authority, in charge of framing basic policy and preserving a common outlook, would mitigate any possible unilateral adventures by a Communist state and even contribute to greater unity.

Future trends within the camp and in relations among Communist states depend on many other factors. There is, first of all, the changing character of the Cold War and of the external pressures on the Communist camp. There is the problem of the nature of the domestic changes in the Communist states and particularly the USSR and China. The emergence of new ruling elites in the Communist states will affect the picture, since they are not likely to have the same feelings of subservience that their predecessors, installed in power by the Soviets, inevitably felt toward Moscow. There is the question of the balance of industrial and technological strength between the East and the West. The future character of the camp also depends on the options available to some of its members. For example, the continuing fear that Germany will desire to reclaim some of its lost territories, as well as a certain identification in Central European thinking of Western policy with the German rejection of the Oder-Neisse line, places Poland and Czechoslovakia in a position of dependence on the USSR, regardless of ideological issues. National interest and geography thus serve to buttress the existing ideological bonds among the party leaderships.

On the other hand, given the fact that some of the European Communist-ruled states identify themselves with European culture and resent the abyss dividing them from Western Europe and driving them farther into the Euro-Asian bloc, efforts to promote the closest all-European links, without directly challenging the power of the regimes and, even more important, the basically socialist organization of their societies, might have the effect of undermining the Communist image of the world. If the Communist states in Europe were to be continuously invited to join in all-European undertakings of social economic, and political character, such Western overtures could eventually have some effect. The present Communist regimes might be expected to reject such invitations out of hand, but they would be likely to prove appealing to the new generation of Communist. less exposed to the Soviet dichotomic perspectives and traditiona suspicions. Not irrelevant to the attractiveness of such Western in itiatives is the considerable gap in the standard of living between the West and East. This all provides the basis for an imaginative and creative Western policy, designed to bridge the existing partition of Europe.[12]

THE COMMUNIST LEARNING PROCESS

Whatever the future of the Soviet bloc may be, one thing i certain: the effort to create stable Communist unity has exposed th Soviet and the other Communist leaderships to a difficult and dis illusioning experience. Writing in 1936 for the American journa *Foreign Affairs,* the brilliant Soviet theoretician N. Bukharin nc only flatly asserted that in an international Communist system ther could not be any "clash of real interests between proletarian state whatsoever" but went on to predict that "there can be no doubt tha after a certain stage of development tremendously powerful cer tripetal tendencies will be revealed — tendencies toward a state unio of proletarian republics."[13] By 1966, it was obvious that the ver opposite development had taken place. Yugoslavia, Poland, Albani China, North Korea, North Vietnam, Rumania, and, abortivel

Hungary, all had demonstrated centrifugal tendencies away from any "state union of proletarian republics."

For the Communist elites — particularly for the Soviet, whose mantle of leadership implied special responsibility for preserving Communist unity — this unexpected development had a profoundly educational impact. The disputes with the Chinese or with the East Europeans could not simply be dismissed, as the Nagy episode initially had been, as relics of narrow-minded nationalism left over from the bourgeois epoch. Moscow thus finally had to realize something that others had earlier perceived about Moscow itself: a revolutionary Communist leadership can be at the same time also a nationalist one. It was not easy for the Kremlin to perceive this verity and even harder to accept it. Accepting it was bound to cause ideological disillusionment and to prompt a basic change in the Soviet world outlook.

The outlook had been shaped by the dichotomic Leninist approach: he who is not with us is against us. This principle governed the initial Soviet reactions to centrifugal challenges. Yugoslavia was condemned as a heretic in 1948–49. Nagy was crushed. Even after the accommodation with Gomulka, brutal economic sanctions were applied against Albania and China. Yet with the exception of the one instance in which actual force was used, that is, against Hungary, Soviet "conflict management" in relations among Communist states was ineffective. This left the Soviet leaders the alternatives either of seeking accommodation or of crushing their opponents. The use of force had at least the advantage of permitting the Kremlin to retain ideological purity, since its application almost automatically entailed the condemnation of the victim as a heretic. But force could not be used effectively either against a powerful opponent like China or a geographically distant one like Albania. Nor did the political cost of the use of force seem justified to Moscow in the case of more limited challenges, such as those posed by Gomulka and, initially at least, by Gheorghiu-Dej.

Faced with this dilemma, Moscow made its decision on more pragmatic grounds. For those states that directly challenged the Kremlin's foreign policy — hence both its ideology and its state interest — the response was political and ideological warfare. But since in the setting of greater diversity Moscow no longer quite dared to proclaim that China or Albania were not "socialist" countries (as it had done with Yugoslavia until 1948),[14] this condition was tantamount to the admission that bitter hostility was possible between "socialist countries," thereby destroying the notion of inherent international harmony based on the similarity of socioeconomic systems.

For those states that did not overtly challenge Soviet foreign policy, even though otherwise they rejected Moscow's supremacy, Moscow recognized the advantage of agreeing to disagree. That was the basis of the Khrushchev-Gomulka accommodation. Rumania was a more marginal case, and in 1964–1965 Moscow apparently was uncertain whether Rumania still belonged in the second category or had moved into the first. However, with some Yugoslav mediation, at least a temporary accommodation was reached. But the cumulative effect of this adjustment, as well as of those with the Poles and the Yugoslavs, was to water down the dichotomic perspective, replacing it with a rather more relative and less utopian standard for evaluating relations among Communist states.

Its practical advantage was that it permitted the Soviet Union to begin also the process of repairing its relations with North Vietnam and North Korea. In the case of North Vietnam, the Soviet effort was facilitated by the Vietnamese dependence on weapons assistance from the more developed Communist states. China alone could neither meet that need nor provide the North Vietnamese with adequate protection against American power. But it was the Soviet willingness to extend this aid, in spite of earlier Vietnamese identification with the Chinese position, that made possible the renewal of political relations between Hanoi and Moscow, gaining by early 1966 for Moscow, at least, something less than outright Vietnamese support for the Chinese. Similarly, in the case of North Korea, the Soviet leadership, particularly after Khrushchev's removal, was able to reestablish contacts and to normalize party and state relations, in spite of North Korean cordiality for the Chinese.[15]

That the Chinese had not yet drawn the same lessons was vividly demonstrated by the simultaneous cooling in Chinese-Korean relations and by the crudeness of the Chinese reactions to any evidence of Communist sympathy for the Soviet position. The most striking example was the unilateral reduction by the Chinese in 1965–1966 of rice deliveries to Cuba, an act of economic pressure notably similar to earlier and equally ineffective Soviet efforts to use economic pressure as a lever in inter-Communist relations. The Chinese action precipitated a violent Cuban condemnation, with the likely result that both Cuban and Chinese revolutionary prestige would suffer in Latin America. Indeed, it could be said that while the Chinese proved themselves excellent in sustained political warfare and enjoyed the upper hand over the Soviets in scoring ideological points, they lagged behind even the relatively slow-learning Russians in appreciating the merits of restraint in relations among Communist states. Nonetheless, under the educative impact of time and necessity, Chinese views also may eventually change.*

Adjustment to the complicated realities of international Communist relations was not merely a matter of learning through trial and error. It was also a question of articulating new principles to replace the old and simplistic utopian notions. In this regard foreign Communists pioneered and Moscow learned by digesting, sometimes with initial reluctance, the principles elucidated by them. The closer those Communists were to Moscow, the more difficult it was for the Soviets to dismiss their views as mere revisionist ramblings. That is why Palmiro Togliatti's statement of April 1964, published posthumously also in *Pravda*, was of such great importance. In effect, by rejecting the notion of "a centralized international organization," opposing any effort to create "exterior uniformity," and by insisting on the freedom of each party to formulate its own policies, with unity limited to the holding of entirely consultative interparty discussions, Togliatti was rejecting the Leninist tradition, binding on the international Communist movement since the Twenty-one Conditions.

Togliatti's views, and Moscow's permissive reaction, stimulated

---

* In this connection, the reader is invited to guess the source of the following statement:
"Contemporary revolutions are an inevitable, historically determined phenomenon. Today the Chinese Revolution is the strongest affirmation of the historical law discovered by Marxism-Leninism. As a result, the Chinese revolution ideologically arms revolutionaries throughout the world. The Chinese revolution showed in practice, on a mighty scale, that today the greater danger for the working-class movement is to overestimate the force of imperialism . . . Overestimating the strength of imperialism is not only seen in fear of it in general but, above all, in fear of imperialist intervention if, in the struggle against the traitorous domestic bourgeoisie, more decisive revolutionary measures should be taken."
It may come as a surprise to learn that the above is not a Chinese, but a Yugoslav statement, made even *after* the Stalin-Tito break. (V. Dedijer, "On the Chinese Revolution," *Komunist*, no. 2, March 1949, p. 172, as cited by A. Ross Johnson, "The Dynamics of Communist Ideological Change in Yugoslavia," unpublished Ph.D. thesis, Columbia University, 1967, ch. vi.)
At that time, the Yugoslavs were still describing Social Democrats as "the most fanatical enemies of the working class, the most despicable lackeys of American imperialism" who promote "the illusion that it is possible to achieve socialism by a road other than the revolutionary road." (R. Colakovic, *Komunist*, no. 3, May 1949, as cited by Johnson.)

a widespread reexamination among East European Communists of the underlying principles guiding relations among Communist states. A remarkably penetrating analysis, published in Czechoslovakia in late 1965 has already been mentioned (p. 436). Its importance was enhanced precisely by Czechoslovakia's past history of pliant conformity with Moscow's policies. Its author, a staff member of the official Czech Institute of International Politics and Economics, made a number of far-reaching observations that were not likely to go unnoticed in Moscow. Rejecting the notion that contemporary Communist diversity reflects a retrogressive step from "the golden age of unity" of the fifties, and dismissing as oversimplified the view restated by the 1960 Moscow Declaration that no conflicts can exist among Communist states, the author pleaded for the recognition of diversity as normal, and on that basis for the formulation of some guiding rules for relations among Communist states. In his view existing ideological categories and organizational forms were no longer adequate.

His own recommendations were bold: parties should be not only organizationally but ideologically independent. They should have that independence not only in domestic policies but also in the formulation of their foreign policies. "Hence it is necessary to discard the fiction of unity meaning absolute identity of views of the Communist and Workers' parties . . ." No country or party can be excluded from the Communist community even "if *the great majority* of parties is convinced that the standpoints of the former are incorrect or non-Marxist." No coercion or pressure of any sort may be applied against such a country. It is particularly pernicious to translate ideological party differences into political or economic state pressures. Bilateral relations are to be preferred.[16]

It is noteworthy that the thrust of the Czech author's argument was more negative than positive. He was quite specific in what was to be avoided. Since much that was mentioned actually involved established Soviet behavior, the analysis represented at least implied criticism of Soviet conduct. His positive recommendations included a plea for compromise, for avoiding the excesses of nationalism, for harmonious discussions. However, perhaps the two most important points he made were his advocacy of the compartmentalization of ideological and state relations, rejecting the intrusion into the latter of any conflicts derived from the former, and his striking recommendation that each party decide entirely on its own what Marxism is, even in the face of the honest conviction of "the great majority" of other parties that a genuine departure from the essentials of Marxism had taken place. The implementation of this principle could result in states labeling themselves Marxist as a matter of convenience, or, conversely, in retaining the external label of Marxism in order to avoid the charge of treason from others, even though quite deliberately abandoning Marxism in practice. Needless to add, the consequence would be to deprive the Communist ideology of any common content whatsoever.

These Czech views were symptomatic of the shift from integral to international relations among Communist states. The emphasis on domestic autonomy and the absence of any general standard was a necessity dictated by the realities of the bloc. But they also made a mockery of the universal claims of the ideology which at least the "integral" relations reflected. That such recommendations were aired in Czechoslovakia was testimony to the ideological crisis produced by conflicts among Communist states.

Indeed, some prominent Communist thinkers openly admitted that their ideology was simply inadequate in responding to the challenge of nationalism when that challenge was raised by a Communist state. In Poland a stormy debate erupted around a book by Adam Schaff, *Marxism and the Individual* (1965). Although primarily concerned with the problem of alienation, Schaff also noted that in his view Communism was running the risk of being submerged by the wave of nationalism which was stimulating acute conflicts among Communist states. (In a revealing comment made during an officially sponsored debate on Schaff's book, one prominent Communist spokesman remarked "It is enough to be reminded how shocking to many were the first manifestations of contradictions within the international Communist movement. It seemed inconceivable . . . At first, as if a feeling of embarrassment dominated, the appearance of these contradictions was treated as something shameful, but today it is an understandable fact . . .")[17] However, Schaff did conclude that although problems of alienation, anti-Semitism, or nationalism did not automatically fade away with the creation of a Communist political order, such an order was better equipped than other systems for coping with these problems.* Schaff's recognition of the persist-

---

* But even this modified optimism about the international Communist system was not shared by all Communists. Commenting on Chinese-Cuban affairs, Castro boldly raised the possibility that "in the world of tomorrow (which the revolutionaries are struggling to establish) the powerful countries will be able to take on themselves the right to blackmail, exercise extortion against, pressure, commit aggression against and strangle other smaller peoples . . ." (Speech of February 6, 1966)

ence and even intensification of nationalism and his conclusion typified the change that was taking place. The argument was no longer that "salvation comes automatically with socialism." Rather, the argument advanced was that socialism offered a better way toward salvation but not salvation itself; in effect, a less utopian, more realistic and relativistic perspective.

Eventually, views such as Kotyk's or Schaff's cannot fail but seep also into the Soviet consciousness, contributing to the further legitimation of the forces promoting pluralism and revisionism within the Communist world. The learning process, however painful and however subject to occasional reverses, nonetheless moves steadily forward, both reinforcing and reinforced by the flux in relations among Communist states.

IDEOLOGICAL RELATIVIZATION AND EROSION

Inherent in both the changes in relations among Communist states and in the Communist ideological conceptions governing these relations was the increasing relativization of the doctrine. Formerly absolute and rigid principles were becoming relative and flexible. With each party increasingly able to insist that its Marxism-Leninism was correct, and with the politically expedient principle of agreeing to disagree gaining broader acceptance in relations among Communist states, the doctrine was becoming diluted and less coherent.

Moreover, in the course of the Sino-Soviet dispute, Leninism has increasingly been exposed to an implicit attack from both the Chinese and the Soviet sides. The Soviets, in stressing the possibilities for a peaceful transition to socialism, have tended to minimize the Leninist stress on revolutionary activism. They have thus argued that their own revolution was "accomplished almost peacefully" and that it had been "the most bloodless of all revolutions." [18] They have also cited the Hungarian revolution of 1918 and the Czechoslovak coup of 1948 as other examples of such peaceful transitions. The Chinese, in response, have charged the Soviets with moving toward Bernsteinism, and have categorically asserted "the inevitability of violent revolution." This has prompted the Soviet spokesmen to argue that the Chinese were replacing the complex Marxist theory of revolution, which allegedly combined both subjective voluntarism with objective dialectics, with a crude "theory of violence," which "is closely linked with the ideology of militarism." [19] The irony of the situation is that while the Soviets had a case in charging the Chinese with the militarization of the Leninist concept of revolution, the Chinese had a point in accusing the Soviets of its pacification.

In their discussion of the role of peasantry, both sides also further undermined the Leninist tradition. The Chinese, by elevating the role of the peasantry to the decisive force in the revolutionary struggle, have been moving toward a form of radical populism, explicitly eschewed by Lenin. The Soviets naturally seized on this point as proof that the Chinese have been straying from Leninism.[20] However, again in their own stress on the potentialities of peaceful transition wherever the proletariat is powerful, the Soviets, too, were jettisoning the Leninist legacy. It is, indeed, a matter of historical paradox to think that the two principal enemies of Leninism were the radical populists and the Mensheviks; and that the debate between the Chinese and the Soviets about the Leninist legacy has pushed them increasingly toward the positions once held by Lenin's opponents.

Symptomatic of the destruction of Leninism was the increasing tendency of East European commentators to use more often the vaguer term "Marxism" rather than "Marxism-Leninism" when discussing ideological questions. It reflected a growing realization that Lenin's contribution was historically limited to a specific society with a peculiar tradition, and that its relevance to the prevailing conditions in East Europe and even in the Soviet Union, as well as perhaps also more broadly to the nuclear age, was questionable.* However, reliance on the much broader and inescapably vaguer term "Marxism" further increased the scope for divergent notions and conflicting opinions.

Moreover, East European Communist views were very susceptible to West European Communist influence. The remarkable Communist-Catholic dialogue in Italy, culminating in a lengthy speech on January 25, 1966, by Luigi Longo, the Party Secretary, extolling the parallelisms between Catholic and Communist thought,[21] was not only embarrassing to Gomulka's anti-Church campaign but was bound to influence East European Communist thought. It, in turn, would serve as a transmission belt, penetrating the Soviet Union. This was all the more likely since in the meantime Soviet practice had begun to veer away from its own theory. Only a mere decade earlier a leading Soviet spokesman had articulated the seven cardinal sins

---

* The Chinese, at the same time, were inclined to stress Mao's creative contributions whenever they mentioned Marxism-Leninism, thereby also diluting Lenin's standing.

of revisionism (Chapter 13, p. 310). It would not be difficult to demonstrate that by the mid-sixties the Soviet leadership was guilty in practice of at least six of these seven cardinal errors (save the one of undermining its own party, although even here that could have been said of Khrushchev's 1962 scheme to divide the CPSU into two parallel hierarchies).

The cohesion of the ideology, furthermore, was not enhanced by topsy-turvy shifts in the views of some of the party leaderships. In the context of the sixties, it is easily forgotten that in 1947 the Yugoslavs were enunciating views strikingly similar to those held later by the Chinese and so explicitly rejected in the 1958 Yugoslav program. Twenty years earlier the Yugoslavs were advocating the intensification of the struggle against imperialism, very much on the basis of a rigid dichotomic perspective; they were stressing the decisive role of the peasant in the revolutionary struggle; they were grandly announcing that their own rapid industrialization would put them on a par with Great Britain in a mere ten years; they were scoffing at the lack of revolutionary commitment among the other parties and stressing the violent, revolutionary pattern of their domestic policies.[22] Indeed, if it were not for considerations of political expediency, the Soviets could score some telling points by drawing parallels between the current views of the Chinese and the earlier views of the Yugoslav "revisionists."

The net result of these developments is that the same doctrine has come to mean different things to its believers in different places. It is no longer an exaggeration to say that the study of Soviet, Yugoslav, and Chinese Marxism-Leninism belongs more appropriately to the discipline of comparative ideologies rather than to the study of Communism. Given the existing political inclination among the Soviet and East European leaderships to blur ideological issues further in order to avert new ideological clashes, the process of the relativization of the ideology is likely to continue.

Changes in doctrine are thus no longer a matter of one elite (or even of one ruler) making conscious (and sometimes unconscious) adjustments with reality while still believing that the universal doctrine remains absolutely right; increasingly, it becomes necessary for several elites or rulers *consciously* to fuzz ideological formulations, at the same time that each side perhaps believes that its own interpretation is the correct one, but that it cannot be expressed because of the higher imperative of unity. In turn, these compromises, with their cynicism and manipulation and consequent relativization, cannot avoid threatening the domestic elite's conviction in the ideology. In some respects the Communist camp may be able to capitalize on this greater internal diversity. By appearing more flexible, the Communists can point to their internal diversity as proof that new states in Africa or Asia need not fear Communist imperialism. In fact, the Soviet Union has already gained from appearing more flexible and reasonable than the Chinese, and perhaps it has done so purposely, trying to derive some advantage from this particular difficulty.

Yet, in the history of ideas, relativization of a hitherto absolute ideology is often the first stage in the erosion of the vitality of the ideology. Erosion involves not mere changes in tactical considerations (the action program) but fundamental uncertainties about the doctrinal component, perhaps even casting a shadow on some of the philosophical assumptions. These uncertainties can be stimulated either by a rigidly dogmatic posture, which causes such a wide gulf between the ideology and reality that even the firmest believers are eventually shaken, or by such flexible compromises in the doctrine that only a label unites the various believers allegedly subscribing to the same doctrine.[23] Cynicism combined with institutional interests can for a while support the corrupted ideological edifice, but inside there develops an emptiness and the corrosive feeling that the structure of power no longer has any justification and legitimacy.

Unlike religion where the ultimate sanction is supernatural, material reality is said to validate the ideological assumptions of Communism. But if Communism fails to expand fast enough, if increasing concessions to the requirements of a particular national situation result in domestic adjustments shattering the basic universal assumptions of the ideology, if the dichotomy said to exist between the Western world and Communism is diluted, and if conflicts between Communist states become even more bitter, then such an erosion will accelerate within individual ruling parties. Factors largely pertinent to the relationship of any given ruling Communist elite to the camp are thus likely to be the source of erosion of the common ideological commitment. Ideological unity requires central ideological and political leadership, as revealed by the various phases of the bloc's development. Yet such unity cannot encompass all the diverse aspirations of the several ruling elites in the setting of inherently growing institutional and ideological pluralism.

Short of subordination based on force, diversity results in a weakening of the ideology or in ideological conflicts. Ideological erosion is hence stimulated as more of the ruling elites begin to see the camp as a brake to the domestic fulfillment of their social goals, although these varying goals might still be identified domestically under the catch-all of Communism. The general commitment to Communism, and even to its domestic dictatorship, might thus continue but the common universal perspective will have fallen victim to the process of erosion. The Communist camp might still persist in form but no longer in content. That at least has been the historical experience both of Christianity and of Islam as state systems, as well as of other movements based on militant secularist, nationalist, or ideological doctrines.

Revisionism was such erosion's harbinger. Its apocalyptic significance was to break through the integrating but distorting myth of the official ideology. The revisionist intellectuals, like the *politiques* in the sixteenth century, were too divorced from power and from the power wielders to avoid defeat in a direct political contest. But politics has a way of catching up with intellectual insight, and some practitioners of power have already realized that their unifying ideology has become a domestic liability to them.

Ideological erosion thus began with doubts about the general desirability of a cohesive bloc and of similarity in action. This then led some to have doubts about the basic, antagonistic dichotomy between the Communist and non-Communist worlds and ultimately may point to the conclusion that social change is an organic, interrelated process which has no winners or losers. In brief, the process of erosion began with the specific assumptions, led to skepticism about the general doctrine, and finally has placed high on the historical agenda the likelihood that the Soviet bloc will soon share the fate of other imperial systems. For the final consummation of this process however, the ideology must first be denied both victories and enemies, a difficult and paradoxical task since denial of one can be construed as the manifestation of the other.

APPENDICES

NOTES

BIBLIOGRAPHY

INDEX

APPENDIX A

Selected Statistics for the Communist Bloc, 1965

Country	Population (thousands)	Geographic area (square km)	Coal production (thousands of metric tons)	Crude steel production (thousands of metric tons)	Electric energy production (millions of kilowatt-hours)
Albania	1,900	28,748	300[b]	—	242[b]
Bulgaria	8,200	110,669	556	588	10,224
China	755,000	9,561,000	350,000[c]	12,000[b]	58,500[d]
Cuba	7,631	114,524	—	—	2,600[c]
Czechoslovakia	14,159	127,869	27,756	8,592	34,188
GDR	17,065	108,299	2,340[a]	4,310[a]	53,544
Hungary	10,146	93,030	4,368	2,520	12,172
Mongolia	1,087	1,535,000	800[b]	—	123[c]
North Korea	10,900[a]	120,538	14,040[b]	1,220[b]	11,770[b]
North Vietnam	17,700	158,750	4,000[b]	—	418[b]
Poland	31,496	312,520	117,360[a]	9,084	43,788
Rumania	19,027	237,500	6,036	3,120	17,196
USSR	230,500	22,402,200	577,904	90,996	507,000
Yugoslavia	19,511	255,804	1,311[a]	1,764	15,528
World	3,335,752	135,773,000	2,900,000	458,600	3,044,000[a]

	Communist bloc		Rest of world	
Population	34.3%	1,144,322,000	65.7%	2,191,430,000
Area	25.9%	35,166,442 square km	74.1%	100,606,000 square km
Coal	38.1%	1,106,765,000 metric tons	61.9%	1,793,235,000 metric tons
Steel	29.2%	134,194,000 metric tons	70.8%	324,406,000 metric tons
Electric Energy	25.2%	767,293,000,000 kilowatt-hours	74.8%	2,276,807,000,000 kilowatt-hours

[a] 1964 figure
[b] 1963 figure
[c] 1961 figure
[d] 1960 figure

Sources: UN, *Monthly Bulletin of Statistics* (New York, March 1966); *1966 Book of the Year* (Chicago: Encyclopaedia Britannica, 1966); *Mirovaia ekonomika i mezhdunarodnie otnoshenia*, no. 8, August 1965.

APPENDIX B

Strength of Communist Parties

Albania	53,000 members (official claim, November 1962)
Bulgaria	550,384 members and candidate members (as of December 31, 1963)
China	17,000,000 members (1961 claim; now estimated at 18–19 million)
Cuba	50,000 members (claim)
Czechoslovakia	1,684,416 members and candidates (official claim; candidates account for 3.4 percent, that is, about 57,000 of total)
GDR	1,610,679 members (official claim on January 1, 1963)
Hungary	540,000 members (official claim, April 1965)
Mongolia	46,000 members (1963 claim)
North Korea	1,600,000 members (1965 claim)
North Vietnam	700,000 members (February 1965 claim; doesn't seem to include party members operating in South Vietnam under label of People's Revolutionary Party)
Poland	1,725,000 members (official claim, July 1965)
Rumania	1,450,000 members (official claim, July 1965)
USSR	12,471,000 members (March 29, 1966)
Yugoslavia	1,030,041 members (official claim, June 30, 1964)

Source: *World Strength of the Communist Party Organizations*, Intelligence and Research Office, U.S. Department of State (Washington, D. C., 1966).

NOTES

1. THE POLITICAL BACKGROUND

1. For a thorough discussion of some of the Western assumptions about Soviet conduct and revealing the extent to which Roosevelt was inclined to believe that a major change in Stalin's thinking could be achieved by a policy of conciliation, see H. Feis, *Churchill, Roosevelt, Stalin* (Princeton, 1957). For a more specific treatment of the Polish aspects which played a crucial role in Anglo-American relations with Stalin, see E. Rozek, *Allied Wartime Diplomacy* (New York, 1958). Revealing materials are contained in the wartime correspondence among the Big Three. See the two volumes entitled *Correspondence between the Chairman of the Council of Ministers of the USSR and the Presidents of the USA and the Prime Ministers of Great Britain during the Great Patriotic War of 1941–1945* (Moscow, 1957).

2. Already by the summer of 1945 the worth of this equipment was officially estimated at half a million United States dollars. *Rzeczpospolita*, August 27, 1945.

3. For a provocative study of the appeal of Marxism to East European intellectuals, see C. Milosz, *The Captive Mind* (New York, 1953). Those who feel that events of 1956 disprove Milosz ought to remember that he was discussing this early period.

4. It is to be remembered that even in prewar East Europe the extent of public ownership and governmental control of economy was considerable and generally accepted. See also Chapter 5.

5. For an interesting account by one of the former underground leaders and a prominent peasant party chief during this period of open struggle with the Communists, see S. Korbonski, *W Imieniu Kremla* (Paris, 1956). For the background of the diplomatic maneuvers leading up to the setting up of this government, see Rozek; and for the particulars of the Communist organization, see M. K. Dziewanowski, *The Communist Party of Poland* (Cambridge, 1959).

6. For some recent revelations, see M. Malinowski, "In the Stormy Era" ("W Wazkim, burzliwym okresie dziejow"), *Polityka* (Warsaw) December 21, 1957; for detailed treatment, see Dziewanowski, *passim*.

7. O. Halecki, ed., *Poland* (New York, 1957), p. 108. For detailed data, see the collection of documents, *P.P.R.* (Warsaw, 1959), pp. 291–292.

8. A. Iwanska, ed., *Contemporary Poland* (Human Relations Area Files, 1955), p. 316.

9. Cf. Korbonski.

10. For his own story, see *The Rape of Poland* (New York, 1948).

11. N. Spulber, *The Economics of Communist Eastern Europe* (New York, 1957), p. 232. This is the best treatment of the subject.

12. *Dziennik Ustaw Rzeczypospolitej Polskiej*, no. 3, item 17, 1946.

13. Spulber, p. 59.

14. Cf. H. Minc in *Zycie Warszawy*, January 3, 1946; *Plan Odbudowy Gospodarczej* (Warsaw, 1947); J. Marczewski, *Planification et croissance économique des democraties populaires* (Paris, 1956), esp. pp. 111–117.

15. L. Dellin, ed., *Bulgaria* (New York, 1957), p. 121; S. Kertesz, ed., *The Fate of East Central Europe* (Notre Dame, 1956), p. 278. For the most comprehensive treatment, see H. Seton-Watson, *The East European Revolution* (New York, 1956).

16. *Pravda*, January 27, 1948.

17. Y. Gluckstein, *Stalin's Satellites in Europe* (London, 1952), p. 15.

18. H. L. Roberts, *Rumania: Political Problems of an Agrarian State* (New Haven, 1951), p. 291. The best study on the subject.

19. *Ibid.*, pp. 294–298.

20. For the Yugoslav account, amply illustrated by alleged conversations between the Soviet and Yugoslav leaders, see V. Dedijer, *Tito* (New York, 1952). See also Chapter 3.

21. V. I. Lenin, *"Left-wing" Communism — An Infantile Disorder* (New York), p. 862.

2. PROBLEMS OF THEORY

1. I benefited a great deal from two excellent studies of this problem: H. G. Skilling, " 'People's Democracy' in Soviet Theory," *Soviet Studies*, July 1951; and R. J. Medalie, "The Policy of Take-Over," *Public Policy*, VII (Cambridge, 1956), originally submitted to my graduate seminar on comparative totalitarianism at Harvard University.

2. *Selected Works* (New York, 1943), VII, 241.

3. "State and Revolution" in *Selected Works*, p. 34 (italics his).

4. *Problems of Leninism* (Moscow, 1940), p. 660.

5. Lenin, p. 341.

6. Stalin, p. 135.

7. See P. A. Toma, "The Slovak Soviet Republic of 1919," *The American Slavic and East European Review*, April 1958.

8. *Kommunisticheskaia Partiia Polshi v borbe za nezavisimost svoei strany* (Moscow, 1955).

9. See Benjamin Schwartz, *Chinese Communism and the Rise of Mao* (Cambridge, 1951), pp. 200–202.

10. Malinowski, "In the Stormy Era," p. 2.

11. "People's Democracy: The Way to the Peaceful Development of Poland," *Glos Ludu*, no. 330, 1946. See also W. Bienkowski, "The Practice and

Theory of the People's Democracy," *Nowe Drogi,* January–February 1948.

12. Quoted in E. Kardelj, *On People's Democracy in Jugoslavia* (New York, no date), p. 14.

13. Quoted in V. Chervenkov, "The Activities of the Bulgarian Workers' Party," *For a Lasting Peace, for a People's Democracy,* no. 3 (December 15, 1947), p. 2; see also T. Dragoicheva, *Politicheska, Organizatsionna i Stopanska Deinost* (Sofia, 1955).

14. W. Gomulka, *W Walce o Demokracje Ludowa* (Warsaw, 1947), I, 303.

15. K. Gottwald, *Deset let* (Prague, 1947), p. 284, as quoted in P. Zinner, "The Strategy and Tactics of the Czechoslovak Communist Party" (unpublished Ph.D. thesis, Harvard University, 1953), p. 127.

16. Bierut, quoted in Kardelj, p. 29.

17. Bierut, *ibid.*

18. This is actually a paraphrase of Gottwald (as quoted in Zinner).

19. Gomulka, I, 199.

20. *Ibid.,* p. 305.

21. Address before the Second Congress of the Hungarian Communist Party, as quoted in Kardelj, p. 9.

22. The following were the most authoritative discussions: E. S. Varga, "Democracies of a New Type," *Mirovoie Khoziaistvo i Mirovaia Politika,* no. 3, 1947; I. P. Trainin, "Democracy of a Special Type," *Sovetskoie Gosudarstvo i Pravo,* nos. 1 and 3, 1947; A. Leontiev, "The Economic Bases of the New Democracy," *Planovoie Khoziaistvo,* no. 4, 1947. Varga's articles represent a reconsideration of some of his views pertaining to East Europe advanced in his book, *Izmeneniia v Ekonomike Kapitalizma v itoge vtoroi mirovoi voiny* (Moscow, 1946), ch. xv.

23. Trainin, no. 1, p. 3.

24. *Bolshevik,* no. 6 (1947), p. 23.

25. L. Gelberg, ed., *Nowe Konstytucje Panstw Europejskich* (Warsaw, 1949).

26. A. Prochazka, "Changes in the Philosophy of Czechoslovak Law" (Microfilm, Library of Congress), pp. 11–12.

27. *Démocratie Nouvelle,* September 1947, p. 463. In his book cited above Varga listed the economies of the People's Democracies as part of the capitalist world.

28. For an interesting comparative discussion, see S. Ossowski, *Struktura Klasowa w Spolecznej Swiadomosci* (Wroclaw, 1957).

29. See Seton-Watson, *The East European Revolution.*

30. Cf. Lenin, "Critical Remarks on the National Question" (1913), "Right of Nations to Self-Determination" (1914), "Revolutionary Proletariat and Right of Nations to Self-Determination" (1915), "Preliminary Theses on National-Colonial Question" (1920); Stalin's *Marxism and the National and Colonial Question.*

31. *Sochineniya* (Moscow, 1947), XXXI/2, 660.

32. *Sochineniya,* 3rd ed., XXV, 290 (italics added).

33. Lenin, quoted in M. Djilas without specific source, "Lenin on Relations between Socialist States," *Komunist* (Belgrade), September 1949.

34. *Sochineniya,* V, 265, from speech to the Twelfth Party Congress.

35. *Sochineniya,* XXV, 624.

36. See Malinowski.
37. E. Kardelj, "On People's Democracy in Yugoslavia," *Komunist* (Belgrade), July 1949; English translation in pamphlet form, cited in note 11, p. 4. This cited view was held from the very beginning and, after the break, the Yugoslav leaders were fond of reminding their Stalinist comrades in East Europe that in the initial period the East Europeans had deviated from true Leninism.
38. *Sluzhebni List*, February 1, 1946; Gelberg.
39. Kardelj, pp. 19–20 (italics added).

3. PROBLEMS OF DIVERSITY

1. Cf. Z. Brzezinski, ed., *Political Controls in the Soviet Army* (New York, 1954).
2. For the full text of the pertinent resolution, see *KPSS v Rezoliutsiiakh i Resheniiakh S'ezdov, Konferentsii i Plenumov TsK*, III (Moscow, 1954), 476–484.
3. *Ibid.*, pp. 485–494.
4. *Ibid.*, pp. 495–501.
5. *Pravda*, November 7, 1946.
6. Malinowski, "In the Stormy Era."
7. See M. Rutkiewicz, "On the 15th Anniversary of the Polish Workers' Party," *Kalendarz Robotniczy 1957* (Warsaw, 1957) for the recollections of a participant in the flight.
8. For an account, see S. Clissold, *The Whirlwind* (New York, 1949) or A. Ulam, *Titoism and the Cominform* (Cambridge, 1953).
9. A comprehensive study of the Hungarian Communist Party is being prepared at Harvard University by C. Stastny. For an informative memoir, see G. Paloczi-Horvath, *The Undefeated* (London, 1959).
10. Zinner, "The Strategy and Tactics of the Czechoslovak Communist Party," p. 84.
11. For the East Germans, see the account of W. Leonhard, *Child of the Revolution* (Chicago, 1958).
12. All these messages are cited by M. Pijade, *About the Legend that the Jugoslav Uprising Owed its Existence to Soviet Assistance* (London, 1950), p. 11.
13. *Ibid.*, esp. pp. 9, 10, 20.
14. For a fuller discussion, see Malinowski. My interpretation of this period differs from that in Dziewanowski, *The Communist Party of Poland*. For an informative account of the ideological confusion that prevailed in the Soviet sponsored Polish Army and of the frequent clashes with the more orthodox Communists, see I. Blum, *Z Dziejow Aparatu Politycznego Wojska Polskiego* (Warsaw, 1957).
15. J. Schoeplin, "The Hungarian Communist Party's Road, 1945–1950," *Latohatar* (Munich), 1955, VI, 241–242. For a skillful unraveling of Soviet and Hungarian strategy of this period, see W. O. McCagg, "Communism in Hungary, 1944–46," (unpublished Ph.D. thesis, Columbia University, 1965).
16. For a fuller discussion of the latter, see Ulam's, *Titoism and the Cominform*.

17. *Trybuna Wolnosci,* December 22, 1944.
18. K. Gottwald, *Statement of Policy* (Prague, 1946), p. 54.
19. I. Nagy, *On Communism* (New York, 1957), p. 239.
20. See H. Ripka, *Le Coup de Prague* (Paris, 1949).
21. *The Soviet-Jugoslav Dispute* (London, 1948).
22. Dedijer, *Tito,* pp. 272, 303.
23. Dedijer, p. 317.
24. *Ibid.,* p. 305.
25. *Pravda,* January 28, 1948.
26. Dedijer, pp. 316–318.
27. *Ibid.,* p. 317.
28. *Ibid.,* p. 291.
29. *Ibid.,* p. 292.
30. *For a Lasting Peace, for a People's Democracy,* no. 1, November 10, 1947.
31. *Ibid.*
32. See speech by E. Kardelj, *ibid.;* good commentary in Ulam.
33. Dedijer, p. 297.
34. Cf. the correspondence between the two Central Committees, published either by the RIIA in London, or the Belgrade publications, and also the discussion by Ulam.

4. THE THEORY RECONSIDERED

1. Radio Prague, December 21, 1952.
2. For the treatment of the ideological dispute, see Ulam, *Titoism and the Cominform;* for historical background, Dziewanowski, *The Communist Party of Poland.*
3. Cf. *For a Lasting Peace, for a People's Democracy,* speeches by V. Chervenkov, "Leading Role of Bulgarian Workers' Party (Communist) in Building the People's Democracy," June 15, 1948; speech by M. Rakosi, April 15, 1948; and Gheorghiu-Dej, March 1, 1948, and so on.
4. Cf. Rakosi's address to the Third Party Conference, *ibid.,* February 15, 1948; and Gheorghiu-Dej, "Consolidating the People's Democracy in Rumania," *ibid.,* January 1, 1948.
5. For example, Chervenkov to the Second Congress of the Fatherland Front, *ibid.,* February 1, 1948.
6. *Ibid.,* April 15, 1948.
7. Revai, p. 147.
8. See Ulam, Dziewanowski.
9. H. Minc, speaking at the Central Committee session, *Nowe Drogi,* no. 11 (1948), p. 57.
10. Bierut, *Nowe Drogi, ibid.,* p. 24. See also B. Bierut and J. Cyrankiewiez, *Podstawy ideologiczne PZPR* (Warsaw, 1952).
11. October 15, 1948.
12. Text in *Pravda,* December 21, 1948; see also M. Rakosi, "What Is a People's Democracy?" *Szabad Nep,* January 16, 1949.
13. For the fullest treatment of the Soviet contribution, see H. G. Skilling, " 'People's Democracy' in Soviet Theory"; for a chronological discussion of

similar processes in East Europe, see R. J. Medalie, "The Policy of Take-Over." The section to follow owes much to both these excellent studies.

14. *Zagadnienia Prawne Konstytucji Polskiej Rzeczypospolitej Ludowej,* I–III (Warsaw, 1954); hereafter cited as *Zagadnienia Prawne.* For an orthodox statement of the legal aspects, see also S. Razmaryn, *Polskie Prawo Panstwowe* (Warsaw, 1951).

15. Among the most authoritative Soviet statements are: N. P. Farberov, *Gosudarstvennoe Pravo Stran Norodnoi Demokratii* (Moscow, 1949); A. Sobolev, "People's Democracy as a Form of Political Organization of Society," a lecture delivered at the Moscow Party Training Center and published in *Bolshevik,* no. 19, 1951, and *Nowe Drogi,* no. 5, 1951; E. Burdzhalov, "Concerning the International Significance of the Historic Experience of the Bolshevik Party," *Bolshevik,* no. 17, 1948; cf. also sources cited in Skilling, pp 17–19.

16. Farberov, p. 27.

17. *Pravda,* April 27, 1949; Skilling, p. 133.

18. *Zagadnienia Prawne,* II, 58 and I, 251.

19. Farberov, p. 35.

20. *Zagadnienia Prawne,* I, 166.

21. *Ibid.,* II, 85.

22. Farberov, pp. 21–24.

23, *Zagadnienia Prawne,* II, 136.

24. See H. G. Skilling, "The Czech Constitutional System," *Political Science Quarterly,* June 1952.

25. Farberov, "On the Character of the People's Democratic State," *Nowe Drogi,* III (1949), 57–58.

26. *Ibid.*

27. *Zagadnienia Prawne,* I, 354.

28. Farberov, *Gosudarstvennoe Pravo,* p. 37.

29. Farberov, *Nowe Drogi,* III, 158.

30. *Bolshevik,* no. 17, 1948.

31. Revai, p. 147.

32. See particularly Gheorghiu-Dej, "Betrayal of Revolutionary Marxism," a violent diatribe in *For a Lasting Peace, for a People's Democracy,* July 1948; and V. Kolarov, "Struggle against Nationalism in the Bulgarian Communist Party," *ibid.,* May 15, 1949. It is noteworthy that at the time Kolarov was competing against Chervenkov for leadership in the party.

33. Sobolev, p. 96.

34. *Ibid.,* p. 95.

35. See *Zagadnienia Prawne,* I, II; *Nowe Konstytucje Panstw Europejskich;* the Mid-European Studies Center volumes on the countries of East Europe; and S. Sharp, *New Constitutions in the Soviet Sphere* (Washington 1950).

36. See *Proiekt za konstitutsia na narodna republika Bulgaria* (Sofia, 1946) For the later version, see Sharp.

37. Farberov, *Sovetskoe Gosudarstvo i Pravo,* no. 4 (1950), p. 83 (above translation taken from Skilling, p. 144). See also Farberov's book for similar assertions, for instance, p. 42.

38. *Zagadnienia Prawne,* I, 115.

39. *Ibid.*, I, 351.
40. *Ibid.*, II, 134.
41. *Ibid.*, I, 256.
42. *Ibid.*
43. *Ibid.*, III, 194. For some broader problems, see M. P. Kareva, *Pravo i Nravstvennost v Sotsialisticheskom Obshchestve* (Moscow, 1954). For the revision of the Bulgarian code on the Soviet pattern, see *News from Behind the Iron Curtain*, April 1952, p. 11.
44. Farberov, *Gosudarstvennoe Pravo*, p. 43. See also his comparisons with bourgeois constitutions, pp. 43–45.
45. *Chronologische Materialien zur Geschichte der SED* (Berlin, 1956), p. 7.
46. From his address in April 1948 to the Party Academy in East Berlin, cited by W. Leonhard, *Die Revolution Entlaesst Ihre Kinder* (Berlin, 1955), pp. 483–484; English translation: *Child of the Revolution.*
47. Otto Grotewohl in *For a Lasting Peace, for a People's Democracy*, March 1, 1949.
48. *Einheit*, no. 4 (1957), p. 400. For some Soviet views on this subject, see D. Melnikov, *Borba za edinuiu, nezavisimuiu, demokraticheskuiu Germaniu* (Moscow, 1951); Akademia Nauk SSSR, *Voprosy stroitelstva edinovo demokraticheskovo germanskovo Gosudarstva* (Moscow, 1951); for an analysis of the earliest period, see M. Croan, "Soviet Uses of the Doctrine of the 'Parliamentary Road' to Socialism; East Germany: 1945–1946," *American Slavic and East European Review*, October 1958.

5. LAYING THE SOCIALIST FOUNDATIONS

1. See M. Fainsod, *How Russia Is Ruled*, rev. ed. (Cambridge, 1963).
2. The following studies, prepared by the Mid-European Studies Center (all New York, 1958) contain special chapters dealing with these matters: S. Skendi, ed., *Albania;* L. Dellin, ed., *Bulgaria;* O. Halecki, ed., *Poland;* V. Busek, ed., *Czechoslovakia;* S. Fisher-Galati, ed., *Romania;* E. Helmreich, ed., *Hungary;* R. F. Byrnes, ed., *Yugoslavia.*
3. *Rude Pravo*, June 28, 1953. For further treatment see *News from Behind the Iron Curtain*, October 1953, pp. 37–46.
4. J. Revai to Budapest architects, *Tarsadalmi Szemle*, September 1951.
5. J. Skrzeszot, *Nowe Drogi*, no. 5, 1953.
6. For a statement of the Communist point of view, see S. Zawadzki, *Rozwoj Wiezi Rad Narodowych z Masami Pracujacymi w Polsce Ludowej* (Warsaw, 1955). The allegedly advanced democratic character of the councils was based on a claim to broad popular representation with each deputy representing a relatively small number of electors. This was compared critically with the Western model and cited as proof of real democracy. However, the consequence was that these huge councils were structurally unable to make policy, not to mention the external pressures for their subservience.
7. For a compact collection of all the plans and some official accomplishment reports, see *Plany Razvitiia Narodnovo Khoziaistva Stran Narodnoi Demokratii* (Moscow, 1952).

8. E. Drozniak, "For Improving and Lowering the Costs of the State Apparatus," *Nowe Drogi*, no. 2, 1955.

9. Spulber, *The Economics of Communist Eastern Europe*, p. 126.

10. *Zycie gospodarcze*, no. 15, 1950.

11. *Zagadnienia Prawne*, II, 281.

12. *Lidova Demokracie*, December 23, 1952.

13. R. Carlton, ed., *Forced Labor in the People's Democracies* (New York 1956): for a Polish Communist account of the use of forced labor in coal mining, and of abuses thereof, see *Trybuna Ludu*, June 6, 1956, p. 4.

14. Z. Brzezinski, *The Permanent Purge* (Cambridge, 1956).

15. *Ibid.*, for an extended discussion; also note on p. 148.

16. In Poland, the secret police even prepared "dossiers" on Politburo members, according to former Politburo member, J. Berman; *Nowe Drogi*, no. 1 (1956), p. 93.

17. December 6, 1951, as quoted in P. Korbel and V. Vagassky, "Purges in the Communist Party of Czechoslovakia" (Radio Free Europe, mimeographed 1952).

18. *Nowe Drogi*, no. 10 (1956), pp. 85–95.

19. *Moscow's European Satellites* (U.S. Department of State, 1955), p. 16 also speech by F. Jozwiak-Witold, *Nowe Drogi*, no. 3 (1953), p. 53, and *New from Behind the Iron Curtain* for the period.

20. *Seria Filozoficzna* (*Nowe Drogi*), II, no. 2 (1949), 24.

21. *Zagadnienia Prawne*, I, 21.

22. *Nowe Drogi*, no. 6 (1954), p. 19. See also S. Skrzypek, "Agricultura Policies in Poland, 1950–1954," *Journal of Central European Affairs*, XVI, no. (1956).

23. See *News from Behind the Iron Curtain*, July 1952, p. 27 and May 1953, p. 31; *Nowe Drogi*, no. 1 (1956), p. 106; Spulber, pp. 254, 261; C. I McVicker, *Titoism* (New York, 1957).

24. B. Bierut, "Poland on the Road to Socialism," *Bolshevik*, no. 21 (1950, p. 23.

25. For a laudatory description of each of the above undertakings, se V. P. Maksakovsky, *Stroiki Sotsializma v evropeiskikh stranakh narodne demokratii* (Moscow, 1952).

26. Spulber, pp. 326–327; J. Wszelaki, "The Rise of Industrial Middle Europe," *Foreign Affairs*, October 1951.

27. H. Minc, "On the Proportions in the Development of the National Economy," *Gospodarka Planowa*, December 1954.

28. J. Hajda, ed., *A Study of Contemporary Czechoslovakia* (New Haven 1955), p. 487.

29. A good graphic illustration is a series of comparative tables on som production items in Spulber, pp. 367–380.

30. Spulber, p. 384. See also Marczewski, *Planification*, pp. 202–206.

31. *Rude Pravo*, January 15, 1952.

6. STALINISM: A PATTERN FOR THE COMMUNIST INTERSTATE SYSTE

1. *Pravda*, June 20, 1950.

2. *Ibid.* (italics added).

3. *Ibid.*

4. *Ibid.*

5. For a good survey, see P. S. Wandycz, "The Soviet System of Alliances in East Central Europe," *Journal of Central European Affairs*, XVI, no. 2 (July 1956). See also G. A. Deborin, *Mezhdunarodnie Otnosheniia i Vneshuaia Politika Sovetskogo Soiuza, 1945–1949* (Moscow, 1958), esp. ch. iii; *Zagadnienie Bezpieczenstwa Zbiorowego w Europie* (Warsaw, 1955), particularly the contribution by C. Berezowski, "Mutual Aid Treaties and the Collective Security"; E. Korovin, *Nerushimaia Druzhba Narodov SSSR i Narodno-Demokraticheskikh Stran* (Moscow, 1955).

6. Wandycz makes the point that only the Bulgarian-Rumanian treaty poke of aid against any aggressor.

7. *Zagadnienia Prawne*, II, 546. On October 12, 1949, Otto Grotewohl's government announced its acceptance of this frontier, but it was a unilateral declaration. In January 1951, a final settlement of frontier delimitation was made by the two regimes (I, 146).

8. For an official discussion, see *Zagadnienia Prawne*, II, 540–599.

9. Dates of formal Cominform meetings: (1) September 22–23, 1947; (2) late January, 1948; (3) around June 20, 1948; (4) November 27, 1949. *Ost-Probleme*, no. 27 (1952), pp. 827–833.

10. Dedijer, *Tito*. See also Chapter 3.

11. For organized Soviet efforts, see A. Inkeles, *Public Opinion in Soviet Russia* (Cambridge, 1950).

12. Halecki, *Poland*, p. 147.

13. Dellin, *Bulgaria*, p. 227.

14. Fisher-Galati, *Romania*, p. 80.

15. A. Gide, *Return from the USSR* (New York, 1937), p. 56.

16. J. Swiatlo, testimony no. 13, "How Poland Is Really Ruled" (unpublished mimeographed material).

17. Nagy again, *On Communism*, cites specific instances of Hungarian reports" to the CPSU (for instance, p. 75).

18. S. Bialer, *Wybralem Prawde*, RFE (New York, 1956), pp. 11–12.

19. Swiatlo.

20. *News from Behind the Iron Curtain*, March 1952, p. 5.

21. Col. Lewikowski and Col. Kuryluk respectively. Information is based on conversations with Polish Communists. Kuryluk is a former Soviet parachutist.

22. Bialer, p. 11.

23. *Nowe Drogi*, no. 10 (1956), p. 88.

24. S. Korbonski, *W Imieniu Rzeczypospolitej* (Paris, 1954), ch. xxiii.

25. Swiatlo.

26. Based on Swiatlo, *Za kulisami bezpieki i partii*, RFE leaflet, pp. 22–25.

27. Dedijer, p. 328.

28. *News from Behind the Iron Curtain*, March 1952, p. 5.

29. Berman, p. 88, cites the case of incriminating materials arriving from Moscow against his personal secretary and others.

30. Swiatlo, *Za kulisami . . .* , p. 4.

31. For the most extended treatment, see I. de Sola Pool, ed., *Satellite Generals* (Stanford, 1955); for material on Soviet officers in the Polish Army,

p. 150. For detailed treatment of the Sovietization of the East European armed forces, see R. Garthoff, *Soviet Military Policy* (New York, 1966), ch. vii.

32. In 1956, after his expulsion, nineteen high officers, all with outstanding war records, were posthumously rehabilitated in Poland. They had been shot several years earlier on trumped-up charges of conspiracy. *Kultura i Spoleczenstwo*, no. 1 (January 1957), pp. 276–277.

33. See recollections of General B. Kiraly, *News from Behind the Iron Curtain*, March 1958.

34. Informal conversations of the author in East Europe.

35. Spulber, pp. 180–181. For an evaluation of the East German, Rumanian, and Hungarian payments, see V. Winston, "The Soviet Satellites — Economic Liability?" *Problems of Communism*, January 1958.

36. This figure is derived from the settlement made by the USSR on November 18, 1956.

37. For a list of properties seized, see Spulber, pp. 207–223.

38. *Ibid.*, p. 191; Roberts, *Rumania: Political Problems of an Agricultural State*, p. 320, observes that "These concerns clearly gave the Soviet Union a controlling position at key points in the Rumanian economy."

39. Spulber, p. 188. See also Columbia Hungarian Interview Project, Interview 202.

40. H. Minc, "The Fruitful Cooperation of the Free Nations," *Zycie Gospodarcze*, no. 20 (1951), p. 1101.

41. Ivanov; *Rude Pravo*, January 1, 1953; Minc; *News from Behind the Iron Curtain*, September 1952, p. 33.

42. For a general discussion, see *News from Behind the Iron Curtain*, September 1952, pp. 28–32.

43. Spulber, p. 430.

44. *Ibid.*, pp. 438–439.

45. See Schwartz, *Chinese Communism and the Rise of Mao*.

46. "On the People's Democratic Dictatorship" (Hong Kong, 1949), as quoted in H. Wei, *China and Soviet Russia* (New York, 1956), p. 264.

47. This was explicitly asserted by covering press editorials: for example *Jen Min Jih Pao* of February 26, 1950 and *Pravda*, same date.

48. Wei, pp. 269–273.

49. *Ibid.*, pp. 273–274.

50. In W. W. Rostow, *The Prospects for Communist China* (New York, 1954), p. 208, M. X. Hsieh's unpublished study is cited for the estimate of 7,000 Soviet military advisers. For the role of Soviet advisers in training the Chinese Air Force, see de Sola Pool, *Satellite Generals*, p. 136.

51. Rostow, p. 194.

52. *Ibid.*, p. 192; Boorman, p. 70.

53. Mao Tse-tung, *Jen Min Jih Pao*, October 8, 1949; Wei, p. 292.

54. For a treatment of this topic, see B. I. Schwartz, "China and the Soviet Theory of People's Democracy," *Problems of Communism*, III, no. 5 (1954).

55. On alleged equality of status between Soviet and Chinese technicians see Wei, p. 292.

56. *Pravda*, October 6, 1952.

57. Nagy, pp. 38–39 (italics added).

58. *Pravda*, October 6, 1952.

7. THE STALINIST LEGACY

1. *On Communism.*

2. Materials cited from this project are listed under the interview number. Interview 563 is particularly interesting since it contains testimony of a party official active in the daily organ of the Central Committee and exposed to the process of disillusionment with the Stalinist legacy as discussed in this chapter.

3. Nagy, pp. 50, 221; see also Hungarian Interviews 152, 563.

4. Nagy, p. 51. See also statement by J. Berman, *Nowe Drogi*, no. 10, 1956, where he pleads guilty to having fallen under the spell of "suspicion psychosis" and concedes the moral degeneration of the secret-police personnel. See also Hungarian Interview 502.

5. Nagy, p. 279.

6. Bienkowski, *Rewolucji Ciag Dalszy* (Warsaw, 1957), p. 36. This is a collection of essays published earlier.

7. *Ibid.*, p. 6.

8. *Ibid.*, p. 20.

9. *Ibid.*, p. 21.

10. The Hungarian Interview Project shows ample evidence of this. Similarly, many statements made in the East European press during 1956 and in China during 1957 refer to this phenomenon.

11. Nagy, p. 60.

12. Bienkowski, p. 146.

13. *Ibid.*, p. 98.

14. Nagy, p. 44.

15. Bienkowski, p. 82.

16. E. Ochab, Radio Warsaw, August 16, 1956; this remark was not reproduced in the *Trybuna Ludu* text of the speech.

17. Bienkowski, p. 61.

18. M. Pohorille, "On the Antagonistic and Nonantagonistic Contradictions between the City and the Countryside," *Nowe Drogi*, no. 5 (1951), p. 57.

19. Bienkowski, p. 48, states this explicitly.

20. For detailed data see Gomulka's address, *Nowe Drogi*, no. 10, 1956; for comparative productivity of the public and private sectors, see Gomulka, *ibid.*, and Spulber, pp. 261–263.

21. For such data, see Economic Commission for Europe, *Economic Bulletin for Europe*, VIII, no. 2, based on cost of food baskets. For a discussion of prevailing concerns among the planners, see the account by F. Schenk and R. Lowenthal, "Soft Goods vs. Hard Goods," *The New Leader*, January 5, 1959. Schenk is a former East German planner. For an extensive critique of the centralized planning system, of the unreliability of the index figures, of the bonus system, of the mishandling of consumer-goods production, of the dogmatic Stalinist planning (pp. 170–171), see the study by a Hungarian economist, J. Kornai, *A Gazdasagi Vezetes Tulzott Központositasa* (Budapest, 1957).

22. For example, testimony of J. Berman, *Nowe Drogi*, no. 10, 1956.

23. J. V. Stalin, "Economic Problems of Socialism in the USSR," *Bolshevik*, September 1952; I use here the translation of L. Gruliow, ed., *Current Soviet Policies* (New York, 1953), p. 9.

24. *Ibid.*, p. 2.

25. *Ibid.*, p. 10.
26. *Pravda*, October 15, 1952, as quoted in Gruliow, p. 235.
27. The Doctors' Plot involved the arrest of a number of prominent Moscow doctors, mostly Jewish. They were charged with plotting to do away with leading Soviet statesmen. *Pravda*, January 13, 1953.

8. THE NEW COURSE: STALINISM DISSIPATED

1. For Soviet reference to a serious lag in the agricultural sector, see M. P. Kim, ed., *Istoriya SSSR* (Moscow, 1957), p. 681.
2. See J. N. Hazard, "Governmental Developments in the USSR since Stalin," *The Annals of the American Academy of Political and Social Science,* January 1956.
3. December 21, 1954.
4. *Pravda*, February 3, 1955.
5. For an account of the uprising, see S. Brant, *The East German Rising 17th June 1953*, translated and adapted by C. Wheeler (Thames and Hudson 1955).
6. This was reiterated at the Twenty-eighth Plenum three years later. *Neues Deutschland*, August 12, 1956.
7. *Economic Survey of Europe since the War* (United Nations, no date) p. 29.
8. Nagy, p. 66.
9. According to Nagy's account, pp. 106–107, the Soviet leaders concentrated their criticisms mainly on the economic aspects of the Hungarian scene.
10. *News from Behind the Iron Curtain*, August 1953, p. 47. (Major part of the speech are translated in that issue; for a broad justification of these policies, see Imre Nagy's book.)
11. *Ibid.*
12. J. Jaroslawski, "Struggle on Two Fronts in Party Work in the Countryside," *Nowe Drogi*, no. 12 (1953), p. 19, cites data with tables on the class distribution of the peasantry in Poland, showing that the medium farmer was the backbone of the peasantry.
13. S. Jedrychowski, "The People's Democracies in the Struggle for More Rapid Increase in the Standard of Living of the Working Masses," *Nowe Drogi*, no. 11 (1953), p. 16.
14. *Ibid.*
15. Jedrychowski, p. 16.
16. *Pravda*, February 20, 1954.
17. M. Fainsod, "The CPSU Since Stalin," *Problems of Communism*, January–February 1958, p. 8. For a detailed analysis of Khrushchev's rise, see Fainsod's "What Happened to 'Collective Leadership'?" *Problems of Communism* July–August 1959; also M. Rush, *The Rise of Khrushchev* (Washington, 1958).
18. See *Pravda*, December 21, 1954 (article by V. Kruzhkov) and January 24, 1955 (article by D. Shepilov) for good statements of the Khrushchev position.
19. *Pravda*, March 21, 1955 (italics added).
20. *Ibid.*

21. For extensive documentation, see "Sino-Soviet Trade," *Soviet Studies*, October 1958; M. L. Sladkovsky, *Ocherki ekonomicheskikh otnoshenii SSSR s Kitaiem* (Moscow, 1957); *Vneshnaia Torgovlia*, no. 8, 1957.

22. The full text is in *The Current Digest of the Soviet Press*, XVI, no. 34, September 16, 1964, p. 7.

23. For instance, Hsiueh Mu-chiao, "China on the Path of Socialist Industrialization," *Pravda*, June 22, 1954; Liao Lu-yen, "Along the Path of Socialist Transformation of China's Agriculture," *Pravda*, July 11, 1954.

24. Boorman, p. 131.

25. See the discussion of this in Chapter 6; and Boorman et al., p. 128.

26. *Pravda*, July 16, 1955.

27. See E. Taborsky, "The 'Old' and the 'New' Course in Satellite Economy," *Journal of Central European Affairs*, January 1958, esp. pp. 383, 387–391.

28. *Moskovskoe soveshchanie* (Moscow, 1954), for the official speeches and communiqué.

29. For texts and speeches, see *Varshavskoe Soveshchanie Evropeiskikh Gosudarstv* (Moscow, 1955); for a semiofficial Communist evaluation, L. Gelberg, *Uklad Warszawski* (Warsaw, 1957).

30. Cf. V. Siroky, "Economic Cooperation on the Level of the Growing Tasks of the Socialist States," *Pravda*, April 6, 1956; R. Fidelski, *Wspolpraca Gospodarcza Polski z Krajami Socjalistycznymi* (Warsaw, 1959).

31. *Pravda*, July 27, 1956.

32. *Ibid*. See also *Trud*, April 3, 1956, for a detailed account of the capacity of enterprises allegedly constructed by the USSR in Eastern Europe.

33. Spulber, p. 432.

34. *Ibid.*, p. 435; see also *Promyshlenno-ekonomicheskaia gazeta*, January 1, 1957. Fuller treatment in Chapter 12.

35. *Trybuna Ludu*, March 28, 1956.

36. For instance, Nagy, p. 143.

37. For instance, *Pravda i Izvestia*, September 17, 1954, citing *Borba*.

38. *Ibid.*, September 22, 1954. For Tito's views on the EDC, see R. B. Farrell, ed., *Jugoslavia and the Soviet Union, 1948–1956* (New York, 1956), p. 163; also *Pravda*, April 22, 1955.

39. *Pravda*, November 29, 1954.

40. *Ibid.*

41. *Izvestia*, January 6, 1955.

42. *Pravda*, May 18, 1955.

43. *For a Lasting Peace, for a People's Democracy*, May 27, 1955.

44. *New York Times*, June 2, 1955; *Pravda* explicitly mentioned the points quoted above in its commentary on the agreement.

45. Our information is based in part on the testimony, written and oral, of S. Bialer, a former member of the Polish Central Committee's staff, who was shown the transcripts of the Moscow proceedings (*Wybralem Prawde*, part 1, pp. 9–16); in part on subsequent Soviet developments, for instance, the July 1957 purge of Molotov, and on pertinent speeches to the Twenty-first CPSU Congress in 1959.

46. *Pravda*, July 16, 1955.

47. *Ibid* (italics added).

48. *Kommunist*, no. 14 (1955), p. 127.
49. *Ibid.*
50. *Ibid.*
51. Text in *Current Digest of the Soviet Press*, VIII, no. 4, 1956.
52. See *News from Behind the Iron Curtain*, April and May 1956, for some reactions; also Chapter 9.
53. *Current Digest*, VIII, no. 8 (italics added).
54. *Ibid.* (italics added).

9. THE IMPACT OF YUGOSLAVIA

1. For example, comments of Radio Zagreb, April 18, describing it as the outmoded appendage of Stalinism.
2. *Borba*, March 20, 1956 (italics added).
3. Early in 1956 Yugoslavia had been granted $110 million credit. *Tanjug*, February 2, 1956.
4. *New York Times*, June 21, 1956.
5. For example, *Borba*, October 3, 1948; for a doctrinaire, anti-Western statement, charging the United States with plotting against the USSR and asserting that the forces of peace are headed by the USSR, see E. Kardelj's report, *The Communist Party of Yugoslavia in the Struggle for New Yugoslavia, for People's Authority and for Socialism* (Belgrade, 1948).
6. Text of speech in Farrell, p. 107.
7. Ulam, p. 138.
8. For comprehensive treatments of the Yugoslav system, see A. Dragnitch, *Tito's Promised Land* (New Brunswick, 1954); McVicker; F. W. Neal, *Titoism in Action* (Berkeley, 1958). The last two are more inclined than Dragnitch to stress the distinctive, less totalitarian features of the Yugoslav system.
9. For instance, M. Bace, "On Critique and Auto-critique in the USSR," *Komunist* (Belgrade), no. 6, 1949.
10. For instance, J. Broz-Tito, *Workers Manage Factories in Jugoslavia* (Belgrade, 1950), pp. 12, 26; or E. Kardelj's speech to the Sixth Congress of the CPJ, quoted in Farrell, esp. p. 138; or M. Djilas, *On New Roads of Socialism* (Belgrade, 1950).
11. Cf. McVicker for a thorough survey.
12. Sixth Congress, Zagreb, 1952.
13. For instance, E. Kardelj, *Borba*, December 9, 1956.
14. L. Stoyovic, "Seven Years of Experience," *Politika*, June 25, 1957; Benj. Ward, "Workers' Management in Yugoslavia," *The Journal of Political Economy*, October 1957.
15. *Borba*, March 20, 1953.
16. E. Kardelj. "Socialist Democracy in Yugoslav Practice," *Borba*, January 1, 1955; part of ch. 5 of McVicker, pp. 245–305, is devoted to an exposition of the official Yugoslav view.
17. Z. Brihta, "One Year Since Stalin's Death," *Vjesnik*, March 4, 1954.
18. Evidence for this is cited by R. Lowenthal in his letter to *The New Leader*, February 9, 1959.
19. A communiqué noted merely that "satisfaction was expressed" by

Gheorghiu-Dej, Novotny, and Rakosi at this turn of events. *For a Lasting Peace, for a People's Democracy*, June 10, 1955.
20. *Borba*, July 28, 1955.
21. For example, Radio Zagreb, August 6, 1955.
22. For example, Tito's speech, including critical references to the East European states, was reprinted in *Pravda*, July 30, 1955.
23. *Ibid.*
24. Tito's speech of October 25, 1954, in Farrell, p. 171.
25. Radio Budapest, August 8, 1955.
26. For details, Radio Zagreb, November 3, 1955; *Politika*, November 1955; *Mlada Fronta*, December 3, 1955.
27. For instance, Radio Sofia, September 8, 1955, speech by Georgi Chankov, the Bulgarian Deputy Chairman of the Council of Ministers.
28. Radio Budapest, November 6, 1955.
29. Radio Bratislava, November 7, 1955.
30. Radio Bucharest, November 6, 1955.
31. This was claimed by Tito personally. See K. Zilliacus, *A New Birth of Freedom* (London, 1956), p. 135. Confirmed to the author by a very high-ranking Yugoslav official.
32. *Borba*, for instance, even stated on April 20, 1957, that "national Communism" was a term invented by Western journalists.
33. *Pravda*, April 18, 1956.
34. *Borba*, April 19, 1956.
35. *Borba*, February 26, 1956.
36. Radio Zagreb, July 26, 1956.
37. *Rabotnichesko Delo*, April 9, 1956.
38. Radio Sofia, April 8, 1956; on friendship with Yugoslavia, see *Rabotnichesko Delo*, April 6, 1956.
39. Radio Sofia, April 18, 1956.
40. *Nova Makedonija*, April 26, 1956.
41. Cf. the data in a *Rabotnichesko Delo* editorial, May 17, 1956, which reported that 282,000 farmers had joined in "the past few months"; also *ibid.*, July 13 and August 9, 1956.
42. "Let Us Study and Apply the 20th Congress Decisions of the CPSU and the April Plenum Decisions of the Bulgarian Communist Party," editorial, *Rabotnichesko Delo*, June 9, 1956.
43. Radio Sofia, September 19, 1956 (italics added).
44. Radio Prague, April 9, 1956.
45. *Rude Pravo*, editorial, "The Force of Truth," April 11, 1956.
46. *Rude Pravo*, May 11, 1956.
47. *Rude Pravo*, September 6, 1956.
48. Full texts, Radio Prague, March 30 and June 15, 1956.
49. Radio Tirana, May 25, 1956.
50. Radio Belgrade, May 28, 1956.
51. *Borba*, June 28, 1956.
52. *Neues Deutschland*, March 4, 1956.
53. *Ibid.*, July 31, 1956.
54. "Useful Contacts," *Pravda*, May 4, 1956.
55. *Pravda*, July 2, 1956.

56. *Current Digest of the Soviet Press,* VIII, no. 38. I am indebted to Miss Gail Warshovsky of Radcliffe College for drawing my attention to this quotation.
57. *Borba,* October 12, 1956.
58. *Ibid.*
59. This was reported by Zilliacus as having been confirmed to him by both Khrushchev and Tito separately (pp. 135, 102–103).

10. HUNGARY: THE TEST CASE OF NATIONAL COMMUNISM

1. *Pravda,* May 26, 1954.
2. See membership table, Chapter 5.
3. *News from Behind the Iron Curtain,* July 1954, p. 53.
4. *Szabad Nep,* July 22, 1953.
5. Nagy's selection by Soviet leaders was admitted by Nagy himself, p. 252.
6. Nagy, p. 283.
7. *Ibid.,* p. 282.
8. *Ibid.,* p. 282; also pp. 280, 281.
9. Quoted in "Research Report: Hungarian Party Congress, May 24–30, 1954" (mimeographed, Radio Free Europe), p. 5.
10. *Ibid.,* p. 24.
11. *Ibid.,* p. 25.
12. *Ibid.,* p. 30.
13. *Ibid.,* pp. 6–10.
14. See testimony of S. Bialer (*Wybralem wolnosc*), who recalls the panic and confusion in Warsaw when the article made its appearance. See *Pravda,* January 24, 1955, "The General Party Line and the Vulgar Marxists"; *Neues Deutschland, Rude Pravo,* January 29, 1955.
15. S. Bialer, "The Three Schools of Kremlin Policy," *The New Leader,* July 29, 1957 (allegedly based on actual reading of the said document while working for the Polish Central Committee).
16. March 21, 1955.
17. *Szabad Nep,* Radio Budapest, April 18, 1955.
18. *Szabad Nep,* May 12 and 13, 1955.
19. The date of his theses dealing with international affairs.
20. Nagy, pp. 26, 28.
21. *Ibid.,* p. 29.
22. *Ibid.,* p. 33 (italics added).
23. *Ibid.,* p. 33; see also p. 244.
24. *Ibid.,* p. 41.
25. For a detailed treatment, see F. Fejtö, *Behind the Rape of Hungary* (New York, 1957) and T. Meray, *Thirteen Days that Shook the Kremlin* (New York, 1959). Hungarian Interviews 563 and 152 provided helpful information on attitudes prevailing in the party, as did a mimeographed study prepared for the Hungarian Project by G. Heltai, entitled "Hungary 1953–1956."
26. For some of their attitudes, see *Proceedings of the Writers Union,* November–December 1955.
27. See *Szabad Nep,* March 27, 1956; Radio Budapest, March 31, 1956.

28. Radio Budapest, May 11, 1956.
29. *Ibid.*, July 9, 1956.
30. *Ibid.*, July 3, 1956.
31. *Szabad Nep*, June 15, 1956.
32. *Ibid.*, June 28, 1956.
33. Radio Budapest, July 7, 1956.
34. *Szabad Nep*, May 28, 1956.
35. *Szabad Nep*, April 13, 1956.
36. *New York Times*, July 9, 1956.
37. Radio Budapest, June 30, 1956.
38. *Szabad Nep*, July 3, 1956.
39. For instance, attacks on the anti-Rakosi literary circles were reprinted by *Pravda*, December 11, 1955.
40. *Szabad Nep*, July 19, 1956. For a purported, and dramatic, account of the Central Committee session (including, for example, Rakosi's vain telephone calls for aid from Khrushchev), see Hungarian Interview 563, pp. 81–82.
41. Zinner, P., ed., *National Communism and Popular Revolt in Eastern Europe* (New York, 1956), p. 346.
42. *Pravda*, October 5, 1956 (100 million rubles, including 40 per cent in cash).
43. *Szabad Nep*, October 7, 1956.
44. Cf. General B. Kiraly's account, "Hungarian Army — Its Part in the Revolt," *East Europe*, June 1958.
45. Speech of October 24, quoted in Zinner, pp. 409–410.
46. Kiraly, p. 7.
47. *Ibid.*, p. 14.
48. Hungarian Interview 152, pp. 88–91. Cf. *Pravda*, "Collapse of the Anti-People's Venture in Hungary," October 28, 1956.
49. *Pravda*, October 31, 1956.
50. *Ibid.*
51. Zinner, pp. 493–494.
52. R. Lowenthal claims that Belgrade considered such a move. See his 'Tito's Affair with Khrushchev," *The New Leader*, October 6, 1958.
53. *Borba*, October 30, 1956.
54. Text in *New York Times*, November 5, 1956.
55. *Borba*, November 24, 1956.
56. Text in Zinner, p. 527.
57. Speech in Zinner, p. 527.
58. *Ibid.*, p. 534.
59. For full translation, see *New York Times*, November 24, 1956, and *National Communism and Popular Revolt in Eastern Europe*, pp. 541–562.
60. *Borba*, November 26, 1956.
61. *Zeri i Popullit*, editorial, "In Connection with the Speech Recently Delivered by Josip Broz-Tito," November 23, 1956.
62. *Pravda*, December 19, 1956, "Who Stands to Gain by This? — On the Speech of Comrade E. Kardelj."
63. For a concise analysis of the Hungarian revolution per se and for its historical background, see P. E. Zinner's excellent piece, "Revolution in Hungary: Reflections on the Vicissitudes of a Totalitarian System," *Journal of*

Politics, March 1959. For fuller treatment, see P. Kecskemeti, *The Unexpected Revolution* (Stanford, 1961); P. Zinner, *Revolution in Hungary* (New York, 1962); F. Vali, *Rift and Revolt in Hungary* (Cambridge, 1961).

II. THE POLISH OCTOBER: THE CHALLENGE OF DOMESTICISM

1. For much more detailed historical treatment, see relevant chapters in Halecki and Dziewanowski; also F. Lewis, *A Case History of Hope* (New York, 1958).
2. For good theoretical treatment see O. Utis, "Generalissimo Stalin and the Art of Government," *Foreign Affairs*, XXX, January 1952; for application in practice, see my *The Permanent Purge*.
3. For instance, *Nowe Drogi*, no. 10 (1953), p. 110.
4. For a partial text in English, see *News from Behind the Iron Curtain*, March 1955.
5. *Nowe Drogi*, no. 10 (1954), pp. 43, 13. See also no. 5, pp. 13–14, for examples of past cultural controls, such as the setting of quotas and themes for painters by a Warsaw office.
6. For a participant's account, see S. Bialer.
7. *Nowe Drogi*, no. 10 (1956), p. 115.
8. *Ibid.*, no. 12 (1954), pp. 10, 12–14.
9. *Ibid.*, no. 2 (1955), p. 2.
10. Bialer, p. 8.
11. *Nowe Drogi*, no. 7 (July 1957), p. 126.
12. D. Zablocka, "Notes on the Intelligentsia," *Nowa Kultura*, September 7, 1958.
13. *Nowe Drogi*, no. 7 (1957), p. 126.
14. S. Zolkiewski, "On Current Literary Discussions," *Nowe Drogi*, no. 6, 1955.
15. For a general account of the clubs, see E. Bryll and J. Garztecki, "Boiled, Burst and Extinguished," *Orka*, November 29, 1957. For a detailed and fascinating history of the Club of the Crooked Circle, see the account by one of its active members, W. Jedlicki, "Klub Krzywego Kola," *Kultura* (Paris 1963).
16. *Nowa Kultura*, March 6, 1955.
17. J. Siekierska, a lecturer at the Central Committee's Institute of Social Sciences, in *Przeglad Kulturalny*, no. 8, 1955.
18. *Zycie Warszawy*, April 19, 1956.
19. Z. Florczak in *Nowa Kultura*, October 1, 1956. See also W. Godek and R. Turski, "Is this the Decline of Marxism?" *Po Prostu*, June 24, 1956. Their title is suggestive of the prevailing mood.
20. *Aktualne zagadnienia polityki kulturalnej w dziedzinie filozofii i socjologii* (Warsaw, 1956).
21. Based on personal sources in Warsaw. According to my information Khrushchev's first choice was F. Mazur (reputedly an agent of the MVD) and Ochab was a "compromise" choice.
22. *Pravda*, April 29, 1956.
23. Radio Warsaw, April 21, 1956.
24. *Ibid.*, April 6, 1956; Warsaw Voievodshi Activ conference.

25. *Trybuna Ludu*, April 24, 1956. Cyrankiewicz, a former socialist, survived all the policy shifts of the regime and retained his post under Gomulka.

26. *Ibid.*, June 17, 1956.

27. Radio Warsaw, May 19, 1956.

28. *Trybuna Ludu*, March 31, 1956.

29. *Zycie Warszawy*, May 29, 1956.

30. For instance, *Nowe Drogi*, no. 2, 1956; J. Rasinski, "A Few Observations on Class Relations in the Countryside," *Nowe Drogi*, no. 5, 1956.

31. For instance, the bitter article by J. Morawski, a party secretary, "The Lessons of the 20th Congress of the CPSU," *Trybuna Ludu*, March 27, 1956; also W. Ulbricht, "Concerning the 20th Party Congress of the CPSU," *Neues Deutschland*, March 4, 1956.

32. *Izvestia*, June 30, 1956; *Pravda*, July 4, 1956.

33. See note on p. 207, Chapter 9, regarding the possible ambivalence in the Yugoslav statement.

34. July 16, 1956 (italics in original).

35. *New York Times*, July 22, 1956.

36. This was preceded by a protocol, signed in February 1956, revising in Poland's favor the Polish-Soviet trade agreement. J. Kobryber, "Polish-Soviet Trade Agreements," *Gospodarka Planowa*, no. 4, April 1956.

37. Information based on personal sources in Warsaw.

38. Radio Warsaw, August 21, 1956.

39. *News from Behind the Iron Curtain*, October 1956, pp. 46–47.

40. Radio Warsaw, August 13, 1956.

41. *Ibid.*, September 22, 1956.

42. *Ibid.*, September 19, 1956.

43. *Po Prostu*, September 30, 1956.

44. *Nowa Kultura*, no. 13, 1956 (W. Woroszylski).

45. Radio Warsaw, September 24, 1956.

46. For Ochab's September objections, see *Nowe Drogi*, no. 10 (1956), p. 112.

47. F. Mazur, one of their leaders and considered in Warsaw to be in the service of Soviet secret police, was at the time in Moscow.

48. For an account of the three-day alert at Zeran, of the numerous Zeran delegations spreading throughout the country to mobilize the workers, and so on, see *Swiat*, November 4, 1956.

49. Radio Szczecin and Gdansk, October 26, 1956.

50. For detailed accounts of the October events, sprinkled liberally with so-called direct quotations from various closed meetings, and such, see K. Syrop, *Spring in October* (New York, 1958), and Lewis, *A Case History of Hope*.

51. According to Ochab, *Nowe Drogi*, no. 10 (1956), p. 16. This issue contains the proceedings of the Eighth Plenum with its startling debates, comments, and rare personal insights. An unusual documentary on the power and ideological processes of a ruling Communist body operating under stress, its publication in English is well merited.

52. *Ibid.*, p. 18.

53. Syrop's book contains the most thorough account (pp. 94–95), based in part on the reports of P. Ben, the *Le Monde* correspondent in Warsaw.

54. *Nowe Drogi*, no. 10 (1956), p. 11.
55. *Ibid.*, p. 113.
56. *Ibid.*
57. *Ibid.*, p. 116.
58. A preferable designation for this particular moment in view of the diverse elements backing Gomulka; see also Chapter 14.
59. *Nowe Drogi*, no. 10 (1956), pp. 12–18.
60. Radio Warsaw, November 6, 1956.
61. Full text in Zinner, pp. 197–239.
62. *Nowe Drogi*, no. 10 (1956), p. 147.
63. Text in Zinner, *National Communism*, pp. 270–284.
64. Full text in *New York Times*, December 19, 1956.
65. *Ibid.*, November 19, 1956.
66. The East European leaders apparently did not expect the attack on Stalin, despite Khrushchev's speech in Sofia in 1955. Thus the East German SED theoretical journal *Einheit* was still praising Stalin in February of 1956 as Khrushchev was delivering his condemnation.

12. THE MAOIST EFFORT TO RECONSTRUCT A CENTER

1. The Chinese were apparently dismayed by the form and extent of Khrushchev's denunciation of Stalin in February 1956. For an able treatment, see Donald S. Zagoria, *The Sino-Soviet Conflict, 1956–1961* (Princeton, 1962), pp. 43–49.
2. *Nowe Drogi*, no. 10 (1956), p. 38.
3. *The Anti-Stalin Campaign and International Communism* (New York, 1957), p. 294.
4. *Nowe Drogi*, no. 10 (1956), p. 39.
5. *Trybuna Ludu*, November 2, 1956.
6. *Pravda*, November 19, 1956 (italics added).
7. For example, M. Bielicki, "Conversations on Politics," *Po Prostu*, December 2, 1956; or the poem by A. Wazyk, "Qui Tacent Clament," *Nowa Kultura*, November 25, 1956.
8. *Trybuna Wolnosci*, November 25, 1956.
9. R. Jurys, "Poznan and Budapest," *Zycie Warszawy*, November 23, 1956.
10. *Izvestia*, November 7, 1956.
11. M. Bibrowski, "Yugoslavia: The Beginning of the Great Debate," *Nowa Kultura*, December 9, 1956.
12. *Pravda*, December 23, 1956. For the Polish follow-up, see note 27.
13. *Neues Deutschland*, November 27, 1956.
14. *Rude Pravo*, December 8, 1956.
15. *Rude Pravo*, editorial, "Shoulder to Shoulder for Peace and Socialism," January 8, 1957.
16. See particularly the illuminating series in *The New Leader*, January 5, 12, and 19, 1959, by F. Schenk and R. Lowenthal, "Politics and Planning in the Soviet Empire."
17. Radio Peking, November 1, 1956.
18. *Jen Min Jih Pao*, November 21, 1956.

19. Quotes from Russian translation, *Pravda*, December 30, 1956.
20. *Pravda*, December 30, 1956 (italics added).
21. For instance, *Rabotnichesko Delo*, January 31, 1957, an article on "Bourgeois Nationalism—Banner of Imperialist Reaction," stated: "The imperialists are trying to drive a wedge into the unity of the world workers' revolutionary movement through various bourgeois ideas which they conceal in a slogan for national independence and equality of rights, or in the term 'anti-Stalinism.' . . ."
22. Both quotations are from P. Avramov, "The Attitude Toward the Soviet Union and the CPSU—Cornerstone of Proletarian Internationalism," *Rabotnichesko Delo*, February 8, 1957.
23. Radio Tirana, February 17, 1957.
24. Radio Belgrade, February 26, 1957 (italics added).
25. For instance, the violent comment on Popovic's speech by *Pravda*, March 11, 1957; replies of *Borba* and *Politika*, March 12; *Rabotnichesko Delo*, March 4, 1957, article on "Guiding Light for World's Proletariat"; Moscow speeches by Bulganin and Kadar on March 27, 1957, strongly condemning the Yugoslavs particularly on the Hungarian issue; and the Yugoslav reassertion of Soviet responsibility for the uprising, *Borba*, April 5, 1957, in a direct reply to Bulganin; and so on.
26. "The Origin and Development . . ." The full text of that document can also be found in W. E. Griffith, *The Sino-Soviet Rift* (Cambridge, 1964).
27. Indicative is the Polish reply of February 10, 1957, to the *Pravda* December 23 article on proletarian internationalism cited earlier: M. Bibrowski, in his "On Internationalism, Stalinism and other Disputed Matters," *Nowa Kultura*, reasserts his previous theses, again attacks Stalinism, gives *Pravda* a lecture on Leninism, and suggests that Azizian, the *Pravda* writer, start practicing true internationalism by ceasing to call those who disagree with his views "bourgeois nationalists," "reformists," "renegades."
28. *Current Background* (translation), no. 439; statement of March 5, 1957 (italics added).
29. See the Schenk and Lowenthal articles.
30. V. Winston, "The Soviet Satellites — Economic Liability?" *Problems of Communism*, January–February 1958, esp. note 15.
31. I. T. Vinogradov, "The Building of Socialism in the European Countries of People's Democracy," *Voprosy istorii KPSS*, no. 3, 1957.
32. Winston; on Soviet loans, see *Mezhdunarodnaia zhizn*, no. 12 (1956), p. 27.
33. "Long Term Planning and Cooperation in Eastern Europe and the Soviet Union," *Economic Bulletin for Europe*, November 1957; see also R. Fidelski, *Wspolpraca Gospodarcza Polski z Krajami Socjalistycznymi* (Warsaw, 1959), esp. pp. 78–90.
34. *Pravda*, July 14, 1957.
35. *Ceteka*, December 14, 1957.
36. For data and tables, see *Vneshnaia Torgovlia*, no. 11 (1957), esp. p. 46.
37. "The GDR and the CSR are the chief exporters of industrial equipment to the USSR. In 1956, approximately 55 per cent of all the imported equipment and some 75 per cent of the equipment imported by Soviet Russia from the socialist countries was from Czechoslovakia and the GDR." *Za-*

hranicny Obchod, January 1958. For ideological as well as economic justification, see V. Keigl, "The Place of Czechoslovakia in the Division of Labor and Economic Cooperation of the Socialist States"; and G. Kolmei, "The Role of Industry and Foreign Trade of the German Democratic Republic in the World Socialist Economic System," *Mirovaia Sotsialisticheskaia Sistema Khoziaistva* (Moscow, 1958).

38. *Probleme Economice,* no. 1, 1958.

39. Text in *New York Times,* January 30, 1957.

40. Moscow Protocol of July 7, 1958.

41. *Rude Pravo,* July 7, 1958.

42. For a detailed treatment of Soviet-Czech trade, with itemized listings, see *Nova Mysl,* June 1958; *Hospodarske Noviny,* July 8, 1958.

43. The most detailed information is contained in two extensive tables in *Zycie Gospodarcze,* October 19, 1958. Other data in *Sztandar Mlodych,* November 6, 1957, and in an interview given by the Polish Minister of Trade, *Przyjazn,* January 19, 1958.

44. "In Unity Lies Strength," *Tvorba,* no. 3, 1957, p. 1.

45. *Pravda,* February 20, 1957.

46. Georges Mond, "A Conversation in Warsaw," *Problems of Communism,* XIII (May–June 1964), pp. 77–82.

47. *Nowe Drogi,* no. 6 (1957), pp. 5, 52.

48. *Ibid.,* p. 8.

49. Text in *New York Times,* September 18, 1957.

50. *Pravda,* June 21, 1957; *Rude Pravo,* June 19, 1957.

51. For instance, *Mezhdunarodnaia zhizn,* no. 5, 1957. p. 49. For an extensive Yugoslav critique of this concept, as well as analysis of the different formulations, see V. Vlahovic, "The Idea and Substance of Proletarian Internationalism," *Socijalizam,* October 1958. (Vlahovic is a Politburo — Executive Committee — member.)

52. For Khrushchev's own justification of Soviet leadership as being "objectively" dictated by history, see *Pravda,* July 12, 1958.

53. *Trybuna Ludu,* November 7, 1957.

54. This writer had an opportunity to observe at the time the strange mixture of optimism, make-believe, and wishful thinking prevalent in Warsaw

55. As confirmed by the Twenty-first CPSU Congress speeches which revealed that domestic Soviet issues were paramount in the attempted anti Khrushchev coup.

56. *Zycie Warszawy,* April 23, 1957 (italics added).

57. For discussion, see R. MacFarquhar, *The Hundred Flowers Campaign and the Chinese Intellectuals* (New York, 1960).

58. See MacFarquhar; also T. Chen, *Thought Reform of the Chinese Intellectuals* (Hong Kong, 1960). For a Soviet account, see V. Lazarev, "The Struggle Against the Rightists in the CPR — the Struggle for Socialism," *Kommunist,* no. 5, April 1958.

59. R. MacFarquhar, "Communist China's Intraparty Dispute," *Pacific Affairs,* no. 4, December 1958; Chao Kuo-chaun, "Leadership in the Chinese Communist Party," *The Annals,* January 1959; Zagoria, pp. 68–71.

60. L. Ilyichev, "The Sputniks and International Relations," *International*

Affairs, no. 3, 1958, p. 7, as quoted in Zagoria, esp. the discussion on pp. 155–160.

61. As later published in Peking, Mao Tse-tung, "Imperialists and All Reactionaries Are Paper Tigers," *Jen Min Jih Pao,* October 27, 1958. For a fuller Chinese account of the strife at the Moscow meeting, see "The Origin and Development . . . ," republished also as a pamphlet.

62. Mao Tse-tung in Moscow, November 1957, as quoted by *Peking Review,* no. 36, September 6, 1963. See also "Two Different Lines on the Question of War and Peace — Comment on the Open Letter of the Central Committee of the CPSU," editorial department of *Jen Min Jih Pao* and *Red Flag,* November 1963, and in *Peking Review,* no. 47, November 27, 1963; particularly the passages dealing with the November 1957 debate between Mao and Khrushchev.

63. Both the Chinese document and the other citations are from "The Origin and Development . . ."

64. For a theoretical discussion of the problem of the deviant who errs by excess, see my "Deviation Control: The Dynamics of Doctrinal Conflict," *The American Political Science Review,* March 1962.

65. See A. L. Hsieh, "The Sino-Soviet Nuclear Dialogue: 1963," *The Journal of Conflict Resolution,* June 1964, esp. pp. 110–113.

66. See speech by Khrushchev, *Pravda,* July 12, 1958.

67. *Pravda,* November 5, 1957.

68. *Pravda,* November 7, 1957.

69. *Pravda,* November 22, 1957.

70. Account of F. Ebert, East German participant, *Neues Deutschland,* November 30, 1957.

71. *Ibid.*

72. *Pravda,* September 15, 1957.

73. *Pravda,* November 22, 1957.

74. *Trybuna Ludu,* November 29, 1957. This reference was omitted from *Pravda's* coverage of his speech, November 30, 1957.

75. For instance, *Izvestia,* December 28, 1957.

76. Personal East European sources.

77. For the distinction, see my "Poland — A Political Glimpse," *Problems of Communism,* no. 5, 1957.

13. UNITY THROUGH THE STRUGGLE AGAINST REVISIONISM

1. For a development of this break-through stage of totalitarian development, see C. J. Friedrich and Z. K. Brzezinski, *Totalitarian Dictatorship and Autocracy* (Cambridge, 1956), ch. xxvii.

2. *V Pomoshch Politicheskomu Samoobrazivaniu,* no. 12, 1957. See also the Collected Essays by V. I. Lenin, *Protiv Revizionizma v Zashchitu Marksizma* (Moscow, 1959).

3. *Nowa Kultura,* no. 4, 1957.

4. Nos. 35–38, 1957; partial translations in *East Europe,* December 1957, February, March, and May 1958.

5. "Old Tunes in a New Key," *Voprosy filosofii,* no. 4, 1957.

6. For some translated condensations, see *Current Digest of the Soviet Press,* IX, no. 38, pp. 3–8, and in no. 52, p. 24.

7. February 5, 1958.

8. Attacks on Polish revisionists always distinguished them from Gomulka. However, this immunity did not extend to those domestic ideologues in Poland who, in supporting the attacks against Kolakowski, themselves appeared to be straying from the fold. For instance, J. J. Wiatr and Z. Bauman, Gomulkaists openly critical of revisionism, were severely admonished for alleging that in the later stages of Stalinism, Marxism as science was dominated by Marxism as ideology. "Is this Marxism?" *Voprosy filosofii,* no. 4, 1957.

9. See his call for "democratic patriotism" in *Deutsche Zeitschrift fuer Philosophie,* March 15, 1953.

10. For Harich's program, see "Die politische Platform Harichs und seiner Freunde," *SBZ-Archiv,* March 25, 1957; for an account of his activities, see the *Neues Deutschland* account of his trial, March 9 and 10, 1957. (I am indebted to my former graduate student, L. G. Stauber, for these references.) The *Neues Deutschland* account was not refuted by West German sources.

11. Radio Moscow, August 4, 1957.

12. *Politika,* May 1957; quoted by S. Lyon, "Czechoslovak-Jugoslav Relations" (mimeographed, Radio Free Europe, no date).

13. *Le Monde* correspondence of Khrushchev's speeches on a visit to Czechoslovakia, July 12, 1956.

14. Radio Prague, July 11, 1957.

15. *Ibid.*

16. On the eve of the Tito-Khrushchev meeting both *Borba* and *Politika* published sharp attacks on the Czech and Bulgarian regimes (July 27, 1957).

17. The most complete accounts are provided by Khrushchev's speech in Sofia, reported in *Pravda,* June 4, 1957, and not refuted by Belgrade.

18. *Pravda,* July 12, 1958; no Yugoslav denial.

19. *Komunist,* August 9, 1957.

20. Text of declaration in *New York Times,* September 17, 1956.

21. Typical was the immediate reaction of the East Germans to the August meeting. *Wirtschaftswissenschaft,* an economic journal, in its October–November 1957 issue, strongly criticized the Yugoslav model, pointing out its inapplicability elsewhere.

22. *Komunist,* January 1, 1958 (views of R. Colakovic, Politburo member).

23. *Ibid.,* January 10, 1958.

24. *Ibid.,* December 13, 1957. Soviet polemics by A. Sobolev in *Kommunist* (Moscow), no. 2, 1958.

25. *Nasa Stvarnost,* January 1958 (views of M. Popovic, head of Yugoslav planning).

26. Hungarian-East German Party Declaration, March 26, 1958.

27. At a Moscow meeting attended by the Bulgarian party delegation he was given a greater ovation than even the First Secretary of the Bulgarian party (*New York Times,* February 20, 1958).

28. *Kommunist,* no. 1, 1958.

29. All quotes from the draft based on *The Joint Translation Service Bulletin,* March 24, 1958.

30. Translation available in *Current Digest of the Soviet Press,* X, no. 16.
31. The final version of the program is available in English, *Jugoslavia's Way,* trans. S. Preibechevich (New York, 1958).
32. Radio Belgrade, April 22–24, 1958, speeches by Tito, Rankovic, and Kardelj.
33. As quoted in *New York Times,* April 23, 1958.
34. *Borba,* April 20, 1958.
35. *Current Digest of the Soviet Press.*
36. *Pravda,* May 8, 1958.
37. For example, *Einheit,* no. 5, 1958; *Ceteka,* citing Novotny, June 18, 1958. For a collected volume of such attacks, see *Protiv Sovremennogo Revizionizma* (Moscow, 1958).
38. *Komunist,* May 9, 1958.
39. For example, *Politika,* May 15; *Borba,* May 16, 1958.
40. *Krasnaia zvezda,* May 17, 1958.
41. Telegram to Tito on his sixty-sixth birthday, May 26, 1958.
42. Text in *Pravda,* July 12, 1958.
43. *Ibid.*
44. For comparative purposes, see E. Bernstein, *Gesellschaftliches und Privat-Eigentum* (Berlin, 1891) and N. Bukharin, *Oekonomik der Transformationsperiode* (Verlag der kommunistischen Internationale, 1922), esp. ch. viii: "System der Produktionsverwaltung in der Diktatur des Proletariats," pp. 138–49.
45. Personal information.
46. *Trybuna Ludu,* April 15, 1958.
47. *Trybuna Ludu,* June 29, 1958.
48. *Pravda,* June 30, 1958; P. Pospelov in *Kommunist,* July 1958.
49. *Pravda,* June 4, 1958.

14. THE POLISH WAY TO SOCIALISM

A condensed version of this chapter appeared in *Problems of Communism,* June–July 1959.

1. For biographical data, see Dziewanowski, p. 340, note 13, or the preface to his collected postwar speeches, *W Walce o Demokracje Ludowa* (Warsaw, 1947), pp. 7–9.
2. S. Mikolajczyk, *The Rape of Poland;* Korbonski, *W Imieniu Kremla.*
3. An excellent comparative treatment is to be found in J. Nowak's "Analysis of Developments in Poland since October 1956," (Radio Free Europe, mimeographed, June 1958).
4. Gomulka, *W Walce,* II, 260.
5. Gomulka, *Przemowienia* (Warsaw, 1957), p. 271.
6. Zinner, *National Communism,* pp. 233–235.
7. *W Walce,* II, 24.
8. *Przemowienia,* p. 86, translation in Zinner, p. 303.
9. *W Walce,* I, 163.
10. *Ibid.,* p. 185.
11. *Przemowienia,* p. 272.
12. *Ibid.,* pp. 278–283.

13. *W Walce*, I, 155.
14. *W Walce*, II, 162 (italics his).
15. *Przemowienia*, pp. 33–34, translation in Zinner, p. 222.
16. *W Walce*, II, 156.
17. *Przemowienia*, pp. 264–271.
18. *Ibid.*, p. 126 (italics his).
19. *Pravda*, November 5, 1957.
20. *Przemowienia*, p. 269.
21. *Ibid.*, p. 305.
22. See *Trybuna Ludu*, December 7, 1956, for a discussion of "fear" among the members.
23. For example, *Zielony Sztandar*, October 20, 1957, October 27, 1957; March 31, 1957.
24. Chapter 11, pp. 242–243.
25. For an excellent discussion of the social disintegration produced by Stalinism and the war, see J. Szczepanski, "An attempted diagnosis," *Przeglad Kulturalny*, September 5–11, 1957.
26. S. Stomma, one of the leaders of the independent Catholic laymen and deputy to the Sejm, *Przeglad Kulturalny*, no. 43, October 25–31, 1956.
27. To be called *Fakty*, quickly prevented by the party.
28. For data on rehabilitations, see *Zycie Warszawy*, June 26, 1957.
29. *Chlopska Droga*, October 17–20, 1957; *Trybuna Ludu*, May 21, 1956
30. Cf. interview with its chairman, Radio Warsaw, January 2, 1957.
31. *Trybuna Ludu*, December 5, 1956.
32. For a good insight into the thinking of the Polish economists, see Edward Lipinski, *Rewizje* (Warsaw, 1958); essentially a collection of his article during late 1956 and early 1957.
33. *Dziennik Ustaw*, November 24, 1956.
34. This writer has been collecting some of them and hopes to publish a short analysis.
35. For some estimates, see my "Poland — A Political Glimpse," *Problem of Communism;* Nowak, "Analysis of Developments in Poland since Octobe 1956"; and R. Staar, "New Course in Communist Poland," *Journal of Politic:* March 1958, p. 76.
36. For instance, L. Kolakowski, "The Ideological Sense of the Concep of the Left," *Po Prostu*, February 24, 1957.
37. Politburo member J. Morawski (closely identified with Gomulka) i *Nowe Drogi*, no. 3, 1957; Politburo member R. Zambrowski (described i Warsaw as spokesman for the central apparat), in *Zycie Partii*, no. 3, 1957.
38. Nowak, p. 54.
39. Leon Kasman, appointed editor, was reported to be a Zambrowski cen trist; for a lengthy list, see Nowak, p. 59.
40. For instance, "Again a 'Cultural Policy?'" *Nowa Kultura*, June 16, 195
41. Apart from a street demonstration by Warsaw youth, other evidenc is suggested by an unpublished analysis of public opinion concerning the events conducted by the Polish Radio (in this writer's possession).
42. For an informed account, see K. Jelenski, "The Rise and Fall of P *Prostu,*" *The New Leader*, December 2, 1957.
43. Specifically, J. Kott, M. Jastrun, P. Hertz, J. Andrzejewski.

44. Speech to the Tenth Plenum, *Trybuna Ludu*, October 26, 1957.

45. Based on personal observation in Warsaw.

46. Account in *New York Times*, August 22, 1957.

47. The purge, conducted without clear ideological guidelines, resulted in the dropping of 200,161 members, of whom only 27,255 were actually excluded, the others being struck from the rolls. The party decreased by 16 per cent, and the vast majority of those dropped had nothing to do with deviation, but had been inactive, or, as in the case of most of those excluded, were guilty of economic offenses. *Sztandar Mlodych*, May 15, 1958.

48. "A Few Remarks on the Leading Role of the UPWP," *Nowe Drogi*, January 1958.

49. As stated by A. Werblan in his secret speech to the Central Committee's Press Commission, May 6, 1958.

50. *Trybuna Ludu*, October 17, 1957.

51. *Ibid.*, October 21, 1957 (Professor A. Schaff).

52. At the end of 1957, this number was estimated at about twenty (*Orka*, September 29, 1957).

53. Nowak, pp. 57–58.

54. *Trybuna Ludu*, November 13, 1957.

55. *Express Wieczorny*, February 15, 1958.

56. Personal interview with a cabinet minister.

57. Speech by Gomulka, *Glos Pracy*, April 18, 1958.

58. In 1492 of 1936 industrial enterprises eligible. *Glos Pracy*, September 20, 1957.

59. *Rada Robotnicza*, no. 12, June 18–20, 1958; for the negative reaction of the Workers' Councils, see *Glos Pracy*, June 17, 1958.

60. Confirmed to the writer by a highly placed member of the Central Committee; explicitly asserted at the Twelfth Plenum in October 1958 by W. Matwin, as recorded on p. 44 of an edited stenographic report designed purely for internal party use.

61. *Biuletyn statystyczny*, no. 4, 1958.

62. For a comprehensive analysis, see P Collins, "The Post-October Agricultural Policy of Wladyslaw Gomulka" (RFE, mimeographed, October 1958).

63. Between 1952 and 1955 only one interpellation had been made. In 1957, fifty-one interpellations were introduced and, it may be noted, only eleven of them came from Communist Party members. *Trybuna Ludu*, November 12, 1957.

64. That distinction was made by Professor T. Kotarbinski, head of the Polish Academy of Sciences. *Trybuna Literacka*, December 1, 1957.

65. For instance, *Przemowienia*, p. 273.

66. S. Frenkel, "The Plan of Economic Offensive," *Przeglad Kulturalny*, November 6, 1958.

67. Confidential transcript, *XII Plenum Komitetu Centralnego* (Central Committee, Warsaw, 1958), p. 198. It is noteworthy that the plenum revealed important defections from the dogmatists' camp, most particularly T. Gede, the ambassador to Moscow

68. *Ibid.*, pp. 160–161.

69. The Congress proceedings were published in a 764-page issue of *Nowe Drogi*, no. 4, April 1959.

70. For a detailed examination of the various alternatives facing Polish agriculture, see the collected essays *O Nowy Program Rolny* (Warsaw, 1957).

71. *Trybuna Ludu*, July 30, 1958.

72. *Nova Svoboda*, December 20, 1957. In the summer of 1959 this writer had considerable difficulty in finding Polish papers in Czechoslovakia.

73. *Trybuna Ludu*, April 4, 1958.

74. *Predvoj*, April 3, 1958.

75. *Tvorba*, December 19, 1957.

76. *Rude Pravo*, January 1, 1958.

77. This writer, in the course of his visits to Poland, was repeatedly told of continuing suspicion on the part of the Soviet rank and file toward Gomulka. That suspicion apparently also existed within the Central Committee and the central *apparat*.

78. *Sovetskaia Litva*, March 22, 1959.

79. For *unusually* warm personal references to Gomulka by Khrushchev (such as "our friend whom we know well and cherish deeply"), see *Pravda*, October 26 and 28, November 4 and 5, 1958.

80. For Poland's influence on the area, see A. Bromke, "Poland's Role in the Loosening of the Soviet Bloc," *International Journal*, Autumn 1965.

81. *Slowo Powszechne*, March 21, 1958.

15. DIVERGENT UNITY

1. See W. E. Griffith, "What Happened to Revisionism," *Problems of Communism*, no. 2, March–April 1960; see also Chapter 13 of this book.

2. For a discussion of this phenomenon of "privatization" in Western Europe, see Otto Kirchheimer, "German Democracy in the 1950's," *World Politics*, January 1961.

3. For a discussion of the problem of ideological adaptation, see Brzezinski, "Communist Ideology and International Affairs," *The Journal of Conflict Resolution*, September 1960.

4. The best deciphering of the dispute during 1956–1961 is in Zagoria, *The Sino-Soviet Conflict*.

5. For discussions of the earlier relations, see B. Schwartz, *Chinese Communism and the Rise of Mao*; C. Brandt, *Stalin's Failure in China* (Cambridge, 1958); C. McLane, *Soviet Policy and the Chinese Communists* (New York, 1958).

6. See V. Dedijer, *Tito*, pp. 321–322.

7. On February 12, 1960, *The Observer* (London) carried a lengthy summary of the 1960 formal exchanges between the CPSU and the CPC, written by Edward Crankshaw and based on a "report, which contains detailed summaries of hitherto secret correspondence" between Moscow and Peking. The accuracy of this report was confirmed by the 1963 Sino-Soviet polemics, especially by the Chinese document "The Origin and Development . . ."

8. For evidence of Chinese uneasiness over the Khrushchev line toward Yugoslavia in June 1955, compare Khrushchev's reference to Yugoslav socialism with Mao's noncommittal phrases; cf. New China News Agency, June 30, 1955, and *Shih-chieh Chih-shih*, July 20, 1955; discussion in R. Hofheinz "China Joins the Bloc," (unpublished research paper, Harvard, 1960).

9. See Choh-Ming Li, "Economic Development," *The China Quarterly*, no. 1, January–March 1960; Wang Kuang-wei, "The Big Leap in China's Economy," *World Marxist Review*, no. 6, June 1960.

10. *Jen Min Jih Pao*, September 10, 1958.

11. *Izvestia*, October 1, 1958.

12. *Leningradskaia Pravda*, October 23, 1958.

13. *Hsinhua*, November 6, 1958.

14. As reported in the Soviet government statement of September 21, 1963; pertinent passages in Griffith, *The Sino-Soviet Rift*, pp. 436–437.

15. *Hung-ch'i*, July 16, 1958.

16. *Ibid.*, August 14, 1958.

17. H. D. Lasswell, *World Politics and Personal Insecurity* (Glencoe, Ill., 1950), p. 128.

18. According to the count of M. Gamarnikow, Polish Desk, Radio Free Europe, Munich.

19. *Hsinhua*, December 18, 1958.

20. *Pravda*, February 8, 1959. For a rosy assessment of Sino-Soviet relations, see M. S. Kapitsa, *Sovetsko-Kitaiskie Otnosheniia* (Moscow, 1958), esp. ch. ix.

21. *Jen Min Jih Pao*, November 19, 1958; lengthy translation in A. Halpern, "The Chinese Communist Line of Neutralism," RAND mimeographed study, July 1960, pp. 19–20.

22. See Brzezinski, "The Challenge of Change in the Soviet Bloc," *Foreign Affairs*, April 1961.

23. For a subsequent critique of this interpretation, presaging the December 1960 declaration by the eighty-one parties, see T. Zhivkov, "Peace: Key Problem of Today," *World Marxist Review*, August 1960.

24. For an analogy with the earlier Menshevik-Bolshevik debate, see Brzezinski, "Communist Ideology and International Affairs," p. 279. For a lengthy statement of the Chinese position, see Yu Chao-li, in *Hung-ch'i*, no. 7, 1960; also Liu Chang-sheng, Radio Peking, June 8, 1960.

25. Halpern, p. 30.

26. Tass statement of September 9, 1959.

27. For sources, see Griffith, *The Sino-Soviet Rift*.

28. "Origin and Development . . ."

29. Khrushchev's address to the Twenty-first CPSU Congress, January 27, 1959.

30. "Origin and Development . . ." and the statement of the Chinese People's Republic government of August 15, 1963.

31. "Origin and Development . . ."

32. D. A. Charles, "The Dismissal of Marshal P'eng Teh-huai," *The China Quarterly*, October–December 1961.

33. For detailed treatment, see Zagoria, chs. xii–xiii.

34. *Hsinhua*, no. 7, 1960; translated in *East Europe*, March 1960.

35. For instance, the Soviets simply ceased citing the Chinese in their press.

36. For East European comments, see *East Europe*, March 1960. For a discussion of Chinese relations with East Europe, see the symposium on "China and the Soviet Satellites," *The China Quarterly*, July–September 1960.

37. G. Fono, "Those From Whom We Can Learn Most," *Nepszabadsag*, November 7, 1957.

38. The Czechs even renewed the publication of Stalin's writings. *Glos Pracy*, September 12, 1958.

39. *Nepszabadsag*, December 15, 1957; see also J. Revai, "Comments on the World Significance of Soviet Culture," *Nepszabadsag*, November 7, 1957.

40. *Rabotnichesko Delo*, February 16, 1958; for conflict with the writers see *Literaturen Front*, November 28, 1957.

41. Editorial, *Nova Mysl*, no. 4, 1958. To ensure unity of thought an Institute for Advanced Study of Marxism-Leninism was opened at Charles University. *Vysoka Skola*, no. 10, 1957.

42. *Rude Pravo*, June 19, 1958.

43. *Nepszabadsag*, May 18, 1958.

44. *Neues Deutschland*, October 22, 1957.

45. *Statistica*, no. 6, 1957; *Rabotnichesko Delo*, December 11, 1957 and April 18, 1958, which states that the increase in "the production of the means of production" is to be 77 per cent by 1962. See also *New York Times*, February 15, 1959.

46. A. Nove, "Problems of Economic DeStalinization," *Problems of Communism*, no. 2, 1957.

47. *Obrana Lidu*, December 4, 1957; see also "Industrial Reorganization in Czechoslovakia," *East Europe*, April 1958 and *Three-Monthly Economic Review of Eastern Europe*, August 1958.

48. For detailed treatment, see D. Floyd, *Rumania: Russia's Dissident Ally* (London, 1965). Also J. M. Montias, "Background and Origins of the Rumanian Dispute with Comecon," *Soviet Studies*, October 1964.

49. *Tvorba*, April 24, 1958.

50. *Pravda* (Prague), July 24, 1958; *Rude Pravo*, June 19, 1958; *Novo Vreme*, July, 1958.

51. For instance, speech by L. Rautu, Politburo member, *Agerpress*, April 22, 1958.

52. For instance, *Romania Libera*, May 11, 1958; *Scinteia*, May 13, 1958.

53. See *New York Times*, February 18, 1959, for some Bulgarian applications; also *East Europe*, February 1959.

54. An English translation appears in *East Europe*, March 1960.

55. For background, see R. Rupen, "Outer Mongolia since 1955," *Pacific Affairs*, December 1957; Rupen, "Outer Mongolia, 1957–1960," *Pacific Affairs*, June 1960; as well as Rupen, "Mongolian Nationalism," *Royal Central Asian Journal*, parts I and II, April and October 1958. See also G. Friters, *Outer Mongolia and Its International Position* (London, 1957).

56. The best treatment of Albania's position in the bloc is W. E. Griffith, *Albania and the Sino-Soviet Rift* (Cambridge, 1963). For some background on the role of ethnic and class considerations in Albanian politics, see R. V. Burks, *The Dynamics of Communism in Eastern Europe* (Princeton, 1961).

57. Dedijer, pp. 321 ff. See also, Burks.

58. *Borba*, February 22, 1961. See also Burks for the discussion of the relationship between the richer Tosks and the more militant and fewer Ghegs. The Tosks had been oppressed by the Turks and feared that any union with

Yugoslavia might alter their domestic relationship with the Ghegs since many Ghegs reside in the Kossovo region. Hoxha and his associates are Tosks.

59. Griffith, *Albania and the Sino-Soviet Rift*, pp. 28, 177.

60. It is noteworthy that the Chinese share of Albanian imports rose from 1/13 of the Soviet share in 1955 to 1/4 in 1957; see Griffith, *Albania and the Sino-Soviet Rift*, pp. 28, 177.

61. T. A. Stepanian, "The October Revolution and the Formation of the Communist System," *Voprosy filosofii*, no. 10, 1958.

62. For a discussion of Khrushchev's views and an explicit rejection of Stepanian's (as cited in note 61), see P. Fedoseyev in *Pravda*, February 9, 1959. Stepanian has long specialized on the subject of transition to Communism, which thus makes the rebuke administered to him all the more significant. See Stepanian, *I. V. Stalin o stroitelstve kommunizma v SSSR* (Moscow, 1950); and "V. I. Lenin on the Building of Communism," *Kommunist*, no. 6, 1954. For emphasis on the difference between Communism, as involving a higher level of industrialization and high productivity, and socialism, as involving a socialist organization of property relations, see *Sovetskaia Moldaviia*, March 17, 1959.

63. For some Soviet discussions, see L. Leontiev, "The Creation of the Material-Technical Basis for Communism," *Pravda*, February 11, 1959; G. Obiedkov, "Theoretical Problems of Communist Construction," *Pravda*, July 31, 1959; B. Ponomarev, "Theoretical Problems of Communist Construction," *Pravda*, March 6, 1959.

64. For some estimates of continued Soviet exploitation, see Chapter 12, p. 286. The growing importance of the "socialist world market" has given rise to special literature dealing with the economic as well as the ideological aspects of this integration, as, for instance, T. Lychowski, *Stosunki Ekonomiczne Miedzy Krajami o Roznych Ustrojach* (Warsaw, 1957); *Sodruzhestvo Stran Sotsializma* (Moscow, 1958); *Mirovaia Sotsialisticheskaia Sistema Khoziaistva* (Moscow, 1958).

16. THE SINO-SOVIET CONFLICT

1. For more detailed treatment than is possible to provide here, the reader would find it profitable to read first for general historical background, K. Mehnert, *Peking and Moscow* (New York, 1963); A. Whiting, *Soviet Policies in China, 1917–1924* (New York, 1954); C. Brandt, *Stalin's Failure in China, 1924–1927*; C. McLane, *Soviet Policy and the Chinese Communists, 1931–1946*; for more recent times: H. Boorman, et al., *Moscow-Peking Axis*; D. Zagoria, *The Sino-Soviet Conflict*; G. F. Hudson, et al., *The Sino-Soviet Dispute* (New York, 1961); W. E. Griffith, *The Sino-Soviet Rift* and *The Sino-Soviet Relations, 1964–1965* (Cambridge, 1966). (I am most grateful to Dr. Griffith for making it possible for me to consult the manuscript of the 1966 book prior to its publication.)

2. For a 1963 summary of these issues, see A. Dallin, ed., *Diversity in International Communism* (New York, 1963), especially the introduction by Dallin and Brzezinski. For a Chinese summary of the divisive issues, see the letter of the Central Committee of the CPC of June 14, 1963; for the Soviet,

the letter of the Central Committee of the CPSU of July 14, 1963. Complete texts of both available in Griffith, *The Sino-Soviet Rift.*

3. "The Leaders of the CPSU Are the Greatest Splitters of Our Times," *Jen Min Jih Pao,* February 4, 1964. Full text in *Peking Review,* no. 6, February 7, 1964.

4. *Ibid.*

5. *Jen Min Jih Pao* editorial, as reported in *Peking Review,* no. 46, November 12, 1965.

6. See Brandt, *Stalin's Failure in China.*

7. This is the general thrust of H. Schwartz's *Tsars, Mandarins and Commissars* (Philadelphia, 1964).

8. For a systematic, detailed, and chronological treatment of these years, see the two volumes by Griffith, *The Sino-Soviet Rift* and *The Sino-Soviet Relations.*

9. See Griffith, *Albania and the Sino-Soviet Rift,* pp. 42–43.

10. Letter of the Central Committee of the CPC of February 29, 1964, to the Central Committee of the CPSU. Text in *Peking Review,* no. 19, May 8, 1964, p. 14.

11. See, for example, Elizabeth Gurley Flynn, "Recollections of the 1960 Conference," *Political Affairs,* November 1963.

12. See, especially, T. Zhivkov (Bulgarian First Secretary), "Peace: Key Problem of Today," which develops many of the points subsequently included in the Moscow declaration; A. Shapiro, "The Contemporary Epoch and Its Characteristics," *Mirovaia ekonomika i mezhdunarodnie otnosheniia,* no. 11, 1960; A. Arzumanyan, "On the Character of the Contemporary Epoch," *Kommunist Vooruzhennykh Sil,* no. 2, October 1960.

13. On the very eve of the conference, the Chinese published a major ideological statement, "A Basic Summary of Experience Gained in the Victory of the Chinese People's Revolution" (*Hsinhua,* November 2, 1960), restating the more radical Chinese position and labeling as "stupid" the failure of some to understand that parliaments are a mere sham and that therefore it is idle to speak of a "parliamentary way" to socialism.

14. See Walter Ulbricht's report in *Neues Deutschland,* December 18, 1960; H. Matern, in *Neues Deutschland,* December 23, 1960; Crankshaw; Osadczuk; and personal interviews.

15. Flynn, p. 29.

16. Zagoria, pp. 367–368.

17. Belgian CP statement, *Le Drapeau Rouge,* February 22, 1962, as quoted by Griffith in his "The November 1960 Meeting," *The China Quarterly,* July–September, 1962. Dr. Griffith's analysis is the best and most complete available, although subject to corrections on some points in the light of evidence available subsequently. See, for example, the document published in January 1963 by the French Communist Party, including hitherto unpublished sections of Thorez's speech to the Moscow conference.

18. Osadczuk, p. 133. He does not list them, but they may have included the Albanian, Vietnamese, Malayan, Spanish, West German (criticized in 1960 for "leftism"), Indonesian, Cuban, Venezuelan, and Peruvian parties. A credible text of Hoxha's vituperative attack on the Soviet position appeared in *The Daily Telegraph* (London), June 9, 1961.

19. For a systematic reconstruction, with fascinating documentary evidence, see Griffith, *Albania and the Sino-Soviet Rift.*

20. Speeches by E. Hoxha and M. Shehu on Radio Tirana, February 13 and 17, 1961.

21. The Yugoslav press, in response to Albanian attacks, began a series on the gruesome history of the Albanian party. See *Borba*, March 19, 20, 21, and 22, 1961, for many hitherto unknown aspects, especially pertaining to the 1956 unrest in Tirana.

22. V. Vlahovic, *A Step Backward*, a report submitted to the Executive Committee of the League of Communists of Yugoslavia on February 10, 1961 (Belgrade, 1961), p. 69.

23. See P. Pospelov in *Pravda*, January 18, 1962, and the editorial in *Jen Min Jih Pao*, January 19, 1962, which referred to American discussion of a split in international Communism and asserted that imperialism would decay in any event — but without directly contradicting the American allegation. For an Albanian attack, see especially the ably argued "Deeper and Deeper in the Mire of Anti-Marxism," *Zeri i Popullit*, January 9, 1962.

24. Statement of March 8, 1963.

25. For a systematic treatment of the history and specifics of the border issue, see D. J. Doolin, *Territorial Claims in the Sino-Soviet Conflict* (Stanford, 1965). Essentially, the territories lost to Russia involved areas north of the Amur River and major portions of what is now Soviet Central Asia, totaling approximately 1.7 million sq. km.

26. Letter of the CC of the CPC of February 29, 1964; see note 10.

27. For example, the account of refugees from China in *Komsomolskaia Pravda*, September 20, 1963. See also Radio Peking, September 30, 1965, for an account of an alleged Soviet effort to subvert the Sinkiang Uighur autonomous region.

28. *Pravda*, September 5, 1964.

29. Open Letter of the Central Committee of the CPSU to all its Members, *Pravda*, July 14, 1963.

30. "The Leaders of the CPSU Are the Greatest Splitters . . ."

31. "Fighting Task of Workers in Philosophy and Social Sciences," *Jen Min Jih Pao*, December 27, 1963; English text in *Peking Review*, no. 1, January 3, 1964.

32. "Two Different Lines on the Question of War and Peace," editorial departments of *Jen Min Jih Pao* and *Hung ch'i*, November 18, 1963.

33. For a good analysis, see B. Bogunovic, *Borba*, February 29, 1964.

34. Statement of the Soviet government, August 20, 1963.

35. *Ibid.*

36. Among the most substantial Chinese ideological elaborations prior to the direct polemics of 1963 were three articles published in the spring of 1962 and dealing, ostensibly, with the revisionist thought of Kautsky, Kardelj, and Bernstein. Available in Dallin, ed., *Diversity in International Communism*, documents nos. 37, 38, and 40.

37. The ruling parties that refused to attend were the Rumanian, North Korean, North Vietnamese, Chinese, and Albanian.

38. "The Leaders of the CPSU Are the Greatest Splitters . . ."

39. "The Proletarian Revolution and Khrushchev's Revisionism," editorial departments of *Jen Min Jih Pao* and *Hung ch'i*, March 31, 1964.

40. The Soviet reaction is described in *Peking Review*, no. 46, November 12, 1965, p. 15.

41. "Carrying the Struggle Against Khrushchev Revisionism to the End," *Peking Review*, no. 25, June 18, 1965.

42. *Ibid.*, also the spring 1965 exchange of letters between Peking and Moscow as reported in E. Crankshaw in *The Observer*, November 14, 1965; also "Refutation of the New Leaders of the CPSU on 'United Action,' " editorial departments of *Jen Min Jih Pao* and *Hung ch'i* as cited in *Peking Review*, no. 46, November 12, 1965.

43. "Refutation of the New Leaders of the CPSU . . ." (italics added).

44. This theme was even more strongly stressed in "The Leaders of the CPSU Are Betrayers of the Declaration and of the Statement," *Peking Review*, no. 1, January 1, 1966.

45. *Pravda*, September 21 and 22, 1963, as cited by Raymond Garthoff in his *Soviet Military Policy: A Historical Analysis* (New York, 1966), ch. ix, note 54.

46. See Uri Ra'anan, "Arms Deals as a Facet of Soviet Foreign Policy, 1955–1964," to be published by the Research Institute on Communist Affairs, Columbia University. For fuller discussions of Sino-Soviet military relations, see Garthoff, *Soviet Military Policy: A Historical Analysis*.

47. Letter of the CC of the CPC of February 29, 1964.

48. *Ibid.*

49. M. Suslov, speech of February 14, 1964.

50. Letter of the CC of the CPC of February 29, 1964.

51. For a fuller discussion, see my "Threat and Opportunity in the Communist Schism," *Foreign Affairs*, April 1963.

52. "Refutation of the New Leaders of the CPSU . . ."

53. For an excellent over-all examination of this trend, see Richard Lowenthal, *World Communism: The Disintegration of a Secular Faith* (New York, 1964).

17. SATELLITES INTO JUNIOR ALLIES

1. Editorial, "The Khrushchevite Revisionists Are Confronted with Difficulties, Failures, and Serious Contradictions," *Zeri i Popullit*, December 10, 1965 (italics added).

2. Conversation with the author.

3. The specifics of internal East European developments will not be treated here, except as they affected inter-Communist relations. For detailed treatment, country by country, of internal developments, see J. F. Brown, *The New Eastern Europe* (New York, 1966). Also Griffith, *Communism in Europe*, 2 vols. (Cambridge, 1966), and Gordon Skilling, *The Governments of Communist East Europe* (New York, 1966).

4. See the account by M. Tatu, *Le Monde* (weekly edition), February 24–March 2, 1966.

5. V. Kotyk, "Some Aspects of the Unity of Socialist Countries at the Present Time," *Slovansky Prehled*, no. 5, 1965.

6. W. E. Griffith, "Yugoslavia," in Brzezinski, ed., *Africa and the Communist World* (Stanford, 1963).

7. For a good over-all account, see M. Gamarnikow, "The Reforms: A Survey," *East Europe*, January 1966.

8. For further discussion, see my *Alternative to Partition* (New York, 1965), pp. 31–38.

9. See Chapter 16, page 419 for Mao's statement already hinting at this; also the speech by Wang Liang "The Peaceful Settlement of Territorial Disputes," delivered in Budapest on April 4, 1964 (Peking, NCNA, April 6, 1964) on renouncing the use of force in resolving border disputes dividing the Communist countries.

10. A good summary of recent Slovak statements is contained in the RFE research paper "Slovak Nationalism Revisited," November 11, 1965. For an official admission of Slovak dislike of the Czechs, see *Rude Pravo*, March 2, 1966.

11. The account that follows is a condensation of my treatment of this subject in *Alternative to Partition*, pp. 16–24, with some additional material. A good over-all summary is in George Gross, "Rumania: The Fruits of Autonomy," *Problems of Communism*, January–February 1966.

12. See particularly the reports by Gheorghiu-Dej, Petre Borila, and Nicolae Ceausescu, *Scinteia*, December 7, 10, and 13, 1961.

13. *Ibid.*, December 7, 1961.

14. H. D. Lasswell, *World Politics and Personal Insecurity*, p. 12.

15. *Ibid.*, p. 121.

16. See the defense of the Rumanian conduct during the Munich crisis by Gh. Matei in *Analele Institutului de Istorii a Partidului*, no. 5, 1965.

17. Gamarnikow, "Comecon Today," *East Europe*, March 1964.

18. I. Rachmuth, "The Importance of Establishing a Rate of Development Which Will Level Off the Economic Progress of All Socialist Countries," *Probleme Economice*, Bucharest, July 1963.

19. C. Murgescu, "Pseudo-theories Which Try to Drain Industrialization of Its Content," *Viata Economica*, August 23, 1963. A year later the Rumanian economist returned to the attack violently criticizing the East Germans again for recommending intensified CEMA specialization, with the Rumanians urging instead a looser structure including even China (*Viata Economica*, June 5, 1964).

20. Letter of the CC of the CPC of February 29, 1964.

21. G. Gross, p. 23.

22. For a criticism of this Gaullist concept, specifically as applied to East Europe, see *Alternative to Partition*, chs. iii and iv. Also for some timid East European criticisms of it as shortsighted, see especially Edmund Osmanczyk, "United Europe, United Germany, and What Else?" *Polityka*, March 5, 1965; and Ludwig Debinski, "A Gaullist Setback," *Tygodnik Powszechny*, April 11, 1965, and "Poland, France, and Germany," *ibid.*, August 29, 1965. For a good analysis of the Polish-French flirtation, see Adam Bromke, "Poland and France: The Sentimental Friendship," *East Europe*, February 1966, pp. 9–15.

23. For a good discussion, see C. Stern's chapter on the GDR in Griffith, *European Communism*, especially pp. 119 ff.

24. *Rabotnicheskoe Delo*, September 19, 1965.

25. Griffith, *European Communism*, p. 8.

26. Both countries had that negative experience in regard to their dealings with Poland and China. See *Alternative to Partition*, p. 17.

27. See the Rumanian declaration of April 27, 1964.

28. This was very frankly admitted by Deputy Premier Jaroszewicz on his return to Warsaw from the twelfth CEMA Executive Committee session, Radio Warsaw, April 26, 1964. For fuller discussion of contemporary CEMA developments, see the next chapter.

29. *Pravda*, March 27, 1959.

30. *Ibid.*, April 4, 1964.

31. See the RFE research report "Novotny on Czechoslovak-Soviet Relations," November 3, 1965.

32. J. Sebesta, "The Basis of Economic Relations Between the CSR and USSR," *Hospodarske Noviny*, October 15, 1965.

33. T. Wolfe, "The Evolving Nature of the Warsaw Pact," RAND Corporation Memorandum, December 1965, p. 7. For fuller discussion of institutional development, see also next chapter.

34. *Pravda*, September 15, 1965. Also Brezhnev's speech to the Twenty-third CPSU Congress, March 29, 1966.

35. *Ibid.*, September 30, 1965. (See also p. 401 of the first edition of this book for some early speculations concerning this development.)

36. For example, GDR Defense Minister, H. Hoffman, *Neues Deutschland*, April 22, 1965, as quoted in Wolfe, p. 43.

37. Wolfe, p. 20.

38. Lasswell, *World Politics and Personal Insecurity*.

18. THE SOVIET ALLIANCE SYSTEM

1. The development of new organizational forms for interrelationships among the European Communist countries at this time was also undoubtedly in part stimulated by the success of the European Economic Community in Western Europe, which raised the question of exclusion from West European markets. Britain, about the same time, came to a similar realization and began its application for admission into the EEC. See Andrzej Korbonski, "The Evolution of Comecon," *International Conciliation*, no. 549, September 1964. See also M. Shulman, "The Communist States and Western Integration," *International Organization*, September 1963.

2. See Kazimierz Grzybowski, *The Socialist Commonwealth of Nations* (New Haven, 1964), pp. 1–57, for a detailed discussion of the uniformity of domestic institutions. See also John N. Hazard, "The Soviet Legal Pattern Spreads Abroad," *Illinois Law Forum*, vol. 1964, Spring Number, pp. 277–298.

3. *Survey of International Affairs* (London, 1962), p. 152.

4. *Izvestia*, January 29, 1956.

5. See, for example, the speech of Marshal Grechko on the Tenth Anniversary of WTO, *Pravda*, May 13, 1965, and other statements at that time. See also *The World Marxist Review*, May 1965, p. 21, in which a Pole and a Czech, in their remarks on WTO, said: "The Soviet Union's nuclear and missile strength affords reliable protection to the achievements of socialism."

6. Chiefs-of-staff (all Soviet officers) have been: A. I. Antonov, 1956–

June 1962; P. I. Batov, June 1962–November 1965; M. I. Kuzakov, November 1965 to the date of the present writing.

7. See Imre Nagy, *On Communism*, p. 189, for a concise statement of the essentially negative role of CEMA.

8. *United Nations Treaty Series* (New York, 1961), pp. 264–285.

9. For an account of what occurred at the meetings of the Executive Committee of the Council through mid-1964, see Michael Kaser, *Comecon* (London, 1965). The Executive Committee met twenty times between July 1962 and December 1965; the Council three times between December 1962 and February 1965.

10. At the July 1963 meeting of party leaders in Moscow, the proposals for a central planning body were dropped and it was said that "bilateral consultations create the best preconditions for a multilateral plan of coordination in the CEMA framework." *Pravda*, July 28, 1963.

11. United Nations Document E/CONF. 46/17, January 8, 1964, p. 5.

12. For a list of these standing commissions, see Kaser, pp. 198–202.

13. *Izvestia*, November 16, 1963.

14. These conversion rubles are usable only with other bloc countries and are not good for foreign exchange. For further on the Bank, see *Pravda*, October 24, 1963; and Kaser, "Socialist Countries' Currency Problems on the World Market"; Adam Zwass, *Finance*, Warsaw, February 1965, translated in JPRS 29, 488, April 6, 1964, U.S. Department of Commerce, as cited by H. Schaefer, "An East European Payments Union?," unpublished manuscript, 1965.

15. *Ibid.* Also M. Senin, "Peace in Europe and Consolidation of Socialist Countries," *International Affairs* (Moscow), August 1965, p. 3. For earlier conventions, see Grzybowski, pp. 130–135.

16. *Izvestia*, July 1, 1965.

17. See *International Affairs* (Moscow), August 1965, pp. 100–101; *Izvestia*, July 15, 1965.

18. A similar organization was set up for cooperation in ball-bearing production. For several years what coordination there was in this field had been handled by the CEMA Standing Commission on Machine Construction. In April 1964 Bulgaria, Hungary, GDR, Poland, and Czechoslovakia concluded an agreement on the creation of the Organization for Cooperation in Ball-Bearing Production (OSPP). The USSR subsequently joined it, but Rumania has remained outside. For a discussion of these organizations as models for future closer coordination, see *Vneshnaia Torgovlia*, November 1965, pp. 21–24.

19. *Izvestia*, March 27, 1948. A fuller discussion of the Danube Commission can be found in Grzybowski.

20. Kaser, pp. 67 and 89–90.

21. *Pravda*, January 8, 1955.

22. The agreements are listed in R. Slusser and J. Triska, *A Calendar of Soviet Treaties 1917–1959* (Stanford, 1959), pp. 326–327. For fuller treatments see George Modelski, *Atomic Energy in the Communist Bloc* (New York, 1959).

23. These organizations are both discussed in more detail in Grzybowski.

24. *Pravda*, March 31, 1965.

25. *Pravda*, July 16, 1965.
26. *Pravda*, June 13, 1964.
27. *Pravda*, April 9, 1965.
28. *Pravda*, January 16, 1966. A similar event took place in December 1963 when Khrushchev sent Brezhnev to Czechoslovakia and Hendrych came to Moscow for the signing of a new friendship and mutual aid treaty. *Pravda*, December 13–14, 1963.
29. V. Matveyev, "Socialist Countries in the International Arena: Constructive Diplomacy that Takes Initiative," *Izvestia*, September 21, 1965.
30. See *Izvestia*, March 14, April 17, and May 28, 1957.
31. See *Pravda*, October 31, 1956.
32. See Slusser and Triska.
33. For example, while Albanian trade with the USSR was cut off from 1962 on, the Chinese and the other bloc countries increased their percentages of Albanian trade to make up for it. Thus in 1962 approximately 95 per cent of Albania's trade remained within the bloc. See the discussion of trade in the third part of this chapter.
34. See Kaser, pp. 71, 72, 105–107. Also B. Ladygin and V. Terekhov, "CEMA: Intergovernmental Specialization and Cooperation of Production," *Mirovaia ekonomika i mezhdunarodnie otnosheniia*, no. 11 (1965), pp. 14–26.
35. Kaser. For a discussion of the various types of bilateral and multilateral organizations for cooperation and production, see the article by the Assistant Polish Permanent Representative at CEMA (G. Ruzhanski), "Production Ties of Fraternal Countries Are Widening," *Vneshnaia Torgovlia*, November 1965, pp. 21–24. Among those organizations discussed are: the Haldex Corporation; the organization for radio-tube production coordination at the factory level between GDR, Poland, and Czechoslovakia; Intermetall; the Organization for Cooperation in Ball-Bearing Production; the Hungarian-Bulgarian joint enterprises: Agromosh and Intrasmash; as well as the means for coordination within the CEMA framework. The author foresees further development of joint enterprises when closer coordination is needed than can be given by the CEMA standing commissions.
36. N. Ptichkin, "To Develop and Perfect Mutually Advantageous Collaboration," *Vneshnaia Torgovlia*, December 1965, pp. 3–6. The author sees CEMA and other forms of bloc economic collaboration increasing since the September Plenum as the various members follow the Soviet lead in removing "voluntarism and subjectivism" from economic planning.
37. For instance, the June 1960 meeting of party leaders at the Rumanian Party Congress, discussed in Chapter 16.
38. See Chapter 16, p. 410.
39. At this time the Albanians were virtually expelled from the bloc. See Chapter 16, p. 414.
40. See Chapters 16 and 17.
41. *World Marxist Review*, April 1965, pp. 3–5.
42. *Pravda*, March 6, 1965.
43. See *World Marxist Review*, December 1965.
44. *Neues Deutschland* (East Berlin), November 30, 1957.
45. See tables 3 and 4 in the original article version of this chapter in *World Politics*.

46. *Pravda,* April 7, 1965; *Izvestia,* October 22, 1965.
47. *Pravda,* May 26, 1965.
48. *Pravda,* June 18, 1965.
49. *Pravda,* November 26, 1965.
50. R. Garthoff, "The Military Establishment," *East Europe,* September 1965, pp. 2–16; *New York Times,* May 19, 1965.
51. *Pravda,* November 27, 1965.
52. *Vneshnaia Torgovlia SSSR za 1959–1963 Gody* (Moscow, 1965), pp. 10–11, absolute figures and p. 22, percentages. *Vneshnaia Torgovlia,* no. 11 (November 1965), p. 9, percentages and absolute figures.
53. All figures, unless otherwise indicated, are from the UN *Yearbook of International Trade Statistics* (New York, 1965), or percentages derived from them.
54. E. Miles and J. Gillooly, *Processes of Inter-Action Among the 14 Communist Party-States: An Exploratory Essay,* Stanford Studies of the Communist System, no. 5 (March 1965), p. 2. Another indication of a difference in the attitudes of certain bloc countries toward Albania was the restoration of a Polish ambassador in Tirana in January 1966. Previously only the Rumanians had been thus represented. (*East Europe,* March 1966.)
55. In other words, in 1956 one out of every nine visitors to the USSR was Chinese; in 1962 it fell to one out of every thirty-two.
56. For a discussion of this problem, see Miles and Gillooly.
57. In speaking of the special agreements on cultural exchange S. D. Sergeev, in his book *Ekonomicheskoe sotrudnichestvo i vzaimopomoshch' sotsialsticheskikh stran* (Moscow, 1964), pp. 376–377, says: "At the present time 70 such agreements have been put into effect defining the bases of regulation of the whole complex of cultural inter-relations between the agreeing sides, and more than 200 agreements on particular questions: on the exchange of movie films, radio programs, books, students, tourists, etc. . ."
58. M. E. Airapetyan and V. V. Sukhodeev, *Novii Tip Mezhdunarodniikh Otnoshenii* (Moscow, 1964), p. 222.
59. S. D. Sergeev, p. 196.
60. *Ibid.,* pp. 191–228, 358–378.
61. *Vestnik An SSSR,* 1965, no. 3, pp. 88–90.
62. *Ibid.,* pp. 88–90: 21 problems with the Czech Academy; 25 problems with the Polish Academy; 22 problems with the Rumanian Academy; 18 problems with the Bulgarian Academy; 22 problems with the East German Academy. In February 1964 an agreement was signed between the Soviet and Yugoslav Academies of Sciences to begin similar joint projects.
63. G. A. Knyazev and A. V. Kol'tsov, *Kratkii Ocherk Istorii Akademii Nauk SSSR* (Moscow, 1964), p. 219. The second conference was in March 1964 in Berlin, the third in April 1964 in Sofia, and the fourth in December 1965 in Moscow.
64. Some of these are: L. I. Abalkin and V. N. Ladygin, *Ekonomicheskie Zakonomernosti Razvitiia Mirovogo Sotsializma* (Moscow, 1963); I. V. Dudinskii, *Mirovaia Sistema Sotsializma i Zakonomernosti Ee Razvitiia* (Moscow, 1961); I. V. Dudinskii, *Rost Ekonomichestogo Moguchestva Mirovoi Sistemy Sotsializma* (Moscow, 1962); I. S. Ikonnikov, et al., *Koordinatsia Narodnohozyaistvennykh Planov Stran SEV* (Moscow, 1965); N. I. Ivanov, *Ekono-*

micheskoe Sotrudnichestvo i Vzaimopomoshch' Stran Sotsializma (Moscow, 1962); B. P. Krasnoglazov, *Ekonomicheskoe Sotrudnichestvo GDR s Sotsialisticheskimi Stranami* (Moscow, 1965); B. P. Miroshnichenko, ed., *Planirovanie v Yevropeiskikh Stranakh Sotsializma* (Moscow, 1962); T. V. Ryabushkin, ed., *Ekonomika Stran Sotsializma* (Moscow, 1964); S. D. Sergeev, *Ekonomicheskoe Sotrudnichestvo i Vzaimopomoshch' Sotsialisticheskikh Stran* (Moscow, 1964); Yu. S. Shiryaev and V. N. Ladygin, *Problemy Sovershenstvovaniia Ekonomicheskogo Sotrudnichestva Stran-Chlenov SEV* (Moscow, 1965); S. Stepanenko, *Nauchno-tekhnicheskoe Sotrudnichestvo Sotsialisticheskikh Stran* (Moscow, 1962); A. D. Stupov, ed., *Ekonomicheskoe Sotrudnichestvo i Vzaimopomoshch' Sotsialisticheskikh Stran* (Moscow, 1962); O. Tarnovskii, *Osnovy Tsenoobrazovaniia v Sotsialisticheskikh Stranakh* (Moscow, 1964).

65. Mention of the Polish work in sociology in the 1950's and 1960's is found in *Marksistsko-Leninskaia Filosofiia i Sotsiologiia v SSR i Yevropeiskikh Sotsialistcheskikh Stranakh* (Moscow, 1965), pp. 484–486. A good summary of work in public opinion is Emilia Wilder, "Opinion Polls," *Survey*, July 1963, pp. 118–129. For Polish sociology, see Leo Labedz, *Survey*, January–March 1960 and Z. Jordan, *Kultura* (Paris), November 1962.

66. For example, in 1960 *Komsomolskaia Pravda* set up its Institute of Public Opinion. However, Soviet sociology did not begin to develop seriously until 1962 and its first real strides were taken in 1964–1965, with the publication of several books on the subject. See George Fischer, *Science and Politics: The New Sociology in the Soviet Union*, Cornell Research Papers in International Studies, no. 1 (Ithaca, 1964), for a discussion of these developments.

67. *World Marxist Review*, February 1962, pp. 78–82.

68. This is shown in the case of Bulgaria by Zhivko Oshavkov's article in G. Ye. Glezerman and V. G. Afkanas'ev, *Opyt i Motodika Konkretnykh Sotsiologicheskikh Issledovanii* (Moscow, 1965), pp. 291–333.

69. On April 4, 1965, it was stated in *Neues Deutschland* that GDR had sociological research organizations at six universities and an Institute for Opinion Research connected with the party Central Committee, *East Europe*, July 1965, p. 42. The Rumanians set up a National Sociological Committee in 1959 but little serious work was done until recently.

70. V. A. Yadov, "What the Experience of the Organization and Execution of Concrete Social Research in Leningrad Indicates," *Nauchnie Doklady Vysshei Shkoly: Filosofskie Nauki*, No. 2, 1965, pp. 157–160.

71. Laszlo Adam, "The Trend of Tourism," *Naplo*, March 13, 1965.

19. IDEOLOGY AND POWER IN RELATIONS
    AMONG COMMUNIST STATES

1. For some of its intellectual antecedents, see the discussion by J. L. Talmon, *The Rise of Totalitarian Democracy* (Boston, 1952); for some of the psychological aspects of modern dictatorship, see Z. Barbu, *Democracy and Dictatorship* (New York, 1956). For a discussion of the implications for the intellectual of such ideology, see W. Kula, *Rozwazania o Historii* (Warsaw, 1958).

2. I have found the following very useful: H. D. Lasswell and A. Kaplan, *Power and Society* (New Haven, 1950); and, especially, H. A. Simon, "Notes

on the Observation and Measurement of Political Power," *Journal of Politics*, November 1953.

3. The above paragraph benefited from D. Comey's formulations and his revision of my original statement on p. 387 of the first edition of *The Soviet Bloc*. See D. Comey, "Marxist-Leninist Ideology and Soviet Policy," *Studies in Soviet Thought* (December 1962), esp. pp. 303–304.

4. H. Kissinger, *Nuclear Weapons and Foreign Policy* (New York, 1957), p. 425.

5. For instance, S. L. Sharp, "National Interest: Key to Soviet Politics," *Problems of Communism*, March–April 1958.

6. V. I. Lenin, *Certain Features of the Historical Development of Marxism* (Moscow, 1955), p. 8.

7. *Kommunist*, no. 14, 1955; for fuller discussion, see Chapter 8.

8. *New York Times*, August 28, 1958 (italics added).

9. J. W. Kaye, *Christianity in India* (London, 1859), pp. 20–21, 30–32.

10. Lowenthal, *World Communism: The Disintegration of a Secular Faith*.

11. See also R. H. McNeal, "The Exhaustion of Diplomatic Techniques in the Sino-Soviet Dispute," *International Journal*, no. 4, Autumn 1963.

12. For a detailed policy discussion and recommendations, see my *Alternative to Partition*.

13. N. Bukharin, "Imperialism and Communism," *Foreign Affairs*, July 1936.

14. The Soviet statement of July 14, 1963, quite explicitly notes that in spite of the break in Albanian-Soviet relations, Albania still remains "a country building socialism."

15. For authoritative treatment, see R. Scalapino, *The Communist Revolution in Asia* (Englewood Cliffs, 1965), and Griffith, *Sino-Soviet Relations*, ch. v.

16. Kotyk, "Some Aspects of the Unity of Socialist Countries at the Present Time" (italics added).

17. J. Jaroslawski, "Discussion on Adam Schaff's Book," *Nowe Drogi*, December 12, 1965.

18. See A. Mikoyan's speech to the Twentieth CPSU Congress, 1956, and F. Konstantinov, "Lenin and Our Own Times," *Kommunist*, no. 5, 1960.

19. For the Chinese view, see particularly, "The Proletarian Revolution and Khrushchev's Revisionism," *Jen Min Jih Pao*, March 31, 1964; for the Soviet view, P. Fedoseyev, "Materialist Understanding of History and 'The Theory of Violence,' " *Kommunist*, no. 5, May 1964.

20. "What are the Chinese Leaders Foisting on the Communist Movement under the Guise of Marxism-Leninism?" Editorial, *Pravda*, May 11, 1964.

21. K. Devlin, "The Catholic-Communist Dialogue," *Problems of Communism*, May–June 1966.

22. These points are well brought out by Ross Johnson, "The Dynamics of Communist Ideological Change in Yugoslavia" (unpublished Ph.D. thesis, Columbia University, 1966). See also M. Djilas, *Conversations with Stalin* (New York, 1962), pp. 29–30, and his April 1947 speech to the Yugoslav Assembly.

23. For a fuller analysis of the various factors prompting erosion, see my *Ideology and Power in Soviet Politics* (New York, 1962), pp. 113–140.

BIBLIOGRAPHY

PERIODICALS

Agricultura Nova. Semiweekly publication on agriculture, issued by the Ministry of Agriculture and Forestry, Bucharest.

The Annals. Quarterly journal of the American Academy of Political and Social Science. Philadelphia.

Bellona. Quarterly of military history. London.

Biuletyn Statystyczny. Monthly reports issued by the Central Statistical Office. Warsaw.

Borba. Daily organ of the Communist Party of Yugoslavia. Belgrade.

Cahiers du communisme. Theoretical and political monthly review of the Central Committee of the French Communist Party. Paris.

Ceteka. Reviews of the daily press and selected topics on domestic events, issued by the Czechoslovak News Agency. Prague.

China Quarterly. A scholarly journal of Chinese and Asian affairs. London.

Chlopska Droga. Weekly periodical of the Central Committee of the Polish United Workers Party. Warsaw.

Current Background. United States State Department publication.

Current Digest of the Soviet Press. Weekly publication of the Joint Committee on Slavic Studies. New York.

Deutsche Zeitschrift fuer Philosophie. Organ of philosophic research and discussion of the German Democratic Republic. Berlin.

Dziennik Ustaw Rzeczypospolitej Polskiej. Gazette of laws issued by the Council of Ministers. Warsaw.

East Europe. A weekly bulletin of seven East European Countries, susperseded *News from Behind the Iron Curtain.* New York.

Economic Bulletin for Europe. United Nations Economic and Social Council, Economic Commission for Europe.

Einheit. Theoretical journal of scientific socialism. Berlin.

Elet es Tudomany. Weekly paper of the Society for Social and Natural Sciences. Budapest.

Express Wieczorny. Daily of the Workers' Publishing Cooperative. Warsaw.

Figyelo. Weekly publication publicizing economic policy. Budapest.

For a Lasting Peace, for a People's Democracy. Organ of the Cominform, originally published in Yugoslavia. After 1948 published in Rumania. Discontinued after 1956.

Foreign Affairs. An American quarterly review. New York.

Glos Pracy. Periodical of the industrial unions, published every other day. Warsaw.

Gospodarka Planowa. Organ of the State Commission for Economic Planning. Warsaw.

Hospodarske Noviny. Weekly publication on economics. Prague.

L'Humanité. Organ of the French Communist Party. Paris.

Hung Ch'i. Theoretical organ of the Chinese Communist Party. Peking.

Information Bulletin of the Central Committee of the Hungarian Communist Party. Budapest.

International Affairs. Soviet foreign-language monthly of political analysis. Moscow.

Izvestia. Organ of the Union of Workers Deputies of the USSR. Moscow.

Jen Min Jih Pao. Organ of the Chinese Communist Party. Peking.

Journal of International Affairs. Semiannual journal of the School of International Affairs, Columbia University. New York.

Journal of Politics. Issued quarterly by the Southern Political Science Association in cooperation with the University of Florida. Gainesville.

Jugopress. Yugoslav Press Agency. Belgrade.

Kommunist. Theoretical and political journal of the Central Committee of the CPSU. Moscow. Previously published under the title *Bolshevik.*

Komunist. Organ of the Central Committee of the Communist Party of Yugoslavia. Belgrade.

Krasnaia Zvezda. Central organ of the Ministry of Defense of the USSR. Moscow.

Kultura i Spoleczenstwo. Quarterly of the Sociological and Cultural History Division of the Polish Academy of Sciences. Warsaw.

Latohatar. Semimonthly political and literary journal issued by a group of exiles. Absorbed *Egesz Latohatar.* Munich.

Leningradskaia Pravda. Daily. Leningrad.

Lidova Democracie. Daily of the Czechoslovak Populist Party. Prague.

Literarni Noviny. Weekly on cultural, political, and artistic questions. Prague.

Lituraturen Front. Weekly issued by the Bulgarian Writers' Union. Sofia.

Magyar Nemzet. Daily of the Patriotic People's Front. Budapest.

Magyar Vilag. Independent Hungarian daily. Budapest.

Mezhdunarodnaia Zhizn. Monthly scientific-political journal. Moscow.

Mirovaia Ekonomika i Mezhdunarodnie Otnosheniia. A scholarly Soviet journal of international affairs. Moscow.

Mlada Fronta. Daily of the Czechoslovak Youth League. Prague.

Le Monde. Daily. Paris.

Nasa Stvarnost. Monthly journal issued by the Central Committee, League of Communists of Yugoslavia. Belgrade.

Nepszabadsag. Central Daily of the Hungarian Socialist Workers' Party. Budapest. Up to November 1956 this newspaper appeared under the title *Szabad Nep.*

Nepszava. Daily of the Central Council of Hungarian Trade Unions. Appeared as *Nepakarat,* November 1956 to January 1958.

Neues Deutschland. Organ of the Central Committee of the SED. Berlin.

The New Leader. Weekly publication of the American Labor Conference on International Affairs. Stroudsburg, Pa.

New Times. Weekly journal published by *Trud.* Moscow.

New York Times. Daily. New York.

Nowa Kultura. Weekly literary journal. Warsaw.

Nova Makedonija. Daily of the Socialist Alliance of Working People of Macedonia. Skopje.

Nova Mysl. Review of Marxism and Leninism. Prague.

Nova Svoboda. Daily of the Communist Party of Czechoslovakia, District Committee of Ostrava. Ostrava.

Novy Zivot. Semiweekly of the Communist Party of Czechoslovakia, District Committee of Presov. Presov.

Nowe Drogi. Theoretical and political monthly organ of the Central Committee of the Polish United Workers' Party. Warsaw.

Obrana Lidu. Daily of the Czechoslovak Army. Prague.

Orka. Polish weekly journal. Warsaw.

Ost-Probleme. Weekly periodical dealing with questions of world Communism. Bad Godesberg, Germany.

Otechestven Front. Daily of the Presidium of the National Assembly and the National Council Fatherland Front. Sofia.

Partiinaia Zhizn. Semimonthly organ of the Central Committee of the Communist Party of the Soviet Union. Moscow.

Peking Review. A weekly magazine of official Chinese views. Peking.

Po Prostu. Weekly journal of students and the young intelligentsia. Warsaw.

Politika. Daily, Politika Printing and Publishing Enterprise. Belgrade.

Polityka. Weekly review on the policy and action of the Polish United Workers' Party in domestic and international fields. Warsaw.

Pravda. Organ of the Central Committee of the CPSU. Moscow.

Prawo i Zycie. Biweekly publication on law, state administration, and socioeconomic problems, issued by the Polish Lawyers' Association. Warsaw.

Predvoj. Weekly publication on politics, culture, and economy, issued by the Central Committee of the Communist Party of Slovakia. Bratislava.

Probleme Economice. Monthly journal of the Economic Institute of the Academy of the Rumanian People's Republic. Bucharest.

Problemy Mira i Sotsializma. A journal reflecting the views of several pro-Soviet Communist parties. Prague.

Problems of Communism. Bimonthly journal published by the United States Information Agency. Washington, D.C.

Przeglad Kulturalny. Weekly of the Council for Culture and the Fine Arts. Warsaw.

Przyjazn. Organ of the Soviet-Polish Friendship Society. Warsaw.

Rabotnicheske Delo. Organ of the Central Committee of the Communist Party of Bulgaria. Sofia.

Rada Rabotnicza. Trade union journal. Warsaw.

Rominia Libera. Daily of the People's Committees of the People's Republic of Rumania. Bucharest.

Rude Pravo. Central Organ of the Communist Party of Czechoslovakia. Prague.

Rzeczpospolita. Daily of the Czytelnik Educational Publications Cooperative. Warsaw.

Scinteia. Organ of the Communist party of Rumania. Bucharest.

Slavic Review. American quarterly of Soviet and East European studies for the American Association for the Advancement of Slavic Studies. New York.

Slowo Powszechne. Daily of the Workers Publishing Cooperative, *Prasa.* Warsaw.

Sluzbeni List. Official federal gazette. Belgrade.

Soviet Studies. Quarterly review of social and economic institutions of the USSR. Oxford.

Sovietskaia Litva. Daily organ of the Central Committee of the Lithuanian Communist Party, the Presidium of the Supreme Soviet of the Lithuanian SSR, and the Council of Ministers of the Lithuanian SSR. Vilnius.

Sovietskaia Moldavia. Organ of the Central Committee of the Communist Party of Moldavia and the Supreme Soviet of the Moldavian Republic. Kishinev.

Sprawy Miedzynarodowe. Bimonthly bulletin of the Polish Institute of International Affairs. Warsaw.

Studia Socjologiczno-Polityczne. Sociological-political journal. Warsaw.

Survey. A scholarly journal on current Communist affairs. London.

Swiat. Illustrated weekly. Warsaw.

Szabad Nep. See *Nepszabadsag.*

Sztandar Mlodych. Daily of the Central Committee, Polish Youth League. Warsaw.

Tarsadalmi Szemle. Theoretical periodical of the Hungarian Workers' Party. Budapest.

Three-Monthly Economic Review of Eastern Europe. Publication of the Economist Intelligence Unit Ltd., London.

Trud. Organ of the All-Union Central Soviet of Professional Associations. Moscow.

Trybuna Literacka. Literary supplement of *Trybuna Ludu.* Warsaw.

Trybuna Ludu. Organ of the Central Committee of the Polish United Workers' Party. Warsaw.

Trybuna Wolnosci. Weekly issued by the Central Committee of the Polish United Workers Party. Warsaw.

Tvorba. Weekly journal for politics, culture, and economics. Prague.

Tygodnik Demokratyczny. Periodical of the Polish Democratic Party. Warsaw.

Tygodnik Powszechny. Weekly magazine for Catholics on religion, social problems, literature, and arts. Absorbed by *Kierunki*, May 1953–November 1956. Volume numbering resumed December 1956 repeats that of 1954 and subsequent years of earlier issuance. Krakow.

Viata Sindicala. Daily of the Central Council of Trade Unions. Bucharest. At present issued under the title *Munca*.

Vneshnaia Torgovlia. Monthly statistical publication. Moscow.

V Pomoshch Politicheskomu Samoobrazivaniu. Journal of the "Popular Library of Marxism-Leninism." Moscow.

Voprosy filosofii. Journal appearing three times annually, published by the Philosophical Institute of the USSR Academy of Science. Moscow.

Voprosy istorii. Monthly of the Historical Institute of the USSR Academy of Science. Superseded *Istoriicheshii zhurnal*. Moscow.

Vysoka Skola. Monthly journal of the National Educational Publishing House. Prague.

Wirtschaftswissenschaft. Bimonthly economic journal of the German Democratic Republic. Berlin.

World Marxist Review. English language edition of *Problemy Mira i Sotsializma*. Toronto.

Zachodnia Agencja Prasowa. Press agency. Warsaw.

Zahranicny Obchod. Organ of the Ministry of Foreign Trade. For economic information. Prague.

Zeri i Popullit. Daily publication of the Central Committee of the Albanian Workers' Party. Tirana.

Zielony Sztandar. Semiweekly issued by the United Peasant Party. Warsaw.

Zycie Gospodarcze. Biweekly journal of the Economic Community. Warsaw.

Zycie Partii. Organ of the Central Committee of the Polish United Workers' Party. Warsaw.

Zycie Warsawy. Daily of the Czytelnik Press Institute. Warsaw.

DOCUMENTS, COLLECTIONS OF DOCUMENTS, SPEECHES

A Magyar-Szoujet Baratsag Diadalutja. Collection of speeches. Budapest, 1958.
The Anti-Stalin Campaign and International Communism. New York, 1957.
Bass, R., and E. Marbury, eds., *The Soviet-Jugoslav Controversy, 1948–1958: A Documentary Record*. New York, 1959.
Bialer, S., *Wybralem Prawde*. Radio Free Europe. New York, 1956.
——— *Wybralem Wolnosc*. Radio Free Europe. New York, 1956.
Bierut, B., and J. Cyrankiewicz, *Podstawy Ideologiczne PZPR*. Warsaw, 1952.
Chervenkov, V., *Otchetnyi Doklad TsK BKP VI S'ezdu Partii*. Sofia, 1954.
Chronologische Materialien zur Geschichte der SED. Berlin, 1956.
Columbia University Hungarian Interview Project. Interview texts.

The Correspondence between the CC of the CPJ and the CC of the AUCP (*b*). Belgrade.

Czechoslovak Ministry of Foreign Affairs, *Statement of Policy of Mr. Gottwald's Government*. Prague, 1946.

Dallin, Alexander, ed., et al., *Diversity in International Communism: A Documentary Record 1961–1963*. New York, 1963.

Documents on Polish-Soviet Relations, 1939–1945, General Sikorski Historical Institute. London, 1961.

"Economic Treaties and Agreements of the Soviet Bloc." Mid-European Studies Center, 1952 (mimeographed).

Eighth National Congress of the Communist Party of China. 3 vols. Peking, 1956.

Farrell, R. B., ed., *Jugoslavia and the Soviet Union, 1948–1956*. New York, 1956.

Gelberg, L., ed., *Nowe Konstytucje Panstw Europejskich*. Warsaw, 1949.

Gerö, E., *The Position of the Hungarian National Economy in 1952*. Budapest, 1952.

Gheorghiu-Dej, G., *Stati i Rechi*. Moscow, 1956.

Gomulka, W. *Przemowienia*. Warsaw, 1957.

——— *W Walce o Democracje Ludowa*. Warsaw, 1947.

Gottwald, K., *Deset Let*. Prague, 1947.

——— *Izbrannie Proizvedenia v Dvuch Tomach*. Moscow, 1957.

Gsovski, V., ed., *Legal Sources and Bibliography of Hungary*. New York, 1958.

Hudson, G. F., Lowenthal, R., and MacFarquhar, R., *The Sino-Soviet Dispute*. New York, 1962.

Kardelj, E., *On People's Democracy in Jugoslavia*. New York, 1949.

——— *The Communist Party of Jugoslavia in the Struggle for New Jugoslavia, for People's Authority and for Socialism*. Belgrade, 1948.

Kommunisticheskii International v Dokumentach, 1919–32. Moscow, 1933.

KPSS v Resoliutsiach i Resheniach S'ezdov, Konferentsii i Plenumov TsK, III. Moscow, 1954.

Kszaltowanie sie Podstaw Programowych Polskiej Partii Robotniczej. Warsaw, 1958.

Left-Wing Sectarianism and the New Course. Radio Free Europe. New York, 1954.

Lenin, V. I., *Certain Features of the Historical Development of Marxism.* Moscow, 1955.

——— *Selected Works*. New York, 1943.

——— *Sochineniya*. Moscow, 1947.

Moskovskoe Sovieshchanie Evropeiskich Stran po Obespecheniu Mira i Besopasnosti v Evrope. Moscow, 1954.

Pieck, W., *Izbrannie Proizvedeniia*. Moscow, 1956.

Pijade, M., *About the Legend that the Jugoslav Uprising Owed its Existence to Soviet Assistance*. London, 1950.

P.P.R. Warsaw, 1959.

Rakosi, M., *Wir Bauen ein Neues Land.* Berlin, 1952.

――― *Valsgatott Beszedek es Cikkek.* Budapest, 1957.

VII S'ezd Bolgarskoi Kommunisticheskoi Partii. Moscow, 1958.

Soveshchanie Predstavitelei Kommunisticheskich i Rabochich Partii Sotsialisticheskich Stran. Moscow, 1957.

Stalin, J. V., "Economic Problems of Socialism in the USSR." Moscow, 1952.

――― *Marxism and the National and Colonial Question.* New York, 1935.

――― *O Stroitelstve Kommunizma v SSSR.* Moscow, 1950.

――― *On the Great Patriotic War of the Union.* Moscow, 1946.

――― *Problems of Leninism.* Moscow, 1940.

Swiatlo, J., testimony no. 13, "How Poland is Really Ruled." Mimeographed, unpublished material.

――― *Za Kulisami Bezpieki i Partii.* Radio Free Europe leaflet.

Tito, J. B., *Borba za Mir.* 3 vols. Belgrade, 1954, 1956, 1957.

――― *Borba za Sotsialistichku Demokratiju.* 2 vols. Belgrade, 1955.

――― *Workers Manage Factories in Jugoslavia.* Belgrade, 1950.

XII Plenum Komitetu Centralnego. Central Committee of the Polish United Workers Party, Warsaw, 1958. Confidential transcript.

Varshavskoie Sovieshchanie Evropeiskich Gosudarstv po Obespecheniu mira i Besopasnosti v Evrope. Moscow, 1955.

Walka o Jednosc Niemiec. Polish Institute of International Affairs. Warsaw, 1953.

Zagadnienia Prawne Konstytucji Polskiej Rzeczypospolitej Ludowej. 3 vols. Warsaw, 1954.

Zagadnienie Bezpieczenstwa Zbiorowego w Europie. Warsaw, 1955.

Zasedania Politicheskogo Konsultativnogo Komiteta Chrezhdennogo v Sootvetstvii s Varshavskim Dogovorom. Moscow, 1956.

Zinner, P., ed., *National Communism and Popular Revolt in Eastern Europe.* New York, 1956.

HISTORY, BACKGROUND, GENERAL WORKS

Agrarian Problems from the Baltic to the Aegean. RIIA. London, 1944.

Almond, G. A., *The Appeals of Communism.* Princeton, 1954.

Amery, J., *Sons of the Eagle: a Study in Guerilla War.* London, 1948.

Andreev, A. M., *Borba Litovskogo Naroda za Sovietskuiu Vlast.* Moscow, 1954.

Avakumovic, I., *History of the CP of Yugoslavia,* vol. I. Aberdeen, 1964.

Barbu, Z., *Democracy and Dictatorship.* New York, 1956.

Barnett, A. D., ed., *Communist Strategies in Asia: A Comparative Analysis of Governments and Parties.* New York, 1963.

Bartlett, V., *East of the Iron Curtain.* New York, 1950.

Beck, J., *The Last Report.* New York, 1957.

Benes, E., *Svetova Krise.* Prague, 1946.

Bernstein, E., *Gesellschaftliches und Privateigentum*. Berlin, 1891.
Betts, R. R., ed., *Central and Southeast Europe, 1945–1948*. London, 1950.
Black, . E., ed., *Challenge in Eastern Europe*. Rutgers University in association with the Mid-European Studies Center of the Free Europe Committee, 1954.
——— *Readings on Contemporary Eastern Europe*. New York, 1953.
Borkenau, F., *European Communism*. London, 1953.
Brandt, C., B. Schwartz, and J. Fairbank, *A Documentary History of Chinese Communism*. Cambridge, 1952.
Brandt, C., *Stalin's Failure in China, 1924–1927*. Cambridge, 1958.
Bromke, A., *Poland's Politics: Idealism vs. Realism*. Cambridge, 1967.
Brown, J. F., *The New Eastern Europe*. New York, 1966.
Bregman, A., *Najlepszy Sojusznik Hitlera*. London, 1958.
Brzezinski, Z., *Alternative to Partition: For a Broader Conception of America's Role in Europe*. New York, 1965.
Buell, R. L., et al., *New Governments in Europe*. New York, 1937.
Buell, R. L., *Poland: Key to Europe*. New York, 1939.
Bukharin, N., *Oekonomik der Transformationsperiode*. Verlag der kommunistischen Internationale, 1922.
Busek, V., ed., *Czechoslovakia*. New York, 1957.
Byrnes, R. F., ed., *Jugoslavia*. New York, 1957.
Cabot, J. M., *The Racial Conflict in Transylvania*. Boston, 1926.
Ciechanowski, J., *Defeat in Victory*. New York, 1947.
Clissold, S., *The Whirlwind*. New York, 1949.
Correspondence between the Chairman of the Council of Ministers of the USSR and the Presidents of the USA and the Prime Ministers of Great Britain during the Great Patriotic War, 1941–1945. Moscow, 1957.
Dellin, L. A. D., ed., *Bulgaria*. New York, 1957.
Douglas, D., *Transitional Economic Systems: The Polish-Czech Example*. London, 1953.
Fainsod, M., *International Socialism and the World War*. Cambridge, 1935.
Feis, H., *Churchill, Roosevelt, Stalin*. Princeton, 1957.
Fejtö, F., *Histoire des démocraties populaires*. Paris, 1952.
Fischer, R., *Stalin and German Communism*. Cambridge, 1958.
Fisher-Galati, S., *Eastern Europe in the Sixties*. New York, 1963.
——— ed., *Romania*. New York, 1957.
Fisher, H. H., *The Communist Revolution: An Outline of Strategy and Tactics*. Stanford, 1955.
Fotich, C., *The War We Lost*. New York, 1948.
Friedrich, C. J., ed., *Totalitarianism*. Cambridge, 1954.
Gluckstein, Y., *Stalin's Satellites in Europe*. London, 1952.
Gross, F., *European Ideologies*. New York, 1948.
Gyorgy, A., *Governments of Danubian Europe*. New York, 1949.
Hajda, J., ed., *A Study of Contemporary Czechoslovakia*. New Haven, 1955.
Halasz, N., *In the Shadow of Russia*. New York, 1959.

Halecki, O., *Borderlands of Western Civilization: A History of East Central Europe*. New York, 1952.
—— ed., *Poland*. New York, 1957.
Healey, D., *The Curtain Falls: The Story of the Socialists in Eastern Europe*. London, 1951.
Helmreich, E., ed., *Hungary*. New York, 1957.
Hogye, M., *The Paris Peace Conference of 1946: The Role of the Hungarian Communists and of the USSR*. Mid-European Studies Center, 1954.
Iwanska, A., ed., *Contemporary Poland*. Human Relations Area Files, 1955.
Jordan, Z., *The Oder-Neisse Line*. London, 1952.
Kerner, D. J., *Czechoslovakia*. Berkeley, 1940.
Kertesz, S., *Diplomacy in a Whirlpool*. Notre Dame, 1953.
—— ed., *East Central Europe and the World*. Notre Dame, 1962.
—— ed., *The Fate of East Central Europe*. Notre Dame, 1956.
Kim, M. P., ed., *Istoria SSSR*. Moscow, 1957.
Kolarz, W., *Russia and Her Colonies*. New York, 1953.
Kommunisticheskaia Partiia Polshi v Borbe za Nezavisimost Svoiei Strany. Moscow, 1955.
Komorowski, Y., *The Secret Army*. London, 1957.
Korbonski, S., *W Imieniu Rzeczypospolitej*. Paris, 1954. English translation: *Fighting Warsaw*. New York, 1956.
Kula, W., *Rozwazania o Historii*. Warsaw, 1958.
Lasswell, H. D., and A. Kaplan, *Power and Society*. New Haven, 1950.
Leites, N., *The Study of Bolshevism*. New York, 1953.
Leonhard, W., *Die Revolution Entlaesst Ihre Kinder*. Berlin, 1955. English translation: *Child of the Revolution*. Chicago, 1958.
Librach, Jan, *The Rise of the Soviet Empire*. New York, 1964.
Lowenthal, R., *World Communism: The Disintegration of a Secular Faith*. New York, 1964.
Lukacs, J. A., *The Great Powers and Eastern Europe*. New York, 1953.
Macartney, C. A., *A History of Hungary, 1929–1945*. Edinburgh, 1956–1957.
—— *Problems of the Danube Basin*. Cambridge, Eng., 1944.
—— and Palmer, A. W., *Independent Eastern Europe: A History*. London, 1962.
Mackiewicz, J., *The Katyn-Wood Murders*. London, 1951
McLane, C. B., *Soviet Policy and the Chinese Communists, 1931–1946*. New York, 1958.
McLean, F., *The Heretic*. New York, 1957.
Mehnert, K., *Peking and Moscow*. New York, 1963.
Meissner, B., *Das Ende des Stalin-Mythos*. Frankfurt, 1956.
Meyer, A. G., *Leninism*. Cambridge, 1957.
—— *Marxism*. Cambridge, 1954.
Mitrany, D., *Marx Against the Peasant*. Chapel Hill, 1951.
Morgan, O. S., *Agricultural Systems of Middle Europe*. New York, 1933.
Mosely, P. E., ed., *The Soviet Union, 1922–1962*. New York, 1963.

Neumann, F., *The Democratic and the Authoritarian State*. Glencoe, 1957.
Nyaradi, N., *My Ringside Seat in Moscow*. New York, 1952.
Oktiabrskaia Revolutsia v Rossii i Mirovoie Osvoboditelnoie Dvizhenie. Gospolitizdat, 1957.
Ossowski, S., *Struktura Klasowa w Spolecznej Swiadomosci*. Wroclaw, 1957.
Politika Sovietskoi Vlasti po Natsional'nym Delam za Try Goda, 1917–1920. Moscow, 1920.
Ripka, H., *Eastern Europe in the Post-War World*. New York, 1961.
Roberts, H. L., *Rumania: Political Problems of an Agricultural State*. New Haven, 1951.
Rostow, W. W., *The Dynamics of Soviet Society*. Cambridge, 1953.
Rothschild, J., *The Communist Party of Bulgaria: Origins and Development, 1883–1936*. New York, 1959.
Rozek, E., *Allied Wartime Diplomacy: A Pattern in Poland*. New York, 1958.
Scalapino, R. A., ed., *The Communist Revolution in Asia*. Englewood Cliffs, 1965.
Schwartz, B. I., *Chinese Communism and the Rise of Mao*. Cambridge, 1952.
Seton-Watson, H., *From Lenin to Malenkov*. New York, 1953.
—— *The East-European Revolution*. New York, 1956.
—— *The History of World Communism*. New York, 1953.
—— *The Pattern of Communist Revolution*. London, 1953.
Sharp, S. L., *New Constitutions in the Soviet Sphere*. Washington, 1950.
Skendi, S., ed., *Albania*. New York, 1957.
Starbinger, W., *Grenzen der Sowjetmacht*. Würzburg, 1955.
Swarup, R., *Communism and Peasantry*. Calcutta, 1954.
Talmon, J. L., *The Rise of Totalitarian Democracy*. Boston, 1952.
Taracouzio, T. A., *War and Peace in Soviet Diplomacy*. New York, 1940.
Thomson, S. H., *Czechoslovakia in European History*. Princeton, 1953.
U.S. Department of State, *Moscow's European Satellites*. Washington, 1955.
Walker, R., *China Under Communism*. New Haven, 1955.
Wandycz, C. S., *Czechoslovak-Polish Federation and the Great Powers*. Bloomington, 1956.
Warriner, D., *Revolution in Eastern Europe*. London, 1950.
Whiting, A. S., *Soviet Policies in China, 1917–1924*. New York, 1954.
Wiley, A., *Tensions Within the Soviet Captive Countries*. Senate Committee on Foreign Relations, 1954.
Wiskemann, E., *Germany's Eastern Neighbours*. Oxford, 1956.
Wolff, R., *The Balkans in Our Time*. Cambridge, 1956.
Zagorski, W., *Seventy Days*. London, 1957.
Zaleski, W., *The Pattern of Life in Poland*. Paris, 1952.
Zamyslova, Z. A., *Kommunisticheskii Internatsional i Ego Rol v Istorii Mezhdunarodnogo Rabochego i Natsional'no-Osvoboditel'nogo Dvizheniia*. Moscow, 1957.

Zinner, P. E., *Communist Strategy and Tactics in Czechoslovakia, 1918–1948.* New York, 1963.

POLITICAL AND IDEOLOGICAL DEVELOPMENTS SINCE 1945

Airapetyan, M. E., and Sukhodeev, U. U., *Novii Tip Mezhdunarodnykh Otnoshenii.* Moscow, 1964.
Akademia Nauk SSSR, *Voprosy Stroitelstva Edinogo Demokraticheskovo Germanskogo Gosudarstva.* Moscow, 1951.
Armstrong, H. F., *Tito and Goliath.* New York, 1951.
Bain, L. B., *Reluctant Satellites.* New York, 1960.
Barnett, A. D., *Communist China: The Early Years, 1949–1955.* New York, 1964.
Beke, L., *A Student's Diary.* New York, 1957.
Bienkowski, W., *Rewolucji Ciag Dalszy.* Warsaw, 1957.
Blum, I., *Z Dziejow Aparatu Politycznego Wojska Polskiego.* Warsaw, 1957.
Boorman, H. L., et al., *Moscow-Peking Axis.* New York, 1957.
Brant, S., *The East German Rising, 17th June 1953.* London, 1955.
Bromke, A., ed., *The Communist States at the Crossroads Between Moscow and Peking.* New York, 1965.
Burks, R. V., *The Dynamics of Communism in Eastern Europe.* Princeton, 1961.
Co sie Dzieje w ZMP? Warsaw, 1957.
Cohen, A., *The Communism of Mao Tse-tung.* Chicago, 1964.
Cretzianu, A., *Captive Rumania.* New York, 1956.
Culbertson, W., *Liberation: The Threat and Challenge of Power.* Atlanta, 1953.
Czechoslovak Academy of Science, *Otazky Narodni a Demokraticke Revoluce v CSR.* Prague, 1955.
de Sola Pool, I., ed., *Satellite Generals.* Stanford, 1955.
Deborin, G. A., ed., *Mezhdunarodnie Otnosheniia i Vneshnaia Politika Sovetskogo Soiuza.* Moscow, 1958.
Dedijer, V., *Tito.* New York, 1952.
Delany, R. F., ed., *This is Communist Hungary.* Chicago, 1958.
Deutschlands Ostproblem. Goettinger Arbeitskreis, Germany, 1957.
Djilas, M., *Conversations with Stalin.* New York, 1962.
——— "On New Roads to Socialism." Belgrade, 1950.
——— *The New Class.* New York, 1957.
Djordjevic, J., *La Yougoslavie, démocratie socialiste.* Paris, 1959.
Doolin, D. J., *Territorial Claims in the Sino-Soviet Conflict.* Stanford, 1965.
Dragnich, A., *Tito's Promised Land.* New Brunswick, 1954.
Dragoicheva, T., *Politicheska, Organizatsionna i Stopanska Deinost.* Sofia, 1945.
Draskovich, S. M., *Tito, Moscow's Trojan Horse.* Chicago, 1957.
Duhnke, H., *Stalinismus in Deutschland.* Cologne, 1955.

Dutt, V. P., *China's Foreign Policy 1958–62.* New York, 1964.
Dziewanowski, M. K., *The Communist Party of Poland.* Cambridge, 1959.
Ekonomika i Polityka Jugoslawii. Collection of essays. Warsaw, 1957.
Esti, B., *Tanulmayok a Magyar Nepi Demokracia Tortenetebol.* Budapest, 1955.
Farberov, N. P., *Gosudarstvennoe Pravo Stran Narodnoi Demokratii.* Moscow, 1949.
Fejtö, F., *Behind the Rape of Hungary.* New York, 1957.
Floyd, D., *Rumania: Russia's Dissident Ally.* New York, 1965.
Friedrich, C. J., ed., *The Soviet Zone of Germany.* New Haven, 1956.
Gabor, R., *Organization and Strategy of the Hungarian Workers Party.* New York, 1952.
Gadourek, I., *The Communist Party of Czechoslovakia in the Post-Stalinist Period.* Chicago, 1957.
———— *Political Control of Czechoslovakia.* Leiden, 1953.
Gelberg, L., *Uklad Warszawski.* Warsaw, 1957.
Gindev, P., *Kum Vuprosa za Kharaktera na Narodno-Demokraticheskata Revoliutsia v Bulgariia.* Sofia, 1956.
Griffith, W. E., *Albania and the Sino-Soviet Rift.* Cambridge, 1963.
———— *The Sino-Soviet Rift.* Cambridge, 1964.
———— ed., *Communism in Europe: Continuity, Change, and the Sino-Soviet Dispute,* 2 vols. Cambridge, 1965–1966.
Grzybowski, K., *The Socialist Commonwealth of Nations: Organizations and Institutions.* New Haven, 1964.
Hallowell, J. H., ed., *Soviet Satellite Nations.* Gainsville, 1958.
Halperin, E., *The Triumphant Heretic.* London, 1958.
Hamm H., *Albania — China's Beachhead in Europe.* New York, 1963.
———— and Kun, J., *Das Rote Schisma.* Cologne, 1963.
Hammond, T. T., *Jugoslavia Between East and West.* New York, 1954.
Hildebrandt, R., *The Explosion.* New York, 1955.
Hoffman, George W., and Neal, F. W., *Yugoslavia and the New Communism.* New York, 1962.
Honey, P. J., *Communism in North Vietnam, Its Role in the Sino-Soviet Dispute.* Cambridge, 1963.
The Hungarian Situation and the Rule of Law. The Hague, 1957.
Hungarian State Publishing House, *The Trial of Josef Mindszenty.* Budapest, 1949.
Imre Nagy: Un Communisme qui n'oublie pas l'homme. Intro. by F. Fejtö. Paris, 1959.
Ionescu, G., *The Breakup of the Soviet Empire in Eastern Europe.* London, 1965.
———— *Communism in Rumania, 1944–1962.* New York, 1964.
Jackson, W. A. D., *The Russo-Chinese Borderlands: Zone of Peaceful Contact or Potential Conflict?* New York, 1962.

Jedlicki, W., "Klub Krzywego Kola," *Kultura* (Paris), 1963.
Jordan, Z., *Philosophy and Ideology.* Dordrecht, 1963.
Justice Enslaved. International Commission of Jurists, The Hague, 1955.
Kanapa, J., *Bulgarie d'hier et d'aujourd'hui.* Paris, 1955.
Kapitsa, M. S., *Sovetsko-Kitaiskie Otnosheniia.* Moscow, 1958.
Kardelj, E., *Socialism and War: A Survey of Chinese Criticisms of the Policy of Coexistence.* New York, 1963.
Kecskemeti, P., *The Unexpected Revolution.* Stanford, 1961.
Korab, A., *Die Entwicklung der kommunistischen Parteien in Ost-mitteleuropa.* Hamburg, 1962.
Korbel, J., *Tito's Communism.* Denver, 1951.
Korbel, P., and V. Vagassky, "Purges in the Communist Party of Czechoslovakia." Radio Free Europe, mimeographed, 1952.
Korbonski, S., *W Imieniu Kremla.* Paris, 1956. English translation: *Warsaw in Chains.* New York, 1959.
Korovin, E., *Nerushimaia Druzhba Narodov SSSR i Narodno-Demokraticheskich Stran.* Moscow, 1955.
Kovacs, I., ed., *Facts About Hungary.* New York, 1958.
Labedz, L., and Urban, G. R., eds. *The Sino-Soviet Conflict.* London, 1965.
Lane, A. B., *I Saw Poland Betrayed.* Indianapolis, 1948.
Lasky, M. J., ed., *The Hungarian Revolution.* London, 1957.
Leonhard, W., *The Kremlin Since Stalin.* New York, 1962.
Lewis, F. *A Case History of Hope.* New York, 1958.
London, K., *Unity and Contradiction in Major Aspects of Sino-Soviet Relations.* New York, 1962.
MacFarquhar, R., *The Hundred Flowers Campaign and the Chinese Intellectuals.* New York, 1960.
—— *Thought Reform of the Chinese Intellectuals.* Hong Kong, 1960.
Maksakovski, V. P., *Stroiki Sotsialisma v Evropeiskich Stranach Narodnoi Demokratii.* Moscow, 1952.
Markham, R. H., *Rumania Under the Soviet Yoke.* Boston, 1949.
Materiali po Istoriia na Bulgarskata Kommunisticheska Partiia. Sofia, 1956.
McVicker, C. P., *Titoism.* New York, 1957.
Melnikov, D., *Borba za Edinuiu Nezavisimuiu Demokraticheskuiu Miroliubivuiu Germaniu.* Moscow, 1951.
Meray, T., *Thirteen Days that Shook the Kremlin.* New York, 1959.
Mikolajczyk, S., *The Rape of Poland.* New York, 1948.
Miles, E. L., and Gillooly, J. S., *Processes of Inter-Action Among the 14 Communist Party-States: An Explanatory Essay.* Stanford, 1965.
Milosz, C., *The Captive Mind.* New York, 1953.
—— *The Seizure of Power.* New York, 1955.
Monin, D. D., *Federatsia ili Edinoe Germanskoie Gosudarstvo.* Moscow, 1947.
Nagy, F., *Struggle Behind the Iron Curtain.* New York, 1948.
Nagy, I., *On Communism.* New York, 1957.

Neal, F. W., *Titoism in Action*. Berkeley, 1958.
Nettl, J. P., *The Eastern Zone and Soviet Policy in Germany*. Oxford, 1951.
O Narodnoi Demokratii v Stranach Evropi. Moscow, 1956.
Pistrak, L., *The Grand Tactician: Khrushchev's Rise to Power*. New York, 1961.
Pod Znamenen Proleterskovo Internatsionalisma. Moscow, 1957.
Prebeichevich, S., tr., *Jugoslavia's Way*. New York, 1958.
Prochazka, A., "Changes in the Philosophy of Czechoslovak Law." Microfilm, Library of Congress, Washington.
Proiekt za Konstitutsia na narodna Republika Bulgaria. Sofia, 1946.
Protiv Sovremennogo Revizionizma. Moscow, 1958.
Reale, E., *Nascita del Cominform*. Milan, 1958.
Reisky-Dubnic, V., *The Communist Propaganda Methods in Czechoslovakia*. New York, 1963.
Research and Publications Service, *The Pattern of the Purge*. New York, 1952.
"Research Report: Hungarian Party Congress, May 24–30, 1954." Radio Free Europe, mimeographed, 1954.
RIIA, *The Soviet-Jugoslav Dispute*. London, 1948.
Ripka, H., *Czechoslovakia Enslaved*. London, 1950.
——— *Le Coup de Prague*. Paris, 1949.
Ritvo, H., *The New Soviet Society* (Final Text of the Program of the CPSU). New York, 1962.
Rostow, W. W., *The Prospects for Communist China*. Cambridge, 1954.
Rothschild, Joseph, *Communist Eastern Europe*. New York, 1964.
Rozmaryn, S., *Polskie Prawo Panstwowe*. Warsaw, 1951.
Rush, M., *Political Succession in the USSR*. New York, 1965.
Scalapino, R. A., ed., *North Korea Today*. New York, 1963.
Schaff, A., *Marksizm a Jednostka Ludzka*. Warsaw, 1965.
——— *Wstep do Teorii Marksismu*. Warsaw, 1948.
Schmidt, D. A., *Anatomy of a Satellite*. Boston, 1952.
Seydewitz, M., *Niemiecka Republika Demokratyczna*. Warsaw, 1955.
Skilling, G. H., *Communism, National and International: Eastern Europe after Stalin*. Toronto, 1964.
Slusser, R. M., and Triska, J., *A Calendar of Soviet Treaties 1917–1957*. Stanford, 1959.
Sobolev, A., *Chto Takoe Narodnaia Demokratia*. Moscow, 1956.
Sodruzhestvo Stran Sotsializma. Collection of essays. Moscow, 1958.
Sovietization of the Czechoslovak Judiciary. Research and Publications Service, New York, 1953.
Staar, R. F., *Poland 1944–1962: The Sovietization of a Captive People*. Baton Rouge, 1962.
Stehle, H., *The Independent Satellite*. New York, 1965.
Stepanian, I. V., *Stalin o Stroitel'stve Kommunizma v SSSR*. Moscow, 1950.
Stern, C., *Die SED*. Germany, 1954.

Stern, C., *Ulbricht: A Political Biography.* New York, 1965.
Stypulkowski, Z., *Polska na Progu 1958 R.* London, 1958.
Sulzberger, C. L., *The Big Thaw.* New York, 1956.
Syrop, K., *Spring in October.* New York, 1958.
Taborsky, E., *Communism in Czechoslovakia.* Princeton, 1961.
Tarantova, L., *Zrada sidli v Belehrade.* Prague, 1952.
Tomasic, D., *National Communism and Soviet Strategy.* Washington, 1957.
The Satellites in Eastern Europe. The Annals (American Academy of Political and Social Science), vol. 317, May 1958.
The Truth about the Nagy Affair: Facts, Documents, Comments. New York, 1961.
Ulam, A., *Titoism and the Cominform.* Cambridge, 1952.
UN Special Committee for Eastern Europe, *Report on the Problem of Hungary.* New York, 1957.
U.S. Department of State, *North Korea: A Case Study in the Techniques of Takeover.* Washington, 1961.
Valev, Le., ed., *Bolgarskii Narod v Borbe za Sotsializm.* Moscow, 1954.
Vali, F. A., *Rift and Revolt in Hungary.* Cambridge, 1961.
Walka Ludu Polskiego o Wolnosc i Socjalizm. Warsaw, 1953.
Wei, H., *China and Soviet Russia.* New York, 1956.
White, L., *Balkan Caesar: Tito versus Stalin.* New York, 1951.
Wint, G., *Communist China's Crusade, Mao's Road to Power and the New Campaign for World Revolution.* New York, 1965.
Zagoria, D., *The Sino-Soviet Conflict, 1956–61.* Princeton, 1962.
Zawadzki, S., *Rozwoj Wiezi Rad Narodowych z Masami Pracujacymi w Polsce Ludowej.* Warsaw, 1955.
Zinner, P., *Revolution in Hungary.* New York, 1962.

ECONOMIC AND SOCIAL DEVELOPMENTS SINCE 1945

Agoston, I., *Le Marché Commun communiste: Principes et pratique du Comecon.* Geneva, 1964.
Aktualne Zagadnienia Polityki Kulturalnej w Dziedzinie Filozofii i Socjologii. Warsaw, 1956.
Alton, T. P., *Postwar Economic Planning in Poland.* New York, 1955.
Bouvier, C., *La Collectivisation de L'Agriculture, URSS-Chines-Democraties Populaires.* Paris, 1958.
Buhler, N., and S. Zukowski, *Discrimination in Education in the People's Democracies.* New York, 1955.
Carlton, R. K., ed., *Forced Labor in the People's Democracies.* New York, 1955.
Chalasinski, J., *Przeszlosc i Przyszlosc Inteligencji Polskiej.* Warsaw, 1958.
Choh, Ming Li, ed., *Industrial Development in Communist China.* New York, 1964.

Chu, Yuan Cheng, *Economic Relations Between Peking and Moscow 1949–63*
New York, 1964.
Csicsery-Ronay, I., "Russian Cultural Penetration in Hungary." Mimeo
graphed, Research and Publications Service, VI, 1950. Vol. II, 1952. Vol
III, 1952.
DeWar, M., *Soviet Trade with Eastern Europe.* London, 1951.
Dyskusja o Polskim Modelu Gospodarczym. Collected Essays. Warsaw, 1957
Economic Commission for Europe, *Etude sur la situation économique de*
L'Europe depuis la guerre. Geneva, 1953.
Economic Survey of Europe Since the War. UN publication, no date.
Fadeyev, N. V., *Sovet Ekonomicheskoi Vzaimopomoshchi.* Moscow, 1964
Feireabend, L., "Agricultural Coops in Czechoslovakia." Mid-European Studie
Center, 1951, mimeographed.
Fidelski, R., *O Radach Rabotniczych.* Warsaw, 1956.
——— *Wspolpraca Gospodarcza Polski z Krajami Socjalistycznymi.* Warsaw
1959.
"Foreign Trade in the People's Democracies of Central and Eastern Europe."
Research and Publications Service, mimeographed, November 1952.
Gabensky, I., "Bulgarian Economy." Research and Publications Service, mime
ographed, 1951.
Gertsovich, G. B., *Razvitie Mirnoi Ekonomiki v Germanskoi Demokratich*
eskoi Respublike. Moscow, 1954.
Goldmann, J., *Planned Economy in Czechoslovakia.* Prague, 1949.
Hlasko, M., *The Eighth Day of the Week.* New York, 1958.
Hoffmann, E., *COMECON: Der Gemeinsame Markt in Osteuropa.* Opladen
1961.
Hungarian Investment Policy Under the New Course. Radio Free Europe
New York, 1954.
Ivanova, N. I., et al., eds., *Razvitie Ekonomiki Stran Narodnoi Demokrati*
Moscow, 1958.
Jahasz, W., *Hungary's Bolshevized Pedagogy in 1951–1952. Research and Pub*
lications Service, New York, 1952.
Jahasz, W., and A. Rothberg, eds., *Flashes in the Night: A Collection o*
Stories from Contemporary Hungary. New York, 1958.
Kalendarz Rabotniczy 1957. Warsaw, 1957.
Karra, V., *Stroitel'stvo Sotsialisticheskoi Ekonomiki v Rumunskoi Narodno*
Respublike. Moscow, 1953.
Kaser, M., *Comecon, Integration Problems of the Planned Economies,* London
1965.
Klochko, M., *Soviet Scientist in Red China.* New York, 1964.
Korbonski, A., *Politics of Socialist Agriculture in Poland, 1945–1960.* New
York, 1965.
Kornai, J., *A Gazdasagi Vezetes Tulzott Kozpontositasa.* Budapest, 1957.
Kracauer, S., and P. Berkman, *Satellite Mentality.* New York, 1956.

Lerski, J., *The Economy of Poland*. The Council for Economic and Industry Research, Inc., Washington, 1954.

Lipinski, E., *Rewizje*. Warsaw, 1958.

Lychowski, T., *Stosunki Ekonomiczne Miedzy Krajami o Roznych Ustrojach*. Warsaw, 1957.

Marczewski, J., *Planification et Croissance Economique des Democraties Populaires*. Paris, 1958.

Mayewski, P., ed., *The Broken Mirror*. New York, 1958.

Mendershausen, H., *Terms of Trade Between the Soviet Union and Smaller Communist Countries, 1955–1957*. Rand Corporation, January 1959.

Michal, J. M., *Central Planning in Czechoslovakia*. Stanford, 1960.

Mirovaia Sotsialisticheskaia Sistema Khoziaistva. Collection of essays. Moscow, 1958.

Modelski, G., *Atomic Energy in the Communist Bloc*. New York, 1959.

Montias, J. M., *Central Planning in Poland*. New Haven, 1962.

Nikolitch, R., "Land Reform and Land Tenure in Jugoslavia." Mid-European Studies Center, mimeographed, 1951.

O Nowy Program Rolny. Collected essays. Warsaw, 1957.

Plan Odbudowy Gospodarczej. Warsaw, 1947.

Plany Razvitia Narodnovo Khoziaistva Stran Narodnoi Demokratii. Moscow, 1952.

Pounds, N., and N. Spulber, eds., *Resources and Planning in Eastern Europe*. Bloomington, 1957.

Przedsiebiorstwo Samodzielne w Gospodarce Planowej. Warsaw, 1957.

Pryor, F. L., *The Communist Foreign Trade System*. Cambridge, 1963.

Report of the FAO Mission to Poland. Washington, 1948.

Rocznik Statystyczny. Polish Statistical Yearbook, Warsaw.

Sanders, I. T., ed., *Collectivization of Agriculture in Eastern Europe*. Lexington, 1958.

Satellite Agriculture in Crisis. Free Europe Committee, Inc., 1954.

Schleiher, H., *Das System der Betrieblichen Selbstverwaltung in Jugoslawien*. Berlin, 1961.

Sergeev, S. D., *Ekonomicheskoi Sotrudnichestvo i Vzaimopomoshch' Sotsialisticheskikh Stran*. Moscow, 1965.

Shuster, G. N., *Religion Behind the Iron Curtain*. New York, 1954.

Sladovsky, M. I., *Ocherki Ekonomicheskich Otnoshenii SSSR s Kitaiem*. Moscow, 1957.

Slusser, R., ed., *Soviet Economic Policy in Postwar Germany*. New York, 1953

Spulber, N., *The Economics of Communist Eastern Europe*. Cambridge, 1957.

Stankiewicz, W., and J. Montias, *Institutional Changes in the Polish Economy*. New York, 1955.

Statisticheski Ezhegodnik Rumynskoi Narodnoi Republiki. Bucharest, 1957.

Statisticheski Godishnik na Narodna Republika Bulgariya. Sofia, 1956.

Szczepanski, J., *Inteligencja i Spoleczenstwo*. Warsaw, 1957.

Tomasevich, J., *Peasants, Politics, and Economic Change in Jugoslavia*. Stanford, 1955.

Tomasic, D., *Personality and Culture in Eastern European Politics*. New York, 1948.

Varga, E., *Izmienienia v Ekonomike Kapitalizma v Itoge Vtoroi Mirovoi Voiny*. Moscow, 1946.

————— *Basic Questions of Economy and Politics of Imperialism after World War II*. Moscow, 1953.

Wellisz, S., *The Economies of the Soviet Bloc*. New York, 1964.

Wszelaki, J., *Communist Economic Strategy: The Role of East Central Europe*. Washington, 1959.

Wykonanie Narodowych Planow Gospodarczych, 1948–1952. Warsaw, 1952.

INDEX

Abrasimov, P. A., 176n, 476
Academies of Social Sciences, 43, 475, 479–480
Adenauer, K., 160
Administration, 426; centralism, East Germany, 80; decline in importance of structure of, 88–89; internal militancy, 89; and Stalin, 105–106; apparatus of, see Bureaucracy; of CPSU, 156; decentralization of Soviet, 157–158; in Poland, 251
Afghanistan, 158
Advisers, Soviet, 118–123, 144, 179, 230, 349; in China, 131, 301, 409, 428
Agricultural policy, 157; Polish, 12, 342, 353, 361, 364–365; Rumanian, 17; Hungarian, 17, 162, 212; postwar Soviet, 43–44; socialist transformation of, 84, 97; size of holdings, 98, 143; and Stalinism, 142–143; East Germany, 160; and Khrushchev, 168; Yugoslav, 191; Chinese, 299, 370
Aid, economic: bilateral, 108; Soviet to China, 133, 374, 376–378, 403, 409, 429; and East Germany, 159; U.S. to Yugoslavia, 188, 316, 363; Soviet to Hungary, 227; Soviet to Poland, 249, 287; Soviet loans to bloc, 285–287; U.S. loan to Poland, 288; Western to Poland, 350; Soviet to Mongolia, 386; political benefits of, 389, 433
Albania, 56, 444; constitution, 32, 37; and CEMA, 128n, 460, 462; and Soviet-Yugoslav rapprochement, 194; aftermath of Twentieth Congress, 204; and Tito, 237, 282, 386–387; and China, 384–385, 386–388, 411–414; and Khrushchev, 387; and Soviet aid, 389; and Sino-Soviet rift, 401, 408–409, 411–412; relations with USSR (1961), 414; suspension of Soviet economic assistance to, 415, 418, 503; suspension of Soviet diplomatic relations, 415, 417, 418, 449; and Warsaw Treaty Organization, 457, 459; trade relations, 477
Albanian Communist Party, 386–387;

purges, 387; 1961 Congress, 414–414, 416. See also Hoxha, E.
Algeria, 373, 380
Alienation, 507; of intellectuals, 200, 204
Alliance system, Soviet, 456–484; formal institutions of, 456–471; informal institutions of, 471–484; obstacles to, 482–484. See also Treaties
Allied Control Commission, 16
All-Union Communist Party, 39; and Gomulka, 62n
Alter, V., 11n
Ambassadors, Soviet, 179, 433; and control of bloc, 118–119; and intraparty coordination, 476
Amnesty, 163, 180, 216, 223, 246
Andreev, A. M., 25n
Andropov, Y. V., 476
Anglo-American relations, 5; Rakosi's analysis of (1945), 50
Anti-colonialism, 411
Anti-Communists, 7–8, 41
Anti-Semitism, 68, 507; and party purges, 93, 95; and Slansky trial, 97; Hungarian, 146; Polish, 251n, 252n; and new elites of mid-sixties, 440
Anti-Stalinism, 193–198; and Bulgaria, 202–203; and internal cohesion of bloc, 206–209; and Hungary, 225
Apel, E., 453
Architecture, 88; repudiation of Stalinist, 180
Arciszewski, T., 11n
Arendt, H., 157n
Armaments, 126; and CEMA, 128. See also Disarmament
Armed forces, 42–43, 137–138; Polish, 45–46, 121–123, 248n, 255, 261, 339, 340; Communization of, 93; Soviet penetration as control of, 120–121; loyalty problem, 122; Soviet advisers in, 122–123; Chinese, 132–133; Hungarian, 226; reorganization of satellite (1952), 457. See also Red Army
Arts, 243–244; party control, 87

577

Association of Polish Youth (Young Communist League), 253, 345
Atlantic Pact, 176. *See also* NATO
Atom-free zones: East Europe, 281n, 365; Far East, 377; Balkans, 450–451, 458n
Austria, 55; and Danube Commission, 463–464
Autarky, economic, 125, 128, 350, 451, 456, 469, 482–483, 498; Nagy on, 128n. *See also* Industrialization, Stalinist
Autonomy, local, 63, 238; and Gomulka, 96, 233, 264, 272–273, 304–305, 335, 343, 358, 359–366, 373, 450; and Stalin, 145–146, 306; in Yugoslavia, 185, 195, 232; post-Stalin, 214; and Soviet primacy, 397; and Sino-Soviet rift, 408, 434; Hungarian, and neutralism, 449; Rumanian, 450
Axen, H., 276; and 1961 Albanian Party Congress, 416
Azizian, A., 275

Balkans, 24n; semi-neutrality, and Rumania, 446; receding Soviet influence in, 449
Balkan Union, 55–57, 62, 93, 114, 124, 194
Baltic states, 24, 33
Bandung conference, 220–221; "spirit" of, 376
Barak, R., 416
Bauer, L., 95, 96
Bavaria, 24
Belgrade declarations, 154, 195, 197, 207, 210, 220–221, 223, 225, 230, 238
Ben Bella, A., 436
Benes, E., 10, 19, 20, 31
Beria, L., 91, 166, 196, 240; and Soviet secret police, 120; significance of execution, 157; and East Germany, 159; arrest, 160
Berlin: blockade, 134; Foreign Ministers Conference (1954), 166; crisis of 1958, 373, 376, 387, 432; Wall, 413, 438
Berman, J., 46, 96–97, 114n, 120, 242; and Stalinism, 113, 165; and Comintern, 119; and Khrushchev's anti-Jewish bias, 171; removed from power (1955), 246; and Natolin faction, 250; expulsion from party, 354
Bessarabia, 439n, 440, 446
Bialer, S., 114n, 120, 167n
Bienkowski, W., 51n; on change, 139; *The Revolution Continued*, 140; on Stalinist legacy, 141; indictment of "lunar economics," 142

Bierut, B., 14, 26, 58, 61, 85, 242, 293n, 392, 500; defines People's Democracy, 27, 28n; and Polish architects, 88; and party purges, 96; and Stalin, 113n, 113, 146; and NKVD, 119; as Party Secretary, 163n; and New Course, 165; death of, 245, 246, 249
Bilateralism, 108–112, 137, 266, 450, 461, 466–471; treaties, 108–109, 282–284, 289, 466–467; informal devices, 113–124; and political control, 117; and interstate relations, 123–124, 144, 497–499; economic, 125–129, 284–291, 446, 498; and Warsaw Pact, 174n; and proletarian internationalism, 272, 292, 325, 328; Polish view, 274–275, 277, 281, 294–295, 304–305; SED's view, 276; Czech view, 276; and emergence of new Soviet-Satellite relationship (1957), 282–284; Yugoslav view, 316, 318, 327–328; and Sino-Soviet rift, 420; increasing Soviet reliance on, 453; and nuclear power, 464–465; joint investment projects, 470; and cultural cooperation, 470–471
Biro, Z., 73
Blum, I., 8n
Bolshevik (CPSU theoretical journal), 76–77
Bolshevik Revolution, 24, 25, 29, 253n, 295, 371; 29th anniversary celebration (1946), 45; 1955 celebration of, 198; 40th anniversary (1957), *see* Moscow Conference of 1957; Gomulka on, 343
Bonapartism, 141
Borba (Yugoslav party paper), 186
Boris, King of Bulgaria, 15
Brezhnev, L., 367, 435, 474; and Warsaw Pact, 453
Broz-Tito, J., *see* Tito, J.
Bukharin, N., 502
Bulganin, N., 169, 284n; Peking visit with Khrushchev, 171; Asian tour with Khrushchev, 181; -Zhukov visit to Poland (1956), 248–249, 252; and reorganization of satellite armies, 457
Bulgaria, 5, 9, 79, 392; postwar position, 14–16, 18, 31; Independent Workers' Party, 15; Fatherland Front, 15–16, 85; terror in, 15–16, 91; land reform, 16, 99; emergence of People's Republic, 27; -Yugoslavia friendship treaty, 56n; castigation by Moscow, 57; and "socialist construction," 69, 70, 73; constitution, 78; Socialist Party, 85n; state administration, 89n; Five-Year-Plan (1949–

1953), 89; nationalization, 100n; Dimitrov Steel Plant, 101; bilateral treaties, 109, 466; friendship societies, 115; Soviet experts in, 121; joint companies, 126; trade with USSR, 127; and CEMA, 128, 460; and China, 130, 384–385; and Stalinism, 146, 203; New Course, 163; and Yugoslavia, 194, 201–202, 202n; High Party School, 201; anti-Stalinism, 203; industrialization (1956), 205; extension of Soviet credit to, 285n; exports, 287n; anti-revisionism, 381; Karl Marx Institute, 381; 1958 Plan, 382; and Sino-Soviet rift, 436; April 1965 military conspiracy, 441; Soviet influence in, 449; and Rumania, 449–450; and Intermetall, 463; tourism, 481

Bulgarian Communist Party, 15; absorbs Social Democrats (1948), 16; Fifth Congress (1948), 72, 98; purges, 93–94, 137, 146; Central Committee, 119; and Titoism, 201–202, 281–282; membership, 202; criticism of leadership, 202n

Bureaucracy, 88–89, 334, 456; Bienkowski on, 141–142; and Khrushchev, 168, 180; and the masses, 181; Soviet, 190, 193; in transition to Communism, 237; Polish, 251. *See also* Administration

Capital development, *see* economic relations, capital-development policy

Castro, Fidel, 507n

Ceausescu, N., 447, 470; bilateral meetings, 474. *See also* Rumania

CEMA (Council of Economic Mutual Assistance), 287–289, 433, 451, 453, 467, 498; and trade, 128–129, 468; invigoration of, 173; and buttressing of political ties, 174–175, 446; and economic integration of bloc, 286–287, 462, 500; and specialization of members, 287, 444–445, 461; and Czechoslovakia, 382; and Yugoslavia, 437; and Rumania, 444–445, 447, 457, 464, 478, 499; Chinese view of, 445, 462n; Bank, 450, 463–464; founding membership, 460; and Marshall Plan, 460; standing commissions, 460, 462; multilateral action, 460; charter (1960), 460, 461; Secretariat, 460–461; Executive Committee, 461; Basic Principles of International Socialist Division of Labor, 461, 472; International Institute of Standardization, 461n; and planning, 461–462, 472; autonomous organizations connected with, 462–463; and multilat-

eral leadership conferences, 472; and autarky, 482–483

Centralists (Centrists), 295–296, 319, 327, 329, 367, 497, 499; neo-Stalinist, 291; Chinese, 297, 306, 329–331, 423; and 1957 Moscow Conference, 302, 304–306, 308; Yugoslav view, 313, 316, 320; and Soviet leadership, 329; and Nagy's execution, 335

Cepicka, A., 122; and cult of personality, 203

Chalasinski, J., 87n

Changchun railroad, 131

Chauvinism, big-power, 190, 280, 433; Chinese fear of, 376; and Soviet-Albanian break, 418

Chervenkov, V., 28n, 70, 94, 202, 322–323, 392; and Bulgarian New Course, 163; party post, 163n; condemnation of, 201; returns to Politburo, 381

Chervonenko, S. V., 476

Chinese Communist Party (CCP), 25–26; and ideology, 156n, 295, 368, 371–373, 390, 508–509; Eighth Congress, 207; National People's Congress (July, 1957), 299; factionalism, 299; victory of 1949, 369; Congress of May 1958, 370; and ideological primacy, 371; Lushan Plenum (1959), 378; "On Khrushchev's Phony Communism and Its Historical Lesson for the World" (1964), 425; misconception of Khrushchev's fall, 425

Chinese Nationalists, 375

Chinese People's Republic (CPR), 3, 444, 498; emergence of (1949), 82, 129, 130, 508; relations with bloc, 129, 279; and Stalinism, 129–134, 144–145; and Poland, 130, 297; status in bloc, 130, 134, 137, 171, 266, 279n, 283, 367, 393; ideological autonomy, 130, 132, 133; and Soviet technical (military) assistance, 131, 301, 409, 428; trade with USSR, 131–132, 477; constitution, 132; Common Program, 132; armed forces, 132–133, 378, 428–429; and Soviet economic aid, 133, 171, 374, 389, 404–405, 409, 429, 503; and Khrushchev, 168, 171, 368, 369, 371, 376–378, 380; joint stock companies, 171; and industry and trade, 183; and Soviet model, 194; and 1956 Moscow declarations, 230; and Polish October, 260, 297; and Soviet-satellite relations, 278–279; and bloc unity, 279–284, 298–308, 367, 397–398; anti-Tito campaign,

281, 329–333, 385, 387, 424; and bloc economic stability, 288; and centralism, 297, 306, 329; Hundred Flowers campaign, 297–299; intellectuals, 298, 368; People's Communes, 299, 370–372, 384–385; agricultural policy, 299; nuclear power, 301n, 376–378, 428; technological agreement with USSR (1957), 301, 376–377, 403, 409; militancy, 301, 307, 397, 399; "rectification campaign," 368; and anti-Stalinism, 369; domestic scene (1957–1961), 370, 392; national goals, 370, 375, 379, 404, 431; "Great Leap Forward," 370, 409; "Concerning the Creation of People's Communes in the Village," 370; "On Some Questions Concerning the People's Communes," 373; Chinese road, 371–373; view of international affairs, 374–375; and India, 375, 376; tenth anniversary of (1959), 378, 380; "go-it-alone" attitude, 378; response of bloc to policies of, 384; anti-Americanism, 398, 428; leadership, 405; Long March, 405; territorial ambitions, 419; bid for primacy (1963), 420–421; "second intermediate zone" proposal, 421; criticism of Soviet foreign policy, 422–424; criticism of Soviet internal affairs, 424–425; disappointment with post-Khrushchev leadership, 426; and CEMA, 445, 462n; and Warsaw Treaty Organization, 457; bilateral agreements, 466–467. See also Sino-Indian dispute; Sino-Soviet relations

Choe Yong-Kun, 392

Chou En-lai, 280–281, 298, 392; and Soviet primacy, 283; on new ideological conception (1957), 284; visits Poland (1957), 297; and CCP factionalism, 299; and Twenty-second CPSU Congress, 417, 472

Chou Yang, 420–421

Churchill, W., 4, 32; Fulton, Missouri speech (1946), 44

Chu Teh, 392

Cieszyn (Teschen) territorial dispute, 54, 440. See also Territorial disputes

Civil Service, international, 460

Clementis, V., 94–95; rehabilitation of, 204

Club of the Crooked Circle, 243. See also Poland, intellectuals

Coexistence policy, 44, 189, 385; Nagy on, 221; Polish concept, 275, 281, 304; and Khrushchev, 300, 319–320; and Tito, 318, 324–325; and China, 379

Colakovic, R., 505

Cold War, 501. See also East-West relations

"Collective leadership," 117, 201; and succession crises, 156–159; and East European power picture, 159, 163

Collectivization, 7, 362–363; Polish, 11, 99, 165, 242, 253, 254, 342–343, 348, 358, 361; Bulgarian, 16, 202; Yugoslav, 2c 188, 191; Soviet, 43–44; and Gomulka 61, 62, 72, 96; and Stalin's "law of development," 98, 100–101; by coercion 98–99; and ideology, 103–104; Stalin' view of, 106–107, 146; Chinese, 134, 172 uneven pace with bloc, 137; and Stalinism, 142; and de-Stalinization, 200 Hungarian, 215, 218

Colonialism, imperialist, 182

Cominform, 31, 58–64, 128, 129, 207, 248 474, 498; founded (1947), 45, 59, 68–70 declaration, 57; theme, 60; opposition 61–62, 302; and Stalinism, 62; and Yugo slavia, 59, 63–64, 68, 109, 177–178, 187 196, 199, 232, 330–332; and socialist con struction, 71, 80–81; and purges, 93 waning of influence of, 112; and Chi nese, 112; disbanded, 186, 187, 199; dis cussion on revival of (1956), 290–291

Comintern, 10, 16, 27, 46, 49, 52, 59, 155 248, 290, 411, 474; Fourth Congress 24n; and bloc leadership, 29, 113; Sec ond Congress (1920), 34, 35n, 426

Committee of Polish Patriots, 10

Common Railway-Wagon Pool, 463. Se also Multilateralism

Communism: postwar appeal of, 147; rev olutionary morale, 300, 487, 504–505 508–509; and China, 370–372; nature of 400. See also International Commu nism

Communist bloc, Eastern Europe, see So viet bloc, Eastern Europe.

Communist International, see Cominter

Communist Manifesto (Marx), 487

Communist Party of the Soviet Union (CPSU): and People's Democracy, 30 37, 47–50; impact of war, 41–45; leader ship, 42, 55, 156, 180, 329–337, 405 membership, 42, 43; Central Commit tee, 43; and Soviet primacy, 70, 75–83 84–91, 111, 113–114, 138, 172, 181, 185 209, 220, 237, 283, 295, 329, 388–393, 406 role of, 70, 73, 85, 105, 172, 263, 399 control of bloc, 114–124; Nineteenth Congress (1952), 117, 135, 149, 391; 195.

Central Committee Plenum, 119; Academy, 120; administrative structure, 156; post-Stalin policy shifts, 167–168; and Khrushchev, 168, 175; Twentieth Congress, 175, 180–184, 185–186, 193, 194, 198–206, 222, 238, 245, 247, 283, 300, 315, 381, 407, 414; Central Committee declaration (June 1956), 206; anxiety over Polish road, 257–258, 295; policy errors, 266–267; expulsion of anti-Khrushchev elements, 296–297, 314–315; and 1957 Moscow conference, 298–308; and 1957 Moscow declaration, 303–304, 317–320, 322, 325; and revisionism, 323; Twenty-first Congress (1949), 364, 373, 374, 390–391; Seven-Year-Plan, 390; Twenty-second Congress, 400, 415, 417, 472; Conference of eighty-one parties, 410–412, 414, 472; formal demotion by Chinese (1963), 420–421; Twenty-third Congress (1966), 427n, 450n, 472, 474; 1965 (September) Plenum, 470; and *World Marxist Review*, 475. *See also* Soviet Union

Congo, 413
Constitutions, 31–37, 73, 89; and theoretical uniformity, 77–83; Chinese, 132
Construction of socialism, *see* Socialist construction
Consumer-goods programs, 157, 158
Controls, 88–89, 137, 456; on education, 87; and national adulation, 115–116; political and economic, 116–127; by Soviet ambassadors, 118–119; by Soviet experts, 120–121; by Soviet secret police, 121; and armed forces, 121–122; sequence of imposition of, 122; of personal contacts and cultural ties, 478
Council of Economic Mutual Assistance (CEMA), *see* CEMA
Criminal codes, 78; Yugoslav revisions in, 191
Croatia, 441
Cuba, 373, 440; missile crisis, 402, 405, 412, 418, 421, 428, 432, 444; Soviet military and technological assistance to, 413; and CEMA, 462; and China, 504–505
Cult of personality, 66, 181; *Borba* on, 186–187; Bulgarian party organ on, 201; and Czech party, 203, 203n; Togliatti on, 273; Gomulka on, 273. *See also* Twentieth Congress, CPSU
Cultural cooperation agreements, 108, 198, 470–471, 479; between bloc and China, 130

Cyrankiewicz, J., 11, 246, 254, 281n, 283n, 354, 364; and Poznan uprising, 248
Czechoslovak Communist Party (KSC), 19; membership, 19; and Poland, 54, 276–277; and Marshall Plan, 55; and controls, 87; purges, 93–95, 97, 137, 194; and proletarian internationalism, 276; -French Party declaration (January 1957), 277; and ideology, 295; and Gomulka, 363; Central Committee, 381; Eleventh Congress, 382. *See also* Novotny
Czechoslovakia, 5, 9, 15, 41, 46–47, 53, 79, 392, 438; postwar position, 18–19; nationalism, 19; nationalization, 19, 100n; Central Trade Union Council, 19; Communist Coup (1948), 19, 69, 75, 508; constitution, 31, 78–79; and Balkan Union, 57; -Polish Economic Collaboration Convention (1947), 57; Socialist Party, 85n; National Front, 85; state administration, 89n; Five-Year-Plan (1949–1953), 89, 164, 288; "White Legion Trials," 90; concentration camps, 91; collectivization, 99, 164; Gottwald Steel Plants, 101; 1952 industrial production, 101; and bilateral treaties, 109, 466; Soviet controls in, 115, 119, 121n; armed forces, 122; trade with USSR, 128, 288; and CEMA, 128, 382, 460; industrial management, 143; internal violence, 146; New Course, 163, 164–165; Pilsen riots (1953), 164; Khrushchev visit, 168; and Yugoslavia, 194, 196; and aftermath of Twentieth Congress, 203–204; Second Congress of Czechoslovak Writers, 204; industrialization (1956), 205; intellectuals, 205; Republics (1938, 1948), 205; exports, 287n, 288; industrial specialization, 288; industrial reorganization (1958), 382–383; and China, 384–386; and Sino-Soviet dispute, 436; economic reform (mid-sixties), 438; and Slovak nationalism, 441; and economic multilateralism, 450, 463; tourism, 480–481; Institute of International Politics and Economics, 506

Dahlem, F., 95; rehabilitation of, 205
Dairen, 131
Damba, D., 392
Danube Commission, 463–464. *See also* Multilateralism
Decentralization, 18; Yugoslav, 191, 356;

Hungarian, 215; Polish, 349–350, 355, 356

Dédijer, V., 55, 63n, 114, 188, 505n; condemns Soviet domestic policy, 190

Defense treaties, *see* Treaties, friendship and alliance

De Gaulle, General C., 44; concept of "European Europe," 447

Democratic centralism, 80–81; in economic affairs, 290

Democratic Party, Poland (SD), *see* Poland, Democratic Party

Democratization, 6, 26; and People's Democracy, 31; Party as mainspring of, 70; and Poland, 249, 251, 251n, 252–253, 274

Dmokhovski, M., 478n

Denisov, G. A., 476

De-Stalinization, 113, 260, 473; Khrushchev's condemnation speech, Twentieth CPSU Congress, 182; *Borba* article, 186–187; and Yugoslavia, 189–193; and anti-Stalinist axis, 193–198; and Titoism, 198–206; and internal cohesion of bloc, 206–209; and Gomulka, 264; and Sino-Soviet rift, 400; and new elites (mid-sixties), 434–442

Deviationism, 185; and Gomulka, 71–72, 75, 195, 239, 241; Yugoslav, 187; and Nagy, 217–218; Chinese view, 297

Dialectic, *see* Marxism-Leninism

Dichotomic view, 32, 44–45, 51, 267–268, 503–504, 511; and Mao Tse-tung, 130; and Tito, 185, 188, 317–318, 325, 510; Stalinist, 218, 283; and Nagy, 221, 231; and Gomulka, 264, 304; and 1957 Moscow declaration, 319; and new elites, 502. *See also* Marxism-Leninism

Dimitrov, G., 16, 58, 70, 93–94, 202, 500; on Soviet model, 27, 72, 73, 74; on People's Democracy, 26, 28n; and Polish Communists, 46, 48; and Balkan Union, 55–57; and nationalization of agriculture, 98; and Stalinism, 113

Disarmament, 315; and Chinese, 379

Djilas, M., 188, 313; condemns Soviet domestic policy, 190

Doctors' Plot, 95, 150. *See also* Anti-Semitism

Dogmatism, 319, 364, 414; and Polish Natolin faction, 249, 252, 254–255, 256, 259n–260n; and Yugoslavia, 284, 321; centralist, 291; and 1957 Moscow declaration, 304; Yugoslav view, 324–325; and Sino-Soviet rift, 399

Domesticism, 51–58, 136, 319, 336, 500; Polish, 53, 245, 263–268, 360; Yugoslva, 63–64, 176, 198–199, 209, 233, 237, 265 (*see also* Balkan Union); and anti-Tito Stalinists, 197; and Nagy, 265; in Rumania, 383, 447; and Sino-Soviet dispute, 434; and new elites, 439–441

Dubois, S., 111n

Dulles, A., 93

Duy Trinh, 416

Eastern Europe, Communist parties of, *see* Soviet bloc, Eastern Europe

East European Pact, *see* Warsaw Pact

East German Communist Party (SED): founding proclamation, 79–80; purges, 95–96, 97, 137; Second Party Conference (1952), 132n; Fifteenth Central Committee Plenum (1953), 160; and proletarian internationalism, 276; and ideology, 295; Fifth Congress, 332. *See also* Ulbricht, W.

East Germany (GDR), 132, 392, 419, 438; and Poland, 53–54; constitution, 79; National Front, 95; Five-Year Plan (1951–1955), 89; and friendship treaties, 108; and Soviet ambassadors, 119; Soviet secret police in, 121; economic exploitation of, 126; and CEMA, 128n, 460; industrial management, 143; New Course, 119, 159, 160–161, 164; East Berlin uprising, 160; and Yugoslavia, 194, 317–318; aftermath of Twentieth Congress of CPSU, 204–205; industrialization (1956), 205; and Soviet credits, 285, 389; exports, 287n; industrial specialization, 288; and revisionism, 312–313, 384; "Economic Tasks up to 1960," 382; industrial administrative reorganization (1958), 382–383; and China, 384–386; economic reform (mid-sixties), 438; and Sino-Soviet rift, 448; and economic multilateralism, 450, 463; Western recognition, 451; bilateral agreements, 467

East-West relations, 8, 81, 330; split, 134–135; détente (1955), 169; and Sino-Soviet affairs (1959), 378–379; détente of 1962–63, 402, 428; Chinese fear of Soviet-American alliance, 421, 424

Economic collaboration: interbloc, 57–58, 109–110, 450n; political significance of, 174–175; Khrushchev's view, 184, 451–452; erosion of organizations of, 433; regional, 451

"Economic Problems of Socialism in the USSR" (Stalin), 148, 150, 158, 371
Economic recovery programs, 7, 18; Polish, 10, 14; Bulgarian, 16
Economic relations, 454–455, 476–477, 497; and Soviet postwar objectives, 4–5; in Poland, 12–14, 247, 285, 382; and planning, 89, 148, 174, 446; and sabotage, 90; and bloc integration, 125, 127, 284–291; and exploitation of bloc, 125–129, 264n, 285–286, 388–389; and ruble as bloc currency, 128; and Stalinist legacy, 140, 142, 144; and "idealistic voluntarism," 142; capital-development policy, 157, 159–160, 168–170, 180; statistics on, 163n, 172; neo-Stalinism, 170; and ideology, 173–176, 278, 284–291; and Hungary, 216–217, 219, 285, 382; extension of Soviet credit to regimes, 285–286, 389–390; USSR-China compared, 372; East Germany, 382; Bulgaria, 382; in Rumania, 383–384; Soviet sanctions against China (1960), 409, 427, 433; internal Soviet, and Sino-Soviet rift, 425–426; and Soviet-Rumanian divergence, 443–446; Soviet dominance in, 477–478
EDC, see European Defense Community
Education: party controls on, 87; and commitment to USSR, 116; of young activists, 120, 148–149; of industrial management, 143, 143n–144n, 356; Polish, 346, 346n; and student exchange, 479
EEC, see European Common Market
Egypt, 231
Eisenhower, D. D., 376
Elections, postwar, 8; Polish, 11; in Bulgaria, 15, 16; Hungarian, 17, 18; Czech, 19; Yugoslav, 19; East German, 313
Elite, 141–142, 145, 433, 455, 503; proletarian, 3; and "collective leadership," 156; and 1955 East-West détente, 169; Czech, 205; Chinese revolutionary, 405; and Sino-Soviet dispute, 434–438, 448; new (mid-sixties), 439–441, 500, 501; parochialism of, 447; similarities among, 495; and formulation of ideology, 510–511
Ende, L., 95
Engels, F., 77
Erlich, H., 11n
Euro-Asian Community, Communist, 446
European Coal and Steel Community, 451
European Common Market (EEC), 433, 464

European Defense Community (EDC), 176
European Economic Commission, see European Common Market
Expansionism, 5. See also Territorial disputes

Fascism, 487
Fadeiev, A., 88
Fadeyev, N. V., 460–461, 461n
Farberov, N. P., 76
Farkas, M., 122, 213n, 216; condemnation of, 218; expelled from party, 227
Fechner, M., 54n; expelled from SED, 160n
Feigin, Colonel, 241
Fidelski, R., 174n–175n
Finland, 258, 419
"First Draft Theses Concerning the National and Colonial Question" (Lenin), 34
Fischer, R., 24n, 35n, 56n
Fisher-Galati, S., 86n
For a Lasting Peace, for a People's Democracy (Yudin), 70, 475
Foreign Affairs, 502
Foreign policy, 157, 198; during Malenkov leadership, 158; and Khrushchev, 168, 170, 180, 214; and Warsaw Pact, 174n; and ideology, 181, 189, 503–504; Yugoslav, 189, 329–330; and Nagy in Hungary, 218; at 1957 Moscow Conference, 298; issues in Sino-Soviet rift, 401–402, 420
Formosa, see Taiwan
France, 44; and 1955 Geneva Conference, 169; and China, 421. See also French Communist Party
Frantsov, G. P., 475
Free Europe Committee, 240
French Communist Party (PCF), 11n, 69; and ideology, 156n, 276, 295; and Stalinism, 200n; -Czech party declaration (1957), 277; and bilateralism, 295n; at Moscow conference of eighty-one Communist parties, 411. See also Thorez, M.
Friedrich, C. J., 157n
Friendship societies, 115, 471; Sino-Soviet, 132, 471
Frunze, M., 217n
"Fuehrerism," 141

Garthoff, R., 458
Gega, L., 387

Geneva Conference (1955), 169, 180, 267
Germany, 4–5; and Poland, 9; Communist Party of, 35n; reparations, 125–126. *See also* East Germany; West Germany
Gerö, E., 298n; on Rakosi and Nagy, 213n; as First Secretary, 225, 228; and the masses, 225; and Mikoyan, 225–226; and Rakosi's legacy, 226–227; Kremlin visit (1956), 227; and Tito, 233–234, 235n
Gheorghiu-Dej, G., 95, 300, 392, 408, 442, 447, 455, 503; and Stalin, 114, 146; and Rumanian New Course, 163; party post, 163n; and domesticism, 383; and establishment of leadership of, 443; death of, 446
Gittings, J., 413n
Goldhammer, B., 95
Gomulka, W., 10, 14, 29, 166, 317, 392, 448, 455, 503; agricultural policy, 12, 342; and Polish road to socialism, 26, 28, 51n, 62, 72–73, 281n, 293, 302; and Red Army presence, 27; on Marxist-Leninist character of PWP, 49; and domesticism, 53, 245, 263–268, 293–294; and Cominform, 61, 303; orientation of, 61n, 68; on personality cult, 66; deviation, 71–72, 75, 195, 239, 241, 246, 250, 251, 339; and party purges, 92, 96, 354; and autonomy, 96, 233, 264, 272–273, 304–305, 335, 343, 358, 359–366; and Stalinist legacy, 140; return to power, 202n, 210, 227, 256; Soviet acceptance of leadership of, 228, 231, 242, 262, 352, 359; and power, 248–252; and Seventh Plenum (1956), 249–254; and Natolin faction, 250, 293; and evolutionists, 250; and Polish-Soviet relations, 251n, 257, 260, 264, 292–293, 342; and the intellectuals, 254, 347–349, 351; domestic policies, 258, 260, 262, 263–265, 350–359; in October 1956 Politburo elections, 259; and October Revolution, 262–263, 338–344; and National Communism, 263–268; ideological views, 264, 273, 274, 339–340; and Khrushchev, 285, 293, 298, 435, 504; and Soviet economic pressure, 290; and the Church, 292, 344, 347, 348, 350–351, 352, 356–357, 360, 509; and neo-Stalinists, 292, 298, 359, 360; and Polish political prisoners in USSR, 293, 349; and proletarian internationalism, 292, 293; principles for building of socialism, 294, 340; at 1957 Moscow Conference, 302–303; and Tito, 314, 333–335;
and principle of Soviet leadership, 335 362, 364; on monolithically united working class, 340; and Workers Councils, 341–342; and revitalization of party, 351–355; as centrist, 352; and Ninth Plenum (1957), 353, 354; Tenth Plenum (October 1957), 353; Twelfth Plenum (1958), 359; denuclearization plan, 451; bilateral meetings, 474. *See* also Poland
Gottwald, K., 19, 29, 46, 61, 85, 392, 447; on national democracy, 27; and Stalin, 54, 114, 146; and Tito, 54; and Poland, 54; on Slansky, 94; and party purges, 94–95. *See also* Czechoslovakia
Gozdzik, L., 253n
Great Britain, *see* United Kingdom
Grechko, Marshal, 459, 476
Greece, 44, 57, 194; Soviet influence in, 449
Griffith, W. E., 387n, 420
Grosz, Archbishop J., 223
Grotewohl, O., 80, 160; and Oder-Neisse dispute, 109
Groza, P., 16
Guinea, 413

Hadzi-Vasilev, M., 321
Hajda, J., 86n
Haldex Corporation, 470. *See also* Joint Companies
Harich, W., 312–313
Herrnstadt, R., 95; expelled from SED, 160n
Higher Party School, 43
Hitler, A., 19, 490; -Stalin Pact, 46
Hochfield, J., 253
Ho Chi Minh, 386, 392
Holzman, F. P., 286n
Hong Kong, 418
Horthy, M., 15, 18
Horvath, M., 27
Hoxha, E., 163n, 204, 300, 313, 392, 455; anti-Yugoslav stand, 282, 387, 414; and 1961 Albanian party Congress, 415
Hungarian Communist Party, 15, 18, 188; and F. Nagy, 17; and intellectuals, 1; 216, 218, 222–223, 226; and People's Democracy, 27–28; party purges, 93, 137; 161, 194, 218, 226; and Stalinist legacy, 140, 212; factions (Nagy-Rakosi), 210; 215; membership, 212; Rakosi phase, 216–219; *apparat* and rank and file, 21; 227; and Gerö, 225–228; anti-revisionism, 381

Hungary, 5, 9, 29, 200, 210–238, 285, 369, 392, 508; postwar conditions in, 14, 17, 18; Smallholders (Peasant) Party, 17, 18; terrorism, 17–18, 91, 219; Soviet Republic, 17, 24; Leftist Bloc, 18; National Peasant Party, 18; nationalization, 18, 100n; intellectuals, 18, 216, 218, 222–223, 226; and Hungarian road, 29; constitution, 31, 78; Soviet postwar policy for, 46; and Rumania, 54; -Yugoslavia friendship treaty, 56n; and intrabloc economic collaboration, 57; and "socialist construction," 69; Socialist Party, 85n; People's Independent Front, 85; Five-Year-Plan (1950–1954), 89, 100n, 128n, 161; dependence on Soviet support, 93; Stalin Works, Dunapentele, 101; and bilateral treaties, 109, 466, 467–468; Soviet military advisers in, 123; reparations to USSR, 125, 126; joint companies, 126; trade with USSR, 127; and CEMA, 128, 460; industrial management, 143, 143n; domestic policy, 146; and collective leadership, 159; New Course, 159, 161–163, 167, 200, 211–213, 215–218, 219, 239; impact of Stalinism on, 161, 167, 200; and Yugoslavia, 194, 196, 197; level of industrialization (1956), 205; revolution, 206, 207, 210, 222–228, 387, 434, 437; and national Communism, 210, 219–222; national Councils, 215n; economic decentralization, 215; Rakosi phase, 216–219; secret police, 216, 219, 226, 228; and international affairs, 221; army, 226, 227, 229; Soviet occupation, 226, 449, 503; role of National Assembly, 227n; restoration of multiparty system, 230–231; and Warsaw Pact, 231; neutrality declared, 231; effect of revolution on Tito, 233–238, 285; and Poland, 262; and post-revolution ideology, 272; and Soviet credit, 285, 389; exports, 287n; Three-Year Plan (1958), 382; and Chinese, 384–386; and Sino-Soviet dispute, 436; de-Stalinization, 438–439; and Intermetall, 463; tourism, 480–481. *See also* Nagy, Imre

Iung Ch'i, 272; on refutation of CPSU leadership, 396

ICBM, *see* Nuclear power

Ideology, 5, 26; and intelligentsia, 7; and People's Democracy, 29–30, 72; postwar diversity, 41–52; and power, 64, 67, 103, 155–156, 211–216, 267–268, 485–512; and Stalinist uniformity, 67, 114, 136–137, 232; reassessment of (1947–1949), 69–70; and Soviet model, 71–77, 389–390; and Soviet control, 120–121; and China, 130, 299, 368, 371–373, 390; decline in importance of, 137, 447; and reality, 139–142; Khrushchev's view of unity in, 172–176, 184; and interstate relations, 180, 485–488; and institutional diversity, 182–183; and Hungary, 226; and Poland, 243–245; tolerable diversity in, 271; and political diversity, 272; 1956 interbloc dialogue, 272–279; economics and politics of unity in, 284–291; Yugoslav new framework for, 321–326; and antirevisionists, 380–384; and Sino-Soviet rift, 405–406, 422, 423–427, 433; and Chinese proposal for "second intermediate zone" in world affairs, 421–422; nationalization of, 434–442; revolutionary, 486–493, 507; and policy, 488–493; relativization, 508–511; erosion of, 511–512. *See also* Marxism-Leninism

Ignar, S., 345

Imperialism, 182; Mao Tse-tung quoted, 379

India, 376; and Sino-Soviet rift, 402, 421; Soviet military aid to, 429. *See also* Sino-Indian disputes

Indo-Chinese War, 166

Indonesia, 415; Soviet military aid to, 429; destruction of Communist Party of, 431

Industrialization, 3, 84, 104, 114, 287; in People's Democracies, 100–101; 163; capital investment for, 100n, 156–157, 180, 216–217, 382; in Poland, 101, 143, 144n, 205, 242, 247, 346, 361; political significance of, 102–103; and youth, 102, 104; and Stalinist exploitation, 127, 142, 143, 156; and Stalin's "testament," 148; and Khrushchev, 168–169, 180; Chinese, 171–172; Yugoslav, 190; and de-Stalinization, 200; statistics on, 211n–212n; Chinese, 370, 372; in 1959, 382; Rumanian, 383–384, 444

Industry: Polish, 12, 13–14, 349; investment in, 126, 158, 162, 168; East German, 160; Nagy on, 162; dependence on Soviet supplies, 175

Information Bureau, *see* Cominform

Intelligentsia (Intellectuals), 6–7, 61n, 207, 512; Polish, 9, 194–195, 242–245, 311–312, 338, 345n, 346–347, 348, 350, 357, 360, 362; Hungarian, 18, 216, 218, 222, 223,

226, 227; and friendship societies, 115; alienation of, 200, 204; Czech, 204, 381–382; East German, 205, 312–313; and Tito, 237, 335–336; Chinese, 279; and Marxism, 310; and antirevisionists, 381; and new elite, 439–441, 500
Interbloc relations, *see* Bilateralism; Multilateralism
Intermetall, 451, 463
International Bank of Economic Cooperation, 463–464. *See also* CEMA; Multilateralism
International Communism, 33, 36, 220; and Tito, 55–56, 315–320; and Gomulka, 62, 345; role of USSR, 130; Chinese relationship to, 130, 378–380; and de-Stalinization, 186; Belgrade declaration, 220; and Nagy's regime in Hungary, 220, 230; dialogue of 1956–1957, 272–279; Soviet hoped-for revival of interparty organization (1956), 290; effect of Sino-Soviet rift on, 397, 420; Chinese propose "second intermediate zone," 421; Twenty-one Conditions, 505
International Union of Students, 385n
Iorga, N., 439
Iran, 158
Italian Communist Party, 11n; at Conference of Eighty-one Communist parties, 411. *See also* Togliatti, P.
Italy, 44, 55, 69; Catholic-Communist dialogue (1966), 509
Ivanov, N. I., 127, 287n
Iwanska, A., 13n, 86n
Izvestia, 158, 167

Japan, 131, 421
Jaroszewicz, A., 197
Jedrychowski, S., 126n, 349n, 359
Jen-min Jih-pao, 272n, 279; critique of Yugoslav program (1957), 330; on U.S. decline in international affairs (1958), 374; on "Refutation of CPSU Leaders," 395; on Khrushchev's "Maligning" of Stalin, 398n; name-calling of Khrushchev, 418
Jews, 19; and party purges, 93, 95; Hungarian and Rumanian, 150; Polish, 250, 259n. *See also* Anti-Semitism
Johnson, A. R., 505n
Joint companies, 126–127, 167n, 171; and Mikoyan, 179; abolition of, 470
Joint Institute for Nuclear Research, 175, 464–465. *See also* Multilateralism

Kadar, J., 113n, 225, 228–229, 392, 408, 449; Kremlin visit (1956), 227; and Tito, 234–235, 235n, 313, 314, 318; socioeconomic policy, 266; and Khrushchev, 435; -Brezhnev meetings (1965), 474
Kaganovich, M., 179; and Polish October, 256; expulsion from CPSU Presidium, 296
Kallai, G., 225
Kardelj, E., 28n, 82, 179, 237, 316, 392, 427; on Yugoslav Revolution, 37; on Socialist roads, 38, 192; early view, 39; and Yugoslav road to socialism, 189; condemns Soviet domestic policy, 190, 315
Kennan, G., 157n
Khrushchev, N. S., 161; and de-Stalinization, 113, 195; on Malenkov's economic policy, 158; view of Communist camp, 168–176, 284n, 297; economic views, 168–170, 286; tandem with Bulganin, 169; foreign-policy views, 170; and Sino-Soviet relations, 171, 368, 369, 371, 434; visits Peking, 171, 371; anti-Jewish bias, 171, 245; on unity, 172, 270; and Yugoslavia, 176–180, 185–187, 193, 195, 233, 247, 329; tours Asia with Bulganin, 180; on interbloc relations, 181, 224, 473; at Twentieth CPSU Congress, 182–184, 408; and institutional diversity, 182–183; de-Stalinization speech, 186–187; and internal cohesion of bloc, 206–209, 367, 376; and Hungary, 214; and Polish October, 256, 259n; and Gomulka, 285, 293, 298, 435, 504; as centralist, 291, 291n; and peaceful coexistence policy, 300; consolidation of power of, 296–297, 314–315; -Tito meeting, Bucharest (1957), 315n, 316–318; domestic popularity (1957), 367; proposes "two-Chinas" formula (1959), 378; at Twenty-first Congress, 391; relationships with leaders of bloc parties, 391; view of international Communism, 397; and eighty-one party conference, 410–411; accuses Chinese of practicing *Lebensraum* theory, 419; "collective mobilization" scheme, 420, 435; fall, 424, 425, 435; Chinese criticism of, 424–425; on role of ideology in relations, 485
Kim Il-song, 392
Kiraly, General, 123n
Kladzko territorial dispute, 54. *See also* Territorial disputes

Kliszko, Z., 256, 353
Klosiewicz, W., 250, 352n
Kniazhinsky, V., 279n
Kolakowski, L., 310–312, 348
Kommunist (CPSU theoretical journal), 180–181, 326, 475
Konev, Marshal, 459
Kopecky, V., 46
Korbonski, S., 8n
Korean People's Democratic Republic, *see* North Korea
Korean War, 128, 129, 133, 135, 403, 405, 429; and industrial development in bloc, 142; armistice (July 27, 1953), 158, 166; and bloc armament industries, 460
Kosmet, 440
Kostov, T., 92, 94, 95, 185n; rehabilitation of, 201
Kotyk, V., 436, 506–507, 508
Kosygin, A., 426n, 435, 467, 473–474
Kovacs, B., 85n, 229; amnesty, 223
Kovacs, I., 198
Kreykemeyer, W., 95
KSC, *see* Czechoslovak Communist Party
Kulaks, 143, 165; Hungarian, 216, 218, 223; Polish, 247; Soviet, 426
Kum-chol, 416
Kun, B., 17; rehabilitation of, 222
Kuusinen, O., 407; and draft for eighty-one party conference, 410

Labor, 190; forced, 90–91; industrial, 102–103; division of, and CEMA, 174; role of, and socialist construction, 341
Ladakh, 373
Lalin, General, 120
Land reform, 7, 12–13, 16–17, 20, 25; in Hungary, 24; and size of holdings, 98
Lange, O., 11; on Polish economic decentralization, 349–350
Laos, 386; Soviet assistance to, 413
Lapot, S., 352n
Lasswell, H., 443
Latin America, 380, 411
Law, 456; Polish, 78; and regulation of labor, 102–103, 144. *See also* Criminal code; Socialist legality
League of Communists of Yugoslavia, 191, 207; and Tito, 19–20; July 1948 party Congress, 188; and People's Front of Yugoslavia, 191; and Workers' Councils, 191; and revisionism, 323; and Sino-Soviet breach, 415. *See also* Yugoslavia
Lebedev, V. Z., 119

Lechowicz, W., 197
"Left-Wing Communism — An Infantile Disorder (Lenin), 50
"Legal Problems of the Constitution of the Polish People's Republic, The," 74
Lenart, 447
Lenin, V. I., 71, 508–509; on revolutionary tactics, 3; on historical framework, 22; on dictatorship of proletariat in transition to Communism, 24, 33; and nationalism, 33–34; *Imperialism*, 487. *See also* Marxism-Leninism
Leningrad affair, 91
Lipset, S. M., 11n
Literacy, 486
Lithuanian Communist Party, 25n
Li Hsien-nien, 416
Liu Shao-ch'i, 370, 392; at conference of eighty-one Communist parties, 411n; and Communist unity, 412
Loebl, E., 94
"Long Live Leninism," 379
Longo, L., 412; and Catholic Communist dialogue (1966), 509
Lowenthal, R., 453
Luca, V., 95, 442; and Gheorghiu-Dej's "patriotic" line, 443
Lukacs, G., 28n
Lukacsi, S., 223
Lu Ting-yi, 309, 379
Luxembourg, R., 53
Lvov, 440

Macao, 418
Macedonia, 440
Machajski, W., 444n
Malaya, 415
Malenkov, G., 60, 161, 241–242; at Moscow Conference (May 1954), 117n–118n; on Korean War, 135; on USSR-bloc relations, 138; succession to leadership, 157–158; and economic innovation, 158; and New Course, 159–168, 217–218; policy outlook (1954), 168–169; ouster (1955), 216, 217, 296, 435n
Maleter, General P., 231; execution of, 333n
Manchuria, 388
Maniu, I., 85n
Mao Tse-tung, 25, 301–302, 307, 317, 371, 372, 377, 392, 411n; concept of revolution, 130, 430, 432; on neutrality, 131; "Contradictions within a Socialist Society," 297; on superiority of socialist

forces, 299, 319; "Hundred flowers" speech, 309, 336–337; anti-American feelings, 319; and Ho Chi Minh, 386; on territorial disputes, 419; on Sino-Soviet reconciliation, 430
Marczewski, J., 101n
Marosan, G., 225, 229, 235n; appeals for Soviet military aid, 228
Marshall Plan, 55, 58; and formation of CEMA, 128, 460
Marxism-Leninism, 189, 248, 295, 509; historical view, 3–4, 67–68, 76, 103, 181, 190, 489, 505n; postwar doctrinal problems, 22–25; dictatorship of the proletariat, 23, 35, 38, 75, 76, 81, 84–91, 132, 188, 237, 272, 280, 400, 489; and People's Republics, 26–27, 71–77; dichotomic view, 32, 44–45, 51, 130, 188; and Gomulka, 49n, 339; class struggle, 67–68, 75, 84, 104, 188, 272, 400; and reality, 68–69; and Soviet primary, 71, 75, 88, 188, 237; "individual characteristics," 76; universality of, 77; decline in importance of, 82; fiscal arrangements, 89–90; and industrialization, 103; base and superstructure, 105–106, 137, 150; and treaties of friendship, 109; and China, 132, 133, 172, 283–284, 509; and Stalin's "testament," 148–149; and Yugoslavia, 177, 190–191, 207, 284, 320, 332; and foreign policy, 181; and Twentieth CPSU Congress, 203; and locally characteristic socialism, 220; and Polish youth, 244; and Peking declaration (April 11, 1957), 283n; and revisionism, 310, 323–324, 336; and de-Stalinization, 367; and Sino-Soviet split, 369–370, 399, 419–420, 497; and recent sociological research, 480; philosophical aspect of, 489; and interstate relations (Czech view), 506–507; relativization of, 508–512. *See also* Ideology
Maslenikov, V., 293
Matwin, W., 273n
Mazur, F., 119, 252, 352n, 360n
Mechanization, 98
Mendershausen, H., 286n
Mensheviks, 426, 509
Merker, P., 95; rehabilitation of, 205
Middle East, 317, 330
Mihailovic, General D., 20
Mijal, K., 352n
Mikolajczyk, S., 10, 11–12, 13, 85n; and Polish Peasant Party (PSL), 345n
Mikoyan, A., 161, 231n; visits Peking, 171;

and Yugoslavia, 176, 179, 186; and Twentieth CPSU Congress, 182; on national peculiarities, 207; and Hungary, 224–225; Kremlin talks with Gerö and Kadar (1956), 227; and Hungarian revolution, 229, 231; and Polish October, 256
Milosz, C., 61n
Minc, B., 89n
Minc, H., 246, 254
Mindszenty, Cardinal, 223
Minorities, 198. *See also* Racism
Missiles, nuclear. *See* Nuclear power, Soviet
Moczar, S., 351
Molotov, V., 39n, 57, 180–181, 371, 476; policy outlook (1954), 168–169; and Yugoslav issue (1955), 176, 178–179, 178n, 492–493; and Polish October, 256; and political diversity of 1956, 291; expulsion from CPSU Presidium, 296
Mongolia, 131, 171, 386, 403, 419; Communist Party of, 408; and CEMA, 451, 460, 462n; and WTO, 457; bilateral agreements, 466
Moscow conference of eighty-one Communist parties (1960), 409, 410–412, 414, 455, 472, 506
Moscow conference of 1957, 290, 298, 303–304, 420, 472; declaration, 296–306; Soviet "neutrality" at, 307; and Tito, 317–320; Peace Manifesto, 319; and *World Marxist Review*, 475
Moscow conference (March 1965), 424, 455, 473
MLF (Multilateral Nuclear Force), 458
Morowski, J., 253, 353; and Yugoslavia, 334
Multilateralism, 108, 391, 446, 450, 456–466, 497–498, 500; and CEMA, 289, 457, 460, 462–463; and leadership conferences, 290, 296–308, 472, 499; and Gomulka, 294, 302, 304–305; and Tito, 318; and Sino-Soviet rift, 420, 422–424; and Warsaw Treaty Organization, 457; and Intermetall, 493. *See also* Bilateralism
Multilateral Nuclear Force, *see* MLF
MVD, 119, 121

Nagy, F., 18
Nagy, I., 28n, 113n, 162n, 194, 331, 383, 447, 449, 503; on State vis-à-vis Party, 105n; on Soviet intervention in political affairs, 117; on isolation of bloc parties, 123n–124n; on CEMA, 128n; on internal

effects of foreign policy, 135–136; on Stalinist legacy, 140, 142; on secret police, 140–141; and New Course, 161–162, 167, 211–213, 215; on too-rapid collectivization, 162; program of action, 162–163; rehabilitation of, 208n; ouster, 210, 218, 219, 222; and Rakosi, 210–215, 222, 224; opposition to policy of, 211, 215; and Soviet leadership, 214; and party *apparat*, 215; illness, 217; condemnation of, 218; *On Communism,* 219n; and National Communism, 220–222, 232; on peaceful coexistence, 221; supporters, 226n; reinstatement (1956), 227, 228; and Hungarian road to socialism, 228; and anti-Rakosi coalition, 230–231; indictment, 232n; and Tito, 237, 313; Polish support for, 262; and Chinese, 278; execution, 333–334, 335; revisionism, 335; and Warsaw Pact, 459. *See also* Hungary

Nasser, G. A., 436

Naszkowski, M., 262n

National Communism, 52, 58, 500; and Poland, 62, 239, 263–268; and Yugoslavia, 64, 176, 198–199, 209, 233–235, 237, 323, 328; and anti-Tito Stalinists, 197; and Hungary, 219–222, 232, 238; Soviet rejection of, 232; and 1957 Moscow declaration, 304

Nationalism, 18, 33–34, 36, 500; in Poland, 14, 343; Bulgarian, 15; Slovak, 19; national democracy, 27–29, 246–247; Yugoslav, 39; national front, 85; and Soviet primacy, 296; Chinese, 370, 375, 431; and Sino-Soviet rift, 404, 419; reemergence (mid-sixties), 439–441; Rumanian, 444; and Soviet military protection, 448–449; and commitment to Communist unity, 450; and ideology, 487–488, 507–508

Nationalization, industrial, 25, 32, 100, 104; Polish, 10, 13–14; Hungarian, 18; Czech, 19; Yugoslav, 20; patterns of, 100n; and trade unions, 102

"National liberation," 401–402, 422, 423; wars of, 34, 37, 379

National peculiarities, 207–208; and Marxism-Leninism, 220; and 1957 Moscow declaration, 303, 305; and revisionism, 309–313; Yugoslavia, 325; Khrushchev's view, 336; and Gomulka, 343, 359, 361

NATO (North Atlantic Treaty Organization), 326, 433; and West Germany, 108, 173

Naushki Station incident, 422n

Nazarkin, K. L., 462

Nazism, 23, 26, 46, 139; as revolutionary ideology, 487

Nehru, J., 235n

Neo-Stalinists, 310; Polish, 259–260; Loyalists, 380–388

Neues Deutschland (SED organ), 95–96, 276

New Course, 217, 263; East Germany, 119, 159, 160–161; and Malenkov, 159–168, 217–218; in Hungary, 161–163, 167, 200, 211–213, 215–218, 219; in Rumania, 163; in Bulgaria, 163; in Czechoslovakia, 163; in Poland, 165–166, 200

Niedzialkowski, M., 11n

1957 Moscow conference, *see* Moscow conference 1957

NKVD (People's Commissariat of Internal Affairs), 11n, 12, 52; and *apparats*, 119–121; and Polish Communist Party leadership, 290

Nobilibus, R. de, 495

North Atlantic Treaty Organization, *see* NATO

North Korea, 392, 415, 504; and CEMA, 128n, 462n; and China, 385, 540; and Soviet economic aid, 389; and Sino-Soviet rift, 408; and WTO, 457; bilateral agreements, 467

North Vietnam, 392, 415, 504; and CEMA, 128n, 462n; and Chinese antirevisionism, 385; and Soviet economic aid, 389; and Sino-Soviet rift, 408, 426, 435; American bombing of (1965), 428; and WTO, 457; and Joint Institute for Nuclear Research, 464–465

Novotny, A., 163n, 300, 392, 408, 448; critique of Stalinism, 203; on Polish October, 276; bilateral meetings, 474. *See also* Czechoslovakia Communist Party

Novy, V., 94

Nowa Kultura (Polish literary journal), 310–311, 355

Nowak, Z., 252, 292, 352; and 1961 Albanian Party Congress, 416

Nowe Drogi, 126n

Nuclear power, 299, 315, 376, 400, 501; Soviet, 298, 374, 376, 458; Chinese, 301n, 376, 422, 428; West Germany, 458, 501; and Joint Institute for Nuclear Research, 464–465

Ochab, E., 114n, 241, 257, 338, 408; be-

comes PWP First Secretary, 245–246; and Pulawska group, 250–251, 351; and factions within party, 252, 254; and Chinese, 254; and Soviet delegation to Warsaw (1956), 257–258; in October 1956 Politburo elections, 259, 261; and Yugoslavia, 334; and agricultural policy, 353
October Revolution, Boshevik. *See* Bolshevik Revolution
Oder-Neisse dispute, 9, 14, 284, 364, 365, 502; and SED, 53–54; and Soviet-Polish treaty, 108; for propaganda purposes, 124; and anti-Communist Poles (1956), 265; and Gomulka, 296–297, 334, 348
"Ode to Adults, An" (Wazyk), 243
Oelssner, F., 313
On Communism (Nagy), 219n
"On Friendship, Cooperation, and Mutual Aid," *see* Warsaw Treaty Organization
"On Friendship and Cooperation between the Soviet Union and other Socialist States," (Moscow, June 1956), 229–230; and withdrawal of Soviet troops, 230; and Yugoslavia, 233–238
"On Proletarian Internationalism" (Azizian), 275
Organization for International Railway Cooperation, 465–466. *See also* Multilateralism
Organization for Socialist Countries in Telecommunication and Posts, 465–466. *See also* Multilateralism

Pak Chon-ae, 392
Paris Commune, 421
Paris Peace Conference: (1960), 54, 378n, 380, 385–386, (of 1946), 463; treaty, 109, 466; failure of, 407, 408
Pasic, N., 326
Patrascanu, L., 92; execution of, 95, 159n
Pauker, A., 95, 442; and Khrushchev's anti-Jewish bias, 171; and Gheorghiu-Dej's "patriotic" line, 442
Peasantry, 6, 23, 509; Chinese, 3; Polish, 10, 11n, 342, 361; Rumanian, 17; and socialism in the countryside, 84, 98, 104, 142–143, 165; resentment toward collectivization, 98–99; alienation of, 99; Hungarian, 226. *See also* Kulaks
P'eng Chen, 407
P'eng Teh-huai, 174; dismissal of, 378
People's Democracy, 25–40, 262; Polish concept, 14, 339–340, 342–343; and coali-

tions, 28–29, 74; and USSR, 30–37, 45–51, 69, 76–77, 80–81; bilateral agreements, 108–112; administrative structure, 31, 80, 89; Yugoslav concept, 37–40; Albanian concept, 37; and domesticism, 52–53; reassessment of, 69–70; ideological base of, 71–77, 88; constitutions of, 78–83, 89; industrialization of, 84–85; and terror, 90–91; as political institution, 107; cultural cooperation agreements, 108; Soviet controls in, 118–119, 121, 144–145, 176; armed forces, 121–123; economic ties with USSR, 125–129, 388–389; and China, 130, 132; differences among, 137; and Stalin's "testament," 148; and Malenkov's New Course, 159–168, 263; and Khrushchev's economic policies, 169–170; and Khrushchev's political policies, 182–184; and Soviet-Yugoslav rapprochement, 194–195, 198; autonomy and stability, 235; and domestic policies, 263; and Soviet policy errors, 266–267; and revisionism, 309. *See also* Soviet bloc, Eastern Europe
People's Front of Yugoslavia, *see* League of Communists of Yugoslavia
Pervukhin, M., 286, 476
Peter, G., 197
Petofi Clubs, Hungary, 222, 224. *See also* Hungary, intellectuals
Petkov, N., 16, 73; execution, 85n
Pieck, W., 54n, 392
Pijade, M., 185n
Pilsudski, J., 122
Planning, 7, 142, 456; Stalin's view, 148; and industrial specialization, 286–288; Polish, 359; and CEMA, 461–462; and Rumania, 461; and bilateral trade agreements, 468–469; coordination, 469. *See also* Economic relations
Pluralism, 396, 499–500, 508. *See also* Centralism
Podgorny, N., 474
Poland, 5, 79, 369, 380, 392, 419
    ECONOMIC FACTORS, 12–14, 247, 285, 287–289, 355–356, 389; collectivization, 11, 99, 165, 242, 292, 342, 349, 358, 361; land reform, 12–13, 342; Marshall Plan, 55; -Czech Economic Collaboration Convention (1947), 57; and USSR, 125–126, 265, 285, 288; trade with USSR, 127–128, 287–289, 290; and CEMA, 128; New Course, 165–166, 167, 239–240, 242; Congress of Polish Economists

(1956), 247; cancellation of debts to USSR, 263; exports, 287n, 289; U.S. loans to, 288; isolation, 335; decentralization, 349–350, 355; Soviet credits, 389
ECONOMIC PLANNING, 359, 382; Three-Year Plan (1947), 14; Six-Year Plan (1950–1955), 89, (1959–1965), 359; Central Planning Commission, 349; Economic Council, 349, 355–356; State Planning Commission, 356; Economic Committee of Council of Ministers, 356
IDEOLOGY: and socialist construction, 69, 165, 273; disputes, 156n; isolation, and bilateralism, 274–275, 277, 280–281, 284, 292
INDUSTRIALIZATION, 12–14, 349; nationalization, 10, 13–14, 100n; Nowa Huta Steel Works, 101; 1952 production, 101; management, 143, 144n; 1956 production, 205
INTELLECTUALS, 9, 194–195, 242–245, 311–312, 338, 345n, 346–347, 350, 357, 360, 362; Academy of Science, 87n; clubs, 243, 347, 355
INTERBLOC RELATIONS, 53–54; Balkan Union, 56, 57; Czechoslovakia, 108; East Germany, 108; bilateral treaties, 108–109; and China, 130, 297, 322, 460; and Yugoslavia, 194–195, 197, 333–335; and Hungarian revolution, 227–229, 262, 273–274; Warsaw Pact, 239; and Hungary, 262–263; multilateral, 294, 302, 304–305, and Sino-Soviet rift, 435; bilateral relations, 450, 466–467; Intermetall, 463; tourism, 481
MILITARY FACTORS: Red Army in, 9–10, 12, 256, 261–262, 448; armed forces, 121–123, 248n, 255, 261, 339, 340; Warsaw Pact, 239; Home Army, 350
NATIONALISTIC FEATURES: nationalism, 14, 343; patriotism, 53, 262; national Communism, 62, 239, 263–268; domesticism, 62, 239, 263–268; National Front, 85, 349n, 358; primacy of domestic issues, 166, 242; Polish road to socialism, 244, 257, 273, 338–366; reforms, 247, 249–251, 253, 438; revisionism, 250, 276, 292, 310–312; and the Church, 292, 344, 347, 348, 350–352, 356–357; censorship, 350–351, 353–354, 355, 358; effect of Western policies and attitudes, 365–366
PARTIES AND ORGANIZATIONS: Communist Party, 10, 33, 46, 48, 62, 96–97, 113, 242, 247, 290; Socialist Party, 11, 33, 53, 85n; Peasant Party, 10, 12, 358n; Central

Trade Union Council, 246; workers' councils, 253, 341–342, 347, 348, 350, 356; Young Communist League, 253, 345; United Peasant Party (ZSL), 345; Democratic Party (SD), 345; Union of Democratic Youth, 347, 348, 354; ZBWiD (veterans' organization), 350, 355; Boy Scouts, 355; Workers' Self-Government Conference, 356. See also Polish Workers' Party
POLISH OCTOBER, 239–268; internal liberalization, 239–245, 350–351; and domesticism, 245–247; Soviet reaction to Polish road, 248–252; and reform, 252–253; and factionalism, 254–256; and Soviet intervention, 256–263; significance of, 265–268; post-revolution ideology, 272–279; post-upheaval political stalemate, 344–349; post-October economic changes, 349–351
POLITICAL FACTORS: terrorism, 9, 11, 12, 14, 90n, 91, 96, 240; People's Republic, 26, 75, 246; constitution, 31-32, 75, 78, 98; state administration, 89n; Warsaw uprisings, 194–195, 348; Poznan uprising, 207, 223, 234–235, 248, 338; Sejm, 246, 253, 292, 345, 349n, 355, 358; post-October stalemate, 344–349
POSTWAR CONDITIONS, 9–14, 18; anti-Communist resistance, 7, 9–10, 340; population, 9n, 89n, 346, 361; Committee of National Liberation, 10; Government-in-Exile, 10, 45; Soviet policy for, 45–46
AND USSR, 249, 251n, 257, 260, 329, 348, 363–365; Soviet Republic (1920), 24; controls in, 115, 119, 120–121; economic relationship, 125–126, 265, 285, 288; trade, 127–128; Stalinist programs, 146, 165, 200; Khrushchev visits, 168; Stalinism, 246, 249, 254, 262; Friendship society, 262; and Soviet primacy, 283; and principle of Soviet leadership, 292–298, 302
Polish United Workers' Party (PWP), 26, 28, 188, 253, 338; founded (1942), 10, 48–49; membership, 10–11, 242–243, 345; and nationalism, 36; First Congress, 61n; and Gomulka's deviation, 71–72, 96; purges, 95, 96, 97, 137; Eighth Plenum (1956), 96, 251n, 256–257, 259n, 273, 283, 344; Soviet penetration, 120–121; Third Plenum (1955), 140, 241; Ninth Plenum (1953), 165; internal conditions criticized, 240–241; "isola-

tion" of Politboro (1954), 241; and
cultural policy, 243, 355; Seventh
Plenum (1956), 249–254, 259n; Natolin
Faction (dogmatists), 249, 252, 254–256,
259n–26on, 292, 293, 351, 352, 359; revisionists (evolutionists), 250, 252, 309–
312, 352; and Polish-Soviet relations,
249, 251; demoralization of, 252; Sixth
Plenum (1956), 259n; status (1956),
264–265; Ninth Plenum (1957), 293,
343, 352, 353; revitalization of, and
Gomulka, 351–355; reduction of party
administration (1957), 352n; Tenth
Plenum (October 1957), 353, 354;
Twelfth Plenum (1958), 359, 361;
Third Congress (1959), 360, 361, 364;
at conference of eighty-one Commu-
nist parties, 411
Politics, modern, 486
Polityka (Polish theoretical journal), 334
Polycentrism, 209, 431. See also Cen-
tralists
Ponomarev, B., 310, 476; and draft for
eighty-one-party conference, 410
Ponomarenko, P. K., 176n
Popov, G. M., 119
Popovic, K., 209n, 282, 284n
Po Prostu, 252n, 253; closing of, 353–354
Popular Front, 49, 50; Soviet response to,
59
Port Arthur, 131; Soviet withdrawal
from, 171
Potsdam Conference, 9, 25, 32
Power: consolidation of Communist, 20–
21, 40, 52–53, 55, 58, 496; planned action for seizure of, 46–47; and ideology,
64, 67, 103, 155–156, 211–216, 267–268,
485–512; and Stalinism, 145, 155; and
succession crises, 156; and Gomulka,
248–252; and balance of world power,
299; and confederation of socialist
states, 307–308
Poznan uprising, 207, 234–235, 338; Yugoslav press on, 207n; effect in Hungary,
223; suppressed by Army, 248; Ochab
on, 257–258. See also Poland, political
factors
Prague Conference of Foreign Ministers
(1950), 111n
Pravda, 57, 114, 158, 167, 330; on repudiation of Malenkov line, 170; on CEMA,
175; on Soviet-Yugoslav rapprochement, 179–180; reports termination of
Hungarian-Yugoslav economic negotiations, 197; Shepilov article after Ma-

lenkov's replacement, 216–217; on Mos-
cow's support of Rakosi, 218; justifies
Soviet intervention in Hungary, 236;
on divisive tendencies within bloc, 248;
"On Proletarian Internationalism," 275;
refutation of Kolakowski, 312; and
Rumyantsev, 474; and Togliatti's "testament," 505
"Problems of Peace and Socialism," see
World Marxist Review
Press, Soviet, 44, 180; and Hungarian
revolution, 229; and Chinese People's
Communes, 371. See also Pravda
Proletariat, 206, 207; dictatorship of, 23,
35, 38, 73, 73n, 75–76, 81, 84, 85–91, 132,
188, 237, 272, 274, 280, 400, 489; and
industrialization, 102–103; Hungarian,
216, 226–
Proletarian internationalism, see Bilateral-
ism
Przeglad Kulturalny, 355
Purges, 15, 43, 87, 91–97, 120, 121, 150–
151, 155, 387, 442; Stalin's view of, 146
Puzak, K., 11n
Puzanov, A. M., 476

Quemoy-Matsu, 428

Rabotnichesko Delo (organ of Bulgarian
party), 94, 201, 202n
Racism, 423, 433
Radkiewicz, S., 120, 241; expulsion from
party, 354
Rajk, L., 92, 93, 94, 95, 185n, 197; rehabilitation of, 223, 227
Rakosi, M., 17, 46, 61, 70, 86n, 105n, 255,
392, 449, 500; on national road to socialism, 29; analysis of world affairs
(1945), 50; and party purges, 93, 140;
and collective leadership, 117n–118n,
163n; and Transylvania, 109; and Stalin,
113n, 113, 146; and Hungary's New
Course, 159, 161, 163, 216, 223; resigns
Premiership, 161–162; and Khrushchev's
anti-Jewish bias, 171; and Tito, 194, 196;
and Nagy, 210–215, 222, 224; and the
masses, 211; personal characteristics,
213, 222; castigation by Moscow, 214,
215; return to power (1955), 216–219;
and Moscow support, 218; and non-
Communist opposition, 218–219, 224;
and Stalinism, 223–224; on anti-Party
views, 224; resignation of, 225; fall of,
229
Rankovic, A., 93, 185n, 315, 316

Rapacki, A., 281n; "denuclearization plan," 365, 451, 458n
Reconstruction, postwar, 4, 496
Red Army, 17, 23, 24, 52, 122, 388; in Poland, 9–10, 12, 256, 261; and emergence of People's Democracy, 27, 37; postwar significance, 42–43; intervention in Hungary, 224, 228–232; in Rumania, 442; and military policy for bloc, 457
Reform, 4, 6, 8–9, 18, 61n, 452; and the peasantry, 7; in Poland, 12, 239–240, 247, 249–251, 253–254, 257, 342, 349; Bulgarian, 16; Economic, 161 (*see also* New Course); Yugoslav, 190; Hungarian, 223, 224. *See also* Land reform
Rehabilitation, 200; posthumous, 201; of Czech leaders, 203–204; in East Germany, 205; in Hungary, 222–223, 227; in Poland, 349
Reparations, 5, 497; and economic exploitation of bloc, 125; and East Germany, 160
Revai, J., 28n, 51n, 74, 211, 213n; on party's attitude toward People's Democracy, 30n; on working class hegemony, 74n; and Hungarian architects, 87
Revisionism, 309–337, 364, 367–368, 508; and Yugoslavia, 178, 284, 309–310, 313–329, 332, 384, 427; Polish, 250, 276, 292, 310–312, 384; and Leninism, 272; Chinese, 297, 298, 377, 378, 424–425; and Gomulka, 302, 352–354; and 1957 Moscow declaration, 304; noninstitutionalized, 309–311; seven cardinal sins of, 310, 510; East German, 312–313; institutional, 320–327; international overtones of, 320; bloc view (1958), 322; and Nagy, 335; Czech, 384; Bulgarian, 384; and Sino-Soviet rift, 399, 400, 426, 434; and local nationalism, 433; and erosion of ideology, 512
Road to socialism, 28–29, 37, 272; Rakosi on, 29; and People's Democracy, 76–77, 80–83, 132n; and China, 132, 371–374; in Soviet-Yugoslav declaration (June 1956), 154; and Soviet leadership, 206–207; multiple, and Yugoslav experience, 207–208; Hungarian, 228; Polish, 244, 257, 273, 305, 338–366; *Pravda* on, 248. *See also* Socialist construction
Roberts, H. L., 100n
Rokossovsky, Marshal K., 122, 123, 255, 259, 259n, 260, 261, 262
Roosevelt, F. D., 32
Rude Pravo (Czech party organ), 94; on

unreserved uniformity, 67; on bilateralism, 276–277
Rumania, 5, 9, 159n, 206, 392, 419, 500; postwar position, 14, 16–17, 18, 31; and Hungarian Communists, 54; -Yugoslavia friendship treaty, 56n; and Balkan Union, 56; proclaims People's Republic (1947), 69; constitution, 78; Socialist Party, 85n; People's Democratic Front, 85; Five-Year Plan (1951–1955), 89; Danube-Black Sea Canal project, 91; nationalization, 100n; bilateral treaties, 109, 466; friendship treaties, 115; reparations to USSR, 125, 126; joint companies, 126; trade with USSR, 128, 383; and CEMA, 128, 444–445, 447, 457, 460, 462, 463; and China, 130; and Stalinist programs, 146; New Course, 163; and Yugoslavia, 194, 204–205; and Twentieth Congress aftermath, 204, 205; economic credit to, 286n; exports, 287n; and ideology, 295; domesticism, 383, 447; during Hungarian revolution, 383; trade with West, 383; Six-Year Plan (1960), 383; and Sino-Soviet dispute, 435–436, 445, 446, 448; de-satellization of, 442–447; and autonomy, 449; and Bulgaria, 449–450; and bilateral relations, 450; armed forces, 454; and WTO, 459; and supranational planning, 461; and natural resources, 478; tourism, 481. *See also* Gheorghiu-Dej, G.
Rumanian Communist Party: purges, 95, 137, 442; membership, 383; November 1958 Plenum, 383; Congress of June 1960 (Bucharest), 407, 409, 414; and Sino-Soviet rift, 422; November 1961 Plenum, 442–443
Ruminski, B., 258–259, 259n, 359, 360
Rumyantsev, A. M., 303, 475
Russia (pre-Revolution), 3, 35. *See also* Soviet Union
Russification, cultural, 115–116

Sabotage, industrial, 90
Saburov, M. Z., 168n; and Soviet bloc credits, 286
Sanakov, S., 279n
Satellites, Soviet, *see* Soviet bloc, Eastern Europe
Schaff, A., 30n, 507–508; on undermining of Marxist ideology, 244; *Marxism and the Individual*, 507
Scherdewan, K., 313
Scinteia (Rumanian party newspaper), 16

Secession, 34–35
Secret police, 42, 91; as control, 118, 120,
    137, 155; Polish, 120, 240–241, 246, 338,
    340, 349, 355; Soviet, in bloc, 120–121;
    and subordination of party, 140; power
    of, under Stalin, 157n; post-Stalinist vi-
    olence, 159; Czech, restraints on, 204;
    Hungarian, 216, 219, 226, 228; weaken-
    ing of, 240
Sectarianism, 304, 323
Security, Soviet, 4–5; and secret police in
    bloc, 120–121; and bloc nuclear arrange-
    ments, 501
SED   (Sozialistiche   Einsheitsparti
    Deutschlands), see East German Com-
    munist Party
Self-determination, 34–35, 220, 442. See
    also Autonomy, local
Semenov, V. S., 119, 159
Sergeev, S. D., 469n
Serov, I., 120
Seton-Watson, H., 439n
Shehu, M., 387
Shelepin, A., 474
Shepilov, D., 114; and Yugoslav issue
    (1955), 179; on priority of industrial
    investment, 216–217, 242, 247; expulsion
    from CPSU Presidium, 296
"Short Course History of the CPSU"
    (Stalin), 72
Sikorski, General W., 46
Silesian basin, 57
Sinkiang, 131, 171, 376, 419. See also Ter-
    ritorial disputes
Sino-Indian disputes, 375; Soviet "neu-
    trality" toward, 378, 418, 421, 428
Sino-Soviet relations, 134, 367–432, 492,
    497, 499; Friendship, Alliance and Mu-
    tual Assistance Treaty (1950), 131, 427–
    432; trade, 131–132, 426n; treaty of 1945,
    131; Friendship Society (1949), 132;
    and diffusion of Soviet authority, 134;
    under Khrushchev, 171–172, 185, 368–
    369, 371, 376–377; and Warsaw Pact,
    174; and November 1957 Moscow Con-
    ference, 298–308; split, 368–380; and
    ideology, 369–370, 399, 419–420, 497,
    508; roots of rift, 369–380; "War and
    Peace" debates (1959–1960), 374–375,
    407; and Taiwan, 375; and Sino-Indian
    border dispute, 375, 378, 418, 421, 428;
    and Sinkiang dispute, 376; reaction of
    East European parties, 384–386; and
    Albanians, 387–388; effect of rift on
    bloc, 393, 432, 434–442, 497; historical

significance of rift, 397–398; issues and
    origins of rift, 398–406; party issues,
    399–401; foreign policy issues, 401–402;
    national (state) issues, 403–406; dy-
    namic escalation of rift, 406–427; open
    confrontation (June 1960), 407; and
    conference of eighty-one parties
    (1960), 409, 410–412, 414; and Soviet-
    Albanian break, 417; overt abuse in,
    418, 421–422; territorial disputes, 418–
    419; Soviet ideological response, 422–
    423; attempts to improve state relations,
    426; intensification with international
    crises, 428; future alternatives in, 430–
    432; and interstate relations, 433; and
    Rumania, 435–436, 445–446; and reentry
    of Yugoslavia into bloc, 436–437; and
    multilateralism, 465–466; and declara-
    tions of unity, 472; and party leader-
    ships' meetings, 472–473
Siroky, V., 164, 204
Skilling, H. G., 76n
Slansky, R., 46, 92, 94–95, 97, 185n; re-
    habilitation of, 204
Slonimski, A., 243n–244n
Slovakia, 19, 109; Soviet Republic, 24;
    Communist Party purges, 94; national-
    ism, 439, 441
Slovenia, 441
Sobolev, A., 74n, 76n
Socialism, 5, 23, 272; "withering away of
    state," 191–192; peaceful transition to,
    300
Socialist construction, 33, 44, 493n; and
    establishment of Cominform, 61, 68–69;
    and Soviet experience, 71, 182–183, 296,
    389–390, 492–493; and Gomulka, 71–72,
    73, 245, 257, 294, 340, 343, 351, 357; and
    People's Democracy's constitutions, 78;
    and Soviet state, 107; and Soviet am-
    bassadors, 118–119; and impoverishment
    of working class, 143; and Czech New
    Course, 164; and Khrushchev, 182–184;
    and Yugoslavia, 190–191; Suslov on,
    275; and Chinese, 280, 371; "general
    laws," 305n–306n; and simultaneous
    transition, 390; stages, according to So-
    viet theorists, 390–391
Socialist legality, 157; consolidation of,
    and Nagy, 162; and restraints on Czech
    secret police, 204; and East German
    intellectuals, 205
Socialist unity, see Unity of Socialist
    camp
Soviet Bloc, Eastern Europe: postwar ob-

jectives, 6–9, 20; consolidation of power, 8, 20, 86n, 90, 496; leadership, 20, 26, 29, 67–68, 85, 329–337; interstate relations, 20, 39, 103–104, 107–112, 182–184, 239, 283, 324–325, 328; Moscow support, 20, 30, 61, 83, 200; relations with USSR, 32–37, 76, 100, 104, 107–113, 145, 155, 181, 213, 221, 230, 236, 285; and nationalism, 33–34, 36; Sovietization, 41, 163; and Cominform, 61–64; view of class struggle, 67–68; membership, 85, 86, 92, 263; authority and control, 85–88, 456; secret police, 91–92; 456; purges, 91–97, 104; and role of state, 105n; friendship treaties, 108–110, 283n; diplomatic relations, 111, 468, 476; emotional commitment of, 115–116, 144; Soviet advisers in, 118–123, 144, 179, 230; and Chinese, 130, 266, 278–284, 298–308, 367, 385–386; Chinese status in, 130, 134, 137, 171, 266, 279n, 283, 367, 393; and West, *see* East-West relations; differences among, 136–137; characteristics of, 137–138, 391–393; Stalinist legacy, 140–147; and stability, 146, 209; and Soviet succession crises, 157–159, 391; effects of Twentieth Congress, 187; and Yugoslavia, 194–198, 208, 314; and Bandung conference, 220–221, 376; and dilemma of Hungarian revolution, 233–238; and Poland, 246; and Soviet policy errors, 266–267; and Soviet leadership, 272, 276, 280; dialogue (1956), 272–279; economic conditions (1956), 285; extension of Soviet credit to, 285n–286n, 389–390; economic dependence on USSR, 287, 448, 477–478, 483, 495; and industrial specialization, 287, 288, 444–445, 461; influence of Western culture on, 368; hierarchy of parties, 392; and Sino-Soviet rift, 393, 432, 434–442, 497; and laws of capitalist mutual relations, 433; desatellization, 434–442; emancipation and interdependence, 447–455; dependence on Soviet military protection, 448–449, 456; regional arrangements, 450-451; military conferences, 457, 476; multilateral meetings of leadership, 471–476; interpersonal contacts, 478–479; scholarly study of bloc development, 480; patterns of interstate relations, 494–502; nuclear status, 501. *See also* People's Democracy

Soviet model, 14, 23–25, 71–77, 381; and emergence of People's Republics, 26–

27; and establishment of Cominform, 58–64; and development of People's Democracy, 71–83; and GDR, 79–80; and arts and sciences, 87–88; and armed forces, 122; and Chinese, 132–134, 171, 384–385; doubt among bloc leaders, 144; and Yugoslavia, 187, 198–199

Soviet Union: postwar objectives, 4–9; incorporation plans, 5, 33, 81–82, 145; relations in bloc, 32–37, 76, 100, 104, 107–113, 145, 155, 181, 213, 221, 230, 236, 285, 472–473, 496–499; constitution (1936), 37; Sovietization of bloc, 41, 163; leadership, 41, 266–267, 272, 280; internal development, postwar, 41–45; secret police, 42, 91; army, 42–43, 173–174, 230–231, 421, 467 (*see also* Red Army); Marshall Plan, 55; domestic affairs of bloc, 69; leading role of, 70–73, 295 (*see also* CPSU, and Soviet primacy); occupation zone, 79; Military Administration, 79, 126; purges of 1936–1938, 93; show trials, 95; Doctors' Plot, 95, 150; emotional commitment of bloc to, 115–116, 144; economic exploitation of bloc, 125–129, 264n, 285–286; and CEMA, 128–129, 174–175, 460; domestic problems after death of Stalin, 156, 266; Council of Ministers, 157; and 1955 Geneva Conference, 169; rapprochement in Yugoslavia, 176–177, 193–197, 220, 295; relations with satellites, 178–180, 194; international stance, post-Stalin, 181–184; internal stability of 1955–1956, 195; and Rakosi-Nagy conflict, 217; intervention in Hungary (1956), 224, 228–232, 233, 235; liberalization in policy (1955), 245; and Poznan uprising, 248; intervention in Poland, 256–263; policy errors (1956), 266–267; extension of credit to bloc, 285n–286n, 389–390; nuclear power, 299, 367, 448–449, 456; technological assistance agreement with CPR (1957), 301, 376–377, 403, 409; post-1955 relations with Yugoslavia, 387; primacy of, and succession problem, 391; 1965 economic reform, 426–427; reduction of leverage of, 437–438, 495, 497; and Intermetall, 463; economic dominance of bloc, 477–478, 483; Academy of Science, 479; Institute of Economics of the World Socialist System, 480; tourism, 481; and bloc nuclear status, 501. *See also* Sino-Soviet relations

Spulber, N., 89n, 100n

Sputnik, 374, 410. See also Nuclear Power
Spychalski, M., 256, 351
Stajakovic, M., 199
Stalinism, 62–64, 67–138, 272, 306, 496–497; and Gomulka, 66, 342; and constitutions, 78; and Soviet model, 84–85, 144; and terror, 90n, 159; and purge trials, 96–97, 104, 120; "economic war communism," 103; as interstate system, 104–138, 166, 186; political superstructure, 104–107, 137; and priority of Soviet interests, 107, 266 (see also Dichotomic view); formal controls of bloc, 107–112, 137, 144, 156, 175; informal controls of bloc, 112–124, 137, 144; economic aspects, 125–129, 138, 142, 156, 164, 166, 179, 382; and trade, 127–128; and China, 129–134, 144–145; and the West, 134–135; and internal pressures, 134–138; Communist condemnation of legacy of, 139–147; and voluntarism, 142, 149; and Stalin's "testament," 147–151; and death of Stalin, 155–156; and post-Stalin ambivalence, 157, 180; and Malenkov's policies, 158–159; 166; 1955 evaluation of, and Yugoslav issue, 179; Khrushchev's view, 181–182; and Twentieth CPSU Congress, 182, 186; and Yugoslavia, 187, 200; domestic, 205; and Hungarian revolution, 233–234; and Polish uprising, 246, 249, 254, 262; 1956 search for replacement for, 272–279
Stalin, J. V., 4, 71, 166, 371, 456; postwar attitudes, 23, 24, 26, 30, 36, 58–59; on self-determination, 35; and Tito, 39n, 40, 55–56, 63–64, 176; Supreme Soviet campaign speech (1946), 44; and party purges, 96–97; and "socialist transformation" of USSR, 105; "Regarding Marxism in Linguistics," 106, charisma of, 112–113, 137, 144; death of, 143, 150, 155; political "testament," 147–151, 157; Istvan Kovacs on, 198; and Sino-Soviet rift, 400; and ideology, 490–492
Standard of Living, 143; under Malenkov, 158; in East Germany, 160; and Nagy, 162; Czech, 164, 204; and Polish, 165, 247, 251, 355, 361; and Khrushchev, 170, 367, 400; gap between East and West, 502
Starewicz, A., 259n, 262n
State, 334; budget, 78, 89, 237; institutions, decline in importance of, 88–89, 191–192, 372; role of, 105–107
Stern, C., 86n

Stevenson, A., 493
Stoica, C., 392
Stoll, L., 382
Students, 87; demonstrations, 204; Hungarian, 226; Polish, 338. See also Universities
Sun Yat-sen, 131
Suslov, M. A., 148n, 387, 474; at Twentieth Congress, CPSU, 182, 207, 291; and condemnation of Nagy, 218; meeting with Kadar and Gero (1956), 227; and Hungarian revolution, 229, 231; on socialist construction, 275, 278, 294, 305n, 437; on CCP leadership, 368; and draft for eighty-one-party conference, 410; report on Communist unity (1964), 422–423; on Soviet aid to China, 429
Sverma, J., 46
Swiatlo, Colonel J., 113n, 120; defection to West, 240
Szabad Nep (Hungarian party daily), 224
Szafer, W., 89n
Szczecin, 440
Szczepanski, J., 147n
Szlai, B., 478n
Szyr, E., 356, 359, 360

Taiwan, 129, 133, 373, 375; and Khrushchev's "two-Chinas" formula, 378
Tarantova, L., 185n
Taxation, 99; turnover tax, 89; and dictatorship of proletariat, 90; in East Germany, 159; in Hungary, 163; Czech, 164; in Poland, 165
Technology, 288; exchange, 469–470; -scientific agreements, 479
Teheran agreement, 32
Territorial disputes, 403–404, 418–419; possible future intensification of, 430; and relations among Communist states, 433, 440, 501; and Rumanian self-assertion, 446
Terror, 104; Poland, 9, 11, 12, 14, 90n, 96; in Bulgaria, 15–16; Hungary, 17–18; as public policy, 90–91; and concentration camps, 90–91; Stalinist, 90n, 159
Teschen, see Cieszyn territorial dispute
Test-ban agreement, 376; as issue in Sino-Soviet rift, 402; Treaty of 1963, 418, 421–422, 424
Thorez, M., 200n, 276; at conference of eighty-one Communist parties (1960), 412
Tibet, 375
Tildy, Z., 229, 231

Titoism, 52, 63–64, 82, 187, 210, 233, 426; and purges, 92; and East European regimes, 194, 199; and Soviet-Yugoslav agreement (1955), 154, 195, 197, 207, 210; and new norms for interstate relations (1956), 198–206; and Bulgarian Party, 201; and internal cohesion of bloc, 206–209, 235; and "capitalist aid," 236

Tito, J. B., 19, 20, 25, 260; and Comintern, 38, 63–64, 68; and Stalin, 39n, 40, 55–56, 63–64, 114, 176; and National Liberation Committee of Yugoslavia, 48; and international Communism, 55–56, 315; domesticism, 55–57; and national Communism, 64, 176, 198–199, 209, 233, 237, 265; expulsion from Cominform, 109 (*see also* Yugoslavia and Cominform); Politburo opposition to, 119; and Khrushchev, 176–180, 186, 193, 233–235, 237, 247, 436; as "capitalist imperialist," 185; and Yugoslav road to socialism, 188–189; bloc fear of Soviet rapprochement with, 194–198; and nonaffiliation with any bloc, 195, 208, 221, 315; September 1956 meetings with Khrushchev, 208; and heterogeneous leadership, 209; and Gero, 226, 227–228; effect of Hungarian revolution on, 233–238, 284–285, 313, 314, 332; and Kadar, 234–235, 235n, 315, 318; and Poznan uprising, 248; and Chinese, 281; and expendability of the camp, 302; -Khrushchev meeting, Bucharest (1957), 315n, 316–318; status in bloc (1957), 317; Chinese attacks (1958), 387; bilateral meetings, 474. *See also* Yugoslavia

Togliatti, P., 248; on personality cult, 273; and conference of eighty-one Communist parties, 411n; "testament," 505

Tonkin Bay, 425

Torré, S., 436

Tourism, *see* Travel

Trade, 127–128, 158; and CEMA, 128–129, 468; Sino-Soviet, 131–132, 426n, 477; Soviet-Yugoslav, 177, 194; agreements, 198, 288, 468–469, 497; Soviet-Polish, 288–289; Soviet-Czech, 453; Soviet-East German, 453; decline of Soviet domination in, 468; Albanian, 477

Trade unions, 102; Polish, 246, 348

Trainin, I. P., 30n

Transylvania, 16, 54, 383, 440, 446

Travel: restrictions on, 124, 198, 350; by party leaderships, 473–474; upsurge in

bloc tourism, 479, 480–481; Western tourism, 481; statistics on, 481n–482n

Treaties, friendship and alliance, 36, 137, 497, 498; and Tito, 56; bilateral, 108–109, 282–284, 289, 466–467, 497; anti-German orientation, 108–109; timing, 109; pattern, 109–112; Warsaw Pact, 173–174; 1957 Sino-Soviet technical assistance treaty, 301, 376–377, 403, 409; and wartime allies, 466; and stationing of Soviet troops, 467. *See also* Alliance system

Treaty of Friendship, Cooperation, and Mutual Assistance, 457. *See also* Warsaw Treaty Organization

Trieste dispute, 55, 122

Tru 'o'ng Chinh, 392

Trybuna Ludu, 124, 353

Tsedenbal, U., 386, 392, 474. *See also* Mongolia

Tulpanov, Colonel, 79

Turkey, 158; Soviet influence in, 449

Tvorba (Czech party weekly), 290

Twentieth Congress CPSU, 175, 180–186, 222, 238, 283, 381, 414; Khrushchev's de-Stalinization speech, 181, 407; and institutional diversity, 181–182; and Yugoslavia, 185–186, 193, 194, 200; aftermath, 198–206, 210; and ideological premises of Polish regime, 245, 247; and peaceful transition thesis, 300, 315. *See also* De-Stalinization

Tzankov, G., 121

Ulam, A., 188

Ulbricht, W., 79, 86n, 160, 300, 313, 392, 408; and party purges, 95–96; and Stalinism, 113, 205, 247; in East German system, 132n; party post, 162n; on Soviet infallibility, 381; seventieth-birthday celebration, 472

Union of Czechoslovak Writers, 382

Union of Polish Patriots, Moscow, 46

United Kingdom, 8, 23, 421; and Geneva Conference (1955), 169. *See also* Anglo-American relations

United Nations, 145; Security Council, 234; and withdrawal of Soviet troops from Hungary, 234

United Peasant Party, Poland (ZSL), *see* Poland United Peasant Party

United Polish Workers' Party, *see* Polish Workers' Party (PWP)

United States, 7, 8, 23, 136n, 300; and Korean War, 135, 405; and Geneva Conference (1955), 169; aid to Yugoslavia, 188; and development of Soviet nuclear capability, 299; recession of 1958, 374; and Chinese Nationalists, 375; and France, 377; per capita production, 391; and space race, 413; and weapons technology, 413; and Bay of Pigs, 413

Unity of the socialist camp, 208–209; Yugoslav view, 39, 314–320; and Cominform, 59–64; and People's Democracy, 80–81; and Khrushchev, 173, 206–209, 367, 376; and Soviet domestic development, 181; and Soviet interests, 219; and Poznan uprising, 249; and Gomulka, 257, 296–297; and CPSU policy errors, 266–267; and Chinese, 271, 279, 283–285, 296–298, 301; 1956–1957 dialogue, 272–279; economics and politics of, 284–291; and Gomulka's Gdansk speech, 335; and principle of Soviet leadership, 335; and Sino-Soviet rift, 407, 433; and emancipation of bloc, 447–455; economic framework for, 451–453, 499, 500; formal institutions of, 456–471; informal institutions of, 471–484; and ideology, 493–496

Universal Postal Union, 46

Universities, 87; Polish, 350, 358; and interpersonal contacts of bloc, 479. See also Education

Urbanization, 102, 205, 206

USSR, see Soviet Union

U-2 crisis, 407, 408, 428

Vali, F., 123n

Varga, Y. S., 30n, 31, 32, 44n

Vietnam, 386; as issue in Sino-Soviet rift, 402. See also North Vietnam

Viner, J., 452

Vishinsky, A., 16

Voprosy istorii, 295

Voroshilov, K., 215, 283n, 365n

Voznesensky, N. A., 91, 148n; execution of, 150

Wander, P., 385n

War: inevitability of, 7–8, 182, 300, 379, 400; of national liberation, 34, 37, 379; Stalin's view of, 84, 149; threat of total, 135; Khrushchev's view, 169n; nuclear, 299–300; Mao quoted on, 379; as issue in Sino-Soviet split, 400

Warsaw Conference of Foreign Ministers (1948), 111n

Warsaw Treaty Organization (WTO),

467, 499; Pact, 173, 230, 231n, 326, 433, 498; Political Consultive Committee, 174n, 457–458; political significance of, 174, 458; Hungarian withdrawal, 231, 239; and Poland, 239, 263, 365; meeting of February 1960, 385; and Yugoslavia, 437; and Rumania, 466, 447; as common political organ of bloc, 453–454, 457; compared to NATO, 457; and military policy for bloc, 457–459; early membership, 457; Committee for Foreign Policy, 458; juridical basis, 458; as forum, 458–459; United Command, 459; and multilateral meetings of leaders, 472; as "Commonwealth Politburo," 500–501

Warsaw uprisings, see Poland, political factors

Wazyk, A., 243

Weiterer, M., 95

Werblan, A., 361n

Western powers, 11, 23; and USSR, wartime alliances, 26; and Soviet hegemony in East Europe, 41; and Yugoslavia, 185, 188, 315, 318; and future bloc policy, 502

West Germany, 79, 97, 101, 448, 453; and NATO, 108, 173; remilitarization, 173; Social Democratic Party (SPD), 313; and China, 421; and nuclear weapons, 458, 501

Wiatr, J., 349n

Williams, D. L., 456n

Williams, P., 111n

Wollweber, E., 313

Workers, 6, 7; Yugoslav, 190–191; alienation of, 200, 211–212; Polish, 244, 249, 253, 338, 346–347

World Congress in Defense of Peace (1948), 88

World Federation of Trade Unions (WFTU), 407

World Marxist Review, 303, 475–476; 1961 conference of sociologists, 480

Writers, 223; Polish, 243; Congress of Soviet (1936), 244n

Wroclaw, 440

Wszelaki, J., 286n

Wyszynski, S., Cardinal, 159n, 250, 448n

Xoxe, K., 204; liquidation of, 387

Yalta Agreements, 10, 25, 32, 44

Yezhov, N., 91

Youth, 87; effects of industrialization on,

102, 104; and commitment to USSR, 116; Hungarian, 223; Polish, 240, 252, 292, 345, 347, 360, 360n–361n
Yu Chao-li, 379
Yudin, P. F., 70, 71, 72, 73; defines People's Democracy, 74
Yugoslavia, 3, 5, 9, 71, 79, 82, 247, 292, 380, 497, 503, 510; postwar position, 7; Fatherland Front (1945), 25; constitution, 32, 37, 38 (1953), 191; Communist take-over, 37–38; ideological orthodoxy, 38–40, 60, 63, 188, 192–193, 207, 281, 327; and nationalism, 39; Soviet postwar policy for, 46; castigated by Moscow, 57, 75; and Cominform, 59, 63–64, 68, 109, 177–178, 187, 196, 199, 232, 330–332, 336; and national Communism, 64, 176, 198–199, 232; abrogation of treaties with USSR, 109; and Paris treaty, 109; Soviet ambassadors in, 119; armed forces, 121, 122; -USSR economic relationship, 126; *White Book*, 127; and CEMA, 129, 462; and China, compared, 130, 133; and Malenkov, 158, 176; Khrushchev's policy for, 176–180; and EDC, 176; rapprochement with USSR (1956), 176–177, 192–198, 315; Marxism-Leninism, 177, 190–191, 207, 284, 328; and revisionism, 178, 284, 309, 310, 313–320, 327–337, 384; and Khrushchev, 183, 185–187, 193, 195; and autonomy, 185, 195, 232; and Twentieth CPSU Congress, 185, 186; and Western support, 185, 188, 236, 316, 318, 363; road to socialism, 187–193; as dictatorship of proletariat, 188; neutralism, 189, 208, 319, 332; and international affairs, 189; economic boycott, 189, 190; Workers' Councils, 190–192, 316, 321–322; reforms, 190–191; terror, 192; normalization of relations in USSR, 194, 295, 297, 329; and Stalinism, 187, 200–206; Socialist Alliance of, 199; and Rumania,

204–205; status in bloc, 266, 327–328; and China, 281, 329–333; and dogmatism, 284; Soviet economic credit, 285n, 331; political orientation (1957), 314–315; and East Germany, 317, 318; and 1957 Moscow declaration, 317–319; and new ideological framework, 321–326; and state capitalism, 334; and Albania, 386–387, 415; post-1955 relations with USSR, 387, 405, 434, 449; and Sino-Soviet rift, 436–437; tourism, 481. *See also* League of Communists of Yugoslavia
Yugov, A., 201, 202
Yur'yev, I. G., 386n

Zauberman, A., 452
Zagoria, D. S., 428n
Zaisser, W., 95; expelled from SED, 160n
Zaleski, W., 11n
Zambrowski, R., 11n, 245, 259n, 354; and Pulawska group, 250–251, 351; in October 1956 Politburo elections, 259, 261
Zawadzki, A., 258, 261, 359, 364
Zhdanov, A., 45, 51, 55, 69; on relations among bloc parties, 59–60, 62; death of, 92; and Slansky, 94; and socialist realism, 244n
Zhivkov, T., 201–202, 208n, 392, 408, 436, 437, 449; and Bulgarian military conspiracy (April 1965), 441; bilateral meetings, 474
Zhujovich, S., 114n
Zhukov, Marshal G., 43, 261n; -Bulganin visit to Poland (1956), 248
Zimyanin, M. V., 476
Zinoviev, G., 35n
ZMP, *see* Poland Young Communists League
Zorin, V., 119
Zycie gospodarcze (Polish economic journal), 356

Russian Research Center Studies

1. *Public Opinion in Soviet Russia: A Study in Mass Persuasion*, by Alex Inkeles
2. *Soviet Politics — The Dilemma of Power: The Role of Ideas in Social Change*, by Barrington Moore, Jr.*
3. *Justice in the U.S.S.R.: An Interpretation of Soviet Law*, by Harold J. Berman. Revised edition, enlarged
4. *Chinese Communism and the Rise of Mao*, by Benjamin I. Schwartz
5. *Titoism and the Cominform*, by Adam B. Ulam*
6. *A Documentary History of Chinese Communism*, by Conrad Brandt, Benjamin Schwartz, and John K. Fairbank*
7. *The New Man in Soviet Psychology*, by Raymond A. Bauer
8. *Soviet Opposition to Stalin: A Case Study in World War II*, by George Fischer*
9. *Minerals: A Key to Soviet Power*, by Demitri B. Shimkin*
10. *Soviet Law in Action: The Recollected Cases of a Soviet Lawyer*, by Harold J. Berman and Boris A. Konstantinovsky*
11. *How Russia is Ruled*, by Merle Fainsod. Revised edition
12. *Terror and Progress USSR: Some Sources of Change and Stability in the Soviet Dictatorship*, by Barrington Moore, Jr.
13. *The Formation of the Soviet Union: Communism and Nationalism, 1917–1923*, by Richard Pipes. Revised edition
14. *Marxism: The Unity of Theory and Practice: A Critical Essay*, by Alfred G. Meyer
15. *Soviet Industrial Production, 1928–1951*, by Donald R. Hodgman
16. *Soviet Taxation: The Fiscal and Monetary Problems of a Planned Economy*, by Franklyn D. Holzman
17. *Soviet Military Law and Administration*, by Harold J. Berman and Miroslav Kerner*
18. *Documents on Soviet Military Law and Administration*, edited and translated by Harold J. Berman and Miroslav Kerner
19. *The Russian Marxists and the Origins of Bolshevism*, by Leopold H. Haimson
20. *The Permanent Purge: Politics in Soviet Totalitarianism*, by Zbigniew K. Brzezinski*
21. *Belorussia: The Making of a Nation: A Case Study*, by Nicholas P. Vakar
22. *A Bibliographical Guide to Belorussia*, by Nicholas P. Vakar*
23. *The Balkans in Our Time*, by Robert Lee Wolff
24. *How the Soviet System Works: Cultural, Psychological, and Social Themes*, by Raymond A. Bauer, Alex Inkeles, and Clyde Kluckhohn†
25. *The Economics of Soviet Steel*, by M. Gardner Clark*
26. *Leninism*, by Alfred G. Meyer*
27. *Factory and Manager in the USSR*, by Joseph S. Berliner†
28. *Soviet Transportation Policy*, by Holland Hunter
29. *Doctor and Patient in Soviet Russia*, by Mark G. Field †
30. *Russian Liberalism: From Gentry to Intelligentsia*, by George Fischer
31. *Stalin's Failure in China, 1924–1927*, by Conrad Brandt
32. *The Communist Party of Poland: An Outline of History*, by M. K. Dziewanowski
33. *Karamzin's Memoir on Ancient and Modern Russia: A Translation and Analysis*, translated by Richard Pipes
34. *A Memoir on Ancient and Modern Russia*, by N. M. Karamzin, the Russian text edited by Richard Pipes*
35. *The Soviet Citizen: Daily Life in a Totalitarian Society*, by Alex Inkeles and Raymond A. Bauer†

36. *Pan-Turkism and Islam in Russia*, by Serge A. Zenkovsky
37. *The Soviet Bloc: Unity and Conflict*, by Zbigniew K. Brzezinski.‡ Revised and enlarged edition
38. *National Consciousness in Eighteenth-Century Russia*, by Hans Rogger
39. *Alexander Herzen and the Birth of Russian Socialism, 1812–1855*, by Martin Malia
40. *The Conscience of the Revolution: Communist Opposition in Soviet Russia*, by Robert V. Daniels
41. *The Soviet Industrialization Debate, 1924–1928*, by Alexander Erlich
42. *The Third Section: Police and Society in Russia under Nicholas I*, by Sidney Monas
43. *Dilemmas of Progress in Tsarist Russia: Legal Marxism and Legal Populism*, by Arthur P. Mendel
44. *Political Control of Literature in the USSR, 1946–1959*, by Harold Swayze
45. *Accounting in Soviet Planning and Management*, by Robert W. Campbell
46. *Social Democracy and the St. Petersburg Labor Movement, 1885–1897*, by Richard Pipes
47. *The New Face of Soviet Totalitarianism*, by Adam B. Ulman
48. *Stalin's Foreign Policy Reappraised*, by Marshall D. Shulman
49. *The Soviet Youth Program: Regimentation and Rebellion*, by Allen Kassof
50. *Soviet Criminal Law and Procedure: The RSFSR Codes*, translated by Harold J. Berman and James W. Spindler; introduction and analysis by Harold J. Berman
51. *Poland's Politics: Idealism vs. Realism*, by Adam Bromke
52. *Managerial Power and Soviet Politics*, by Jeremy R. Azrael
53. *Danilevsky: A Russian Totalitarian Philosopher*, by Robert E. MacMaster
54. *Russia's Protectorates in Central Asia: Bukhara and Khiva, 1865–1924*, by Seymour Becker
55. *Revolutionary Russia*, edited by Richard Pipes
56. *The Family in Soviet Russia*, by H. Kent Geiger
57. *Social Change in Soviet Russia*, by Alex Inkeles
58. *The Soviet Prefects: The Local Party Organs in Industrial Decision-making*, by Jerry F. Hough
59. *Soviet-Polish Relations, 1917–1921*, by Piotr S. Wandycz
60. *One Hundred Thousand Tractors: The MTS and The Development of Controls in Soviet Agriculture*, by Robert F. Miller
61. *The Lysenko Affair*, by David Joravsky
62. *Icon and Swastika: The Russian Orthodox Church Under Nazi and Soviet Control*, by Harvey Fireside
63. *A Century of Russian Agriculture: From Alexander II to Krushchev*, by Lazar Volin
64. *Struve: Liberal on the Left, 1870–1905*, by Richard Pipes

* Out of print.
† Publications of the Harvard Project on the Soviet Social System.
‡ Published jointly with the Center for International Affairs, Harvard University.

Publications Written under the Auspices of the Center for International Affairs Harvard University

BOOKS

The Soviet Bloc, by Zbigniew K. Brzezinski (jointly with the Russian Research Center), 1960. Harvard University Press. Revised edition, 1967.

The Necessity for Choice, by Henry A. Kissinger, 1961. Harper & Bros.

Strategy and Arms Control, by Thomas C. Schelling and Morton H. Halperin, 1961. Twentieth Century Fund.

Rift and Revolt in Hungary, by Ferenc A. Váli, 1961. Harvard University Press.

United States Manufacturing Investment in Brazil, by Lincoln Gordon and Engelbert L. Grommers, 1962. Harvard Business School.

The Economy of Cyprus, by A. J. Meyer, with Simos Vassiliou (jointly with the Center for Middle Eastern Studies), 1962. Harvard University Press.

Entrepreneurs of Lebanon, by Yusif A. Sayigh (jointly with the Center for Middle Eastern Studies), 1962. Harvard University Press.

Communist China 1955-1959: Policy Documents with Analysis, with a Foreword by Robert R. Bowie and John K. Fairbank (jointly with the East Asian Research Center), 1962. Harvard University Press.

In Search of France, by Stanley Hoffmann, Charles P. Kindleberger, Laurence Wylie, Jesse R. Pitts, Jean-Baptiste Duroselle, and François Goguel, 1963. Harvard University Press.

Somali Nationalism, by Saadia Touval, 1963. Harvard University Press.

The Dilemma of Mexico's Development, by Raymond Vernon, 1963. Harvard University Press.

Limited War in the Nuclear Age, by Morton H. Halperin, 1963. John Wiley & Sons.

The Arms Debate, by Robert A. Levine, 1963. Harvard University Press.

Africans on the Land, by Montague Yudelman, 1964. Harvard University Press.

Counterinsurgency Warfare, by David Galula, 1964. Frederick A. Praeger, Inc.

People and Policy in the Middle East, by Max Weston Thornburg, 1964. W. W. Norton & Co.

Shaping the Future, by Robert R. Bowie, 1964. Columbia University Press.

Foreign Aid and Foreign Policy, by Edward S. Mason (jointly with the Council on Foreign Relations), 1964. Harper & Row.

Public Policy and Private Enterprise in Mexico, by M. S. Wionczek, D. H. Shelton, C. P. Blair, and R. Izquierdo, ed. Raymond Vernon, 1964. Harvard University Press.

How Nations Negotiate, by Fred C. Iklé, 1964. Harper & Row.

China and the Bomb, by Morton H. Halperin (jointly with the East Asian Research Center), 1965. Frederick A. Praeger, Inc.

Democracy in Germany, by Fritz Erler (Jodidi Lectures), 1965. Harvard University Press.

The Troubled Partnership, by Henry A. Kissinger (jointly with the Council on Foreign Relations), 1965. McGraw-Hill Book Co.

The Rise of Nationalism in Central Africa, by Robert I. Rotberg, 1965. Harvard University Press.

Pan-Africanism and East African Integration, by Joseph S. Nye, Jr., 1965. Harvard University Press.

Communist China and Arms Control, by Morton H. Halperin and Dwight H. Perkins (jointly with the East Asian Research Center), 1965. Frederick A. Praeger, Inc.

Problems of National Strategy, ed. Henry Kissinger, 1965. Frederick A. Praeger, Inc.

Deterrence before Hiroshima: The Airpower Background of Modern Strategy, by George H. Quester, 1966. John Wiley & Sons.

Containing the Arms Race, by Jeremy J. Stone, 1966. M.I.T. Press.

Germany and the Atlantic Alliance, by James L. Richardson, 1966. Harvard University Press.

Arms and Influence, by Thomas C. Schelling, 1966. Yale University Press.

Political Change in a West African State, by Martin L. Kilson, 1966. Harvard University Press.

Planning without Facts: Lessons in Resource Allocation from Nigeria's Development, by Wolfgang F. Stolper, 1966. Harvard University Press.

Foreign Policy and Democratic Politics, by Kenneth N. Waltz (jointly with the Institute of War and Peace Studies, Columbia University), 1967. Little, Brown & Co.

Contemporary Military Strategy, by Morton H. Halperin, 1967. Little, Brown & Co.

Sino Soviet Relations and Arms Control, ed. Morton H. Halperin (jointly with the East Asian Research Center), 1967. M.I.T. Press.

Export Instability and Economic Development, by Alasdair MacBean, 1967. Harvard University Press.

Africa and United States Policy, by Rupert Emerson, 1967. Prentice-Hall.

Elites in Latin America, ed. Seymour M. Lipset and Aldo Solari, 1967. Oxford University Press.

Europe's Postwar Growth, by Charles P. Kindleberger, 1967. Harvard University Press.

The Rise and Decline of the Cold War, by Paul Seabury, 1967. Basic Books.

Student Politics, ed. Seymour M. Lipset, 1967. Basic Books.

Pakistan's Development, by Gustav F. Papanek, 1967. Harvard University Press.

Strike a Blow and Die: A Narrative of Race Relations in Colonial Africa, by George Simeon Mwase. Edited with an Introduction by Robert I. Rotberg, 1967. Harvard University Press.

Aid, Influence, and Foreign Policy, by Joan M. Nelson, 1968. Macmillan.

Party Systems and Voter Alignments, ed. Seymour M. Lipset and Stein Rokkan, 1967. Free Press.

Agrarian Socialism, by Seymour M. Lipset, revised edition, 1968. Doubleday Anchor.

Revolution and Counterrevolution, by Seymour M. Lipset, 1968. Basic Books.

Korea: The Politics of the Vortex, by Gregory Henderson, 1968. Harvard University Press.

International Regionalism, by Joseph S. Nye, 1968. Little, Brown & Co.

The TFX Decision: McNamara and the Military, by Robert J. Art, 1968. Little, Brown & Co.

Development Policy: Theory and Practice, ed. Gustav F. Papanek, 1968. Harvard University Press.

Political Order in Changing Societies, by Samuel P. Huntington, 1968. Yale University Press.

Political Development in Latin America, by Martin Needler, 1968. Random House.

The Precarious Republic, by Michael Hudson, 1968. Random House.

The Brazilian Capital Goods Industry, 1929–1964, by Nathaniel H. Leff, 1968. Harvard University Press.

Economic Policy-making and Development in Brazil, 1947–1964, by Nathaniel H. Leff, 1968. Wiley.

German Foreign Policy in Transition, by Karl Kaiser, 1968. Oxford University Press.

Turmoil and Transition: Higher Education and Student Politics in India, ed. Philip G. Altbach, 1968. Lalvani Publishing House, Bombay 1.

The Process of Modernization, by John Brode, 1969. Harvard University Press.

Lord and Peasant in Peru: A Paradigm of Political and Social Change, by F. LaMond Tullis, 1970. Harvard University Press.

OCCASIONAL PAPERS, PUBLISHED BY THE CENTER

FOR INTERNATIONAL AFFAIRS

1. *A Plan for Planning: The Need for a Better Method of Assisting Underdeveloped Countries on Their Economic Policies,* by Gustav F. Papanek, 1961.*
2. *The Flow of Resources from Rich to Poor,* by Alan D. Neale, 1961.
3. *Limited War: An Essay on the Development of the Theory and an Annotated Bibliography,* by Morton H. Halperin, 1962.*
4. *Reflections on the Failure of the First West Indian Federation,* by Hugh W. Springer, 1962.
5. *On the Interaction of Opposing Forces under Possible Arms Agreements,* by Glenn A. Kent, 1963.
6. *Europe's Northern Cap and the Soviet Union,* by Nils Orvik, 1963.
7. *Civil Administration in the Punjab: An Analysis of a State Government in India,* by E. N. Mangat Rai, 1963.
8. *On the Appropriate Size of a Development Program,* by Edward S. Mason, 1964.
9. *Self-Determination Revisited in the Era of Decolonization,* by Rupert Emerson, 1964.
10. *The Planning and Execution of Economic Development in Southeast Asia,* by Clair Wilcox, 1965.
11. *Pan-Africanism in Action,* by Albert Tevoedjre, 1965.
12. *Is China Turning In?* by Morton H. Halperin, 1965.
13. *Economic Development in India and Pakistan,* by Edward S. Mason, 1966.
14. *The Role of the Military in Recent Turkish Politics,* by Ergun Özbudun, 1966.
15. *Economic Development and Individual Change: A Social-Psychological Study of the Comilla Experiment in Pakistan,* by Howard Schuman, 1967.
16. *A Select Bibliography on Students, Politics, and Higher Education,* by Philip Altbach, 1967.
17. *Europe's Political Puzzle: A Study of the Fouchet Negotiations and the 1963 Veto,* by Alessandro Silj, 1967.
18. *The Cap and the Straits: Problems of Nordic Security,* by Jan Klenberg, 1968.
19. *Cyprus: The Law and Politics of Civil Strife,* by Linda B. Miller, 1968.
20. *East and West Pakistan: A Problem in the Political Economy of Regional Planning,* by Md. Anisur Rahman, 1968.
21. *Internal War and International Systems: Perspective on Method,* by George A. Kelly and Linda B. Miller, 1969.
22. *Migrants, Urban Poverty, and Instability in New Nations,* by Joan M. Nelson, 1969.

* Out of print.